THE NEW INTERNATIONAL COMMENTARY ON THE OLD TESTAMENT

R. K. HARRISON, *General Editor*

The Book of
JOSHUA

by

MARTEN H. WOUDSTRA

WILLIAM B. EERDMANS PUBLISHING COMPANY
GRAND RAPIDS, MICHIGAN

Library of Congress Cataloging in Publication Data

Woudstra, Marten H.
The book of Joshua.

(New international commentary on the Old Testament)
Bibliography: p. 44.
Includes index.
1. Bible. O. T. Joshua—Commentaries.
I. Bible. O. T. Joshua. English. Woudstra.
1981. II. Title. III. Series.
BS1295.3.W68   222'.2077   80-23413
ISBN 0-8028-2356-4

To the Memory of my Parents:
JAN WOUDSTRA (1883–1957)
and
ADRIANA GOODIJK (1880–1951)

AUTHOR'S PREFACE

The invitation to write this commentary was received many years ago. Heavy involvement in other major projects, such as the preparation of the *New International Version*, prevented a speedy completion of the work. A choice had to be made between Bible translation, itself a form of Bible exposition, and Bible commentary. The commentary took precedence part of the time, but at other times the translation simply had to take priority.

A well-known French OT scholar, upon hearing that I was preparing a commentary on the book of Joshua, told me the task would not be an easy one. In the course of these many years I have had ample opportunity to experience the truthfulness of that remark. OT studies today are in a state of flux as never before. There is a great variety of opinion concerning almost any matter of importance. The book of Joshua seems to be at the crossroads of this animated discussion. Deep-seated differences in the scholarly world surface in the many studies devoted to this book.

Throughout this work it has been the writer's objective to take account of the various viewpoints concerning a given issue and to benefit from them where possible. But there were also occasions where disagreement was called for. This disagreement was sometimes of a fundamental sort, especially in matters regarding revelation, inspiration, and the implications of biblical theism for scientific endeavor. Nevertheless, an attempt has been made to carry on some dialogue with those whose opinions were reviewed. My only regret is that this could not be done more. The impasse in which OT scholarship often finds itself could perhaps become less severe if scholars were able to listen to each other more. It is my hope that in presenting divergent opinions I have been fair. If this may not always be evident, because of the brevity of the comments made, I hereby express my sincere regrets. Too much is at stake in this area of biblical interpretation. We are all equally involved in this challenging task. Nevertheless, the scholarly differences that exist are often of such magnitude that an early solution cannot be expected.

When work on the commentary began, I was not necessarily expecting much evidence of structure and design in the book of Joshua. However, as the work progressed, I thought I discovered various instances in which it appeared that the material had been arranged so as to support the book's total message. I have presented some of this evidence in the Introduction and have also called attention to it at appropriate points in the commentary. Finding this evidence of structure and design has led to the conclusion that one may legitimately speak of a basic unity of composition of the book as it now lies before us.

Throughout the commentary I have attempted to listen to what the narrator(s) had to say. The words "narrator," "account," etc. are meant to call attention to the fact that the work of interpreting a body of literature such as Joshua consists of eliciting from the work the meaning that is already there. The interpreter's task is a humble one. Although creativity and even intuition may play a role, his task is essentially that of listening to what someone else is trying to say. Ultimately (one could also say, primarily), that someone else is the great Someone Else. Exegesis, properly engaged in and done under the Spirit's guidance, gives access to what God says on the sacred page.

Whether the present work has been at all successful in accomplishing its avowed purpose will be for the reader to judge. It has been the writer's experience that the task of interpreting, besides being a constant exercise in humility, also offers satisfaction and contentment. The satisfaction arises from the fact that the interpreter has the privilege of perceiving meaning. This *perceived* meaning is at the same time *received* meaning. It is received as a gift, and since the gift is precious it causes contentment and joy. This gift is handed on across the centuries, yet it is able to illumine the present.

The notion of meaning had best be understood in as comprehensive a sense as possible. To be sure, there are time-bound elements in ancient literature such as the Bible. There is a distance between the book of Joshua and ourselves. Nevertheless, meaning in the comprehensive sense inevitably involves contemporary relevance. There simply is no such thing as irrelevant meaning. Properly understood, meaning makes a "bell ring," it "gets through" to a person, and thus it carries its own application.

The above can be said about any literature that is properly called classic, no matter of what age or origin. It is particularly true of that literature which purports to be the living Word of God. This Word the OT prophets experienced as a fire burning in their bones, and as a hammer that breaks the rock in pieces. They also experienced it as a word of life and of peace. It is with this meaningful Word that the biblical interpreter is concerned. As he or she faithfully passes on the meaning of that Word to those eager to receive it, there would seem to be little need for concern with the question of how to draw a line from the Bible to the present world. The line will already be there. Moreover, exegesis as presently understood should not preempt the task of the preacher, the teacher, or of any other person ready to take to hand the Word of God and to understand its contemporary relevance. So may it be the desire of all of us together to listen obediently to what the literature studied actually says. Only when this is done dare we be confident that God's Word will make its wholesome effect known and felt in our time.

The translation of the basic Joshua text offered in this commentary generally adheres quite closely to the original, with due observance of English style and diction. No attempt at stylistic finesse has been made. Considerations of economy of time and effort seemed to make such refinement inadvisable. Greater polish in matters of style usually involves a rendering farther removed from the literal order of words in the original, yet in a commentary one is often called upon to give a more literal rendering. To provide both types of translation would involve double work.

Nearly thirty years ago, in 1949, Paul Auvray remarked that the "definitive commentary" on Joshua had not yet been written. Since that time, several Joshua commentaries have appeared. The present work now joins their ranks. Were Auvray with us today he would probably reiterate his opinion. Still, the task of interpreting the Scriptures remains, and each generation of interpreters benefits from what has been accomplished by its predecessors. It is hoped that the present work shows to some degree its great indebtedness to what others have contributed.

Among the academic institutions whose library facilities were put at my disposal the following should be mentioned: the Harvard Divinity School, the University of Hamburg (Germany), the Theologische Hogeschool der Gereformeerde Kerken, Kampen (the Netherlands), the Provinciale Bibliotheek of Leeuwarden (the Netherlands), and my own seminary. To the personnel of all these institutions goes a word of heartfelt thanks.

A word of sincere thanks goes also to the editor of this Commentary series, Dr. R. K. Harrison, for his careful scrutiny of the manuscript, as well as to Mr. Mark Vander Hart, M.Div., for preparing the maps that appear in this volume and for rendering some assistance in the preparation of the subject and proper name indexes.

I am dedicating this work to the memory of my parents, who first taught me to love the Scripture and to appreciate its central message. And to God be all the glory.

MARTEN H. WOUDSTRA

CONTENTS

PRINCIPAL ABBREVIATIONS

ANET	J. B. Pritchard, ed., *Ancient Near Eastern Texts* (³1969)
AOTS	D. W. Thomas, ed., *Archaeology and OT Study*
ASV	American Standard Version (1901)
ATD	*Das AT Deutsch*
BA	*Biblical Archaeologist*
BAR	*Biblical Archaeology Review*
BASOR	*Bulletin of the American Schools of Oriental Research*
BDB	F. Brown, S. R. Driver, and C. A. Briggs, *A Hebrew and English Lexicon of the OT*
BH	*Biblia Hebraica*
Bibl	*Biblica*
BJRL	*Bulletin of the John Rylands Library*
BK	*Biblischer Kommentar*
BWANT	*Beiträge zur Wissenschaft vom Alten und Neuen Testament*
BZAW	*Beihefte zur ZAW*
CBQ	*Catholic Biblical Quarterly*
CTM	*Concordia Theological Monthly*
DNV	Dutch New Version (*De Bijbel in Nieuwe Vertaling*, 1952)
DOTT	D. W. Thomas, ed., *Documents from OT Times*
EV	English Versions
GB	W. Gesenius and F. Buhl, *Hebräisches und aramäisches Handwörterbuch* (¹⁷1921)
GKC	E. Kautzsch and A. E. Cowley, *Gesenius' Hebrew Grammar*
GTT	J. Simons, *The Geographical and Topographical Texts of the OT*
HAT	*Handbuch zum AT*
HTR	*Harvard Theological Review*
IB	*Interpreter's Bible*
IDB	G. A. Buttrick, ed., *Interpreter's Dictionary of the Bible*
IEJ	*Israel Exploration Journal*

ISBE	*The International Standard Bible Encyclopedia* (³1979–)
JAOS	*Journal of the American Oriental Society*
JB	Jerusalem Bible (1966)
JBL	*Journal of Biblical Literature*
JETS	*Journal of the Evangelical Theological Society*
JQR	*Jewish Quarterly Review*
JSS	*Journal of Semitic Studies*
JTS	*Journal of Theological Studies*
KB	L. Koehler and W. Baumgartner, *Lexicon in Veteris Testamenti Libros*
KD	C. F. Keil and F. Delitzsch, *Commentary on the OT* II (E. T. repr. 1973)
Knox	R. Knox, *The Holy Bible* (1944)
KS	A. Alt, *Kleine Schriften zur Geschichte des Volkes Israel*
LXX	Septuagint
MT	Masoretic Text
NAB	New American Bible (1970)
NBD	J. D. Douglas, ed., *New Bible Dictionary*
NEB	New English Bible (1970)
OTL	*OT Library*
OTS	*Oudtestamentische Studien*
PEQ	*Palestine Exploration Quarterly*
RB	*Revue Biblique*
RSV	Revised Standard Version (1952)
SBT	*Studies in Biblical Theology*
TB	*Tyndale Bulletin*
TDNT	G. Kittel and G. Friedrich, eds., *Theological Dictionary of the NT*
TDOT	G. J. Botterweck and H. Ringgren, eds., *Theological Dictionary of the OT*
VT	*Vetus Testamentum*
VTS	Supplements to *VT*
WTJ	*Westminster Theological Journal*
ZAW	*Zeitschrift für die alttestamentliche Wissenschaft*
ZDPV	*Zeitschrift des Deutschen Palästina-Vereins*

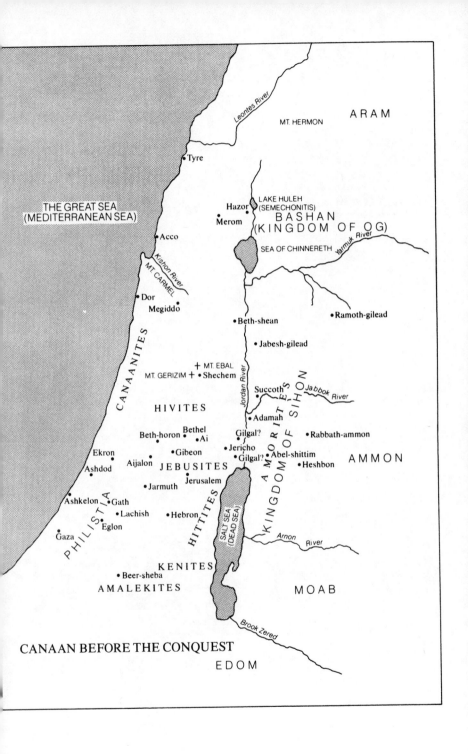

CANAAN BEFORE THE CONQUEST

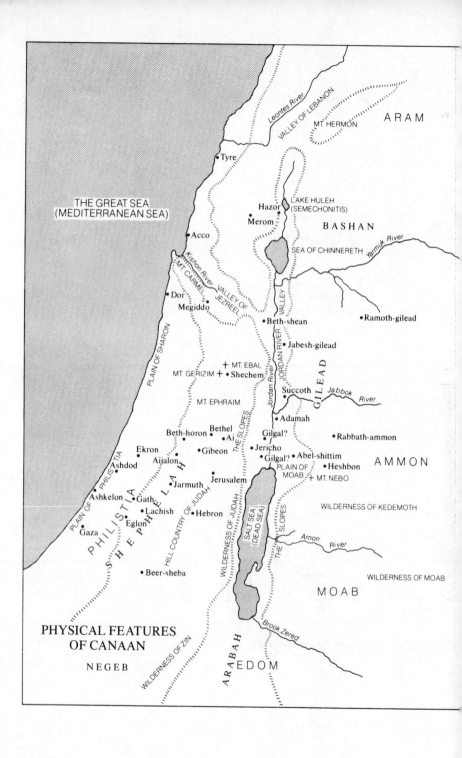

PHYSICAL FEATURES OF CANAAN

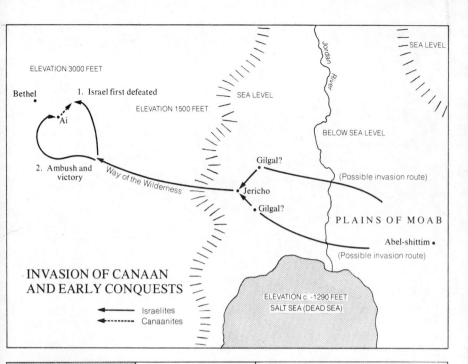

ELEVATION 3000 FEET

Bethel

1. Israel first defeated

Ai

ELEVATION 1500 FEET

SEA LEVEL

2. Ambush and
victory

Way of the Wilderness

Jordan River

SEA LEVEL

BELOW SEA LEVEL

Gilgal?

Jericho

Gilgal?

(Possible invasion route)

PLAINS OF MOAB

Abel-shittim •

(Possible invasion route)

INVASION OF CANAAN
AND EARLY CONQUESTS

→ Israelites
⤙---- Canaanites

ELEVATION c. -1290 FEET
SALT SEA (DEAD SEA)

+ MT. EBAL
MT. GERIZIM + • Shechem

Jordan River

Succoth

Jabbok River

• Adamah

Beth-horon •
• Bethel
• Ai

Gilgal?

• Rabbath-ammon

Ekron

Aijalon

• Gibeon

• Jericho
• Gilgal? • Abel-shittim
• Heshbon

AMMON

Ashdod

Jarmuth

Jerusalem

Ashkelon
• Gath
• Lachish
Eglon

• Hebron

SALT SEA (DEAD SEA)

Arnon River

Gaza

PHILISTIA

• Beer-sheba

MOAB

GIBEON CAMPAIGN

→ Israelites
⤙---- Canaanites

Brook Zered

EDOM

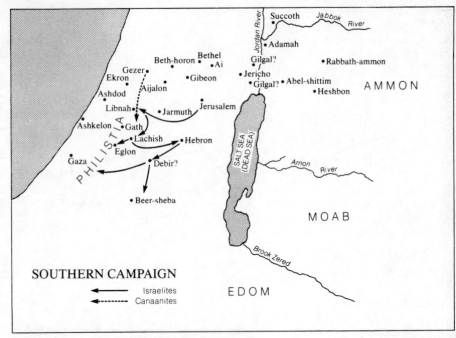

SOUTHERN CAMPAIGN

→ Israelites
╌╌→ Canaanites

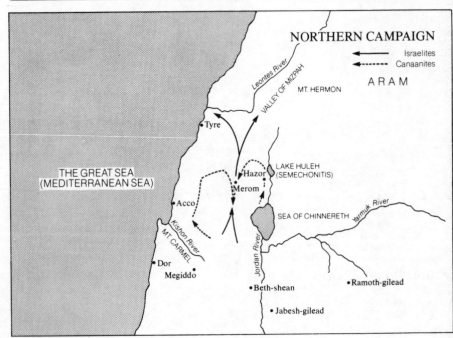

NORTHERN CAMPAIGN

→ Israelites
╌╌→ Canaanites

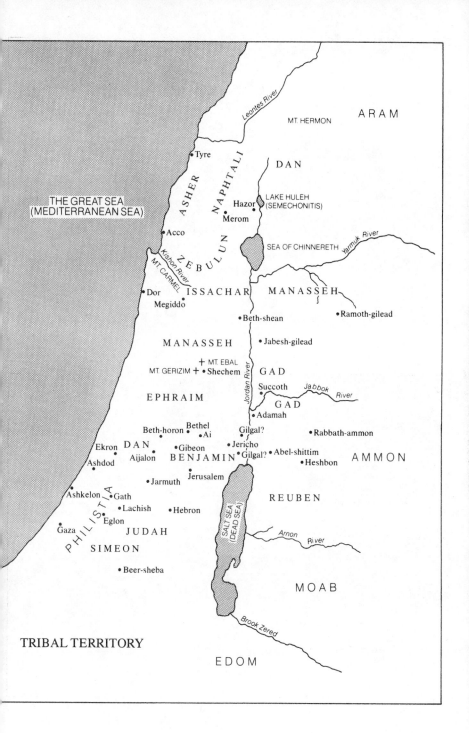

TRIBAL TERRITORY

The Book of
JOSHUA

INTRODUCTION

I. TITLE AND PURPOSE

In the Hebrew canon the book of Joshua heads the second division of the OT, "The Prophets." This division includes the "historical books" (Joshua through 2 Kings, minus Ruth), as well as the books of the writing prophets (Isaiah through Malachi, minus Daniel). Traditional Jewish scholarship distinguishes between the "Former Prophets" and the "Latter Prophets," with Joshua and the other historical books assigned to the "Former Prophets." Christian scholars have gladly adopted this terminology. Indeed, it can be used to good advantage, for it provides insight into the true nature and purpose of the books.

The intent of the Former Prophets is to present an interpretative (prophetical) history of God's dealings with his covenant people Israel, from the time of Moses' death until the Babylonian captivity. Thus viewed, these books let the light of divine revelation fall upon the events recorded and so enable us to perceive the line of development that holds these events together and gives them their true meaning.

The book of Joshua received its name from its principal character. The most common Hebrew form of the name Joshua is $y^ehôšu'a$ (cf. Josh. 1:1), although other forms also occur (cf. Deut. 3:21; Neh. 8:17). An earlier form of the name was Hoshea (cf. Num. 13:8, 16; Deut. 32:44, MT). In the LXX the name is rendered *Iēsous*, also the form in which it occurs in the NT (cf. Acts 7:45 and Heb. 4:8). Joshua, which means "the Lord is Salvation," was also the name the Savior bore.

No attempt will be made to present an extensive sketch of Joshua the man, although the book does permit a picture of Israel's leader during the Conquest. Focusing on "Bible characters" does have merits, but the danger exists that in doing so one overlooks the fact that the aim of biblical historiography is not to focus on the human agents of the redemptive

3

drama, or to exploit their good and evil deeds for purposes of moral example or deterrent. How sacred history must be viewed is well illustrated in the book of Joshua itself. In ch. 24 the book offers an overview of God's past dealings with his people (vv. 2–13). This is a prophetic survey, introduced by the customary formula: "Thus says the Lord." Throughout this summary the emphasis is on what God, the covenant Lord, has done. It is this emphasis, not that of moral example, that causes the people to respond with an expression of loyalty to their Lord and demonstrate their willingness to serve only him (vv. 16–18).

It is the sincere belief of the commentator that as one reads the Former Prophets, including the book of Joshua, a resolute effort should be made to avoid putting mankind in the center. "Bible stories" tend to be weighted too much on the anthropocentric. Biblical narrative all too often is searched for moral examples that can be followed or shunned, as the case may be. Biblical history thus is dissolved into a number of instances of human conduct, moral or immoral. The historical context within which the events are placed by the biblical author tends to be ignored. When a straight line is drawn from the "then" to the "now," the uniqueness of the biblical events as instances of God's self-revelation is in danger of being overlooked. The nuances of meaning placed in the biblical account by the inspired authors fail to get their due, for everything turns around the supposed "lesson." Biblical events tend to be lifted out of their redemptive-historical context by being made into timeless paradigms of moral behavior.

But this is not in keeping with Scripture's own design and purpose. Scripture presents historical facts in order to show that history is en route to a goal: that there is dynamic movement, and that the earlier leads to a later and a last. Even those NT chapters often considered to be patterned after the example-model, 1 Cor. 10 and Heb. 11, speak of the facts in terms of an "already" and a "not yet" (cf. 1 Cor. 10:11b and Heb. 11:39–40.) Another example of theocentric rather than anthropocentric recounting of history in the OT may be found in 1 Sam. 12:6–11.

The common "Bible story approach," replete with moral lessons taken out of context, inevitably leads to widespread moralism. The example method is also found in current Liberation theology, where the Exodus motif is considered to be the mainspring for change. But in the Bible the Exodus is viewed as redemption, not just in the sense of physical deliverance from oppression, but also in the sense of freedom from the bondage of sin. When God triumphs over Pharaoh, he also manifests his superiority over the gods of Egypt. Words used to describe the Exodus

4

release of enslaved Israel enter the vocabulary of redemption in its more comprehensive, Christ-effected, sense.[1]

Thus the example method effectively cuts us off from the true scriptural meaning of books such as Joshua and the other Former Prophets. Morality becomes the watchword. But morality as such cannot save. Only when it is woven into the fabric of redemption and flows from the redemptive work which God accomplishes for his people can morality receive its due.

II. AUTHORSHIP AND DATE

Experts are divided about few books in the OT as they are about the book of Joshua. Both the date and the authorship (editing) of the book are subjects of continuing controversy.

According to the Talmud, "Joshua wrote his own book," although the Talmudic tradition posited that the death of Joshua had been recorded by Eleazar son of Aaron, and the latter's own death by his son Phinehas. Jewish medieval expositors such as Rashi and David Kimchi believed that most of the book came from Joshua's time, but matters mentioned in 19:37 and 15:14–19 were thought to be from a later hand. Abrabanel, on the other hand, held that the book was probably from the hand of the prophet Samuel, who believed that the expression "until this day" (4:9; 5:9; 7:26, etc.) was an indication of a considerable lapse of time between the events and their description in the book. The reference to the book of Jashar (10:13) was also thought to be an indication of a date no earlier than the time of David (2 Sam. 1:18). A good many of these arguments continue to surface in modern discussion.

In the current phase of Joshua criticism two views "stand opposed to one another without compromise."[1] The one is a primarily literary-

---

1. That Liberation theology is not consistent in its use of OT materials has been pointed out by R. H. Preston, "From the Bible to the Modern World: A Problem for Ecumenical Ethics," *BJRL* 59 (1976), p. 185. Preston urges care in the use of the OT as a model, warning against "sudden darts from a Biblical text to a specific conclusion" (example: Karl Barth!) and pointing out that Liberation theology, while making much of the Exodus as the model of God's activity for today, is silent on the events of the Settlement or of the Exile. "Why," Preston asks, "is that central event [the Exile] in Old Testament history not made a key model of interpretation?" His remark that this "all savours of covering subjectivity in using the Bible with a mask of objectivity" appears to be well taken; see also M. H. Woudstra, "A Critique of Liberation Theology by a Cross-Culturalized Calvinist," *JETS* 23 (1980), pp. 3-12.

1. See O. Kaiser, *Introduction to the OT* (Minneapolis: 1977), p. 135.

critical view; the other, while not rejecting literary criticism, believes that it must be combined with the traditio-historical view.

Following in the footsteps of J. Wellhausen (1844–1918) a group of contemporary scholars continues to believe that Joshua, together with the Five Books of Moses, must be regarded as part of a six-book unit called the Hexateuch. They therefore hold that the alleged sources of the Pentateuch, the so-called Jehovist (Yahwist), Elohist, Deuteronomist, and the Priestly document can be detected in the book of Joshua as well. But there is no consensus of opinion about how to divide the book among the various sources.[2]

Since Wellhausen, the basic form of the narrative of chs. 2–11 has usually been thought to derive from the Elohist source. This assumption, however, is based on the opinion that this presentation of the events of the Conquest differs from a supposedly parallel description of the same events in Judg. 1. Since the latter is believed to represent the J source, the conclusion was drawn that the Joshua materials came from the E source,[3] but doubts have arisen as to the propriety of this assignment. W. Rudolph argues strongly that the first twelve chapters of the book belong to J, not to E.[4]

The second part of the book, especially chs. 13–22 dealing with the distribution of the land, has been frequently ascribed to the P source. The role of the Priestly editor, however, has been variously described. Moreover, most scholars adhering to some form of Wellhausian source hypothesis are agreed that the book in its present form owes its existence to a Deuteronomistic redaction. The fact that not P but D is believed to have been the final hand at work in Joshua's redaction should actually come as a source of embarrassment to the adherents of the documentary hypothesis, for in the Pentateuch itself P is considered to be the foundational document.[5]

A commentary on Joshua is not the place to deal extensively with the broader question of Pentateuchal criticism and the documentary hy-

---

2. E. M. Good, *IDB* II, p. 990, writes: "The results are so inconclusive that it seems justifiable to doubt that the Pentateuchal documents continue into Joshua."
3. Cf. Kaiser, *op. cit.*, p. 136.
4. For a summary of divergent opinions that is still very useful, cf. N. H. Snaith, "The Historical Books," in H. H. Rowley, ed., *The OT and Modern Study* (London: 1951), pp. 84–86.
5. Cf. R. K. Harrison, *Introduction to the OT* (Grand Rapids: 1969), p. 668; see also E. J. Young, *Introduction to the OT* (Grand Rapids: ²1960), p. 156. Young also presents some cogent reasons why the assumption of a Hexateuch lacks sufficient support.

pothesis. Suffice it to say that we are unable to accept that hypothesis. If, as P. C. Craigie has demonstrated satisfactorily,[6] the book of Deuteronomy may be assigned confidently to the Mosaic age, the very foundation of the documentary hypothesis has been removed.

The traditio-historical approach to the authorship of Joshua abandons the literary-critical solution with regard to chs. 1–12. M. Noth holds that there are three sources in chs. 2–12, namely a group of etiological legends (chs. 2–9) along with two hero legends (ch. 10 and 11:1–9). According to Noth, some of these stories were not originally national in scope. Rather, they were handed down in connection with a sanctuary in Benjaminite Gilgal and were originally Benjaminite in scope.[7] As Saul became Israel's national king, however, this Benjaminite material became the property of the nation and was broadened so that Joshua grew in stature as a national hero. A collector is believed responsible for the combination of these materials in chs. 2–9; 10; and 11. He was active about 900 BC.

Noth argues for a continuing history-work in the OT from Deuteronomy through 2 Kings, written by the Deuteronomist. His approach, therefore, represents an important modification of the documentary hypothesis but does not break radically with it.

O. Kaiser has asked some searching questions regarding Noth's approach to chs. 2–11.[8] One of them concerns the choice of Gilgal as the presumed site for the handing down of these early Joshua materials. Kaiser suggests that the choice of this site may simply be a fiction and points out, rightly so we believe, that 9:27 is more likely to be connected with Gibeon and ultimately with Jerusalem than with Gilgal.

Another critical question arises with respect to the relation between Judg. 1, which supposedly gives a true picture of the course of events during the Conquest, and Josh. 2–11, which is thought to present a fictional account of an all-Israelite conquest. The question is how this fic-

6. *The Book of Deuteronomy.* NICOT (Grand Rapids: 1976), *passim*.
7. See M. Noth, *Das Buch Josua. HAT* VII (Tübingen: ²1953), pp. 7–17. Noth follows A. Alt who also wrote extensively on the date and authorship of Joshua. See Alt, "Judas Gaue unter Josia," in *KS* II (Munich: 1959), pp. 276–288; cf. also "Das System der Stammesgrenzen im Buche Josua," in *KS* I (Munich: 1953), pp. 193–202. In the same volume see also "Josua," pp. 176–192.
8. See Kaiser, *op. cit.*, p. 138. Kaiser's questions must be seen as based on assumptions essentially similar to those of Noth and are intended as intrinsic criticism. Although we do not share these basic assumptions, we would note the ongoing debate around Noth's hypothesis, which has been widely followed; see, e.g., J. A. Soggin, *Joshua. OTL* (Philadelphia: 1972), *passim*, which adopts many of Noth's positions.

tional account could have been put forward at a time when the tradition incorporated in Judg. 1 was already known.

Noth believes that chs. 13–19, which the literary critics frequently assign to the Priestly source, are made up of two documentary sources: a system of tribal boundaries reflecting the time of the Judges, and a list of places in the kingdom of Judah, supposedly reflecting the period of the Judahite king Josiah. In this respect Noth, following Alt, has been instrumental in claiming a higher degree of antiquity for the various boundary and city lists than was accorded them by earlier scholars.[9]

Alt's position, however, is not held universally. S. Mowinckel believes that chs. 13–19 are postexilic,[10] composed by the P editor from earlier traditions. The Scandinavian scholar is of the opinion that some of the details of these lists, e.g. the relation between Ephraim and Manasseh (chs. 16–17), actually reflect the Samaritan schism and must therefore be quite late.

What is to be noted in all these attempts at dating the boundary and city lists to a time other than that of Joshua himself is that most scholars grant these lists a "strongly theoretical stamp."[11] Certain regions by the Mediterranean Sea, while assigned to some of the tribes, were actually never in the possession of Israel. Yet the attempt is made to fit these boundary descriptions and city lists into some period of Israel's actual geographical and political development. Is it not more natural to suppose that these lists are indeed what they claim to be, namely, descriptions of what happened at the time when Israel had just entered into Canaan, when it had conquered the land at least in principle, and then had started to *allot* the territory to the tribes? Such an allotment involved a *programmatic* element: certain areas were yet to be subjugated, and slackness in doing so is duly noted (13:13; 15:63; 17:12).[12] This argues for dating the lists in the time of Joshua himself.

We are not unaware of the argument from archaeology sometimes

---

9. G. C. Aalders, *Oud-Testamentische Kanoniek* (Kampen: 1952), generally a very conservative work, speaks with appreciation of the work of Alt, whom Noth follows, and calls it a "step forward" (p. 170).

10. Cf. *Zur Frage nach dokumentarischen Quellen in Josua 13–19* (Oslo: 1946), *passim*.

11. Cf. Alt, *KS* I, p. 196. This belief is echoed by Soggin, *Joshua*, p. 11, who speaks of "territorial aspirations not yet fulfilled," and by Kaiser, *op. cit.*, p. 140: "The drawing of the boundaries is in part (on this all sides are agreed) completely theoretical." Kaiser speaks in this regard of a "theory of religious entitlement." Does not this comport with the reality of an allotment during Joshua's day?

12. Note should also be taken of Y. Kaufmann's vigorous opposition to Alt in *The Biblical Account of the Conquest of Palestine* (Jerusalem: 1953), e.g., pp. 13ff.

used to propose a later date, nor are we unsympathetic to such reasoning. The city of Secacah, so it is pointed out, while assigned to Judah (15:61), was actually a site whose single occupational level is dated to the 9th century BC.[13] But archaeological arguments of this sort must be used with caution. Much remains unknown about the identity of biblical sites. Opinions concerning some of them continue to differ. In our commentary on chs. 13–19 it will be necessary to list more than one suggested location for a particular site mentioned. Even the identity of ancient Gibeon, held by many to be ej-Jib, is not accepted by all (see the commentary on 9:3). Moreover, experts in the field of biblical topography and historical geography have not been able to agree on some of these matters.[14] This would seem to be another reason for not questioning the basic reliability of the biblical representation.

It is to be granted, of course, that to place the system of tribal boundaries in the premonarchic period, as does Alt, virtually makes it develop from approximately the same time that the book of Joshua may well have received its present shape (see below). Yet, it would seem precarious to endorse Alt's relatively early date for some of the materials in chs. 13–19 if this endorsement involved a question of the biblical record's intrinsic reliability.[15]

Regarding the broader question of date and authorship, Kaiser rightly observes that the theories presently prevailing need further examination.[16] There appears to be uncertainty among scholars concerning this question. Would this not be a reason to examine afresh the biblical data and then draw some tentative conclusions?

One argument widely used to assign a relatively late date to the final composition of Joshua is drawn from what is believed to be a divergent view of the Conquest in Judg. 1. The latter, so it is held, presents the view

13. Cf. *NBD*, s.v. Secacah, p. 1157.
14. For other divergent opinions on the date of these materials see Z. Kallai-Kleinmann, "The Town Lists of Judah, Simeon, Benjamin and Dan," *VT* 8 (1958), pp. 134–160; and Y. Aharoni, "The Province List of Judah," *VT* 9 (1959), pp. 225–246. Kallai-Kleinmann attempts to show that the boundary description reflects the period of David and Solomon, the list of the cities of Judah the period of Hezekiah, and that of Benjamin the time of Abijah, but Aharoni considers the city lists of Judah to reflect the time of Jehoshaphat.
15. This commentary has been written from the standpoint of the Bible's basic reliability. This standpoint springs from faith in the Bible's own claims, and is not as such subject to external verification. It is not opposed to the use of historical and archaeological arguments, provided these do not presuppose holding in abeyance the Bible's reliability until the "proof" has been rendered by outside sources.
16. Kaiser, *op. cit.*, pp. 137, 141.

of a piecemeal conquest by individual tribes, whereas the former pictures a unified onslaught by all the tribes under Joshua. What should be noted first is that Judg. 1 purports to describe events after Joshua's death (Judg. 1:1).[17] Those who would hold the Judges material to present just a divergent view of the Conquest would have to eliminate Judg. 1:1 from consideration. But if Judg. 1 does present events subsequent to Joshua, as we believe it does, then the two views of the Conquest need not be contrasted as more or less true to the actual course of events. Both could be equally true.

But what about the view of the Conquest as found in Joshua itself? Is it as optimistic and unrealistic as often alleged? On the one hand, a repeated emphasis is upon the fulfilment of God's promises to the fathers and upon the complete subjugation of the land (11:23; 21:43–45). But the unfinished nature of the Conquest also receives attention (cf. 13:13; 15:63; 16:10; 17:12–13; 23:4–5; cf. 23:9). Thus the picture drawn in Joshua is more composite than is sometimes acknowledged in critical discussion.

As for participation in the Conquest, the book does contain indications of individual and tribal efforts (14:6–15; 17:14–18; 19:47–48). It could be supposed that these features were due to a divergent tradition, or that they had entered into the record by editing done out of a variety of motives. Yet the final shape of Joshua presents a fairly realistic narrative involving a united Conquest despite the need for further supplementation. On that basis, therefore, there appears to be no need to consider that the final form of the book is due to a late and unhistorical view of the events.

Having surveyed some of the more comprehensive questions bearing on date and authorship, we now proceed to some of the specific data which appear to be pertinent.

According to 16:10 the Canaanites still live in Gezer, a city which was subsequently conquered during Solomon's days by an Egyptian Pharaoh who destroyed the native population. Jebus is as yet unconquered, a feat to be accomplished by David (cf. 15:63 with 2 Sam. 5). It may also be that 9:27 precedes the time of Saul, who subsequently violated the terms of the covenant made with Gibeon (2 Sam. 21:1ff.).

The appeal that is made to 5:1, where according to one Hebrew manuscript tradition a first plural pronoun is used, thus suggesting an

---

17. A. E. Cundall considers Judg. 1:1a to be the title and introduction to the whole book; Cundall and L. Morris, *Judges and Ruth*. Tyndale OT Commentary (Downers Grove: 1968). This means that 1:1b–2:5 actually describe events during Joshua's lifetime. K. A. Kitchen, *The Bible in Its World* (London: 1978), p. 91, argues, more correctly we believe, that not everything in Judg. 1 is to be placed after Joshua's death. Some verses contain "flashbacks" to Joshua's time (1:10–15, 20).

eyewitness account, is not as strong as it seems. Not only is there a diversity in the Hebrew textual tradition, but one could also account for the "we" form in terms of a feeling of corporate solidarity. A much stronger argument for a relatively early date can be derived from 13:6, where there is no mention of Tyre, a city which in later times certainly rivaled Sidon in importance. Kaufmann has also made a good case for the high antiquity of the list of Levitical cities in ch. 21.[18]

An argument from style may be taken from the vividness with which various details of the narrative are described (cf. 14:6–12; 15:16–19; 17:14–18; cf. also 2:21; 7:21; 8:26, etc.). This suggests anything but a late, remote, and postexilic account. Of course, some of these features may have survived in ancient documents which subsequently were woven into the present book; but it is doubtful whether the good independent evidence necessary for such a process has been presented.

As noted above, the expression "until this day" was believed at an early stage of Joshua studies to be an indication of a date considerably later than the time when the events recorded had actually occurred (see 4:9; 5:9; 7:26; 8:28–29; 9:27; 10:27; 13:13; 14:14; 15:63; 16:10).[19] However, this expression is not as clear an indication of late composition as is sometimes thought. Looking back into the recent past was done even within the lifetime of Joshua himself (cf. 22:3; 23:9–10). If the writer of the book lived some 40 to 50 years after Joshua's time, could he not have used this expression to inform his readers of the continuing presence of a given landmark or memorial?[20]

An explicit reference to a written source used by the author is found in 10:13. The book of Jashar is also cited in 2 Sam. 1:18, but it does not follow that the Joshua reference must therefore be at least as late as David's time. This book may well have been a steadily growing collection of noteworthy sayings dating from various periods of Israel's history including that of Joshua. No clear conclusion as to the date of Joshua can thus be derived from the use of such a source.

The contention of several scholars that the connection in 8:33 of the sojourner with the homeborn suggests a time considerably later than

18. Cf. Kaufmann, *op. cit.*, p. 40.
19. There is no unanimity, even among those favoring a relatively early date, about the import of 6:25. Did Rahab actually live among Israel when this was written or was she believed to be present through her posterity?
20. This is convincingly argued by C. J. Goslinga, *Het Boek Jozua*. Korte Verklaring der Heilige Schrift (Kampen: ³1955), p. 16. See also 22:17 where Phinehas looks into the recent past and states that its results are still felt at the time of his speaking.

Joshua, when strangers had begun to settle in Israel's midst, does not take into account the fact that the same expression occurs in passages such as Exod. 12:19, 48. If, as we believe, the Exodus passages go back to the times of Moses, then it would not be surprising for an author of Joshua's day to use identical words.

The opinions of conservative scholarship are not wholly unanimous as to the approximate date of Joshua's composition. R. K. Harrison suggests a date at the beginning of the Monarchy, perhaps 1045 BC.[21] G. C. Aalders believes that the book received its present form sometime during the period of the Judges,[22] whereas C. J. Goslinga, who at one time held that the book was predominantly Joshua's own work, has subsequently come to think that the author may be among the circle of the officers mentioned in 1:10; 3:2; 8:33; 23:2; 24:1.[23] The author would then have been a younger contemporary of Joshua himself. J. H. Kroeze, on the other hand, contends that we do not know how the book came into existence, but that we now have it in its final form; this is how God has given it to us and it is so to be used as a part of his redemptive revelation. Natural factors in the origin of biblical books must be recognized (cf. Luke 1:1–3), but these factors were used by God and the Holy Spirit, and whatever the human authors wrote, they did so as impelled by God's Spirit (2 Pet. 1:21).[24]

These are in themselves excellent observations. Whether there is cause to be quite as skeptical about date and authorship as Kroeze, however, is open to question. The lack of unanimity among those who argue for a late date, though paralleled somewhat by a similar deficiency among those favoring an early date, is nevertheless a just reason to examine the data afresh and to maintain a healthy skepticism with respect to some of the critics' claims. Is this not ample justification for taking the presentation of the book to be more true to fact than has long been allowed? Would not that also have some bearing on its date of composition? Could not the

---

21. *Op. cit.*, p. 673.
22. *Op. cit.*, p. 168.
23. *Op. cit.*, p. 20.
24. *Het Boek Jozua*. Commentaar op het OT (Kampen: 1968), p. 13. Kroeze continues with an enumeration of a great many "rough spots," as he calls them, supposedly to be found in Joshua, such as repetitions, insertions, interruptions of the flow of the narrative, etc. We have not been impressed by this list and have attempted to account for many of these seeming inadequacies in terms of the peculiar nature of Hebrew narrative, with its anticipations, succinct summaries, to be followed by further elaborations, etc. Examples may be found in the commentary proper.

view of history developed in Joshua have been the product of the days in which Israel, according to the book's own testimony, "served the Lord" (24:31), i.e., in the days of Joshua himself and of the elders who outlived him? The spirit of joyful optimism which pervades the book by and large could perhaps be accounted for best by that assumption.

III. UNITY OF COMPOSITION

The discussion about date and authorship has pointed up the variety of opinion with respect to Joshua's composition. Some continue to consider the book to be a composite of the alleged documents believed to underlie the present form of the Pentateuch, while others prefer to regard Joshua as part of a "deuteronomic" history work. This position often assumes the use of a variety of materials in the composition of the book: etiological tales in the early chapters; lists of boundaries and cities dating from various periods of Israel's history, and the like.

It will be readily understood that the possibility for composite authorship increases as the date of writing is pushed farther forward. When the date is placed close to Joshua's own time this possibility decreases correspondingly.

That a variety of materials was used cannot well be denied on any theory. The book itself acknowledges use of the "book of Jashar" (10:13). Another reference to a written record probably at the writer's disposal is found in 18:9. One may assume that similar records were kept of the allotments to the tribes as described in chs. 15–17.

If the date of composition may be put as early as suggested above, eyewitness accounts of the actual Conquest would have been available. Writing activity on Joshua's part is referred to in 8:32; 24:26, although neither explicitly states that he recorded the events that transpired during the Conquest.

As for the many "rough spots"[1] which some think they have discovered in the book, we have attempted to show at several places in the commentary that what now looks like an insertion, a duplicate, or an interruption may well be due to the unique manner in which Hebrew narrative is constructed. Such material tends to be episodic in nature. It centers now on this, then on that phase of an event. It tends to use prolepsis, offering a provisional summary of what was done to conclude the matter discussed, but at some later point to take up this issue in some

---

1. Cf. p. 12, note 24.

detail. Thus the matter of the pursuit of the spies by the men of Jericho is mentioned in 2:7, but only briefly, and is picked up again in v. 22. Rahab's conversation with the men as reported in 2:16ff. appears to happen at a rather inconvenient time and place, for just before the writer has recorded that she let the men down through a window by a rope (v. 15). But that information can again be understood as a provisional conclusion of one part of the story which proceeds episodically, and need not be taken chronologically.

Similar explanations may be offered for details of the story of the fall of Jericho, the attack upon Ai, etc. (see commentary). With regard to the burning of Ai (8:19, 28), the two accounts are not merely duplicates. The two burnings served different purposes. The first was meant to be a signal, and was possibly partial; the second was final and complete.

At the same time, it is well to remember that chronology is not the chief concern of the "prophetical" historiography contained in this book. The words spoken by Joshua and reported in 3:7–13 may not have been uttered at the point where they now occur. One should allow for thematic interests to have shaped the materials. A suspense element may also be detected (see 3:8 and commentary). By means of prolepsis the reader is alerted to certain significant and dramatic occurrences which will take place; the actual unfolding of the drama is sometimes postponed until later in the narrative. The author's ability to make his narrative live dramatically is beyond question (see 3:15; 5:13–15; 6:11, and commentary). The narrator also knew how to change the pace of his narrative. A certain sequence of events, such as the preparation for and the actual encirclement of Jericho, receives a drawn-out description, followed by a few succinct statements of the final denouement: the falling of the walls, the entry of the city, and the extermination of the people (see 6:20–21, and commentary).

The question of unity of composition goes inseparably with that of unity of conception and theme. A thoughtful reading of the book reveals that underlying all the materials is a unity of theme to which everything has been made subordinate.[2]

Worthy of notice are several features demonstrating design in the book's final composition. Some are enumerated here at random. Perhaps closer scrutiny could discover even greater orderliness than might now appear from this survey.

2. See H. W. Hertzberg, *Die Bücher Josua, Richter, Ruth. ATD* IX (Göttingen: [5]1974), p. 8, who remarks that Joshua appears a compact work, designed for unity of conception, with everything in it made subordinate to its purpose.

1. Both the first and last chapters have a hortatory tone. This provides a fitting "prophetical" setting for the book's chief contents.

2. The stories of the burials of Joshua, Joseph, and Eleazar, significantly placed at the book's conclusion, serve to underscore the book's thematic concern, fulfilment of the promise. All these persons were laid to rest in the land which was now Israel's. What a blessed contrast with the patriarch Abraham who had to bargain for a burial place for his loved one (Gen. 23; cf. Joseph's words in Gen. 50:25)!

3. Certain smaller units of narrative are placed within a "frame" all of their own (cf. 1 above).

a. The story of the southern campaign begins with the frantic preparation of Israel's (and Yahweh's) foes in 9:1-2 and concludes with the summary in 10:40-43.

b. There is a clear correspondence between the promise of 1:3, 6 and the summary in 11:16ff. A further correspondence may be detected between 1:12-18 and 22:1-6.

c. The story of the actual Conquest is preceded by an account of Israel's breach of faith through Achan's sin (ch. 7). The story of the settlement begins (one might also say that the story of the Conquest ends) with the account of a threat of a similar breach of faith (22:9-34). The second account (see vv. 16 and 20) recalls the earlier one by using the same word (Heb. *ma'al*) as that used to describe Achan's offense.

d. The last significant event among the Conquest stories is Joshua's expulsion of the dreaded Anakim, 11:21-22, the same Anakim whom Israel had dreaded earlier (Num. 13:33). Thus Joshua's act of expulsion is viewed as the happy conclusion to a narrative sequence which begins before the book of Joshua: disbelief and fear on one end, subjugation of the dreaded foe on the other.

e. The same Anakim motif probably prompted the placement of the Caleb materials in 14:12. These materials now stand as a frame around the allotment of Judah (compare 14:6-15 with 15:13-19).

f. At the same time, the story of how Caleb obtains his inheritance corresponds with the story of Joshua receiving his inheritance (19:49-50). The account of Caleb's inheritance opens the story of the allotment, while that of Joshua closes it. The men, who as spies had rendered a good report during the wilderness period (Num. 13), open and close the account of the allotment in Joshua. That which Israel in the desert had deemed impossible, the conquest of the promised land, had become a reality.

g. A negative correspondence may be noted as one compares 14:6-12 (the beginning of the allotment's first phase marked by faith), with

18:2–3 (the beginning of the second phase of allotment is marked by hesitation).

h. There may also be a negative correspondence intended by putting the story of Caleb's claim by faith to a portion of enemy territory at the beginning of Judah's allotment and contrasting it with Judah's failure to conquer Jebus, placed at the conclusion of Judah's allotment (15:63).

4. The fact that the material of Achan's trespass is given such extensive treatment at the beginning of the story of the Conquest (ch. 7) is probably due to the writer's design. The holy land must be inhabited by holy people.

5. An analysis of the Achan story in itself reveals the interaction of two motifs: God's blazing anger (to which the reader is alerted at the outset, even though Israel is as yet unaware) and the people's responsibility.[3]

Although some of these structural data may be open to question, nevertheless there would appear to be too many to be completely accidental. They suggest thematic concerns, skilfully worked out in the book.[4] These concerns have been touched on only briefly in the body of this commentary. Attention to style, manner of narration, and structural data force us to be occupied intensely with the text we are seeking to understand. That, after all, is the purpose of reading and interpreting any kind of literature, including the Bible.[5]

In light of the evidence presented above, it appears that a strong case can be made for unity of composition, not to the exclusion of the use of diverse sources, but by means of them.

IV. OCCASION

A tentative case has been made for a date not too far removed from the events described in the book. Nevertheless, the question of the occasion

---

3. For a careful analysis of a similar "predestination" motif hovering in the back of human action and intrigue, cf. J. P. Fokkelman's discussion of Gen. 25:19–34, in *Narrative Art in Genesis* (Assen: 1975), pp. 115–121.

4. M. Kessler, "Narrative Technique in 1 Sm 16:1–13," *CBQ* 32 (1970), p. 545, rightly urges his readers to recognize the "independent, creative enterprise of the final compiler," reminding that the oldest writers in the OT "composed much more themselves than is usually assumed."

5. Cf. J. P. Fokkelman, *op. cit.*, p. 4: "Before using the text as a transparency we should recognize its intrinsic values and give it a chance to speak for itself." This commentary has attempted to do just that. Cf. also Fokkelman's quotation of E. Staiger, a specialist in E. Mörike's poems: "I love them; they speak to me; and in the confidence in this encounter I venture to interpret them" (p. 8, note 22).

for writing this book is not absolutely dependent on settling the precise date of authorship. In a broader sense, the occasion of Israel writing its "prophetical" history lies in Israel's concern to keep alive the memory of the acts of its covenant God for future generations (cf. Ps. 78:1–4). This concern is also God's own concern. It is he who orders that various memorials be set up so later generations may dwell on what he did for his chosen people (Josh. 4:1–9, 20–24).

One might say, therefore, that the occasion for the writing of the book of Joshua was the covenant between God and Israel and the need, flowing from that covenant, to keep alive the memories of the past in order both to perceive thereby the significance of the present, and to open up vistas of the future.

Some prefer to make a close connection between covenant and covenant document. This has been done skilfully by M. G. Kline,[1] who on the basis of a comparison with treaties[2] from the cultures of Israel's neighbors, concludes that making a covenant always involves preparing a corresponding covenant document. This approach has been combined with a defense of the early date of many of the OT books which scholars had always considered to be late. But on the question of how precisely to use the treaty materials for dating OT books no consensus has as yet arisen.[3]

Apart from such close reliance on extrabiblical sources such as ancient Near Eastern treaties, one can safely say that the covenant provided the occasion for, and the underlying unity of, the various historical narratives that the OT now contains.[4] Since God was in covenant with Israel

1. Cf. M. G. Kline, "Canon and Covenant," *WTJ* 32 (1969/70), pp. 49–67, 179–200; 33 (1970/71), pp. 45–72; also *The Structure of Biblical Authority* (Grand Rapids: 1971).

2. The treaty/covenant literature is very vast. We mention a few titles: G. E. Mendenhall, *Law and Covenant in Israel and the Ancient Near East* (Pittsburgh: 1955); K. Baltzer, *The Covenant Formulary in OT, Jewish and Early Christian Writings* (E.T. 1971); D. J. McCarthy, *Treaty and Covenant* (Rome: 1963). See also Craigie, *Deuteronomy*, pp. 22–24.

3. At stake is the precise form of the extrabiblical treaties during successive periods from which they have come. Some hail from the second and others from the first millennium BC. Those who defend a second-millennium date for books such as Deuteronomy and Joshua argue that certain covenant features exhibited in the biblical books were no longer found in the first-millennium treaties but are found in those of the second millennium only. See K. A. Kitchen, *Ancient Orient and OT* (Downers Grove: 1966), pp. 90–102; and M. G. Kline, *Treaty of the Great King* (Grand Rapids: 1963).

4. Cf. C. Vonk, *Inleiding op de Profeten: Jozua*. De Heilige Schrift (Barendrecht: 1972), p. 10; and A. Van Daalen, *Simson*. Studia Semitica Neerlandica 8 (Assen: 1966), pp. 10–11. Says Van Daalen: "Gradually the insight is growing that the

17

he wanted them to know how the promise made to the forefathers was fulfilled during the Conquest so his chosen people would trust and obey him in future generations. God wanted Israel to know of the possibility of covenant disobedience and of his displeasure at such an act. Providing an extensive and detailed account of how the promised land was apportioned and settled, he wanted to impress upon them the realization that the covenant, while spiritual in its core, became concretely manifested in the "here and now" of Israel's existence during the old dispensation. Thus he alerted them to the future dimension of a much wider fulfilment of the covenant promise, the new heaven and the new earth (compare Ps. 37:9 with Matt. 5:5).

V. HISTORICAL BACKGROUND

A knowledge of the historical background of the events described in the book of Joshua may be helpful, although not absolutely essential, for understanding the book. Biblical historiography, though firmly anchored in space and time, pursues its own unique aims. It means to set forth God's dealings with his people Israel and with the nations around Israel. It does not mean to present a general history of the nation of Israel but has as its focus the progress of God's revelation and the establishment of his kingdom on earth.[1]

Since this is so, biblical narrative may not be judged by standards that are alien to its genius. Such an approach does great harm, and the biblical writings are put on the defensive. Some biblical scholars frankly assume a cleavage between the faith picture that Israel wove of its past and the allegedly scientific picture which the historian reconstructs. G. von Rad's *Theology of the OT*[2] proceeds upon that basis. Von Rad seeks to

---

OT is not a loose collection of stories, traditions and additions, edited by several redactors, but that behind this opus there is one conception . . . which, while using many motifs and data, directed all of these toward that one entity, the covenant. . . ."

1. The unique nature of OT narrative has long been recognized by those who defended its veracity and trustworthiness against the attacks of the higher critics. Cf. W. H. Green, *The Higher Criticism of the Pentateuch* (New York: 1895, repr. 1978), p. 19: "The Pentateuch has one theme . . . viz., the theocracy in Israel, or the establishment of Israel to be the people of God." KD, p. 7, observe that the "Former Prophets trace the history of the people of God, or Israel, in its theocratic development as a covenant nation, and as the channel of that salvation which was to be manifested to all nations in the fulness of time."
2. (E.T. New York: 1962–65).

examine the traditions of Israel's faith, while admitting that historically things may have been different from what the Bible says. Others have tried to maintain some objective-historical foundation for the faith narratives of the Bible.[3] At stake in this whole debate is the question of whether there is a truly Christian method of "doing" history or science in general, or whether there is but one "objective" scientific method which can be used by all indiscriminately. The present writer believes that the Bible's authoritative claims are regulatory for all human endeavor, including the scientific enterprise. The Christian theism which the Bible teaches is the ideal basis for all scientific pursuit.[4]

This does not mean there is no common ground between those who pursue the science of history from a Christian and biblical point of view and those who do not. Nevertheless, a basic cleavage exists between those who recognize God's intervention in history and those who ignore such intervention as a meaningful and regulatory factor in constructing scientific hypotheses. The "common ground" can therefore concern only secondary matters. In the basic approach is a divergence that cannot be bridged. At issue here is method only, not personal beliefs or commitment. In many cases there may be a personal commitment that is not carried forward in the method employed in historical research.

Because of the unique claims the Bible makes for being the revelation of God to man, claims which are accepted on faith and not on the basis of "external" proof, the exegetical understanding of the Bible is a work no less theological than historical and literary. The interpretation of the Bible in the ultimate sense aims at understanding the mind of the Divine Author. Therefore, although the historical, the literary, and the theological may be distinguished, they may not be separated.[5]

Other considerations should be kept in mind as one seeks to evaluate the historical background of the book of Joshua and similar narrative

3. See R. de Vaux, "Method in the Study of Early Hebrew History," in J. P. Hyatt, ed., *The Bible in Modern Scholarship* (Nashville: 1965), p. 16; W. Eichrodt, *The Theology of the OT* I. *OTL* (Philadelphia: 1961), pp. 512–520.
4. See M. H. Woudstra, "Event and Interpretation in the OT," in S. Kistemaker, ed., *Interpreting God's Word Today* (Grand Rapids: 1970), esp. pp. 58–68; cf. also Craigie, *Deuteronomy*, pp. 73–78.
5. J. Bright, *The Authority of the OT* (Grand Rapids: 1967), p. 94, comes close to making this kind of separation when saying: ". . . one can make an exegesis of texts, but one cannot make an exegesis of the Holy Spirit's intention." But if the Spirit's intention found a perfect expression in "texts," why cannot the interpreter exegete this intention? For a similar skepticism as expressed by Bright, cf. G. E. Mendenhall, response to de Vaux, in Hyatt, *op. cit.*, p. 36, who posits that there is no academic method for understanding the mind of the Bible's Ultimate Author.

books. Because of biblical history's unique aim, one cannot expect a complete and exhaustive record of all the major events that occurred during a given period. Instead, one may expect that selections and combinations of facts have been made. Moreover, certain events may be treated at great length for thematic purposes, while others are passed over quickly and in summary form. This is true in Joshua, where the events of the spying out of the land, the crossing of the Jordan, and the capture of certain cities (Jericho and Ai) are given a significant amount of space, while other events are passed over quickly (see 10:28–43).[6]

Biblical narrative is likely to be more concerned with God's activity than with the relation between cause and effect. To be sure, the book of Joshua does highlight the significant role Joshua plays as general (e.g., 10:9, 10b; 11:7). Yet the emphasis lies chiefly on God's "giving" the land to his people.

Recent decades have witnessed a pleasing amount of attention paid to the structure of Hebrew narrative. It has been recognized increasingly that the application of source and form criticism to biblical narrative has tended to obscure the intrinsic structure of the narrative or cycle of narratives. Stylistic and rhetorical categories are given greater emphasis than has hitherto been the case. This can only help to bring out more fully the unique nature of biblical narrative, a uniqueness which earlier conservative writers such as W. H. Green and C. F. Keil and F. Delitzsch recognized in their own way.[7]

What should be kept in mind in evaluating the historical background of a book such as Joshua is that the biblical events are presented within their own interpretative context. They are not described for their own sake. To focus on these events without seeing their biblical context would do them an injustice. Such injustice is not merely experienced in the "theological" realm. Rather, the interpreted facts as they occur in the written context are the data for the historian to work with and to explain. All dualism between faith and history, and between theology and exegesis, should be avoided. The biblical text itself, in its integrity, is a prime datum of history. It must be understood *in toto*, or it will not be understood at all.

To say that biblical events are interpreted events does not mean that

---

6. For a helpful enumeration of some of the distinctive features of biblical narrative, cf. Aalders, *Oud-Testamentische Kanoniek*, pp. 161–63.

7. Examples of rhetorical criticism applied to OT narrative are Fokkelman, *Narrative Art in Genesis*; and M. Kessler, *CBQ* 32 (1970), pp. 543–554. Cf. also C. H. Giblin, "Structural Patterns in Jos 24:1–25," *CBQ* 26 (1964), pp. 50–69.

apart from this interpretation they would be of no value, or that they could have a variety of meanings, not necessarily those that the Bible attributes to them. M. Noth, for example, argues that Israel's history, like all human history, is enigmatic and capable of more than one meaning *(vieldeutig)*, as far as its outward appearance goes.[8] But this can be maintained only if one stands outside the world of authoritative scriptural thought. Scripture does not know of mute facts. Neither does it allow that facts be given more than one interpretation. The frame of reference within which Scripture places the facts is that of Christian theism. Within that frame of reference the facts are related to God, who uses them to manifest himself in them. This is not to say that the meaning of the facts can always be ascertained readily. This applies especially to the facts of "general history." But this is something different from saying that they are mute or that they are capable of more than one interpretation. Man's inability to read the facts rightly is due to the obscuring effect that sin has had on man's cognitive and rational functions.

A discussion of the historical background of the book of Joshua inevitably involves the question of how to evaluate the data taken from archaeology and the use of these data in verifying the biblical record. Well known in this connection is the protracted discussion and controversy between those who hold a rather high view of the use of archaeology (W. F. Albright, J. Bright, G. E. Wright, and others) and those who warn against overvaluing such use (Noth and others).

It cannot be denied that archaeological discoveries have yielded great results for the general appreciation of the authenticity of many of the traditions retained in the biblical narrative. Social customs, cultic practices, domestic and temple architecture, agricultural practices, modes of warfare, and many more such cultural and social facts have come to light through archaeological discovery. Significant advances have been made in the appreciation of ancient literary forms and conventions, and wholesale epics and mythological texts have been discovered. All these have made great contributions to understanding biblical literature, and may be expected to do so in the future.

Archaeology also has its limitations, however, and today's archaeologists are the first to point them out. The identification of ancient sites continues to be as vexing a problem as ever. Inscriptional evidence which establishes such identity beyond the shadow of a doubt is often rare, especially in Palestine. Even when it is present it may be read in more than one way. Thus one finds scholars divided on the question which tell rep-

8. M. Noth, *The History of Israel* (E.T. [2]1960), pp. 48–49.

resents a particular ancient city, as with Albright's identification of Tell Beit Mirsim as ancient Debir (10:38; 12:13).

A related problem concerns the exact chronological sequence of the various layers of occupation. There appears at present no doubt about the identification of ancient Samaria with modern Sebastiyeh, but controversy does center on the precise manner in which individual layers are to be linked to particular reigns of Israel's kings.[9]

A huge number of archaeological sites is known today, yet only relatively few are completely or partially excavated. Thus one is led to approach any claim made by archaeology with necessary reserve, while acknowledging the tremendous service this science has rendered in a general way for elucidating the biblical "world." For the time being our preference lies more with the "German" school than with the archaeological school.[10] The former, so it would seem, would allow greater concentration on the biblical texts, which, after all, it is the interpreter's duty to understand. This is not to say, however, that the important auxiliary services which can be rendered by archaeology should not be received gratefully.

Expressing a preference for the "German school" does not mean that one accepts their negative stance toward the veracity of the biblical traditions in Joshua. It only means that one approaches the archaeological argument with greater caution than is sometimes shown by those who defend the Bible's veracity. For example, I believe that there was such a thing as a conquest of Palestine. This differs from the position of Alt, Noth, and others, who see evidence of a more gradual interpenetration of the Israelite tribes into Canaanite settlements.[11] Yet, believing the biblical representation concerning a military conquest to be true, it is difficult to regard the archaeological evidence as having been furnished to the satisfaction of all.

9. See Kitchen, *The Bible in Its World*, p. 13.
10. These are the terms used by G. E. Mendenhall, " 'Change and Decay in All Around I See': Conquest, Covenant, and *The Tenth Generation*," *BA* 39 (1976), p. 155. Mendenhall states bluntly that the "German school" and the "biblical archeology school" "cancel each other out." In this respect he speaks of "an impasse in biblical studies for at least the past thirty years."
11. Cf. A. Alt, "Erwägungen über die Landnahme der Israeliten in Palästina," in *KS* I, pp. 126–175; and "The Settlement of the Israelites in Palestine," in *Essays on OT History and Religion* (E.T. 1967), pp. 133–169. See also M. Weippert, *The Settlement of the Israelite Tribes in Palestine*. *SBT* 21 (E.T. 1971); and S. Herrmann, *A History of Israel in OT Times* (E.T. 1975), pp. 86–111. In addition to the "conquest model" and the "interpenetration model" is also the "revolt model," as examined in N. K. Gottwald, *The Tribes of Yahweh* (Maryknoll, N.Y.: 1979), pp. 192-219. This study was not available to the author when the chief work on this commentary was being done.

This leads to a more direct discussion of some problems pertaining to the historical background of the book of Joshua. Most vexing is the approximate date of the Conquest. This is naturally related to the corresponding question of the time of the Exodus. At this point the chief focus of discussion will be upon the data pertaining to the Conquest. Since for a proper understanding of Joshua little is to be gained from a discussion of the date of the Conquest, only a brief summary of the pertinent data will suffice here.

The two divergent dates for the Conquest held by biblical scholarship today are c. 1400 BC (the "early date") and c. 1250 BC (the "late date"), with corresponding dates for the Exodus of c. 1440 BC and c. 1290 BC.[12]

OT data bearing on the question are 1 K. 6:1; Judg. 11:26 and Exod. 12:40 (showing a difference between the Masoretic Text and the LXX). When taken at face value these data point toward the early date. Those favoring the late date consider the figure 480 in 1 K. 6:1 to be based on oriental symbolism, representing twelve generations of forty years each. However, a generation would be closer to twenty-five years, so twelve generations would total 300 years. Since Solomon's building of the temple began in 961 BC, this reckoning would bring the Exodus into the mid-thirteenth century BC. One does not wish to rule out the use of symbolical numbers in the Bible, but in the approach evaluated here the matter is traced a step forward. The number twelve, deduced from the figure 480 (twelve times forty), is now applied to a more "realistic" view of a generation (twenty-five years), yielding the figure 300. The question arises as to whether such secondary use of the allegedly symbolical value of 480 in 1 K. 6:1 is warranted and justified.

Judges 11:26 would seem even more difficult for those favoring a late date. Jephthah may be placed c. 1100 BC. In his diplomatic message to the Ammonite king he would most likely have sought to be correct, or approximately so. It is perhaps significant that the extensive textual register of Noth's *History* does not refer to this text, nor does Bright.[13] Those who do cite it while favoring the late date consider the figure 300 to be due to a computation by the author of Judges, based on the approximate number of years of the Judges preceding Jephthah. Again, this is rather ingenious, but not quite convincing.

Many of the other arguments for or against a certain date for the

12. For a defense of the early date in light of recent discussion see L. Wood, "Date of the Exodus," in *New Perspectives on the OT*, J. B. Payne, ed. (Waco: 1970), pp. 66–87. See also R. K. Harrison, *Introduction to the OT*, pp. 315–325, where the late date is favored.
13. *A History of Israel* (Philadelphia: ²1972).

Conquest are taken from historical and archaeological data as far as they are known and interpreted. For quite some time it was held, on the basis of J. Garstang's excavation at Tell eş-Şultan (Jericho), that the early date was supported by evidence of the destruction of Jericho. Dame K. Kenyon, however, claims on the basis of subsequent excavations that Garstang's conclusions were wrong and that the evidence for any conquest at all at Jericho is scanty and inconclusive. This has prompted scholars to suggest that the Jericho story may have been invented. Because of the prominence of Jericho at other points in Israel's history, Israel came to believe that if it had crossed into Palestine the way it did, the city of Jericho would have been the first to be conquered.[14] For those who do not wish to follow this road of last resort nothing remains but to conclude that archaeology in the case of Jericho (and likewise Ai, if equated with et-Tell) fails to bear out the veracity of the biblical account. Its witness is silent where its eloquence would have been appreciated.

Important support for the late date is believed to come from the destruction layers caused by burning that are evident in various Palestinian cities such as Lachish, Debir, and Hazor, all dating from the thirteenth century BC. However, two things may be observed in this connection. First, archaeology has not been able to prove that the destruction of these cities was inflicted by Israel under Joshua's leadership. Other possibilities would be an invasion of the Egyptian Pharaoh Merneptah, c. 1234 BC; invasion by the "Sea Peoples," also in the 13th century; or destruction by inter-city warfare. Second, there is no evidence that Joshua burned all the cities he conquered, nor any report in the book that Lachish and Debir were destroyed by fire. Indeed, it is stated explicitly that Joshua did not burn most of the cities (11:13). This is why O. Tufnell has refused to assign the destruction of Lachish, evidenced by layers of thirteenth-century burned debris, to Joshua.[15]

Those who favor an early date frequently have appealed to the Amarna tablets and their mention of Habiru invading Canaan. The tablets consist of letters by Canaanite kinglets to their Egyptian overlords Amenhotep III and Akhenaten between c. 1400 and 1367 BC. The letters reflect a rather chaotic situation in Canaan. Their frequent reference to a group called Habiru was thought to reflect the Hebrew invasion under Joshua, but the fact that later discoveries have shown the Habiru phenomenon to

14. This is the position tentatively developed by J. L. Koole, *Verhaal en Feit in het OT*. Cahiers voor de gemeente 1 (Kampen: 1967).
15. "Lachish," in *AOTS*, p. 302; and cf. Mendenhall, *BA* 39 (1976), p. 154: ". . . there is no evidence that those Late Bronze Age destruction levels had anything at all to do with the so-called Israelite conquest."

be far more widespread than Palestine has resulted in a more cautious approach. The question is far too large to be dealt with within the scope of this introductory chapter.[16]

Another argument used in defense of the late date is N. Glueck's exploration of Transjordan showing an alleged absence of sedentary occupation between 1900 and 1300 BC. This would include the time when, using the early date, Israel would have encountered kingdoms existing in that region (cf. Num. 20:14–21; 21:21–35; 22–25). Glueck's findings have been questioned extensively by others.

In summary, one may say that the arguments for or against a certain date of the Conquest have long reached a stalemate, and little new material has come to light recently to break this deadlock.

An advantage in holding to a late date is that it enables use of the evidence of sudden destruction to counter the "German school" position regarding an alleged slow infiltration of Israel into Palestine. But what if the very appeal to the archaeological evidence is open to serious question at precisely that point? The picture that emerges from the ongoing debate is not an attractive one. In the matter of chronology archaeology has thus far proven less than an adequate guide.

What, then, of the picture of a concerted onslaught upon Canaan by Israel under Joshua's leadership? Must we surrender it in favor of a slow interpenetration of Israelite and Canaanite elements? Is the piecemeal Conquest reflected in Judg. 1 to be preferred as a more authentic representation than that of Joshua?

We believe the picture drawn by the book of Joshua to be true and reliable. Obviously, the nature of biblical narrative must be kept in mind constantly when epithets such as "true" and "reliable" are used to describe it. The yardstick of scientific historiography must not be applied injudiciously to books such as Joshua, but in the realm of reporting for the purpose of exhortation, warning, and encouragement, we believe Joshua to be a reliable record of real events.

In Joshua, some events of the Conquest were highlighted, others passed over quickly, and some probably not recorded at all. The precise length of time it took for Joshua and the Israelites to accomplish their task can only be determined by means of inference from the biblical data. Such matters were not the narrator's chief concern. The cities that Joshua con-

---

16. For a survey of the Habiru question cf. F. F. Bruce, "Tell el-Amarna," in *AOTS*, pp. 6–15; cf. also M. G. Kline, "The Ḥa-BI-ru—Kin or Foe of Israel?" *WTJ* 19 (1956/57), pp. 1–24, 170–184; 20 (1957/58), pp. 46–70. See also Gottwald, *The Tribes of Yahweh*, pp. 401-409, and *passim*. Gottwald's learned work bears the subtitle: "A Sociology of the Religion of Liberated Israel."

quered in his southern campaign (ch. 10) apparently were not occupied. Occupation was to follow later and would take more time. Again and again the book of Joshua itself indicates that work remained to be done in future years (cf. 13:1; 15:63; 16:10; 17:12, 16). Thus the picture of Judg. 1 ought not to be contrasted with that of Joshua.[17]

The above discussion has admittedly been sketchy. The magnitude of the subject when treated fully would far exceed the limits set here. Moreover, as stated above, the relative value of such discussion for understanding the real purpose of the book of Joshua is rather small. Hearing God's voice in Joshua is the interpreter's chief task. To be able to do so in a book that purports to describe certain historical events presupposes that one affirms the basic historicity of these events. Beyond that the biblical record was not concerned to enlighten us. As yet the comparative materials from extrabiblical sources appear too subject to divergent interpretations to be of much use.[18]

VI. THEOLOGY

1. Terminology and Method

The term "theology" is here retained for the purpose of uniformity with other volumes in this commentary series. The term is not entirely clear

17. Cf. K. A. Kitchen's valuable discussion *The Bible in Its World*, pp. 90–91. See also a much earlier discussion of Joshua's "credibility" in J. P. Lange, ed., *A Commentary on the Holy Scriptures* 4 (E.T. 1875; repr. 1949), pp. 14-17, a work that still has great value.

18. Although I would probably support the first of the three categories of reactions to archaeological findings condemned by J. M. Miller, I share somewhat his impatience with the way the archaeological evidence has been treated thus far; "Archaeology and the Israelite Conquest of Palestine: Some Methodological Observations," *PEQ* 109 (1977), pp. 87–93. For recent defenses of an early date of the Exodus (Conquest), cf. also B. Waltke, "Palestinian Artifactual Evidence Supporting the Early Date of the Exodus," *Bibliotheca Sacra* 129 (1972), pp. 33–47; and S. H. Horn, "What We Don't Know about Moses and the Exodus," *BAR* 3 (1977), pp. 22–31. The uncertainty encountered with respect to the chronology of the Exodus and Conquest is paralleled by a similar uncertainty with respect to the chronology of the patriarchal period, with theories varying from 2500 BC to 1200 BC (see C. Westermann's comprehensive survey in *Genesis* II, fasc. 1–2. BK I (Neukirchen: 1977), pp. 1–90, with literature pp. 91–115; cf. also Kitchen's discussion in *The Bible in Its World*, pp. 56–74). As one ponders these perplexing facts, it is well to keep in mind N. M. Sarna's words: ". . . there is no field of human endeavor more strewn with the debris of discarded theories than that of Biblical scholarship" (*BAR* 4 [1978], p. 52).

and is understood variously by those who use it. A word of clarification would therefore appear to be in order.

In our opinion, biblical exegesis consists of the following three major components: the grammatical and literary, the historical, and the theological. Since the object of biblical exegesis is a body of literature which purports to be God's very word to mankind, it is evident that the theological element is not one that follows upon exegesis but, rather, is an integral element of exegesis. It should be the biblical interpreter's aim to understand the literature at hand, with the objective of comprehending the mind of the Spirit who speaks in and through the Scriptures. In reading and interpreting, the biblical student seeks to acquire the knowledge of God which the literature imparts to the reader who is guided by the Spirit. Thus understood, the word "theology" as a designation of what a given book of the Bible comprises is perfectly suitable.

There are also other uses, however, to which this term is put. The opinion is widespread that "theology," when used of the message of a biblical book, is really no more than a summary of the "theological intention" of the book's secondary author.[1] With regard to Joshua, this is often understood to be the theological intention of the "deuteronomistic school." The writer, or writers, are said to have shaped the material to fit the particular theology they held. This suggests actually that the biblical theologian today is called upon to theologize, not upon the Word and revelation of God, but upon some individual's theology. The question of inspiration and revelation is left out of consideration. The result is a theology of the second degree which can never be dignified by the term "theology." Theological reflection must concern that which God says about himself. When it concerns that which someone else has already expressed by way of human reflection about God, it ceases to be theological reflection. At best it is a form of history of ancient doctrine.

The above is not meant to deny that biblical books such as Joshua offer a viewpoint which is as much man's as the Spirit's. Calling this position a form of theology might be justified, although the term is not particularly felicitous. Whatever theological viewpoint the author (or authors) of a biblical book, this viewpoint ceased to be merely such when used by the Spirit to convey God's will to man. When the "theological intention" of the author is taken up into the process of inspiration and revelation, it is thereby transformed into the expression of God's will. Only thus can it become the object of truly theological speculation.

1. Cf. J. Bright, *The Authority of the OT*, p. 244, where the term is so used. This is but one example of many.

Another related use of the word "theology," as commonly understood, calls for comment. All too often one gets the impression that in using the word "theology" interpreters focus on the "faith" of Israel, on its "religion." When this is done, the interpreter is again not truly engaging in his own theology, but is offering the reader a type of phenomenology of religion, a history of the religious experience of ancient Israel. Such an approach has its merits and a definite right to exist. But it should not be called "theology." Moreover, when Israel's faith becomes the object of analysis and study, an attempt should be made to recognize, at every point in the analysis, the factor of divine revelation which lay behind that faith and made it what it was. This is not to deny that much in the OT resembles phenomena found in the ancient Near Eastern world, knowledge of which is enhanced through ever-widening discoveries. Israel's faith and religion developed and took shape within that broader context. Nevertheless, in the course of its religious history Israel received a revelation from God that was uniquely its own (Ps. 147:20; 79:6). To say this is not to engage in a narrow exclusivism as is sometimes alleged. It is simply accepting the Bible's own testimony and making it the foundation of one's scientific endeavor.

A question which has been widely discussed concerns the proper method and role of biblical theology as distinct from other disciplines, e.g., systematic theology, history, and the phenomenology of religion. The scope of this introduction does not permit an extensive analysis and resumé of this discussion.[2]

As stated above, we hold biblical theology to be an outflow of, and integral to, the exegetical process comprehensively understood. This does not mean that we thereby assign to biblical theology a normative role. No theology, being the product of human speculation and reflection, is normative. In other words, one need not accept the dilemma posed by K. Stendahl: descriptive or normative-systematic.[3] In a certain way biblical

---

2. Among the earlier literature, cf. C. T. Craig, "Biblical Theology and the Rise of Historicism," *JBL* 62 (1943), pp. 281–294; C. Gamble, Jr., "The Literature of Biblical Theology: A Bibliographical Study," *Interpretation* 7 (1953), pp. 466–480. See also K. Stendahl, "Method in the Study of Biblical Theology," in Hyatt, *The Bible in Modern Scholarship*, pp. 196–209, with a response by A. Dulles, pp. 210–16. Many of these studies suffer from a defective view of the correlation between faith and history, and of the role of revelation in the historical process. While attempting to accommodate a subjective element in biblical theology, they also hold to the would-be objectivity of a scientific method equally acceptable to believers and nonbelievers. For a recent appraisal of the trends in biblical theology see also W. Kaiser, *Toward an OT Theology* (Grand Rapids: 1978), *passim*.
3. *Op. cit.*, p. 199.

theology is descriptive. It seeks to describe, with due regard to the historical progress of revelation and redemption, the contents of God's self-revelation in a given book of the Bible or in the Bible as a whole. This is not to say that biblical theology consists in a "study of the actual theology and theologies to be found in the Bible," as Stendahl maintains.[4] The Bible, so we believe, does not contain a theology or theologies. One can only derive a theology from the Bible by reflecting in faith on its revelation-contents. Stendahl is right when warning against investing biblical theology with a normative function. But he is wrong in allowing systematic theology to have that normative function. No theology should ever be granted such a function. Neither would the distinction between "what it meant" (biblical theology) and "what it means" (normative-systematic theology) appear to be particularly helpful. The total exegetical process, including all of its three components mentioned above, aims at the total understanding of the literature studied, and it does so with a view to the present and the future no less than to the past. The seventeenth-century exegetes did not consider their task finished until they had explored the full implications of their text for doctrinal and moral purposes. Today we do well to draw the line somewhat more narrowly. To be sure, the preacher's exegesis is not really done until he mounts the pulpit and delivers God's Word to God's people at a certain juncture in time. Nevertheless, the task of an exegetical commentary such as this is not to provide ready-made sermonic material. This is not to say, however, that exegesis must be content only with what "it meant." An attempt should be made to set forth something of the abiding teachings of a book such as Joshua. Keeping in mind Scripture's Primary Author, one may be confident that his intentions were fully realized when he chose to express them in a Scripture whose every page is time-bound. This allows ample scope for studying the intentions of the secondary authors. Indeed, no exegesis would be responsible without due regard for their intentions. Nevertheless, the interpreter's goal must be to ascertain what the Spirit was saying through the words of these time-bound utterances.

The task of the theologian-exegete is a humble yet a significant one. It begins with listening; it continues and ends with listening. In seeking to understand the text of Holy Scripture, the interpreter may be aided by the many auxiliary disciplines that have contributed to the understanding of the Bible: anthropology, sociology, psychology, history of religions, botany, zoology, geography, and more. Yet all of them must be made subordinate to the interpreter's primary task, to understand the sacred text.

4. *Idem.*

That text, though conditioned by history at every step of its development, claims to be the authoritative Word for all times and circumstances. There are no normative and non-normative parts to Scripture. Properly understood, it is pervasively normative. This is true, even though there is a progress from the less to the more, from promise to fulfilment, from the "shadows" to the reality. While certain practices, such as the wholesale extermination of enemy populations by the *ḥerem*, have ceased to be normative, the revelation contained in the written record regarding such practices does not cease to be normative. It is not the interpreter's task to analyze customs, religious attitudes, or psychological states of mind. Rather, it is to understand the scriptural record within which these are given their interpretative context. It is that record which constitutes the revelation that God has given his people, then and now.

Thus viewed, the auxiliary sciences which have contributed so much to understanding Scripture may receive their due, but they will not tyrannize biblical studies by foisting upon them a methodology alien to the very object the biblical interpreter investigates. One must recognize the value of historical science, but to attempt to assign to historical science a restricted role as do some scholars, without breaking with that science's rationalistic tenets, is an illusory undertaking. The historical method, as commonly understood, cannot be satisfied with a limited role. It must dictate to all the sciences, including theology and the study of revealed religion.

The current state of OT studies does not foster a high opinion of what present-day methodology has accomplished in terms of a usable and generally accepted understanding of biblical truth. Biblical theologians differ sharply as to method and approach. In the realm of historical and archaeological studies the picture is no more promising.[5] In this light, would it not be wise to raise with renewed insistence the question of theological and exegetical method? H.-J. Kraus concludes his monumental work on the history of OT historical-critical studies with reference to the "dark horizon" with respect to OT proclamation and investigation. These

5. Pessimistic opinions abound as to the state of affairs in OT science. J. Bright, "Modern Study of OT Literature," in G. E. Wright, ed., *The Bible and the Ancient Near East* (1961; repr. Winona Lake: 1979), pp. 13–14, states that the whole field of biblical criticism is "in a state of flux." It is his impression that "it is moving in several mutually canceling directions at once. Even upon major points there is often little unanimity to be observed"; see also G. E. Mendenhall, "Biblical History in Transition," *idem*, p. 33; cf. M. Kessler, *CBQ* 32 (1970), p. 543, who speaks of a "crisis" in OT studies.

words were first written in 1956,[6] but have circumstances improved since that time?

We must also raise in conclusion the question of the relation between the Old and New Testaments, and the bearing of that relation on our theologico-exegetical method. Are there, as J. Bright alleges, "pre-Christian" or even "sub-Christian" sentiments in the book of Joshua?[7]

One needs first a proper understanding of what makes a sentiment Christian. The Church has always held that the entire Bible, both Old and New Testament, was God's Word. Some have denied it, as did Marcion and A. von Harnack. Nevertheless, on the basis of the Bible's own testimony we would maintain that the mainline understanding of the Church was indeed correct. The Church did not "take over" a "Jewish canon" as is sometimes alleged. Instead, the Church saw itself delineated in, and its Savior set forth by, the OT Scriptures. The fact that in doing so it sometimes used unjustifiable methods of exegesis should not blind us to the other fact that within the authoritative pages of the NT itself the essential link with the OT is already laid. The early Church did not "take over" the OT. Instead, there was a growing recognition that the historical roots of what the Church experienced lay back there in the pages of the OT. The alleged "Jewishness" of the OT canon is subject to severe misunderstanding. Judaism and Jewishness, at least today, mean something far more than, and far different from, a believing acceptance of the OT Scriptures. Modern Jews will freely admit that the final arbiter of their faith and practice is the Jewish writings *subsequent* to the conclusion of the OT canon. Moreover, the very words "Old Testament" suggest the existence of a New Testament. If one rejects the existence of the latter, one does not really "have" the former. The OT is not exclusively a Jewish book. Christianity did not spring from the "mother-religion" of Judaism. Thoughtful Jews, especially those of orthodox persuasion, eschew the term "Judaeo-Christian," so widely used today. They sense rightly that such a compound does injustice to the distinctiveness of either component, for it is exactly the "Christ" of the second part that is denied by those who represent the first part.

Therefore, to call a biblical sentiment "pre-Christian" injects into the discussion an element that is less than helpful. To be sure, strictly speaking the Christian phase of revelation commences with the coming of Christ and the establishment of the NT Church. It is also true that Chris-

---

6. *Geschichte der Historisch-Kritischen Erforschung des ATs* (Neukirchen: 1956), p. 444.
7. *The Authority of the OT*, p. 245.

31

tians should avoid reading back into the OT their full-fledged religious consciousness, nurtured as it is by the total revelation of God and by the Church's reflection throughout the ages. Yet the term "pre-Christian" as a characterization of the message of Joshua or of any part of it is imprecise. The Church acted correctly in accepting the entire canon as God's revelation for all times. The entire canon is now the criterion of what is and is not Christian. God's revelation in Christ and the subsequent illumination of that event in the epistles and gospels do constitute the culmination of all that God said and did. Nevertheless, books such as Joshua, and all of their parts, when properly understood, are also part of the Christian message.

Even greater strictures should be placed on the use of the term "sub-Christian" as a fitting description of the book of Joshua. This term implies the notion of a canon within the canon. But to call parts of Joshua sub-Christian also involves hermeneutical questions. What is the biblical interpreter expected to do in reading Joshua as ancient and inspired literature? He is to listen to the inspired record and to elicit the meaning which it contains. Within this record the events of the past, including that of the Conquest and the slaughter of the Canaanites, have received their interpretative context. This record is neither pre-Christian nor sub-Christian, but God's Word for the ages.

2. Substance

An air of joyful optimism pervades the book of Joshua. Its keynote is the fulfilment of the promise made to the forefathers regarding the possession of the land of Canaan. From the opening of the book, which records God's words regarding the impending crossing of the Jordan, to its end, with the burial of various persons in the soil of the longed-for promised land, sustained emphasis is given the accomplishment of God's "words." One of the most central passages in this regard is 21:43–45; cf. also 11:23.

Joshua has been compared by several commentators with the book of Acts. One should use due caution in such comparison. The earlier and the later in God's dealings with his people should be recognized. No mere equation between the two should be attempted. Yet an unmistakable similarity can be seen. Joshua depicts the Conquest of the land promised to the fathers, whereas Acts shows the Church moving forward in conquest of the then known world. Both books pause from time to time to sum up what has already been accomplished (cf. Acts 6:7; 9:31; 12:24).

Earlier in this Introduction attention has been called to certain features of the book which may be helpful in finding the theological significance of what the author of Joshua[8] means to say to us (see "Unity of Composition" and "Occasion"). These features need not be enumerated again.

While the predominant note of the book is God's faithfulness to promises made long ago, another emphasis is made also. It concerns the "not yet" of the complete fulfilment of these promises. The author's reminders that much remains to be done appear side-by-side with the theme of the fulfilment of God's promises. The allotment section, chs. 13–19, clearly speaks of land not yet possessed (see 13:1–7). Within this section are recurring notes concerning the failure of certain tribes to possess a part of their allotment (cf. 15:63; 17:12, etc.). This gives the book a certain open-endedness. It reaches toward the future and suggests to the readers the feeling that their task is not yet done.

It would be unfortunate, however, if for hortatory and homiletic purposes only Joshua's emphasis on incompletion should receive attention, for though by no means negligible, it is not the predominant emphasis. In the present age of insecurity and fear, of staggering world-wide problems and challenges, the primary need is to stress the truth of the everlasting faithfulness of God as set forth in Joshua. This was, so we believe, the primary purpose of the book. Israel was yet to go through many perilous times. Enemy armies would sweep through the land. Apostasy would often be rife. Yet to come would be devastation, deportation, and captivity. In those times the faithful needed to know the joyful word of confidence and of hope, that God remains loyal to the word once spoken.

The explicitly hortatory parts of the book are chiefly found at its end (chs. 23–24), although chs. 1 and 18 also contain some exhortation. Covenant obedience will be richly rewarded. Covenant disobedience will bring the punishment which God has laid down in the curses of the covenant (8:34; 23:12–13, 16). The danger of apostasy is therefore clearly delineated. Yet the book ends on a very affirmative note in stating that Israel served the Lord all the days of Joshua and of the elders who outlived Joshua (24:31). This comment by the author is all the more remarkable in light of his earlier report of Joshua's stern words to Israel: "You cannot serve the Lord, for he is a holy God; he is a jealous God" (v. 19). In other words, the author is concerned to end on an optimistic note. Israel, he says, was doing the seemingly impossible. It served the very God of whom

---

8. We refer to the "author of Joshua" in order to distinguish between him (them) and the person of Joshua, and also to focus on the interpreter's main task, that of reading a body of literature, rather than interpreting events or the *ipsissima verba* of Joshua or God.

Joshua had said in absolute terms that this could not be done. Any interpreter who overlooks this positive statement does a basic injustice to the author's intention. Of course, the author's comment does contain a hidden note of future trouble. But this is not Judges, where the same statement occurs in quite a different context (Judg. 2:7). Each book must be permitted to make its own contribution to the ongoing revelation of God.

A major component of the book, and one with rich theological implications, is the focus on the land. Israel is to cross over to possess the land (1:2). Lengthy chapters are devoted to the distribution of the land (13:8–19:48). The promise of the land had been a fixed element in all the promises to the patriarchs. It is evident, therefore, that the author means to emphasize the fulfilment of that covenant promise.

The land is elsewhere often called "the Lord's inheritance" (RSV "heritage"; Exod. 15:17; 1 Sam. 26:19; Jer. 2:7; 16:18; 50:11). The author of Joshua calls it the Lord's "possession" (22:19), a word closely akin to that of "inheritance." Fundamental for the understanding of the role the land played in Israel's religious life is the statement made in Lev. 25:23: "The land is mine; and you are strangers and sojourners with me." The terms "inheritance" and "stranger" have been taken up into NT vocabulary (1 Pet. 1:4; Heb. 11:13; Rom. 8:17; cf. 1 Pet. 2:11). This NT use is not due to a spiritualization process. On the contrary, the OT idea itself, linked to the very heart of the covenant promise, is already spiritual to the core. The OT believer grasped the true meaning of this in his most exalted moments: cf. Ps. 16:5–6, where other terms also pertaining to the division of the land are used to express the height of covenant fellowship between believer and God.[9]

Due care should be taken not to carry over the promise of the land into the modern era, as if somehow today the possession of the land is still part of what the people of the ancient covenant may claim. In the OT land possession and covenant blessing go hand in hand. But this possession of the land may be forfeited, as the author of Joshua indicates (23:16). Although the Latter Prophets contain many promises concerning a return to the land after the period of punishment, the NT, while holding out some promise of ultimate restoration to the people of the ancient covenant (Rom. 11:25–26), does not combine this promise with a repossession of the land of the fathers.

9. In light of the close connection between covenant promise ("I will be their God and they will be my people") and land possession, there is no need to call Ps. 16 a "totally spiritualized" view of the division of the land. Land possession itself was already "spiritual" to the core; cf. G. von Rad, *OT Theology* I, p. 300, for the other view.

As suggested elsewhere in this Introduction, a possible line may be drawn between the land of Canaan, possessed by Israel, and the whole earth, possessed by the people of God in the New Dispensation (compare Ps. 37:11 with Matt. 5:5). There is an eschatological side to the notion of "inheritance" (cf. Rev. 21:7). These lines may be inferred naturally from the OT materials and brought forward into the NT without forcing the OT materials.

Once the essentially spiritual dimension of the possession of Canaan is seen clearly, the symbolico-typical significance of the promised land can be more easily grasped. In Christian hymnody and devotional literature Canaan has long typified the rest of heavenly glory. The lines of the hymn

> When I tread the verge of Jordan,
>   Bid my anxious fears subside;
> Death of death, and hell's destruction,
>   Land me safe on Canaan's side

express this sentiment beautifully. In modern Liberation theology Canaan has assumed the meaning that at some particular time all wrongs will be righted and freedom will be granted to the oppressed of the earth.

Traditional typology should be used with due caution. The early Christian church went to extremes in its typological use of the OT. Yet this excess should not prevent the Church from using typology where Scripture permits or suggests it. The book of Hebrews draws a parallel between Joshua and Jesus, and between that which Joshua accomplished and that which Jesus has accomplished (Heb. 4:8). The common context is that of "rest," a term which is very significant theologically (see 1:13 and commentary; cf. Deut. 12:9–10; 25:19; 2 Sam. 7:1). The very OT materials, when properly understood, lend themselves to the extended use that the NT makes of them. Such typology rests squarely in the symbolical meaning which the land already possessed for the ancient Israelites. Only when typology is undergirded by symbolism can one draw the lines forward in typological fashion. This is not to say that the first recipients of this revelation understood the full dimension of meaning; but that is not the sole consideration in establishing the typological meaning of a certain event, person, or cultic practice. With proper caution and restraint, some typological use may be made of the revelation the author imparts in Joshua, provided that this is not the one and only use to which this revelation is put for the present.[10] The typological meaning of the OT must not be

10. For a difference between "heaven typology" and "eternal life typology" in regard to Jordan and Canaan, see C. J. Goslinga, *Het Boek Jozua*, p. 31. Goslinga disagrees with S. G. de Graaf, *Verbondsgeschiedenis* I [1952], p. 277; E.T. *Prom-*

overrated. It is only one of the several ways in which the link between the two Testaments can be established.[11]

3. Some Details

a. God and his revelation

The God whom the author of Joshua introduces is like the God of the rest of the OT. His existence is assumed. He communicates his will to Joshua, as he did earlier to Moses (1:1, 7). Sometimes he makes his revelation known by means of the lot (7:14). He also sends his heavenly emissary to impress upon Joshua his nearness to help (5:13–15).

God gives the land to Israel, but this does not preclude the activity of Israel in conquering the land (1:3; 10:7–9). God's providence does not interfere with man's freedom to act as a moral agent. He hardens the heart of the Canaanites that he may destroy them (11:20), but the author clearly notes that some of the Canaanite population made peace with Israel (v. 19).[12]

God wants Rahab and all her house spared from the destruction of Jericho, to reward her for her kindness toward Israel (6:17), and he punishes Achan and his house for their trespass against the devoted things (ch. 7).

God performs miracles (lit. "things to be wondered at"; 3:5) and controls the forces of nature to bring about victory for Israel (10:12–14). He is faithful to the word he speaks (11:23; 21:43–45), and makes his people enter into the promised "rest." He demands loyalty to himself, and love and fear, which must be expressed by keeping his commandments and "cleaving" to him (22:5; 24:14).

To the obedient and covenant-keeping God promises blessing and continued help in completely occupying the promised land (23:5); to the disobedient he will send destruction (vv. 12, 16). His hand has been in all of previous redemptive history (24:3). This history must not be viewed in human-centered fashion, but from God's perspective. It is this perspective,

---

ise and Deliverance I [1977], p. 397), who holds that the crossing into Canaan does not typify entering into heaven but entering into eternal life with Christ. De Graaf's view is more this-worldly. Properly understood, it could be used to support a wholesome Liberation theology, i.e., one in which the vertical dimension is not lacking.

11. For a helpful discussion of the relation between the Testaments cf. P. A. Verhoef, "The Relationship between the Old and the New Testaments," in J. B. Payne, ed., *New Perspectives on the OT*, pp. 280–303.

12. For other views of the reason for the punishment of Canaan, cf. Gen. 15:16; Lev. 18:24–25.

rather than that of human "example," that prompts Israel to express its readiness to be loyal to the Lord (v. 17).

While primarily the God of Israel (9:18), he is also the Lord of all the earth (3:11); he is so recognized by a woman who does not as yet belong to the covenant nation (2:11). He is a holy and jealous God (24:19). The service of such a deity, when viewed in absolute terms, is impossible. Yet he is the God who under the emblem of his ark of the covenant marches ahead of his people to the brink of Jordan (3:3, 14–16).[13] And in spite of his holiness and jealousy, Israel does serve him (24:31).

b. Cultus

The book of Joshua shows regard for the cultic ceremony of circumcision (5:2–9) by recording the mass circumcision as Joshua's very first act after the crossing. This leads to the celebration of the Passover, the most solemn of Israel's cultic celebrations (vv. 10–12). The author is also much concerned with the proper mode of worship by reporting extensively the altar controversy between the west Jordanian and the east Jordanian tribes (cf. 22:10–34). The cultic ceremony on Mount Ebal and Mount Gerizim (8:30–35) involves building an altar and bringing sacrifices. The casting of the lots for the division of the land takes place at Shiloh, where the tent of meeting had been set up (18:1, 6). Not only Joshua but also Eleazar the priest are said to have had a part in this distribution of the land (19:51).

The cultus, with all that it stood for, had important theological and typological implications. These are not developed by the author of Joshua, but one may assume that he was aware of them to the extent possible for OT believers. The present reader of the inspired account may feel free to draw the necessary implications from this emphasis on the cultus, within the limits of proper restraint.[14]

c. Israel and the nations

Many have recoiled at the severity which was shown to the native population of Canaan by Joshua and the Israelites. Some would rate the book

13. The author's heavy emphasis on the ark shows the significance he attaches to it. In view of the close association of ark and Yahweh (e.g., Num. 10:35–36), one may call the ark one of the Lord's self-manifestations. A typological meaning of the ark (ark = Christ) would appear to be legitimate. See also M. H. Woudstra, *The Ark of the Covenant From Conquest to Kingship* (Philadelphia: 1965), *passim*.
14. There is a need to study the cultus more intensively than has sometimes been done, especially by Protestants. Apart from any typological meaning, the cultus is a living, redemptive-historical datum in the Scriptures, opening helpful eschatological vistas. Cf. Woudstra, "The Tabernacle in Biblical-Theological Perspective," in Payne, ed., *New Perspectives on the OT*, pp. 88–103.

of Joshua quite low in the biblical canon, or would rather not include it at all.[15]

The author makes clear that the extermination of the Canaanites by Joshua and the Israelites was at the Lord's behest (cf. 6:2; 8:1–2; 10:8, 40, 42). At the same time, while stressing the sovereign design expressed in the hardening of the Canaanites' hearts (11:20), he also points out the resolve of the Canaanites to destroy the invading Israelites (9:1–2; 11:1–5). He even highlights this aspect of human responsibility by using it as part of his "frame" around the account of the Conquest (see "Unity of Composition"). This emphasis is in keeping with other OT passages (Gen. 15:16b; Lev. 18:24–25; Deut. 9:1–6; 12:29–30). Apparently, the sins of the Canaanites were such as to demand exemplary punishment. Instead of using the forces of nature, as he did with the destruction of Sodom and Gomorrah, God used the sword of the Israelites to accomplish his punitive purpose. The iniquity of the Amorites now being "full" (Gen. 15:16), God ceased to be long-suffering with respect to them.

God's promise to Abraham that in him all the families of the earth would be blessed (or would "bless themselves") must be seen in the proper context. It is preceded by the words: "I will bless them that bless you and curse them that curse you" (Gen. 12:3). Canaan, by its frantic preparations for war against Israel, is clearly shown to belong to those who "cursed" Abraham and his offspring. This same line of thought runs through the prophecies against the nations, found in many of the Latter Prophets, some of which are devoted exclusively to a prophecy of judgment against a given nation (cf. Nahum and Obadiah). Such prophecy cannot be explained away as an utterance of reprehensible nationalism, as do some commentators. That God is "a consuming fire" is a truth taught equally in both the NT and the OT (see further the commentary on 23:1 concerning Israel's "enemies"). Both lines, Israel as a blessing for all the nations and the enemy relationship between Israel and the nations, ought to be recognized as equally valid. The one cannot be subordinated to the other without doing injustice to the full message of the Bible.

d. Joshua's view of sin

Sin is viewed from its objective side. The sin of Achan involves the whole community of Israel (7:1). This agrees with other "objective" treatments of sin (Gen. 20:3; 26:10; Deut. 21:1–9; Exod. 21:12–14; sinning in "ignorance," Lev. 5:1–6; etc.). It shows the power of sin as a force with

15. This attitude stems from a failure to understand the practice of the *ḥerem*, the wholesale curse upon the land, its people, and possessions (see commentary on 6:17).

which to be reckoned, but does not as such militate against regarding sin as proceeding from personal motivation (cf. 7:21).[16]

Sin is viewed as having a communal dimension (7:15). It is tantamount to committing "folly in Israel" (cf. also Gen. 34:7; Judg. 19:23; 20:6, 10; Jer. 29:23). This is similarly recognized in Israel's laws (Deut. 22:21). But the OT also knows of the need not to put the son to death for the iniquity that his father has committed, or vice versa (Deut. 24:16; Ezek. 18:20). When the corporate element involved in sin becomes a reason for self-excuse (cf. Jer. 31:30; Ezek. 18), then the other side of the truth concerning individual responsibility must be highlighted. The NT teaches both the communal and the individual aspect of sin.

VII. TEXT

The Hebrew text of Joshua as represented in the Masoretic tradition is generally in good condition and emendations are seldom called for. This commentary is based on the MT, with only occasional reference to the ancient versions (LXX, Vulgate, and Syriac Peshitta).

Scholarly opinion regarding the value of the LXX tradition as compared with the Masoretic tradition is divided. Some consider the LXX to be superior (J. Wellhausen,[1] C. Steuernagel,[2] and S. Holmes),[3] while others believe the LXX to be inferior (J. Holzinger[4] and G. A. Smith[5]).

H. Orlinsky concludes on the basis of his study of "a dozen or so

16. W. Eichrodt, *The Theology of the OT* II. *OTL* (Philadelphia: 1967), p. 240, points out that "the far-reaching clan responsibility found among the Hittites is unknown in Israel."

1. Cf. J. Wellhausen, *Die Composition des Hexateuchs und der historischen Bücher des AT* (Berlin: ³1899), pp. 116–134, cited in H. Orlinsky, "The Hebrew *Vorlage* of the Septuagint of the Book of Joshua," *VTS* 17 (1969), pp. 187–195.

2. Cf. C. Steuernagel, *Das Buch Josua*. Hand Kommentar zum AT (Göttingen: ²1923), p. 204.

3. Cf. S. Holmes, *Joshua: The Hebrew and Greek Texts* (Cambridge: 1914). Orlinsky, *op. cit.*, p. 190, calls this an "unusually fine study" which has suffered neglect all these years.

4. Cf. H. Holzinger, *Das Buch Josua*. Kurzer Hand-Commentar zum AT (1901), pp. xiv–xv: "Es geht daher nicht an, LXX ohne Weiteres den Vorzug vor MT zu geben." Whether correction of the MT by means of the LXX must be undertaken can only be settled on a case-by-case basis. The danger of subjectivity must be the inevitable risk.

5. Cf. G. A. Smith, "Joshua," in J. Hastings, ed., *A Dictionary of the Bible* II (New York: 1906), pp. 779–788, cited in Orlinsky, *op. cit.*

words and phrases" in Joshua that the LXX translator was not guilty of omission but that the Hebrew *Vorlage* lacked the word or phrase in question.[6] This applies, for example, to the phrase, "Moses the servant of the Lord," which occurs seventeen times in the Hebrew text and is lacking four times in the LXX. Orlinsky concludes that "the fidelity of the translator to his Hebrew text can be questioned only on the basis of other cogent arguments to the contrary."[7] Although thinking at the beginning of his study that a completely fresh investigation of the LXX of Joshua in relation to the preserved Hebrew text would be necessary, Orlinsky concludes that this would not be the case after all.[8]

The discussion concerning the role of the LXX for textual emendation probably will continue for a long time. The discoveries of the Dead Sea Scrolls have swung the pendulum in favor of a higher regard for the LXX as representing an independent Hebrew tradition next to that found in the MT, but this does not mean that therefore the LXX tradition must generally be preferred. Holzinger continues to be correct in stating that alteration of the MT in terms of the LXX can only be undertaken on a case-by-case basis. From time to time this commentary refers to the LXX and its merits are evaluated briefly.

In general, it may be said that the Codex Vaticanus of the LXX represents an independent textual tradition from that of the MT.[9] The Lucianic recension, on the other hand, appears to have been corrected by reference to Palestinian Hebrew sources. Among the discoveries at Qumran are two manuscripts of the Vaticanus. These have not been used in this work, since no adequate study of them has as yet been made.[10]

VIII. CANONICITY

The canonicity of a biblical book is a datum that follows from its divine inspiration. Canonicity is not dependent on external proof of a book's veracity, or on the dictum of the Church. The Church can only recognize as canonical that which is inherently canonical. A biblical book presents itself as a sufficient and authoritative "rule for faith and practice," and

6. *Op. cit.*, p. 193.
7. *Op. cit.*, p. 194.
8. *Op. cit.*, p. 195.
9. Cf. R. K. Harrison, *Introduction to the OT*, p. 678.
10. Cf. J. A. Soggin, *Joshua*, p. 19.

consequently the believing community accepts it as such. In doing so it is guided by the Spirit.[1]

This does not mean that one cannot distinguish between canonicity (a datum) and canonization (a historical phenomenon involving human recognition and acceptance).

Jewish tradition recognized Joshua as the first book of the Former Prophets. Joshua was not counted with the books of the Pentateuch. Among the Samaritans only the Pentateuch was accepted. These two facts provide a convincing argument against the critical position of an alleged Hexateuch.[2]

The Christian Church accepted Joshua as part of the Word of God, together with the other books of the OT. As pointed out above, this was not the "taking over" of a "Jewish canon." Instead, it was the inevitable recognition that the God who had revealed himself in Christ had spoken beforehand through the prophets (Heb. 1:1). This recognition took place during a gradual process of growth, and it was guided by the Spirit for as long as the NT came to be written.[3]

It would be tempting at this point to engage in a short survey of how the book of Joshua, accepted as canonical by the Church, actually fared in interpretation and homiletic use. To give formal recognition to a biblical book's canonical status is one thing, but to understand and use it truly as a rule for faith and practice is quite another. However, the scope of this Introduction does not permit such an examination. Suffice it to say that Joshua has had its critics, and continues to have them until the present time. J. G. Eichhorn, writing in the period of rampant rationalism, called Joshua an "impious" book,[4] and J. Bright reports that "now and then one hears the wish expressed that [Joshua] was not in the Bible at all."[5]

1. An appreciated aspect of some recent OT commentaries (e.g., B. S. Childs, *Exodus. OTL* [Philadelphia: 1974]) is the fact that the authors take as their point of departure the "canonical shape" of the book. In probing further, however, one discovers that this term means no more than to call attention to the book in "its final shape," that in which synagogue and church "accepted" it. In other words, the emphasis lies on the empirical aspect rather than that of self-authentication. It is the latter, not the former, which makes a book canonical.
2. For a refutation of the idea of Hexateuch, cf. E. J. Young, *Introduction to the OT*, pp. 157–58.
3. For the writer's opinion concerning the canonicity of the OT, cf. "The Continued Recognition of the OT as Part of the Christian Canon" (inaugural address, Grand Rapids: 1963).
4. Cited in J. P. Lange, ed., *A Commentary on the Holy Scriptures* 4, p. 14. Lange's work is excellent as a source of the earlier critical study of Joshua.
5. *The Authority of the OT*, p. 243.

At appropriate points in both Introduction and Commentary we have addressed ourselves to the difficulties that people have had with this book. Joshua records some of the most astounding miracles God ever performed on behalf of his people. Here also one reads of the divine command to slaughter the Canaanite population, a people whose heart had been "hardened" by God, but also a people who did their utmost to thwart the onward march of God's people into the land of promise. Part of the problem interpreters have had with this book derives from the insoluble question of how to square the sovereignty of God with the teaching concerning human freedom and responsibility. Both concepts are taught clearly in the book of Joshua.

Hence the argument for canonicity in its more comprehensive sense rests on the reader's willingness to come to terms with the miraculous as well as with the question of the divine will working itself out in human history. Purely rational arguments will not suffice. The old adage *"fides quaerit intellectum"* should be kept in mind. This is not to say that faith means the sacrifice of the intellect. Rather, without faith the intellect is subject to the results of sin, and even with faith the intellect knows and sees only in part.

IX. ANALYSIS OF CONTENTS

The following extensive outline will serve to acquaint the reader with the contents of the book.

I. The Promised Land Conquered (1:1–12:24)
   A. Introduction and Main Themes (1:1–18)
       1. Exhortation and Encouragement (1:1–9)
       2. All Israel to Participate in the Conquest (1:10–18)
   B. Spies Sent to Jericho; Canaan Dismayed at the Power of Israel's God (2:1–24)
   C. Crossing into the Promised Land: Remembering God's Acts (3:1–4:24)
       1. The Crossing (3:1–17)
       2. The Memorial Stones (4:1–24)
   D. Covenant Sign and Covenant Meal (5:1–12)
   E. The Captain of the Lord's Army (5:13–15)
   F. Jericho Taken and Cursed; Rahab Spared (6:1–27)
   G. Covenant Disobedience, Defeat, and Punishment (7:1–26)
   H. Ai Conquered and Burned (8:1–29)
   I. Blessings and Curses Proclaimed in Canaan (8:30–35)

X. SELECT BIBLIOGRAPHY

To present here an exhaustive bibliography would require an independent publication of considerable size. It is hoped that what is offered will be somewhat representative of the various viewpoints encountered in a study of the book of Joshua.

G. C. Aalders, "Jozua," in F. W. Grosheide and E. P. van Itterzon, eds., *Christelijke Encyclopaedie* IV (Kampen: ²1959), pp. 116–19.
Idem, Oud-Testamentische Kanoniek (Kampen: 1952).
F.-M. Abel, *Le Livre de Josué*. La Sainte Bible (Jerusalem: ²1958).
Y. Aharoni, "Book of Joshua," in C. Roth, ed., *Encyclopaedia Judaica* 10 (Jerusalem: 1971), pp. 271–77.
Idem, The Land of the Bible (Philadelphia: 1967).
Idem, "The Negeb of Judah," *IEJ* 8 (1958), pp. 26–38.

Idem, "The Province List of Judah," *VT* 9 (1959), pp. 225–246.

W. F. Albright, *From the Stone Age to Christianity* (Garden City: ²1957).

Idem, "The List of Levitic Cities," in *Louis Ginzberg Jubilee Volume* I (New York: 1945), pp. 49–73.

Idem, "The Israelite Conquest of Canaan in the Light of Archaeology," *BASOR* 74 (1939), pp. 11–23.

Idem, "The Role of the Canaanites in the History of Civilization," in G. E. Wright, ed., *The Bible and the Ancient Near East* (1961; repr. Winona Lake: 1979), pp. 328–362.

B. J. Alfrink, *Josué*, 1952.

A. Alt, "Josua," in *KS* I (Munich: 1959), pp. 176–192.

Idem, "Festungen und Levitenorte im Lande Juda," in *KS* II (Munich: 1959), pp. 306–315.

Idem, "Judas Gaue unter Josia," in *KS* II, pp. 276–288.

Idem, "The Settlement of the Israelites in Palestine," in *Essays on OT History and Religion* (E.T. 1966), pp. 133–169.

G. W. Anderson, "Israel: Amphictyony; 'Am; Ḳāhāl; 'Ēḏāh," in H. T. Frank and W. L. Reed, eds., *Translating and Understanding the OT* (Nashville: 1970), pp. 135–151.

D. S. Attema, "Het Boek Jozua," in J. H. Bavinck and A. H. Edelkoort, eds., *Bijbel in de Nieuwe Vertaling* (Baarn: 1958), pp. 117–167.

P. Auvray, in L. Pirot, ed., *Dictionnaire de la Bible*, Suppl. 4 (1949), s.v. "Josué."

O. Bächli, "Von der Liste zur Beschreibung: Beobachtungen und Erwägungen zu Jos. 13–19," *ZDPV* 89 (1973), pp. 1–14.

Idem, "Zur Lage des alten Gilgal," *ZDPV* 83 (1967), pp. 64–71.

K. Baltzer, *The Covenant Formulary in OT, Jewish and Early Christian Writings* (E.T. 1971).

J. R. Bartlett, "Sihon and Og, Kings of the Amorites," *VT* 20 (1970), pp. 257–277.

M. A. Beek, *Wegen en Voetsporen van het OT* (Baarn: ²1969).

I. Ben-Shem, *The Conquest of Trans-Jordan* (Tel Aviv: 1972). [Hebrew with English summary]

J. Blenkinsopp, *Gibeon and Israel* (Cambridge: 1972).

J. Bright, *The Authority of the OT* (Grand Rapids: 1967).

Idem, "The Book of Joshua," in *IB* II (Nashville: 1953).

Idem, *Early Israel in Recent History Writing*. *SBT* 19 (London: 1956).

Idem, *A History of Israel* (Philadelphia: ²1972).

H. Burgman, "Der Josuafluch zur Zeit des Makkabäers Simon (143–134 v.Chr.)," *Biblische Zeitschrift* 19 (1975), pp. 26–40.

J. A. Callaway, "New Evidence on the Conquest of 'Ai," *JBL* 87 (1968), pp. 312–320.

Idem, "The 1964 'Ai (et-Tell) Excavations," *BASOR* 178 (1965), pp. 13–40.

J. Calvin, *Commentaries on the Book of Joshua* (E.T. 1949).

K. M. Campbell, "Rahab's Covenant: A short note on Joshua ii 9–21," *VT* 22 (1972), pp. 243f.

B. S. Childs, "A Study of the Formula 'Until This Day,' " *JBL* 82 (1963), pp. 279–292.

Idem, "The Etiological Tale Re-examined," *VT* 24 (1974), pp. 385–397.

Idem, "A Tradition-historical Study of the Reed Sea Tradition," *VT* 20 (1970), pp. 406–418.

P. C. Craigie, *The Book of Deuteronomy*. NICOT (Grand Rapids: 1976).

F. M. Cross and G. E. Wright, "The Boundary and Province Lists of the Kingdom of Judah," *JBL* 75 (1956), pp. 202–226.

A. E. Cundall, Jr., and L. Morris, *Judges and Ruth*. Tyndale OT Commentary (Downers Grove: 1968).

J. J. De Vault, *The Book of Josue*. Pamphlet Bible Series 2 (New York: 1960).

S. J. De Vries, "Temporal Terms as Structural Elements in the Holy-War Tradition," *VT* 25 (1975), pp. 80-105.

P. Diepold, *Israels Land*. BWANT 95 (Stuttgart: 1972).

H. Donner and W. Röllig, eds., *Kanaanäische und aramäische Inschriften*. 3 vols. (Wiesbaden: 1962–64).

J. Dus, "Die Analyse zweier Ladeerzählungen des Josuabuches (Jos. 3–4 und 6)," *ZAW* 72 (1960), pp. 107–134.

Idem, "Gibeon: Eine Kultstätte des ŠMŠ und die Stadt des benjaminitischen Schicksals," *VT* 10 (1960), pp. 353–374.

W. Eichrodt, *The Theology of the OT*. 2 vols. OTL (Philadelphia: 1961–67).

Idem, "Hat die alttestamentliche Theologie noch selbständige Bedeutung innerhalb der alttestamentlichen Wissenschaft?" *ZAW* 47 (1929), pp. 83–91.

O. Eissfeldt, *The OT: An Introduction* (E.T. 1965).

Idem, "Israel und Seine Geschichte," in *KS* III (Tübingen: 1966), pp. 159–167. (Review of M. Noth, *Geschichte Israels*).

Idem, "Von Joseph zu Josua," *op. cit.*, pp. 151–58. (Review of H. H. Rowley, *From Joseph to Joshua*)

F. C. Fensham, "The Treaty Between Israel and the Gibeonites," *BA* 27 (1964), pp. 96–100.

J. P. Fokkelman, *Narrative Art in Genesis* (Assen: 1975).

H. J. Franken, "The Problem of Identification in Biblical Archaeology," *PEQ* 108 (1976), pp. 3–11.

Idem, "Heilig Land en Heilige Huisjes" (inaugural address, 1962).

H. Freedman, *Joshua*. In A. Cohen, ed., *Joshua and Ruth*. Soncino Books of the Bible (London: 1950).

J. Garstang, *The Foundations of Biblical History, Joshua, Judges* (London: 1931).

A. Gelin, *Josué*. La Sainte Bible (Paris: 1955).

C. H. J. de Geus, *The Tribes of Israel*. Studia Semitica Neerlandica 18 (Assen: 1976). (Excellent bibliography)

C. H. Giblin, "Structural Patterns in Jos 24, 1–25," *CBQ* 26 (1964), pp. 50–69.

W. H. Gispen *et al.*, eds., *Bijbelse Encyclopaedie* (2 vols. ²1975).

F. Golka, "Zur Erforschung der Ätiologieen im AT," *VT* 20 (1970), pp. 90–98.

C. J. Goslinga, *Jozua*. Korte Verklaring der Heilige Schrift (Kampen: ³1955).

N. K. Gottwald, *The Tribes of Yahweh* (Maryknoll, N.Y.: 1979).

S. G. de Graaf, *Promise and Deliverance* I (St. Catharines: 1977).

J. Gray, *Joshua, Judges and Ruth*. Century Bible (London: 1967).

Idem, "Hazor," *VT* 16 (1966), pp. 26–52.

M. Greenberg, "The Biblical Conception of Asylum," *JBL* 78 (1959), pp. 125–132.

J. M. Grintz, "The Treaty of Joshua with the Gibeonites," *JAOS* 86 (1966), pp. 113–126.

Idem, "Ai which is beside Beth-Aven," *Bib* 42 (1961), pp. 201–216.

J. de Groot, *Het Boek Jozua*. Tekst en Uitleg (Groningen: 1931).

H. H. Grosheide, "Hazor," *Gereformeerd Weekblad* 31 (1975–76), pp. 307, 315, 323; 32 (1976–77), pp. 3–4.

K. Gutbrod, *Das Buch vom Lande Gottes*. Die Botschaft des AT 10 (Calwer: 1951).

J. Halbe, "Gibeon and Israel," *VT* 25 (1975), pp. 613–641.

A. Haldar, *Who Were the Amorites?* Monographs on the Ancient Near East 1 (Leiden: 1971).

B. Halpern, "Gibeon: Israelite Diplomacy in the Conquest Era," *CBQ* 37 (1975), pp. 303–316.

M. Haran, "The Gibeonites, the Nethinim and the Sons of Solomon's Servants," *VT* 11 (1961), pp. 159–169.

R. K. Harrison, *Introduction to the OT* (Grand Rapids: 1969).

J. Heller, "Die Priesterin Raab," *Communio Viatorum* 8 (1965), pp. 113–17.

S. Herrmann, *A History of Israel in OT Times* (E.T. 1975).

H. W. Hertzberg, *Die Bücher Josua, Richter, Ruth. ATD* IX (Göttingen: ⁵1974).

D. R. Hillers, *Treaty Curses and the OT Prophets*. Biblica et Orientalia 6 (Rome: 1964).

H. A. Hoffner, "The Hittites and Hurrians," in D. J. Wiseman, ed., *Peoples of OT Times* (Oxford: 1973), pp. 197–228.

J. S. Holladay, Jr., "The Days the *Moon* Stood Still," *JBL* 87 (1968), pp. 166–178.

S. Holmes, *Joshua, the Hebrew and Greek Texts* (Cambridge: 1914).

B. Holwerda, "De Heilshistorie in de Prediking," in *". . . Begonnen Hebbende Van Mozes . . ."* (Terneuzen: 1953), pp. 79–118.

Idem, Jozua (Seminariedictaat), n.d.

H. Holzinger, *Das Buch Josua*. Kurzer Hand-Commentar zum AT (Freiburg: 1901).

A. R. Hulst, "Der Jordan in den Alttestamentlichen Ueberlieferungen," *OTS* 14 (1965), pp. 162–188.

J. P. Hyatt, "Was There an Ancient Historical Credo in Israel and an Independent Sinai Tradition?", in H. T. Frank and W. L. Reed, eds., *Translating and Understanding the OT* (Nashville: 1970), pp. 152–170.

G. H. Jones, " 'Holy War' or 'Yahweh War'?" *VT* 24 (1975), pp. 642–658.

O. Kaiser, *Introduction to the OT* (Minneapolis: 1977).

W. Kaiser, *Toward an OT Theology* (Grand Rapids: 1978).

Z. Kallai-Kleinmann, "The Town Lists of Judah, Simeon, Benjamin and Dan," *VT* 8 (1958), pp. 134–160.

Y. Kaufmann, *The Biblical Account of the Conquest of Palestine* (Jerusalem: 1953).

C. F. Keil and F. Delitzsch, *Joshua, Judges, Ruth.* Biblical Commentary on the OT II (E.T. 1950).

K. M. Kenyon, *Digging up Jerusalem* (New York: 1974).

M. Kessler, "Narrative Techniques in 1 Sm 16, 1–13," *CBQ* 32 (1970), pp. 543–554.

K. A. Kitchen, *Ancient Orient and OT* (Downers Grove: 1966).

Idem, "Historical Method and Early Hebrew Tradition," *TB* 17 (1966), pp. 63–97.

Idem, The Bible in Its World (London: 1978).

M. Kline, "The Ḥa-BI-Ru—Kin or Foe of Israel?" *WTJ* 19 (1956/57), pp. 1–24, 170–184; 20 (1957/58), pp. 46–70.

Idem, Treaty of the Great King (Grand Rapids: 1963).

J. L. Koole, *Verhaal en Feit in het OT. Cahiers voor de gemeente* 1 (Kampen: 1967).

E. G. Kraeling, *The Rand McNally Bible Atlas* (New York: 1956).

H.-J. Kraus, "Gilgal, ein Beitrag zur Kultusgeschichte Israels," *VT* 1 (1951), pp. 181–199.

J. H. Kroeze, *Het Boek Jozua.* Commentaar op het OT (Kampen: 1968).

A. Kuschke, "Kleine Beiträge zur Siedlungsgeschichte der Stämme Asser und Juda," *HTR* 64 (1971), pp. 291–313.

J. P. Lange, ed., *A Commentary on the Holy Scriptures* (E.T. 1875; repr. 1949).

C. à Lapide, *Commentarius in Iosue, Iudicum* (Antwerp: 1642).

P. Lapp, "The Conquest of Palestine in the Light of Archaeology," *CTM* 38 (1967), pp. 283–300.

J. Lindblom, "Die Vorstellung vom Sprechen Jahwes zu den Menschen im AT," *ZAW* 75 (1963), pp. 263–288.

J. Liver, "The Literary History of Joshua ix," *JSS* 8 (1963), pp. 227–243.

D. Livingston, "Location of Biblical Bethel and Ai Reconsidered," *WTJ* 33 (1970–71), pp. 20–44.

Idem, "Traditional Site of Bethel Questioned," *WTJ* 34 (1971–72), pp. 39–50.

N. Lohfink, "Die deuteronomistische Darstellung des Übergangs der Führung Israels von Moses auf Josue," *Scholastik* 37 (1962), pp. 32–44.

M. R. H. Löhr, *Das Asylwesen im AT* (Halle: 1930).

B. O. Long, *The Problem of Etiological Narrative in the OT. BZAW* 108 (Berlin: 1968).

D. J. McCarthy, "Some Holy War Vocabulary in Joshua 2," *CBQ* 33 (1971), pp. 228–230.

H. McKeating, "The Development of the Law on Homicide in Ancient Israel," *VT* 25 (1975), pp. 46–68.

A. Malamat, "Hazor the Head of All Those Kingdoms," *JBL* 79 (1960), pp. 12–19.

M. L. Margolis, *The Book of Joshua in Greek*. 4 vols. (Paris: 1931–38).

W. J. Martin, " 'Dischronologized' Narrative in the Old Testament," *VTS* 17 (1969), pp. 179–186.

B. Mazar, "The Cities of the Priests and the Levites," *VTS* 7 (1960), pp. 193–205.

G. E. Mendenhall, "The Hebrew Conquest of Palestine," *BA* 25 (1962), pp. 66–87.

J. M. Miller, "Archaeology and the Israelite Conquest of Palestine: Some Methodological Observations," *PEQ* 109 (1977), pp. 87–93.

J. M. Miller and G. M. Tucker, *The Book of Joshua*. Cambridge Bible Commentary (New York: 1974).

T. C. Mitchell, "The OT Use of Nᵉšāmā," *VT* 11 (1961), pp. 177–187, esp. pp. 182–83.

J. C. de Moor, "Rāpi'ūma-Rephaim," *ZAW* 88 (1976), pp. 323–345.

W. L. Moran, "The Repose of Rahab's Israelite Guests (Jos 2, 1–24)," in *Studi sull' Oriente e la Bibbia*. Festschrift G. M. Rinaldi (1967), pp. 273–284.

J. Muilenburg, "The Site of Ancient Gilgal," *BASOR* 140 (1955), pp. 11–27.

R. North, "The Hivites," *Bibl* 54 (1973), pp. 43–62.

M. Noth, "Der Beitrag der Archäologie zur Geschichte Israels," *VTS* 7 (1960), pp. 262–282.

Idem, The History of Israel (E.T. ²1960).

Idem, Das Buch Josua. HAT VII (Tübingen: ³1971).

Idem, The OT World (E.T. 1966).

B. van Oeveren, *De Vrijsteden in het OT* (Kampen: 1968).

B. J. Oosterhoff, *Feit of Interpretatie* (Kampen: 1967).

H. M. Orlinsky, "The Hebrew *Vorlage* of the Septuagint of the Book of Joshua," *VTS* 17 (1969), pp. 187–195.

J. Pedersen, *Israel: Its Life and Culture* I-II (E.T. 1926; ⁵1963).

J. B. Pritchard, "Culture and History," in J. P. Hyatt, ed., *The Bible in Modern Scholarship* (Nashville: 1965), pp. 313–324.

Idem, Gibeon Where the Sun Stood Still (Princeton: 1962).

G. von Rad, *OT Theology*. 2 vols. (E.T. 1962–65).

A. F. Rainey, "Bethel Is Still *Beitîn*," *WTJ* 33 (1970–71), pp. 175–188.

P. Renard, "Achan," in L. Pirot, ed., *Dictionnaire de la Bible* (Paris: 1926), Suppl. I, col. 129.

R. Rendtorff, *Das Überlieferungsgeschichtliche Problem des Pentateuch. BZAW* 147 (Berlin: 1977).

H. H. Rowley, *From Joseph to Joshua* (London: 1950).

R. Savignac, "La Conquète de Jéricho," *RB* 7 (1910), pp. 36–53.

P. P. Sayden, "The Crossing of the Jordan, Jos. chaps. 3 and 4," *CBQ* 12 (1950), pp. 194–207.

J. Schirmann, "Joshua," in C. Roth, ed., *Encyclopedia Judaica* 10, pp. 270f.

H. H. Schmid, *Die Steine und das Wort* (1975).

H. Schrade, *Der Verborgene Gott: Gottesbild und Gottesvorstellung in Israel und im alten Orient* (Stuttgart: 1949).

F. Sierksma, "Quelques Remarques sur la Circoncision en Israel," *OTS* 9 (1951), pp. 136–169.

J. Simons, *Opgravingen in Palestina* (Roermond: 1936).

Idem, *The Geographical and Topographical Texts of the OT*. Studia Francisci Scholten 2 (Leiden: 1959).

Idem, "The Structure and Interpretation of Josh. xvi–xvii," *Orientalia Neerlandica* (Leiden: 1948), pp. 190–215.

J. A. Soggin, *Joshua*. *OTL* (Philadelphia: 1972).

J. Steinmann, *Josué*. *Connaître la Bible* (Bruges: 1960).

C. Steuernagel, *Deuteronomium und Josua*. Hand Kommentar zum AT (Göttingen: ²1923).

S. Talmon, "The Town Lists of Simeon," *IEJ* 15 (1965), pp. 235–241.

D. W. Thomas, ed., *Documents from OT Times* (New York: 1961).

J. A. Thompson, *The Ancient Near Eastern Treaties and the OT* (London: 1964).

A. Tricot, "La Prise d'Aï (Jos. 7,1–8,29)," *Bibl* 3 (1922), pp. 273–300.

A. C. Tunyogi, "The Book of the Conquest," *JBL* 84 (1965), pp. 374–380.

J. Van Seters, "The Conquest of Sihon's Kingdom: A Literary Examination," *JBL* 91 (1972), pp. 182–197.

Idem, "The Terms 'Amorite' and 'Hittite' in the OT," *VT* 22 (1972), pp. 64–81.

R. de Vaux, *Ancient Israel: Its Life and Institutions*. 2 vols. (E.T. 1961).

Idem, *The Early History of Israel* (E.T. 1978).

Idem, "Les Hurrites de l'histoire et les Horites de la Bible," *RB* 74 (1967), pp. 481–503.

Idem, "Method in the Study of Early Hebrew History," in J. P. Hyatt, ed., *The Bible in Modern Scholarship* (Nashville: 1965), pp. 15–29.

Idem, "On Right and Wrong Uses of Archaeology," in J. A. Sanders, ed., *Near Eastern Archaeology in the Twentieth Century* (Garden City: 1970), pp. 64–80.

Idem, "The Settlement of the Israelites in Southern Palestine and the Origins of the Tribe of Judah," in H. T. Frank and W. L. Reed, eds., *Translating and Understanding the OT* (Nashville: 1970), pp. 108–134.

Idem, "La Thèse de l'amphictyonie israélite," *HTR* 64 (1971), pp. 415–436.

J. G. Vink, "The Priestly Code in the Book of Joshua," *OTS* 15 (1969), pp. 63–80.

E. Vogt, "Die Erzählung vom Jordanübergang Josue 3–4," *Bibl* 46 (1965), pp. 125–148.

C. Vonk, *Inleiding op de Profeten: Jozua*. De Heilige Schrift (Barendrecht: 1972).

G. Vos, *Biblical Theology* (Grand Rapids: 1948).

T. C. Vriezen, *An Outline of OT Theology* (E.T. 1958).

B. Waltke, "Palestinian Artifactual Evidence Supporting the Early Date of the Exodus," *Bibliotheca Sacra* 129 (1972), pp. 33–47.

P. Weimar, "Die Jahwekriegserzählungen in Exodus 14, Josua 10, Richter 4 und 1 Samuel 7," *Bibl* 57 (1976), pp. 38–73, esp. 51–62.

M. Weippert, *The Settlement of the Israelite Tribes in Palestine: A Critical Survey of Recent Scholarly Debate*. SBT 21 (E.T. 1971).

G. J. Wenham, *The Book of Leviticus*. NICOT (Grand Rapids: 1979).

Idem, "The Deuteronomic Theology of the Book of Joshua," *JBL* 90 (1971), pp. 140–48.

J. A. Wilcoxen, "Narrative Structure and Cult Legend; A Study of Joshua 1–6," in J. C. Rylaarsdam, ed., *Transitions in Biblical Scholarship* (1968), pp. 43–70.

D. J. Wiseman, ed., *Peoples of OT Times* (Oxford: 1973).

L. T. Wood, "Date of the Exodus," in J. B. Payne, ed., *New Perspectives on the OT* (Waco: 1970), pp. 66–87.

M. H. Woudstra, *The Ark of the Covenant From Conquest to Kingship* (Philadelphia: 1965).

Idem, "A Critique of Liberation Theology by a Cross-Culturalized Calvinist," *JETS* 23 (1980), pp. 3–12.

Idem, "Event and Interpretation in the OT," in S. Kistemaker, ed., *Interpreting God's Word Today* (Grand Rapids: 1970), pp. 49–72.

Idem, *Calvin's Dying Bequest to the Church*, *A Critical Evaluation of the Commentary on Joshua*. Calvin Theological Seminary Monograph 1 (Grand Rapids: 1960).

G. E. Wright, "A Problem of Ancient Topography: Lachish and Eglon," *BA* 34 (1971), pp. 76–86.

Idem, "The Literary and Historical Problem of Joshua 10 and Judges 1," *JNES* 5 (1946), pp. 105–114.

Idem, *The OT and Theology* (New York: 1969).

Y. Yadin, "Hazor," in *AOTS*, pp. 245–263.

S. Yeivin, *The Israelite Conquest of Canaan* (1973).

E. J. Young, *The Study of OT Theology Today* (London: 1958).

TEXT AND COMMENTARY

I. THE PROMISED LAND CONQUERED
(1:1 – 12:24)

A. INTRODUCTION AND MAIN THEMES (1:1 – 18)

1. EXHORTATION AND ENCOURAGEMENT (1:1 – 9)

1 *After the death of Moses the servant of the Lord, the Lord said to Joshua, son of Nun and Moses' aide:*

2 *"My servant Moses is dead. Now therefore, prepare to cross this Jordan, you and all this people, into the land I am about to give to them, to the Israelites.*

3 *Every place the soles of your feet will tread upon I give to you, as I promised to Moses.*

4 *From the desert and from the Lebanon there, as far as the great river, the river Euphrates, all the land of the Hittites, and to the Great Sea in the west will be your territory.*

5 *No one will be able to hold his ground before you all the days of your life; as I have been with Moses, so I will be with you; I will not leave you nor forsake you.*

6 *Be strong and courageous, for you are the one who will cause this people to inherit the land which I promised by oath to their fathers to give to them.*

7 *Only be strong and very courageous and act strictly according to the whole law which Moses my servant imposed upon you. Do not depart from it to the right or to the left, that you may prosper wherever you go.*

8 *Let not this book of the law ever be out of your mouth, but meditate on it day and night, that you may act strictly in accordance with all that is written in it, for then you will happily achieve your goal and then you will prosper.*

9 *Have I not commanded you: Be strong and courageous? Do not*

tremble, neither be dismayed, for the Lord your God is with you wherever you go."

This first chapter serves as an introduction to the book. It contains several elements and motifs which will be developed more fully in subsequent chapters.[1] As such the following may be mentioned. Vv. 1, 2, 5, 17 speak of Joshua's role as Israel's new leader[2] and of his intimate connection with the former leader, Moses. This connection is made explicit in 4:14.[3] Other introductory elements are the Jordan crossing (v. 2), the conquest of the promised land (vv. 5, 9, 11, 14), and the "all Israel" motif (vv. 12–16).[4] To be noted further is the theme of required covenant obedience (vv. 3, 7–8, 13, 17–18). This theme is developed in ch. 7 (Achan's covenant transgression) and recurs in 23:16 and ch. 24, *passim*. Also, attention may be called to the allotment theme (v. 6; cf. chs. 13–22) and to that of the land as God's gift (vv. 3, 9; cf. 6:2; 10:42; 21:43; 23:3).[5]

1 *After the death of Moses.* This verse links the book of Joshua closely with Deuteronomy, which precedes in the Hebrew canon.[6] Moses' death is recorded in Deut. 34. Joshua was designated as Moses' successor in Num. 27:15–23 and in Deut. 3:21–22; 31:1–8. He was the one to complete Moses' unfinished mission and lead Israel into the promised land. Thus the continuity of leadership is assured.[7]

1. To call this introduction "deuteronomic" as, e.g., J. Steinmann, *Josué*. Connaître la Bible (Bruges: 1960), p. 31, carries implications for authorship and composition which should be avoided. But deuteronomic elements in this section may be recognized. C. Steuernagel, *Das Buch Josua*, mentions Deut. 11:25a and 31:8 with v. 5, and Deut. 31:7 with v. 6.
2. For a study of a possible leadership "theology" in Joshua see D. J. McCarthy, "The Theology of Leadership in Joshua 1–9," *Bibl* 52 (1971), pp. 165–175.
3. The Jordan crossing offers striking parallels between the experiences of these two leaders. Compare 3:13 with Exod. 15:8 and 3:17 with Exod. 14:21–22. Another similarity is the solemn encounter both have at the beginning of their mission (5:15 and Exod. 3:5).
4. Many examples are given by G. J. Wenham, "The Deuteronomic Theology of The Book of Joshua," *JBL* 90 (1971), pp. 144f.; cf. 3:7; 4:14; 7:23; 8:21, 24; 23:2. The Transjordanian tribes are to take part in the Conquest with their brothers (1:12–15; cf. also ch. 22). Further instances of this motif are found in 8:3; 10:7, 29, 31, 36, 38, 43.
5. Closely associated with the idea of the land as God's gift is that of the land as "inheritance" (11:23) and that of "rest" (1:15). For a development of some of these themes with emphasis on Deuteronomy cf. P. Diepold, *Israels Land. BWANT* 95 (Stuttgart: 1972), pp. 81–84 (on "inheritance").
6. In Hebrew the connection is expressed by *wayᵉhî* ("and it came to pass"), which points to the closeness of the link.
7. See also N. Lohfink, "Die deuteronomistische Darstellung des Übergangs der Führung Israels von Moses auf Josue," *Scholastik* 37 (1962), pp. 32–44.

The reference to the death of Moses may also serve to remind the reader of Moses' disobedience which had forfeited for this great man of God the entry into Canaan (cf. Heb. 3:18–19; 4:1). However, there is no slighting of Moses' role as leader. He is referred to by the title *servant of the Lord*[8] (cf. Deut. 34:5 and Josh. 1:2, 7, 13, 15; 8:31; 12:6; 13:8; etc.).[9] This title is also given to Abraham (Gen. 26:24), David (1 K. 8:66), as well as non-Israelite rulers such as Nebuchadnezzar (Jer. 25:9). In the book of Isaiah the term assumes a very special meaning in the so-called "Servant Songs" (42:1–4; 49:1–7; 50:4–11; 52:13–53:12). Joshua will not receive this significant title until the end of the book (Josh. 24:29). For the time being he is called *Moses' aide*.[10]

Frequent Pentateuchal references to Joshua, here called *son of Nun* (cf. Exod. 17:9; 24:13; 33:11; Num. 11:28; 13:8, 16; 14:6, 30, 38; 27:15–23; Deut. 3:21, 28; 31:7–8, 14, 23; 34:9) make further identification superfluous. *The Lord said*—there was a direct communication between the Lord and Joshua, but its exact nature is not disclosed.[11] Underlying this expression is the biblical assumption of a personal God whose existence is not proved but forms the tacit starting point of all biblical revelation.[12] In Num. 27:21 the military actions of Joshua and Israel (their "going out" and "coming in") are made dependent on priestly mediation by means of the Urim, but this does not preclude more direct revelations on God's part.[13] In general it may be said that Joshua, no less than his great predecessor, receives his orders directly from God[14] (see also 3:7;

8. These words are lacking in the LXX (B A). They are considered secondary by some commentators (e.g., Steuernagel and Gelin), but retained as genuine by others (Noth and Kroeze).

9. Cf. also 1 K. 8:56; 2 K. 18:12; Ps. 105:26; Rev. 15:3.

10. Heb. $m^e\check{s}\bar{a}r\bar{e}\underline{t}$, rendered "minister" in RSV. The term denotes personal service from man to man (Gen. 39:4; 1 K. 19:21), but it is also used for man's service (ministry) in the sanctuary (Num. 4:12; 2 Chr. 24:14). The Hebrew root implies honorable service to which one is called or which is undertaken voluntarily; cf. GB s.v. $\check{s}\bar{a}ra\underline{t}$, and see also Exod. 24:13; 33:11; Num. 11:28.

11. For a helpful analysis of the Lord's "speaking" to man, see J. Lindblom, "Die Vorstellung vom Sprechen Jahwes zu den Menschen im AT," *ZAW* 75 (1963), pp. 263–288.

12. Gods of Israel's neighbors also claimed to speak to their devotees, e.g., the Moabite god Chemosh; cf. *DOTT*, p. 197.

13. J. H. Kroeze, *Het Boek Jozua*, pp. 26f., holds the opposite view and sees a discrepancy between Numbers and Joshua.

14. J. A. Soggin, *Joshua*, p. 28, stresses, we believe unduly, the second-hand nature of Joshua's ministry compared with that of Moses.

5:9; 8:1; 10:8; 11:6).[15] This means that in all instances Israel's true Leader is the Lord.[16]

2 The Lord's words to Joshua begin by making reference to Moses' death. This death becomes the occasion (*Now therefore*[17]) for the Lord's command to cross the Jordan and enter Canaan. These are two of the leitmotifs of the book of Joshua (see introduction to this chapter).

Prepare to cross this Jordan. This was a formidable command, and everybody acquainted with the local geography, as also later readers of this book, would have understood it so. The river Jordan had a separating rather than a connecting function, running through a deep gorge which may be called the earth's deepest valley.[18] The Jordan flows into the Dead Sea, which lies 1286 feet below sea level. The river runs through a wider trough called the Ghor, within which is a narrower depression of one hundred feet or more in depth, forming the actual river bottom. In addition to these forbidding features the absolute level of the river valley is greatly enhanced by the mountains on both sides. The slopes are generally steep and sudden, sometimes forming huge precipices.[19] Also note 3:15, which points to the river's swollen condition at the time of the crossing. Thus the miracle of the Lord's giving of the land is anticipated effectively by the writer's recalling of the Lord's command.[20]

I am about to give.[21] This is the "theme" of the giving of the land

15. The frequency of the Lord's speaking to Israel often depends on the nation's moral and spiritual fitness (cf. 1 Sam. 3:10; Ezek. 7:26; Ps. 74:9; 1 Sam. 28:15). In some instances the Lord speaks, but only to "deceive" the wilfully disobedient who have repudiated his true word (Ezek. 14:7, 9; 1 K. 22:19–20; in an eschatological setting: 2 Thess. 2:11).

16. Lindblom, *op. cit.*, p. 287, points out that in this respect Israel differed from its neighbors. Some of the great legislators of antiquity, such as Lipit-Ishtar and Hammurabi, view themselves as the actual legislators of their subjects even though they claim to have received a divine command to write down their laws. On the question of the claims of other gods compared with that of the true God, cf. also E. J. Young, *The Study of OT Theology Today* (London: 1958), pp. 21ff.

17. Heb. w^e '*attâ*. Kroeze, *op. cit.*, p. 28 takes this in an adversative sense ("maar nu"), but this is not likely. M. Noth (*Das Buch Josua*) renders it "*nun also,*" and C. J. Goslinga (*Het Boek Jozua*, p. 36) "*nu dan.*"

18. E. G. Kraeling, *Rand McNally Bible Atlas* (1956), p. 26. This does not mean that the Jordan could not be forded at all. See G. E. Wright and F. V. Filson, eds., *The Westminster Historical Atlas* (Philadelphia: ²1956), p. 20.

19. See Y. Aharoni, *The Land of the Bible* (Philadelphia: 1967), p. 29.

20. The use of the demonstrative "this" points to the river's proximity. LXX (BA) omits the pronoun; Vulgate "*Jordanum istum.*"

21. Heb. *nōṯēn*, pres. part., of impending action. Not all interpreters take it this way. Kroeze: "De HERE is daar nu mee bezig"; Goslinga: "het land dat ik hun . . . geef." But Soggin: "I propose to give," and Hertzberg, *ATD* IX: "zu geben im Begriff bin." See also P. C. Craigie, *The Book of Deuteronomy*, p. 100, note 1.

of promise. The patriarchal narratives already employ the verb "to give" with respect to what God will do with the land of promise (Gen. 12:7; 13:15; 15:18; 26:3–4).[22] The book of Joshua thus means to inform its readers of the fulfilment of the ancient promise,[23] although a comparison of 13:1 with 11:23 indicates that the promise is only partially fulfilled. This constitutes the "already-not yet" dimension, so typical of the entire OT, and provides an eschatological aspect which is more fully developed in Ezek. 48.[24] *To them, to the Israelites.* The last three words are not represented in the LXX,[25] but a good case for retaining them can be made on material grounds. Properly understood these words remind the reader of Israel's earlier rebellion which had caused the previous generation to die in the desert. However, though these did not enter into the "rest" (Deut. 12:10), the Lord's promise to his people had not come to naught (cf. also Josh. 21:43–45). The present "remnant" is truly and fully Israel.

3 *Every place . . . I give to you.* This verse repeats the notion that the land will be God's gift (see previous verse).[26] Equally significant is the emphasis on the Lord's promise to Moses. Joshua is Moses' successor and will complete his mission. God's work is continuous. See Deut. 11:24 and other repeated references to a future possession of Canaan (Exod. 3:8, 17; 6:4, 8; 23:23, 27, 31; 34:11).

4 The boundaries of Canaan as presented here are listed in their

---

22. The patriarchal narratives use either the imperfect or the perfect of the verb. The latter is also used in 1:3.

23. N. M. Sarna, *Understanding Genesis* (New York: 1966), p. 124, speaks of a transference of ownership into possession.

24. On the eschatological dimension of some of Joshua's message see also J. Bright, *The Authority of the OT*, p. 246.

25. A word of caution is in order with respect to the use of the LXX for textual emendation. R. Pfeiffer's words are very much to the point: "Strictly speaking, the Septuagint (LXX) about which we have been speaking is an unknown entity. It is uncritical to speak of the printed editions of the Greek Bible or even of the Greek text preserved in manuscripts as 'the LXX', although this practice is well-nigh universal!" (*Introduction to the OT* [New York: ²1948], p. 107). Cf. also H. Orlinsky, "Textual Criticism of the OT" in G. E. Wright, ed., *The Bible and the Ancient Near East* (1961; repr. Winona Lake: 1979), pp. 113–132. Orlinsky points to the significance of the manuscript discoveries at the Dead Sea caves, but also states that "it is clear that much work remains to be done by the textual critic of the Hebrew Bible and its LXX version and recensions" (p. 121). See also "Text" in the Introduction.

26. The Heb. here uses the perfect: *nᵉtattîû*, which may also be rendered "I have given." According to Soggin, *op. cit.*, p. 29, this expresses "a divine decree" in which the future is "already irrevocably decided." Cf. also Hertzberg, *op. cit.*, p. 14. B. Holwerda, *Jozua* (Seminariedictaat, n.d.), considers this to be a declarative perfect ("I hereby give"). Whatever the case, the Israelites are here reminded that the promised land is theirs because God graciously wanted it that way.

widest extent (cf. also Gen. 15:18; Deut. 1:7; 11:24). Only during the period of Israel's greatest territorial expansion, under David and Solomon, were these boundaries approximated.[27] The description is not without some difficulties.[28] The *desert* is probably the region which borders the cultivated land of Palestine to the south and east.[29] The description then moves northward to the Lebanon, which at this point appears to be included in the boundaries of the land.[30] The *great river* constitutes the eastward extension in the direction of the Euphrates (cf. Gen. 15:18; Deut. 1:7).[31] The expression *all the land of the Hittites* may reflect the fact that both Babylonia and Egypt, between which Canaan was a buffer state, referred occasionally to Canaan-Syria as "the land of Hatti." At this point it may mean little more than that the land is still in the hand of the "natives."[32] This would then correspond to Gen. 12:6. The Hittites are frequently mentioned as one of the ethnic entities inhabiting Canaan prior to the Conquest (cf. 3:10; 9:1; 11:3; 12:8; 24:11).[33] *The Great Sea in the west* (lit. "the going down of

27. In view of the fact that the Lord is here considered the speaker, the remark of A. Gelin, *Josué*. La Sainte Bible (Paris: 1955), that this represents "the Hebrew imperialist dream" seems inappropriate. One may allow for a viewpoint to have affected the narration, but not to such an extent.
28. There is no clear-cut pattern of boundary lines drawn "from" one point "to" another as, e.g., in Deut. 11:24; see Y. Aharoni, *op. cit.*, pp. 61ff.; and Kroeze, *op. cit.*, pp. 28ff.
29. The text could also refer to the Syrian desert. This is the way J. H. Kroeze takes it.
30. In Josh. 13:5 the Lebanon belongs to the as yet unconquered but allotted regions. Cf. further 11:17; Judg. 3:3 (the Hivites in Lebanon are tribes not yet subdued); and Deut. 1:7. The pronoun *zeh* with Lebanon, lit. "this," is surprising, when the southern location of the Israelites at this moment is considered. The rendering "the Lebanon there" reflects what other versions have done (e.g., Moffatt, Zürcher Bibel), and can be defended in light of the Hebrew. R. North ("The Hivites," *Bibl* 54 [1973], pp. 43–62) considers the inclusion of Lebanon as well as that of the Euphrates "a vague rhetorical exaggeration," which must be "dismissed."
31. Another designation of the Euphrates is simply "the River" (see Gen. 31:21 [Heb.]; Exod. 23:31 [Heb.]; Num. 22:5). David's exploits toward the Euphrates are mentioned in 2 Sam. 8:1–12.
32. For further study see O. R. Gurney, "Boğazköy," in *AOTS*, pp. 105–116; H. A. Hoffner, "The Hittites and the Hurrians," in D. J. Wiseman, ed., *Peoples of OT Times* (Oxford: 1973), pp. 197–228; R. North, *op. cit.*, pp. 57f. Says North: "It seems warranted to conclude that the *whole* population of Canaan or *any part* could loosely be called 'Hittite', and this not entirely without relation to the northern empire of that name" (p. 57).
33. There is no unanimity among experts as to the relation of the biblical Hittites (cf. also Gen. 10:15; 23:3; 26:34) and the Hittite empire which had its center in what is presently Turkey and lasted from c. 1680–1190 BC. R. de Vaux, "Les Hurrites de l'histoire et les Horites de la Bible," *RB* 74 (1967), pp. 481–503,

the sun") is the Mediterranean Sea. The entire enumeration contains a certain programmatic element. This is God's description of the land which he has chosen for his people, and which they will obtain through conquest.

5 If Joshua, or the later readers of his book, should feel faint and disheartened vis-à-vis the coming events, the Lord's words are there to encourage and reassure. This verse reflects assurances given in Deut. 7:24. The Lord's words imply future opposition, but this opposition will come to naught. The divine assistance will be rendered to Joshua no less than to Moses. Thus the note of the continuity of leadership (see introduction to chapter) is struck again (cf. vv. 7, 13, 15). *I will be with you*: primarily a word of assistance and help in the coming battles, this word is capable of being deepened in the sense in which the Psalms use it. *I will not leave*[34] *you nor forsake you*: the guarantee of success will be the Lord's unfailing presence and aid.

6 *Be strong and courageous*. As Moses had done previously (cf. Deut. 1:38; 3:28), so the Lord himself now encourages Joshua in his future task. Joshua will be the one to bring to fruition the promise solemnly made to the forefathers.[35] This is one of the main themes of the entire book. It pertains both to the first and the second part of Joshua, to the Conquest as well as the allotment. The word "inherit," used to describe the future possession of the land, is of rich theological significance. It has subsequently become a NT term for the enjoyment of the spiritual blessings of salvation (e.g., 1 Pet. 1:4). The word[36] is used in 11:23; 14:13; 16:4; 17:6 (cf. also Deut. 1:38; 12:10). It suggests that Israel has a claim upon the land vis-à-vis its former inhabitants. It also suggests the durative aspect

---

explicitly states that there were never any proper Hittites in Palestine. Both North and Hoffner, *op. cit.*, occupy a mediating position (see previous note). Another view is that "the land of the Hittites" represents a number of smaller Hittite states in the northern region; see Kroeze, *op. cit.*, p. 29. N. K. Gottwald, *The Tribes of Yahweh*, pp. 560f., concludes that the various references to "Hittites" as living in Canaan "remains an enigma," but he allows for a sizeable influx of Hittites and other northern peoples into Palestine in the thirteenth-twelfth centuries BC.

34. Heb. lit. "making someone sink." Hertzberg, *op. cit.*: "ich will mich dir nicht entziehen"; M. Noth, *Das Buch Josua*: "ich will dich nicht preisgeben"; RSV: "I will not fail you."

35. For this promise to the forefathers cf. Gen. 12:3, 7; 13:14–16; 15:7–8; 22:17; 24:7; 26:3; 35:10–12; 48:3–4; 50:24. See G. von Rad, *OT Theology* I (E.T. 1962), pp. 170f.

36. Heb. *naḥal* (verb), *naḥᵃlâ* (noun).

37. See the discussion of P. Diepold, *Israels Land*, pp. 81–84. The notion of "inheritance" is also used of God's possession of Israel (Deut. 32:9), and may even be used for what the nations receive from God as he apportions to them the

of the possession of the land, and that of individual apportionment.[37] Connected with this are the words "portion" and "lot" (see 22:25).[38] To call these words "theological" does not mean that they would have sprung from the brain of Israel's theologians. On the contrary, it is *God* who uses these terms. Their theological meaning rests squarely in the reality of the promised land which Joshua will cause Israel to inherit.[39]

7   In view of the impending Conquest the repetition of the exhortation to *be strong and very courageous* is not superfluous (cf. also vv. 9, 18). The new element is the divine injunction to *act strictly*[40] *according to the whole law* of Moses. God's law (Torah)[41] is his revelation word, interwoven with Israel's salvation history and steeped in God's redemptive acts on his people's behalf. This word is used at times as a synonym for a code of law (8:31; Deut. 4:44; 17:18), but the English word "law" does not completely capture the meaning of Heb. *tôrâ*.[42] Again, the writer emphasizes the connection between Joshua and Moses (see commentary on vv. 1, 5). By not departing from the law *to the right or to the left* Joshua will be the prototype of the happy man described in Ps. 1.[43] The language is reminiscent of Deut. 5:32; 17:20; 31:29. The general assumption of the OT is that the law can be kept, although occasionally another note is struck (see 24:19; Ps. 143:2). Moreover, the history of God's OT people testifies to the fact that the law, the keeping of which was so solemnly enjoined, was constantly broken.

Law observance in the above sense will cause Joshua and the people

---

world (Deut. 32:8). When God calls Israel his inheritance, a note of loving attachment may be detected (see Jer. 2:7; 16:18). To defile this "inheritance" was a heinous sin.

38. These words are given a more "spiritual" application in Ps. 16:5–6, although already the possession of the land itself is part of the covenant promise (Gen. 12:3, 7) and this covenant was essentially spiritual.

39. A proper understanding of the full implications of the land as "inheritance" could well be the means of coming to a better insight into the prophecies concerning the land, which are now so diversely understood by Christians.

40. Heb. *lišmôr la'ăsôṯ*, lit. "observe to do." NAB: "taking care to observe"; Gelin: "agir soigneusement"; Goslinga: "om nauwlettend waar te nemen."

41. The derivation of Heb. *tôrâ* is disputed. It has been suggested that its basic meaning is that of "pointing," "direction," "indication."

42. The Greek translation of *tôrâ* was *nomos*, which in turn gave rise to Latin *lex*, from which it is but one step to "legal" and "legalistic." The Hebrew word is more comprehensive; cf. Ps. 19:7 (Eng. v. 8).

43. It would be a mistake to regard Ps. 1 or Josh. 1:7 as setting forth work-righteousness. The law is God's covenant statute, and the covenant is one of grace.

to *prosper*.[44] The OT, more than the NT, places a direct connection between law observance and prosperity. But the book of Job and Ps. 73 show that this must not be seen as an automatic connection. The essence of OT religion is spiritual, although there are relative differences in outlook between the Testaments.

8–9 The idea of law observance as a condition for happiness is enlarged here. *Let not this book of the law ever be out of your mouth.* That which in the previous verse was simply called "law"[45] is now referred to as "the book of the law." This book is not to be out of Joshua's mouth,[46] a characteristically emphatic way of speaking. Joshua is to speak of this book and meditate[47] on it, as later the blessed man of Ps. 1 will do.[48] Daily meditation on the Book, and a strict observance of its gracious provisions for a life in covenant fellowship with the Lord, will mean a happy achievement of life's goal[49] and prosperity. Thus the assurance of success already given in v. 7 is here confirmed and enlarged upon. Later

---

44. Heb. *hiskîl*. The root means "to have success," and also "to be prudent," "to act circumspectly." It is frequently used in the Psalms (Ps. 2:10; 14:2; 119:99) and in Proverbs (1:3; 10:5; 14:35). In a religio-ethical sense it means that someone seeks God and lets himself and his thought be guided by God; see J. Pedersen, *Israel: Its Life and Culture*, Vol. I–II (E.T. 1926; ⁵1963), p. 198.

45. There is a difference of opinion about the originality of the word "law" in v. 7, but the reference in v. 8 is undisputed although generally regarded "late" by scholars adhering to some form of Wellhausianism.

46. This negative way of speaking implies a strong positive. Zürcher Bibel: "Von diesem Gezetzbuch sollst du allzeit reden." Knox: "The law thou hast in writing must govern every utterance of thine." The mouth is here seen as the organ of speech (cf. Exod. 4:11; Ps. 37:30 ["mouth" and "tongue" parallel]).

47. Heb. *hāgâ*, "meditate," suggests a barely audible murmur.

48. This concern with the written word is not late, nor is it an evidence of a growing petrifaction of living religion, or of a more "rigid" view of the canon as suggested by T. C. Vriezen, *An Outline of OT Theology* (E.T. 1958), pp. 94ff. Although the danger of a mere book-religion is always present, the biblical concern for the Book is not opposed to vital religion. Soggin, *op. cit.*, p. 32, correctly observes that "we are faced here with something which rather resembles the *sola scriptura* of the Reformation, in the sense of a concrete basis . . . opposed to all romantic and mystical enthusiasm and to all human traditionalism."

49. Lit. "for then you will make your way prosper." The Hebrew word for "prosper" at this point is *ṣālaḥ*. Pedersen defines it as "the power, the ability to live. . . . It designates the efficiency as an inner power to work in accordance with its nature, and at the same time success, prosperity and the carrying out of that for which one is disposed" (p. 196). F.-M. Abel translates: "C'est alors que tu seras heureux dans tes enterprises" (*Le Livre de Josué*. La Sainte Bible [Jerusalem: ²1961], p. 221). Hertzberg renders it: "dann wirst du deinen Weg glücklich vollenden."

readers of the book of Joshua are hereby also assured that in keeping God's law there is great reward.

With another exhortation to *be strong and courageous* this beautiful passage draws to a close. Again, this is more than a mere repetition. The thought is enhanced (*Do not tremble, neither be dismayed*) and a final assurance of the Lord's presence is given.

2. ALL ISRAEL TO PARTICIPATE IN THE CONQUEST (1:10–18)

10 *Then Joshua gave the officers of the people the following command:*
11 *"Go through the camp and tell the people: Get provisions ready, for in three days you will cross the Jordan here to go and take possession of the land which the Lord your God is about to give you to possess."*
12 *To the Reubenites and Gadites and half the tribe of Manasseh Joshua said:*
13 *"Remember the charge which Moses, the Lord's servant, gave you: The Lord your God grants you rest and gives you this land;*
14 *your wives, your little ones, and your cattle may remain in the land which Moses gave you beyond the Jordan; but you are to cross in formation in front of your kinsmen, all your valiant men, and you are to help them,*
15 *until the Lord gives your kinsmen rest as he has done you and they also have taken possession of the land which the Lord your God is giving them. Then you may go back to the land you own and take possession of it, which Moses, the Lord's servant, has given you beyond the Jordan, in the East."*
16 *And they answered Joshua: "Whatever you have commanded us we will do, and wherever you will send us we will go.*
17 *Just as we have obeyed Moses in everything, so we will obey you; only let the Lord your God be with you as he was with Moses.*
18 *Anyone who rebels against your orders and does not obey your words, whatever you may command him, shall be put to death. Only be strong and courageous."*

10–11 Joshua here assumes the leadership which the account has been concerned to stress (see chapter introduction). He hands on to the people and their *officers*[1] the command received from the Lord and tells them to gather provisions for the time when the people will cross the Jordan. This

---

1. Heb. *šōṭᵉrîm*. This word "probably indicates a more administrative than purely military function" (P. C. Craigie, *The Book of Deuteronomy*, p. 98; R. de Vaux, *Ancient Israel: Its Life and Institutions* [E.T. 1961], p. 155). See Exod. 5:14–15, 19; Deut. 1:15; 20:5, 8–9.

will be in three days.[2] What these provisions are to consist of is not stated. Probably the manna had already ceased to fall. This is a plausible assumption in light of the people's willingness to buy food on their journey through Edom (Deut. 2:6; cf. also Exod. 16:35; Josh. 5:12). Even if the manna was still available, it could not be stored for several days in advance (Exod. 16:19). The account at this point is not concerned to enter into the martial aspects of what lies ahead for the people. All that is to be done is to *cross* and *take possession*.[3] The language is reminiscent of Deut. 3:18; 4:5, 14. The author is only concerned to indicate that Israel is now about to convert ownership by promise into actual possession (see commentary at v. 2).[4] Another recurring feature is the emphasis on the fact that the land will be God's gift (cf. vv. 2–3, 6, 13, 15).

12–13   In keeping with his concern to stress the participation of a united Israel, the writer now reports Joshua's words to the tribes who had already obtained their land from Moses on the east of the Jordan (cf. Num. 32; Deut. 3:18–20).[5] The *Reubenites and Gadites and half the tribe of Manasseh* are reminded of Moses' words to them. Thus another link is forged between Joshua and Moses. Moses had spoken of the *rest* which the tribes beyond Jordan had already obtained. This theologically significant term[6] (discussed in the Introduction to the Commentary) is one of the key words for understanding the book of Joshua as well as later revelation.

2. The exact temporal reference is not clear. C. J. Goslinga, *Het Boek Jozua*, p. 42, states that the expression does not mean that the crossing as such will take place in three days, but rather that within three days the people must be on their way to cross the Jordan, an event which will take place later. B. J. Alfrink, *Josué. De Boeken van het OT* (Roermond: 1952), p. 21, believes that 1:12–3:1 took place before the command issued in v. 11. *De Statenvertaling* (Haarlem: 1937) uses a pluperfect in 2:1. A. Gelin, *Josué*, may be right when asserting that the number "three" need not be taken exactly (cf. Hos. 6:2; Esth. 4:16; Exod. 19:11).

3. Heb. *yāraš*. GB link the notion of violence with this root ("mit Gewalt"). The root also has a close association with "inherit," v. 6. The LXX renders it with *kataschein*, but in Deuteronomy *klēronomein* is used for *yāraš*.

4. The absence of warlike terminology is thus lessened somewhat in light of the lexical data in note 3. There is no reason to see this transaction as nothing more than a liturgical, cultic crossing, as does Hertzberg, and to some extent Soggin.

5. See on the "unity of Israel" as *leitmotif* in Joshua, G. J. Wenham, *JBL* 90 (1971), pp. 144f., where many examples of this motif are given.

6. Heb. *mēnîaḥ*, hiph. part. of *nûaḥ*; cf. 21:44; 23:1; Deut. 12:10; 25:19. This notion plays a significant role in Ps. 95; cf. Heb. 3–4. From 2 Sam. 7:1, 11 it becomes clear that "rest" may be enjoyed in principle but can be deepened and enriched (cf. also 1 K. 8:56).

14–15 The rest already granted may not be enjoyed fully until all Israel has achieved it together. Hence the command for these Transjordanian tribes to cross in front of their brothers while leaving their wives, children, and cattle behind. They are to do so *in formation*,[7] a word which suggests preparedness for war. Those who must do so are designated *valiant men*, a word which sometimes means "men of strength," "men of efficiency." Here it stands for the fighting men whose number, according to 4:13, was forty thousand (cf. also Num. 26:7, 18, 34). Once the conquest of the land is fully accomplished these men may return to the region beyond Jordan.[8]

16–17 The "all Israel" motif comes to beautiful expression in the readiness of those addressed to heed Joshua's summons.[9] The response is warm and complete (*whatever . . . wherever*), and again the link between Moses and Joshua is explicitly expressed.[10] Thus Joshua's leadership is recognized and the continuity of God's dealings with his people demonstrated. Later reluctance on the part of some tribes to come to the aid of their oppressed brothers (Judg. 5:16–17) will be justly rebuked, but this does not yet cast its shadow over this joyful scene.

18 The readiness of the tribes to follow Joshua is so great that those who may want to disobey him are threatened with death. The word used for this act of disobedience is "rebel," a word employed often for disobedience toward the Lord's commandments (Deut. 1:26, 43; 9:23; 1 Sam. 12:14). This use underscores the seriousness of the rebellion contemplated and explains the harshness of the penalty to be applied.

B. SPIES SENT TO JERICHO; CANAAN DISMAYED AT THE POWER OF ISRAEL'S GOD (2:1– 24)

1 *Joshua, son of Nun, secretly sent two men from Shittim on a mission*

7. Heb. *ḥᵃmušîm*. The word may mean lit. a five-fold arrangement of army troops; see de Vaux, *Ancient Israel*, p. 216. Other translations: "with your weapons" (JB), "armed" (ASV and RSV), "ten strijde toegerust" (DNV), "kampfgerüstet" (Steuernagel).

8. This expression is used here of the region east of Jordan; cf. Deut. 1:1.

9. Gelin, *op. cit.*, p. 26; and J. Steinmann, *Josué*, p. 31, suppose that those responding are the twelve tribes in their entirety. The response, however, is more naturally linked to what immediately precedes, although it also expresses a unanimity beyond the occasion which prompted the response.

10. The words: *"Only let the Lord . . . be with you . . . "* may also be understood in the sense of a question: "The Lord . . . is with you, is he not?" Thus understood these words would indicate a slight uncertainty which is removed by the Lord himself at a later point (cf. 3:7).

to gather information, with the following charge: "Go, reconnoitre the country and especially Jericho." They went and came to the house of a harlot whose name was Rahab, and there they went to sleep.

2 The king of Jericho was told: "Look, men from the Israelites have come here this night to gather intelligence about the country."

3 Then the king of Jericho sent to Rahab to tell her: "Bring out those men who have come to you, who have entered your house, for they have come to gather intelligence about the whole country."

4 But the woman had taken the two men and hidden them. So she answered: "True, these men did come to me, but I did not know where they were from;

5 and when the gate was about to be shut, at the onset of darkness, these men went off. I do not know where the men went. Pursue them quickly; you will surely overtake them."

6 But she had brought them upstairs on the roof and hidden them under the stalks of flax which she had lying piled up on the roof.

7 As to the men, they chased after them in the direction of the Jordan, near the fords, and the gate was shut, right after those had left who pursued them.

8 The others had not yet lain down when she came up to them on the roof.

9 She said to the men: "I know that the Lord has given you the land, and that the dread of you has fallen on us, and that all the inhabitants of the land have lost heart because of you.

10 For we have heard how the Lord dried up the water of the Red Sea before you when you went out of Egypt, and what you have done to the two kings of the Amorites who were on the other side of the Jordan, Sihon and Og, to whom you applied the curse.

11 When we heard that, our heart dissolved and because of you there was no courage left with anyone, for the Lord your God is a God in heaven above and on the earth beneath.

12 Now then, do swear to me by the Lord! As I have shown faithfulness to you, you on your part will show faithfulness to my family, and give me a sure sign,

13 and save alive my father and mother, my brothers and my sisters, and all who belong to them, and save us from death."

14 Then the men answered her: "Our life for yours! Unless you tell of this agreement of ours! When the Lord will have given us the land then we will show you faithfulness and loyalty."

15 She let them down through a window by a rope, for her house was on the outside of the wall and in that wall she lived.

16 She said to them: "To the mountain country you must go, in order that those who pursue you do not reach you, and hide yourselves

*for three days till the pursuers have gone back; then you can go on
your way."*

17 *The men said to her: "We will be free from this oath of yours which
you have made us swear—*

18 *look, when we enter the country, you must tie this scarlet cord in
the window through which you have let us down, and you must
gather your father and your mother, your brothers and your entire
family with you into the house.*

19 *This means that whoever will go outside through the doors of your
house, his blood will be on his own head and we will go free. But
as concerns anyone who will be with you in the house, his blood
will be on our head if a hand is laid on him.*

20 *If you should report this matter of ours then we will be free of your
oath which you have made us swear."*

21 *She replied: "As you have spoken, so will it be." She let them go
and they left.*

And she tied the scarlet cord in the window.

22 *They went, and came to the mountain country and stayed there three
days, till the pursuers had gone back. The pursuers looked everywhere and did not find them.*

23 *So the two men came down again out of the mountain country; they
crossed over and came to Joshua son of Nun and told him everything
that had befallen them.*

24 *They said to Joshua: "The Lord has given the whole country into
our power and all the inhabitants have lost heart because of us."*

Chapter 2 illustrates vividly one of the truths set forth in the previous
chapter: God will "give" the land of Canaan to Israel. Rahab's confession
and the spies' report (2:9–11, 24) demonstrate that even the mightiest
cities will not be able to resist the power of the God of Israel. Another
connection between the two chapters may be found in the note of encouragement to Joshua struck in both (cf. 1:7, 9, 18b).

There is no reason to regard ch. 2 as originally embodying a version
of the Conquest different from that presented in ch. 6.[1] It is true that
Joshua sends out spies as if the city and the land must be conquered by
force, whereas in actual fact Jericho's wall will fall miraculously (but cf.
24:11). However, at no point thus far has the account indicated that such
a miracle will take place. Joshua's sending of the spies, therefore, is simply
evidence of his foresight as a general. It does not conflict with the miracle

1. See, e.g., J. A. Soggin, *Joshua*, p. 38: "ch. 2 presents a version of the conquest parallel to, but different in substance from, the narrative actually given in
ch. 6."

that is to follow; neither is it a sign of lack of faith in God's promises. The story of the spies must be seen in this light. The spies act and speak as if the city will be taken by force. This is why the "sign" of the red cord is agreed upon. Whatever other secret agreements and inside information may have been carried back to Joshua's camp, the later developments of the actual events have made superfluous their report. This accounts for some of the unanswered questions which the story of the spies leaves. As to the chronological question of the "three days" (1:11), see the commentary at that point.[2]

1 Joshua sends *two men*[3] *from Shittim*[4] *on a mission to gather information* concerning the country and especially[5] concerning Jericho.[6] The two men take up lodging in the house of a certain Rahab,[7] who is called a harlot (Heb. *zônâ*) both here and in Heb. 11:31; Jas. 2:25 (Gk. *pornē*). A house like that could be expected to be frequented by men. This

2. Those who hold to the tenets of the documentary analysis as applied to the Pentateuch are not agreed as to the basic unity of this account. Steuernagel, *Das Buch Josua*, p. 212, views the chapter as basically "einheitlich," with the exception of vv. 17-21. H. Holzinger, *Das Buch Josua*, p. 4, thinks he can detect JE in this chapter (Steuernagel sees E only). M. Noth, *Das Buch Josua*, p. 29, does not doubt the "literary unity" of the account.

3. The LXX calls them "young men," as does the MT in 6:23. Does the LXX mean to lessen the moral problem of the spies' going to the house of a harlot?

4. Shittim, probably the same as Abel-shittim (Num. 33:49), was the place where Israel had sinned with Baal-peor (Num. 25:1). It has been identified with Tell el-Kefrein, a cone-shaped hill guarding the Wâdī Kefrein. Others think of Tell el-Hammâm as the possible site (see E. G. Kraeling, *The Rand McNally Bible Atlas*, 124; and Y. Aharoni, *The Land of the Bible*, p. 32). The word Shittim means "acacia trees."

5. The addition "and especially Jericho" (lit. "and Jericho") is deemed suspect by Noth and others. Several translations (RSV, Moffatt, Gelin, Hertzberg) treat the "and" (Heb. *waw*) as signifying "especially," "also." The fact that Jericho would have been an obvious goal of the fact-finding mission does not make the mention of it by Joshua superfluous.

6. Jericho ("moon city?" from Heb. *yārēaḥ*, "moon") has frequently been identified with Tell eṣ-Ṣultan. Excavations took place at that site in 1907–09, 1930–36, and 1952–53. See K. M. Kenyon, "Jericho," in *AOTS*, pp. 264–275. But the question of identification must be left open. There are still various unexplored tells in the vicinity. See also the article on Jericho in W. H. Gispen *et al.*, eds., *Bijbelse Encyclopaedie* (Kampen: ³1979), pp. 395f.

7. Rahab's name is not to be confused with the name of the sea monster mentioned in Job 9:13. It may have a connection with the root *rāḥab*, "to be broad," and be an abbreviation of a theophoric name, Rehabiah in 1 Chr. 23:17; 24:21. Josephus maintained Rahab was an innkeeper. It is possible to hold that she was both that and a harlot. The Targums call her a *pundeqita*, which means innkeeper. But, as Kroeze indicates (*Jozua*, p. 36), this word in the Targums always receives an unfavorable sense.

probably was the reason why the spies turned in there in order to escape detection.[8] The word *šāḵaḇ*, "sleep," does indeed have an ambiguous meaning and may be used of sexual intercourse, but in v. 8 it seems to be used without such connotation. There is no reason to understand it otherwise in v. 1. Some read v. 3, "who have come to you," as having sexual overtones (cf. Gen. 38:16; Judg. 16:1). This is indeed a possible meaning of the phrase, but the addition "who have entered your house" would seem to be against that understanding here.[9]

2–3 Jericho's king[10] is apprised of the arrival of the two Israelite men. Although this arrival took place before nightfall (see v. 5), it was apparently toward the evening ("this night"; cf. Gen. 19:1, 5). The king demands, by means of messengers, the surrender of the two spies. On the phrase *who have entered your house* (lacking in the Syriac translation) see the commentary on the previous verse.[11]

4–7 In this section the customary Hebrew word order (and – verb form – subject) is frequently changed to a more vivid style of narration with the subject preceding the verb.

The woman has taken[12] the two men to a hiding place[13] on the roof (see v. 6). She admits that strangers have come to her, that she does not know their identity, and that they have already left the city before nightfall and the shutting of the city gate. With the advice to the messengers of the king that a hot pursuit be organized, she concludes her remarks with a

8. A. Gelin is quite positive that sexual intentions ("illicit commerce") played a part in the men's choice; *Josué*, p. 27.

9. Some commentators, e.g., Noth (*op. cit.*, p. 24), believe that the words "who have entered your house" are an addition designed to prevent a misunderstanding of the previous words. But why add these words here, in the speech of the king's messengers? Would there be a need for such "attenuation" (see F.-M. Abel, *Le Livre de Josué*, p. 20) precisely on that point?

10. From the so-called Amarna tablets, 14th century correspondence between Canaanite kinglets and Egyptian pharaohs, it is known that Canaan at this time consisted of city states each with its own king (cf. also 12:9; Judg. 1:7).

11. The Hebrew verb translated "gather intelligence" means lit. "dig, search." Knox translates: ". . . come to search out every corner of the land."

12. The pluperfect is a possible reading of the Hebrew. It is employed in the translations of C. J. Goslinga and the DNV. This explains more easily why the king's messengers did not show suspicion. The woman may have sensed possible danger, and she took measures accordingly. See note 17.

13. The Hebrew form for "she had hidden them" is unusual (*wattiṣpᵉnô* for *wattiṣpᵉnēm*). Some (e.g. J. de Groot, *Het Boek Jozua. Tekst en Uitleg* [Groningen: 1931], p. 75) suggest that this is an old dual form. It may also be that the suffix must be treated distributively: she had hidden each of them. Cf. also GKC § 60d.

recommendation for immediate pursuit.[14]

Verse 6 supplements the reference of v. 4. The woman had hidden the men on the flat roof *under the stalks of flax*[15] she kept there. The narrative does not state explicitly that the spies were the recipients of special divine care. Yet it is strange that the king's messengers were so quickly persuaded of the accuracy of this woman's words and that no search of her house was instituted. The Bible is often sparing with indications of divine guidance over against human intrigue (cf. Gen. 50:20; 2 Sam. 17:14). Yet this guidance may well be implied by the narrator of this account.

Hebrew narrative often proceeds episodically. V. 7 reports the pursuit of the men *in the direction of the Jordan, near the fords*[16] and of the shutting of the city gate. The topic of the pursuit is not resumed, however, until v. 22. The reader is first invited to concentrate on what goes on inside Rahab's house. In the meantime the narrative conjures up the fruitless chase by the king's men.

8–11   After Rahab has rid herself of the king's men she ascends to the roof where the men *had not yet lain down*; they had not yet gone to sleep (Gen. 19:4).[17] The woman expresses her conviction *that the Lord has given you the land*. Thus she confirms what ch. 1 had stated repeatedly (1:2–3, 11, 15). She also speaks of the *dread* that has fallen upon Canaan's inhabitants. Her words bear out the truth of Exod. 15:14–16; 23:27. The

14. Several commentators call Rahab's words a lie. Others point out that the account does not contain a value judgment, which is left to the reader to supply from the wider biblical context. B. Holwerda (*Jozua*, p. 8) argues that "truth" in Israel is something different from "agreement with fact." It means "loyalty toward the neighbor and the Lord." Thus viewed, Rahab's words need not be called a lie.

15. Flax is seldom mentioned in the OT. It is referred to in the Gezer calendar, dating from between the 11th and 9th centuries BC (see *DOTT*, p. 201). H. Donner and W. Röllig, eds., *Kanaanäische und aramäische Inschriften* II (Wiesbaden: 1964), p. 181, date it "with some degree of certainty" to the second half of the 10th century.

16. Heb. *'al hammaʿbᵉrôṯ*. Other translations: "as far as the fords" (Soggin, with appeal to Ugaritic); "auf die Furten zu" (Hertzberg); "vers les gués" (Abel). KD, p. 36, list a number of fords where the Jordan could be crossed. However, the conditions described in 3:15 would still make crossing hazardous at this time.

16. Heb. *'al hammaʿbᵉrôṯ*. Other translations: "as far as the fords" (Soggin, with appeal to Ugaritic); "auf die Furten zu" (Hertzberg); "vers les gués" (Abel). KD, p. 36) list a number of fords where the Jordan could be crossed. However, the conditions described in 3:15 would still make crossing hazardous at this time.

17. This bit of information would seem strange if the hiding of the men had taken place just as the king's messengers were at the door. It is more natural if this hiding had taken place earlier; see our translation of v. 4.

Canaanites are portrayed as having *lost heart* (lit. "been seized with anxiety").[18] Dread accompanies God's march through the world on behalf of his people (cf. 4:24; 5:1). The prophets link the Lord's acts in time with his eschatological acts of redemption and judgment (compare Isa. 9:4 [Eng. 5] with Judg. 7; Isa. 28:21 with 2 Sam. 5:20, 25). Rahab's words thus form a link in a real chain of events which will some day usher in the end time (see also Deut. 2:25; 11:25). What was promised there is now being fulfilled. Even the memory of the crossing of the Red Sea[19] has not faded. It has become vivid again due to Israel's proximity, opposite Jericho. A more recent event is Israel's defeat of *Sihon and Og*, here called *kings of the Amorites*.[20] To them Israel had *applied the curse*[21] (Num. 21:21–35). Again Rahab speaks of the dismay which has befallen her people in Canaan. Their *heart dissolved*, and *there was no courage left with anyone*. All this leads her to confess that the Lord, Israel's God, is *a God in heaven above and on the earth beneath*. At this point Rahab's words resemble those of Moses in Deut. 4:39. Are these words of Rahab's "confession," so strongly resembling various thoughts expressed in the

18. For a treatment of this word (Heb. *môg*) and other words in this chapter as evidence of "holy war" terminology see D. J. McCarthy, "Some Holy War Vocabulary in Joshua 2," *CBQ* 33 (1971), pp. 228–230. On the "holy war" motif in general and on the "dread" this entails on the part of Yahweh's enemies see G. von Rad, *OT Theology* I, p. 205. This motif may be recognized, provided it is not used to cast doubt upon the reality of the phenomena which occurred during Israel's wars. The motif derives its *raison d'être* from the historical facts it describes. It is more than just a "theological" schematization. This opinion differs from the current critical view. See, e.g., G. H. Jones, " 'Holy War' or 'Yahweh War'?" *VT* 25 (1975), who states that "there is no proof that the Holy War scheme in its entirety was ever put into action historically." The Holy War formula "does not represent what actually happened historically" (p. 657). The last three words constitute the real problem. Is Jones still working with the methodology of Leopold von Ranke?

19. In spite of the modern trend toward "Reed Sea" as the translation of Heb. *yām sûp*, we believe a good case can be made for "Red Sea." According to L. Koehler-W. Baumgartner (*Lexicon in Veteris Testamenti Libros* [Leiden: ²1958], p. 652), *sûp* means "rushes," "waterplants," such as were also wrapped around the face of Jonah who was thrown into the Mediterranean Sea (Jon. 2:5). Kraeling, *The Rand McNally Bible Atlas*, p. 103, states that *yām sûp* "is most definitely identifiable" when it refers to the Gulf of Aqabah (1 K. 9:26). This gulf was an arm of the *Red* Sea, not of some body of water called *Reed* Sea. The point is not essential to the thought expressed here and will not be pursued further.

20. This term is used in a variety of ways in the OT. Amorites occur in the Table of Nations (Gen. 10:16). The term also stands for all the inhabitants of Canaan (Gen. 15:16). Sometimes it "is the most generic name for the populations here envisioned" (R. North, *Bibl* 54 (1973), p. 48. However, in this case and elsewhere, it is reserved for dwellers on the east side of the Jordan (9:10; 24:8).

21. For this expression see commentary on 6:17.

Pentateuch, simply a fabrication of the author of this account?[22] We believe the substance of these words to be truly that of Rahab. However, her conversation with the spies may well have been longer than actually reported. If so, a summary by the Israelite writer had to be supplied. In such an outline various thoughts of the Pentateuchal books may have influenced the report, but not to such an extent as to cast doubt on the basic veracity of the words and on the sentiments expressed. A closer comparison with Exod. 15:15–16; Deut. 2:25; 11:25 shows that Rahab's words are not verbatim quotes.

In some ways her words reflect clearly that she is just beginning to emerge from her pagan environment. Calling God *the Lord your God* who *is a God in heaven above and on the earth beneath*, Rahab expresses a thought which is also biblical; but similar utterances may be found also in pagan literature.[23]

12–13 Rahab now demands that the spies take a solemn oath that they will return her *faithfulness*[24] with similar faithfulness toward her and her family. This oath, once taken, will serve as a *sure sign*[25] that she and her entire family – father, mother, brothers, sisters, and all who belong to them – will be saved alive at the time of the attack upon Jericho which both she and the spies assume will be made (see introduction to this

22. C. Steuernagel, *op. cit.*, p. 213, sees 9b–11 as "Zusatz des Rd [Redaktors, MHW], durch den er die erbauliche Wirkung der Erzählung steigern will."

23. Cf. the Egyptian "Hymn to Aten" and the "Hymn to Amun"; see *DOTT*, pp. 147, 149. These hymns contain expressions such as "Thou sole god, there is no other like thee!" and "The only sole one, who has no peer." For a pagan reaction to the Lord's acts on behalf of Israel see also 1 Sam. 4:8. The thought that Israel's God acts "in the sight of the nations" is frequently expressed in Ezekiel, e.g. 20:22. The Alalah inscriptions contain an invocation of "the gods above and the gods beneath," language similar to that used by Rahab; see D. J. Wiseman, "Alalakh," in *AOTS*, pp. 131, 135.

24. Heb. *ḥeseḏ*, a word hard to translate by one English equivalent. Koehler-Baumgartner, *Lexicon*, translates it with: "Gemeinschaftspflicht, Verbundenheit, Solidarität." The word means principally that one is loyal to a covenant relationship, but it also contains the notions of mercy and of kindness. Many translations use the notion of "kindness" at this point: ASV, RSV, American Translation, Moffatt, Jerusalem Bible; Abel "bonté"; Zürcher Bibel "Barmherzigkeit"; Noth "Treue"; Holwerda similar; DNV "Weldaad."

25. Some commentators wish to omit these words, which do not occur in the LXX, e.g., Noth. Gelin puts them in brackets. Perhaps the LXX, thinking that these words must be understood in terms of the scarlet cord, considered them out of place here. We prefer to take them as referring to the oath which Rahab requested (with Keil and Delitzsch, B. Alfrink, and Kroeze). A solemn oath in oriental context might well be referred to as a "sign." For the LXX text at this point, cf. also Holzinger, *op. cit.*, p. 5, who thinks he can detect more than one point where the LXX has smoothed out ("Glättungen") the text.

chapter). Rahab thinks in terms of family and clan. This is in keeping with the thought patterns of the ancient Near East. It is also an indication of her unselfishness.

14–15 The men respond with a strong assurance that they will guarantee with their very lives (*Our life for yours!*[26]) the safety of Rahab and her kin. See also vv. 17, 20; 6:22. But they insist that utter secrecy must be observed, and that *this agreement of ours*[27] should not be told to others. But *faithfulness and loyalty* will surely be shown when the Lord will have *given the land* to Israel. "Faithfulness and loyalty" is the standard expression for acts done and kindness shown in connection with covenantal agreements (Gen. 24:27, 49; 32:10). The spies as well as Rahab previously (v. 9) express their conviction that the Lord will "give" the land to Israel, thus confirming a repeated emphasis of ch. 1; see 1:2–3, 11, 13.

It seems best to regard the information of v. 15, of how Rahab *let them down through a window by a rope*, as a proleptic summary of the final action whereby the spies are permitted to leave the city.[28] This is better than to assume the ensuing conversation (vv. 16–21a) to have taken place at the moment when the men were being let down from the house in the wall.

The narrator is concerned to bring one part of the narrative to a conclusion, and already at this point reports the mode of escape employed. Rahab's house is *on the outside of the wall*, but it may also be said to be *in that wall*.[29] Those familiar with houses built on (against) the massive dikes protecting the Netherlands lowlands from the sea may see a parallel here.

16 In her advice to the men (*To the mountain country you must go*), the woman may have thought of Jebel Qaranṭal, a prominent mountaintop northwest of Jericho, identified by the Crusaders as the scene of Jesus' temptation. This area is full of crevices and caves, and would thus provide a likely hiding place.

17–20 Before taking leave, the two spies state more precisely than they had previously the conditions under which the oath of v. 14 will be binding on them. The declaration beginning *we will be free of this oath* is not brought to its grammatical conclusion,[30] but is followed by the

26. Heb. lit. "our life instead of you to die."
27. This can also be rendered: "This business of ours." Heb. *dāḇār* here can mean both "word" and "matter."
28. So with Soggin, Hertzberg, and others. See also W. J. Martin, " 'Dischronologized' Narrative in the *OT*," *VTS* 17 (1969), pp. 179–186.
29. The Hebrew for these two expressions is *beqîr haḥômâ* and *baḥômâ* respectively. Cf. 1 K. 6:5, where the preposition is *'al*, "against."
30. The element left out would be "if you break the agreement." Cf. Hertzberg, who supplies: "bei folgender Sachlage."

74

conditions the men now impose on Rahab and her family. She is to *tie this scarlet cord in the window*,[31] and to make sure that those whom she hopes to include in this agreement will be with her in the house. The whole conversation reflects the expectation that the city will be taken by force, that breaches will be made and houses destroyed and taken in combat (see introduction to this chapter).

Some of the Church Fathers considered the red cord that Rahab used as a sign whereby she and her family would be spared from death to be a symbol of the blood of Christ. Rahab herself was considered a symbol of the Church, since she by her faith and kindness secured the safety of her family.[32] Typological connections of this sort must be handled with great care. Indeed, a real typological connection between the Testaments should be recognized in the light of the Bible's own consciousness. But due care should be taken to detect whether there is in fact a real line of continuity running from the "type" to that which it is supposed to typify. No mere coincidence such as the sameness of the color or other externalities will suffice.[33] The men state precisely what will be the case. He who is not in Rahab's house at the time of the capture of Jericho, *his blood will be on his own head*,[34] i.e., he will be responsible for his death, whereas the men themselves will assume responsibility for the death of any who will be with Rahab in the house. Rahab, as they have stated before, is sworn to complete secrecy.[35]

31. If, as we suggest, the conversation takes places before the actual letting down through the window, then "this" cord must refer to one which the men, who probably came prepared for various eventualities, had brought with them.
32. Cf. JB footnote at this point.
33. The question of what constitutes a correct typology is too vast to be treated here. In recent decades higher-critical studies have attempted to salvage typology for Biblical Theology, but the end product of these attempts is not to be equated with the traditional typology of the Church. While the latter's excesses should be granted (cf., e.g., G. Vos, *Biblical Theology* [1948], p. 162), the newer substitute is not to be welcomed. Cf. also W. Eichrodt, "Is Typological Exegesis an Appropriate Method?" in C. Westermann, ed., *Essays on OT Hermeneutics* (E.T. 1979), pp. 224–245. Perhaps some connection between the cord and the blood on the doorpost at the Exodus passover exists, but due care is called for in seeing such connection.
34. Cf. Lev. 20:9; 2 Sam. 1:16; 1 K. 2:37; Ezek. 18:13; 33:4; Matt. 27:25.
35. These verses contain some unusual Hebrew constructions, such as the use of the masc. *hazzeh* with the feminine word for "oath." BH suggests this be read *hazzōt*, a rare feminine form; but see GKC § 34a (note 2). Another irregularity is the verb forms in vv. 17–18, 20, where Rahab is addressed. In recent decades Hebrew linguists have shown some reluctance to streamline unusual-looking forms. Wider knowledge of comparative Semitics has urged caution; cf. W. L. Moran, "The Hebrew Language in Its North Semitic Background" in G. E. Wright, ed., *The Bible and the Ancient Near East*, p. 65.

21 Rahab agrees to these conditions. She then lets them go in the manner stated in v. 15 (see commentary). The narrator, again in the fashion more often observed in Hebrew narrative, completes the story of the scarlet cord, reporting that Rahab tied it in the window. Thus the narrative is brought to a conclusion so far as this sign is concerned, although the actual event probably took place later.[36] Note a similar prolepsis in the first part of v. 22.

22-24 The men heed Rahab's advice. They stay three days in the *mountain country*, and though one may assume a careful search on the part of Jericho's men there is no detection. This constitutes another tacit admission that divine guidance is favoring the mission of Joshua's men; see also vv. 3-7.

The men then come down and ford the Jordan, a perilous undertaking under the prevailing circumstances (cf. 3:15), and tell Joshua, their chief, *everything that had befallen them*. The message carried back to Joshua contains that which thematically is the most important element of this chapter. It reiterates that *the Lord has given the whole country into our power* (cf. 1:3, 6, 11; 2:9) and stresses at the same time the panic-stricken condition[37] of Canaan's inhabitants.

After these somewhat introductory chapters, the narrative is now ready to pick up the main thread of the story.

C. CROSSING INTO THE PROMISED LAND: REMEMBERING GOD'S ACTS (3:1 – 4:24)

1. THE CROSSING (3:1–17)

1 *Joshua arose early in the morning, and he and all the Israelites broke camp from Shittim and went to the Jordan and lodged there before they crossed over.*

2 *Three days afterwards the officers went through the camp*

3 *and gave the people the following orders: "As soon as you see the ark of the covenant of the Lord your God and the Levitical priests bearing it, then you yourselves are to set out from your place and follow behind it.*

4 *However, there shall be a distance between you and it of about two thousand cubits. Do not come close to it so that you may know the*

---

36. This solution appears preferable to that of the LXX, where the phrase is omitted entirely. The MT at this point is clearly the "more difficult" reading and should for that reason be given due consideration.
37. The verb *môg* is used here as also in v. 9. About possible "holy war" associations see commentary on v. 9.

way you are to go, for you have not been over this way before."

5 *And Joshua said to the people: "Sanctify yourselves; for tomorrow the Lord will do miracles among you."*

6 *Then he said to the priests: "Take up the ark of the covenant and pass over in front of the people." So they took up the ark of the covenant and went in front of the people.*

7 *And the Lord said to Joshua: "This day I will begin to exalt you in the eyes of all Israel, that they may know that as I was with Moses so I will be with you.*

8 *As for you, give orders to the priests who bear the ark of the covenant: when you come to the edge of the water of the Jordan you shall stand in the Jordan."*

9 *And Joshua said to the Israelites: "Come near to me and hear the words of the Lord your God."*

10 *Then Joshua said: "By this you will know that a living God is among you and that he will certainly drive out from before you the Canaanite, and the Hittite, and the Hivite, and the Perizzite, and the Girgashite, and the Amorite, and the Jebusite.*

11 *Behold, the ark of the covenant, the Lord of all the earth, crosses before you into the Jordan.*

12 *Now then, take twelve men out of the tribes of Israel, one man from each tribe.*

13 *When the soles of the feet of the priests who bear the ark of the Lord, the Lord of the whole earth, come to rest in the waters of the Jordan, the waters of the Jordan will be cut off, namely the waters flowing from upstream, and they will stand in a single heap."*

14 *Now when the people broke camp to cross the Jordan, with the priests bearing the ark of the covenant preceding the people,*

15 *and as soon as the bearers of the ark came to the Jordan and the feet of the priests bearing the ark dipped into the edge of the waters (the Jordan being full above all its banks, all the days of the harvest),*

16 *then the waters coming down from above stood; they rose up in one heap, a great distance, from Adam, a city beside Zarethan; while those flowing down to the Sea of the Arabah, the Salt Sea, were completely cut off. So the people crossed over opposite Jericho.*

17 *And the priests bearing the ark of the covenant of the Lord stood firm on dry ground in the midst of the Jordan, while all Israel crossed over on dry ground, until the whole nation had finished crossing over the Jordan.*

Chapters 3–4 belong close together. Both describe Israel's crossing of the Jordan. However, ch. 4, while providing some further details of the crossing not given in ch. 3, focuses especially on the erection of the memorial

77

stones which must keep alive the memory of this great event for future generations; see 4:1–9; 20–24.

It will be well, in reading these chapters, to keep in mind the Hebrew narrative technique employed here. Some examples of this technique were given in the preceding chapter; see commentary on 2:15, 21b. In this technique the narrator concludes a certain matter (3:17; 4:1), stating that the crossing was completed; yet at a later point (4:5, 15ff.), he resumes his description of the crossing when necessary for the development of his topic. We prefer this manner of reading the account to that adopted by those who see these chapters as a composite of various traditions woven together by a redactor.[1] The element of suspense which this narrative technique injects into the account should also be duly noted. Examples will be furnished in the commentary below.[2] Of great importance is the use of certain terms throughout chs. 3–4; "to cross," used on no fewer than twenty-two occasions, and "to stand," used five times, indicate that "this narrative appears first of all as a uniform whole, theologically exhibiting a definite concern, and literarily held together by certain leading words."[3]

The materials of chs. 3–4 could be divided along the following lines: 3:1–6, preparation for the miracle; 3:7–17, the divine miracle; 4:1–14, specific details of the crossing; 4:15–24, the erection of the memorial stones. Each of these sections begins with a command to Joshua,

1. C. Steuernagel (*Das Buch Josua*, p. 216) considers ch. 3 to be made up of a basic source, called D², to which a later redactor added occasional fragments from the E source. He suggests a similar approach to ch. 4. M. Noth (*Das Buch Josua*, pp. 31–33) believes that chs. 3–4 mean to report two traditions, one dealing with the erection of a monument in the river bed (3:12; 4:4–7, 9) and another dealing with a similar monument at the sanctuary of Gilgal (4:1–3, 8, 20–24). See also J. A. Soggin, *Joshua*, who holds that these chapters represent an ancient liturgy in which a Jordan "crossing" was symbolically enacted in a cultic ceremony. This cult act was subsequently "historicized" and became the story of the crossing; see also H.-J. Kraus, "Gilgal, ein Beitrag zur Kultusgeschichte Israels," *VT* 1 (1951), pp. 181–199; and Noth's criticism of this approach, *op. cit.*, p. 33.
2. This suspense element is also noted in the commentary by D. Baldi, *Giosué*. Bibbia Garofalo (Turin: 1952) (not available to the present writer) and too quickly dismissed as without solid foundation by Soggin, *op. cit.*, p. 59.
3. So H. W. Hertzberg, *ATD* IX, p. 25. Hertzberg does note the various attempts to unravel supposed narrative strata in these two chapters, but also observes that the literary analysis of the materials has often left further questions which could not be answered satisfactorily. He has a valid concern to see the main purpose of the story recounted here: to highlight God's gracious guidance of his people who, through the Jordan crossing, are now at last being ushered into the land promised to the fathers.

followed by an indication that the command was transmitted to the people and carried out subsequently.

1 Having heard the encouraging report of the two spies, Joshua now carries out without delay the divine command recorded in 1:2. He rises *early in the morning*,[4] and *he and all the Israelites* break camp from Shittim, the same place from which the spies had been sent (2:1). Thus the people move close to the Jordan River, ready to cross it when the command is given. Though the words *lodged there* could refer to just one night's stay, they can also be taken of a stay slightly longer in duration (cf. 2 Sam. 12:16 where the word means repeated lodging and Zeph. 2:14 where a more permanent lodging is envisaged). This accounts for the *three days* of v. 2. In light of the subsequent dramatic developments one senses in the words *before they crossed over* something of the suspense element discussed above. This crossing will be the means whereby the "giving" of the land, so prominently mentioned in the preceding chapters (1:11; 2:9, 24), will become a reality.

2 The reason why the *officers* did not give further orders for the crossing until *three days afterwards* may lie in the fact that the Lord meant to impress upon Israel the seeming impossibility of that which he had commanded them to do. The Jordan, under any circumstance a formidable barrier (see commentary on 1:2), was at this time filled with the spring waters (3:15). Several days at Jordan's banks would thus have served the purpose of trying the people's patience.

The chronological connection between the *three days* in this verse and those of 1:11 has been given more than one interpretation. It appears best not to identify the two.[5] The three days of 1:11 may have been an indefinite period (see commentary), allowing for the mission of the spies to have occurred in the meantime. This mission may have taken as many as four or five days. The three days here begin with Israel's departure from Shittim.[6]

3 The officers tell the people to take their clue from the movement of *the ark of the covenant of the Lord your God* and from *the Levitical priests bearing it*. This ark, emblem of the Lord's indwelling amongst

4. For this phrase cf. also 6:12; 7:16; 8:10.
5. This is also the position of C. F. Keil and F. Delitzsch, C. J. Goslinga, and B. Holwerda.
6. J. H. Kroeze, *Het Boek Jozua*, p. 50, believes that 3:2, 4–5 must be linked with 1:10–11, and that together these verses speak of what immediately precedes the crossing. Kroeze believes that the author at this point did not have a precise chronological order in mind and simply reported the story of the spies at the point where he needed it.

Israel, dominates the entire account of the crossing (see vv. 6, 8, 11, 13–14, 17; 4:7, 9, 11, 16, 18). Thus the Lord, to whom the ark belongs, is presented as the One who actually enters Canaan ahead of the Israelites. As *ark of the covenant* the sacred chest is viewed as the container of the law tablets, the covenant statutes par excellence (Exod. 25:21; Deut. 10:1; cf. Num. 10:33). This was one of several designations of the ark, but one well suited to express the idea that Israel's privilege as God's people was linked with the sacred obligation to keep the covenant that God in his grace had made with them.

The name *ark of the covenant* should not be taken as a later rationalization of an earlier, supposedly more "primitive" ark concept which conceived of the Lord as more directly associated with his cult object.[7] Some passages do stress the close link between the Lord and his ark (e.g., Num. 10:35–36), but Num. 10:33 indicates that such a conception is compatible with the use of the term *ark of the covenant*.[8] In fact, even in Josh. 3 the great significance of the ark is duly recognized. Its first mention *precedes* the mention of its bearers; cf. also 4:11. This agrees with other references (cf. Num. 10:33) where the ark is viewed as acting in an almost autonomous fashion, although nowhere does the OT suggest a magical or fetishistic understanding of the ark, apart from superstitious contexts such as 1 Sam. 4:3–4.

Those bearing the ark are called *the Levitical priests*, both here and in 8:33. Elsewhere in the account they are simply called priests, with or without the addition: "Those bearing the ark." The explanatory adjective "Levitical" (lit. "the priests, the Levites") serves to distinguish these priests from others who were non-Levitical; see Exod. 19:22, 24. The restriction of the priesthood to the tribe of Levi, more particularly to Aaron's family, dates from the desert period; see Exod. 32:26–29; Num. 25:7–13; Deut. 18:5).[9]

---

7. This view is widespread; cf. J. Steinmann, *Josué*, p. 37.
8. For a further elaboration of the many views concerning the ark, and an alleged development of its "theology," cf. also M. H. Woudstra, *The Ark of the Covenant from Conquest to Kingship, passim*; see also "The Ark of the Covenant in Jeremiah 3:16–18," in J. Cook, ed., *Grace upon Grace*. Festschrift L. J. Kuyper (Grand Rapids: 1975), pp. 117–127. There is no good biblical reason to deny, or be embarrassed by, the more "numinous" elements in the passages dealing with the ark. Only upon the tenets of comparative religion do such passages become embarrassing because such study is so often pursued from the viewpoint of evolutionism.
9. According to J. Wellhausen and his latter day disciples the expression "the priests the Levites" is a late, deuteronomic clarification, added after Josiah's cultic reforms as described in 2 K. 22–23; for a rebuttal cf. O. T. Allis, *The Five Books of Moses* (Philadelphia: ²1949), pp. 184, 193.

It was the Levites, especially the sons of Kohath, who had been entrusted with the duty of carrying the ark (Num. 4:4, 15). This custom is observed in Deut. 10:8; 31:25; 1 Sam. 6:15; 2 Sam. 15:24; 2 Chr. 5:4; 35:3. On other occasions, however, the priests were assigned to perform that duty (Deut. 31:9; 1 K. 8:3, 6).[10]

The people at the bank of the Jordan are told to *follow behind* the ark and its bearers.

4 To impress upon the Israelites the ark's great sanctity they are instructed that *there shall be a distance between you and it of about two thousand cubits*. Thus the sacred object is to proceed in full view of the people. There should not be any rash handling or inadvertent touching (cf. 1 Sam. 6:19; 2 Sam. 6:7). The ark was the symbol of the indwelling of the Holy One; cf. Num. 7:89. The distance of 2000 cubits was approximately that of the outer bank of the Jordan to the inner bed, from el-Ghôr to ez-Zôr. Thus the people would still be on the outer bank while the feet of the priests touched the water's edge (see v. 8).[11]

By seeing the ark descend to the Jordan the people would *know the way you are to go*. It will be an unusual way, one not previously used as a crossing. Perhaps there is already a hint here of the miracle that is to occur.

5–6 To prepare for the coming events the people are to *sanctify*,[12] or consecrate themselves. What this entailed may be seen from Exod. 19:10, 14–15; Num. 11:18. Outward rites were meant to further inward openness toward God and his acts. These acts will be performed *tomorrow*. They are called *miracles*, lit. "things to be astounded at"[13] (see Exod.

---

10. A comparison of parallel accounts in Kings and Chronicles points up certain differences in the respective functions of priests and Levites which have not yet been sufficiently explained.
    The LXX reads "the priests and the Levites," as do the Syriac and Targum. However, the Vulgate reads *sacerdotes stirpis leviticae*, enhancing and strengthening the thought of the MT.
11. The distance of 2000 cubits was used later to mark off an allowable sabbath day's journey (cf. Acts 1:12). This was fixed by Jewish rabbis on the basis of Exod. 16:29; Num. 35:5. Some interpreters have appealed to this correspondence to suggest that the account of the crossing breathes a cultic spirit, but without sufficient ground.
12. From the Hebrew root *qdš*, the derivation of which is not completely clear. Some hold it to be from a root meaning "to cut," others: "to be bright."
13. Heb. *niplā'ôṯ*, Gk. *thaumastá*. Another Hebrew word used to describe a miracle is *môrā'*, emphasizing the fear and dread which a miracle produces in the beholder; cf. Deut. 10:21; 2 Sam. 7:23.

3:5). It is these marvelous acts of God which the believer is to celebrate (Ps. 9:2 [Eng. v. 1]; 26:7; 40:6 [Eng. v. 5]; 71:17). They are the very foundation of Israel's redemptive history.

The sequence between vv. 5-6 shows that chronology is not the narrator's chief concern. Verse 6 reports the command by Joshua that the priest *take up the ark of the covenant and pass over in front of the people*. This command must have been issued on the day which is called "tomorrow" in the immediately preceding verse. No recognition of the time lapse between these verses is given. The report of the one event follows immediately upon that of the other. The same may be said about the execution of Joshua's command by the priests. Verse 6b reports that the priests did what Joshua told them to do. Yet it would seem best to hold that the substance of what is reported in vv. 7-13 took place and was spoken prior to the priests' departure. Not until v. 14 is there an actual description of the sequel to 6b. This shows that the order in which the events are reported is material rather than chronological.

The priests *took up the ark*. In the light of Num. 10:35 this was tantamount to the Lord's own "arising." He identified himself with the ark. Its movements were his movements also.

7 Having reported, by way of prolepsis, the lifting up of the sacred ark by the priests, the narrator now reports words which the Lord speaks to Joshua, probably prior to the actual departure of the ark (see above). The Lord *will begin to exalt* Joshua through the events that are now taking place. Joshua will know that as the Lord *was with Moses* so he will be with him. This confirms what was said in ch. 1, where constant stress was placed on Joshua's close connection with his predecessor (see 1:3, 5, 7, 17). The continuity of leadership which God himself had arranged already during Moses' lifetime (Deut. 1:37-38) will now become realized in Joshua's exaltation. Earlier, attention was called to certain striking parallels in the careers of Moses and Joshua (see commentary on 1:5, 14, 17). The parallel that comes to mind here is Exod. 14:31. Joshua's exaltation will take place *in the eyes of all Israel*; see commentary on 1:2, 12-15. Cf. 4:14; 7:23; 8:21, 24; 23:2; and related phrases in 18:1; 22:12, 14, 18; 24:1.

8 Whatever the exact chronology of the events, the manner in which the narrative proceeds clearly contains an element of suspense. Joshua is now to *give orders to the priests who bear the ark* that when they *come to the edge of the water of the Jordan* they *shall stand in the Jordan*. Thus, in the narrative at least, one is brought to the dramatic point of the approach to Jordan's bank. However, the execution of this command is delayed; in fact the command itself is not actually given until the events themselves begin to unfold. Nevertheless, the effect upon the reader is one of anticipation.

Joshua's role with respect to the impending miracle of the parting of Jordan's water is less direct than that of Moses at the Red Sea. Moses was himself instrumental in the miracle (Exod. 14:16, 21), but Joshua merely is to give orders. It may be that the Lord's presence in the ark also plays a role in this difference. The ark had not been made when Israel left Egypt.

Verse 8 does not specify what will happen when the priests actually do stand in the Jordan. This may well be another feature of suspense in this narrative. It would seem that this verse means to call attention to the initial planting of the feet in the river. What will happen then is not reported until v. 13.[14] Verse 8 thus becomes another prolepsis of what will be explained more fully at a later point.

9–10   Joshua now summons the people to him so that they may *hear the words of the Lord your God*. Although there has been no previous indication that the words following in vv. 10–14 had been imparted to Joshua, we may assume that this was so. At any rate, Joshua is God's authorized spokesman; see also v. 7.

By this anticipates what will not be explained until v. 13. Again the account moves slowly. The announcement of the coming miracle without a complete statement of its nature serves to create a feeling of suspense.

Joshua's explanation of the miracle's meaning should not be used to argue that miracles are in themselves neutral and mute, subject to more than one interpretation. Nor does Joshua's explanation give meaning to the miracle which otherwise it would not have. Rather, it only calls attention to that which is inherent in the miracle. True, miracles can be interpreted in several ways, but within the biblical view miraculous events have one unambiguous and clear meaning. Those who do not accept them as such fly in the face of evidence which all can see. Only blindness of mind caused by sin makes people misinterpret miracles.[15]

The coming miracle will make people know that a living God is among them. This will be an experiential knowing (Heb. *yāḏaʿ*). The

---

14. The very cadence of the Hebrew shows an awareness of the solemnity of the moment. See, e.g., the last few words of the verse: *mê hayyardēn bayyardēn taʿamōḏû*. Note the somewhat chiastic connection, and the use of the pausal form of the verb. Verse 9 also shows an unusual verb form in *gōšû hēnnâ* (lit. "approach ye hither"); see GKC § 66c. The change of pace attracts the attention.

15. There is a diversity of opinion about this point even among orthodox Christians. What is set forth above is, so we believe, the Christian theistic approach to reality and fact without which biblical scholarship will fall into many a pitfall.

people will find out in a very practical manner, and will perceive[16] that there is *a living God* among them. As *living God*[17] God stands opposed to, and is different from, the gods of the nations who are always portrayed as unable to act or to save (Ps. 96:5; 115:3–7). These other gods are idols (Heb. *'elîlîm*; Lev. 19:4). They are nothing but breath (Heb. *h*ᵃ*bālîm*; Deut. 32:21; Jer. 8:19). This living God is *among* Israel, which indicates his active presence with his people (Deut. 6:15).

This living God, the Lord of history, will *certainly drive out*[18] *from before you* the present inhabitants of Canaan. The inhabitants of Canaan are frequently enumerated in lists of various length in the books of the Pentateuch (Gen. 15:19–21; Exod. 3:17; 23:28; Deut. 7:1, etc.). Without being directly aware of it, they are awaiting the time when their iniquity will be full (Gen. 15:16; Deut. 32:8). The order in which they are listed differs. Here the order is: *the Canaanite, and the Hittite, and the Hivite, and the Perizzite, and the Girgashite, and the Amorite, and the Jebusite.* They are viewed here as seven in number (cf. Deut. 7:1), possibly a number symbolic of fullness (Josh. 9:1; Exod. 3:17 list only six; Gen. 15:19–21 ten). The term *Canaanite* is frequently used as a collective for all the inhabitants of Canaan regardless of racial origin. Here it stands for those living "by the sea" (5:1; Num. 13:29; cf. 11:3). This name most frequently heads the list of the nations to be dispossessed.[19] For the *Hittite* see the commentary on 1:4. Gibeon belonged to the ethnic group of *Hivites* (9:7; 11:19). They also lived in Shechem (Gen. 34:2; cf. Josh. 9:7; 11:3). Scholarly opinion is not united as to their precise identity.[20] *Perizzites* lived in central Palestine during the patriarchal period (Gen. 13:7; Exod. 3:8, 17; 23:23). Their name does not occur in extrabiblical sources, and little

---

16. Hertzberg translates: "Daran werdet ihr merken"; Noth: "Daran werdet ihr erkennen." These words suggest inward perception of truth which is part of the meaning of *yāḍa'*.
17. Heb. *'ēl ḥay*; also *'ᵉlôhîm ḥayyîm* (Deut. 5:26; 1 Sam. 17:26; 2 K. 19:4).
18. Heb. *yāraš*. In the Qal this word also means "to possess." Used in the Hiphil it assumes the meaning "to dispossess," "to drive out."
19. For a complete discussion of the various lists see R. North, *Bibl* 54 (1973), pp. 43–62. Cf. also P. C. Craigie, *Deuteronomy*, on Deut. 7:1; and C. H. de Geus, *The Tribes of Israel*. Studia Semitica Neerlandica 18 (Assen: 1976), *passim*.
20. The LXX sometimes replaces "Hivites" with "Horites," e.g., 9:7; Gen. 34:2, but no clear pattern emerges; compare the MT of 11:3 with LXX. North concludes that there is no "evidence within the Bible of the genuine existence of an otherwise unknown clan called Hivites" (p. 61). R. de Vaux maintains that it is entirely arbitrary to correct Hivites everywhere to Horite or imagine them a branch or synonym; *RB* 74 (1967), p. 499. According to 11:3; Judg. 3:13, the Hivites came from the north.

is known about them. In 17:15 they are connected with forested country
(see also Judg. 1:4–5). It has been suggested that the *Girgashites* lived in
the region where later the Gadarenes (RSV Gerasenes) lived, i.e. in Transjordan, near the Sea of Galilee (Luke 8:26), but little is known for certain
about this.[21] As for the *Amorites*, the Bible uses this term in both a wider
and a narrower sense. In the wider sense it denotes the entire population
of Canaan (24:15; Gen. 15:16; Judg. 1:34–35),[22] but it also stands for the
inhabitants of Canaan's mountain regions (Num. 13:29; Deut. 1:7).[23] In
all but one instance in Joshua (11:3) the *Jebusites* are placed at the end of
the list. Like the Amorites they appear to have lived in Canaan's mountain
regions (11:3; Num. 13:29). In 15:8, 63 they are connected with the region
of Jerusalem (cf. Judg. 1:21; 19:10–11; 2 Sam. 5:6).[24]

Joshua tells the Israelites that the living God will drive out all these
nations before them. This will happen *certainly*, as the use of the infinitive
absolute indicates.

11–13 Joshua now calls attention to *the ark of the covenant* (see
v. 3) which will cross before the people into the Jordan. The ark was such
an intimate symbol of the Lord's indwelling (cf. Num. 10:35) that to speak
of the ark is tantamount to speaking of the Lord whose ark it is. This is
probably why the words *the Lord of all the earth* stand in apposition to
the ark.[25] The phrase, which is also found in Mic. 4:13; Zech. 4:14; 6:5,
is a fitting one at this point. God's sovereignty over the earth offers Israel,
God's people, a rightful claim to the land they are about to enter (cf. Deut.

21. The Girgashites have also been linked with the Hittite term *Qaraqashi*, which
means the clients of the Sumerian god of light, *Gesh*. But no real relevance to the
Girgashites seems to be established.
22. Before Joshua's time the Amorites, called *amurru* in Mesopotamian documents, were a powerful people. Hammurabi the great legislator belonged to them.
The debate concerning their identity and origin continues; see A. Haldar, *Who
were the Amorites?* Monographs on the Ancient Near East 1 (Leiden: 1971); and
the critical review by J. R. Bartlett in *Bible Bibliography* (1974), p. 475.
23. Sihon and Og are also called "kings of the Amorites"; 2:10; 9:10; Ps. 135:10–
12.
24. The suggestion has been made that the Jebusites were Hurrian. See, e.g.,
C. J. M. Weir, "Nuzi," in *AOTS*, pp. 80–83, where the possible connection between Hurrians and other names mentioned in the Canaanite tribal lists is also
explored. See also D. R. Ap-Thomas, "Jerusalem," *idem*, p. 286; J. M. Miller,
"Jebus and Jerusalem: A Case of Mistaken Identity," *ZDPV* 90 (1974), pp. 115–
127.
25. There appears to be no need, from our understanding of the phrase, to replace
the word "covenant" with that of "Lord" as many do; the LXX reads "covenant,"
but cf. v. 13.

32:8–9).[26] Already at this point (v. 12), Joshua orders the setting apart of *twelve men*. This is another instance of anticipation and will be more fully developed in 4:2.[27] These men are to be taken *out of the tribes of Israel, one man from each tribe*, thus providing another support of the "all Israel" emphasis (see commentary on 1:2, 12–16; 3:7). The narrative now moves to a decisive climax by giving the specific details of the miracle that will occur, as reported by Joshua to the Israelites. The fact that this can be announced ahead of time constitutes part of the miraculous element, whatever natural causes may have played a part in bringing it about. Everything will center on *the ark of the Lord, the Lord of all the earth*. Exactly at the time when the feet of the ark-bearing priests will *come to rest in the waters of the Jordan*, the parting of the Jordan waters will become a fact. Thus further information is given about what had been hinted at proleptically in v. 8. The ark's prominence should be noted, though this ought not to be considered in terms of magic.[28] There is a certain way in which it is not the ark but the faith of those who carry and follow it that will bring about the miracle. The stories in 1 Sam. 4ff. show clearly that a superstitious belief in the ark's potency does not bring about the desired end.

Jordan's waters *will be cut off, namely the waters flowing from upstream, and they will stand in a single heap*. The language here is somewhat reminiscent of Exod. 15:8; cf. also Ps. 78:13. The two events in which Moses and Joshua each played such a prominent role are thus closely connected. They also lie in each other's redemptive historical extension.

14–16a The English translation of these verses is an attempt to follow closely the lengthy Hebrew constructions employed here.[29] This is now the resumption of the main line of action, anticipated in v. 6. The

26. F.-M. Abel, *Le Livre de Josué*, p. 26, considers the phrase "Lord of all the earth" to have been introduced here to counteract a tendency toward territorial particularism which he sees in Deut. 32:9 and elsewhere. If Deut. 32:9 is read in conjunction with the preceding verse, it is far from particularistic in a narrow and objectionable sense; v. 9 does not require an antidote.

27. Abel translates (paraphrases) correctly: "Dès maintenant, choississez douze hommes. . . ." There appears to be no need, therefore, to think of two independent stone traditions, each speaking of a different monument, of which this would be a misplaced remnant (as, e.g., Noth, *Das Buch Josua*, p. 35).

28. For a "magical" understanding of most of the ark stories, cf. H. Schrade, *Der Verborgene Gott: Gottesbild und Gottesvorstellung in Israel und im alten Orient* (Stuttgart: 1949). For a critical evaluation of this approach see Woudstra, *The Ark of the Covenant from Conquest to Kingship*, pp. 55f.

29. The sentence of 14–16 is continuous, consisting of three protases (vv. 14–15), the first and third of which are more precisely defined by a circumstantial clause, and of three apodoses (v. 16). See KD, p. 44.

ark's central role is again stressed.[30] The narrative returns to the very beginning, when *the people broke camp* (lit. "when the people set out from their tents"). The master narrator, who has been using prolepsis and suspense to such good advantage, is again at work here. The reader is brought to the water's brink, and sees the priests' feet dip *into the edge of the waters*, but at that point another delay occurs by means of a lengthy parenthesis (v. 15b). Before reporting the actual parting of the waters, the narrator must note the condition of the Jordan at this time of year, it *being full above all its banks, all the days of the harvest*.[31] This accomplishes two things: it delays once more the crucial point of the actual miracle, and it focuses on the seemingly impossible situation under which the miracle will be performed.

Finally, the description of the miracle is given: *the waters coming down from above stood*. Anticipations of this had been given in vv. 4–5, 8, 13. The words rendered *from Adam* may also be read "at Adam."[32] The city of Adam is probably to be identified with Dâmiyeh, 19 miles upstream from Jericho. If "from Adam" is indeed the correct understanding, then the account says that the Jordan waters were piled up over the entire distance from Adam to the point where the crossing took place. Taking the alternate reading, the waters *stood* and *rose up* at a point not visible to the Israelites. This would have resulted in a very wide stretch of river bottom suitable for crossing.[33] The city of Zarethan, beside which

---

30. The Hebrew expression here is *hā'ārôn habbᵉrît*, with a definite article in front of *bᵉrît*, which rules out a construct-absolute relation. This may be read as "the ark, i.e., the covenant," stressing the close association between the two. The tablets of the covenant contained in the ark are also called "the covenant." GKC § 127 g judges that the word *habbᵉrît* has been added by a redactor. Some of the earlier phraseology concerning the ark (see v. 11) should caution against such an approach.

31. The phrase is not without certain difficulties. There is some question about Heb. *gᵉdôt*, translated "banks" by several, but "uitlopers" ("small side arms") by Kroeze. And what about "all" of Jordan's banks? A river has two banks, not many. Hertzberg omits "all"; JB "the Jordan overflows the whole length of its banks . . ."; DNV "Now the Jordan had gone entirely outside its banks. . . ." The difficulty may be connected with the geographical features of the Jordan, with its several sets of banks. See also Keil and Delitzsch, where three banks are mentioned: the upper and outer banks, the lower or middle banks, and the true banks of the river bed.

32. The difference is between the Qere *mē'ādām*, and the Ketib *bᵉ'ādām*.

33. Most commentaries call attention to certain natural causes which may have contributed to the occurrence of the miracle at this time. An Arab historian reports that in A.D. 1267 landslides dammed the river for several hours. A similar occurrence took place in 1927.

Adam is said to be situated, is mentioned in 1 K. 7:46. There is no agreement as to its precise location.[34]

Of the waters *flowing down to the Sea of the Arabah*,[35] *the Salt Sea*—also known as the Dead Sea (a name not used in the OT)—it is said that they were *completely cut off*. According to one opinion the waters flowing down were other streams which were kept from entering the Jordan at points below the actual stoppage of the main flow.

16b–17 The account now comes to a provisional conclusion by reporting how *the people crossed over opposite Jericho*, with some further remarks about *the priests bearing the ark of the covenant of the Lord* who *stood firm on dry ground in the midst of the Jordan*. This type of concluding statement concerning a certain aspect of an event reported agrees with the narrative style observed earlier (see vv. 6, 12; cf. 2:21b). Thus a provisional rounding-off of this great account of the crossing is achieved. Ch. 4 will resume the story of the crossing to the extent necessary for the author's further purposes.

Until the very end of the account, due stress is given to ark and priests (vv. 3, 8, 13). The ark, the supreme symbol of God's indwelling, is viewed as directing silently the whole proceedings as the priests *stood firm*[36] *on dry ground*. The narrator's chief concern with this chapter has been to focus attention upon the stupendous miracle, wrought under the watchful eye of the Lord, whose ark led the way into the waters and then stood in the river bed while *the whole nation*[37] *had finished crossing over the Jordan*.

Later generations of readers would be encouraged by the recollection of this great act of God. The entry into the promised land with all its truly spiritual implications would thus be etched indelibly upon their hearts. Already during the OT period their minds would be "raised to Christ,"[38] who, typically, had accompanied them on their trek through the desert (1 Cor. 10:4) and who, in the symbol of the ark, had stood by them in the

---

34. For a useful discussion see Soggin, *Joshua*, pp. 61f.

35. The Arabah is the continuation of the Jordan rift between the Dead Sea and the Gulf of Elath (Aqabah).

36. Heb. *hākēn*, inf. abs. of *kûn*, used adverbially.

37. The word used is *gôy*, used also in 4:1; 5:6, 8; 10:13. In the rest of the chapter *'am* is used (vv. 3, 5–6, 14, 16). *'am* stands for the people as an ethical religious community; *gôy* views them as a totality.

38. J. Calvin, *Commentaries on the Book of Joshua* (E.T. Grand Rapids: 1979), p. xxii; see Woudstra, *Calvin's Dying Bequest to the Church: A Critical Evaluation of the Commentary on Joshua.* Calvin Theological Seminary Monograph Series (Grand Rapids: 1960), pp. 24–28, 40.

death-like experience of Jordan's crossing until they were safe on the other side.[39]

2. THE MEMORIAL STONES (4:1-24)

1 *When the whole nation had finished crossing the Jordan the Lord said to Joshua:*

2 *"Take twelve men from the people, one from each tribe,*

3 *and give them this command: take up here, from the middle of the Jordan, from the place where the feet of the priests stood firm, twelve stones and carry them with you and put them down at the campsite where you will spend the night."*

4 *Then Joshua called the twelve men whom he had selected from the Israelites, one for each tribe.*

5 *And he said to them: "Go over to the middle of the Jordan, to the place where the ark of the Lord your God is, and each of you take up one stone on his shoulder, according to the number of the tribes of the Israelites,*

6 *so that this may be a sign among you. For when later your children ask you: What do these stones mean for you?*

7 *then you must tell them: They mean that the waters of the Jordan were cut off before the ark of the covenant of the Lord; when it crossed the Jordan the waters of the Jordan were cut off. Therefore these stones are to be a memorial to the Israelites forever."*

8 *So the Israelites did as Joshua had commanded; they took up twelve stones from the middle of the Jordan, according to the number of the tribes of the Israelites, as the Lord had told Joshua; and they carried them with them to the campsite and put them down there.*

9 *And Joshua set up twelve stones in the middle of the Jordan at the place where the feet of the priests who carried the ark of the covenant had stood, and they have been there to this day.*

10 *The priests who carried the ark remained standing in the middle of the Jordan until everything was finished which the Lord had instructed Joshua to tell the people to do, in accord with all that Moses had commanded Joshua; and the people hurried over.*

11 *And as soon as all the people had finished crossing over, the ark of the Lord and the priests crossed over before the eyes of the people.*

12 *And the Reubenites, Gadites, and the half-tribe of Manasseh marched over in formation, ahead of the Israelites, as Moses had said to them.*

39. About the typical meaning of the crossing of the Jordan cf. C. J. Goslinga, *Het Boek Jozua*, p. 31; S. G. De Graaf, *Promise and Deliverance* I (St. Catharines: 1977), p. 397.

13 *About forty thousand of them, equipped for war, crossed over before the Lord to the plains of Jericho for battle.*

14 *In that day the Lord made Joshua a great man in the sight of all Israel, and they feared him as they feared Moses, all the days of his life.*

15 *The Lord said to Joshua:*

16 *"Command the priests carrying the ark of the testimony to come up out of the Jordan."*

17 *So Joshua commanded the priests: "Come up out of the Jordan."*

18 *When the priests carrying the ark of the covenant of the Lord came up out of the bed of the Jordan, the feet of the priests had no sooner been raised to the dry ground than the waters of the Jordan returned to their place and ran full-flood along its banks as before.*

19 *The people came up from the Jordan on the tenth of the first month and made camp at Gilgal on the east side of Jericho.*

20 *And those twelve stones which they had taken up from the Jordan Joshua set up at Gilgal.*

21 *And he said to the Israelites: "When your children in the future will ask their fathers: What do these stones mean?*

22 *then you must tell your children: On dry ground Israel crossed over this Jordan.*

23 *For the Lord your God dried up the waters of the Jordan before you until you had crossed, just as the Lord your God had done to the Red Sea, which he dried up before us until we had crossed,*

24 *so that all the people of the earth may know that the hand of the Lord is strong, in order that you may fear the Lord your God all the days."*

If the chief purpose of ch. 4, the erection of the memorial stones, is kept in mind, the apparent lack of order and of composition,[1] which many have thought to characterize the account at this point, ceases to be a pressing problem.[2] (See introduction to ch. 3.)

1-3 After *the whole nation* (Heb. *gôy*, as in 3:17) *had finished crossing.* The situation is that envisaged in 3:17 which had presented the crossing in summary form. At that point, *the Lord said to Joshua;* in other words he repeated the command given and recorded in 3:12. The emphasis of the command lies in the participation of all Israel in the ritual of the ceremonial stones (see 1:2; 3:1, 12). *Twelve men . . . one from each tribe,*

1. J. de Groot, *Het Boek Jozua*, p. 79, thinks he detects a lack of talent in composition, but prefers that view rather than accept the weaving together of two documents.
2. See E. J. Young, *An Introduction to the OT*, pp. 174f., where the various data of chs. 3-4 are harmonized.

are to be taken. These men are ordered to *take up here, from the middle of the Jordan*, twelve stones to be carried to the campsite on the other side. Joshua is portrayed as actually standing at the spot where the stones must be taken up. It is *from the place where the feet of the priests stood firm* (see 3:17). This agrees with the continued emphasis upon the role of the ark in the story of the crossing (see 3:3, 14–15; 4:5, 7). Verse 9 adds to this concern the further information of the erection of a twelve-stone monument in the river bed itself, at the spot where the ark had been during the crossing (see also vv. 10–11, 15–18). The memorial to be erected is thus seen as a reminder of what the Lord had done by means of his ark in bringing about the miracle of the crossing.

4–7   Joshua carries out the divine command by taking *the twelve men* already *selected* (see 3:12).[3] In vv. 4–5 the emphasis lies again on the participation of the twelve tribes in this ceremony (v. 2). This concern also dominates all of ch. 22. The place from which the stones must be fetched is described elaborately: *the middle of the Jordan . . . the place where the ark of the Lord your God is*. The ark's role is crucial.

To symbol-oriented easterners the action commanded would hardly need further elucidation. Nevertheless, the account adds an immediate explanation, thereby showing the great significance it would have for future generations. The stones will be *a sign among you*. The word "sign" (Heb. *'ôt*) can mean "pledge," "omen," "miracle"; here it is used as "memorial." This sign will be *among you*; its function will be active, not remote or inoperative. Its primary purpose is for the future, *when later your children ask you*. The language is reminiscent of Exod. 12:26–27; Deut. 6:20–25. God's acts of salvation on his people's behalf must be perpetuated in the memory of coming generations. The immediate scope of the injunction seems to be that of the current generation; yet it is clear that more is meant than the immediate future (v. 7b). The explanation parents are to give their children regarding the significance of the memorial stones recalls briefly the great miracle of damming the waters *before the ark*. Again the ark's role, so prominent in both chs. 3 and 4, is central. The ark is the very symbol of *the covenant of the Lord*. Thus the full light falls on the redemptive significance of the event. No mere recalling of a miracle is envisaged. The miracle is to be viewed as an expression of covenant fidelity. By repeating the reference to the cutting-off of the waters the explanation highlights its tremendous significance. The purpose in setting up the stones is finally summed up in the word "memorial" (Heb.

3. The words "whom he had selected" may also be rendered "whom they had selected," thus stressing the people's choice.

zikkārôn). The notion of remembering in Hebrew is more than a calling to mind. It involves a remembering with concern; it also implies loving reflection and, where called for, a corresponding degree of action. (See Jer. 2:6–7 for a neglect of this duty on Israel's part.) The memorial is meant for *the Israelites*, all without exception, whether on this side of Jordan or on the east side.

8–9 The narrative technique employed throughout these chapters now makes the narrator round off his account provisionally. At a later point the matter will be resumed (v. 14). At present the author is concerned to speak of the execution of Joshua's orders. Due stress is placed on the fact that *they took up twelve stones from the middle of Jordan*, and that this was done *according to the number of the tribes of the Israelites* (see also vv. 4–5; cf. the "all Israel" emphasis of 1:12ff.). This is also expressed in the fact that the story speaks of *the Israelites* who *did as Joshua had commanded*, while in actual fact it was Israel's twelve-man delegation that performed the task. Verse 9 mentions still other stones which *Joshua set up . . . in the middle of the Jordan*. In view of the fact that the role of the ark at the crossing is so consistently emphasized in the account, it comes as no surprise that the very spot where the priests' feet had rested during the crossing should also receive a memorial, even though the account has not prepared the reader for this development. The author reports that these stones *have been there to this day*. This phrase, often considered a typical expression of an etiological tale, is in reality meant as a confirmation of the veracity of the account.[4] The stones described here were probably visible when the Jordan ran low.[5]

10–11 Having given a summary of certain actions which he deemed essential for the construction of his account the narrator now returns to details of the crossing. Again the account is concerned to stress the ark's central role at the crossing. *The priests who carried the ark remained standing in the middle of Jordan* (cf. 3:17). In the meantime the people had the opportunity to carry out Joshua's instructions, which he

4. See B. S. Childs, "A Study of the Formula 'Until This Day,' " *JBL* 82 (1963), pp. 279–292: *idem*, "The Etiological Tale Re-examined," *VT* 24 (1974), pp. 387–397. On this same subject: F. Golka, "Zur Erforschung der Ätiologieen im AT," *VT* 20 (1970), pp. 90–98.
5. The LXX uses Gk. *állous* here to indicate that these stones were indeed different from those already mentioned. Modern commentators prefer to think of two stone traditions which somehow ended up in a combined narrative the "seams" of which still show. The Vulgate reads: *alios quoque duodecim lapides*.

had received from the Lord. These instructions also agreed *with all that Moses had commanded Joshua*.[6] This corresponds to the author's concern to link Joshua with his great predecessor (1:5, 14, 17; 3:7; 11:23).

The words *the people hurried over* may also be rendered "the people crossed over quickly," as by the NAB. In view of the constant emphasis on the marvelous acts of the Lord, the latter rendering may be more consistent with the account. Everything went without hindrance and was completed in a short time. Verse 11 indicates that the priests left the river *as soon as all the people had finished crossing over*. The words *all the people* have a pregnant meaning, as becomes clear from v. 12. This is another element of the "all Israel" theme. One should note the order of crossing: *the ark of the Lord and the priests*. This agrees with 3:3, and with the prominence of the ark in the account of the crossing.[7] All this then takes place *before the eyes of the people*,[8] who stand on the west bank of the river.

12–13   The participation of the tribes of Reuben, Gad, and the half-tribe of Manasseh and their going *ahead of the* (other) *Israelites*, is another feature of the "all Israel" concern. They march *in formation*[9] (v. 12) and *equipped for war* (v. 13), both terms anticipating the battles which must be fought with the native population.[10]

Again the writer is concerned to link this participation of the Transjordanian tribes with that which Moses had commanded Joshua (v. 10; cf. 1:17). While from 1:14 the impression might be gained that all the men of the Transjordanian tribes were to go along, this account indicates that their number is confined to 40,000. See Num. 26 for the total number of Reuben and Gad, each of which numbered in excess of that.

14   The link between Moses and Joshua, already made in the preceding verse, is made even stronger at this point. The miracle of the

6. Heb. lit. "all the word (or "thing") which the Lord commanded Joshua." The various "words" (e.g., 1:2, 11; Deut. 3:28; 31:3, 7, 23) could also be viewed as a single unit, one "word."
7. For a further discussion of the ark's representative function and how not to view it, see M. H. Woudstra, *The Ark of the Covenant From Conquest to Kingship*, pp. 13–57.
8. This has also been rendered "at the head of the people," which conveys a different meaning of the actual events. We take Heb. *lipnê* in its literal sense here.
9. Heb. $h^a m u \check{s} î m$, as in 1:14.
10. This is the most natural explanation. It makes the positing of two "traditions," one presumably more peacelike, the other warlike, unnecessary. Both thoughts are consistent with the story as a whole. Jericho falls without a fight; other cities must be fought for.

crossing is the occasion for the Lord to make *Joshua a great man in the sight of all Israel, and they feared him as they feared Moses*. The parallel with Moses' position after the Red Sea crossing is striking (cf. Exod. 14:31b). Joshua, like Moses, is accepted as God's accredited spokesman. The fear and the respect the people had felt for Moses is transferred to Joshua.

15–18 Here the narrative of the ark's coming up out of the bed of Jordan is brought to its conclusion. Again the focus is on the ark, here called *the ark of the testimony*. For other designations, see, e.g., 3:3, 6, 17; 4:7, 11. The word translated "testimony" (Heb. *'ēḏûṯ*) also means "monitory sign," "reminder." The ark contained the testimony (Exod. 31:18), i.e., the tablets of the covenant (see also Exod. 27:21; Lev. 24:3). Covenant and testimony sometimes are interchangeable (compare Exod. 31:18 with Deut. 9:11). It was the ark of this testimony which was now to be taken out of the Jordan where, borne by the priests, it had majestically directed the crossing. The ark's departure *out of* the Jordan is described in terms equally as dramatic as those of the ark's approaching the Jordan (3:14–16). The same elaborateness and the same scoring of effect are used, especially in v. 18, which is parallel to 3:15. So Joshua, upon receiving the divine command, orders the priests to leave the river. *When the priests . . . came up out of the bed of the Jordan, the feet of the priests had no sooner been raised to the dry ground than the waters of the Jordan returned*. Obviously the writer wants to inculcate the lesson that truly a miracle had occurred.[11] This lesson was to be handed down to posterity by means of this marvelous narrative.

19 *The people came up from the Jordan on the tenth of the first month*.[12] This information ties in the event of the crossing with the selecting of the passover lamb (Exod. 12:3), which took place prior to the Red Sea crossing explicitly recalled in v. 23. It also prepares the reader for the events depicted in 5:10.[13] Henceforth the commemoration of the first pass-

11. Cf. Calvin at this passage: "There cannot be a doubt that this wonderful sight must have been received with feelings of fear, leading the Israelites more distinctly to acknowledge that they were saved in the midst of death" (p. 65).
12. This month, also known by the name Nisan, coincides with March–April. See F. F. Bruce, "Calendar," in *NBD*, pp. 176–79. R. de Vaux, *Ancient Israel*, p. 185, considers v. 19 to be from the hand of a redactor, but no ground for this is given. An ancient copy of an agricultural calendar dating from the 10th century BC was found at the Canaanite city of Gezer; see *DOTT*, pp. 201–3.
13. Those following the cultic approach to this entire account see in this information concerning the date a connection with an alleged spring festival celebrated at Gilgal; see J. A. Soggin, *Joshua*, p. 66.

over will therefore coincide with the commemoration of the entry into the promised land. God's calendar has different dates (cf. Jer. 23:7–8), but the dates belong to the same time frame, and that calendar shows the dates of God's redemption of his people.

The town of *Gilgal*, where *Joshua set up camp*, has not been identified with certainty. Its general location is sought to the east of Jericho, between the former city and the Jordan.[14] Much has been made, and continues to be made, of Gilgal as a supposed seat of a shrine, probably antedating the arrival of Israel at that spot, and hence of Canaanite origin. But the sober information which the OT itself provides hardly leaves room for such an elaborate theory.[15] What does appear is that in the days of Saul and Samuel a town by this name served as a center for sacrifice and worship (1 Sam. 10:8; 11:15), but it is not entirely certain that this was the same Gilgal[16] (see also Hos. 4:15; Amos 4:4).

20–24   The chapter now returns to the main theme (see commentary on vv. 1ff.) with the report that the *twelve stones which they had taken up from the Jordan* were *set up at Gilgal*. That this ceremony is of great importance to the narrator becomes clear from the fact that for the second time (see vv. 6–7) he records what parents must tell[17] their children in connection with these memorial stones. The fathers are to instruct their children: *on dry ground Israel crossed over this Jordan*. This reply, though shorter than that in v. 7, does not differ from it in substance. One must assume that other details of the crossing were meant to be included as well. Moreover, the account is written not only for the benefit of Joshua's contemporaries, but also has in mind those who at a much later time, and often under much different circumstances, would need this reminder of God's mighty acts.

---

14. See K. A. Kitchen, "Gilgal," in *NBD*, pp. 469f. For other Gilgals, see 2 K. 2:1; 4:38; cf. Deut. 11:30. The word Gilgal may come from *galgal*, "wheel," thus indicating a circle of stones. But in 5:9 it is connected, at least by popular etymology, with *gālal*, "to roll."
15. On a supposed cultic celebration at Gilgal see H.-J. Kraus, "Gilgal, ein Beitrag zur Kultusgeschichte Israels," *VT* 1 (1951), pp. 181–199. For a critique of this approach see B. S. Childs, "A Traditio-historical Study of the Reed Sea Tradition," *VT* 20 (1970), p. 415; a far more radical critique is offered in Y. Kaufmann, *The Biblical Account of the Conquest of Palestine*, pp. 67–69.
16. J. H. Kroeze, *Het Boek Jozua*, p. 63, believes that the Gilgal of Deut. 11:30, which was near Shechem, played a part in the stories of Saul and Samuel.
17. The Hebrew uses the verb form *hôḍaʿtem*, "cause to know," from the root *yāḍaʿ*, "to know," used of an experiential knowing, a knowing with both head and heart at one and the same time.

Verses 23–24 may be taken as an additional comment by Joshua in reflecting upon the crossing and its meaning.[18] It may also be a part of that which the parents are to tell their children. If the latter is true, then the passage must present an identification between the Israel of Joshua's days and that of later times, including our own. Verse 23 clearly states that *the Lord your God dried up the waters of the Jordan before you*, but the "you"[19] addressed will also include later generations of inquirers (cf. also the "us" at the end of the verse). Such personal involvement with events long past reflects the corporate aspect of OT thought, and is quite typical of the covenant spirit which pervades the book of Deuteronomy.[20]

Whatever the case, an explicit link is now laid between the Jordan crossing and the crossing of *the Red Sea*,[21] *which he dried up before us until we had crossed*.

After this reminder of God's continued work of redemption (Red Sea–Jordan–future commemoration), the scope of this event is broadened to include *all the people of the earth*. This may be a parallel to the song of Moses (Exod. 15:14–16), where a similar effect is associated with the Red Sea crossing. On the parallels between Moses and Joshua see also the commentary on 1:5. The purpose of the Jordan miracle is *that all the people of the earth may know that the hand of the Lord is strong*. God, according to a pervasive emphasis of the OT, performs his acts before the forum of the peoples. Indeed, Moses mentions that fact when the Lord is determined to destroy Israel (Num. 14:13–19). This emphasis is very strong in Ezekiel (e.g., Ezek. 20:9, *passim*). The *strong hand* of the Lord[22] was also evident in the wonders of the Exodus (Exod. 3:19; 6:1; 13:9; Deut. 6:21; 7:8; 9:26). Thus another link between these two events is deliberately laid. When this recognition is found among the nations, Israel

---

18. This is C. J. Goslinga's approach in *Het Boek Jozua*, p. 63. Kroeze considers this to be part of what the parents are to say; *op. cit.*, p. 63.

19. The Syriac translation uses "them" and "they" at the beginning of the verse but retains "us" and "we" at the end.

20. See also B. Holwerda, *Jozua*, p. 14, who also calls attention to the prayers of Nehemiah (Neh. 1:4–11; cf. Ezra's prayer, Neh. 9:6–37) and of Daniel (Dan. 9:3–19). The Bible knows of only one people of God, and God works for and with them throughout their history.

21. For this translation, see the commentary on 2:10. Cf. also the doubt expressed by M. Noth, *The History of Israel*, pp. 115f., n. 3: " 'Reed Sea' (provided *yām sûp* really means that)."

22. Here the LXX, avoiding the anthropomorphism, renders Heb. *yāḏ*, "hand," with *dýnamis*.

too will *fear*[23] *the Lord your God all the days*. "Fearing the Lord" is the most fundamental expression in the OT for faith or religion. That fear, which is not slavish dread but rather contains an element of recognition of God's glory and majesty along with trust (cf. Ps. 130:4), will be felt by Israel as it witnesses the nations' recognition of its God and his acts of redemption and judgment.[24] In Rahab's case this recognition led to her rescue; in the case of her fellow Canaanites this same recognition led to their doom.

Thus the purpose and meaning of the miracle of the crossing is stated clearly and can be perceived by future readers of the book of Joshua.

D. COVENANT SIGN AND COVENANT MEAL (5:1–12)

1 *And when all the kings of the Amorites west of the Jordan and all the kings of the Canaanites along the seacoast heard how the Lord had dried up the waters of the Jordan before the Israelites until they had crossed over, their hearts sank and there was no longer any spirit in them to face the Israelites.*

2 *At that time the Lord said to Joshua: "Make stone knives and circumcise the Israelites again."*

3 *So Joshua made stone knives and circumcised the Israelites at the Hill of the Foreskins.*

4 *Now this is the reason why Joshua had the circumcision: All the people leaving Egypt, that is, all the men of military age, had died in the desert on their trek out of Egypt.*

5 *For all the people who came out were circumcised, but all the people born in the desert on the way in their trek out of Egypt had not been circumcised.*

6 *For the Israelites traveled in the desert forty years until all the generation of those of military age when leaving Egypt were gone, since they had not obeyed the voice of the Lord and the Lord had declared to them by oath that he would not let them see the land which he promised on oath to their fathers to give them, a land flowing with milk and honey.*

---

23. We have retained the MT $y^e r\bar{a}'tem$ as an unusually pointed form of $y\bar{a}r\bar{e}'$, "to fear." Many prefer to emend to $yir'\bar{a}t\bar{a}m$, which is an infinitive construct with masculine plural suffix. See K. Arayaprateep, "A note on YR' in Jos. IV 24," *VT* 22 (1972), pp. 240–42.

24. Heb. *'ereṣ*, translated "earth," could also be rendered "land." The meaning of the clause would not differ basically, and perhaps would move even closer to Exod. 15:14ff.

7 *But he put their children in their place. It was these Joshua circumcised, for they were uncircumcised, since they had not been circumcised on the way.*

8 *When the circumcising of the whole nation was done they stayed in their places in the camp until they were healed.*

9 *And the Lord said to Joshua: "Today I have rolled away the shame of Egypt from you." So the place has been called Gilgal to this day.*

10 *While the Israelites were encamped at Gilgal they kept Passover on the evening of the fourteenth of the month, on the plains of Jericho.*

11 *On the day after the Passover they ate from the produce of that land, unleavened bread and roasted grain, that same day.*

12 *On the day after they ate of the produce of that land the manna stopped; the Israelites did not have manna any more but they ate that year from the produce of the land of Canaan.*

This section deals with the observance of two important ceremonies, both related to God's covenant with his people, namely circumcision and the Passover. The word "covenant" is not mentioned explicitly, but when this section is read in the larger context of Gen. 17 and Exod. 12 (see Exod. 12:48b), the connection is obvious.[1] Though circumcision was essential to the celebration of the Passover (Exod. 12:48), the signal manifestation of God's goodness as shown in the Jordan crossing was not as such dependent on the nation's circumcised or uncircumcised state. Insistence upon the observance of law under the Old Covenant, though in a very real sense a condition of the covenant, was not to be construed along the lines of righteousness by works. For after all, the very code of the covenant had been given to Israel after the people had been redeemed from Egyptian bondage.[2]

1 The report of *how the Lord had dried up the waters of the Jordan* reaches *all the kings of the Amorites west of the Jordan and all the kings of the Canaanites*. This verse closely links up with 4:24, where a similar effect is predicated, and it restates the sentiments attributed to Rahab (2:10–11; cf. also 1:5). Thus the emphasis is once again on the miraculous side of the possession of the promised land, although there will also be a time when this dread on the Canaanites' part will prompt them to hostile action against God's people (see 9:1–2; 10:1–4). The terms *Amorites* and *Canaanites* are here broad designations for the total popu-

---

1. J. A. Soggin, *Joshua*, p. 71, argues that the absence of a reference to Exod. 12 means that the account did not know of its condition or that it had no link with the Passover. Both are unlikely arguments from silence.
2. See G. Vos, *Biblical Theology*, p. 127.

lation of Canaan west of the Jordan, Amorites designating the tribes who lived in the mountains, and Canaanites those by the Mediterranean Sea. The words *west of the Jordan* (lit. "beyond the Jordan[3] to the west") serve to distinguish between the Amorites mentioned here and those in 2:10. The effect of the crossing upon the kings of Canaan was one of the "sinking[4] of the heart" and a loss of *spirit* (see 2:11). The heart in the OT is the seat of the intellect, will, and emotion. It is the great collective for the spiritual activities of man. This failure of heart results in a loss of spirit or breath.[5]

2–3   The story of the circumcision presented here may have been intended as another parallel between the lives of Joshua and of Moses (see commentary on 1:17; and compare 3:13 with Exod. 15:8; 3:17 with Exod. 14:21–22, 29). Just as before fully entering upon his task as the people's deliverer Moses was reminded of the need to circumcise one of his sons (Exod. 4:24–26), Joshua receives the command to circumcise all those who had not received this rite. This command precedes his role as the captain of the Lord's people during the Conquest.

We take *at that time*, though a rather broad chronological term, to refer to the time just described in chs. 3–4 (esp. 4:19).[6] Therefore the time lapse between this mass circumcision and the Passover, held on the fourteenth of the month (v. 10), was no more than three days. The painful effects of circumcision were still felt at that time (cf. Gen. 34:25), but this need not have precluded participation in the Passover.[7]

The Lord wants Joshua to make *stone knives* (see Exod. 4:25). This may reflect the antiquity of the ceremony, dating back to times when stone (lit. "flint") was more commonly used for cutting than metal. With these knives Joshua is to *circumcise the Israelites again* (lit. "again a

---

3. This is the well-known b^e'*ēber hayyardēn*, used in Deut. 1:1 of "Transjordan." Here it obviously refers to the West Jordan country.
4. Lit. "melting."
5. Several commentators prefer to take this verse with the preceding chapter. However, as part of ch. 5 it probably serves to explain indirectly why Israel at this point could safely risk circumcision of its uncircumcised males with the physical incapacity that accompanied this rite.
6. J. H. Kroeze, *Het Boek Jozua*, p. 66, argues for a more indefinite understanding of the phrase and allows for the circumcision to have been earlier (before the crossing) or later. It was then simply recorded here for material, not chronological reasons.
7. KD, pp. 57f., present reasons why one may hold this ceremony to have taken place after the crossing and before the Passover.

second time").[8] The rite of circumcision, referred to metaphorically in Deut. 10:16; 30:6, was instituted as a sign of Israel's covenant relationship with the Lord (Gen. 17:11).[9] It consisted in the cutting-away of the foreskin of an eight-day-old Israelite male. Its religious import is grasped clearly already in OT times (see Deut. 10:16; Jer. 4:4; 6:10 (RSV "closed"); Jer. 9:24–25 (Eng. 25–26).[10]

According to v. 5 the Israelites who had left Egypt in the Exodus had been circumcised, and the command to *circumcise the Israelites again* probably should be read in light of that verse.[11] This also explains that the Israelites to be circumcised at this time consisted of a certain number. Carrying out the divine command, Joshua *made stone knives*[12] *and circumcised the Israelites at*[13] *the Hill of the Foreskins*.[14] The narrator may have used this name proleptically, indicating that the hill received this name upon this occasion.[15]

4–7 The account now adds reasons for this mass circumcision.

8. The LXX appears to have read *šēb* ("sit down") instead of MT *šûb* ("again"). As it stands the MT is a bit redundant but not ungrammatical. With J. Bright, "Joshua," *IB* II (Nashville: 1953), we see no reason to prefer the LXX here.
9. It is often alleged that these verses along with Gen. 17; Exod. 4:24–26 offer three different accounts of the origin of the rite. But Exod. 4 does not claim to present the origin of the practice, and Josh. 5 clearly states that those who left Egypt were circumcised; see J. A. Motyer, "Circumcision," in *NBD*, pp. 233f.
10. Circumcision was practiced also outside Israel. Egyptian bas-reliefs bear witness to the custom from the 3rd millennium B.C. It may not have been a universal practice, and was often used as a puberty rite. Jer. 9:24–25 (Eng. 25–26) mentions a number of nations which practiced circumcision. See R. de Vaux, *Ancient Israel*, pp. 46f.; and cf. F. Sierksma, "Quelques Remarques sur la Circoncision en Israel," *OTS* 9 (1951), pp. 136–169.
11. Others, e.g., A. Gelin, *Josué*, think of the circumcision of Abraham's family to have been the first one meant here. KD consider this a "farfetched" view. The LXX of vv. 4b, 6a makes it appear that the majority of those leaving Egypt were *un*circumcised. The MT appears to be preferable.
12. Cf. KD for a possible explanation of the logistics of this operation. A sizeable number of men were already circumcised and could therefore assist in the completion of this mass ceremony within one day.
13. The Hebrew preposition is *'el*, probably = *'al*, although Gelin, *op. cit.*, translates literally "vers" (i.e., "toward"). ASV, RSV use "at," JB "on."
14. RSV (and ASV mg.) treat this as a proper name, "Gibeath-haaraloth." This favors the view which considers this to have been a hill already known by that name prior to Israel's circumcision; see also following note.
15. Kroeze, *op. cit.*, who follows a different chronology of events (see earlier note), thinks this name may be connected with mass circumcisions practiced among Canaanite tribes; see also Jer. 9:25. The view adopted above would seem more natural and less complex.

It reminds the reader that *all the people leaving Egypt, that is, all the men of military age, had died in the desert*. This already anticipates what will be explained more fully in subsequent verses. It recalls the sad result of rebellion and disobedience (Num. 14:28–32). The tone of this section is admonishing and hortatory, but this is no reason to deny its originality in this context.[16] Biblical historiography often exhibits such features.

Verse 5 must be read in close conjunction with v. 6, which supplies the notion of the forty years' wandering in the desert. During this time those who had left Egypt as adults had died. There is also a reference to disobedience of *the voice of the Lord*, recalling Num. 14 and the story of the twelve spies. Perhaps the writer means that this period of wandering, caused by the people's disobedience, was a time of wrath during which the sign of the covenant between God and Israel could not be applied.[17] As to the general way in which the desert period is viewed in the OT, sometimes positively, then again negatively, compare Hos. 2:16 (Eng. 14); 13:4; Jer. 2:2, with Ezek. 20:6–26; Ps. 106.

A very striking statement affirms that the same Lord who had *promised on oath to their fathers to give them a land flowing with milk and honey* is also the One who declares *by oath that he would not let them see the land*. This shows the conditionality of God's covenant promises, a conditionality which as such is not in conflict with the principle of sovereign grace.

God's oath to the fathers is recorded in Gen. 15; 22:16–18; 26:3; Exod. 32:13. The principle of grace in God's dealings with Israel clearly appears in the fact that *he put their children in their place*. Thus viewed, the remnant idea, so prominent in the prophets, is already found incipiently in the stories of the Exodus and the Conquest. Verse 7 concludes by elaborating that *it was these Joshua circumcised, for they were uncircumcised*.[18]

8 It is obvious from what the writer has said earlier that *the circumcising of the whole nation* must be read in a restricted sense. The

16. H. Holzinger, *Das Buch Josua*, p. 11, holds that vv. 4–7 have been "patched up and improved" at a later date; cf. also M. Noth, *Das Buch Josua*, p. 39. Such views do not do justice to the peculiar nature of "prophetical" historiography presented in the Former Prophets; see introduction to the commentary.

17. Another view is that the Israelites omitted circumcision out of a spirit of rebellion, but this view is less likely. F.-M. Abel, *Le Livre de Josué*, p. 30, rightly rejects the view that the Israelites on their incessant wanderings had not a moment's rest to perform the rite. This is not what the Hebrew text says, although Abel so alleges.

18. The hortatory, admonishing element throughout vv. 5–7 should be kept in mind. This explains also its elaborateness.

painful effects of the ceremony (cf. Gen. 34:25) caused the people to stay in their places for a certain period of time.[19]

9 The Lord declares: *"Today I have rolled away the shame of Egypt from you."* Israel's bondage, which at the Exodus had been broken in principle, was finally and definitively removed now that the people were safely on Canaan's side, no longer subject to the words of shame of which Num. 14:13–16; Deut. 9:28 speak hypothetically.[20]

So the place has been called Gilgal to this day. Hebrew *gālal*, "to roll," is connected here with the place name Gilgal.[21] For the location of Gilgal, see the commentary on 4:19.

10–12 Circumcision was a necessary precondition for participation in the Passover festival (Exod. 12:48b). Although the account does not explicitly link the two at this point, the connection between vv. 2–7 and v. 10 is obvious. The reader also has been prepared for a commemoration of the great event of the Exodus by the comments made in 4:23. Thus *while the Israelites were encamped at Gilgal they kept Passover.* The biblical significance of the Passover is explained in Exod. 12:13, 23, 27. It commemorated the passing over of the angel of destruction which had come to slay the firstborn of the land of Egypt.[22]

This Passover was kept *on the evening of the fourteenth of the*

19. On the chronology of the sequence of events of the crossing, the circumcision, and the Passover, see notes 7, 12.

20. Since the Egyptians themselves practiced circumcision the "shame" of Egypt cannot have reference to shameful words which Egyptians spoke about the circumcision or noncircumcision of the Israelites.

21. The "etymologies" given in the OT should not be judged by exact scientific standards. However, they do establish a real and trustworthy link between a given name and the event which occurred. This is certainly more than mere etiology. See P. Auvray, "Josué," in L. Pirot, ed., *Dictionnaire de la Bible*, Suppl. 4 (Paris: 1949), col. 1140: "Does one not know that nothing resembles an etiological legend as much as an authentic memory attached to a site and to a thing?" The Gilgal-*galal* connection must be viewed as such an "authentic memory." For a view directly opposite, cf. Soggin, *op. cit.*, p. 72.

22. This is the sufficient, though not necessarily the scientifically adequate, explanation of the word "passover," Heb. *pesaḥ*. Opinion differs as to the exact meaning of the verb *pāsaḥ*. Does it mean (1) "to limp" (2 Sam. 4:4; 1 K. 18:21, 26) and hence "to leap past," (2) "to pass something by," or (3) "to protect, save, spare?" For the third opinion appeal may be made to Isa. 31:5; Exod. 12:23. Naturalistic explanations of the Passover have been proposed. It is thought to signify the sun's passage through the equinox into the sign of the Ram, or it is held to be a form of spring festival. Whatever earlier meaning the festival may have had, its present biblical meaning is the only legitimate one for the interpreter. See also R. A. Stewart, "Passover," in *NBD*, p. 936.

month. This was the first month of the year, called Abib, also known as Nisan (4:19; Exod. 13:4; Neh. 2:1). The place of the celebration is called *the plains of Jericho* (cf. 4:13). These "plains" (Heb. *'ăreᵇbôt*) are the steppe-like regions west of the river Jordan. The same word is used of the "plains of Moab" on the east of the river (cf. Num. 22:1).

The desert period now had definitely come to an end. *On the day after the Passover they ate from the produce of that land, unleavened bread and roasted grain, that same day.* According to Lev. 23:6 the Feast of Unleavened Bread began on the fifteenth of the month and lasted for seven days. Before the firstfruits of the harvest could be consumed the priest was to dedicate them (Lev. 23:10-11, 14). No exhaustive report of all the details of the celebrations is given here. The author was chiefly concerned to let the light fall on three significant developments: the celebration of Passover, the eating of Canaan's produce, and the stopping of the manna which had supported the Israelites during their trek through the desert. Thus he means to mark the new beginning which has now occurred.[23] Verse 12 adds the significant point of the ceasing of the manna and, again rather elaborately, states that *the Israelites did not have manna any more but they ate that year from the produce of the land of Canaan*. The lesson taught by the manna (Deut. 8:3) had been sufficient. God's pedagogy could now resort to other means, namely those of ordinary providence.

The precise sequence of events is construed variously by the commentators. If it is correct to assume a connection between Lev. 23 and the celebration of Josh. 5, then the following reconstruction suggests itself. The *day after the Passover* (v. 11) is the same as that mentioned in Lev. 23:11. According to traditional Jewish beliefs this was the sixteenth day of the month, for the Feast of Unleavened Bread began on the fifteenth, according to Lev. 23:7. The new harvest of Canaan could not be eaten until the priest had waved a sheaf of it before the Lord. But this does not preclude eating the produce of the previous harvest prior to that ceremony. Unleavened bread, for that matter, was prescribed also during the Passover, not only after its conclusion.

E. THE CAPTAIN OF THE LORD'S ARMY (5:13-15)

13 *When Joshua was near Jericho he raised his eyes and discovered a*

---

23. This appears to be the most organic way to deal with alleged discrepancies which scholars think they can detect between the Feast of Unleavened Bread specified in the Pentateuch and the Gilgal celebration. For these discrepancies see de Vaux, *op. cit.*, p. 488.

man standing in front of him holding a drawn sword in his hand. Joshua stepped up to him and said to him: "Do you belong to us or to our enemies?"

14 *He replied: "No, I am the captain of the army of the Lord. I have now come." Then Joshua fell on his face to the ground and worshipped and asked: "What does my lord have to say to his servant?"*

15 *The captain of the army of the Lord said to Joshua: "Take off your shoes from your feet, for the place on which you stand is holy ground." And Joshua did so.*

Some interpreters consider this pericope to be incomplete, assuming that part of the original tradition has no longer been preserved. Some judge that v. 15 should contain more instructions than it does now. Others[1] prefer to read 5:13–15 in conjunction with 6:2–5, thus making 6:1 a parenthetical statement. A third view considers these verses to be sufficiently self-contained as to make further supplementation superfluous. We believe that the inherent drama of the encounter described makes this last view plausible, and it is adopted here.

A connection between this appearance to Joshua and a similar appearance to Joshua's predecessor, Moses (Exod. 3:1–22), is evident.

13–15 *Joshua was near Jericho*[2] when *he raised his eyes and discovered a man standing in front of him.* The description is dramatic, recalling similar moments in the description of the crossing (e.g., 3:14–16). The appearance is unexpected (for similar language, cf. Gen. 22:13). The mysterious person is *holding a drawn sword in his hand.* This suggests combat readiness,[3] but Joshua's reaction to the appearance (*"Do you belong to us or to our enemies?"*) suggests that there is something ambiguous about it. Joshua's question serves to enhance the air of mystery surrounding

1. E.g., E. J. Young, *An Introduction to the OT*, p. 161.
2. Heb. lit. *bîrîḥô,* "in Jericho." Some suggest this may have been a visionary experience during which Joshua found himself in spirit within Jericho. The immediate context suggests a point near Jericho (RSV "by"; F.-M. Abel "près de").
3. M. Noth, *Das Buch Josua*, p. 39, views this story as a remnant of an original tale concerning the establishment of a sanctuary, probably in Jericho. As A. Gelin, *Josué*, p. 41, correctly points out, however, the sword which the mysterious visitor holds is not directed against Israel for its alleged failure to establish a sanctuary. Rather, it is directed against Israel's enemies. J. A. Soggin, *Joshua*, p. 77, considers this story to have belonged originally to a tradition in which Jericho had to be captured. Thus Joshua might have been pictured as being in Jericho, taking stock of the conquered city, perhaps the ruins of a sanctuary. The view of two divergent Jericho traditions, however, does not stand up under close scrutiny; see commentary on ch. 2.

the event and helps to prepare the reader for the significant disclosure that is to follow in v. 14.

Joshua's alternative, proceeding perhaps from the assumption that the mysterious visitor is no more than human, is negated by a simple *"No."* The visitor does not fit Joshua's categories exactly. He identifies himself as *the captain of the army of the Lord*. The Lord's army (Heb. ṣābā'; see Gen. 21:22; 2 Sam. 3:23) is sometimes viewed as composed of the angels (1 K. 22:19; Ps. 103:20–21; 148:2; Luke 2:13). The word translated *captain* (Heb. śar) is used of princes (Gen. 12:15; Num. 22:13) and of prominent officers of a royal court. In Gen. 21:22 it is used in the sense of a military captain (cf. 1 Sam. 17:18, 55). In Dan. 10:13, 20–21; 12:1 it occurs in connection with the angelic host, translated "prince" in ASV, RSV. It would seem that an angelic figure is intended here, in the sense of the Angel of the Lord (see Gen. 16:7–14; 21:14–21; Judg. 2:1; 6:12, 22).

Joshua's reaction to this solemn announcement is one of deep respect. He *fell on his face . . . and worshipped*.[4] Although Joshua's use of the words *my lord* indicates a recognition of superiority, it falls short of ascription of deity.[5] Nevertheless, the total impact of the scene, also in the light of v. 15, is such that a superhuman presence is indicated. The visitor says to Joshua, *"I have now come."* Do these words require further definition of a goal: I have come to do such and such?[6] Has something been lost from the account? Was the speaker interrupted?[7] The book of Psalms knows of a "coming" that is pregnant with redemptive meaning; see Ps. 40:8 (Eng. 7); 50:3; 96:13 = 98:9. Such instances are sufficient to treat the words of the visitor to Joshua as in need of no further definition.[8]

If there was still any doubt about the essentially superhuman nature of this mysterious appearance, v. 15 removes it. Joshua is told: *take off your shoes from your feet, for the place on which you stand is holy ground*. Moses (Exod. 3:5) and Joshua have an identical experience. Holiness in the OT has its basis and origin in God. Things, places, and people can be called holy only insofar as they have been set aside for God or claimed

---

4. Soggin, *op. cit.*, p. 78, correctly observes that "the angel is not a being distinct from Yahweh, but in a sense is one of his hypostases, to the extent that the worship paid to him is directed to Yahweh himself."

5. Heb. 'ᵃdōnî, not 'ᵃdōnay; neither is the word "worship" by itself an indication of respect shown to deity.

6. Abel, *op. cit.*, p. 32, claims it does; see, e.g., 2 Sam. 14:15. But is it clear that there are no exceptions?

7. This is what KD maintain.

8. See J. H. Kroeze, *Het Boek Jozua*, p. 75.

by him.[9] We believe, therefore, that the theophany as reported here is self-contained and needs no further supplementation. Joshua has been made aware of the presence of One greater than man whose drawn sword clearly speaks of combat readiness, and whose army is nothing less than that of the Lord himself. What more is there to know before the Conquest is to begin in earnest?

F. JERICHO TAKEN AND CURSED; RAHAB SPARED (6:1–27)

1 *Meanwhile Jericho had shut the gate and was so completely closed to the Israelites that no one could go out or in.*

2 *Then the Lord said to Joshua: "See, Jericho with its king, these mighty warriors, I have given into your power.*

3 *March around the city with all the men of war going around the city once. Do this for six days.*

4 *Meanwhile seven priests shall each carry a signal horn in front of the ark. On the seventh day you must march around the city seven times and then the priests shall sound the horns.*

5 *When they prolong the blast of the horn and you hear it sound, then all the people shall raise a great cry and the wall of the city shall fall flat and the people shall climb over it, each man going straight ahead."*

6 *Then Joshua son of Nun called the priests and said to them: "Take up the ark of the covenant and let seven priests each carry a signal horn in front of the ark of the Lord."*

7 *And he said to the people: "Advance and march around the city and let the armed men go in front of the ark."*

8 *As soon as Joshua had spoken to the people seven priests each carrying a signal horn before the Lord advanced while sounding the horns, the ark of the covenant of the Lord following them.*

9 *The armed men went in front of the priests who sounded the horns and the rear guard followed the ark, with the horns sounding all the while.*

10 *But Joshua commanded the people: "Do not raise a shout, nor let your voice be heard, nor let a word come from your lips until the day I say to you: Shout! Then shout."*

11 *So Joshua made the ark of the Lord go round the city, circling it once. Then they went to the camp and they lodged in the camp.*

---

9. See G. von Rad, *OT Theology* I, pp. 204ff.

12 *The next morning Joshua arose early; the priests took up the ark of the Lord.*

13 *The seven priests each carrying a signal horn in front of the ark of the Lord moved on and sounded the horns, the armed men going before them and the rear guard following the ark of the Lord, with the horns sounding all the while.*

14 *So they marched around the city once on the second day and returned to the camp. This they did six days.*

15 *On the seventh day they arose at daybreak and marched around the city in the same manner seven times, only on that day they marched around the city seven times.*

16 *At the seventh time, when the priests sounded the horns, Joshua said to the people: "Shout! for the Lord has given you the city.*

17 *The city with all that is in it is to be put under the curse and given up to the Lord, but only Rahab the prostitute and all who are with her in the house are to be spared, for she hid the agents we sent.*

18 *As for you, keep yourselves absolutely clean of the accursed things, so that you do not, while carrying out the curse, take of the accursed things and so put the curse on the camp of Israel and bring trouble on it.*

19 *All the silver and gold and everything of bronze or iron are to be set apart for the Lord; they shall go into the treasury of the Lord."*

20 *Then, while the horns sounded, the people shouted. As soon as the people heard the sound of the horn they gave a loud cry and the wall fell flat, and the people stormed the city right from where they were and took it.*

21 *And they carried out the curse by putting to the sword all that was in the city, man and woman, young and old, ox, and sheep, and donkey.*

22 *But to the two men who had reconnoitred the land Joshua said: "Go into the house of the prostitute and bring out of it the woman and all who belong to her in keeping with your oath to her."*

23 *So the young men who had served as spies entered and brought out Rahab, together with her father, her mother, her brothers, and all who belonged to her. They brought out all the members of her family and assigned to them a place outside the camp of Israel.*

24 *The city and everything in it was put to the torch, except that the silver and the gold and everything of bronze and iron were put into the treasury of the house of the Lord.*

25 *But Rahab the prostitute together with her family and all who belonged to her Joshua spared, and she has lived among the Israelites to this day, because she hid the agents whom Joshua sent to reconnoitre Jericho.*

26 *At that time Joshua laid down this oath:*

"Cursed before the Lord be the man

Who undertakes to build this city, Jericho;

At the cost of his oldest he will lay its foundation,

And at the cost of his youngest he will set up its gates."

27 *And the Lord was with Joshua and the report about him spread through the whole country.*

Within the scope of the book of Joshua, this chapter means to celebrate the most outstanding instance of God's "giving" of the land to Israel. This motif runs through the entire book. The story of the fall of Jericho, although beset by certain difficulties both as to the exact order of events and its basis in historical fact, must not be treated as a mere product of Israel's faith. It is, we believe, historical narrative as well as "theological" presentation.[1] On the difficulties of fact just referred to, see the introduction to this commentary. Difficulties as to the order of events will appear less significant when the special nature of Hebrew narrative technique is kept in mind.[2]

1 *Meanwhile Jericho*[3] *had shut the gate.* The purpose of this verse is to describe the seemingly hopeless situation confronting Israel, a people unskilled in the kind of warfare that was now required. Thus the miracle of God's giving of the city would stand out all the more clearly (see v. 2).

1. H. H. Schmid, *Die Steine und das Wort* (Zurich: 1975), p. 161, treats these two as mutually exclusive. The story of ch. 6, according to Schmid, is not "Geschichtbericht sondern eine theologische Erzählung"; but biblical theology, if it is to be theology at all, must have a basis in fact. See also R. de Vaux in J. P. Hyatt, ed., *The Bible in Modern Scholarship*, p. 16; and cf. the introduction to this commentary.

2. B. J. Alfrink, *Josué*, in his comments on vv. 6–7 rightly calls attention to Hebrew narrative style which tends to supplement what is at first incompletely reported. See also G. C. Aalders, *OT Kanoniek*, p. 166, who notes "the peculiarities of OT historiography." In spite of the obvious solution of supposed difficulties and contradictions in this narrative, commentaries continue to call attention to them, e.g., J. M. Miller and G. M. Tucker, *The Book of Joshua*. Cambridge Bible Commentary (New York: 1974), pp. 53f. It is far better to emphasize the independent, creative enterprise of the final compiler. An example of this approach may be found in M. Kessler, *CBQ* 32 (1970), pp. 543–554.

3. Jericho is usually identified with Tell eṣ-Ṣultan, on the western outskirts of the modern city of Jericho, but questions of identification of ancient sites continue to concern scholars. The question remains whether the Jericho that has been excavated is that of Joshua. Several other tells can be found in the vicinity. See "Jericho," in W. H. Gispen *et al.*, eds., *Bijbelse Encyclopedie*.

Jericho was not open to penetration from the outside, neither could those inside communicate with the enemy (but cf. ch. 2).[4]

2 This chapter contains an interesting interplay of word and act. The chief emphasis lies on God's act of giving the city into Israel's hand, but much verbal explanation precedes and surrounds the act. When Jericho falls it will be an act of faith (Heb. 11:30) as well as an act of God. Faith will lay hold on the veracity of God's word concerning the act he is to perform.[5] God assures Joshua that he will give (has given; cf. 1:3) the city of Jericho, its king, and its mighty warriors[6] into Israel's power (see commentary on 1:2, 13; 2:9, 24; cf. Deut. 2:24; 3:2). This is a feature common to narrative of the "holy war" (see commentary on 2:8–11).

The fact that the king of Jericho (cf. 2:2) is mentioned, plus the mighty warriors, may be an indication that armed resistance was planned, and probably offered, after the city walls fell (see 24:11). All this serves to stress the Lord's sovereign power in giving Jericho to Israel.

3–5 *March around*[7] *the city.* Verse 3 states the basic idea of the march around Jericho, with various details supplied in following verses. The cities of Palestine in this period were not large. Jericho measured c. 225 by 80 meters and its circumference was 600 meters.[8] The length of the column that marched around the city is not known. This would depend also on its depth. In view of the large numbers of marchers one must assume that the head of the column had long returned to the camp when the others were still marching.

There is no need to think of the magical rites of circumambulation, rituals which, upon the magical view, would bring about the desired end efficaciously.[9] The biblical world view stands opposed to that of magic,

---

4. The Hebrew uses two participles, one Qal active, the other Pual passive. (NEB "bolted and barred"; A. Gelin "Hermétiquement close.") The words "closed to" could also be rendered "closed on account of."

5. See the worthwhile discussion in K. Gutbrod, *Das Buch vom Lande Gottes. Die Botschaft des AT* 10 (Stuttgart: 1951), p. 52.

6. The same expression (Heb. *gibbôrê heḥāyil*) is used in 1:14; see H. Eising on *ḥāyil* in *TDOT* IV (Grand Rapids: 1980).

7. The Hebrew imperatives "march around" and "do this" are in the second person plural and singular, respectively. Israel is alternately viewed as a single unit or as a plurality. It may also be that Joshua's responsibility is stressed in the second instance.

8. Jerusalem, captured by David from the Jebusites, measured 400 by 100 meters, Shechem 230 by 150 meters. See M. Noth, *The OT World* (E.T. 1966), p. 147.

9. A. Gelin, *Josué*, p. 43, calls attention to such a magical rite as a possible background to the command given; but he also points out that the intended malediction is expected to take effect in the Lord's name. Thus magic is ruled out.

THE BOOK OF JOSHUA

although the popular mind of the Israelite may at times have shown traces of magical thinking. Superficial similarities must be checked carefully as to their true nature. In this instance the command to march around the city comes from the Lord. This precludes magical manipulation.[10]

This is also clear from the role of the ark in this whole episode.[11] The number seven (*seven priests each carry a signal horn*) is doubtless symbolical, recalling God's works at creation. The Lord who creates also works in the history of redemption. On the seventh day he will act on his people's behalf.[12]

The priests are to blow the signal horns[13] which they carry with them. This may be meant as a reminder of the theophany at Mount Sinai (Exod. 19:16, 19; cf. also 2 Sam. 6:15). It has martial overtones and suggests war and victory (cf. also Rev. 8:6).

What v. 4 does not state can be supplied readily from vv. 6–11. A military contingent goes around the city once each day. The heavily armed go first (vv. 7, 9), followed by the priests with the horns on which they blow constantly (v. 8), the ark (also borne by priests), and finally a rear guard.[14]

The people are to shout when the priests *prolong the blast of the horn*. As becomes clear from the later description (vv. 16, 20), the horns will fall silent after the seventh turn around the city. Joshua will then give an explicit signal to raise the shout, but Israel will not begin to shout until the horns blow again. The *great cry* (Heb. *terû'â*) is the battle cry raised for intimidation of enemies and for encouragement of the friendly forces (see Num. 10:9; 23:21). It is used in connection with the ark in 1 Sam. 4:5; 2 Sam. 6:15 (see also Num. 29:1; Ps. 33:3). In Ps. 89:16 (Eng. 15) those who "know" this triumphant cry are called "blessed," but a false trust in the Lord and his ark may result in defeat (1 Sam. 4:5ff.).

---

10. The LXX translates Heb. *sābab*, which we have rendered "march around," by "surround," "station around." Although this rendering is possible, it is less likely here in view of what follows. More is meant than a mere encirclement.
11. It is true that scholars have often placed the ark within the orbit of semi-magical operations; see, e.g., J. Dus, "Die Analyse zweier Ladeerzählungen des Josuabuches (Jos. 3–4 und 6)," *ZAW* 72 (1960), pp. 107–134. For a critique, cf. M. H. Woudstra, *The Ark of the Covenant From Conquest to Kingship*, *passim*.
12. On the Talmudic understanding of this, and a possible reference to the sabbath, cf. H. Freedman, *Joshua*. Soncino Books of the Bible (London: 1950), p. 27.
13. The account uses different terms for the horns: *šoperôt hayyōbelîm* (4a); *šōpārôt* (4b); *qeren hayyôbēl* (5). None of these words corresponds exactly to Eng. "trumpet," Heb. *hasōserâ*.
14. See S. Attema, "Het Boek Jozua," in J. H. Bavinck and A. H. Edelkoort, eds., *Bijbel in de Nieuwe Vertaling* (Baarn: 1958), p. 127.

At the cry of the people the wall will fall flat, not outward or inward, but downward. It will collapse. Wherever the people will be at that time they will climb over[15] the collapsed wall, *each man going straight ahead*.

6–7   Joshua carries out the divine command by giving charges to the priests (v. 6) and the people (v. 7).[16] In keeping with Hebrew narrative style these verses contain details not mentioned in the report of the Lord's words to Joshua. This narrative technique, skilfully using the same elements and adding new points as the narrative goes along, serves to build up to an effective climax which will not occur until v. 20, when the wall's collapse is actually reported. The ark is called alternately *ark of the covenant* and *ark of the Lord* (see commentary on 3:3). Both terms, when properly understood within their context, should guard against a magical understanding of this solemn procession around Jericho.

On account of the ark's central significance, it is mentioned first, then the priests who are to carry a signal horn in front of it. Verse 7 speaks of the armed contingent[17] which is to precede the ark. Although the city would be taken without regular combat the symbolical presence of these armed men was meant to cause fear in the hearts of Jericho's inhabitants. Moreover, the application of the curse (v. 21) would require the presence of armed personnel; see also 24:11.

8–14   Verse 8 speaks first of the ark's role in the procession, even though v. 7 reports that the armed men are to head the column. This narrative feature highlights the importance of the ark in this event. Moreover, the narrator is conscious of the close association between ark and deity: the priests who carry the seven horns do so *before the Lord*, for the ark is the Lord's ark, and he is as if identified with it (cf. Num. 10:35–36; 2 Sam. 6:14). The ark, moreover, follows the priests as if by locomotion, although actually borne by priests (see commentary on 4:11; cf. Num. 10:33).[18]

---

15. Heb. verb '*ālâ*, also used for a cultic "going up" to a sanctuary. This is used as support for understanding this story in terms of "a ritual of a seven day festival"; see Schmid, *op. cit.*, p. 150. However, the verb need not mean more than a climbing up to a higher location. It is also used in the sense of assault upon an enemy; see Num. 13:31; Judg. 1:1; 12:3; 1 Sam. 14:10.

16. The Hebrew Ketib reads "and they said," i.e., the priests; so ASV.

17. Heb. *ḥālûṣ*, lit. "stripped" for action; cf. 4:13; cf. R. de Vaux, *Ancient Israel*, p. 216.

18. The opening words of v. 8 are not found in the LXX, which continues the imperative mood of v. 7: "and let seven priests advance." With C. J. Goslinga, *Jozua*, p. 69, we prefer the MT.

Verse 9 introduces the presence of a rear guard. Thus bit by bit the details of the order of march are supplied; they are not secondary elements supplied by a later hand. The procession will take place in complete silence, with only the horns giving forth their sound. The people are to wait for a signal from Joshua, whereupon they are to raise the shout.

The emphasis upon the ark's role is continued in v. 11. Joshua makes the ark go round[19] the city; all other elements must take second place. When the march is done the people return to the camp at Gilgal (see 5:10). Since the city was small it must be assumed that the vanguard had long returned when the others were still marching. To make the most of the dramatic buildup before the actual climax of the story, the account now describes the events of the second day. Again one sees the prominence of the ark and reads of the solemn sounding of the horns as priest, vanguard, and rearguard march around the city. The very style of narration suggests the inexorable fate which will soon befall the doomed city, "given" beforehand into Israel's hand by the Lord. One can almost see it happen. Day after day the same line of march, the same awe-inspiring sounding of the horns. In the midst of it all is the Lord, invisibly present under the symbol of the ark.

15–19 A sudden acceleration in the narrative begins in v. 15. The reader is now brought close to the dramatic moment of the collapse of the wall. Instead of a lengthy description of the seven circuits of the march around the town only a terse statement that this sevenfold encirclement took place is given. Still, there is another masterful delay of the action (vv. 16–19) in a manner comparable to the account of the crossing (see commentary on 3:14). Perhaps Joshua had spoken the words recorded here at an earlier time. At any rate, their insertion at this point increases the suspense upon the reader.[20]

Joshua tells the people to raise the shout (see vv. 5, 10). Again there is a reminder of God's "giving" of the city (v. 2; cf. 8:1, 18; Judg. 3:28; 4:7; 7:9, 15; 1 Sam. 23:4, etc.). The symbolical nature of Jericho's fall, historical though it be, should not escape the reader. The very first city of the promised land was to be Israel's by a mere shout raised at the command of Joshua, the Lord's servant. The symbolical nature of this event is also expressed by the fact that the *curse* applied to Jericho and its

19. The LXX, Syriac, and Vulgate translate: "and the ark went around," thus stressing once again the ark's semi-independence of movement.
20. Alfrink, *op. cit.*, suggests that at the end of the sevenfold encirclement the entire marching column, with the heavily armed contingent closest to the city, may have stood around Jericho's walls, ready to raise the shout. This is a plausible reconstruction of events.

inhabitants is to be most severe. This curse (Heb. *ḥerem*) meant that something or someone was absolutely and irrevocably consecrated so that it could not be redeemed (Lev. 27:28–29). It also meant that the object (person) was sentenced to utter destruction (Deut. 13:16). Both connotations are intended here.[21] The *ḥerem* was applied in various degrees (cf. Deut. 13:16; 20:10–18; 1 Sam. 15:3). In Jericho's case the most rigorous form would apply, by way of example. Transjordan had also experienced this curse (Josh. 2:10; Num. 21:21–35; Deut. 2:34; 3:4). The temporal destruction by the curse must be seen as a prelude and a foreshadowing of a more final judgment that God will mete out to those whose unrighteousness will be full (cf. Gen. 15:16) in the end of days (see Jer. 51:63–64; Rev. 18:20–21). Since the *ḥerem* originates as a general rule from an order given by the Lord, one cannot correctly call it an expression of a "sub-Christian" sentiment,[22] lest he involve God in a gradual evolution from cruel to benign.[23]

Though the judgment of God is uppermost in the fate that will befall Jericho, Rahab's rescue from this judgment, in keeping with the promises recorded in ch. 2, is a singular instance of God's goodness shown to a member of the Canaanite population, whose doom had been foretold as early as Gen. 15:16. Rahab will be saved because of what she did for the agents sent to Jericho. Her faith (Heb. 11:31), which "worked" (Jas. 2:25), will "justify" her. Her *house* will share in this rescue from disaster (see 2:13).

The report of Joshua's words concerning the curse and what it entails is completed in vv. 18–19. Israel is to keep itself clean from the accursed things, which had been devoted to the Lord (Lev. 27:28). As

21. The Arabic root *h-r-m* means "to prohibit," "to declare unlawful"; cf. the English word harem.
22. J. Bright, *The Authority of the OT*, pp. 243–251, rightly links the "holy war" concepts of the book of Joshua, including the *ḥerem*, with the eschatological battle enjoined upon the Christian (Eph. 6:10–20; 2 Tim. 2:1–4), but his use of the term "sub-Christian" (p. 245) in connection with the OT curse is unfortunate and confusing. Gutbrod, *op. cit.*, p. 56, rightly states that the *ḥerem* teaches that God, the Creator, may also destroy his creatures (Jer. 18:6; 45:4; Rom. 9:20; see Jesus' words in Matt. 10:28; Luke 13:3). Also in the NT God continues to be the God who is to be feared (2 Cor. 5:11). Cf. J. Calvin, *Commentaries on the Book of Joshua*, pp. 96f.; M. H. Woudstra, *Calvin's Dying Bequest to the Church*, pp. 31–33.
23. W. F. Albright's comments on this practice (*From the Stone Age to Christianity* [Garden City: ²1957], pp. 279f.) are useful but do not come close to doing justice to the theological implications of the *ḥerem*.

executors of the curse[24] Israel itself would become subject to the curse and thus bring trouble[25] on the camp, if it partook of the devoted things. This strict prohibition explains the story to follow in ch. 7. The only things that were to be kept from destruction were the metals—silver, gold, and everything of bronze and iron. These were to go into *the treasury of the Lord* (see Num. 31:54; cf. 1 K. 7:51; 1 Chr. 29:8). This expression is general enough to designate all that is required for carrying out the Lord's service. All these materials would be set apart (Heb. *qōdeš*, lit. "a holy thing"; see commentary on 5:15).[26]

20–21 The narrative now comes to its decisive point. On the exact sequence of events see also the commentary on 6:4, 5. The people shout while the horns sound. Joshua's signal as well as the long blast upon the horn makes them raise the war cry. Just as in v. 15, there is now a sudden acceleration of the pace of the narrative, showing the master's hand. The slow, deliberate description of the city's seven-day encirclement, coupled with a lengthy exposé of what the people are to do when the miracle occurs, makes place for the quick strokes of the brush applied in v. 20: the horns, the shout, the falling flat of the walls, the storming of the city and its capture; all is recited in just a few brief words.[27]

The people make a frontal assault upon the city and put to death everything living. The fall of the walls had been predicted (v. 5). Josh. 24:11 suggests a measure of resistance within Jericho. What happens to the king of Jericho is not stated here, but may be inferred from 8:2, 29; 10:1.

22–25 The contrast noted in the report of Joshua's words (see

24. Many prefer to read *taḥmᵉḏû* ("you covet") in place of *taḥᵃrîmû* ("You carry out the curse"). But, as J. H. Kroeze points out (*Het Boek Jozua*, p. 84), this destroys the pun.

25. Heb. *'āḵar*; see 7:26b, "valley of Achor."

26. Life in Israel was divided into "holy" and "profane" (i.e. common, accessible) zones. Zech. 14:20–21 sees this line of demarcation disappear in the great future. All will be permeated with the spirit of the holy. This time, however, has not yet arrived in Joshua's day. Things devoted to destruction will be holy to the Lord.

27. Did natural causes (earthquake, heavy rainfall?) have anything to do with this sudden collapse of the walls? Belief in miracle does not rule out the interplay of natural causes. Nevertheless, the story is silent about this. It means to celebrate God's act. On the archaeological controversy regarding the remains of Jericho, see commentary on 6:1, 2; cf. K. M. Kenyon in *AOTS*, pp. 264–275; K. A. Kitchen, "Jericho," in *NBD*, pp. 611–12. P. Auvray is no doubt correct when assigning to archaeology a valuable but limited role; see L. Pirot, ed., *Dictionnaire de la Bible*, Suppl. 4, col. 1138: "L'archéologie ne répond pas à toutes les questions."

vv. 17–18), in which there is an alternation between curse and rescue, is also present here. In the midst of the scene of destruction, exemplary of what would happen to Canaan as a whole, is the description of Rahab's rescue. As noted above, the life of a person put under the curse ordinarily could not be redeemed. Thus the sparing of Rahab and her family takes on unusual significance. The signal of the red cord, agreed upon in 2:12–21, no longer plays a part in this rescue. It had been chosen when the precise nature of Jericho's capture was not yet known. Rahab's rescue is connected with two things: the oath the two men had sworn to her (v. 22; cf. 2:12), and the kind act she had performed (6:17). The two are obviously related and are already connected in ch. 2.

The narrative alternates between a description of Jericho's destruction and the story of Rahab. The interweaving of these two motifs serves to give added emphasis to the contrast.

As indicated in 2:12–13, not only Rahab herself but also her "house" is rescued from the curse. A similar solidarity between individual and family, but in the opposite sense, is found in the next chapter. The reason why Rahab and her family are assigned *a place outside the camp of Israel* lies in their ceremonial uncleanness (Lev. 13:46; Deut. 23:3), aggravated in this instance by the curse to which they ordinarily would have been subject.

In the meantime the story of Jericho's complete destruction is continued (v. 24). Fire is applied to the doomed city to wipe its memory from the earth. The metals specified in v. 19 are *put into the treasury of the house of the Lord*.[28] By way of conclusion, v. 25 states explicitly that Rahab (here called *the prostitute*; see also 2:1) is spared and that she and her family have lived among Israel *to this day*. Many take this expression to be an indication of the etiological nature of the story (see commentary on 4:9; 5:9). Rather, it is used to confirm the historical veracity of the event just reported.[29] The purpose of this verse is to celebrate the goodness

---

28. The LXX omits "house of." Is it anachronistic? J. Bright (*IB* II, p. 582) thinks so, as do many others. However, see 9:23. The structure where the sacred tent was housed was called "house" (1 Sam. 1:7). Moreover, Ps. 27:4, 6 makes clear that "house" and "tent" are sometimes used interchangeably. Hence the expression means no more than that these metal objects were stored for the purpose of maintaining the worship at the sanctuary.

29. On the implications of the use of this recurrent phrase for questions of authorship and date cf. Aalders, *op. cit.*, p. 164. Goslinga, *op. cit.*, p. 14, believes that the expression as used here must mean that Rahab was still living when this was written. The NEB understands the words to mean no more than that Rahab "settled permanently among the Israelites."

of God exhibited in Rahab's rescue.[30] Perhaps the writer also means to remind later readers that at some significant points in Israel's history, other non-Israelite stock was added to the nation's life. Purely racial components have never defined the people of God under the "old dispensation." What Israel was it had because of God's grace (cf. Deut. 7:6–8).[31]

26–27 By means of a solemn oath[32] Joshua finally pronounces a curse upon Jericho so that it will never be rebuilt. This rule of permanent desolation of a wicked city applied also to any city in Israel that had departed from the covenant (Deut. 13:16). Curses and blessings must be seen as potent and efficacious means whereby the Lord intends to affect the weal and woe of those who fear him and those who do not.[33] This must not be viewed in the sense of a magical incantation.[34] Nevertheless, the effect of curses and blessings is no less great than that which magic ascribes to them. Bearer of the powerful "word" is the Lord, who created the world by speaking only a word (Ps. 33:6). No one can curse if the Lord does not curse (Num. 23:8a). In that conviction Joshua now pronounces a curse on Jericho. The city's fall was symbolical of what would happen to Canaan as a whole.

In this instance, a curse is pronounced on him who builds, i.e., fortifies and renders strong (cf. 1 K. 15:17; 2 Chr. 11:5; 14:5–6 [Eng. 6–7]) the once destroyed city.[35] This curse is not meant for those who, as is known from 18:21; Judg. 3:13; 2 Sam. 10:5, used the site of Jericho for habitation. Only he who will use Jericho as a city with a "foundation" and "gates" will be affected by the curse. Of him it is said that *at the cost*[36] *of his oldest he will lay its foundation, and at the cost of his youngest*

---

30. In all likelihood the Rahab mentioned in the genealogy of Jesus (Matt. 1:5) is the one of the Joshua story; see the discussion in KD, pp. 72f. Jewish tradition held that Rahab was married to Joshua and that she became the mother of eight prophets; see C. Cohen, "Rahab," in C. Roth, ed., *Encyclopedia Judaica*, XIII (Jerusalem: 1971), col. 1513.

31. See Gutbrod, *op. cit.*, p. 54.

32. Heb. Hiphil, "Joshua caused to swear," probably with participation of the people who were to say, "Amen" (Deut. 27:15).

33. On the significance of oaths in Israelite society, cf. J. Pedersen, *Israel: Its Life and Culture* I–II, p. 441. Pedersen's work is useful as an analysis of the psychological background of OT revelation, but it never actually recognizes the revelation factor. It also fails to estimate correctly the maturity of religious thought in Israel.

34. Some biblical theologies consider the lines between religion and magic to be fluid; e.g., T. C. Vriezen, *An Outline of OT Theology*, p. 20.

35. The structure of the Hebrew is rhythmically poetic. The curse formula may have had wider application.

36. Heb. preposition *be*, "at the price of."

he will set up its gates. The exact meaning of this curse is disputed. It is clear that 1 K. 16:34 reports the fulfilment of the curse.[37] Some have held that foundation sacrifices were practiced at that time, but others question this.[38] Even if in Ahab's days such sacrifices were practiced, this may have been due to Phoenician influences. The translation "at the cost of" leaves the question open as to the precise mode in which the sons of the builder of Jericho ended their lives.

The account of Jericho's fall concludes with a reference to the Lord's being *with Joshua* and to the spreading of his fame through the whole country. This agrees with one of the recurring emphases of the book (see 1:5; 3:7; 4:14; see also 2:10–11; 5:1). There is a certain triumphant note to the book of Joshua. Israel's leadership is in good and firm hands. This is attested to by God's great act in bringing about Jericho's fall. No hero-worship is intended, however, as can be seen from the frank exposé of Joshua's weakness in ch. 7; cf. also 9:14–15.

G. COVENANT DISOBEDIENCE, DEFEAT, AND PUNISHMENT (7:1– 26)

1 *But the Israelites trespassed with respect to the accursed things. Achan, son of Carmi, son of Zabdi, son of Zerah, of the tribe of Judah, took of the accursed things; and the Lord's anger blazed against the Israelites.*

2 *Now Joshua sent men from Jericho to Ai which is near Beth-aven, east of Bethel, and said to them: "Go up and spy out the region." So the men went up and scouted Ai.*

3 *Then they returned to Joshua and said to him: "All the people need not go; let about two or three thousand men go up and take Ai. Do not weary all the people, for there are only a few of them."*

4 *So about three thousand men of the people went up; but they were routed by the men of Ai,*

5 *for the men of Ai killed about thirty-six of them. They chased them from the city gate to the Breaks, killing them at the descent. And the hearts of the people melted and turned to water.*

6 *Then Joshua tore his garments, and prostrated himself before the ark of the Lord till evening; the elders of Israel did so with him, and they all heaped dust upon their heads.*

37. The LXX already reports this outcome in ch. 6, though with some difference in the names employed.
38. See de Vaux, *op. cit.*, p. 442.

7 *And Joshua said: "Ah, Sovereign Lord, why did you ever bring this people across the Jordan, to give us into the hands of the Amorites and destroy us? Had we only been of a mind to remain on the other side of the Jordan!*

8 *Oh, Lord, what can I say after that Israel has turned tail before its enemies?*

9 *When news of this reaches the Canaanites and all the inhabitants of the country, they will surround us and wipe the memory of our name off the earth. What then will you do for your great name?"*

10 *Then the Lord said to Joshua: "Stand up! Why are you lying on your face?*

11 *Israel has sinned; they have transgressed my covenant which I have commanded them. They have taken from the accursed things. They have stolen; they have deceived; they have put it among their own stuff.*

12 *That is why the Israelites cannot stand before their enemies; they turn their backs to them because they have become an accursed thing. I will not be with you again unless you completely destroy the accursed thing from among you.*

13 *Go, sanctify the people. Say to them: Sanctify yourselves for tomorrow; for thus the Lord, the God of Israel, says: A curse is among you, Israel! you cannot stand before your enemies until you remove the accursed thing from among you!*

14 *In the morning you shall present yourselves tribe by tribe; then the tribe which the Lord marks shall come forward clan by clan. And the clan which the Lord marks shall come forward family by family. And the family which the Lord marks shall come forward man by man.*

15 *Then he that is marked as the accursed one shall be burned with fire, together with all that belongs to him, because he has broken the covenant of the Lord and has committed folly in Israel."*

16 *Early next morning Joshua rose and had Israel come forward tribe by tribe; the tribe of Judah was marked.*

17 *He had the clans of Judah come forward, and the lot marked the clan of the Zerahites. He had the clan of the Zerahites come forward man by man, and Zabdi was marked.*

18 *He had that family come forward man by man, and Achan son of Carmi, son of Zabdi, son of Zerah, of the tribe of Judah, was marked.*

19 *Then Joshua said to Achan: "My son, give glory to the Lord the God of Israel and make confession to him. Tell me what you have done. Do not hide it from me."*

20 *Then Achan answered Joshua: "Indeed, it is I who have sinned against the Lord, the God of Israel, for this is what I have done:*

21 *When I saw among the spoil a beautiful robe from Shinar, and two hundred shekels of silver, and a bar of gold weighing fifty shekels, I coveted them and took them. They are hidden there in the earth, in my tent, and the silver is at the bottom."*

22 *Then Joshua sent messengers. They ran to the tent, and indeed, it was hidden in his tent, and the silver was at the bottom.*

23 *They took the things from the tent and brought them to Joshua and all the Israelites, and laid them out before the Lord.*

24 *Then Joshua, and all Israel with him, took Achan son of Zerah, and the silver, and the robe, and the bar of gold, and his sons and his daughters, and his oxen, and his donkeys, and his sheep, and his tent, and all that he had, and they brought them up to the valley of Achor.*

25 *Joshua said: "Why have you brought trouble on us? The Lord will trouble you this day." And all Israel stoned him with stones; they burned them with fire and stoned them with stones.*

26 *And they piled up over him a large heap of stones, until this day. And the Lord turned from the blazing of his anger. For this reason the name of that place was called the valley of Achor, until this day.*

The purpose of this chapter, to be read in close conjunction with ch. 8, is easy to recognize. The Lord, who "gives" the promised land to his people, and who has just furnished a striking instance of this in the capture of Jericho, demands of his people loyalty to the covenant he has made with them. When the covenant is violated (see v. 11), Israel receives a setback before Ai, God's wrath blazes, and his pardon must be gained. Only then will Israel again be assured of victory (8:1).[1]

It is also clear from this chapter that the book of Joshua, and Hebrew historiography as a whole, means to do more than offer a chronicle of events. It wishes to let the light of revelation fall upon the events so that through them the principles by which God writes redemptive history will become clear for later generations of readers and for the church through the ages.[2]

---

1. More than one commentator (e.g., K. Gutbrod, *Das Buch vom Lande Gottes*, p. 61; J. de Groot, *Het Boek Jozua*, p. 95) draws a parallel with Acts 5:1–11; see also C. J. Goslinga, *Het Boek Jozua*, p. 8. This parallel is apt, but it should not be drawn at the expense of the historical distance which separates the church of the old dispensation from that of the new.
2. Cf. M. H. Woudstra, "Event and Interpretation in the OT," in S. Kistemaker, ed., *Interpreting God's Word Today*, pp. 49–72.

1 The chief point of the story[3] is made clear at the outset. The writer informs his readers of what the Israelites of Joshua's day would only discover through defeat, humiliation, and the laborious casting of lots before the Lord. He reports immediately that *the Israelites trespassed with respect to the accursed things*, and the name of the violator is mentioned, complete with a long list of his ancestors. The word used to describe the offense, *trespass* (Heb. *mā'al*),[4] means lit. "to act under cover," hence "treacherously," "secretly." It indicates a breach of trust (Lev. 5:15), generally against the Lord, as here, by purloining or withholding what was sanctified to him. The sin is called here by its proper name, although psychological elements in the process of its commission are not unknown to the writer (see v. 21). In Achan's confession the same frank admission of sin as an offense against God is found (v. 20).

The offense is committed *with respect to the accursed things*, i.e., the *ḥerem* which Joshua had pronounced on everything pertaining to Jericho and its inhabitants (6:17–19). The description of the offense is based on the healthy principle of solidarity. One man is the offender but the entire people are viewed as having committed the trespass, and the Lord's anger blazes against them. The individual functions within the larger context of the community of which he is a part. Achan robbed the whole nation of the purity and holiness which it ought to possess before God.[5] This sense of corporate solidarity[6] is also found in the designation of sin as a "folly in Israel" (v. 15). Corporate guilt and individual responsibility

---

3. M. Noth, *Das Buch Josua*, p. 43, claims to detect two originally independent stories in ch. 7, each with its own local background: the Achan story (Judahite), and the Ai story (Benjaminite). A subsequent "collector" combined the two and used the Achan story to explain the defeat at Ai. This interpretation fits Noth's basic approach to Joshua's composition. However, the interweaving of the two motifs of Ai and Achan is so close that much ingenuity is needed to unravel the two; for a critique see also Y. Kaufmann, *The Biblical Account of the Conquest of Palestine*, pp. 76f.

4. Other translations of this phrase are JB "incurred guilt by violating the ban"; H. W. Hertzberg, *ATD* IX "broke faith with the thing banned"; F.-M. Abel "se rendirent coupables d'une violation de l'anathème." See 22:16, 20, 22, 31; Lev. 5:15, 21 (Eng. 6:2); Num. 5:6. The phrase is also frequent in Ezekiel (14:13; 15:8; 17:20; 18:24, etc.). Cf. also G. J. Wenham, *Leviticus*, 1979, p. 106.

5. See KD, p. 74; Gutbrod, *op. cit.*, p. 61, points out that the congregation of God, Israel, cannot be indifferent to the sin of one of its members.

6. There is really no need to introduce here the idea of "corporate personality," an idea which H. W. Robinson applied to the OT: "The Hebrew Conception of Corporate Personality," *BZAW* 66 (1936), pp. 49–62; see also the critique of this approach in J. W. Rogerson, "The Hebrew Conception of Corporate Personality: a Re-examination," *JTS* 21 (1970), pp. 1–16.

go hand in hand in this story. Though all Israel is involved, Achan[7] is singled out as the perpetrator of the sinful act. His genealogy is traced back four steps, indicating the author's concern to expose the sin and point out its full seriousness.

Achan's sin arouses the Lord's anger, which is said to *blaze* against the Israelites. The expression "his anger blazed" ("was kindled") is used of humans (Gen. 4:5; 2 Sam. 12:5), but especially of God (Num. 11:1, 10; 22:22). God is portrayed as a devouring fire (Deut. 4:24; 9:3). It is not possible on this point to contrast the OT and NT view of God (see Heb. 12:29; Rom. 1:18).[8] This anger of God had been felt in the desert (Deut. 9:19). Now it is felt again.[9]

2–5 Unaware of what the reader already knows, namely that the covenant has been violated, Joshua proceeds to send out men from Jericho to Ai. This mission of the spies is not an independent unit of tradition. On the contrary, a human agency is operating here against the background of the divine displeasure that is bound to bring about a foolish report on the part of those who reconnoitre the city. Joshua's first serious attempt to master the country which the Lord said had been given to Israel (1:3) is thus doomed to fail, not by a blind, whimsical fate, but by God's righteous anger, caused by the people's concrete sin. God's promise was based on covenant obedience (1:7–8), and this obedience had been withheld.

The city to be explored by Joshua's men is *Ai*[10] *which is near Beth-aven, east of Bethel*. Much has been written about the archaeological aspects of this site.[11] The usual identification of Ai with et-Tell has led to the conclusion that, during the time Israel entered Palestine, Ai was not

---

7. The name occurs as Achar in 1 Chr. 2:7, probably a play on the meaning of the Hebrew root *'ākar*, "to trouble"; see vv. 25–26.

8. Some of the prophets who speak most eloquently of God's love, viz. Hosea and Jeremiah, also use the most explicit terms to describe his anger; cf., e.g., Hos. 13:7–8.

9. The biblical notion of the divine wrath should be distinguished from that of the ancients, for whom wrath was something whimsical, unmotivated, and capricious. It is not like the Roman *ira deorum*, though at times it is mysterious and inexplicable (see Num. 1:53). Cf. R. V. G. Tasker, "Wrath," in *NBD*, p. 1341.

10. The Hebrew name always occurs with the definite article, *hā'ay*. It is widely held that this word actually means "the mound," "the ruin," so that the OT itself would suggest that Ai was a ruin-heap. But Kaufmann, *op. cit.*, p. 77, disagrees. Related names, so he maintains, always refer to inhabited places (15:29; Num. 21:11; 33:44–45; Isa. 10:28). J. H. Kroeze, *Het Boek Jozua*, p. 91, points out that the equation Ai = "ruin" is not supported by stringent proof; see also 18:23.

11. For a summary see, e.g., R. de Vaux, *The Early History of Israel* (E.T. 1978), pp. 614f.

an inhabited city at all.[12] Various solutions of this problem have been offered by those who wish to maintain the basic veracity of the biblical account of Ai's capture by Joshua and his forces.[13] In general, what was said about Jericho in the commentary on 6:1 should also be kept in mind here. The limitations of archaeological research together with its valuable contributions to the science of biblical interpretation should be kept equally in mind.[14]

Biblical Ai is said to be *near Beth-aven*, lit. "house of vanity" or "house of nothingness."[15] The name is used for Bethel in Hos. 4:15; 10:5; Amos 5:5 (see also 1 Sam. 13:5). No firm identification has been proposed.[16] Ai was also *east of Bethel*. This is probably present-day Beitîn, which has been excavated. Houses from the Middle Bronze period have been discovered there.[17]

The point from which the men who are to explore the region of Ai are dispatched is said to be Jericho. In light of 5:10 this must be the camp of Gilgal which was near Jericho. In its present context, which we believe to be original, this story of the spies' counsel unfolds itself against the background of the Lord's blazing anger (v. 1). The advice of the spies sets the stage for Israel's defeat, but behind it, as the reader knows, is God's displeasure. Perhaps a certain lightheartedness plagued the men as they reported back to Joshua. Possibly Joshua himself should have consulted the divine will more explicitly, but the account does not say. Its chief purpose is to portray human planning against the background of the divine displeasure (see also 2 Sam. 17:14b; 24:1).

The facts are presented succinctly in v. 4, thus accelerating the

12. The possibility that Ai is not the modern et-Tell is suggested by Kaufmann, *op. cit.*, p. 77. It has been raised in recent years by D. Livingston, "Location of Biblical Bethel and Ai Reconsidered," *WTJ* 33 (1970–71), pp. 20–44; cf. also "Traditional Site of Bethel Questioned," *WTJ* 34 (1971–72), pp. 39–50; A. F. Rainey, "Bethel is Still *Beitîn*," *WTJ* 33 (1970–71), pp. 175–188.

13. Some of the possibilities suggested: Ai is not et-Tell; Ai served as a camp for the people from Bethel; the story of Bethel's capture was transferred to the Ai location in course of the tradition of the Conquest. Since the king of Ai is mentioned explicitly, theories concerning a transfer of traditions run into difficulty.

14. Cf. P. Auvray's observation cited above, p. 114, n. 27; see also M. Noth's strictures on the argument from archaeology in his dispute with J. Bright and W. F. Albright, summarized in de Vaux, *Early History*, p. 489.

15. J. M. Miller and G. M. Tucker, *The Book of Joshua*, p. 62, take it to mean "house of taboo." The name is considered a gloss on the text, an insulting substitute for Bethel where false worship was later conducted. However, the juxtaposition of Beth-aven and Bethel should caution against such an approach.

16. One suggestion is Burqa, east of el-Bireh, north of Tell en-Naṣbeh.

17. See A. R. Millard, "Bethel," in *NBD*, p. 143.

flow of the narrative and moving quickly to the dramatic result of the defeat, Joshua's dismay and his prayer to God. Three thousand men go against Ai to do battle, but they are routed and *about thirty-six* of them are killed (v. 5). Joshua had dispatched the maximum number of men mentioned by the spies, who had suggested *two or three thousand*. This force still seems considerable in view of the facts reported. However, it was much smaller than the entire Israelite manpower, and since Ai was a fortified city a substantial number of military men was called for despite the city's small population and fighting force. It might seem that the relatively small number killed[18] would not warrant the dismay shown by Joshua and the elders upon hearing of the defeat, but this was the first regular attempt to take one of the cities of Canaan. Defeat at this juncture was symbolically as significant as had been the miraculous capture of Jericho.[19]

The account uses several local details in describing Israel's rout before the men of Ai.[20] The Israelites are chased *from the city gate to the Breaks*,[21] and they are killed *at the descent*.

The language chosen to describe the effect of the defeat upon the people of Israel is similar to that used for the disheartened condition of the Canaanites vis-à-vis Israel (2:11; cf. 5:1). The tables have turned, the result of the people's disobedience of God's command.

6–9 Joshua is grief-stricken. He demonstrates his dismay by engaging in customary expressions of sadness such as the tearing of his clothes and the heaping of dust on his head.[22] The narrator's vivid description adds to the poignancy of the scene. It thus enhances the portrayal of the seriousness of the offense which brought about this stunning defeat. The ark, which had played such a central role in the events described in chs. 3–4, 6, is again the center of the people's concern, but now in quite

18. One would expect a round number after the word "about" rather than "thirty-six." Perhaps the sexagesimal system which was in use would make this equivalent to one hundred in our mode of reckoning; so Kroeze, *op. cit.*, p. 93; Hertzberg, *op. cit.*, p. 51, suggests it is closer to three hundred in our reckoning.
19. The defeat at Ai also shows how seriously God takes the *ḥerem* which was imposed on Jericho.
20. See also 8:9, 11, 14, all of which use terminology which seems to betray the insider; cf. Noth, *op. cit.*, p. 48.
21. The Vulgate treats this as a proper name, Sabarim; Heb. *šᵉbārîm*. The LXX understands this word in the sense of a "breaking" of the Israelites by the men of Ai: *kaí synétripsan autoús*. The Hebrew word can also be rendered "quarries."
22. For other oriental utterances of grief cf. Deut. 9:18; Judg. 20:23; 1 Sam. 7:6; Isa. 32:11; Lam. 2:10; Ezek. 27:30, etc. See also R. de Vaux, *Ancient Israel*, p. 59.

a different sense. Israel's leader and its elders prostrate themselves before the sacred chest.[23] The grief displayed must be seen not just in the light of the numerical loss, which may have been comparatively small. It derives rather from the fact that this first attempt to conquer a Canaanite city in the country promised as Israel's future habitation had met with utter failure.

The prayer Joshua offers uses language similar to that used by Moses under similar circumstances.[24] By addressing God as *Sovereign Lord* (Heb. *'ᵃdōnāy yhwh*) Joshua expresses a note of perplexity shown elsewhere by the use of this dual address to God (cf. Jer. 1:6; Ezek. 4:14; also Deut. 3:24).

Blind to the great things the Lord had done at the time of the crossing and at the fall of Jericho, Joshua raises the daring question of the "why" of it all.[25] Did God mean to bring Israel into Palestine only to destroy it by the hands of the Amorites?[26] These are bold words and can be explained only as an utterance of supreme grief. Out of context these words resemble the murmuring of Israel in the desert (Num. 14:3),[27] but there is also an element close to self-reproach. Israel could have stayed on the other side,[28] and Joshua now wishes that they had done so. As it is, Israel has *turned tail* before its enemies, and this leaves Joshua speechless. Complaints of this kind must have struck a responsive chord in the hearts of the readers for whom these words were recorded (cf. Pss. 44, 74). Israel's historiography is not aimed at celebrating the great accomplishments of a super-people, even though Israel could rightly claim to be God's

23. Apparently the chest had not been carried to the battle scene itself. This argues against the theory that the ark's most original function was as a palladium of battle for the Lord of hosts; cf. also the scene in 1 Sam. 4, where initially the ark had been left at home. In Judg. 20:27 the ark is at Bethel, but the battle scene is Gibeah.
24. On the Moses-Joshua parallel cf. 1:17; 4:14; see G. J. Wenham, "The Deuteronomic Theology of the Book of Joshua," *JBL* 90 (1971), pp. 145f.
25. Cf. O. Eissfeldt, *The OT: An Introduction* (E.T. 1965), p. 114, who treats this prayer as exhibiting elements of the songs of national complaint (cf. Jer. 4:1–2; Hos. 14:5–9).
26. On the Amorites, cf. 3:10; 5:1. Here the term stands for those inhabiting the mountain country. In v. 9 "Canaanites" is used in the wider sense of all inhabitants of Canaan.
27. It is possible also in light of v. 10 to see Joshua's words as an utterance of sheer unbelief, but boldness of this sort need not be so interpreted. It is probably best to understand these words as exhibiting a mixture of despondency and searching faith.
28. Lit. "had we only been of a mind," Heb. *lû hô'alnû*. Cf. Vulg. *utinam ut coepimus*, "had we only begun"; cf. Luther, "wie wir angefangen hatten." But *yā'al* also means "to show willingness," "to determine"; see BDB.

elect. Israel's failures and frustrations are frankly set forth in the sacred record.

In Exod. 23:22 God had promised that when Israel did his will its enemies would be his enemies,[29] but that defeat would be the price for covenant disloyalty. Of the latter Joshua had not yet been apprised, although he might have concluded from the facts that the covenant had been broken (but cf. Ps. 44:18–27 [Eng. 17–26]). The "name" of the covenant people may be connected correctly with the "name" of the Lord himself, as is done by Joshua in v. 9. But when Israel's name is wiped off the earth, what will happen to the Lord's name? God acts on behalf of his people, and he does so for his name's sake (Ezek. 20:9, 14, 22; cf. Ps. 79:4, 10; Jer. 14:7).

God's choice of Israel is entirely voluntary and gracious (see Deut. 7), but this choice involves a mutual obligation and commitment. It therefore also involves, humanly speaking, the possibility of a loss of "face" on the part of him who had committed himself as sovereign to assist his people (3:10).[30] Joshua had a right to plead as he did, for he did not yet know what the readers know, namely that the covenant, the very basis of God's gracious help to Israel, had been violated. Moses' prayers in Exod. 32:11–13; Num. 14:15–16 may have served as models for Joshua.[31]

10–12 The Lord's reply to Joshua is curt. Joshua is told to stand up and no longer lie on his face. If our understanding of Joshua's prayer has been correct, the Lord's displeasure with Joshua's grief arises not from the nature of his plea but from the Lord's great anger which blazes toward all Israel on account of its sin (v. 1). Corporately they are all involved in the offense of Achan.

The nature of the sin is clearly stated: a breach of *covenant*. Israel itself, not God, is the cause of the present misfortune. Prosperity and success had been promised Israel (1:8), but only if the people acted according to what had been written in the law of the Lord. The *ḥerem* rules also belonged to that law (Deut. 20:10–18). Contamination with the practices of the Canaanite peoples was thus to be avoided and the Lord's claim to the promised land clearly demonstrated.

---

29. Cf. W. Foerster, ἐχθρός, ἔχθρα" in *TDNT* II (E.T. 1964), pp. 811–15.

30. The fact that the covenant link between God and Israel was often taken for granted and became a reason for false security on Israel's part should not lead to the mistake of voiding all reference to a true security which flows from a proper understanding of covenant.

31. The use of the respectful *Oh, Lord* (Heb. *bî 'ᵃḏōnāy*, lit. "let the guilt be on me if I speak wrongly") in v. 8 would seem to lend support to a favorable interpretation of Joshua's plea.

Verse 11 uses two typical words to describe the situation: "sinned" (Heb. *ḥāṭā'*) and "transgressed" (Heb. *'āḇar*).[32] This is followed by a long list of descriptions of the sinful act.[33] The main thing is put first: *they have taken from the accursed things* (cf. 6:18). The rest of the indictment enlarges upon the act, calling it concealment, theft, deceit, and finally selfishness. That which belonged to the Lord as his exclusive property had been put to selfish use, and throughout the entire indictment runs the thought of corporate guilt (see v. 1): the Israelites have sinned and done all these things. This is the cause of their defeat. By partaking of the accursed thing they themselves have become accursed.[34]

Verse 12 uses the expression *accursed thing* in two slightly different senses. Israel itself has become an accursed thing, but also among them is an accursed thing that must be completely destroyed if the Lord is ever to be *with* Israel again. Thus the corporate and the individual go hand in hand in this verse.

13-15 Achan's sinful act, not yet known to either Joshua or the people, and the people's involvement in this act mean that Israel's sanctity as covenant people (Exod. 19:6) has been violated. For this reason the people under Joshua's leadership are to sanctify themselves for tomorrow (see 3:5). Thus the distinction between the holy and the common (Lev. 10:10) which had been obliterated could again be observed. The narrative is rather explicit at this point. The Lord's words to Joshua (v. 12) are repeated in what Joshua is told to communicate to the people. This gives the narrator the chance to stress the need for complete purity among God's people as a prerequisite for covenant fellowship between the people and their God. There could be no victory over the enemy without removal of

---

32. Heb. *ḥāṭā'* is numerically the most frequent word used in the OT for an act contrary to God's will. Just as *'āḇar*, it is used of transgressing the covenant and stresses the formal aspect of the sinful act. There is a goal, a line, which must guide man's actions. When that goal is missed and that line crossed, man's communion with God is broken. This formal aspect of sin must not be contrasted with a more "religious" sin notion which the OT is somehow supposed to lack because of its preoccupation with law and covenant (as suggested in G. Quell, "ἁμαρτάνω, ἁμάρτημα, ἁμαρτία," *TDNT* I (E.T. 1964), pp. 267–286.
33. The Hebrew links the various phrases five times with *gam*, "also," probably for climactic effect.
34. This has not come about by a kind of "sacred contagion, conceived in an almost physical sense," as A. Gelin, *Josué*, p. 50, suggests. There may be an external similarity here between taboo notions and contamination with the curse, but the OT thought world differs basically from that of taboo and mana. Israel's contamination stems from transgression of a command.

the curse. As *the Lord, the God of Israel*, God places this sovereign demand before his people.

Instead of informing the people directly about the identity of the offender,[35] the Lord chooses the indirect means of the lot.[36] This serves to awaken in the people an awareness of their involvement in the sin committed, and at the same time it lets the full light fall upon the individual who committed it.

The people are to present themselves[37] at the sanctuary by their various divisions, tribes,[38] clans, and finally as family and individual. The Hebrew terms used for these divisions fluctuate (e.g., Num. 4:18; Judg. 20:12). In each case the Lord himself will mark (lit. "catch") the guilty party. By a slow process of elimination the guilty person will finally appear. That person, together with all that belongs to him, is to *be burned with fire*. Certain crimes in Israel were punished in this way (cf. Gen. 38:24; cf. Lev. 20:4). Verse 25 mentions stoning as another form of punishment. The two do not exclude each other.[39] Again the reader is reminded of the central significance of the sin committed. It is a transgression of the covenant (see v. 11). The author also uses another term to describe the sin:

---

35. J. Calvin realizes that God does not always use this method of the lot; *Commentaries on the Book of Joshua*, p. 113. God, according to Calvin, "has taught us by this example [*exemplum*] that there is nothing so hidden as not to be revealed in its own time."

36. The precise way in which God will "mark" (Heb. *lākaḏ*, "catch") the offender is not indicated. Some think of the Urim and Thummim (see Num. 27:21); so J. Bright, *IB* II, p. 587. The word *lākaḏ* is used in 1 Sam. 14:42, where Urim and Thummim are definitely used.

37. Heb. *niqrab*, lit. "make oneself come near," i.e., to the sanctuary. In vv. 16–18 the Hiphil of this verb is used; cf. Exod. 22:7.

38. The Hebrew uses two words for "tribe," here and elsewhere. The word *šēḇeṭ* designates the tribe in its political cohesion; *maṭṭeh*, on the other hand, views the tribe as the multitude of those that compose it; see P. Renard, "Achan," in F. Vigouroux, ed., *Dictionnaire de La Bible*, I (Paris: 1895), col. 130. This meaningful distinction, as Renard correctly observes, "reduces to nothing the system of the rationalists who wish to ascribe two different authors to the book of Joshua" on the basis of the use of these two terms. According to de Vaux, *Ancient Israel*, p. 8, *šēḇeṭ* and *maṭṭeh* are said to be "two words with the same meaning," but this overlooks the point to which Renard calls attention.

39. Jewish writings claimed that Achan was stoned because he had sinned on the sabbath, but that he was burned because of his crime; see A. Menes–M. Soloweitschik, "Achan," in J. Klatzkin, ed., *Encyclopaedia Judaica* (Berlin: 1928), cols. 699f. The sin of sacrilege, e.g., that of heresy and witchcraft according to medieval church officials, had to be punished by burning—a fearful application of this passage.

a *folly in Israel*.[40] The use of this term again stresses the corporate aspect of the sinful act.

16–18 Now follows a description of the elaborate process by which the offender, who remains silent during it all, is found (cf. also 1 Sam. 10:20–21). The very manner of the description, although typical of Hebrew narrative, nevertheless serves to highlight the crime committed (see also vv. 14–15). The order followed is the same as that set out in v. 14[41] and the reverse of that of v. 1. Achan belongs to the tribe of Judah, the descendants of which are listed in Num. 26:19–22; 1 Chr. 2:3–55. After one of its clans, that of the Zerahites, has been marked, the family of Zabdi[42] is taken. Achan, although himself head of a family (in the western sense), was nevertheless a part of the larger "family" of Zabdi. Again (v. 18) Achan's full line of descent is enumerated as in v. 1. All this serves to emphasize that what had been done was most serious in the writer's eyes.

19–21 Joshua charges Achan to *give glory to the Lord the God of Israel and make confession to him*. Joshua's tone is that of a father speaking to a wayward child.[43] He summons Achan to confess the truth before God, which will mean giving glory to the Lord. The word translated *confession* (Heb. *tôḏâ*) can also be rendered "praise."[44] At certain times in Israel's history a song of thanksgiving which accompanies an admission of sin develops into a confession (cf. Ezra 10:11, where the same Hebrew word is used). The whole account from beginning to end is thoroughly

40. "Folly" (Heb. *neḇālâ*) designates sin as something deliberately pursued. It is often used of sexual sins (Gen. 34:7; cf. Judg. 20:6, 10). Some prefer to translate "shameful deed" (cf. also Ps. 14:1). This "folly" attacks the very foundations of life, and stands opposed to the "wisdom" of which the book of Proverbs speaks. Cf. G. von Rad, *OT Theology* I, pp. 267, 428f.

41. In our translation of v. 17 we have read *mišpeḥôṯ*, "clans," instead of MT *mišpaḥaṯ*, singular.

42. In v. 17b the clan of the Zerahites is to come forward "man by man," Heb. *laggeḇārîm*. Here this must mean the heads of the families and not yet the individual members of the unit concerned. The Vulgate translates *domos*, "families," thus solving the problem in a different way. Abel follows this approach, *op. cit.*, p. 40; as does Gelin, *op. cit.*, p. 51. Materially this is correct, but the MT renders an acceptable sense.

43. For this language cf. John 9:24.

44. The Vulgate renders the word by *confitere*. The LXX also stresses the confession element with *dós tén exomológēsin*, although *homologéō* also contains the element of praise. See Kroeze, *op. cit.*, p. 99; and cf. von Rad, *op. cit.*, pp. 356–370. Von Rad believes that the Heb. *hôḏâ*, "which we generally translate as 'to praise,' properly means 'to confess,' 'to accept,' and always refers to a preceding divine datum."

God-centered. The sin is committed against God; it is a violation of his covenant, and only through giving glory to him can the evil be eradicated. Hiding the sin would be a form of self-assertion.[45] Achan, who for an unknown reason has remained silent through the painful process of the lot, now makes a full confession. He admits that he is the offender, and that his offense has been against no one else but God himself.[46]

Achan's confession shows a sin consciousness that is different from that of Israel's neighbors. In Egypt, for example, evil was not viewed as a rebellion against the divine will but merely as an aberration from the cosmic order. As such, sin was only evidence of ignorance on the part of the sinner. Contrition is, therefore, a sentiment not found among the Egyptians.[47]

Not only is the sin called by its proper name, but the psychological process which led to the sinful act is set forth masterfully. Achan's actions were inspired by the desire for the beautiful things he encountered. The robe[48] he saw was a beautiful one, from Shinar, which is Babylon (cf. Gen. 10:10; Isa. 11:11; Dan. 1:2; Zech. 5:11).[49] Then there were two hundred shekels[50] of silver and a bar of gold weighing fifty shekels. These Achan *coveted*, which is the root of sin (see Exod. 20:17; Deut. 5:21,

---

45. Jewish sages held that since Achan made a confession he became the recipient of the world to come; cf. M. Guttmann, "A. in Talmud und Midrasch," in Klatzkin, *op. cit.*, I, p. 700. This belief was shared by H. Grotius; cf. L. Diestel, *Geschichte des AT in der Christlichen Kirche* (Jena: 1869), p. 520.

46. The words "this is what I have done," Heb. $w^e\underline{k}\bar{a}z\hat{o}'\underline{t}\ w^e\underline{k}\bar{a}z\hat{o}'\underline{t}\ '\bar{a}\hat{s}\hat{\imath}\underline{t}\hat{\imath}$, are so he holds, is only making a general confession here ("I have done such and such"). The account had already reported the details of the crime, but this element was lost. However, the Hebrew expression when used in 2 Sam. 17:15; 2 K. 5:4; 9:12 refers to what is to follow, not to something already reported.

47. See *DOTT*, p. 151.

48. The Hebrew word used also means "splendor," e.g., Zech. 11:3 (RSV "glory"). It designates a king's robe in Jon. 3:6. Elijah's robe was also called by this term (1 K. 19:13); though made of hair it may have been a beautiful article of clothing. Vulgate *pallium coccineum* ("scarlet robe"); LXX *psilḗ poikílē*, a multicolored cloak.

49. Shinar appears to be the biblical counterpart of cuneiform Sumeru, and is believed to be the lower part of Mesopotamia. Some hold that it represents Shanhar, found in certain Egyptian historical texts; cf. *ANET*, pp. 243, 247.

50. "Shekel" means lit. "weight." Coined money was not used until after the Babylonian Exile. Earlier, gold and silver were weighed. One shekel of gold was equal to 13⅓ shekels of silver. For modern equivalents, cf. de Vaux, *Ancient Israel*, p. 205, who maintains that the shekel weighed 0.30 ounces (8.4 grams), but that in a series derived from the royal talent all the units weighed double. Goslinga, *op. cit.*, p. 82, equates 200 shekels with 3 kilograms. However, all such estimates are conjectural.

where the same Hebrew word is used). The coveted things were then taken, hidden in the tent, and buried in the earth.

22–26 From this point on the story moves swiftly to its dramatic conclusion. Again the hand of the master storyteller, observed in earlier chapters, is evident. Messengers are dispatched, and they find the stolen objects just as indicated in Achan's confession.[51] The items are carried back to Joshua and to the assembled Israelites (the LXX speaks only of the "elders"), and they are spread out[52] for all to see. However, the main purpose of this transaction is to return the objects to the Lord whose they were by virtue of the curse (6:18–19).

According to v. 12, the accursed thing, in this case Achan through whom the curse had come upon all Israel, had to be destroyed. Verses 24–26 report that this was done. The enumeration of v. 24 sounds like a litany. *Joshua and all Israel* participate in the final act. Although all Israel had been implicated in this sin (vv. 1, 11), the curse which Achan had violated is applied to himself (cf. Deut. 13:16–17). The OT system of sacrifice made ample provision for atonement for offenses, but sins with an upraised hand (Num. 15:27–31) could not be atoned for by means of sacrifice.

The place where the execution takes place is called proleptically *the valley of Achor*. The symbolism of this name is explained in Joshua's words in v. 25. It will be a valley devoted to the memory of the one who "troubled" Israel (see also the name Achar in 1 Chr. 2:7).

Although v. 15 had spoken only of burning, v. 25 also speaks of stoning. Moreover, v. 25 uses alternately the third person singular and the third person plural for the object of the punishment. It may well be that the stoning was done to enable "all Israel" to participate in the act. The use of both singular and plural probably indicates that Achan was put to death separately, to make an example of him. The fact that his family also shared in that fate may be due to their common knowledge of the crime. After all, the goods were hidden in the parental tent. The element of corporate guilt is here also. Deut. 24:16 is held in balance by Deut. 5:9.[53] The former should not be seen as representing a more individualistic, less "sacral" view than the latter. Properly understood the Bible does not teach

51. The words "it was hidden" (v. 22) represent a Hebrew passive participle which occurs without corresponding determinant.
52. Heb. lit. "poured out." This word is held by some to be evidence that the original story knew only of a theft of money, coins which could be poured out. But the expression "pour" could well be used for the laying out of several articles, including a robe.
53. For an overview of opinions as to the role of Deut. 24:16 at this point, see J. P. Lange, *A Commentary on the Holy Scriptures* 4, p. 79.

individualism anywhere. Care should also be taken not to view the corporate element as only a remnant of a primitive mode of thought that is inconsistent with modern thinking.[54]

Achan, his family, and all their belongings are *brought up* to the valley of Achor. The use of this verb (Heb. *'ālâ*) is a strange one when used with reference to a *valley*. Not enough is known about the geographical situation to make a definite judgment.[55]

In a final summary Joshua speaks of Achan's having *brought trouble*, and concludes by saying that *the Lord will trouble you this day*. This is not vindictiveness. Joshua acts in keeping with the divine command (v. 15); and God, the God of the covenant, acts in keeping with the covenant (cf. Ezek. 16:59). A violation of the covenant causes covenant retribution. Physical death as punishment for sin was given prominence in OT times. This shows God's displeasure with sin. Conclusions as to the eternal destiny of individuals so punished had better not be made rashly. As revelation progresses the true nature of the relationship between sin and punishment becomes clear (compare 2 K. 1:9–16 with Luke 9:51–55). Jesus rejects the suggestion of an Elijah-type judgment, but, as Luke 10:8–12 indicates, he at the same time speaks of a more ultimate judgment on those who knowingly reject him.

The Hebrew uses two different words for "stoning," *rāgam* (v. 25a) and *sāqal* (v. 25b). The former is used here for the act of stoning as a form of capital punishment. The latter refers to the casting up of stones upon the bodies after they had been burned, for the purpose of erecting a memorial pile (see also v. 26).[56]

The account concludes with a statement that the pile of stones erected over Achan has remained there *until this day*.[57] Achan's death

---

54. Cf. von Rad, *op. cit.*, I, p. 265.
55. The use of the word *'ālâ*, which can also be used for "going up" to a cultic center, has led to the supposition that the basis of the Achan story is cultic; see, e.g., Hertzberg, *op. cit.*, p. 56. This is then tied in with an etiological understanding of the story. The etiological approach, however, is problematic in light of the intentions of OT historiography. To suspend a cultic approach to this story from the use of the verb *'ālâ*, which can also have noncultic meanings, is precarious.
56. Neither the LXX nor the Vulgate refers to the second stoning. The LXX mentions only Achan's stoning and omits everything else. The Vulgate states that Achan was stoned and that everything which belonged to him was burned. These may be attempts to solve the apparent problem which the MT presents.
57. For the meaning of this phrase see the commentary on 4:9; 5:9; cf. B. Childs, *JBL* 82 (1963), pp. 279–292. Childs concludes that this formula only rarely functions etiologically. Most often it is added by way of a personal testimony to confirm the reliability of the event reported.

caused the Lord's blazing anger to cease. The name of the valley, *valley of Achor*, continued throughout Israel's history (see also Hos. 2:17).

H. AI CONQUERED AND BURNED (8:1–29)

1 *Then the Lord said to Joshua: "Do not fear and do not be dismayed. Take with you all the warriors and go, march up to Ai. See, I hereby give into your power the king of Ai and his people and his city and his land.*

2 *And you shall do to Ai and its king as you have done to Jericho and its king. You may take as booty for yourselves its spoil and its cattle, but nothing more. Set an ambush against the city on its backside."*

3 *So Joshua and all the warriors made preparations to march up to Ai. Joshua chose thirty thousand men, picked troops, and sent them out by night.*

4 *And he gave them these orders: "Attention! you are to lie in ambush against the city, on its backside; do not go very far from the city, and all of you be ready.*

5 *But I, and all the troops that are with me, will approach the city. Then, when they come out against us as at the first time, we will flee before them.*

6 *Then they will go out following us till we have drawn them away from the city. For they will say: They are fleeing before us as at the first time. So we will flee before them.*

7 *Then you must rise up from ambush and take possession of the city. The Lord your God will give it into your power.*

8 *Once you have seized the city you are to set fire to the city. According to the word of the Lord so shall you do. See, I have given you orders."*

9 *So Joshua sent them off, and they went to the place of ambush, and took up their position between Bethel and Ai, on the west of Ai. But Joshua lodged that night among the people.*

10 *Rising up early in the morning Joshua mustered the people, and he and the elders of Israel marched up in front of the people to Ai.*

11 *All the people, the warriors that were with him, marched up and approached and went right in front of the city, and then they encamped on the north side of Ai. Now there was a valley between him and Ai.*

12 *He took about five thousand men and placed them in ambush between Bethel and Ai, on the west of the city.*

13 *Thus they assigned a place to the people, namely the whole camp that was on the north of the city, and their ambush on the west of the city. And Joshua went that night into the midst of the valley.*

14 *Now when the king of Ai noticed it, the men of the city hurried and got up early and went out to meet Israel for battle, he and all his people, to the place of the encounter facing the Arabah; but he did not know that he had an ambush on the backside of the city.*

15 *And Joshua and all Israel pretended to be beaten at their approach, and they fled along the way to the wilderness.*

16 *Then all the men that were in the city were called up to pursue behind them; they pursued Joshua and were drawn away from the city.*

17 *Not a man was left in Ai and Bethel who did not go out in pursuit of Israel. They left the city open and pursued after Israel.*

18 *Then the Lord said to Joshua: "Point the javelin which is in your hand toward Ai, for into your hand shall I give it." So Joshua pointed the javelin which was in his hand toward the city.*

19 *Now as to the men in ambush, they rose up in a hurry from their place, and as soon as he pointed his hand they ran and came to the city and seized it, and they quickly set fire to the city.*

20 *When the men of Ai looked behind them they saw to their surprise that the smoke of the city rose up toward heaven, and they had no chance to flee in one direction or in another. For the people that were in flight toward the wilderness turned around to face their pursuer.*

21 *When Joshua and all Israel saw that the ambush had taken the city and that the smoke of the city rose up, they turned and attacked the men of Ai.*

22 *And the others came out of the city to meet them. And they got right in the middle of Israel, with some being on the one side and others on the other. They smote them, so that they let none of them remain or escape.*

23 *The king of Ai they seized alive, and they brought him to Joshua.*

24 *When Israel had finished killing all the inhabitants of Ai in the field, in the wilderness in which they had pursued them, and they had fallen by the edge of the sword till the last man, then all Israel turned back toward Ai and smote it with the edge of the sword.*

25 *The total of those fallen on that day, including men and women, was twelve thousand, all inhabitants of Ai.*

26 *Joshua did not withdraw his hand with which he was pointing the javelin, until he had executed the curse upon all the inhabitants of Ai.*

27 *The cattle, however, and the booty of that city Israel took as spoil for itself, according to the word of the Lord which he had commanded Joshua.*

28 *And Joshua burned Ai and made it into a permanent ruin, a desolation, until this day.*

29 *And the king of Ai he hung on a tree until the evening, but when the sun went down Joshua ordered his body to be taken down from that tree, and they cast it at the entrance of the city gate, and they raised over him a large pile of stones, until this day.*

Chapter 8, like its predecessors, should be evaluated and understood in terms of the historiography of the book of Joshua. It is therefore neither theological propaganda nor an exact, scientific description of a sequence of events. To apply the canons of scientific historiography to such a chapter would do it an injustice.[1] At the same time, the difficulties presented by this chapter[2] do not appear to be such as to warrant the assumption of pure etiology as basis for the events narrated. Nor does the theory that the chapter is a composite of two somewhat contradictory or at least parallel sources commend itself. An attempt will be made here to treat the chapter as a unit and the events narrated as factual and nonfictitious.

1–2 The chapter opens with a word of encouragement to Joshua which recalls words spoken earlier (1:6, 9; cf. Deut. 1:21; 31:8).[3] By reporting these words of the Lord the writer means to indicate that circumstances are again as they used to be. God's promises of divine assistance had been jeopardized by the people's disobedience as reported in ch. 7. The Lord's anger, however, had been turned away (7:26). The object of the present chapter, therefore, is to show what can be done (and what *was* done) when God's people act in accordance with his will.

Joshua is told to take *all the warriors* with him. This is distinct from the advice given him by the men who reconnoitred Ai (7:3) and must be understood in that light.[4] Joshua and the men are to *march up to Ai*, which was situated on higher ground compared to the Gilgal area where the command was given. The account does not indicate explicitly whether the earlier expedition against Ai (ch. 7), which had not been commanded in so many words by the Lord, was therefore condemned. At that time

1. The specific nature of the "history" of the book of Joshua does not rule out all historical criticism, but P. Auvray, in L. Pirot, ed., *Dictionnaire de la Bible*, Suppl. 4, col. 1140, rightly states that "to reject as pure legend the stories of Jericho, Ai, and Gibeon is not only arbitrary, it is to renounce the work of a historian and render less intelligible what one is called upon to elucidate: Le travail historique est une construction, non une déstruction."
2. Commenting upon the differences between vv. 3 and 12, and offering his solution E. J. Young, *An Introduction to the OT*, p. 176, admits "I grant that it is extremely difficult."
3. The exhortation not to fear is frequent in the Bible; see 10:8, 25; 11:6; Gen. 15:1; 26:24; 46:3; Exod. 14:13; 20:20; Num. 21:34; also Jer. 1:8; Ezek. 2:6.
4. A comparison of 1:14–15 with 3:12–13 shows that "all" may sometimes mean a certain limited number.

Joshua no doubt acted on his own accord, since the capture of Ai after that of Jericho naturally suggested itself to him as Israel's military leader. The defeat at Ai was due to other reasons.

As upon previous occasions, the Lord assures Joshua that the city of Ai is *given* into Israel's power (for this emphasis cf. 1:2–3; 2:24; 6:2; cf. Judg. 3:28; 4:7; 7:9, 15; 1 Sam. 23:4; 24:5, etc.). It would be theologizing to see in this phraseology (Heb. *nātattî*, perfect tense) a reference to a divine decree in which all things have already been accomplished,[5] although references of this sort should be taken into account in considering and formulating the doctrine of the decrees. However, the very sequel to the story indicates that the emphasis upon the giving of Canaan (Ai) goes hand in hand with careful planning and even the employment of a ruse.[6]

Ai's king, his people, and his city and land are given into Israel's power. God's declaration is solemn and reassuring, with nothing left out.[7] Ai's capture, though different from that of Jericho, will nevertheless continue the pattern then set. Its king must be treated in the way that Jericho's king was treated. Ch. 6 does not spell out what this treatment was, so one must infer this from 8:29. Also the entire population is to be treated like that of Jericho (cf. 6:17). This means that, though the term *ḥerem* is not used, the idea is present (see Deut. 3:2, 7; Num. 21:34), although the curse is not to be applied quite as strictly as in the case of Jericho (see commentary on 6:17–19, 21). The pattern in Ai's case will be that laid down in Deut. 2:34–35; 3:6–7:[8] Israel may take the spoil and the cattle.[9]

One detail of the attack upon Ai is mentioned specifically in the Lord's word to Joshua. It concerns the ambush[10] which is to play an

---

5. This is how J. A. Soggin understands the phrase, *Joshua*, p. 29; cf. also H. W. Hertzberg, *ATD* IX, p. 56: "Es *wird* überhaupt nicht erobert, sondern es *ist* erobert, durch das nunmehr dekretierende Gotteswort." Such an approach appears unduly theological on the part of scholars who otherwise celebrate the historical method. Moreover, it obstructs the construction of a wholesome doctrine of the decrees.

6. On Calvin's discussion of God's employing a ruse, see KD, p. 84.

7. The LXX omits "his people" and "his city." The land of Ai's king is probably the territory referred to in vv. 11, 13, 15.

8. Deut. 20:10–16 permits a more lenient attitude toward cities outside Canaan than toward Canaanite cities. The saving alive of Ai's livestock was done by specific divine injunction.

9. It may be that K. Gutbrod, *Das Buch vom Lande Gottes*, pp. 73f., is right in suggesting that the permission to take spoil was also intended to remove the temptation which had presented itself to Achan at Jericho. Israel will receive symbolically the possessions of Canaan in loan from the Lord to use them for him.

10. Heb. *'ôrēḇ*, a collective noun designating those in ambush. In v. 9 a different word (*ma'ªrāḇ*) is used. Literally it stands for the place of ambush.

important part in the subsequent account. This ambush is to be placed at the *backside* of the city; v. 9 makes clear this is the west side. Does this explicit command mean to indicate that Israel's wars of conquest are fought ultimately under the "generalship" of none other than the Lord himself? See also the appearance to Joshua in 5:13–15.

3–9 The narrative now proceeds to report in great detail the preparations made by Joshua for the attack upon Ai. The actual battle between Ai and Israel is not described until vv. 14ff. The circumstantial nature of this account recalls similar features in ch. 3. The fact that Ai's capture is given so much attention also indicates the concern of the book of Joshua as a whole. Its historiography is episodic, with the light focused on salient details. The capture of most of the other cities of south-Canaan will only be summarized briefly in ch. 10.

Although the main features of the account are clear, some of the details appear somewhat confusing at first. These difficulties have long prompted interpreters to hold that two or more narrative traditions were woven into one consecutive account,[11] but this inevitably means that, since the "seams" are still showing, the storyteller was less than proficient in putting the account together.[12] We prefer to treat the narrative as a basic unity. At any rate, the account should be interpreted in its present form and its meaning ascertained.

At least two approaches toward a proper understanding of vv. 3–9 (cf. v. 13) suggest themselves. One can take the verses as describing the sending of an ambush one day ahead of the movement of the main force from Gilgal to the vicinity of Ai. When that is done one must consider vv. 12–13 to be a recapitulation, and the verb tenses should be pluperfect (v. 12, "He had taken . . . etc.").[13] This of course assumes that the ambush

11. For a list of the alleged "duplicates" in the account (vv. 3 and 10; 9 and 12; 3 and 12, etc.) see J. M. Miller and G. M. Tucker, *The Book of Joshua*, p. 68. M. Noth, *Das Buch Josua*, pp. 49f., holds that though the account is materially composite it is literarily a unity. He discovers only two "doublets," i.e., in 8:12–13.

12. Lately it has become customary not to heed these "seams" but to hold that oriental narrative composition simply was not concerned to iron out all seeming discrepancies. In fact, narrators are said to have had a high regard for their traditions and thus to have been reluctant to smooth over differences between them. Scholars who hold to a certain theory of inspiration try to incorporate this approach into their inspiration theories. The present author is not inclined to support such views unless every other avenue leading toward a suitable solution appears to be closed completely.

13. This is how several interpreters understand these verses, e.g., C. J. Goslinga, *Het Boek Jozua*, pp. 85, 185f. (but he also allows for a different approach); B. J. Alfrink, *Josué*, pp. 49f.; cf. also D. S. Attema, "Het Boek Jozua."

mentioned in v. 3 is the same as that of v. 12, and that the difference in number must be due to scribal error, with the figure five thousand preferred rather than thirty thousand.

The other approach is to regard vv. 3–9 as a proleptic description of an action that did not take place until the whole force had marched from Gilgal to Ai and had taken up camp near the city to the north (vv. 11–13). Upon this approach v. 10 describes the march of the entire army, including the ambush which is yet to be stationed. The first view is burdened with the difficulty that the ambush, which was then sent ahead of the chief force by one whole day and night, had to remain invisible to the people of Ai for so long a period. For this reason we follow the second approach, but the passage remains a difficult one.[14]

Then Joshua and *all the warriors*[15] make preparations to go up to Ai. Because Ai is higher than Gilgal, where the preparations are made, the verb *march up* is accurately chosen. Joshua selects thirty thousand men, who were thus *picked troops*.[16] Since in vv. 4ff. these men are addressed as to their prospective duty in the ambush, the question arises as to how to understand the difference between the figures used in vv. 3, 12. Moreover, even if the figure in v. 3 should be retained, the large number of troops used for a mere ambush causes wonderment, and not least in light of Ai's total population, which is said to be twelve thousand (v. 25). Perhaps the best solution is to assume a scribal error in one of the two entries.[17] Since at an earlier point in the scribal tradition numerals were indicated by the letters of the Hebrew alphabet, such an error could have

14. Young, *Introduction*, p. 176, while granting that the question is "extremely difficult," suggests that the events may have been as follows: Joshua picks thirty thousand men (v. 3) and sends them away (v. 9); v. 9b relates what Joshua himself did. Verses 10–11 begin a detailed account. Thus, v. 9 is a general summary statement of the execution of the divine command, the details of which begin in v. 10.
15. Heb. *'am hammilḥāmâ*, used in the OT only here and in v. 11; 10:7; 11:7. Other translations: NEB "army"; RSV "fighting men"; Noth "Kriegsvolk"; NAB "soldiers"; Abel "gens de guerre."
16. Heb. *gibbôrê haḥayil*; see also 1:14; 6:2.
17. This is done by Keil and Delitzsch, Goslinga, etc. B. Holwerda, *Jozua*, p. 26, holds there were two ambushes, but he allows for the Heb *'elep*, ordinarily translated "thousand," to stand for an indefinite "unit" which could have been much less than a thousand; cf. G. E. Mendenhall, "The Census Lists of Numbers 1 and 26," *JBL* 77 (1958), pp. 52–66. Thus the logistical problem would be lessened. Cf. also G. J. Wenham, *JBL* 90 (1971), p. 142.

occurred quite easily. In light of what was said earlier, the lower of the two figures would be the accurate one.[18]

The instructions given to the men who are to lie in ambush are clear, but not all the details of what was agreed upon are given immediately, as becomes apparent as the story unfolds. This mode of narration was also followed in chs. 3, 6.[19] Joshua's main force will move toward the city while the ambush is at its backside. This will cause the men of Ai to undertake a sally and a pursuit. Israel will pretend to be in flight as before. The ambush is then to *take possession of the city*. The sign of the extended javelin (vv. 18–19) is not mentioned here. To encourage the men Joshua again refers to the fact that *the Lord your God will give it into your power* (see v. 1). After the city is seized (v. 8) it is to be set on fire. The narrator distinguishes carefully in the verbs he uses between this fire and the burning mentioned later in v. 28. The former was meant as a signal to the men of Ai that their cause was desperate, while the latter was a final destruction.

The ambush is to act *according to the word of the Lord*. The Lord's word to Joshua, as reported in v. 2,[20] had spoken of the ambush only, with no further instructions. This may be another instance in which the narrative gradually supplies details (compare also 3:7–8, 9–13). The final words of Joshua to the men of the ambush (*See, I have given you orders*) must be understood in the light of other emphases such as 3:9–10. Joshua is the Lord's authorized spokesman. Throughout the account are repeated features stressing Joshua's leadership (cf. also 4:14).

If our understanding of this passage is correct then v. 9, which mentions the dispatch of the forces of ambush, is a summary statement which anticipates a subsequent action reported later in v. 12. The ambush was laid *between Bethel and Ai, on the west of Ai*. Features in the landscape such as the presence of large rocks on the hills would make a suitable hiding place for the men.

Verse 9b indicates that Joshua spent the night among the people. If, as we have supposed, v. 9 is anticipatory of what will be reported in greater detail in the following verses, then this night which Joshua spends among the people is that during which the ambush is sent out, and the "people" among whom it is spent is the chief force located, as will be

---

18. J. H. Kroeze, *Het Boek Jozua*, p. 106, too easily assumes the existence of two parallel traditions listing differing figures.

19. For this piecemeal reporting of the various details of the story compare 3:7–8 with 3:9–13; and 6:4–5 with 6:16, 20.

20. The LXX apparently understood v. 2 more narrowly and omitted a reference to the word of the Lord in v. 8. F.-M. Abel, p. 228, and JB follow the LXX at this point; Abel: "Tels sont les ordres que vous exécuterez."

seen, at the north of Ai. Such "dischronologized" narrative is not uncommon in the OT.[21]

10–13 These verses report the sequence of events as they actually occurred. Joshua musters the troops and marches to Ai, together with the *elders*. These elders were the heads of clans and families, representing a tribe upon special occasions (see Exod. 3:16, 18; 18:12; 24:1; Lev. 4:13–15; 9:1; Num. 11:16). Their participation in this significant march to Ai may have been recorded by way of contrast with the lamentation before the ark in which they had also taken part (7:6). The continuation between vv. 10–11 in Hebrew is not the usual narrative sequence.[22] However, this does not mean that the events reported in v. 11 do not actually follow those of v. 10. It does mean that the narrative places stress upon those participating in the march to Ai (lit. "Now as to the people, the warriors, they marched up," etc.).[23]

After approaching the city and going right in front of it, the Israelite army moved northward, where it encamped. The forces of Israel and Ai were now separated by a valley (Heb. *gay*).[24] The valley into the midst of which Joshua went[25] (v. 13) is designated by a different Hebrew word (*'ēmeq*). Apparently these were two distinct features of the landscape. As pointed out earlier, the description of this event shows acquaintance with local terrain.

Verse 12 reports the dispatching of the ambush (see commentary on vv. 3–4). If, as we have assumed, only one ambush of five thousand troops is involved, then the locations mentioned in vv. 2, 9, 12 are one and the same.[26] Verse 13a sums up the situation without adding any new

---

21. Cf. W. J. Martin, *VTS* 17 (1969), pp. 179–186.
22. In other words, rather than the *wayyiqtôl* form, the *we . . . qātal* form is used. This allows for placing the subject of the verb first, contrary to common usage.
23. Alfrink, *op. cit.*, p. 50, correctly calls attention to the change in tense, but it is not clear that this necessitates the use of the pluperfect in English as he contends.
24. The LXX is considerably shorter in 11b–12: ". . . they came over against the city to the east, and the ambush of the city to the west." This abbreviated form certainly simplifies the problem which the MT presents, but does it explain how the MT came to be so complicated? A. Gelin, *Josué*, considers vv. 11b–13 to be a later addition; the NEB omits all of v. 13.
25. With a slight change of consonants the Hebrew can also be made to read: "Joshua lodged in the midst of the valley."
26. Those who hold to the presence of two ambushes prefer to think that the "backside" (vv. 2, 4) is a southwestern location, exactly opposite to the northeastern location of the main force, whereas the other ambush would then be due west of the town, thus designed to cut off escape toward Bethel.

information. Joshua and the elders *assigned a place to the people*. This is the camp on the north side, with the ambush[27] on the west side. The statement that *Joshua went that night into the midst of the valley* probably means that Joshua with the main force traversed the valley and thus positioned himself close to Ai, ready for the attack.[28]

14–17 After an extended description of the preparation for the attack upon Ai the narrative suddenly accelerates and comes to a dramatic description of the main action.[29] Having received intelligence of Israel's movements, the king of Ai and all his people go out to meet Israel. Apparently there was a suitable place, translated here *place of the encounter*,[30] where the king seeks to engage Israel in battle. It is said to be *facing the Arabah*, a term which usually stands for the valley in which the river Jordan runs. Here it probably designates the uncultivated area called *wilderness* in v. 15 (Heb. *miḏbār*).

As noted previously (e.g., in ch. 3), the narrator knows how to build suspense into the story. He informs the reader that the king of Ai undertook the attack, unaware of the ambush on the backside of his city.

Joshua and the Israelites act as if they are beaten a second time (cf. 7:2–5), and take flight *along the way to the wilderness*.[31]

Apparently some of the people of Ai had still been left behind in the city, which means that v. 14 should not be read too literally.[32] These are now called up to join the pursuit of the fleeing Israelites. Verses 16–17 describe dramatically how the inhabitants of the doomed city of Ai (see v. 1: it was "given" into Israel's hands) spare no effort in what turns out to be a reckless pursuit of the enemy, meanwhile leaving their ambushed city defenseless and unattended. This is Hebrew narrative at its best.

Hitherto the city of Bethel, although mentioned previously (v. 9),

27. Heb. *'āqēḇ*, lit. "heel."
28. This is how, e.g., Alfrink, *op. cit.*, pp. 50f., understands the phrase. He renders it "Joshua went straight across the valley," and refers to Exod. 14:29; Ezek. 9:4. Others prefer to read, with slight consonantal change: Joshua *lodged* in the valley. The Syriac reads "people" for "valley."
29. This is comparable to the flow of the narrative in chs. 3, 6.
30. Heb. *mô'ēḏ*. It also means "appointed time." ASV so renders it, but the margin reads "appointed place"; BDB allows for that meaning also. The term may be one more instance of allusions indicating a close acquaintance with local terrain. J. Bright, unable to accept the idea of a prearranged place, suggests a tentative emendation *môrēḏ*, "descent" (*IB* II, p. 592).
31. Y. Aharoni, *The Land of the Bible*, p. 56, thinks of a definite "route," from near Bethel to the Jordan Valley; cf. Judg. 20:42.
32. The LXX omits vv. 15b–16a, thus avoiding the difficulty of how to combine vv. 14, 16. The Vulgate understands v. 16a quite differently from the MT.

had not been regarded as participating in these events. Here it suddenly is introduced as supplying people for the pursuit and thereby leaving itself as exposed as neighboring Ai.³³ This reference to Bethel is mysterious and cannot be fully explained. The king of Bethel is mentioned among those slain by Joshua (12:16), but there is no reference to Bethel's capture anywhere in the book of Joshua. Since the ambush mentioned in v. 12 was stationed between Bethel and Ai, to the west of Ai, the men of Bethel had to pass close by the ambush in order to come to Ai's assistance.

18–23 At this point in the battle the Lord takes charge directly. Just as he did in v. 2, where specific directions were given for the laying of the ambush, so here the Lord orders Joshua to extend the javelin toward Ai. Was this a prearranged sign to those in ambush? One could obtain that impression from v. 19, but was the javelin in Joshua's hand visible to those west of the city? Perhaps the pointing of the javelin was followed by another sign which was communicated to the ambush. More probably, the javelin's use was symbolical, a gesture of doom and destruction (cf. v. 26, where Joshua is seen to extend the javelin until the destruction of Ai was complete). Just as the javelin was in Joshua's hand, so the city toward which it was extended was in Israel's hand (v. 18). Nevertheless, the account does connect Joshua's pointing of the weapon and the ambush's action in taking the city and setting fire to it (v. 19).

As is more often the case in Hebrew narrative, the events described are juxtaposed as so many flashes appearing upon a screen. Verse 19 speaks of the activities of the ambush. Verse 20 mentions the bewilderment of the men of Ai as they see their city taken and find the way of escape closed off. That same verse tells of the fleeing Israelites turning around to face their pursuers; v. 21 supplies a further description of this turning about. Then, in v. 22 we apparently³⁴ are invited again to take a step back in the narrative, for this verse mentions once again that *the others came out of the city to meet them* (cf. v. 14).

The total effect of the narrative is clear and telling. The men of Ai are trapped, and the Israelites, acting upon divine orders, do not let anyone escape. Only Ai's king is brought alive to Joshua so that he may do to him

---

33. The reference to Bethel is lacking in the LXX. Some, e.g., Noth, favor omitting it. Soggin, *op. cit.*, p. 95, points out that it is the *lectio difficilior* and should therefore be retained. Some scholars have held that the story of an original capture of Bethel (not Ai) was subsequently transferred to Ai; see commentary on 7:2.

34. The verse begins with Heb. *wᵉˀēlleh*, lit. "and these." This could also refer to the men of the ambush. ASV, correctly we believe, renders "the others." The Luther Bible puts it explicitly: "and they in the city also came to meet them."

as he did to the king of Jericho (v. 2). The episodic nature of the narrative is evident again in the juxtaposition of vv. 22b (*they let none of them remain*) and 23 (*The king . . . they seized alive*).

24–29 Verse 24b states more explicitly than had been done in v. 22b that none of the people of Ai who had come out to pursue Israel escaped death. They were struck down *in the field* (an additional designation of locale), *in the wilderness* (see vv. 15, 20). This was part of the *ḥerem* which was to be applied to all of Canaan and had already been applied to Jericho (6:17).[35] The same ban was then applied to those still left in the city. The name of Bethel, introduced in v. 17, is not mentioned again in this respect. The total number of those slain amounts to twelve thousand, the entire population of Ai.[36]

As another Moses,[37] Joshua continues to stretch out his hand, holding the javelin until the ban is executed fully upon Ai. Since it was the Lord who originally ordered the extending of this weapon, the narrative means to say that the ban was carried out at the Lord's behest.[38]

Despite the extensive destruction, cattle and booty were spared and became Israel's possession (see v. 2; cf. Deut. 2:34–35; 3:6–7). The city is then put to the torch. Cf. v. 19, where an initial burning is reported, but for other purposes, and described with a different Hebrew verb.

The story of Ai ends with the report of the erection of two monuments which recall the event *until this day* (for this expression see commentary on 4:9). The first monument is the ruin heap of Ai itself, the other is the pile of stones over the dead body of the city's king (v. 29). God's past acts of deliverance for Israel and of judgment on those who disobey him, be they Israelite (Achan) or non-Israelite, could thus be recalled by generations to come.

35. The expression *edge of the sword* (lit. "mouth of the sword") may serve to point to the devouring, voracious character of the sword. For another view, linking it with the use of a long-bladed, curved sword, see Y. Yadin, *The Art of Warfare in Biblical Lands* I (New York: 1963), p. 79. This sickle sword has only one cutting side, the "edge."
36. Hertzberg, *op. cit.*, p. 60, sees a certain contrast between this number and the information of 7:3. Canaanite cities of this period were small; see commentary on 6:3–5; and cf. Noth, *The OT World*, pp. 129f. Yet the contrast which the modern interpreter senses was apparently not felt by the writer (collector) of the book of Joshua.
37. For other similarities between the stories of Joshua and Moses, see 5:15 and related passages; and cf. Wenham, *JBL* 90 (1971), p. 146.
38. The destruction of the Lord's enemies must be viewed in the light of eschatology; cf. Judg. 5:31; Rev. 18:20. God's kingdom cannot come unless those who oppose it are silenced.

If one wishes to call these stories etiological, namely in the sense of providing the later generation with the true cause (Gk. *aitia*) of these ruins, piles of stones, etc., such use of language need not be rejected in itself. The current understanding of the term "etiology," however, makes such use of language less than suitable for this purpose. Israel's "sense of history," celebrated in many books on OT theology, and frequently contrasted with that of other nations, did not spring from purely subjective experiences. These experiences had been nurtured by a series of facts in which God had truly acted on Israel's behalf.

It was not the monuments which remain "until this day" that triggered the stories which speak of them. Rather, the events mentioned in the stories are the true cause of the monuments. However much the reader should be conscious of the viewpoint which affects the Bible's historiography, he should never let the biblical facts become a mere product of Israel's religious genius. The Bible presents a reliable record of what the God of history did in space and time. For this reason the Israel of Joshua's days and later had good reason to treasure the memories attached to the monuments of the past.

Verse 28 emphasizes the desolateness of Ai, which now becomes a permanent heap of ruins. The account of the death of the city's king follows in v. 29. Thus the story reverts back, as it were, to its starting point (cf. vv. 1–2). First the king was killed, and then his body was hung on a tree.[39] This disgrace symbolically expresses the curse of God (Deut. 21:22–23). The dead body was not left hanging overnight but was taken down; the rules of Deuteronomy were applied not only to Israelites but also to this Canaanite king.[40] A pile of stones is then cast up over the dead body, as had been done over Achan's body (7:26).

I. BLESSINGS AND CURSES PROCLAIMED IN CANAAN (8:30–35)

30 *Then Joshua built an altar to the Lord, the God of Israel, on Mount Ebal,*
31 *as Moses the servant of the Lord commanded the Israelites, as it is written in the book of the law of Moses, an altar of unhewn stones,*

---

39. This may have been an impalement, but 10:26 suggests that the king had first been killed.
40. Thus the newly conquered promised land is to be kept free from the curse. See Gutbrod, *op. cit.*, p. 76, where also a line is drawn forward to the "accursed" One, Jesus Christ, who also was put upon a tree.

upon which no man had lifted up any iron. And they offered on it burnt offerings to the Lord, and sacrificed peace offerings.

32 *He also wrote there on the stones a copy of the law of Moses, which he had written, before the eyes of the Israelites.*

33 *And all Israel, and their elders and officers, and their judges, stood on both sides of the ark over against the Levitical priests, who carried the ark of the covenant of the Lord, both the sojourner and the born Israelite, the one half over against Mount Gerizim and the other half over against Mount Ebal, as Moses the servant of the Lord had commanded earlier, to bless the people of Israel.*

34 *And afterwards he read all the words of the law, the blessing and the curse, according to all that is written in the book of the law.*

35 *There was no word of all that Moses had commanded, which Joshua did not read before the whole assembly of Israel, and the women and the little ones and the sojourners who were among them.*

The story of the building of an altar on Mount Ebal and of the solemn reading of the blessings and curses of the covenant at that site is strategically important for understanding the message of the book of Joshua.[1] No sooner has the significant victory at Ai been won, so the narrator means to suggest, than the claims of the covenant Lord of Israel have to be published abroad. The story of the erection of the altar, the setting up of the stones inscribed with Moses' law, the reading of blessing and curse to which the people respond by a solemn "Amen" (see Deut. 27:11–26), all shed significant light upon the message of Joshua. In unmistakably clear symbolism the reader is told that the right of possessing the promised land is tied to the proclamation of, and subjection to, God's covenant claims upon his people (and upon the world).[2] Whatever questions the interpreter may face in reading these many stirring words, this basic lesson should not be lost.

30–35 Joshua builds *an altar to the Lord, the God of Israel*,[3] on Mount Ebal. Altar building, during the patriarchal period, often had ac-

1. A. Gelin, *Josué*, p. 57, states that this "solemn episode is as it were the summit of the book of Joshua."
2. A story in the Talmud claims that the law was written in seventy languages so that all the peoples of the earth might read; see J. P. Lange, ed., *A Commentary on the Holy Scriptures* 4, p. 85. While the story is apocryphal, the sentiment it expresses of the worldwide claims of God's Torah is not.
3. For this expression cf. 24:2, 23; cf. also Gen. 33:20. H. Ringgren, "*ᵉlōhîm*," in *TDOT* I (E.T. ²1977), p. 278, points out that the expression is frequently used in the so-called "holy war" passages, such as 7:13; 10:40, 42; 14:14; Judg. 4:6; 5:3, 5; 6:8. It is also used when non-Israelites speak of God: 1 Sam. 5:7–8; 6:3, 5. C. Steuernagel, *Jahwe, der Gott Israels*, BZAW 27 (1914), pp. 329–349, holds that it was a cultic epithet which was at home at Shechem, designating the god of

companied theophanies in the land of Canaan (Gen. 12:7–8; 13:18). These altars were an expression of the symbolical claim which the patriarchs, themselves "strangers and sojourners" in the land of promise, were laying to the land of Canaan which had been given to them (Gen. 12:7). The promise made to the fathers had now been realized. Hence this altar on Mount Ebal.

The ceremony of the building of the altar continues a pattern established earlier. Several of the significant events thus far recorded were followed by solemn ceremonies:[4] the placing of the stones at Gilgal, the circumcision and the Passover, the curse upon ruined Jericho, the hanging of Ai's king, and the erection of a monument over his body. All these are meant to inspire absolute confidence in victory, though they also serve other, redemptive-historical purposes within the present narrative.

Mount Ebal, where the ceremony was held, is identified by most interpreters with Jebel Eslāmîyeh, north of Shechem (modern Nablus). Deut. 11:30, which specifies the site of the proclamation of blessings and curses, places it and Mount Gerizim "over against Gilgal, beside the oaks of Moreh" (ASV).[5]

If the location near Shechem[6] is correct, then the conquest of Ai

a group of tribes called Israel; cf. also M. Noth, *The History of Israel*, p. 92. But Ringgren remarks that this hypothesis can hardly be proven and that it does not explain all the occurrences. The expression is also used in introductory formulas in Jeremiah and Ezekiel.

4. This is pointed out by Y. Kaufmann, *The Biblical Account of the Conquest of Palestine*, p. 93.

5. Eusebius and Jerome thought of two small hills in the vicinity of Jericho and of the traditional Gilgal. See also K. A. Kitchen, *NBD*, p. 470, who believes Deut. 11:30 may refer to the Gilgal near Jericho.

6. Though Shechem is mentioned explicitly in 24:1, in the present story its name is not recorded. Noth, *History*, pp. 88ff., holds that Shechem was the center of a cultic amphictyony patterned after those of other nations. In early Greek civilization certain cities would band together for the support of a central sanctuary, thus forming an amphictyony. Noth's theory has found widespread support, but it has also encountered opposition; see, e.g., G. E. Wright, *The OT and Theology* (New York: 1969), pp. 128f. G. W. Anderson, "Israel: Amphictyony; ʿAm; Ḳāhāl; ʿĒḏāh," in H. T. Frank and W. L. Reed, eds., *Translating and Understanding the OT*, p. 148, rightly observes: "As a technical term drawn from environments very different from those of ancient Israel, its use [i.e., of the term amphictyony] in relation to Israel begs questions rather than answers them"; cf. Herrmann, *A History of Israel in OT Times*, states: ". . . the theory of the amphictyony has only a semblance of truth about it" (p. 105). For a critique of Noth's theories, cf. also M. H. Woudstra, *The Ark of the Covenant from Conquest to Kingship*, pp. 122–25. Among the recent critics of Noth's theory may also be listed N. K. Gottwald, *The Tribes of Yahweh*, who ascribes a "limited merit" to this "model" but wishes to be freed from its "tyranny" (pp. 356f.). Gottwald's approach and that of the author of this commentary differ radically in terms of presuppositions.

had made it possible for Joshua to move the entire Israelite camp, including women and children (v. 35), to that vicinity, which was considerably to the north, without encountering opposition. Perhaps those are right who assume that Ai's fate had inspired fear in the Canaanites.[7] Perhaps also the events described in Gen. 34, even though initially resulting in hostility between Jacob's family and the local inhabitants, may have left some traces of a friendly relationship.[8] The problem is a difficult one.[9]

It may well be that considerations of composition led the author of Joshua to place the story here. Such arrangement of historical material would not be out of accord with the principles of biblical historiography,[10] but no strong objections can be raised against a chronological understanding of this episode.[11]

Questions such as the above are important, but the purpose of the

7. So, e.g., C. J. Goslinga, *Het Boek Jozua*, p. 90.
8. Indeed, the taking of Shechem is not explicitly recorded anywhere in Joshua. But the biblical records do not mean to be exhaustive chronicles of all that happened; see K. A. Kitchen, *Ancient Orient and OT*, p. 71. Widespread among scholars following A. Alt is the theory that the "conquest" of Palestine was in effect a much more gradual penetration into Canaan than now appears in the record; see Alt, *Essays on OT History and Religion*, pp. 133–169. For a defense of the traditional understanding of the Conquest, see Kaufmann, *op. cit*. M. Greenberg's comments are worth noting: ". . . when the entire tradition speaks of general hostility between the Israelites and the natives—the exception of Shechem being accounted for in the tradition itself (the Dinah episode, Jacob's blessing of Joseph) — I cannot comprehend why a peaceful, gradual interpenetration of populations (as the Israelite occupation is sometimes alleged to have been) should have been so contrarily represented"; cf. J. P. Hyatt, ed., *The Bible in Modern Scholarship*, p. 39.
9. If Shechem was indeed as central a point for the amphictyony as Noth and others believe, the absence of any mention of it in this story surely causes surprise. Noth suggests that this silence is to be explained in light of the fact that, when this bit of "tradition" began to circulate, the central sanctuary at Shechem (the existence of which he postulates but does not prove) had ceased to function (*History*, p. 93, note 1)! This is a curious bit of circular reasoning. For the archaeological situation at the site of ancient Shechem, cf. G. E. Wright, "Shechem," in *AOTS*, pp. 355–370; see also W. G. Dever, "The MB IIC Stratification in the Northwest Gate Area at Shechem," *BASOR* 216 (1974), pp. 31–52.
10. See M. H. Woudstra in S. Kistemaker, ed., *Interpreting God's Word Today*, pp. 54f.
11. The LXX puts this episode after 9:2, a rather unlikely place. Others suggest it happened toward the close of the conquest events, but would an event of such crucial importance have to wait that long? J. H. Kroeze, *Het Boek Jozua*, p. 111, rejects the chronological view and suggests a possible parallel between what Moses did after Amalek's defeat (Exod. 17:15) and Joshua's activities here, after Ai's capture.

story does not necessarily depend on their solution one way or the other. On the one hand, the actual occurrence of the event recorded should be maintained. On the other, one must recognize that biblical narrative performs a function beyond that of the chronological recording of history. It means to teach the reader by means of the events it narrates.

The altar is built according to Moses' commands to Israel. Moses is again given the honorary title *servant of the Lord* (see 1:1–2). All is done according to what was written *in the book of the law of Moses*, particularly the book of Deuteronomy (see Deut. 27:2–26). The altar is built *of unhewn stones* as specified (see Exod. 20:25). Various interpretations of this requirement have been offered. Possibly this was done to avoid even the semblance of the making of "graven images," forbidden in the Decalog.[12] In general, it may have served to indicate the non-Canaanite nature of Israel's worship.[13]

The sacrifices brought upon the altar were *burnt offerings*[14] and *peace offerings*.[15] These two were offered also at Mount Sinai when the law was first given to Israel (Exod. 20:24). Their use on Mount Ebal signifies that Joshua meant this to be a solemn reminder of the covenant made at Sinai.

The stones on which a copy of the law was written were probably not the stones of the altar.[16] Deut. 27:1–8 prescribes that large whitewashed stones should be inscribed. This was an Egyptian technique rather than Palestinian or Mesopotamian.[17] Just who wrote the copy of the law which Joshua inscribed upon the stones is not quite clear. Perhaps it was

12. See W. H. Gispen, *Het Boek Exodus* II (Kampen: 1939), *ad loc*.

13. Other views: 1. Worship tends to favor archaic customs. Unhewn stones suggest the times before the use of metal instruments; see also 5:2. But this is God's command. Does God favor archaic customs for his worship? 2. "Holy" things must be kept free from the influence of human crafts; so, e.g., H. W. Hertzberg, *ATD* IX, p. 61. 3. The stone was regarded as the deity's domicile. Cutting the stone would remove the deity forcibly. This view does not do justice to the fact that Exod. 20:25; Deut. 27 are said to be God's words to Israel.

14. These were holocausts, given completely to God through burning; see Exod. 29:38–46; Lev. 1; 6:1–6 (Eng. 8–13).

15. Also called "communion sacrifices" (Heb. *šᵉlāmîm*). This sacrifice speaks of wholeness and of restored relations between God and man; see Lev. 3; 7:11–21. A communal meal accompanies it (Deut. 27:7); cf. G. J. Wenham, *The Book of Leviticus*, pp. 74-81.

16. The Hebrew does use the definite article here, as customary in Hebrew when designating objects to be used. It need not mean "the just named stones"; cf. GKC § 126 q.

17. See P. C. Craigie, *Deuteronomy*, p. 328, and the literature mentioned there.

Moses[18] or Joshua himself. What is evident is that the writing of this copy on the stones was done in the sight of the assembled Israelites. The narrative does not specify the extent of the "law" which was written. It could be the Ten Commandments, or the blessings and curses of Deut. 28.[19]

The solemn ceremony of the recording of the law on Mount Ebal, besides serving the purpose of establishing the claim of the Covenant Lord over all of Canaan, may have served to recognize Joshua as Moses' lawful successor (see 1:16–18).

Ceremonies of covenant renewal are now known from nations other than Israel. These ceremonies often consisted of two successive parts. One could think of Deut. 31:3 as constituting the first part (cf. Deut. 31:9–13). The Ebal ceremony would then be the final phase of Joshua's formal succession to the office of leader of Israel.[20] At such covenant renewal ceremonies the basic covenant document would be copied so that all might read it. By way of ratification a series of blessings and curses would be pronounced. All this appears to be the background of what is recorded in this pericope.

The ark, the sacred emblem of the Lord's presence with his people,[21] forms the center of the following ceremony, the reading of the law's blessings and curses. *All Israel*[22] participates in this ceremony (see also v. 35), but stress is placed first upon the representatives of the people, the elders, officers, and judges. The *elders* and *officers* were also mentioned in 7:6 (cf. 8:10) and 1:10 respectively (see commentary). *Judges* are mentioned here for the first time in Joshua (but cf. 23:2; 24:1; Num. 25:5). The word does not yet have the specific meaning it acquires when later used to designate the saviors and deliverers that God sent in times of

18. JB "There Joshua wrote . . . a copy of the Law which Moses had written . . ."; likewise Zürcher Bibel and NIV. RSV leaves the matter open.
19. The Jews believed that the written law contained the 613 commandments which the rabbis claimed to find in the Pentateuch. See also n. 2.
20. This is more fully worked out in M. G. Kline, *Treaty of the Great King*, pp. 36, 121ff. Cf. also D. R. Hillers, *Treaty-Curses and the OT Prophets*. Biblica et Orientalia (Rome: 1964), p. 84.
21. See commentary on 3:3. The stipulations of Deut. 27 do not mention the ark. Noth, *History*, p. 93, n. 1, suggests that it is mentioned here solely because of the role it played in chs. 3–4, 6, but this is a rather subjective judgment.
22. The "all israel" concept has often been tied in with Noth's amphictyony theories; see n. 6. Along with the literature mentioned reference must also be made to C. H. J. de Geus, *The Tribes of Israel*, *passim* and esp. pp. 193–95, where the notion is critically examined and rejected. De Geus' study is comprehensive and scholarly, but it breathes a spirit of radical criticism with respect to the veracity of the biblical stories.

Israel's apostasy and oppression (see Judg. 2:16). But the function of judge should not be thought of exclusively in juridical terms.[23]

All these stand around the *Levitical priests* (see 3:3) who carry the ark, in order that, as Calvin says so well, "The Lord might be surrounded on all sides by his own people."[24] The assembly includes not only those born as Israelites but also the sojourners (see Exod. 12:19, 48–49; Lev. 16:29; 17:15; 18:26; 19:34, etc.). This is not a distinction between home born, i.e., those born inside Palestine, and foreign born, for that would obviously be an anachronism.[25] The distinction is rather between those native to Israel and those who were not. Just as similar laws apply to both (see Exod. 12:19, 48–49), so they must both be present at the solemn reenactment of the covenant ceremonies.

The two mountains where the people arrange themselves are Ebal (see v. 30) and Gerizim.[26] Investigations have indicated that the acoustical qualities of that site are excellent for such a ceremony.[27] Verse 33 again emphasizes that all is done according to Moses' commandment. Moreover, that verse speaks only of the blessing.[28] In actual fact, as is clear from v. 34, both *blessing and curse* were read. This shows that the blessing was of paramount importance, although it would be erroneous to relegate the curses to a second-rank position.[29] Both belong to the pattern of covenant-

23. For a good discussion see *ibid.*, pp. 204–207.
24. J. Calvin, *Commentaries on the Book of Joshua*, p. 134.
25. An incorrect understanding of this distinction has led some commentators to consider this passage to be late, inasmuch as the distinction between native and foreign born would not be in effect so early after the entry into Canaan.
26. Gerizim is located opposite Ebal, south of ancient Shechem. It is 869 meters high (Ebal, 938 meters). Later, the Samaritans had a temple there; cf. John 4:20. The Samaritan reads Gerizim in v. 30 instead of Ebal. It has been suggested that this is the correct reading and that the present MT reading is due to Jewish anti-Samaritan feelings; cf. H. H. Rowley, *From Joseph to Joshua* (London: 1950), p. 127, n. 3. Hertzberg, *op. cit.*, p. 61, thinks likewise, but such an allegation cannot be proved.
27. Cf. J. de Groot, *Het Boek Jozua*, p. 98, who, however, questions whether this acoustical quality was sufficient to allow for a reading of the law. It would seem that this is pressing the question of the intended audience too far. One need not suppose that the entire multitude understood all that was read.
28. Calvin's remark concerning the prominence of blessing is appropriate: ". . . as it was the purpose of God to allure the people to himself by sweetness and winning condescension"; *idem*. The curses, according to Calvin, are secondary (*accidentales*); *idem*. The blessings are to turn the people to obedience.
29. Much has been written about the role of curses and blessings in covenant context; see, e.g., F. C. Fensham, "Maledietion and Benediction in Ancient Near Eastern Vassal-Treaties and the OT," *ZAW* 74 (1962), pp. 1–9.

making and covenant renewal. A covenant cannot be conceived of without an oath confirming the relationship. In turn, the oath is a form of conditional self-cursing.[30] Blessing and cursing are the two poles around which the history of the covenant revolves (see Deut. 11:26; 30:1). The blessing means life, the curse death (Deut. 30:19). God may also turn a curse into a blessing (Deut. 23:5).[31] The words of blessing and cursing are not to be conceived of as mere words. Within the biblical context they are true vehicles of power, not in a magical sense but because they were uttered on behalf of him whose Word is powerful (Ps. 33:9). To bless is to "put" the "name" of the Lord upon the people (Num. 6:27). To curse is to invoke that name by way of self-malediction or in order to curse others.[32]

As made clear in v. 34, *the law* and its reading must be seen in immediate conjunction with *the blessing and the curse*, which are mentioned in one breath. To read the one means to read the other. Deut. 27:14–26 supplies further details as to the manner in which the reading was done.[33] The law that is read is that which *Moses had commanded* (v. 35; see also vv. 31, 33); but Moses' words are also the Lord's words (see Deut. 4:2). The reading of the law takes place *before the whole assembly of Israel*. This assembly (Heb. *qāhāl*) is Israel as it is called together in assembly.[34] Everyone takes part, including women, little ones, and sojourners. They are all confronted with the demands of the Lord of the covenant as they enter upon a new phase of their existence in the land of promise. If these demands are responded to in covenant obedience, Israel's future happiness will be secured.

---

30. See also J. Scharbert, "'ālāh; ta'ᵃlāh," *TDOT* I (E.T. ²1977), pp. 261–66; "brk; bᵉrākhāh," *TDOT* II (E.T. ²1977), pp. 279–308; and the literature listed there. For a comparison between biblical and extrabiblical "covenants," cf. also J. A. Thompson, *The Ancient Near Eastern Treaties and the OT* (London: 1964).
31. This indicates that curses and blessings must not be viewed in a magical context. God alone is the originator of the powerful word; cf. H. W. Beyer, "εὐλογέω, εὐλογητός, εὐλογία, ἐνευλογέω," *TDNT* II (E.T. 1964), pp. 754–765.
32. See also M. Weinfeld, "bᵉrîth," *TDOT* II (E.T. ²1977), 253–279.
33. Deut. 27:14–26 mentions only the curses, although vv. 12–13 speak explicitly of both blessing and curse; see also Deut. 11:29. Extrabiblical treaties were more explicit in listing curses in case of disloyalty than in enumerating blessings.
34. The other Hebrew word designating the people of Israel is 'ēḏâ. The qāhāl is the assembly as called together for cultic duty, military action, or covenant-making. The 'ēḏâ views the people as they engage in the Lord's service in daily life. Heb. qāhāl is also used for the assembly at Mount Sinai (Deut. 9:10). The LXX frequently translates it with ekklēsía, but also with synagōgḗ.

J. SOUTHERN CANAAN SUBDUED (9:1– 10:43)

1. ISRAEL'S TREATY WITH GIBEON (9:1–27)

1 *When all the kings who were beyond the Jordan in the hill country and in the lowland and all along the coast of the Great Sea to over against Lebanon, the Hittites, the Amorites, the Canaanites, the Perizzites, the Hivites, and the Jebusites heard this,*

2 *they banded together to fight with one accord against Joshua and against Israel.*

3 *But as for the inhabitants of Gibeon, when they heard what Joshua had done with Jericho and Ai,*

4 *they too acted with craftiness; they acted as ambassadors. They took old sacks on their donkeys and worn-out wineskins, torn and tied together again,*

5 *with worn-out, patched sandals on their feet and worn-out clothes on their bodies; and all the bread of their travel ration was dry; it was nothing but crumbs.*

6 *They came to Joshua in the camp at Gilgal and said to him and to the men of Israel: "We have come from a far country. Now then, make a treaty with us."*

7 *Then the men of Israel said to the Hivites: "Perhaps you live among us. How then can we make a treaty with you?"*

8 *Then they said to Joshua: "We are your servants." And Joshua said to them: "Who are you, and where do you come from?"*

9 *They said to him: "From a very far country have your servants come because of the name of the Lord your God. For we have heard of his fame, all he did in Egypt,*

10 *and all he did to the two kings of the Amorites, who were beyond Jordan, Sihon the king of Heshbon and Og the king of Bashan, who was at Ashtaroth.*

11 *Our elders and all the inhabitants of our country spoke to us, saying: 'Take with you provisions for the journey, and go to meet them and say to them: We are your servants. Now then, make a treaty with us.'*

12 *This is our bread. It was still warm when we took it from our houses as our food for the journey, the day we left to go to you, and now, see, it is dry and has become crumbs.*

13 *And these are our wineskins which were new when we filled them. Look, they have burst. And these clothes and shoes of ours have become worn out because of the very long journey."*

14 *The men took of their provisions, but they did not ask the Lord's counsel.*

151

15 *Joshua then made peace with them and concluded a treaty with them to guarantee their lives. And the princes of the congregation ratified it with an oath.*

16 *Now it happened when three days had passed after they had made this treaty with them that they heard that they were neighbors and lived among them.*

17 *The Israelites broke camp and came to their cities on the third day. Now their cities were Gibeon, Chephirah, Beeroth and Kiriath-jearim.*

18 *But the Israelites did not kill them, for the princes of the congregation had made them an oath by the Lord the God of Israel. And the whole congregation murmured against the princes.*

19 *But all the princes said to the whole congregation: "We have made an oath to them by the Lord, the God of Israel; therefore we may not touch them.*

20 *This we can do with them and let them live, that there be no wrath on us, because of the oath which we swore to them."*

21 *And the princes said to them: "Let them live." So they became hewers of wood and drawers of water to the whole congregation, as the princes had spoken of them.*

22 *Joshua summoned them and spoke to them as follows: "Why have you deceived us by saying: We live very far away from you, while you are living among us?*

23 *Therefore you are cursed. A steady stream of servants will come from you—woodcutters and water carriers for the house of my God."*

24 *They answered Joshua: "It had indeed been reported to your servants what the Lord your God had commanded his servant Moses, to give to you the whole country and to destroy all the inhabitants before you. So we feared greatly before you, for our very lives, and we did this thing.*

25 *Therefore, see, we are in your power; what looks good and right in your eyes, do that to us."*

26 *And he did so with them, and delivered them out of the power of the Israelites so that they did not kill them.*

27 *And Joshua made them that day woodcutters and water carriers for the congregation and for the altar of the Lord, to this day, in the place which he would choose.*

1–2 These verses may be regarded as the introduction to chs. 9–10 (one may also include ch. 11). They speak of the determined opposition of Canaan's kings against Israel, the people of God who are now taking possession of the land God had promised to give to them at a time when the "iniquity of the Amorites" would be "full" (Gen. 15:16). The author uses the motif of the fear of Canaan's inhabitants in more than one way.

152

In 2:8–11, 24b; 5:1 the emphasis is on the paralyzing effect of Israel's entry upon Canaan's people. At this point, however, the kings band together against God's people, and, as becomes clear from the testimony of the Gibeonites in 9:9, against Israel's God. Within the context of the theocratic viewpoint which imbues biblical historiography one may truly say that the spirit of Ps. 2 comes to expression here.

These verses also have a particular bearing upon ch. 9. The spirit of resistance, which is doomed to failure already at the outset in the light of the events at Jericho and Ai, is contrasted here with the spirit of fearful submission displayed by the people of Gibeon who come to ask for a treaty. The relationship between Israel and the Canaanites appears to be the leading concern of the entire chapter (vv. 7, 18, 26). In reading this chapter one is advised to keep in mind the author's later comment in 11:19–20. In the light of the total teaching of the Bible, however, it does not exonerate the human agents from their share of the responsibility.

Verses 1–2 appear to speak of a grand coalition of all the Canaanite forces. In actual fact this coalition did not come into being. The southern kings did not combine their forces with those of the north (compare ch. 10 with ch. 11), as one might expect from the enumeration of geographical areas in v. 1. With this apparent discrepancy the author probably meant to do two things. He wanted to let the full light of revelation fall upon the one spirit of resistance which began to take possession of all Canaan's leaders, with the exception of Gibeon. On the other hand, he may also have wished to indicate that the intent of the kings to combine *all* of their forces somehow became frustrated by a higher hand.

The kings who plan a concerted assault upon Israel are said to be *beyond the Jordan*. At this point the expression designates the area west of the river.[1] The geographical description includes the three major zones into which Palestine is divided toward the west. The *hill country* (Heb. *hāhār*) stands for the central mountain region of Palestine, so named in contrast to the lowland (cf. 10:40; 11:2, 16; Num. 13:17; Deut. 1:7). The

---

1. The expression "beyond the Jordan" (Heb. b^e'$\bar{e}ber$ $hayyard\bar{e}n$) occurs seventeen times in the book, referring to east Jordan (1:14; 2:10; 9:10; 14:3, etc.) and also to west Jordan (5:1; 9:1; 12:7; 22:7). In some of these instances an additional qualification is added: "toward the west" (5:1; 12:7) or "toward the east" (1:15; 12:1; RSV "toward the sunrise"). The term cannot be considered to reflect the geographical locale of the writer at any given moment. The variety of its use may be due to the fact that Israel had recently moved from a location east of the Jordan to one west of the Jordan, thus accounting for a certain ambiguity of the term which needed further clarification at times. So C. J. Goslinga, *Het Boek Jozua*, p. 184.

lowland (Heb. *šᵉpēlâ*)² refers always³ to the region between the Philistine plain and the mountains in the center. It is a rocky plateau, which, although higher than the plain, is low in comparison with the much more elevated mountains to the east. *The coast of the Great Sea* is the Mediterranean sea-coast (cf. 1:4; 15:12, 47; 23:4). This plain is said to reach *to over against*⁴ *Lebanon*. Apparently the author intends to draw the circle of Israel's opponents as wide as possible, just as he had drawn the circle of Israel's boundaries as wide as possible (see 1:4 and commentary).

The stage is thus set for the campaigns described in chs. 10–11. Six nations are enumerated. For their identity and approximate location, see 3:10 and commentary. The nations of Canaan to be dispossessed by Israel are frequently enumerated in the Pentateuch (Gen. 15:18–19; cf. also Exod. 23:23, 28; 33:2; 34:11; Deut. 7:1; 20:17). In light of these Pentateuchal references, the doom of the nations is sure. Cf. also Deut. 32:8–9, which presents an intriguing bit of insight into the true nature of the distribution of the nations of the world, with Israel as its center. This sheds an interesting light on what the author of Joshua is attempting with this enumeration of the kings of Canaan. What begins as resistance and organized opposition will end in defeat (see 11:16–18). Truly, the nations "plot in vain" (Ps. 2:1).

3–5 Contrasted with the activities of most of Canaan's kings, who prepare for war, is the conduct of *Gibeon*, which prepares for peace (Heb. *šālôm*; see v. 15), i.e., a relationship of harmonious understanding based on a covenant or treaty. Gibeon's exact location continues to be a matter of dispute, although many scholars accept its identification with modern ej-Jib, a site about 8 miles north and slightly west of Jerusalem. However, according to the ancient list of Palestinian cities prepared by Eusebius (called *Onomasticon*), Gibeon lay four Roman miles west of Bethel. This would exclude ej-Jib as a possibility. One support for this identification is that recent excavations at ej-Jib have uncovered a number of jar handles inscribed with the ancient Hebrew name of Gibeon. But this does not establish identity beyond all doubt.⁵ Jar handles inscribed with

2. The expression occurs twenty times in the OT, seven of which are in Joshua (cf. 10:40; 11:2, 16 [twice]; 12:8; 15:33).
3. The possible exceptions are 11:2, 16.
4. Heb. is *'el mûl*, which BDB renders "towards the front of, on the front of." Other renderings are JB "towards Lebanon"; Zürcher Bibel "bis an den Libanon hin."
5. One reason for caution is that no remains of a Late Bronze settlement, which might be considered contemporary with Joshua, have been discovered at ej-Jib. Even those scholars prepared to accept the identification express themselves care-

other names such as Hebron and Socoh have also been discovered at this site. A feature which would appear to be of greater weight for identification is the discovery of imposing water works in the ruins of ej-Jib (see 2 Sam. 2:12–17; Jer. 41:12).[6]

No mention is made of Gibeon's king, but only its elders (v. 11). Apparently the city's form of government differed from that of other Canaanite cities.[7] The reason for Gibeon's readiness to make a treaty with Israel lies in what the Gibeonites have *heard* concerning *what Joshua had done with Jericho and Ai*. To be noted is the contrast between the reactions of the kings (who also have *heard* these reports) and those of Gibeon. Foolish and wise reactions are thus contrasted finely. Apparently the ruse employed by Joshua at Ai's capture leads the Gibeonites themselves to employ *craftiness*. They resort to the scheme of being *ambassadors*[8] from a faraway country. The storyteller recounts vividly the preparations for the intended deception of Israel and its leaders. Does not the narrator's skill at such points argue against considering this chapter to be the composite of a variety of traditions, patched together so that the seams show at several points?[9]

---

fully, e.g., R. de Vaux, *Early History*, p. 626; J. Blenkinsopp, *Gibeon and Israel* (Cambridge: 1972), p. 5: ". . . these [jar] handles were uncovered" in circumstances which strongly suggested that they were original to the site." Blenkinsopp adds: "Perhaps the site of the Late Bronze city lies elsewhere on the tell only a relatively small area of which was excavated"; p. 6.

6. J. Simons, *The Geographical and Topographical Texts of the OT*. Studia Francisci Scholten 2 (Leiden: 1959), pp. 175f., opposes the identification with ej-Jib; see also in W. H. Gispen *et al.*, eds., *Bijbelse Encyclopaedie* I (^{2}1975), s.v. "Gibeon."

7. For further study on Gibeon and its treaty cf. F. C. Fensham, "The Treaty Between Israel and the Gibeonites," *BA* 27 (1964), pp. 96–100; J. M. Grintz, "The Treaty of Joshua with the Gibeonites," *JAOS* 86 (1966), pp. 113–126; J. Blenkinsopp, *op. cit*. The latter suggests Gibeon may have been within the jurisdiction of the king of Jerusalem so that a treaty with Israel was tantamount to a renunciation of Gibeon's allegiance to Jerusalem. As to the possible date of the events described in 9:1–10:5, he suggests that it is "not too far removed from the Amarna period" (p. 32).

8. Another translation, involving a slight emendation of the Hebrew, and followed by many recent versions is: "they made ready provisions." It is held that "acted as ambassadors" is redundant to the story, but is it really? The author could well have put this summary statement first.

9. It has been widely alleged that the seemingly dual role of Israel's leaders and of Joshua, as well as the apparently different attitude displayed toward Gibeon— one benign, the other hostile—argues for the compositeness of the narrative. However, attempts to unravel the "traditions" supposedly woven together are far from unanimous in their result. De Vaux, *Early History*, pp. 621f., lists no fewer than six different approaches and concludes: "The very fact that scholars who have

6 The telling is highly elaborate and not without humor. The place where the men meet with Joshua and the Israelites is said to be *the camp at Gilgal*. Did Joshua, after the events recorded in 8:30–35, return to the site near Jericho? Or must this be a location closer to the mountains where the law had just been proclaimed? Scholars show no great unanimity about this question, nor about the location of Gilgal in general[10] (see also commentary on 4:19). Several interpreters[11] believe that the Gilgal which is meant here was close to Ebal and Gerizim. But the fact that the account does not so much as hint that this camp was located at a different site appears to support the view that this Gilgal is the same as that mentioned earlier.

Regarding the allegedly dual focus of responsibility—that of Joshua, and that of the men of Israel and of the princes of the congregation (see vv. 6–7, 14–15, 18–19, 21–22, 24; see n. 9), one should observe that the story makes the would-be ambassadors of a far country come to Joshua first (v. 6). This is the narrator's way of saying that Joshua was ultimately responsible for the subsequent events and that he was aware of the Gibeonites' mission from the outset. It is therefore incorrect to say that the story does not make plain who was acting for Israel. Ultimately, it is Joshua. He also takes the leading role in making the treaty with Gibeon (v. 15). At that point the princes of the congregation take an oath of ratification, but the treaty is made by Joshua.[12] In all this the peculiar nature of Hebrew historiography should be kept in mind. It does not always aim at completeness, and its presentation of the facts may sometimes seem deficient in clarity when judged by western standards.

The Gibeonites make it appear that they come *from a far country*

---

concerned themselves with Jos 9 have come to such different conclusions points to the complexity of the problems of literary criticism and the history of traditions"; p. 622. Could not the alleged differences in the story be explained more felicitously and harmoniously in light of the style of Hebrew narrative, which often proceeds somewhat episodically, as seen in previous chapters?

10. On the basis of BDB, the OT distinguishes between at least four different locations named Gilgal: (a) near Jericho: 4:19–20; 5:9–10; and, according to BDB, also in 9:6; 10:7, 9; (b) near the border of Judah and Benjamin (15:17), same as Geliloth (18:17); (c) in North Israel (2 K. 2:1), (d) near Mount Gerizim and Ebal (Deut. 11:30).

11. E.g., C. F. Keil and F. Delitzsch, C. J. Goslinga, B. Holwerda. C. H. J. de Geus, *The Tribes of Israel*, p. 32, mentions two prominent OT scholars, R. Kittel and E. Sellin, who both believed that Gilgal was situated near Shechem.

12. For a contrary view cf. J. M. Miller and G. M. Tucker, *The Book of Joshua*, p. 78, where the alleged "inconsistencies and duplicates" are enumerated; cf. also Noth, *Das Buch Josua*, p. 55.

(*very far*, in v. 9).[13] It is not necessary to suppose that they were acquainted with the stipulations of Deut. 20:10–15, which permitted Israel to make treaties with distant peoples, in distinction from the Canaanites who had to be destroyed and with whom no alliances of any sort were allowed (Deut. 7). The reference to the great distance they had traveled was probably meant to lure the Israelites by means of false pride to enter into an alliance. Moreover, the treatment meted out to Jericho and Ai had made it abundantly clear that they could not hope for a conciliatory attitude if they presented themselves as part of Canaan's population. The information contained in vv. 1–2 would also make it prudent to conceal the fact that they lived within Canaan. This information had no doubt been conveyed to Joshua, and would make him even less prepared to enter into an alliance for fear of foul play.

The Gibeonites request a *treaty* (Heb. $b^e r\hat{\imath}t$; another translation would be "covenant"). See vv. 15, 18 for a further elaboration of what was desired and actually granted. Joshua probably was naive in not perceiving that the Gibeonites, if from such a distance as they claimed, were not actually in need of a treaty. The account does not say so explicitly, although it does add a word of criticism in v. 14b. As, for example, in the story of David's conflict with Absalom, the biblical narrative often simply lets the facts speak for themselves, though within the larger context of biblical morality.

7–10   The naiveté of which mention was made above was not so great as to remove all suspicion. The *men of Israel* (lit. "man of Israel")[14] cautiously raised the possibility[15] that the Gibeonites might be part of Canaan's population. The Gibeonites are identified as *Hivites*[16] at this point

13. Because of this feature de Vaux, *Early History*, pp. 622f., believes that the story of the ruse of Gibeon cannot be historical. He asks: if Gibeon was as far away as it claimed to be, why seek Israel's protection? This, however, leaves out the possibility of a naive acceptance by Joshua of the facts as presented.
14. The Hebrew language tends to think of people in terms of corporate entities requiring singular nouns and verbs, though this can be combined with the use of plurals. See, e.g., Num. 20:14–21, where Israel and Edom are alternately referred to in singular and plural terms. In light of this usage there is no reason, therefore, to hold v. 7 to be the remnant of an older piece of narrative, as is suggested by H. W. Hertzberg, *ATD* IX, p. 66.
15. The Ketib has *wayyô'm^{e}rû* ("and they said"), the Qere *wayyô'mer* ("and he said") to agree with singular subject. The subject, however, has a collective force. There is no need to abandon the Ketib.
16. Heb. "Hivite" (singular); see previous note. See Blenkinsopp, *op. cit.*, p. 21: " 'Hivite' is not identical with 'Horite' and must not be made so by arbitrary

(see commentary on 3:10). The use of this name on the part of the narrator may be intentional, for Hivites were among those to be driven out by the Lord. Here, however, negotiations are under way between them and Israel. The anomaly of the situation in which Israel will soon involve itself is thus hinted at.[17]

The Gibeonites respond by indicating to Joshua, who continues to play a central role, that they are his servants. This expression may be nothing more than a form of common oriental politeness (Gen. 50:18), although with a view to the treaty that is desired the words may express future subservience (see also v. 11). Joshua now desires further information as to the identity and place of origin of the "ambassadors." Apparently the discussion thus far has not yielded sufficient results to proceed directly with the treaty.

In their reply the Gibeonites repeat their previous contention that they are from a very far country. Psychologically they strike a responsive chord in Joshua's heart by referring to the great *name of the Lord your God* (see 7:9). In the biblical context the name of the Lord is that by which he makes himself known (cf. Ps. 5:12 [Eng. 11]; 9:11 [Eng. 10]; 91:14; Isa. 56:6). God, according to Ps. 54:3 [Eng. 1], saves by his name (cf. Ps. 124:8; 44:6 [Eng. 5]). In the ancient Near East the name of a deity was often the key to power and success. It could be used for casting spells on enemies.[18]

The Gibeonites refer (v. 9) to God's acts of deliverance in Egypt (see 2:10; Exod. 15:15-16) and to what he did to Sihon and Og[19] across the Jordan[20] (see Num. 21:21-35; Deut. 2:26-3:17). These events would be celebrated later in Israel's sacred songs (see Ps. 78:51; 135:8-11;

---

textual emendation. A relationship does, however, exist between Hivites and Horites (Hurrians), though its precise nature cannot be established at present."

17. "You live among us"; lit. "thou livest in my midst." This is consistent with the singular subject "man." The expression "among us" anticipates the full possession of Canaan by the Israelites. There is no need to hold this to be evidence of the late origin of this tradition, as some do.

18. For an English translation of an Egyptian myth concerning "The God and His Unknown Name of Power," cf. *ANET*, pp. 12-14.

19. For a critical examination of the stories of Sihon and Og resulting in a near denial of their "historicity" cf. J. R. Bartlett, "Sihon and Og, Kings of the Amorites," *VT* 20 (1970), pp. 257-277; and J. Van Seters, "The Conquest of Sihon's Kingdom: A Literary Examination," *JBL* 91 (1972), pp. 182-197.

20. On this expression see v. 1. Apparently it is used without respect to the place where the speaker (writer) finds himself.

136:10–22). Thus without wanting to do so, the Gibeonites pay homage to Israel's God.[21]

11–13 The story continues to relate how the Gibeonites tell their version of the events leading up to their mission to the camp of Israel. They refer to their *elders* but no king is mentioned. Apparently the Gibeonite political organization differed from that of other cities of Canaan, which were ruled by kings.

The storyteller, who in vv. 3–5 had already shown obvious delight in telling of the cunning ruse to which Gibeon had resorted, now shows equal mastery in reporting the words of the Gibeonites. It all looks so genuine. How could Joshua and his fellow Israelites ever think that the Gibeonites were trying to deceive them? They are invited to take a good look at the provisions: the bread—warm and crisp when packed into the bags for the journey, but now dry and reduced to crumbs! Likewise the wineskins, the clothes and the shoes—they were fresh and new when the journey started, but the long trek has taken its sad toll.

Thus the narrator knows how to paint with his words or, if he drew on an oral tradition of shorter or longer duration, how to use this tradition skilfully. The "sacred" history of the Bible surely is of a most unusual sort.

14–15 The beginning of v. 14 can be understood in different ways. *The men* who *took of their provisions* could be the Gibeonites; having concluded their little speech, they now exhibit some of their provisions to substantiate their words. This view, however, involves a sudden change in subject between 14a and 14b. In v. 14b it is the Israelites, not the Gibeonites, who *did not ask the Lord's counsel*. It is also possible to understand *the men* to be Joshua and Israel, who took the provisions in order to inspect them. A third view, which has had some currency, and which already is briefly mentioned in Calvin's commentary (though not accepted), is that the taking of the provisions (NEB "accept") was tantamount to a covenantal ritual involving a communal eating of bread, intended to seal an agreement. This is an intriguing suggestion; Gen. 31:46–47 also speaks of a meal that concludes a covenant ceremony. But is this brief reference here sufficient to justify this covenantal understanding of the phrase? The second option appears to be the preferred one.[22]

---

21. The Gibeonites wisely are silent about that which had most recently happened (Jericho and Ai), though that had prompted their mission (v. 3). A reference here would have betrayed their secret.

22. Hertzberg, *op. cit.*, is correct in stating that the immediate context suggests the second option. He allows for an earlier tradition underlying the present account

An interpretative comment (*but they did not ask the Lord's counsel*) clearly shows the narrator's concern.[23] This advice could have been sought through Urim and Thummim (Num. 27:21). In the case of the detection of Achan's crime the lot had been used, or so it appears (see 7:16–18).

In v. 15 the story comes to its dramatic climax. It speaks of the peace (Heb. *šālôm*) which Joshua extended to the Gibeonites. This peace, indicating a harmonious relationship between two covenanting parties, accompanies a treaty relationship. The word may also be rendered "friendship" at this point.[24] The other expression used to describe the new relationship between Gibeon and Israel is the familiar *kāraṯ bᵉrîṯ*, which is one of the terms used to describe the making of a covenant or treaty. This expression implies a relationship of subordination, with the prominent party imposing certain conditions on the other party (cf. 1 Sam. 11:1).[25] Such action, however, is not explicit here. The chief concern of the narrative is to make clear that life was guaranteed by one party (Joshua) to the other (Gibeon). This is important for understanding what follows, and hence is the only thing mentioned in the account.

Treaties and covenants in ancient cultures were accompanied by a solemn oath.[26] This oath is here sworn by the *princes of the congregation*.[27] Whether this whole transaction must be viewed as essentially similar to the concluding of a suzerainty treaty as known from related cultures, especially Hittite, is a matter of doubt. It would seem to put too much weight

---

which meant to speak of a covenant ceremony, but the interpreter must seek to interpret the text in its present context. See also KD, p. 98, who observe that, if a meal in mutual friendship had been meant, more explicit mention should have been made by means of a clause "with them." The LXX renders "men" with *árchontes*, thus ruling out the first option.

23. Biblical narrative does not always supply such interpretation, often simply permitting the reader to read between the lines. See 11:20; 2 Sam. 17:14 for other explicit comments upon the events as recorded.

24. This is the word used by Hertzberg and the Zürcher Bibel. It is obvious that a mere cessation of hostilities cannot be indicated, for hostilities had not yet existed; cf. J. Pedersen, *Israel: Its Life and Culture* I–II, pp. 263ff.

25. Cf. M. Weinfeld, *TDOT* II, p. 256.

26. The word "oath" is not used explicitly, but is implied by idea of swearing (Heb. *nišba'*). An oath is a conditional self-curse (cf. the modern "So help me God" [if I break the oath]); see also J. Scharbert, *TDOT* I, pp. 261–66.

27. On practices followed in the making of treaties in the ancient Near East, see also G. Mendenhall, "Covenant Forms in Israelite Tradition," *BA* 17 (1954), p. 52. Oath and covenant are also closely related in Ezek. 16:59.

upon this transaction.[28] The *princes* referred to were chiefs and representatives of the tribes (cf. Num. 1:16, 44; 2:3).[29]

16 Having called attention to the ill-advised rashness with which the treaty had been entered, the narrator now points to the evil consequences resulting from this carelessness. The chief consequence will be the presence of a Canaanite enclave in Israel's midst, which Deut. 7 had expressly forbidden. Three days[30] after the conclusion of the treaty the truth comes to light: The Gibeonites are neighbors.[31] It is probably best to take the three-day interval to consist of the day the Gibeonites left, followed by a day of preparations for the breaking of camp (v. 17) plus a day's journey to Gibeon.[32] The distance between Gilgal and Gibeon was only 19 miles.

17–21 For the first time in the narrative the reader is informed of the fact that Gibeon was part of a larger group of cities to which belonged Chephirah,[33] Beeroth,[34] and Kiriath-jearim.[35]

28. See Fensham, *BA* 27 (1964), who argues that Gibeon wanted a safe position within Israel's commonwealth by entering into a vassal-suzerain treaty with Joshua. De Vaux considers Fensham's attempt "an exaggeration" (*Early History*, p. 624) and adds: "The most that can be said is that this is a case of international law in the Ancient Near East" (p. 625). In other words, all that needs to be said is that certain customs of ancient oriental law practice were being observed.
29. On the scope of the word "congregation" (Heb. *'ēḏâ*) see p. 150, n. 34 and cf. p. 163, n. 41. The making of treaties with other nations was not as such prohibited (see Deut. 20:10–11, 15). But by permitting himself to be easily misled Joshua committed a grave error, which tended to threaten the separateness and holiness of the covenant nation as commanded in Deut. 7:1–5.
30. For a similar lapse of time cf. also 1:11; 2:22; 3:2. Since part of a day was probably reckoned to be one day, the actual period may have been shorter than seventy-two hours; see H. W. Hertzberg, *op. cit.*, p. 67; see also 10:9 for the time it took to march to Gibeon.
31. The Hebrew switches between plural and singular forms at this point; see also v. 7. The words "they heard" need not mean that during this time Israel was still in its camp at Gilgal. The same could be said if Israel had already broken camp and, upon arriving in Gibeon's vicinity, had heard of the truth.
32. This is said on the assumption that the three days of v. 16 are the same as those mentioned in v. 17.
33. Usually identified with Khirbet Kefireh, "an impressive hilltop location of four to five acres, southwest of ej Jib"; E. Kraeling, *The Rand McNally Bible Atlas*, p. 137. It lies "on a spur 5 miles west of Gibeon, dominating the Wadi Qatneh, which leads down to Aijalon"; J. P. U. Lilley, "Chephirah," *NBD*, p. 207.
34. There is no unanimity about this site. Blenkinsopp, *op. cit.*, p. 8, believes that

Verse 18 reports, by anticipating the final outcome of this incident, that *the Israelites did not kill them*. The verse must be understood as introductory to all that transpires subsequently.[36] The sparing of the Gibeonites' lives is attributed to the sanctity of the oath taken (v. 15), a sanctity which was apparently felt even though the oath had been based on the false presentation of facts by one of the parties to the treaty.[37] This oath had been sworn by *the Lord the God of Israel* (see 7:13, 19–20; 8:30) and therefore could not be broken.

The reaction of the congregation is one of murmuring.[38] Apparently the people felt that violence was being done to the rules laid down in Deut. 7. Joshua's role at this point is not immediately apparent. It is the *princes of the congregation*, who had sworn to the treaty (v. 15) and who seem to bear the brunt of the people's complaint, who now reply.

When compared to v. 18a, v. 19 makes clear the nature of the Hebrew narrative at this point. That which the preceding verse had stated in summary form is now elaborated. The princes emphatically assume responsibility for the oath taken. (The Hebrew uses the independent personal pronoun: "we ourselves have sworn.") Note also the repetition of the phrase *the Lord, the God of Israel* (see v. 18). The princes see no reason to violate this oath, to which God has been witness, by killing[39] the Gibeonites.

The alternative to "touching" the Gibeonites is to let them live (v. 20). One might paraphrase v. 20a as follows: "We must do something of the following to them, which will result in letting them live." The princes' true reason for maintaining the oath is to avoid the *wrath* of God

its identification with el-Bireh "has achieved a greater degree of probability with the elimination of its principal rivals." But de Vaux, *Early History*, p. 626, considers the arguments for identification of the two "not convincing."

35. This is the present Deir el-Azhar, 2 miles south of Chephirah; see 18:11–20 for their location in Benjamin's territory.

36. For similar summary anticipations in the Joshua narrative, see examples in commentary on chs. 2, 8.

37. Many commentators, e.g., Calvin, Keil and Delitzsch, and Lange, discuss the rightness or wrongness of this attitude on the part of Israel. This may be a fruitful topic of discussion for one interested in the somewhat elusive subject of "OT ethics," but a commentary such as this does not appear to be the proper place.

38. The verb (Heb. *lûn*) is the same as used for Israel's complaining in the desert (see Exod. 15:24; 16:2; Num. 14:2, 36). Does the use of this verb here mean to give a hint that also in the promised land the basic attitude of the people has not changed?

39. "Therefore we may not touch them": "touch" often connotes violence; cf. Gen. 26:11; 2 S. 14:10; Ps. 105:15. Not touching the Gibeonites means that they will become inviolate and their lives will be spared.

which otherwise would strike them. For the concept of wrath (Heb. *qeṣep*) see 22:20; Num. 1:53; 18:5; 2 K. 3:27. The wrath of God in the Bible is always morally conditioned and represents a holy reaction on God's part toward a human infraction upon his holiness.[40]

The verdict of the princes is to let the Gibeonites live, in keeping with the oath recorded in v. 15. Immediately, anticipating what is yet to be reported in vv. 22–23, the narrator reports that the Gibeonites became hewers of wood and drawers of water (v. 21). Further details of these functions, as well as the addition *for the whole congregation*,[41] are supplied later (see v. 27, which makes this more specific). The final words of v. 21 (*as the princes had spoken of*[42] *them*) presuppose that this decision was not communicated directly to the Gibeonites by the princes but that this was left for Joshua to do.

22–27   Joshua now summons the Gibeonites (probably the same people who had originally come to him for a treaty) and openly rebukes them for their deceitful actions. This treachery deserves an appropriate penalty. After the summary of the misdeed follows, in typical fashion (*therefore you are cursed* (v. 23), Heb. *weʿattâ ʾarûrîm ʾattem*), the pronouncement of the verdict.[43] In this curse formula the one cursed occupies a position of subordination to the one cursing. Such a person is thus

40. A tendency to treat this wrath as a somewhat separate entity seems to be expressed by the translation of F.-M. Abel, *Le Livre de Josué*, who capitalizes the word (*la Colère*); cf. JB: *the* wrath. Care should be taken not to draw the OT wrath concept within the orbit of primitive religion, even though some features may show outward similarities.

41. Heb. *ʿēḏâ*. Grintz, *op. cit.*, p. 118, makes the following observation about the period in which this term functioned: "By its very nature it functioned in a 'republican' period, at a time when the tribal organization was still alive. . . . Thus in scope and functions, the *ʿeda* comes very near the Roman *comitia*, especially the *comitia centuriata*." This judgment is a significant corrective of the views of those who adhere to traditional source hypothesis as applied to the Pentateuch and Joshua. The source hypothesis considers the occurrence of the term *ʿēḏâ* an evidence of lateness. C. Steuernagel, *Das Buch Josua*, p. 241, states that the conception of Israel as *ʿēḏâ* is characteristic for P, an alleged document which certainly does *not* date from the tribal period of Israel's history.

42. Heb. preposition *leʿ*, which may mean "concerning"; see BDB, s.v. *leʿ*; and cf. Gen. 20:13; Deut. 33:12. H. Freedman, *Joshua*, renders v. 21a "And the princes said *concerning* them. . . ." This is grammatically possible; see BDB, s.v. *ʾel*. The LXX presents an easier reading, omitting the first words of v. 21; v. 21b–c thus become part of what the princes were saying, and the whole is a continuation of the word of vv. 19–20. See the footnotes in NEB, where the LXX is followed.

43. Many of the prophetic oracles imply this formula when introducing God's judgment upon wayward Israel, e.g., Isa. 5:3, 5; see also Gen. 3:22.

expelled from a communal situation which previously had guaranteed security, justice, and happiness.[44] While the Gibeonites' lives are spared, they are reduced to the position of perennial serfhood instead of remaining allies. *Servants* should be taken in the most pejorative sense here. As *woodcutters and water carriers* the Gibeonites will perform only menial services (see Deut. 29:11).

Apparently the story serves more than one purpose. In v. 14b the author makes clear that Joshua and the Israelites were at fault in not consulting God's counsel. By this omission they unquestionably endangered the sanctity of Israel, for they allowed a segment of Canaan's population to live. However, another side to this can be shown. The Gibeonites, through their deceit, have brought about this situation. The oath sworn to them cannot be undone, but the anomaly which has resulted must be clearly marked as another indelible reminder (for other "monuments" in the Joshua stories, cf. 4:9, 20; 6:26; 7:26; 8:28–29) of what has happened. Thus the need for complete separateness between Israel and its idolatrous neighbors would be felt and called to mind in the very treatment that the Gibeonites received. Those of the Canaanite population that were spared from the *ḥerem* (see 6:17) would nevertheless live as accursed ones among Israel. This curse also recalls Gen. 9:25, where Canaan was reduced to perpetual servitude to his brethren.

What had been said in general terms in v. 21 (*to the whole congregation*) is now repeated more specifically. The service rendered will be with respect to *the house*[45] *of my God* (v. 23). In v. 27 the elements of communal and cultic service are combined, and the altar is mentioned instead of the house. The sacrifices and the ritual washings at the sanctuary required a great deal of wood and water. To supply these, the *Gibeonites* would henceforth be used.[46]

In their reply, the Gibeonites speak, in a way similar to earlier sentiments reported in the book (see 2:9; 5:1), of the fear the Canaanites

44. See J. Scharbert, "'*rr*," *TDOT* I, pp. 408f.
45. The use of this word in v. 23 need not be an indication of lateness (see 6:19, 24 and commentary). It could well apply to the tabernacle service and only secondarily to that at the Jerusalem temple. Gibeon itself also had a sanctuary in David's days (see 1 K. 3:4; cf. 2 Chr. 1:3). Others (e.g., Noth) think of a shrine at Gilgal.
46. How the Gibeonites performed their task is not clear from the sacred record. 2 Sam. 21:1–14 refers to them again, but in a different context. Some think they are the later *netinîm* of Ezra 2:43–54, 58, but no good reason exists to associate these with the Gibeonites; see also de Vaux, *Early History*, pp. 625f., and cf. M. Haran, "The Gibeonites, the Nethinim and the Sons of Solomon's Servants," *VT* 11 (1961), pp. 159–169.

have felt at the coming of the Israelites. They show an acquaintance with the Lord's promise to Moses (see Deut. 7:1–5; 20:16–17) that he would give the land to Israel and destroy its inhabitants.[47] Led by fear, they resorted to the ruse which has now caused them to be cursed. Without any further defense they surrender fully to Joshua and give him a free hand. The narrative hereby gives a third instance of Canaan's submission to Israel, in addition to Jericho and Ai, both of which had been subjected involuntarily. Gibeon, an important city (see 10:2), submits voluntarily. This emphasis agrees with what had been stated in 1:5, and confirms the triumphant note which characterizes the book of Joshua throughout.[48]

Joshua carries out the word spoken earlier (v. 23). By making the Gibeonites temple servants for the rest of their existence as a people, he delivers them from the hand of the Israelites. The murmuring of the latter (see v. 18) had been with the intent of putting the Gibeonites to death in accord with Deut. 7. Therefore, the emphasis of the story is a negative one. The Gibeonites are not put to death. That this also may have resulted in a later inclusion of the Gibeonites in the circle of the covenant is not spelled out, although the possibility for such inclusion has now been created. That, however, does not appear to be the point of the story.[49]

The story concludes with a final statement that the Gibeonites were indeed assigned the task of *woodcutters and water carriers*. Their task appears to have been twofold, non-cultic (*for the congregation*) and cultic (*and for the altar*).[50] For the customary phrase that this condition continued

47. For the fear of the Canaanites cf. also 24:16–18; Exod. 15:14–16. For other indications that non-Israelites may have been acquainted with Canaan's doom as ordained by God, cf. Num. 23:24; 24:8. There is no need, therefore, to consider the words of the Gibeonites as nothing but a "deuteronomistic" representation.
48. The question of Israel's relationship to the "nations" cannot be examined here to any degree. For a biblical "philosophy" of history cf. Deut. 32:8–9. The OT knows on the one hand of foreigners coming to the sanctuary (see Lev. 17:8; Num. 15:14–16), but it also continues to speak of their permanent exclusion (Ezek. 44:6–8; Zech. 14:21). Both elements are legitimate strands of revelation (cf. also Rev. 19:15–16; see Exod. 15:18).
49. C. Vonk, *Inleiding op de Profeten: Jozua*, p. 143, stresses the future blessing of which the Gibeonites partook (1 Chr. 16:39; 21:29; Neh. 3:7), but this is not perfectly clear, and the story itself says nothing about it.
50. Another possibility: "congregation" forms the cultic part of the *qᵉhal yhwh*. If so, then the words "and for the altar" are only epexegetical for the congregation and, more particularly, for the altar. This is the view of J. P. Lange, ed., *A Commentary on the Holy Scriptures* 4, p. 90. Upon this view the Gibeonites were only temple servants.

to this day, see 4:9; 5:9; 7:26; 8:29.[51] The author wishes to explain that the well-known custom of using Gibeonites for these menial services dates back to this time. Their functioning in that capacity, moreover, may serve as yet another "monument" which will help Israel to remember what God had commanded concerning its relationship to the people of Canaan.

In order to define the locale of the Gibeonites' service even more precisely, the author concludes by adding the customary phase *in the place which he would choose* (lit. "for the place which the Lord will choose"; see Deut. 12:5, 11, 14, 18, 21, 26; 14:23, etc.). This phrase shows the anti-Canaanite thrust of Israel's cultic legislation.[52] Exod. 20:24 permits the building of altars where God grants a special theophany. In Moses' days the theophany came to be associated with the presence of the cloud over the tabernacle. However, the phrase does not as such forbid the building of altars other than at the location of the central sanctuary. In the days of Joshua and the Judges it came to be used for all those places where the tabernacle would be stationed. This lasted till the erection of Jerusalem's temple (1 K. 8:16, 44, 48; 11:13, 32, 36). Hence it would include Shiloh (18:1) and Gibeon (1 Ch. 16:39; 21:29; 2 Ch. 1:5).

The use of this phrase at the conclusion of the Gibeon narrative[53] shows the writer's concern with the legitimate worship of God. The Gibeonites, who themselves were a living embodiment of Israel's difference from the population of Canaan, were to serve only at such cultic centers as were clearly Israelite and hence non-Canaanite.

2. THE LORD'S BATTLES AT GIBEON AND IN SOUTHERN CANAAN (10:1–43)

a. The Battle at Gibeon (10:1–27)

1 *When Adoni-zedek king of Jerusalem heard that Joshua had taken*

---

51. The phrase is definitely more than, and other than, an etiological expression, as Noth contends. Apart from the objections to this position elsewhere in this commentary, the following may be pointed out: (1) the story of the Gibeonites is linked immediately with the coalition of the other Canaanite kings (10:1ff.), and there is no reason to deny the historical basis of that story; (b) the treaty with Gibeon is also referred to in 2 Sam. 21:1–14. This story is considered to be an "independent and solid tradition" also by those who might not as such object for more general reasons to the etiological approach; see de Vaux, *Early History*, p. 622; (c) the phrase "to this day" is not etiological; rather it serves as a confirmation of what the author has just reported as fact.
52. Cf. P. C. Craigie, *Deuteronomy*, p. 217.
53. The phrase follows somewhat haltingly at the end of the verse.

Ai and had applied the curse to it—as he had done to Jericho and its king, so he had done to Ai and its king—and that the inhabitants of Gibeon had made peace with Israel, and were among them.

2 *he and his people feared greatly; for Gibeon was as big as one of the cities that had a king; it was bigger than Ai, and all its men were valiant men.*

3 *So Adoni-zedek king of Jerusalem sent a message to Hoham king of Hebron, to Piram king of Jarmuth, to Japhia king of Lachish, and to Debir king of Eglon, as follows:*

4 *"Come with your forces to help me, that we may beat Gibeon, for it has made peace with Joshua and the Israelites."*

5 *So the five Amorite kings drew up with their combined forces, namely the king of Jerusalem, the king of Hebron, the king of Jarmuth, the king of Lachish, the king of Eglon, they and all their armies. They laid siege against Gibeon and opened the attack against it.*

6 *Then the men of Gibeon sent word to Joshua, to the camp at Gilgal: "Do not abandon your servants. Hurry and come to our aid and give us rescue, and help us, for all the kings of the Amorites who dwell in the mountain region have gathered against us."*

7 *Joshua marched up from Gilgal, he and all the warriors with him and all the valiant men.*

8 *And the Lord said to Joshua: "Do not fear them. For I have given them into your power. Not a man of them shall be able to stand his ground before you."*

9 *And Joshua fell upon them suddenly—the whole night he marched from Gilgal—*

10 *and the Lord caused panic among them before Israel so that it inflicted a smashing defeat on them at Gibeon. And it pursued them in the direction of the ascent of Beth-horon and killed them all the way to Azekah and Makkedah.*

11 *And as they fled from the Israelites and were on the descent of Beth-horon the Lord cast on them large stones from the sky as far as Azekah, so that they died. More people died through the hailstones than the Israelites killed with the sword.*

12 *Then Joshua spoke to the Lord on the day when the Lord delivered the Amorites to the men of Israel, and he said, with Israel as eyewitness:*

*"Sun, stand still at Gibeon,
and moon, at the valley of Aijalon."*

13 *And still stood the sun, and the moon—it halted, until the people had avenged itself upon its enemies. This is, as you know, written in the book of Jashar. The sun halted in the middle of the sky, and did not hasten to go down for about a whole day.*

14 *A day like that there has not been before or after, for the Lord to listen to the cry of a man. Surely the Lord fought for Israel.*

15 *Then Joshua and all Israel with him returned to the camp at Gilgal.*

16 *Those five kings, however, took to flight and hid themselves in the cave at Makkedah.*

17 *And it was reported to Joshua: "The five kings are found, hidden in the cave at Makkedah."*

18 *Then Joshua said: "Roll large stones before the mouth of the cave and post men by it to keep watch.*

19 *As for you, do not stand still, but pursue your enemies and attack their rear guard. Do not let them enter their cities, for the Lord your God has delivered them into your power."*

20 *When Joshua and the Israelites had inflicted a shattering defeat on them till they were fully wiped out, and those who had been able to escape had come into their fortresses,*

21 *all the people returned safe to Joshua in the camp at Makkedah. No one had dared to move his tongue against any of the Israelites.*

22 *Then Joshua said: "Open the mouth of the cave, and bring the five kings out to me from the cave."*

23 *And they did so, and brought out to him those five kings from the cave, the king of Jerusalem, the king of Hebron, the king of Jarmuth, the king of Lachish, and the king of Eglon.*

24 *When they had brought the five kings to Joshua, Joshua summoned all the men of Israel and said to the chiefs of the warriors who had gone with him: "Come near and put your feet on the necks of these kings." So they came near and put their feet on their necks.*

25 *And Joshua said to them: "Do not fear, neither be dismayed. Be strong and courageous, for thus the Lord will do to all your enemies against whom you fight."*

26 *Thereupon Joshua struck and killed them and had them hung on five trees. And they remained hanging on the trees till the evening.*

27 *But at the time of sunset Joshua issued an order, and they took them down from the trees and threw them into the cave where they had hidden themselves. Some large stones were put in the mouth of the cave, and they are there to this day.*

1–2 The chapter begins by mentioning once again the fear which has come over the Canaanites, both because of what Joshua had done and because of what Gibeon had done in making a treaty with Israel. The reader is by now familiar with this recurring motif (see 2:10–11; 5:1; 9:1–2, 24). The cumulative effect of these references is great. Israel, though originally nothing but a band of desert people, inspires fear into the hearts of those who live in their walled villages.

The story focuses first on *Adoni-zedek*[1] *king of Jerusalem*. This is the first time the name Jerusalem occurs in the OT (Gen. 14:18; 22:14 refer to it indirectly but not by name).[2]

The *peace* (Heb. *šālôm*) which Gibeon had made with Israel was the treaty described in the previous chapter. The special reason for Adonizedek's fear was Gibeon's size and prominence among the cities of Palestine. The city was clearly bigger than Ai, so that the latter's capture had not necessarily spelled defeat for Gibeon. Yet Gibeon had entered into a treaty with Israel and was now *among them* (see 9:7, 22), which means that the city had entered the Israelite community (so JB) and had been taken up into the midst of Israel, even though in a strictly subordinate role.[3]

3–5 There now follows a description of the alliance between a number of Palestine's kings (see also 9:1–2) for the purpose of punishing Gibeon. Adoni-zedek is the instigator, inviting four other kings in the vicinity to a joint campaign. The emphatic enumeration of the names of these kings, in vv. 3, 5, is impressive. It serves to point out the threat posed to Gibeon and thereby also to Gibeon's newly-won treaty partner, Israel. But cf. v. 23 for the final outcome! The author is sure of his material and knows how to use it effectively: frantic preparation for war at the

---

1. The name is a compound of "Adon," a name which also occurs in extrabiblical sources (see *DOTT*, p. 252) and means Lord (see also Adonijah, 1 K. 1:5), and "-zedek," a root which in Hebrew and common Semitic means "just" (cf. Gen. 14:18, Melchizedek). Adoni-zedek means "my lord (i.e., my god) is just (righteousness)." Some have suggested that Zedek was originally the name of a deity. The name would then mean "my lord is Zedek," but there is no sufficient evidence for this suggestion. See M. A. MacLeod, "Adonijah," *NBD*, p. 15. The LXX reads "Adoni-bezek" (see also Judg. 1:5–7).
2. Jerusalem is referred to by the name Urusalim in the Amarna tablets, Akkadian correspondence between officials in Western Asia (Palestine) and Egyptian pharaohs, c. 1400–1360 BC; see *ANET*, pp. 487–89. The meaning of this word has not been explained satisfactorily. KB suggest it means "the foundation of (y^eru) (the god) Shalem." Others suggest "dwelling of peace," or "founded in safety." The name "Salem" also occurs in the Ebla tablets, which antedate other references by at least a millennium. See also *AOTS*, pp. 277–295; D. F. Payne, "Jerusalem," *NBD*, pp. 614–620. J. Blenkinsopp, *Gibeon and Israel*, p. 29, suggests that Gibeon may have been within the jurisdiction of the king of Jerusalem, as Bethlehem was according to the Amarna letters. Gibeon's treaty with Israel would thus be a renunciation of its allegiance to Jerusalem.
3. We have rendered k^eʾaḥaṭ ʿārê hammamlāḵâ "as one of the cities that had a king." From 9:11 it may be concluded that Gibeon had a "republican" form of government. Another translation would be "as one of the royal cities," with the word "royal" designating a city of prominence.

outset, shameful defeat and total submission resulting in death at the end. These instances of military threat against Israel's very existence may well form the background of some of the Psalms (cf. Ps. 2).

The four other cities involved in this anti-Gibeon coalition are Hebron, Jarmuth, Lachish, and Eglon.[4] *Hebron*, whose name means "confederacy" or "association," lay 19 miles south-southwest of Jerusalem. It is also called Kiriath-arba (20:7; Gen. 23:2; 35:27).[5] *Jarmuth*, today known as Khirbet Yarmûk, is sixteen miles west of Jerusalem, and occupies a dominant position commanding a view of the coastal plain and the sea. *Lachish*, now known as Tell ed-Duweir, also is an ancient city dating back to the eighth millennium BC. From 1550 to 1200 BC it was a provincial capital of the Egyptian empire. At the beginning of the twelfth century it was destroyed by fire.[6] *Eglon* is generally identified with Tell el-Ḥesī,[7] one of the first sites excavated in Palestine. The fortified city dates from the Middle Bronze Age (2100–1550 BC) and survived until the fourteenth century BC.[8]

The coalition against Gibeon is another test of Israel's willingness to stand by the treaty it had made. The first test is reported in ch. 9, when the Israelites themselves had intended to kill the Gibeonites for their treachery (v. 26), but Joshua prevented the action.

The result of the anti-Gibeon coalition is threatening. Perhaps the narrative means to give added emphasis by enumerating a second time (see v. 3) the names of the five cities whose kings now come against Gibeon. This assault, it should be recognized, is the first serious attempt at resistance on the part of Canaanite kings to be recorded in Joshua. The ensuing battle will therefore be a crucial test of the Lord's faithfulness toward his people as promised in the words recorded in 1:3, 5.

The kings of the coalition are designated Amorite (v. 5; cf. also v. 6). The term Amorite can have a wider and a narrower application (see

---

4. Hebron does not appear in the Amarna correspondence, but the other three cities do. Y. Aharoni suggests that Hebron may have been within the boundaries of the Jerusalemite kingdom (*The Land of the Bible*, p. 195).

5. Hebron was built "seven years before Zoan in Egypt" (Num. 13:22). Egyptologists speak of the "Era of Tanis" (c. 1720 BC; Tanis is another name for Zoan). Hebron is already mentioned in Abraham's days (Gen. 13:18).

6. This destruction by fire cannot have been inflicted by Joshua and Israel, as O. Tufnell correctly remarks (*AOTS*, p. 302). Joshua did not burn any cities except Hazor (11:13).

7. For other possible identifications see J. P. U. Lilley, "Eglon," *NBD*, p. 337.

8. The names of three of the kings, Hoham, Piram, and Debir, occur only here as proper names. The first two names show Arab influence; see J. de Groot, *Het Boek Jozua*, p. 104. For Japhia cf. also 2 Sam. 5:15.

also 3:10 and commentary), often referring to the people living in the mountain regions of Canaan (see also v. 6; cf. Num. 13:29; Deut. 1:44). But not all the cities of the coalition were mountain cities. Perhaps because of Jerusalem's initiative they were so referred to by the people of Gibeon.

The kings came, *laid siege against Gibeon and opened the attack against it.*[9]

6–8 The Gibeonites manage to get an urgent appeal for help out of the besieged city to Joshua who is in the camp at Gilgal (see 5:9–10; 9:17). No explicit reference is made to the treaty just concluded (ch. 9), but it is natural to suppose that the treaty nevertheless forms the judicial ground for the request.[10]

Joshua responds without delay. He marches up from Gilgal, *he and all the warriors with him and all the valiant men.*[11]

Because of the unusual nature of this conflict a special word of reassurance and encouragement on the Lord's part is now recorded. The exhortation not to *fear*, the assurance that the enemy has been *given into* Joshua's *power*, and the promise that none will *be able to stand his ground before you*—all have been given before (1:5; 6:2; 8:1, 18). At this crucial point in the narrative, however, they assume a special significance.

9–10 The account of the battle alternately stresses man's activity and God's supernatural help and intervention.[12] First, there is the night's march from Gilgal to Gibeon, a distance of some 35 kilometers, and a movement from lower to higher terrain.[13] Having probably reached the

---

9. Lit. "and made war (or "fought") against it." From the subsequent context what is meant clearly is a siege with accompanying assault.

10. To what extent one should appeal here to Hittite suzerainty treaties by way of explanation of Joshua's response is open to question; see also p. 161, n. 28. J. H. Kroeze, *Het Boek Jozua*, p. 130, rightly warns against exaggerated use of these extrabiblical materials and observes that Joshua certainly "did not have to learn the morality of treaty-loyalty from the Hittites."

11. One could argue that "all the valiant men" (Heb. *kōl gibbôrê heḥāyyil* [cf. 1:14; 6:2; 8:3]) is explicative of "all the warriors" (Heb. *'am hammilḥāmâ*). This is how the DNV treats the two phrases. But the present approach has also been followed in recent versions: NAB "his picked troops and the rest of his soldiers"; NEB "all his forces and all his fighting men"; NIV similarly.

12. See also K. Gutbrod, *Das Buch vom Lande Gottes*, p. 89, who rightly calls vv. 8–11 a "masterpiece of Biblical narrative" whose total thrust is to emphasize the truth that "God gives and Israel takes."

13. It is possible that a full moon favored this otherwise arduous undertaking. So, e.g., B. J. Alfrink, *Josué*, p. 60, who appeals for this opinion to Joshua's later reference to the moon (v. 12).

vicinity of Gibeon in the morning,[14] Joshua falls upon the united Amorite forces *suddenly*. However, *the Lord caused panic among them before Israel*. The verb used here (Heb. *hāmam*) often occurs in descriptions of God's aid to Israel in defeating its foes. It appears to be used of various meteorological phenomena put into service by God at the proper moment (Exod. 14:24; cf. Ps. 77:16–18 [Eng. 17–19], thunder and lightning; Judg. 4:15, probably heavy rain [see Judg. 5:20–21]; 1 Sam. 7:10, thunder; cf. also 2 Sam. 22:15; Ps. 18:14 [Eng. 15]; 144:6).

It appears best to take this statement as an anticipatory summary of the entire course of the battle, including that which is reported in vv. 12–15. Similar summaries have been encountered in the earlier narratives of this book (e.g., 9:6).[15] The use of such features in the description may well be due to a certain schematic presentation of various battles Israel fought in the course of her history and thus part of the so-called "holy war" vocabulary.[16] Due care should be taken, however, not to let these features become merely a mode of representation of what in reality may have been quite otherwise.[17]

Israel[18] is now in the position of inflicting *a smashing defeat*. This defeat took place first of all *at Gibeon* but was followed by a pursuit in the direction of *the ascent of Beth-horon* (called descent in v. 11).[19] The flight of the foe was in a westerly direction toward the coastal plain. The road was a particularly dangerous one for a defeated army since its retreating files could be assailed from the slopes above the road.[20]

14. Since Joshua's words to the sun (vv. 12ff.) speak of the sun "at Gibeon" and the moon "at the valley of Aijalon," it is best to assume Joshua's position to be such that, looking eastward toward Gibeon, he would see the sun standing in the eastern sky over Gibeon. He himself was already engaged in pursuit of the enemy westward from Gibeon.

15. See C. Vonk, *Inleiding op de Profeten: Jozua*, p. 149.

16. On possible "holy war" vocabulary in Joshua cf. G. J. Wenham, *JBL* 90 (1971), pp. 141–42.

17. The question has wider ramifications. Some of this "holy war" language recurs in passages which have for their ultimate reference point the eschatological battle of the end time, e.g., Ps. 76:7, 9, 13 (Eng. 6, 8, 12).

18. The verb forms in v. 10 are masculine singular throughout. "It inflicted" could therefore also be rendered "He (i.e., the Lord) inflicted," but this would be less suitable for the activity of pursuing. The LXX does translate "the Lord inflicted."

19. There were two Beth-horons, an Upper and a Lower Beth-horon. The road from Gibeon to Upper Beth-horon first goes up from 710 to 776 meters. It then descends to Beth-horon. From Upper Beth-horon the road drops off downhill to Lower Beth-horon.

20. Thus E. G. Kraeling, *The Rand McNally Bible Atlas*, p. 138. Y. Aharoni, *op. cit.*, p. 55, calls the ascent (descent) of Beth-horon the "most obvious weak point" of the entire route from Gibeon to the plain.

There is another anticipation in this story (v. 10c). Israel is said to have killed the enemy *all the way to Azekah and Makkedah*,[21] whereas in v. 11 the scene of action is still at Beth-horon.

11 The panic caused by the Lord among the enemy (v. 10a) is due, among other things, to the *large stones* which he *cast from the sky as far as Azekah*. This happened just as the enemy found itself in that most difficult location of the descent of Beth-horon.[22] By this hailstorm[23] of unusual severity the Lord caused more deaths among the Amorites than the Israelites killed with the sword. Once again the account confirms that the military courage of Joshua and the Israelites, which is not belittled in any way, is operating within the larger context of God's miraculous intervention whereby in a real sense the enemy is "given" (v. 8) into Israel's power. For hail as an instrument of judgment in God's hands cf. Isa. 30:30 (on Assyria, the leading world power at that time); 28:2 (on the drunkards of Ephraim); and 32:19; see also Job 38:22-23, where hail is said to be "reserved" against the day of battle in God's treasuries.

12-15 Focusing in rapid sketches on various phases of this stupendous battle, the author proceeds to tell of the miracle of the long day. This adds another detail to what, in v. 11, already appears to be a somewhat finished story. Joshua speaks to the Lord at a moment described first in general terms: *Then* (Heb. '*āz*) *Joshua spoke to the Lord*. This is a rather indefinite indication of time. It may well be that these words were spoken in the morning of the battle (see above concerning the position of the sun "at Gibeon," viewed from a location west of Gibeon). The episodic nature of Hebrew narrative does not even demand that the casting of the large stones (v. 11) has already occurred at the time of Joshua's words to the Lord. What the narrative does say by way of further chronological

21. Azekah is Tell ez-Zakarîyah, a bold site filling a strategic position below Jarmuth (Kraeling, *op. cit.*, p. 138). It lies in the Shephelah, about 30 kilometers south of Beth-horon. Makkedah's location remains unknown.
22. The circumstantial clause by which the enemy's presence on the descent is indicated gives emphasis to the coincidence (divinely brought about) of two unusual difficulties.
23. KD, p. 106, clearly opt for the view that these were hailstones, which seems like the most acceptable interpretation. Others, e.g. Vonk, following Velikowsky, prefer to think of a rain of meteorites. The Hebrew uses *bārāḏ*, "hail," but Vonk calls attention to passages where this phenomenon is combined with a fire phenomenon, e.g., Exod. 9:23-24; cf. also Ps. 78:47-48 (thunderbolts); 105:32 (lightning); and see Ps. 18:14 (Eng. 13); Ps. 148:8; 2 Sam. 22. Since, however, natural hail is often accompanied by thunder and lightning, the passages cited do not necessarily support the meteorite theory.

precision is that these words were offered *on the day when the Lord delivered the Amorites to the men of Israel*.

There is no unanimity among interpreters as to the precise point where the quotation from the book of Jashar (v. 13b) begins and ends. Some believe that the reference to the source concludes the quote.[24] Others believe that all of vv. 12–15 is in effect a quotation from said book, with the exception, of course, of the reference to the book itself, which would be by the writer of Joshua.[25] The second position appears most tenable, and explains the sudden intrusion of v. 15. Thus, Joshua returned to the camp at Gilgal, an action which cannot have taken place until after the episode of the kings in the cave as well as the campaign in south Canaan (vv. 22–39).[26] Taking the other view, which restricts the quotation to vv. 12b and 13a, one would have to regard v. 15 as a summary anticipation of what took place later in time.[27]

Joshua speaks first to the Lord, but he also utters his words audibly *with Israel as eyewitness*.[28] This means not only that his words could be heard but that his very posture may have been expressive of prayer. The words Joshua speaks are not in the form of a prayer. They are an apostrophe addressed to the sun and the moon.[29] What Joshua bids the sun to do is to "stand still." The Hebrew uses an imperative of *dāmam*, which may also mean "be still," "be dumb." V. 13 indicates that the sun did Joshua's bidding. At that point another form of *dāmam* is used, but of the moon it is said that it halted (Heb. *'āmad*, "to stand"). From this parallelism

24. So Kroeze, *op. cit.*, p. 133.
25. KD, p. 107, believe the quotation begins with "in the day when . . ." and includes v. 15. Likewise Vonk, *op. cit.*, p. 153, although he includes all of v. 12 in the quotation. On the other hand, C. J. Goslinga, *Jozua*, p. 102, considers only part of v. 12 and the first part of v. 13 to be quotation. He believes that v. 15 was inserted by a copyist who wanted to write v. 43 but put it at the wrong place (the end of v. 42 is verbally almost identical to that of v. 14).
26. Alfrink, *op. cit.*, p. 65, believes vv. 12–15 belong at the end of the chapter, after what is now v. 42. This would mean that v. 15 would coincide with v. 43.
27. This is how C. à Lapide took it, *Commentarius in Iosue, Iudicum, Ruth, IV. Libros Regum et II. Paralipomena* (Antwerp: 1642): *"Hic ergo versus per anticipationem hic ponitur et quia per parenthesis interiicitur."* J. Calvin, *Commentaries on the Book of Joshua*, states that v. 15 is "not inserted in its proper place"; p. 157. It has been put here *"neglecto temporis ordine"* ("without regard to the order of time").
28. This phrase is omitted by F.-M. Abel, *Le Livre de Josué*, following the LXX, which here differs from the MT at more than one point.
29. The LXX treats Joshua's words as a prayer to God: "Then Joshua spoke to the Lord . . . and said: Let the sun stand. . . ."

one would be led to conclude that *dāmam* in both verses also has the general meaning of "standing still," "being motionless."[30]

The language that Joshua uses in addressing the sun and moon is the language of ordinary observation still used today in the scientific age. Probably Joshua and his contemporaries thought of the sun as moving around the earth, but his language should not be pressed to construct a "view of the universe" any more than should today's reference to the rising and setting of the sun.

The respective locations of the sun and the moon[31] at the time that Joshua addressed them are *at Gibeon* and *at the valley of Aijalon*. This means that, as Joshua looked in the direction of the sun, he saw it standing in the sky over Gibeon. Likewise the moon could be seen standing over the valley of Aijalon which was west of Beth-horon.

The sun and the moon did Joshua's bidding *until the people had avenged itself upon its enemies*.[32] It is obvious from this additional comment, as well as from the words at the end of v. 13, how the reader understood the event described here. There was a halting of the sun (Heb. *'āmaḏ*) and a delay in its going down. This allowed Israel to complete its campaign against the fleeing enemy.[33]

---

30. Blenkinsopp, *op. cit.*, p. 47, calls attention to 1 Sam. 14:9, where the same two verbs, *dāmam* and *'āmaḏ*, are used in the sense of a nonparticipation in battle. Sun and moon are supposed to have been the tutelary deities of Gibeon and Aijalon, respectively, and they are enjoined here not to take part in military action. For a similar view cf. J. Dus, "Gibeon: Eine Kultstätte des ŠMŠ und die Stadt des benjaminitischen Schicksals," *VT* 10 (1960), pp. 353–374. But cf. R. de Vaux, *Early History*, p. 634, who points out (a) that we have no indication that these cities were centers of the cult of sun and moon; (b) that it is unlikely for Joshua to have addressed pagan deities; (c) that Gibeon was not an enemy city but that Joshua was fighting for its defense.

31. The reason why the moon is also mentioned here is not so much because of the needs of Hebrew parallelism, but because the moon in oriental society was used to regulate times and seasons as well as the sun. J. S. Holladay, Jr., "The Day(s) the *Moon* Stood Still," *JBL* 87 (1968), pp. 166–178, argues that the reason for the moon's mention lies in Assyrian astronomical practices which considered it a good omen when sun and moon were both visible together. See de Vaux, *Early History*, p. 634, for a critique of this suggestion.

32. The Hebrew word for "people" is *gôy*, without article. It is here used of Israel, elsewhere often of non-Israelites. Its use here may be due to the somewhat poetic, at least rhythmic, nature of the words of v. 13a. This may also account for the unusual construction of *nāqam*, "to avenge oneself," which ordinarily requires a preposition.

33. Alfrink, *op. cit.*, pp. 66ff., presents a complete survey of the many attempts that have been made to explain the events recorded here. Alfrink himself thinks that the word *dāmam*, "to be silent," is used here in the sense of the Babylonian-

The *book of Jashar*[34] from which this information is taken is also mentioned in 2 Sam. 1:18, where it is introduced by exactly the same formula as here. The work appears to have been a collection of odes in praise of certain heroes of the theocracy, interwoven with historical notices of their achievements.[35]

Verse 14 provides another clue as to how the writer of the book of Joshua understood the episode recorded here. He sees in it an extraordinary answer to prayer.[36] The stature of Joshua, whose prayer was so singularly answered, is thus enhanced. See also 1:17; 4:14, and commentary. On the place and function of v. 15 see above.

The long day must be seen as one of several instances of the fact that *the Lord fought for Israel* (v. 14b; see also vv. 8, 10–11; cf. Exod. 14:13; Deut. 20:4). It is not the task of a work such as this to provide further explanatory comment as to the precise nature of the event recorded here and its relationship to the world of time and space as observed today. The reader should be open to any attempt to explain the text on the basis of proper philological considerations, but rationalizing attempts for the purpose of satisfying the modern scientific mind should be avoided. In general it may be said that the biblical view of the world as created by God, who assigned to each heavenly body its place and function (Gen. 1:16), permits a rather literal view of the events reported here. Positivistic and evolutionistic science has of course long challenged this biblical view of the world as out of accord with the actual state of affairs. This broader question as to the proper relation between Bible and science cannot be entered into at this point.

16–21 The narrative now focuses on another facet of the battle

---

Assyrian *nabû*, "to rest," which stands for the darkening of sun and moon, both in an atmospheric and an astronomical sense. In Hab. 3:11 the writer uses *'āmaḏ* in an atmospheric sense to describe a darkening of sun and moon. The event described in the quotation from the book of Jashar is therefore the same as that described in vv. 10–11.

34. The LXX does not have this reference here. The word *yāšar* can either be left as a proper name, Jashar, or it may be rendered "just," "upright." Moffatt's translation renders it "heroes," apparently treating the singular as a collective. It has also been taken as a reference to believing Israel, or to one or more believing Israelites. Some have seen a reference to Jeshurun here (cf. Deut. 32:15; 33:5, 26.) See also A. van Selms, "Book of Jasher," *NBD*, p. 600.

35. Gutbrod, *op. cit.*, p. 89, sees in this reference to the just one(s) a witness of the expectation of a Savior in whom God will fight for Israel in a most unique way.

36. In like manner Moses (Num. 12:8) and David (2 Sam. 7:13) are singled out above their contemporaries. See also 2 K. 18:5; 23:25.

with the Amorite coalition. This style of narration resembles that observed elsewhere in the first part of the book. The preceding verses seemingly present a fairly well-rounded whole. What remains is to furnish some further particulars concerning the way in which Israel inflicted a humiliating defeat upon its enemies. This gives the needed balance to the structure of the account as a whole. Having begun with a vivid description of the alliance of the five kings and the threat this posed to Gibeon (and Israel), the story ends with a description of the kings' death.[37] For this reason the narrator retraces his steps and shows how the pursuit of the enemy is still in full swing (see vv. 10–11). During their flight on this fateful day the five kings have taken refuge in *the cave*[38] *at Makkedah*.[39] The narrative is very vivid at this point and contains a definite element of suspense. When Joshua is told[40] that the five kings are hidden in the cave he orders large stones to be rolled in front of the cave's mouth and guards to be stationed by it. Thus what had been sought as a refuge becomes a place of incarceration and ultimate doom. In the meantime, the Israelites are told not to *stand still, but pursue your enemies* (v. 19). Again, the narrative highlights the fact that the Lord, Israel's God, has *delivered them into your power* (see v. 8; cf. 1:3; 2:24 and elsewhere), but this does not rule out Israel's participation in battle. It is Israel that is not to let the enemy *enter their cities*, and Israel that is to attack the enemy's *rear guard*.

Neither is it true that the story presents an altogether unrealistic portrait of the defeat that Israel inflicts on the allied forces. For although v. 20 emphasizes the greatness of the *shattering defeat* inflicted, it does not conceal the fact that not all of the enemy were slain. On the one hand is the statement that *they were fully wiped out*, but on the other hand the account refers to *those who had been able to escape*. This feature lends credibility to the story. This is not just an epic or a saga. This is historiography, written with a special theocratic purpose to be sure, but history

---

37. Keeping in mind the narrative technique employed we do not need to see the episode of the five kings in the cave as an originally separate and independent tale told for etiological purposes, as is the view of M. Noth, *Das Buch Josua*, pp. 60, 65f.

38. The Hebrew employs the definite article. However, Hebrew sometimes uses the definite article where in our estimation an indefinite article is called for; see GKC § 126 q. One could therefore also say "a cave." At any rate, no etiological associations should be made here.

39. Also mentioned in vv. 10, 21, 28, its precise location is unknown; see *GTT*, p. 273; and J. P. U. Lilley, "Makkedah," *NBD*, p. 773.

40. Joshua was probably in pursuit of the enemy over the widespread field of battle. He had not yet returned to Gilgal, as some suppose. Verse 15 is an anticipation of what takes place later.

just the same. Joshua's charge to the people not to *let them enter into their cities* (v. 19) cannot prevent some Canaanites from doing so (v. 20). But about the total victorious outcome there can be no doubt. Israel returns safely to Joshua, who is in the camp at Makkedah. The phrase *no one had dared to move his tongue against any of the Israelites*[41] (v. 21) is similar to Exod. 11:7 and may have been chosen deliberately to indicate the continuity in God's work of deliverance.

22–27 The story of the defeat of the five Amorite kings now moves swiftly to its dramatic conclusion. (Concerning the suspense element built into the story, see above.) The five kings are released from the cave. The narrator repeats once again the names of the cities over which they were king, probably by way of solemn contrast to v. 5. The threat to Israel's life and safety has now been turned into victory over its enemies. Before the enemy kings are put to death a symbolical action is undertaken to assure the people that Israel's God will likewise humiliate all other enemies (v. 26). Joshua summons *the chiefs*[42] *of the warriors* to place their feet upon the necks of the five kings. A widespread ancient custom called for victorious kings to put their feet upon the necks of conquered enemies (see also Deut. 33:29; 1 K. 5:3; Ps. 110:1). This symbolical action, clear enough by itself, is accompanied by words of encouragement. These words (*be strong and courageous*) had also been spoken to Joshua himself (1:6). Joshua here repeats them to the representatives of the people (see also 8:1). This note of encouragement in the face of threatening danger is one of the keynotes of the book of Joshua. The chiefs of the warriors do as they are bidden. Canaan has now become a servant to Shem (see Gen. 9:25–27).[43] The sacred writer indeed may have thought of the ancient oracle as he wrote these words.

After Joshua has put to death the five kings he has their bodies hung[44] on five trees. The same had been done to Ai's king (8:29; see also Deut. 21:22–23). The kings thus are presented to the people as accursed by God. At sunset, however, the dead bodies are taken down from the trees to prevent a defilement of the land (Deut. 21:23). The kings' bodies are then thrown into the cave in which they had earlier taken refuge. The story ends with the erection of yet another monument whereby the Israelites

41. The verb form *ḥāraṣ* means lit. "to point." In Exod. 11:7 it is used of dogs. So, e.g., KD: "There pointed not (a dog) its tongue. . . ." NEB understands this differently.
42. Heb. *qāṣîn*, "chief, ruler, commander." This is its only occurrence in Joshua; it occurs also in Judges and some of the prophets.
43. For this association of thought see H. W. Hertzberg, *ATD* IX, p. 75.
44. This hanging probably was carried out by means of impalement.

will be able to remember the great events of the conquest of the land (cf. 7:26; 8:29). In conclusion, the narrator reports that the stones *are there to this day*[45] (see 4:9 and commentary). This expression is not to be regarded as an indication of an etiological tale but serves to confirm the veracity of the report rendered.[46]

b. The Southern Campaign (10:28–39)

28 *Joshua took also Makkedah on that day and struck it with the edge of the sword, also its king. He applied the curse to it and to all that lived therein. He did not let anyone escape and did with the king of Makkedah as he had done with the king of Jericho.*

29 *From Makkedah Joshua and all Israel passed on to Libnah and warred against Libnah.*

30 *The Lord gave it also into the power of Israel together with its king, and he struck it and all that lived therein with the edge of the sword. He did not let anyone in it escape and did with the king of Libnah as he had done with the king of Jericho.*

31 *From Libnah Joshua and all Israel with him passed on to Lachish; he besieged it and warred against it.*

32 *And the Lord gave Lachish into the power of Israel. On the second day Joshua took it and he struck it and all that lived therein with the edge of the sword, just as he had done with Libnah.*

33 *At that time Horam the king of Gezer marched up to help Lachish, but Joshua struck him and his people, until he had left him none remaining.*

34 *From Lachish Joshua and all Israel with him passed on to Eglon. They besieged it and warred against it.*

35 *They took it on that day and struck it with the edge of the sword;*

---

45. The Hebrew expression at this point is strengthened by means of *'eṣem*, "to this very day." KD understand the phrase to mean here only that the stones which Israel had placed at the mouth of the cave had remained there until that very day, i.e., until the day the kings were taken out and executed. This understanding appears forced and is not shared by the majority of translations and commentaries.

46. Noth, *op. cit.*, p. 60, considers the story of the five kings at Makkedah to be etiological, particularly in light of the phrase "to this day." But see B. S. Childs, *JBL* 82 (1963), pp. 279–292; *VT* 24 (1974), pp. 385–397. Childs rightly pleads for a clearer definition of the term etiology than is presently given by authors who work with this concept, and urges "extreme caution" in the employment of the term when applied to the stories of Israel's past. "Far more likely is a position which takes seriously Israel's attempt to describe a genuine sequence of events, even when the attempt is not always successful according to the canons of modern historical criticism" (p. 397). For a critique of Noth's etiological approach see also Y. Kaufmann, *The Biblical Account of the Conquest of Palestine*, pp. 72f.

he applied the curse on that day to all that lived therein, just as he had done with Lachish.

36 *From Eglon Joshua and all Israel with him marched up to Hebron and they warred against it.*

37 *They took it and struck it with the edge of the sword, also its king and all its cities and all that lived therein. He let no one escape, just as he had done with Eglon. And they applied the curse to it and to all that lived therein.*

38 *Then Joshua and all Israel with him turned toward Debir and warred against it.*

39 *And he took it and its king and all its cities. They struck them with the edge of the sword and applied the curse to all that lived therein. He let no one escape. Just as he had done to Hebron so he did with Debir and its king, as he had also done with Libnah and its king.*

These verses provide in summary fashion a brief description of the victories which Joshua and the Israelites obtained over a number of cities situated in southern Canaan. Some of the cities conquered belong to the coalition mentioned in the earlier part of the chapter, for though the kings of that coalition suffered defeat and death, not all of their cities were taken. Others, Jerusalem, for example, are not mentioned again. The location of most of the cities is in the Shephelah, but Hebron is in the hill country. There is no unanimity about the location of Debir.

The narrative of the book of Joshua, which thus far has given rather explicit accounts of single events, suddenly quickens its pace. There is much repetition, to be sure, but this is due to the Hebrew mode of presentation. Only the scantiest of details of the conquest of each city is given, however. The description uses a number of stereotyped expressions which recur in the successive accounts, but variations also occur. These variations, together with the omission of the names of two of the cities that were part of the earlier coalition, show that the account is reliable historically and is not the product of some later streamlining of traditions that were originally quite different, as some scholars allege.[1] Among the variations in the individual accounts the following may be noted: (i) No mention is made of the slaying of the kings of Lachish and Eglon whereas, in the case of the other four cities, the fate of the kings is mentioned; (ii)

1. A good deal of the critical scepticism with respect to the veracity of the present account stems from scholarly doubt concerning a single "Conquest" of Palestine under Joshua's leadership. Y. Aharoni, *The Land of the Bible*, p. 197, n. 64, believes that the conquest of Hebron and Debir was actually accomplished by Caleb and Kenaz (15:13–19; Judg. 1:12–15). In the course of time these conquests were associated with Judah (Judg. 1:10–11), and finally with all Israel under Joshua (Josh. 10:36–39). Similarly, F.-M. Abel, *Le Livre de Josué*, p. 51.

the language used to describe the various phases of the campaign differs, depending on the geographical locale. Thus Joshua is said to have "passed over," "marched up," and "turned"; (iii) the aid offered by the king of Gezer to the king of Lachish is a special feature which occurs only at that point.

Though the record of the southern campaign under Joshua's leadership must be deemed reliable historically, this record does not simply intend to supply historical information. Its purpose, within the larger context of the book of Joshua, is to report by means of a few bold narrative strokes that what the Lord had promised Joshua (1:3) was being fulfilled increasingly. The interpretative clue to this passage lies in what is stated in vv. 40–43 (see commentary).

28 The first town captured is *Makkedah*. It was near Azekah (see v. 10), but its exact location is unknown. Joshua had his camp there during the campaign against the five kings (v. 21). Several of the elements which also occur in the description of the rest of the campaign are found here: Joshua *struck it with the edge of the sword*. Its king was slain and his body was treated as that of the king of Jericho (see also 8:2, 29). The curse (Heb. *ḥerem*) was applied to the city[2] and *to all that lived[3] therein*. None escaped.

29–30 The next town to be taken is *Libnah*.[4] A new feature in the description of its capture is the reference to the participation by *all Israel* (see also vv. 31, 34, 36, 38). Stress upon the unity of Israel is a special concern of the book (see 3:7, 17; 4:14; 7:23f.; 8:21, 24; 23:2). Two other features may be noted. First, Joshua *warred* against Libnah. This word occurs also in the subsequent descriptions. Second, the Lord gives Libnah and its king into Israel's hands. This is consistent with the emphasis of the entire book thus far (see 1:2; 2:24; 8:1; 10:8). The entire conquest of Canaan, including this part, is to be seen as the result of God's granting of the land to the people of his choice.

31–33 Going in a southerly direction Joshua comes to *Lachish*.[5]

---

2. The exact expression does not occur in the case of either Libnah (vv. 29–30) or Lachish (vv. 31–32), but the idea is present in each instance. On the theological meaning of this term see 6:17 and commentary.

3. Heb. *kol-hannepeš*, lit. "every soul."

4. This is either Tell eṣ-Ṣâfî, or Tell Bornat.

5. Lachish is now generally identified with Tell ed-Duweir. From 1550–1200 BC it was a provincial capital of the Egyptian empire. Evidence of sudden destruction by burning c. 1200 BC is often ascribed to Joshua's campaign, but in the light of

At this point in the description of the campaign another variant occurs (see introduction to this section). Lachish is *besieged* (also Eglon, v. 34) and is taken *on the second day*. Nothing is said about the king of Lachish. He was one of the anti-Gibeon coalition (v. 3) and had been executed by Joshua (vv. 23, 26). The fate of Lachish and its inhabitants is similar to that of Libnah. A further detail concerning the capture of this city is the attempt on the part of *Horam*[6] *the king of Gezer*[7] to come to its aid. This city lay considerably farther north, about a day's march. Additional details about this rescue effort are not given. Was Horam already on his way before Joshua lay siege to Lachish? All we learn is that Horam was thoroughly defeated and perhaps put to death. The city itself was not taken (see Judg. 1:29; 1 K. 9:15–17).

34–35 Joshua then moved in a southwesterly direction, to *Eglon*.[8] He *besieged it* and *took it on that day* (as distinct from Lachish, which was taken on the second day, v. 32). Eglon was treated the same as the other cities. The curse was applied to it, indicating complete devotion to God in a punitive sense (see v. 28). The slaying of Eglon's king is reported in vv. 23, 26.

36–37 *Hebron* is the next city taken. Together with Lachish and Eglon it had belonged to the Amorite coalition (vv. 3, 5). Though the city was a place of real consequence, it has not been possible thus far to determine definitively where it was situated. Its general location was 19 miles south-southwest of Jerusalem (see also 14:15;[9] Judg. 1:10). It was the center of the Anakim (11:21), but the latter's expulsion and utter destruction are not yet explicitly mentioned at this point. The writer reserves that information for a more appropriate moment (11:21–22).

Although the king of Hebron had been slain together with his allies

---

11:13 this must be doubted; see also O. Tufnell, *AOTS*, p. 302, who observes that the Philistines or the Egyptians themselves may have burned the city in a punitive raid.

6. The LXX calls him *Ailam*, which is the same as the LXX name for the king of Hebron (v. 3).

7. Identified with Tell Jezer. In the Amarna period Lachish and Gezer had close connections; see Aharoni, *op. cit.*, p. 199. Gezer is mentioned several times in Egyptian inscriptions, including the famous Merneptah stele (c. 1220 BC), which mentions its capture.

8. Presently identified with Tell el-Ḥesī (formerly thought to be Lachish). Its name also occurs in the Egyptian Execration Texts of the 20th–19th centuries BC.

9. Hebron is also called Kiriath-arba, lit. "city of Four." But in 15:13; 21:11, the word *arba* is treated as a proper name. E. A. Speiser, *Genesis*. Anchor Bible I (Garden City: 1964), p. 169, has suggested that *arba* is "merely a popular adaptation of another name, perhaps non-Semitic."

at the cave of Makkedah (v. 26), the narrative speaks here of a new king of Hebron.[10] From this it is obvious that Joshua's campaign thus far, though briefly summarized, had occupied a certain period of time, long enough at any rate for the people of Hebron to choose a new king for themselves. Hebron is subjected to the curse (*ḥerem*) together with *all its cities*.[11]

38–39 The last city mentioned is *Debir*. Joshua *turned toward* it since Debir was 11 miles southwest of Hebron. It was strategically located between the southland (Negeb) and the Shephelah. Its earlier name had been Kiriath-sepher, "city of books."[12] Like Hebron, Debir had to be recaptured at a later point in Israel's history (cf. 14:6–15; 15:15–17; Judg. 1:10–13). The fate of Debir is like that of the other cities. The narrator links explicitly what happened to Debir with the fate of Hebron and Libnah. This enhances the sombre monotony of destruction which characterizes this passage.[13]

c. Summary Comment and Concluding Statement (10:40–43)

40 *So Joshua conquered the whole region, the hill country, and the southland, and the lowland, and the slopes, and all their kings. He let no one escape, but he applied the curse to all that breathed, as the Lord, the God of Israel, had commanded.*

41 *Joshua defeated them from Kadesh-barnea to Gaza, and the whole region of Goshen as far as Gibeon.*

42 *And Joshua mastered all these kings and their land in one stroke, for the Lord, the God of Israel, fought for Israel.*

43 *Then Joshua and all Israel with him returned to the camp at Gilgal.*

40–42 These verses present a provisional conclusion to the section begun in 9:1–2. At that point mention had been made of a combination of Canaanite forces ready to thwart the Israelite invasion. Here is the record of what has come of this effort. A more definite summary and conclusion is offered in 11:23; see also 11:19–20.

10. The LXX omits any reference to Hebron's king at this point. It also omits "all its cities" (see below).

11. The subjects of the verbs in vv. 34–39 are sometimes third masculine singular, then again third masculine plural. The latter refers to Israel. The former could also refer to Israel viewed as a single unit, or it could allude to Joshua, Israel's captain.

12. Debir's exact location is still a matter of dispute; see E. G. Kraeling, *The Rand McNally Bible Atlas*, p. 146. Many accept W. F. Albright's identification with Tell Beit Mirsim; cf. *AOTS*, pp. 207–220. This is denied in W. H. Gispen *et al.*, eds., *Bijbelse Encyclopedie*, p. 224. J. Simons, *GTT*, p. 149 regards the location at Tell Beit Mirsim "far from certain."

13. The LXX does not have the reference to Libnah and its king.

Of the four parts of the country mentioned in v. 40, namely *the hill country, and the southland, and the lowland, and the slopes*, two had also been mentioned in 9:1–2: the hill country and the lowland. The addition of the southland at this point is obvious since this is the conclusion of the southern campaign. What is meant by *the slopes* is not entirely certain. On the basis of 12:8 it would appear that these are the slopes going down toward the lowland (the Shephelah) in the west. Another view is that these are the slopes that descend from the Judean mountain region toward the Dead Sea in the east.

As appears from other parts of the book (11:22; 13:2–3; 15:63), the conquest of this territory and of the cities in it was not final in all respects. Nevertheless the author of this section is at pains to draw a provisional conclusion which indicates that enough had been accomplished to pause and reflect on the very substantial progress that had been made toward subjugation of the land. Once again there is a reference to the curse (*ḥerem*) that was applied to the inhabitants of the region.[1] This had been done in accordance with the commandment of *the Lord, the God of Israel* (see 8:30 for this solemn designation of Israel's God; for the command referred to, cf. Deut. 7:1–4; 20:16–18).[2] The Israelites were not to become involved with the Canaanite population lest they be corrupted by them, religiously and morally. Later history proved how real such contamination would be.

Verse 41 mentions the extreme boundaries of the region conquered. This makes the claim of v. 40 more concrete and also agrees with ancient custom.[3]

The southernmost point mentioned is *Kadesh-barnea*, located in

---

1. The expression in v. 40 is *kol-hannᵉšāmâ* (lit. "all the breath," i.e., breathing things) in distinction from *kol-hannepeš* used in vv. 28–39.
2. J. Calvin, *Commentaries on the Book of Joshua*, remarks: "Here the divine authority is again interspersed in order completely to acquit Joshua of any charge of cruelty"; p. 163. The heavenly tribunal, according to Calvin, must not in the least be subjected to human laws. Reflecting on the death of women and infants Calvin observes that we ourselves, upon due examination, find things worthy of a hundred deaths. "Why, then, should the Lord not perceive just ground for one death in any infant which has only passed from its mother's womb?" (p. 164).
3. See Y. Aharoni, *The Land of the Bible*, p. 77. In ancient treaty documents borders were fixed according to the four points of the compass in two ways. The first is the fixing of terminal points (cf. 13:26; Exod. 23:31; 2 Sam. 24:2; cf. Josh. 11:17; 12:7). The second method involves the recording in sequence of points along the border. It is used in the Bible in only two contexts: the ideal boundaries of the promised land (Num. 34:1–12) and the actual territorial allotments (Josh. 15:1–12; 16:1–9; 17:7–9; 18:12–20; 19:10–14, 26–30, 33–34).

the wilderness of Zin (cf. Num. 20:1; cf. 13:26). In Josh. 15:3 it is part of the southern boundary of Judah. The line is then drawn northward to *Gaza* (see 13:3 and commentary). *The whole region of Goshen as far as Gibeon* is the broad intermediate zone designated as a border region between the hill country and the Negeb.[4] The name *Goshen*, which also occurs in 11:16, is not to be confused with the Goshen in Egypt. *Gibeon* is meant to designate a northern limit of the territory described here.

In his concluding comments the narrator stresses first that all this happened *in one stroke*, i.e., in one campaign.[5] Secondly, he again emphasizes the divine assistance Joshua and Israel received. This had been particularly evident in the battle of Gibeon (vv. 8, 10–11, 14), but it apparently was true of the entire southern expedition (see also v. 25; cf. 1:5).

All in all, the summary at the end of this chapter may indicate that more campaign activity took place than is actually recorded in the preceding verses. Whatever the case, the events recorded in ch. 10 are a significant step toward the complete subjugation of the land of Canaan.

43 The information about Joshua's return to Gilgal where the camp was, is repeated here (see v. 15 and commentary).

K. NORTH CANAAN DELIVERED INTO ISRAEL'S HANDS (11:1–15)

1 *When Jabin the king of Hazor heard of this, he sent messengers to Jobab the king of Madon, and to the king of Shimron, and to the king of Achshaph,*

2 *and to the kings in the north in the mountain district, in the valley south of Chinneroth, and in the lowland, and in Naphoth-dor on the west,*

3 *to the Canaanites in the east and west, the Amorites, the Hittites, the Perizzites, and the Jebusites in the hill country, and the Hivites under Hermon, in the region of Mizpah.*

4 *They marched out with all their troops, a huge army, in number like the sand that is on the seashore, and a great many horses and chariots.*

---

4. So Aharoni, *op. cit.*, p. 38. KD, p. 118, however, state that it "defines the extent from south to north on the eastern side." J. Simons, *GTT*, p. 273, also looks for a location "in the south or south-east."

5. This does not prevent the campaign from having taken a considerable time; see 11:18.

5 *All these kings met at an agreed place, and came to set up camp unitedly at the waters of Merom, to fight against Israel.*

6 *Then the Lord said to Joshua: "Do not fear before them, for tomorrow at this time I will be he who will hand all of them over to Israel as dead men. Then you can hamstring their horses and burn their chariots with fire."*

7 *So Joshua with all his warriors came suddenly upon them by the waters of Merom and fell on them.*

8 *And the Lord gave them into the power of Israel, who struck and pursued them as far as Great Sidon and Misrephoth-maim and eastward to the valley of Mizpah. They struck them till they left none that could escape.*

9 *Joshua treated them as the Lord had said to him: he hamstrung their horses and burned their chariots.*

10 *At that same time Joshua turned back and took Hazor and struck its king with the sword. (Hazor was formerly the head of all those kingdoms.)*

11 *And they struck all that lived therein with the edge of the sword, applying the curse to them. Nothing that had breath was left over, and he burned Hazor with fire.*

12 *And all the cities of these kings and all the kings themselves Joshua took, and he struck them with the edge of the sword; he applied the curse to them as the Lord had given orders to his servant Moses.*

13 *However, the cities that stood on their mounds Israel did not burn, with the exception of Hazor alone; that did Joshua burn.*

14 *And all the booty of these cities and the cattle the Israelites took as spoil for themselves. But they struck all the people with the edge of the sword until they had destroyed them. They left nothing that breathed.*

15 *As the Lord commanded his servant Moses so Moses commanded Joshua, and so Joshua acted. He left nothing undone of all that the Lord had commanded Moses.*

The account of the conquest of Palestine by Israel under Joshua's military leadership is brought to a conclusion with the events reported in this chapter. Ch. 9 opens with a reference to the determination of Canaan's kings to offer united resistance against the Israelite onslaught. Ch. 10 presents the southern phase of this Canaanite coalition war. The present chapter depicts Israel's military exploits in the north (vv. 1–15) and is concluded by a more general summary of the Conquest (vv. 16–23).

Both formally and materially a close parallel exists between 11:1–9 and 10:1–27.[1] In both instances a coalition seeks to thwart the Israelite

---

1. Cf. C. Steuernagel, *Das Buch Josua*, p. 250.

invasion. Both accounts also speak of the divine help experienced during Israel's battle with the enemy (e.g., v. 8), although this element is far more prominent in the earlier account. Each passage includes first a decisive battle, followed by further military activity that was meant to establish a more permanent foothold in this part of the country. Each account speaks of a single main instigator of the coalition: the king of Jerusalem in ch. 10, and the king of Hazor in ch. 11.

1 The opening words of this chapter are identical to those of chs. 9–10 (Heb. *wayyᵉhî kishmōᶜᵃ*, lit. "when (so and so) heard"). In this instance it is *Jabin the king of Hazor* who hears *this*, i.e., the success of Joshua's military operations in the south.[2] The city of Hazor[3] was an important center in the north of Palestine, situated on the "way of the sea," which ran from Egypt across Megiddo to Qatna in the north. In v. 10 it is called "the head of all these kingdoms" (see also Judg. 4:2, 23, 24, where King Jabin of that later period is called "king of Canaan"). Hazor has been identified with Khirbet Waqqâṣ (Tell el-Qedaḥ),[4] located to the south and west of Lake Huleh in northern Palestine. Its size was much larger than that of other prominent cities in Canaan. The site of ancient Hazor is composed of two elements: (a) the tell proper, covering about 30 acres, and (b) a large rectangular enclosure to the north, about 175 acres in area. In comparison, the site of Megiddo measures less than 20 acres.[5]

Jabin, Hazor's king, is the one who heard of Joshua's successes and sought to form a coalition against him. Since the story of the battle of Barak and Deborah also refers to Jabin (Judg. 4), frequent attempts have been made to connect the two stories and to consider them as two versions of one event. Some scholars believe that the name Jabin does not originally belong in the Deborah story but only that of Sisera. Others think that the only battle which actually took place in the north was the one fought under Deborah, but that in the course of time the victory won under

2. Nothing is reported about a conquest of the central parts of Palestine. The biblical account does not aim at being exhaustive. See also 8:30–35 and commentary.
3. On the excavations at this city see Y. Yadin, "Hazor," in *AOTS*, pp. 245–263; cf. J. Gray, "Hazor," *VT* 16 (1966), pp. 26–52.
4. Hazor was excavated from 1955–58 and also in 1968–69; cf. Y. Yadin, "The Fifth Season of Excavations at Hazor, 1968–69," *BA* 23 (1969), pp. 50–71; see also Gray, *op. cit.*
5. Hazor is the only Palestinian city mentioned in the Mari tablets, archives from the Amorite city of Mari on the middle Euphrates, dating from the 18th century BC. The name also occurs in the Amarna tablets of the 14th century BC in an accusation by the king of Tyre against the king of Hazor; cf. Aharoni, *op. cit.*, p. 137.

her was actually ascribed to Joshua because of his prominence in Israel's traditions.[6] The biblical record, however, presents the two battles as two distinct events. The name Jabin may well have been a hereditary title adopted by successive kings of Hazor.[7] The city itself, though destroyed by Joshua, may have been rebuilt subsequently.[8] Its strategic location would have prompted such rebuilding.

Jabin sends *messengers to Jobab the king of Madon*. This city is probably to be identified with Qarn Ḥaṭṭīn (the "Horns of Hattin"), west of Tiberias. A strong city was located there at one time, especially in the Late Bronze Age. The following two cities, the kings of which received messengers from Jabin, are mentioned by name, but their kings are not identified. The cities are *Shimron*[9] and *Achshaph*.[10]

2 The narrator now begins to be less specific.[11] Having mentioned

6. Still another version is that of Aharoni, *ibid.*, p. 203, who would put both stories at a later time. But R. de Vaux, *Early History*, pp. 659f., and Yadin, "Hazor and the Battle of Joshua," *BAR* 2 (1976), pp. 3ff., oppose Aharoni's views on archaeological grounds.

7. See also A. E. Cundall, *Judges*, p. 81. Various kings of Damascus bore the name of Ben-hadad at a later time.

8. Hazor's archaeological record as fixed by the excavators indicates that it was destroyed for the last time in the second part of the 13th century, never to be rebuilt. The scholars who attempt to shift the description of ch. 11 to the time of Deborah must place her well into the 13th century, a rather impossible date if one adopts the supposition of the "late" date of the Exodus. In general, caution is urged in accepting archaeological conclusions regarding possible dates of destruction. See also H. H. Grosheide, "Hasor," *Gereformeerd Weekblad* 31 (1975–76), pp. 307, 315, 323; 32 (1976–77), pp. 3f. The archaeologist is the one who draws the conclusions, and the connections he sees may not always be explicit. The record of excavations is as yet very fragmentary. The Holy Land has yielded relatively few written documents. Moreover, it is a great temptation to lay a connection between the Bible and a given archaeological find, and to do so without sufficient warrant from the available facts.

9. Called Shimron-meron in 12:20; perhaps Marun, on the road from Tyre to Dan.

10. This city's name occurs several times in extrabiblical documents, e.g., the Egyptian Papyrus Anastasi I, 13th century BC (cf. *ANET*, p. 477), the Amarna tablets, and the Execration Texts (cf. Aharoni, *op. cit.*, pp. 103, 133). E. G. Kraeling, *The Rand McNally Bible Atlas*, p. 139, assumes that it is the same city as that mentioned in 19:25, located in the plain of Acre. A probable site appears to be Tell Berweh at the foot of the hills and commanding a road coming down from near Safed. It has also been identified with Tell Harbaj and with Tell Keisân. See also *GTT*, pp. 189ff.; and M. Weippert, *The Settlement of the Israelite Tribes in Palestine*, pp. 35f.

11. Some have alleged that this description has undergone a corruption and can be restored by means of the LXX; e.g., *GTT*, p. 274. The present commentary, however, attempts to maintain the MT and to give it a reasonable sense.

the rulers of some of the key points on the commercial highways in northern Palestine, he now refers more broadly to several regions to the north, south, and west. He mentions *the kings in the north in the mountain district* and *in the valley south of Chinneroth*. The valley mentioned is the deep rift along which the Jordan flows. Chinneroth was probably situated near the Sea of Chinnereth, the Sea of Galilee (cf. 12:3; 19:35). The *lowland* (Heb. $\check{s}^e p\bar{e}l\hat{a}$) is the area between the Judean mountain country and the seacoast to the west. The narrator draws a rather wide circle at this point.[12] *Naphoth-dor*, also rendered "hills of Dor," is puzzling. Dor lies on the Mediterranean coast and was an ancient port and trade center. The word "naphoth" is usually connected with a Hebrew root meaning "to be high," hence "hills of," but there are no hills near Dor. Perhaps the extension of Mount Carmel in this direction has given rise to the idea of elevation.[13]

3 Apparently the northern coalition must be seen as a last comprehensive effort on the part of the inhabitants of Canaan to undo the onslaught of Israel's armies under Joshua. This is why the narrative at this point enumerates once more (see also 3:10; cf. 9:1) the tribes of Canaan who participate in the coalition headed by Hazor's king. (For the possible identity of the tribes enumerated see 3:10 and commentary.) The enumeration differs from other similar ones in that at certain points geographical determinants are given. For *Canaanites in the east and west* see Num. 13:29; Isa. 23:11. For the *Amorites* cf. 5:1; Num. 13:29; Deut. 3:9. The *Hivites* are assigned a place at the foot of Mount Hermon, the highest mountain in the region of northern Palestine. This is called *the region of Mizpah* (or valley of Mizpah, v. 8). The name Mizpah, from the Hebrew root *sph*, "to look out," was used for several localities of Palestine (see Judg. 10:17; 20:1). At this point the region of Mizpah must be regarded as a parallel designation for the boundary of the Israelite occupation of Mount Hermon.[14] The occurrence of *Jebusites* in this northern region is surprising. They are usually associated with the city later called Jerusalem, in the southern region. Their mention may result from the same attempt to represent the coalition as being very comprehensive (as noted in v. 2 above). Much of ancient history remains obscure. The biblical record at this point may well have preserved an isolated reference that represents a historical fact no longer known from other sources.

---

12. A. Gelin, *Josué*, p. 75, suggests two other possible identifications for the lowland, viz. a region near modern Haifa, or the valley of Esdraelon. This would make the total region more limited.
13. Thus *idem*.
14. See Aharoni, *op. cit.*, p. 217.

4 This verse contains a vivid description of the powerful threat posed to Israel by the amassed Canaanite forces: *all their troops, a huge army, in number like the sand that is on the seashore*. This probably serves to impress the reader with the seemingly impossible situation from which the Lord, the God of Israel, will presently rescue his people. An additional factor is the use by the Canaanite forces of *a great many horses and chariots*. From about 1500 BC, chariotry had become the essential, and at times the principal, arm of the military forces in the Near East.[15] Each little Canaanite state had its chariots and charioteers. These latter were troops in chariots, not mounted cavalry, which were a phenomenon of a much later period, and in some countries such as Egypt were never a prominent feature of warfare. By contrast, Israel's king was not to multiply horses (Deut. 17:16). The messianic king of the future (Zech. 9:9) will be seated on an ass, implying his peaceful nature, and not on a horse. At times in Hebrew history, the use of chariots and horses by its enemies proved to be a great obstacle to Israel (cf. 17:16–18; Judg. 1:19; 4:13). In its better moments, and under the influence of divine inspiration, Israel knew that reliance on chariots and horses was vain (see Ps. 20:8 [Eng. 7]).

5 The purpose of this verse is to show the deliberateness and united nature of the Canaanite attempts at resistance. The kings *met at an agreed place*.[16] A coalition of this sort required careful advance planning. Naturally there is a common point where camp is set up. This is said to be *at the waters of Merom*. Long assumed to be Lake Semechonitis, these waters are now considered to have been near Meron (another form of Merom; see 12:20), to be identified with the city Meiron, which lies west-northwest of modern Safed.[17]

6–9 The description of the actual encounter between Israel and the Canaanites is brief and lacking in specific detail. It begins with the customary assurance on the Lord's part[18] that he will *hand over*[19] the enemy into Israel's power. For this reason Joshua is urged not to fear, an element also found in earlier accounts (1:9b; 8:1; 10:8, 25). Only one day will elapse (*tomorrow*) before the complete victory over the enemy. Taking

---

15. See de Vaux, *Ancient Israel*, p. 222.

16. Heb. *wāʿaḏ* appears to imply a previously agreed-upon place; cf. Gelin, *op. cit.*, p. 75: "tous ces rois fixèrent un lieu de rassemblement." Other translations are less specific.

17. Merom is known from 2nd millennium Egyptian sources as well as from Tiglath-pileser III's account of his Galilee expedition; cf. *ANET*, p. 283; and Aharoni, *op. cit.*, p. 205.

18. On possible "holy war" teminology, see 10:9–10 and commentary.

19. The Hebrew is quite specific: "It will be I who will give." On the "giving" of the land, see also 1:2 and commentary.

this chronological indication literally[20] we are led to assume that Joshua, whose camp had been in Gilgal (see 10:43), had already moved northward and was now in the general vicinity of the new field of battle. Since the taking of cities such as Taanach and Megiddo, both in the northern part of the central region, is presupposed in the lists furnished in 12:21, a number of other military operations performed by Joshua must have been passed over in silence.

A specific injunction is given with respect to the horses, which must be hamstrung, and the chariots, which are to be burned. In view of what was said above concerning the prohibition of the use of horses, the command to hamstring the horses in order to render them unusable for further combat can be easily understood.[21] This rule was also applied later (2 Sam. 8:4; but not in 1 K. 10:26). The burning of the chariots serves a similar purpose. Israel is to rely on the Lord, although the more common forms of combat are not thereby ruled out (see also v. 7; cf. 10:9).

Joshua proceeds to the attack, swiftly and suddenly. The area of combat, the district of the waters of Merom, is about 4000 feet above sea level, therefore an area in which chariots would find no room for maneuvering.[22] The author, however, is concerned chiefly to stress the divine assistance rendered to Israel during the combat. *The Lord*, so he states, *gave them into the power of Israel* (see v. 6 and related passages). The enemy's line of retreat after having been beaten extends toward *Great Sidon and Misrephoth-maim*. This was the westward line of withdrawal. Sidon lay on the Phoenician coast at Ṣaidā.[23] Misrephoth-maim (lit. "Misrephoth of the waters") is possibly 'Ain Mesherîfeh, south of the so-called Ladder of Tyre. Eastward the pursuit of the Canaanite forces extended as far as *the valley of Mizpah* (v. 3).

20. S. J. De Vries, "Temporal Terms as Structural Elements in the Holy-War Tradition," *VT* 25 (1975), p. 81, argues that phrases such as "tomorrow" (see also 3:5; Exod. 10:4) give "the entire event a theological dimension." Were it not for such a phrase, "all that is recounted would seem to occur on the horizontal plane." With some reservations about DeVries' terminology "secular-theological," the present writer appreciates the concern to read this story as part of the special history which Joshua purports to be throughout.
21. This "theocratic" motivation should be given preference to the suggestion that Israel was as yet unaccustomed to the use of horses and chariots and hence was told to render them inoperable. This second consideration need not have been absent from the Lord's command. However, one should remember that Israel's historiography is "prophetical" in character.
22. For further details of the area of combat cf. J. Gray, *op. cit.*, pp. 49f.
23. This city is also referred to in the Ras Shamra literature, in the Papyrus Anastasi (a 13th century Egyptian document), and in the Egyptian Wen Amon story (11th century). Asher's boundary extended as far as Sidon (19:28). "Great Sidon" may refer to the city with its subordinate territories.

The description of the enemy rout resembles that of 10:28–43. Emphasis is placed on the completeness of the victory. As seen earlier, this need not preclude the survival of some of the enemy forces, but by and large the enemy resistance must be judged to have been broken. From v. 11 it becomes clear that the curse (*herem*) was also applied to these northern enemies. At the conclusion of this brief description the author reports that Joshua carried out the divine command with respect to the horses and chariots.[24] His faithfulness in executing the Lord's command is also stressed elsewhere in the account of the Conquest (see 10:40; 11:15 [mentioned twice]).

10–15 This section closely parallels 10:28–38, just as vv. 16–20 parallel 10:40–42. Having spoken of the complete rout of the forces of the Canaanite kings, the author now gives certain details concerning Joshua's further activities. The capture of Hazor is mentioned first. The words rendered *Joshua turned back and took Hazor* may also be read: "Joshua again went into action and took Hazor." (For the significance of Hazor, see v. 1 and commentary.) The expression *Hazor was formerly the head of all those kingdoms* means that the writer is looking back to a time already past when he records the event, and noting the city's prominence at the time when Joshua conquered it.[25] Thus the account stresses the great significance of Hazor's capture, and implicitly of the whole northern campaign which is meant as the concluding part of the conquest of Canaan.

Not only is Hazor's king put to death with the sword (v. 10), but the curse (*herem*) is also applied to all that lived in the city (v. 11; cf. 6:17). There were various degrees of the curse. Jericho was placed under a complete curse (6:21), which included killing the cattle. In the case of Ai, however, the Israelites could keep the cattle (8:2, 27). As is clear from v. 14, Joshua treated the cities other than Hazor less severely than Hazor itself. Thus this great northern city was made into an example. Like Jericho and Ai it was burned, but no curse was put upon one who would rebuild it, as had been done in the pronouncement upon Jericho (6:26).

24. H. Freedman, *Joshua*, p. 64, states that the practice of hamstringing horses "does not seem to have been unusual, its purpose being to make them unfit as warhorses and employable only for domestic occupations" (cf. Gen. 49:6). Others hold that the horses were thus doomed to a slow and painful death, probably to teach Israel and its enemies that a horse is a vain thing for safety (Ps. 33:17).
25. This opinion agrees with that of Yadin, *AOTS*, p. 261, and differs from that of Aharoni, *op. cit.*, p. 207; see also n. 6 above. Aharoni holds that these words refer to a period in Hazor's history which had already come to an end by the time the events recorded here took place, but it is unlikely that the author would give such prominence to the capture of a city, the decline of which had occurred some time previously. See also J. A. Soggin, *Joshua*, p. 136, about the relationship between the battle of Deborah (Judg. 4–5) and the battle described here.

Just as he did in 10:40, so here also the author links the application of the curse to an explicit command given by the Lord through *his servant Moses* (vv. 12, 15). (About Moses' significance for the future destruction of Canaan see also 9:24; cf. 1:3, 5, 7.[26] About Moses' designation as *servant* of the Lord see 1:1 and commentary.) The link between Canaan's destruction and the Lord's design will be made even more explicit in v. 20.

The burning of Hazor was an exception. Other cities *that stood on their mounds*[27] were not burned[28] (v. 13). This seems to mean, among other things, that the Israelites took possession of the other cities and lived in them. Such a procedure would bear out the truth of the promise made in Deut. 6:10, where Israel is said to be living in cities they had not built.[29] The booty and the cattle of these cities were kept by the Israelites (v. 14); cf. Deut. 3:7.

Verse 15 concludes with another reference to the exemplary faithfulness with which Joshua carried out the Lord's commands as given originally to Moses (see v. 12).

L. SUMMARY CONCERNING THE CONQUEST: GOD'S HAND (11:16–23)

16 *So Joshua took this whole land, the hill country, the whole southland, the whole land of Goshen, the lowland, the valley, and the hill country of Israel with its lowland,*

17 *from Mount Halak which rises toward Seir, as far as Baal-gad in the valley of Lebanon at the foot of Mount Hermon. All their kings he seized, struck them down, and put them to death.*

18 *For a long time Joshua made war with all these kings.*

19 *Not a city was there which made peace with the Israelites, except the Hivites who lived at Gibeon. They took everything in battle.*

26. Cf. G. J. Wenham, *JBL* 90 (1971), pp. 145f. Some parallels between Moses and Joshua were noted earlier (5:15). In this and later chapters note the following: just as God had hardened Pharaoh's heart, so he hardens that of Joshua's enemies (11:20); 12:1–6 lists Moses' victories; 12:7–24 lists those of Joshua. The same is true for the allotments; compare 13:8–32 with 14:1ff.

27. Heb. *tel*, also rendered "ruins," "tells" (Gelin), "raised sites" (NAB). KB and Noth render the word with *Schutthügel*, "mound," "ruin heap."

28. For the significance of this in the identification of cities showing destruction by burning, cf. O. Tufnell, *AOTS*, p. 302. Not all interpreters agree as to the scope of this statement. Did it include all of Canaan's cities, or only those of the north? Probably the former is accurate.

29. See also the worthwhile comments by C. Vonk, *Inleiding op de Profeten: Jozua*, pp. 176f. Israel could live in Canaan's cities. Ascetic abstinence from that which unbelievers have produced and made is not called for, provided there is abstinence from idolatrous practice.

20 *For the Lord had ordained that with a stubborn heart they should go out to battle with the Israelites, so that they could strike them with the curse without mercy, and destroy them, as the Lord commanded Moses.*

21 *And Joshua came at that time and wiped out the Anakim from the hill country, from Hebron, from Debir, from Anab, from the whole hill country of Judah, and from the whole hill country of Israel. Joshua applied the curse to them and to their cities.*

22 *No Anakim were left in the land of the Israelites; only in Gaza, in Gath, and in Ashdod did some remain.*

23 *Joshua took the whole country, according to everything the Lord had spoken to Moses, and Joshua gave it to Israel as an inheritance according to their divisions by tribes. And the country had rest from war.*

The author now comes to a provisional conclusion to his narrative of the Conquest. Though at later points (e.g., 13:1; 15:63; 16:10) he will point to the incompleteness of the Conquest, at this stage he emphasizes that, from a certain viewpoint, one could say that the whole land was taken. Having begun his account with a reference to the promise made to the patriarchs (1:3, 6), the narrator is fully justified in presenting this glowing summary. Compared to those early times, when Abraham did not possess more than just a grave in Canaan, it could indeed be said that the whole land was taken (see also 21:43–45). The viewpoint here is that of the "rest" which Israel has now obtained, a rest capable of being extended and deepened (see also 1:13 and commentary; cf. 2 Sam. 7:1). Note also Deut. 1:7, where the various parts of the promised land yet to be conquered are enumerated (cf. Josh. 12:8). These summary enumerations serve to stress that God's promises have been fulfilled (see Gen. 15:18–20).

16 Four of the regions mentioned here are also found in the enumeration of 10:40: the *hill country* (of Judah), the *southland* (Negeb), the *lowland* (Shephelah), and *Goshen*. On the latter's location see 10:41. The *valley* is mentioned in v. 2. The *hill country of Israel*[1] designates the central mountain region. It, too, had its corresponding *lowland*(s),[2] the area extending toward the Mediterranean shore. The enumeration does not refer explicitly to the north country just conquered. Perhaps the author did not

1. That this difference between the two hill countries (Judah and Israel) does not mean a late date for the final redaction of the book of Joshua is extensively argued in KD, pp. 124f., n. 1.
2. This lowland is "more narrow and especially less characteristic as an intermediate area than the Judaean Shephelah" (*GTT*, p. 104). The author of Joshua does not use geographically precise language. His purpose is to present general descriptions.

deem this necessary since the account had just been given. It may also be that he meant the hill country of Israel to include the Galilee district.

17a The total extent of the country conquered is given in terms of a southern and a northern point. The southern point is formed by *Mount Halak which rises toward Seir*. In 10:41 the southern outpost of the country is Kadesh-barnea, which lay further west than Mount Halak.[3] This mountain is probably modern Jebel Halâq, west of the Ascent of Akrabbim. It is said to rise *toward Seir*,[4] which is to say toward the country of Edom on the other side of the Arabah. This may mean that its broad side faced in that direction. Actually Mount Halak was low compared to the Edomite mountain crags.[5]

The northern point mentioned[6] is *Baal-gad in the valley of Lebanon* (cf. 12:7; 13:5). The *valley* is that between the Lebanon and Anti-Lebanon. The latter terminates in the massif of Mount Hermon, at whose foot Baal-gad was located. Identification with Hasbeiyah or with Tell Haus has been suggested.[7]

17b–18 Verses 17b–18 contain one of the few indications about the approximate time it took Joshua to subjugate Canaan. After reporting that Joshua seized and put to death the kings of Canaan, the author states that *for a long time Joshua made war with all these kings* (v. 18). This shows that the rather enthusiastic reports about the Conquest given in the preceding chapters must be seen in the light of an extended campaign. The final redaction of the book of Joshua, whether by the author, or by a later hand,[8] does not see a conflict between the two. What should be kept in mind is the peculiar nature of Hebrew "prophetical" historiography (see introduction to the commentary).

How much time the subjugation of Palestine by Joshua and his forces actually took cannot be stated precisely. With an appeal to 14:12,

---

3. Lit. "smooth," "bald."
4. The word Seir defines a mountain (Gen. 14:6), a land (Gen. 32:3; 36:9; Num. 24:18), and a people (Ezek. 25:8) in the general area of Edom (see J. A. Thompson, "Seir," *NBD*, p. 1157). According to *GTT*, p. 257, it included regions both west and east of the Arabah.
5. So E. G. Kraeling, *The Rand McNally Bible Atlas*, p. 140.
6. The extent of the promised land again is given in the most generous terms (see also 1:4). Such descriptions were meant to be "programmatic" for later generations which, through covenant disobedience, might have lost possession of certain parts of the land thus described.
7. M. Noth, *Das Buch Josua*, suggests a possible identification with Baalbek.
8. There is no absolute need to think of a "later author," as does J. H. Kroeze, *Jozua*, p. 147, although this possibility may be entertained. As matters now stand, the two viewpoints appear compatible within the one book.

read in light of the thirty-eight years' wandering in the desert (Deut. 2:14), it has been suggested that the period of the Conquest was seven years. However, this cannot be certain.

The statement that Joshua *seized all their kings* and *put them to death* anticipates the rather triumphant enumeration in ch. 12 and is probably also meant as a fulfilment of God's promise in Deut. 7:24 (see also Josh. 1:5).

19–20 Just as v. 18 affords a look behind the scenes in terms of the actual course of events, so vv. 19–20 afford another perspective, that of God's design and purpose. The conquest of Canaan must be viewed as the working out of this intent (cf. also Gen. 15:16; Deut. 9:4). Still, the example of what *the Hivites who lived at Gibeon* did also points to human responsibility within history (cf. 9:1–2; 10:1–5; 11:1–5). Of course, this is not necessarily the primary purpose of the reference to Gibeon. The desire of the Gibeonites to make a treaty is presented as an exception in order to show the need for Israel to take *everything in battle* (v. 19b). Nevertheless, Gibeon's attitude is contrasted with that of the other Canaanite cities. The latter had shown *a stubborn heart* (v. 20).

The narrator is not concerned to analyze the motives that may have persuaded these Canaanites to offer resistance, although he is fully aware that it was not blind fate but active planning that led to the anti-Israelite coalitions of chs. 10–11. Rather, he affords here a glimpse behind the scenes.[9] The stubborn heart is due to God's hardening[10] process. This hardening had for its ultimate purpose the destruction of the Canaanites, who, in the light of Gen. 15:16, had become increasingly iniquitous during the period of Israel's sojourn in Egypt and the trek through the desert.

Thus the destruction of the Canaanites is due to God's hardening them,[11] but this in no way exonerates the Canaanites. The other way was

9. Hebrew historiography does so sparingly (but cf. 2 Sam. 17:14; 1 K. 12:15; 2 Sam. 24:1; 1 Chr. 21:1). Akin to this way of looking at history is the thought of Isa. 6:10, often quoted in the NT (cf. Rom. 1:24; 2 Thess. 2:11). God gives up to their own wickedness those who have shown that they prefer the lie to the truth. Nevertheless, the sovereignty and majesty of the divine counsel is not limited by the will of man.

10. Verse 20a can be rendered more literally: "For it was the Lord's doing to harden their hearts. . . ." On the concept of "hardening" see Exod. 4:21 and related passages. The Hebrew uses the Piel of *ḥāzaq*, which can also be used intransitively, in the Qal (Exod. 7:13, 22).

11. The biblical view of good and evil is monistic. Good and evil are not two eternally opposing principles. Ultimately evil functions under God's dominion (compare 2 Sam. 24:1 with 1 Chr. 21:1), but God is not the author of sin; cf. W. Eichrodt, *The Theology of the OT* I, p. 286.

open, as is shown by what the Gibeonites did. Ultimately, however, the whole course of events serves to carry out the command to Moses that Israel was to show no mercy to its Canaanite foes (Deut. 20:16), in order to safeguard Israel against Canaanite idolatry (Deut. 7:2–4; 12:1–4).[12] A merely human way of measuring God's actions in history proves inadequate in understanding a passage such as this.[13] Nevertheless, it would be improper to eliminate this presentation of God or to modify it in any way.

21–22 These verses disclose Joshua's success in wiping out *the Anakim*, those dreaded early inhabitants of Canaan, whose presence in Canaan caused Israel to rebel in the desert more than forty years earlier (Num. 13:28; 32:33). The account of their elimination forms a fitting conclusion to the story of the Conquest. This is probably why it occurs at this point (see also p. 15). The time element is left rather indefinite: *Joshua came at that time*. Similar time designations are found in 5:2; 11:10. These events may have taken place during the "long time" of which v. 18 speaks. From 10:36–39 it is known that two of the cities inhabited by Anakim, *Hebron* and *Debir*, were taken in the southern campaign. Did Joshua have this encounter with the Anakim at that time? The author is not concerned to give precise information.

A further factor touching on the chronology of events is the information contained in 14:13–15; 15:13–19; Judg. 1:9–15. These passages mention Hebron and Debir and speak of the Anakim. In one of them Caleb is credited with having driven out the three sons of Anak from Hebron. In the present passage Joshua is said to have wiped them out so that none remained in the land of the Israelites except in some of the cities of the Philistines. Biblical historiography does not always give clear-cut answers to problems of this sort, for its purpose is not to present a mere chronicle of events. One cannot always reconstruct the exact course of events from the biblical record.[14] This does not mean that questions of historical sequence and historical detail cease to be important, because biblical events

12. G. von Rad, *OT Theology* I, p. 74n., calls this the more "didactic" explanation of Canaan's destruction as compared with the relatively "older" view of the hardening of the Canaanites, but this is a value judgment stemming from a certain view of the history of religions.
13. Cf. K. Gutbrod, *Das Buch vom Lande Gottes*, p. 98; see Rom. 9:14ff.; Isa. 45:9.
14. Some suppose that two mutually independent traditions are permitted to stand unreconciled side by side, but this is unlikely. Perhaps Joshua's thorough destruction of these cities was followed by later reconstruction so that Caleb had to repeat the work done earlier. It is also possible that Caleb's exploits, being done under Joshua's overall leadership, were put to Joshua's account.

always occur in history. Their historicity is thus important for the understanding of the biblical message. When clarity of detail is lacking, however,
the interpreter must be content to look at the events reported within their
given literary context in order to ascertain the author's purpose.

The *Anakim*[15] which were wiped out by Joshua belonged to Canaan's oldest inhabitants. (For their fear-inspiring character cf. also Deut.
1:28; 9:2). Their stature and formidable nature were almost proverbial, for
they were taken as a standard for comparison to stress the size of such
other peoples as the Emim (Deut. 2:10) and the Rephaim (Deut. 2:21).[16]
The cities and regions from which Joshua expelled them were *Hebron*,
Debir, *Anab*, the *whole hill country of Judah*, and *the whole hill country
of Israel*.[17] (For the location of Hebron and Debir see 10:36, 38.) Anab
has been identified with a site 14 miles from Hebron (cf. 15:50), Khirbet
'Anâb.

The wiping out of the Anakim also involved the application of the
"curse" (*ḥerem*) to them (see 6:17). Thus the most dreaded inhabitants
of Canaan suffered the fate that God had reserved for them. The author
also knows of some surviving remnants, however. Hence his concern to
paint a picture of a completed Conquest does not lead him to gloss over
this point. Anakim were still to be found *in Gaza, in Gath, and in Ashdod*.
Throughout most of OT history these cities belonged to the Philistines.
Gaza was at least temporarily in Israelite hands (Judg. 1:18; cf. also Josh.
13:3; Judg. 3:3). However, *the land of the Israelites* itself was rid of the
Anakim.

23 Keeping in mind the purpose of this concluding summary (see
above), one may understand how the author can truly say that *Joshua took
the whole country*. The enemy's chief resistance had been broken, though
much work remained to be done (13:1). For purposes beneficial to Israel,
the driving out of the Canaanites was meant to take a long time (see Exod.
23:29–30; Deut. 7:22; but cf. Judg. 2:20–23 for a different application of
this same thought).[18]

---

15. The name may mean "the long-necked ones." Arba was the "father" of Anak,
and Anak's three sons were Sheshai, Ahiman, and Talmai (15:13). The word
"father" may indicate an ultimate ancestor.
16. See T. C. Mitchell, "Anak, Anakim," *NBD*, pp. 34f. On the Rephaim see
also J. C. de Moor, "Rapi'ūma-Rephaim," *ZAW* 88 (1976), pp. 323–345.
17. On the distinction between these two "hill countries" see v. 16 and note.
18. The completeness of the Conquest is stressed in 12:7–8; 21:43–45; 23:1, 4.
Its incompleteness appears from 13:2–6; 14:12; 17:12–18; 18:2–3; 23:5, 7, 12–
13. In 23:4–5 these two viewpoints, both equally legitimate depending on immediate context, occur side by side.

Again the author is concerned to stress the faithful execution on Joshua's part of what the Lord had spoken to Moses (see also vv. 15, 20). This is meant to endorse Joshua's leadership. It also indicates that the taking of the land must be seen as the fulfilment of the divine word spoken to Moses.

The last part of the verse anticipates what follows in chs. 13–19. It speaks of the giving of the land *to Israel as an inheritance according to their divisions by tribes. Inheritance* is a theologically significant word (see 1:6). The same is true of the statement that *the country had rest*[19] *from war*. These concluding sentences show the interpretative element in Israel's historiography. When Israel had completed the Conquest it thereby entered into its promised inheritance and enjoyed the rest which was the concomitant of inheritance.

M. GOD'S KINGSHIP VICTORIOUS OVER CANAAN'S KINGS (12:1–24)

1. EAST OF THE JORDAN (12:1–6)

1 *Now these are the kings of the land whom the Israelites defeated and of whose land they took possession on the other side of the Jordan in the east, from the Arnon Valley to Mount Hermon, with the whole valley, eastward:*
2 *Sihon king of the Amorites who lived at Heshbon and who ruled from Aroer which lies on the edge of the Arnon Valley, and over the center of the valley and over half of Gilead till the Jabbok Valley, the boundary of the Ammonites,*
3 *and over the valley to the Sea of Chinnereth eastward, and to the Sea of the Valley, the Salt Sea, eastward, toward Beth-jeshimoth, and southward to the foot of the slopes of Pisgah;*
4 *and the territory of Og king of Bashan, one of the remnant of the Rephaim, who lived at Ashtaroth and at Edrei*
5 *and ruled over Mount Hermon and Salecah and all Bashan to the boundary of the Geshurites and the Maacathites, and over half of Gilead to the boundary of Sihon king of Heshbon.*
6 *Moses, the servant of the Lord, and the Israelites defeated them. And Moses, the servant of the Lord, gave the land as a possession to the Reubenites, the Gadites, and the half tribe of Manasseh.*

---

19. Heb. *sāqaṭ*. The more common root to describe the "rest" of God's people in Canaan is *nûaḥ*, *mᵉnûḥâ*. The two are materially related in thought; see 5:31; 8:28.

The purpose of this chapter is obvious. Structurally it is closely related to 11:16–17, especially v. 17. By enumerating the kings conquered by Joshua and Israel, the writer gives eloquent testimony to the fact that Israel's enemies, who had banded together with hostile intent (11:19–20; cf. 9:1–2; 11:1–5), had been unable to stand against Israel and its God. Thus seen, this list is a song of praise to the Lord's honor. If Israel was to carry out its God-given task of being God's people in Canaan, it was necessary that those who could seduce it by their pagan practices should be eliminated from the land. Joshua was the man destined by God to carry out this program. He is not to be blamed for the severity with which he acted. Not only did he show exemplary faithfulness to the divine command, but he also remained true to his given word in the case of Rahab and the Gibeonites, and without partiality applied the curse to Achan, one of Israel's own.

The events recorded in the first part of Joshua form a prelude to a more final victory which God will win over the enemies of his cause. At that future time, God will purge the world of those who have refused to accept him as Lord and will give this purified world to his people as their inheritance forever (Ps. 37:9; Matt. 5:5).[1]

1 The chapter begins with a description of the kings defeated on the east side of the Jordan, perhaps because the author is concerned to draw a parallel between Moses and Joshua. It was Moses who had accomplished the conquest of the Transjordanian kings and had allotted their territory to two and a half of the tribes.[2] Another obvious reason for beginning with the Transjordanian kings is the writer's concern to stress the unity of all Israel (see 1:12–15 and commentary). Transjordan properly belongs to Israel, and the tribes living there are as much part of the nation as are those living in the west (see also ch. 22). Thus the emphasis is not only on the defeat of the kings but also on the possession which Israel takes of their territory (vv. 1, 6; cf. v. 7).

The southern boundary of the Transjordanian country occupied and possessed by Israel was *the Arnon Valley*.[3] This is as far as the kingdom

1. The eschatological dimension of the book of Joshua is stressed also by J. Bright, *The Authority of the OT*, p. 246; cf. also C. J. Goslinga, *Het Boek Jozua*, pp. 113f.
2. See also p. 193, n. 25.
3. The four great rivers in this eastern region are, from south to north, the Zered, the Arnon, the Jabbok, and the Yarmuk. These rivers flow at their upper courses near the border of the desert in a south-north direction, breaking suddenly to the west, and finally reaching the Jordan or the Dead Sea through deep gorges; cf. Y. Aharoni, *The Land of the Bible*, p. 34. The word rendered "valley" (Heb. *naḥal*) may also be rendered "wadi," "brook," "torrent."

of Sihon (v. 2) extended southward (Deut. 2:19). South of the Arnon was Moab's domain (Deut. 3:8, 16). To the east lay Ammon, which shared as a border with Israel the Jabbok in its upper course (Num. 21:24).[4] The northern limit was *Mount Hermon*[5] (see vv. 3, 17). This means that the northeast border is drawn rather more modestly than in 1:4, where the river Euphrates is mentioned. But at that point the Lord is speaking "programmatically," while here the actual extent of conquered lands is given. The eastern boundary of Transjordan was fluid, being formed by desert lands. Toward the west this area had the *Jordan* for its boundary.[6]

2 The story of *Sihon king of the Amorites*[7] *who lived at Heshbon* is found in Num. 21:21–35 (see also Deut. 2–3). Sihon lived in Heshbon,[8] a city he had taken from the Moabites (Num. 21:26). It was located to the east of the northern tip of the Dead Sea. Sihon *ruled from Aroer . . . till the Jabbok Valley.* Aroer was considered a traditional border city of Israelite Transjordan in later times (see Jer. 48:19). It overlooks the passage of the highway which runs through the Arnon Valley. Sihon also ruled over *the center of the valley*[9] and over *half of Gilead.* The term "Gilead"

---

4. At many points in this description are parallels to passages in Numbers (ch. 21) and Deuteronomy. For the latter see also P. C. Craigie, *Deuteronomy*.

5. The Hermon is a majestic mountain, rising to 9232 feet. Although outside Palestine proper it dominates the country as an immense landmark; see E. G. Kraeling, *The Rand McNally Bible Atlas*, p. 25.

6. For the geographical features of the Jordan Valley, see 1:2 and commentary. The Hebrew word translated "valley" is *ᵃrābâ*. In biblical times this term was used for the entire rift valley, which runs from the Sea of Tiberias to the Gulf of Aqabah. Here it is used in a more restricted sense for the Jordan Valley plus the deep rift in which the Dead Sea is located. This sea is called "Sea of the Valley," v. 3. For a general description of the area east of Jordan see N. Glueck, "Transjordan," in *AOTS*, pp. 428–453.

7. The victory over Sihon (and Og) is often recalled in Israel's sacred writing and song (2:10; 9:10; Deut. 31:4; Judg. 11:19–21; Neh. 9:22; Ps. 135:11; 136:19). A certain type of OT scholarship, the starting-point of which is not shared by the writer of this commentary, considers the story of Israel's defeat of these two kings to be a "deuteronomistic construction of history" (M. Noth, *Das Buch Josua*, 1953, p. 71). For other studies written along this line see J. Van Seters, *JBL* 91 (1972), pp. 182–197; cf. J. F. Bartlett, *VT* 20 (1970), pp. 257–277. Bartlett believes that the material of these two kings had a liturgical origin and that it was the "Deuteronomist" who linked Og of Bashan to Sihon, an Amorite.

8. Excavations at the supposed site of ancient Heshbon have been conducted in recent years, but these yielded no results pertaining to the period of the Conquest. It may be that Tell Ḥesbân is not the site of the biblical Heshbon; cf. K. A. Kitchen, *The Bible in Its World*, pp. 14, 88.

9. Hebrew lit. "From Aroer which (is) upon the lip of the valley of Arnon and the middle of the valley (brook)." Some translations supply the word "from"

is used loosely in the Bible.[10] In general, it is a mountain region both north and south of the river Jabbok, reaching altitudes of more than 3000 feet. Sihon's part lay south of the river. It extended *till the Jabbok Valley, the boundary of the Ammonites*.[11] The Jabbok ran through Gilead, dividing it into southern and northern parts, and it emptied in the Jordan at Adam (3:16). Its upper course, the part where it ran from south to north, comprised the border with Ammon (see Deut. 3:16–17).

3 In the Jordan Valley Sihon's domain extended farther north, beyond the Jabbok as far as *the Sea of Chinnereth* (the Sea of Galilee or Tiberias), but on the east side of the valley only. Southward, it extended toward *the Sea of the Valley, the Salt Sea*, again on the east side only. The words *toward Beth-jeshimoth* have also been rendered "the way of Beth-jeshimoth." This reading would indicate one of numerous roads, to the presence of which the OT bears witness. In this case it would be a continuation of the road which ran from Jericho and ascended from Beth-jeshimoth toward Heshbon.[12] Beth-jeshimoth was probably the modern Tell el-'Azeimeh near the northeastern shore of the Dead Sea. The southern border of Sihon's kingdom also consisted of *the foot of the slopes of Pisgah*.[13] Their general location was at the northeastern end of the Dead Sea (see 13:20; Deut. 3:17; 4:49). Moses was permitted to see the promised land from its heights (Deut. 34:1).

4–6 Now follows the description of Og's territory. (See above for the significance of Sihon and Og in Israel's sacred literature.[14]) Og is called the *king of Bashan*. Bashan is the northern part of Transjordan, situated mainly north of the Yarmuk River, although it is not clear whether this river was actually its border. Og was *one of the remnant of the Reph-*

---

before "the middle." Our translation makes "the middle" dependent on "ruled" (Heb. *môšēl*).

10. See Glueck, *op. cit.*, pp. 450–52.

11. Some interpreters, e.g., J. Simons, *GTT*, p. 120, consider this to be a reference not to the boundary of the Ammonites at that time but to the "original Ammonite realm," captured by Sihon from the Ammonites; n. 82. See also J. R. Bartlett, *op. cit.*, p. 260.

12. See Aharoni, *op. cit.*, p. 57. Heb. *derek* can mean "way," "road"; it can also mean "in the direction of," "toward."

13. Wherever *pisgâ* occurs in the Hebrew text it is accompanied by the definite article, showing that it is a common noun; see G. T. Manley, "Pisgah, Ashdoth Pisgah," *NBD*, p. 1000. A number of scholars have identified Pisgah with the mountain range of which Nebo was the summit; see Craigie, *op. cit.*, p. 123, n. 9.

14. Deut. 3:21–22 indicates that the defeat of these two kings was considered a promissory sign of the conquest of the land of Canaan west of the Jordan.

aim,[15] a prehistoric people which once inhabited Palestine. One of the places where Og is said to have lived (or ruled) is *Edrei*, a city located on one of the eastern tributaries of the Yarmuk. Perhaps Bashan's southern border was not far from the modern border between Syria and Jordan. This coincides with the Yarmuk in its lower course and follows its southern tributaries farther east. The other place where Og lived was *Ashtaroth* (Gen. 14:5: Ashteroth-karnaim),[16] situated east-northeast of the Sea of Galilee. Og's territory extended over *Mount Hermon* (see v. 1) and included *Salecah and all Bashan*. Salecah was a town in the extreme east of Bashan, southeast of Ashtaroth.

Og's territory ran to *the boundary of the Geshurites and the Maacathites* (v. 5). The land of Geshur lay to the northeast of the Sea of Galilee (Deut. 3:14). Maacah was in the same region, with Hermon to the north, Geshur in the south, Bashan to the east, and the wadi es-Hasbani (one of the tributaries of the Jordan) to the west (13:13). Corresponding to what is said about Sihon's territory in v. 2, that of Og is said to extend *over half of Gilead to the boundary of Sihon* (v. 5). The final verse of this pericope (v. 6) places emphasis on the distribution of the conquered territory to *the Reubenites, the Gadites, and the half tribe of Manasseh*. First, however, the author reiterates the fact that *Moses and the Israelites defeated* these kings of Transjordan. Twice in this verse Moses is referred to as *the servant of the Lord* (see 1:1), perhaps to emphasize the legitimacy of the claim that could be laid to these Transjordanian lands by the tribes mentioned. The actual distribution of Transjordan to the tribes is set forth more fully in 13:8-32, to provide a pendant to Joshua's distribution of the land to the remaining tribes.

2. WEST OF THE JORDAN (12:7-24)

7 *And these are the kings whom Joshua and the Israelites defeated on the other side of Jordan in the west, from Baal-gad in the valley of Lebanon to Mount Halak, which rises toward Seir, the land which Joshua gave to the tribes of Israel as a possession, according to their divisions,*

8 *in the hill country, in the lowland, in the valley, on the slopes, in the desert, and in the southland: the land of the Hittites, the Amorites, the Canaanites, the Perizzites, the Hivites, and the Jebusites:*

---

15. See J. C. de Moor, *ZAW* 88 (1976), pp. 323-345.

16. It is not completely certain whether these two Ashtaroths are the same. Simons, *GTT*, p. 124, calls the two "more probably distinct than identical." See also Bartlett, *op. cit.*, p. 265, n. 3. Ashtaroth may be the same as Beeshterah (21:27).

9 *the king of Jericho*	*one*
the king of Ai, beside Bethel	*one*
10 *the king of Jerusalem*	*one*
the king of Hebron	*one*
11 *the king of Jarmuth*	*one*
the king of Lachish	*one*
12 *the king of Eglon*	*one*
the king of Gezer	*one*
13 *the king of Debir*	*one*
the king of Geder	*one*
14 *the king of Hormah*	*one*
the king of Arad	*one*
15 *the king of Libnah*	*one*
the king of Adullam	*one*
16 *the king of Makkedah*	*one*
the king of Bethel	*one*
17 *the king of Tappuah*	*one*
the king of Hepher	*one*
18 *the king of Aphek*	*one*
the king of Lasharon	*one*
19 *the king of Madon*	*one*
the king of Hazor	*one*
20 *the king of Shimron-meron*	*one*
the king of Achshaph	*one*
21 *the king of Taanach*	*one*
the king of Megiddo	*one*
22 *the king of Kedesh*	*one*
the king of Jokneam in Carmel	*one*
23 *the king of Dor in Naphath-dor*	*one*
the king of Goiim in Galilee	*one*
24 *the king of Tirzah*	*one.*

Together thirty-one kings.

7–8 Verse 7a corresponds to vv. 1, 6. Just as Israel (v. 1) or Moses *and* Israel (v. 6) had defeated the kings in Transjordan, so *Joshua and the Israelites* defeated the kings *on the other side of Jordan*[1] *in the west*. The concern of this section is the same as that which precedes it. A final summary must be given of what Israel has accomplished under Joshua's leadership. That this is ultimately the Lord's leadership should have become clear to all who have read the first part of the book (see 1:3, 9; 2:24,

---

1. Sometimes used for Transjordan (1:14; 2:10; also with the addition "eastward," as in 1:15; 12:1); sometimes with reference to Cisjordan (9:1); and at three places with the addition "in the west" (5:1; 12:7; 22:7).

etc.), although this is not the author's immediate concern (see introduction to vv. 1–6).

This description of the boundary lines of the land west of the Jordan agrees with 11:17, except that the north (*Baal-gad*) is mentioned first, and the south (*Mount Halak*) last. *Joshua gave* this land to the tribes, *according to their divisions*[2] (see 11:23), just as Moses had done in Transjordan (12:6). It is clear from this repeated emphasis upon the distribution of the land that the author wishes to present the conquest of the territory as the basis for Israel's present and future possession of it. This is also the reason why he takes another look at the land in its entirety (see for other enumerations in a different context 9:1; 10:40; 11:16). The author means to say that the land given for a possession to Israel is commensurate with the land of Palestine. However, some new elements occur in this list. The land of Goshen (11:16) is omitted. The *slopes* (10:40), mentioned in the present catalog, are omitted in 11:16. A new element is the reference to *the desert*. Judah would occupy some cities in the desert later on (15:61). See also 8:15 for the region near Ai. A recurring feature is the enumeration of the various tribes inhabiting Canaan (cf. 3:10; 11:3). This repetition may have served as a reminder of the fulfilment of the promise already made in Gen. 15:19–21, where the Canaanite tribes were mentioned also.

9–24 The list of defeated kings follows roughly the order in which the events of the Conquest have been told in the preceding chapters, but expanded by some additional names such as Taanach and Megiddo (v. 21). The new names represent cities in the central and northern regions, an area about which the narratives have been relatively brief. The list begins with the kings of the two cities, the capture of which has been related most extensively, namely *Jericho* and *Ai*. Ai is said to be *beside Bethel* (see 7:2 and commentary; cf. Gen. 12:8; 13:3; Ezra 2:28; Neh. 7:32). Then follow (vv. 10–12) the names of the five cities which formed the southern coalition mentioned in 10:3, 23. For *Gezer* (v. 12b) see 10:33, and for *Debir* (v. 13a) see 10:38. The three following names, *Geder* (v. 13b), *Hormah*, and *Arad* (v. 14), do not occur earlier in Joshua. Hormah and Arad are mentioned in the Pentateuch (Num. 21:1; 33:40; Deut. 1:44; cf. Judg. 1:17). Hormah may be Tell es-Sebeta, a site about 3 miles east of Beer-sheba. Arad must be sought in the same vicinity.[3] *Geder* is

---

2. These were the smaller units of the tribe (see 7:14–18). One term of such subdivisions may sometimes be used for another.

3. Y. Aharoni, "The Negeb," in *AOTS*, p. 389, suggests that the two sites may possibly be identified with Tell el-Milḥ and Khirbet el-Meshash, respectively.

THE BOOK OF JOSHUA

unknown.[4] With *Libnah* and *Makkedah* (vv. 15–16) the list reverts to events mentioned in 10:28–30. *Adullam* (v. 15b) is an additional name. It has been identified with Khirbet esh-Sheikh Madhkûr, midway between Jerusalem and Lachish (cf. 1 Sam. 22:1). *Bethel*[5] (v. 16b) and *Tappuah* (v. 17b) were cities in the Ephraimite mountains. *Hepher* (v. 17b) and *Aphek* (v. 18a) were located in the Sharon Valley, the largest of the coastal plains in northern Palestine. The next name, *Lasharon*, can also be read as "to Sharon," i.e., belonging to Sharon. This is how it was understood by the LXX. It would then be a means of distinguishing Aphek of the Sharon Valley from other cities by that name. The rest of the list,[6] with the exception of *Tirzah* (v. 24), which belongs with the cities of the central district, concerns kings in northern Palestine. For *Madon* and *Hazor* (v. 19) and *Achshaph* (v. 20b), cf. 11:1. *Shimron-meron* may be the same as Shimron of 11:1, but there are other suggestions.[7]

Taanach and *Megiddo* (v. 21) are not mentioned in the actual conquest narratives. They were two strategically located cities in the valley of Jezreel, dominating the southwestern pass from that valley to the Plain of Sharon. From 17:11; Judg. 1:27 it is apparent that the Canaanite inhabitants of these cities were not entirely expelled. *Kedesh* (v. 22a) may have been the city mentioned in Judg. 4:6 as belonging to Naphtali, or that in Issachar (1 Chr. 6:57 [Eng. v. 72]).[8] *Jokneam in Carmel* (v. 22b) has been identified with Tell Qeimûn, located by the Kishon stream. It belonged later to Zebulun's territory (19:11; 21:34). For *Dor* cf. 11:2. *Goiim in Galilee* (see n. 6) may be the same as the "Galilee of the Gentiles" of Isa. 8:23 (Eng. 9:1); Heb. *gôyim* means "peoples," "Gentiles." Another suggestion connects this name with Harosheth-haggoyim of Judg. 4:2.

---

4. Some suggest the name be read as Gerar, requiring only a slight change in the Hebrew text, but in 1 Chr. 27:28 one of Solomon's officials is called a Gederite.
5. The name of Bethel does not occur in the LXX. Bethel's capture during the period of the Judges, some time after Joshua (Judg. 1:22–26), has been suggested as a possible reason for this reading of the LXX.
6. The LXX exhibits the following three variants. (a) Instead of reading "the king of Madon—one; the king of Hazor—one; the king of Shimron-meron—one," the LXX reads "the king of Hazor, the king of Symoon, the king of Marron." Hazor is placed first, Symoon corresponds to Shimron of 11:1, and Marron may be Madon of 11:1, though it also reflects the element -meron of Shimron-meron. (b) The MT order Taanach-Megiddo-Kedesh is reversed to Kedesh-Tanaach-Megiddo. (c) Goiim in Gilgal (Hebrew text; v. 23b) is rendered Goiim in Galilee in the LXX, a reading which has been adopted in the above translation.
7. See *GTT*, p. 279.
8. *Idem*: "Judging by the context this name refers to the city in Issachar."

Finally, *Tirzah* is Tell el-Fâr'ah, a few miles northeast of Nablus in central Palestine.

The total of these names in the Hebrew listing is thirty-one; in that of the LXX it is twenty-nine.

This concludes the description of the Conquest as described by the author of Joshua. It has been his concern to present some highlights of this conquest, interspersed and concluded with summary statements intended as a condensed version of historical occurrences, leading to the point where Israel is able to enter into its promised "inheritance," and into the "rest" that is the concomitant of the enjoyment of this inheritance. The Conquest is to be seen as the result of God's "giving" of the land to his covenant people. The land and its people will henceforth be the source from which God's plan of salvation will unfold.

II. THE PROMISED LAND DISTRIBUTED (13:1– 22:34)

A. GOD'S COMMAND TO DISTRIBUTE THE LAND (13:1– 7)

1 *When Joshua had reached old age the Lord said to him: "You have reached old age, and the country still remains to be occupied to a very large extent.*
2 *This is the land that remains: all the districts of the Philistines and all [the country of] the Geshurites;*
3 *from the Shihor east of Egypt to the boundary of Ekron northward; it is reckoned as Canaanite territory; the five lords of the Philistines: those of Gaza, Ashdod, Ashkelon, Gath, and Ekron; also the Avvim*
4 *on the south; the whole land of the Canaanites and Mearah which belongs to the Sidonians, as far as Aphek, as far as the territory of the Amorites;*
5 *then the country of the Giblites and the entire Lebanon eastward from Baal-gad under Mount Hermon to Lebo-hamath;*
6 *all the inhabitants of the mountain regions from the Lebanon to Misrephoth-maim; all the Sidonians. I myself will drive them out from before the Israelites. Just allot it to Israel as an inheritance as I have ordered you.*
7 *And now, divide this country as inheritance to the nine tribes and the half tribe of Manasseh."*

This chapter begins the second part of the book of Joshua. On the one hand, the book presents the Conquest as essentially completed (see 11:23; ch. 12). Compared to the promise made to the forefathers, from Gen. 12 onward, this was a proper point of view from which to describe the events. However, the book features another emphasis particularly in the section at hand. It speaks of a task yet undone and of a land yet to be occupied and possessed. There remains an assignment that is unfulfilled (see, e.g., 15:63; 17:12). At the end of the story of the allotment the writer again stresses the complete fulfilment of all that God ever promised concerning the land

208

(21:43), but in 23:4–5 reference is made to a task not yet done. Apparently these two emphases are meant to complement each other. The one is "theologically" as valid as the other. Neither should be sacrificed in the interest of logical order or coherence. Israel may rest in the work accomplished by its covenant Lord, but the nation is also made to look forward to greater dimensions of the rest now enjoyed. This latter emphasis should not be turned into one of works-righteousness. Of that the OT is as devoid as the NT. The land is and remains a land of promise, "given" to the patriarchs within the context of a covenant of grace. Note also in this section the promise of God's role in driving out Israel's enemies (13:6), stated emphatically: "I myself will drive them out."

The allotment of the land was essentially a deeply spiritual occurrence and was so understood by the believing Israelites. See, for example, the terms used in Ps. 16:6 to describe the believer's happiness and joy. At the same time, this happiness, especially in the OT phase of the covenant, attached itself to such "material" things as land and trees, houses and vineyards.

A final comment should be made on the typological significance of Canaan. Isa. 11:14–15 speaks of the great future in terms of a possession of Canaan up to the limits described here: Philistia and the River of Egypt.[1] Thus the minute description of the boundary lines of the land yet to be occupied may serve to direct the eye of the believer to the ultimate limit of the fulfilment of God's promises to his people.[2]

1 Joshua's advanced age is given as the reason for commanding the allotment of the land. Apparently the authority of Joshua makes it necessary to perform this task during his lifetime. His age at this time is not stated. He took a leading role in the fight with Amalek (Exod. 17:8–16), which was almost fifty years earlier (cf. 11:18). Caleb, one of Joshua's companions during the events described in Num. 13–14, was by this time eighty-five years old (14:10). Probably Joshua's own age was approximately the same. Joshua had been called to finish Moses' work that still needed to be done (Deut. 31:1–8; cf. Josh. 1:1). Joshua is to see that the country which *still remains to be occupied to a very large extent*[3] is allotted

1. For this thought cf. H. W. Hertzberg, *ATD* IX, p. 86.
2. One should avoid undue theologizing. But Josh. 13 is more than, and different from, a mere geographical record. To observe that 13:1-6a "deals largely with extra-Palestinian territories" (N. K. Gottwald, *The Tribes of Yahweh*, p. 197) leaves unsaid the reason why this is so. It ignores Joshua's programmatic emphasis.
3. Some translations understand the words rendered "to be occupied" as "to be conquered" (e.g., NAB). The Hebrew verb is *yāraš*. KB give as the meaning "unterwerfen, in Besitz nehmen" ("subdue, take possession of"). The word "oc-

to the tribes (v. 7). For the connection between this thought and that of a completed Conquest, as found, for example, in 11:23, see the introduction to this chapter.

2 *The land that remains*⁴ consists first of *all the districts of the Philistines*. The Philistines were a non-Semitic people inhabiting the coast of Palestine, which derives its name from these inhabitants. Their original dwelling place was probably Crete, also called Caphtor. Their chief migration took place in connection with the movement of the so-called Sea Peoples in the twelfth century BC. Traders from the Aegean, however, may have been present in this area during patriarchal times, which accounts for a reference to Philistines in Gen. 21:32; 26:1.⁵

The country of the Geshurites, mentioned next, is a region in southern Palestine, not to be confused with a similar area in the northeast (vv. 11, 13; Deut. 3:14).

3 The area of land yet to be occupied had for its southern border *the Shihor east of Egypt*. What is meant is probably the "brook (wadi) of Egypt," i.e., the modern Wâdī el- 'Arîsh (see 15:4, 47).⁶ The northern border was *Ekron*, first assigned to Judah (15:11), and on further distribution to Dan (19:43), but captured by Judah (Judg. 1:18). It was one of the five principal Philistine cities (see later in v. 3), identified probably with modern Khirbet el-Muqenna', about 3½ miles west of Tell Batashi. The city is biblical Timnah, south of the brook Sorek, known from the Samson stories.⁷ This Philistine country was nevertheless *reckoned as Canaanite territory*, a remark made necessary for two reasons: (a) the Philistines themselves were not descendants of Canaan (Gen. 10:14) but were intruders who replaced the original Avvim (Deut. 2:23); (b) since this was Canaanite country it

---

cupied" could be understood both of conquest and of allotment, which is a form of taking possession. In actual fact, Joshua is not expected to conquer the lands enumerated, but he is to take possession of them by means of the allotment. The other form of possession, that of actual settlement in conquered cities and districts, may yet take many years (see also Exod. 23:29; Judg. 1).

4. M. Noth, *Das Buch Josua*, pp. 73f., argues that vv. 2–6 are obviously secondary, an addition by a later hand who did not understand v. 1. Noth's reasoning, followed by J. A. Soggin, H. W. Hertzberg, and others, appears strained. The connection between vv. 1 and 2 is quite natural, and v. 2 does not give the word *šā'ar* ("remain") more prominence than it has in v. 1, as Noth alleges.

5. See T. C. Mitchell, "Philistines, Philistia," *NBD*, pp. 988–991.

6. See K. A. Kitchen, "River of Egypt" in *NBD*, pp. 353f. Shihor means "black (or dark) river." Another interpretation is "water of Horus," an Egyptian deity.

7. Judg. 16:4; 14:1. Ekron has also been identified with 'Aqir, ten miles northeast of Ashdod.

rightfully belonged to Israel by divine promise (Gen. 12:7; Exod. 3:8–9; Num. 33:53; 34:1–12).

The five principal cities of the Philistines are now enumerated: *Gaza, Ashdod, Ashkelon, Gath, and Ekron.* The first three lay near the Mediterranean coast, the other two farther inland in the foothills. The account speaks of the *lords*[8] *of the Philistines.* This may be a concrete form representing an abstract, "lordly domains," but it may also be that the emphasis lies on the personal element. These lords would give the Israelites much to worry about in later history. They are listed here among the lands yet to be occupied. The *Avvim* also appear in Deut. 2:23 (see above). The words *in the south* at the beginning of v. 4 can best be taken with this preceding material. The Avvim were located in this southerly region.

4 The description now turns its attention northward. The land that remains includes *the whole land of the Canaanites* (for "Canaanites" see 3:10). The name is used here to designate the inhabitants of the Syro-Palestinian coastland, especially Phoenicia proper[9] (see also Gen. 10:19). Considerable discussion has been focused on the next two words, *and Mearah.* This commentary understands it as a proper name, although some take it to mean "cave." No town by the name of Mearah is known.[10] Mearah is said to belong *to the Sidonians,* who lived on the Phoenician coast. This area extends *as far as Aphek,* probably modern Afqa near the sources of the Nahr Ibrahim, southeast of Byblos, some 23 miles north of modern Beirut. A further limit in the north is *the territory of the Amorites* (on the name "Amorites," see 3:10). Used here in a rather unusual sense, the designation refers to territory beyond the limits of the land to be possessed by Israel, and may stand for the kingdom of Amurru in the Lebanon region, well known from 14th and 13th century Egyptian and

8. Heb. *seren.* It has been suggested that Gk. *týrannos* was derived from this. J. A. Soggin, *Joshua,* translates "five 'tyrannies,' " using an abstract form for a concrete subject.

9. For a discussion of the name Canaan and Canaanites see Y. Aharoni, *The Land of the Bible*, pp. 61–63; W. F. Albright, "The Role of the Canaanites in the History of Civilization," in G. E. Wright, ed., *The Bible and the Ancient Near East* (repr. Winona Lake: 1979), pp. 328–362. See also N. K. Gottwald, *The Tribes of Yahweh, passim,* a work which appeared after the manuscript for this commentary was completed.

10. Some translations take the first part of Mearah to stand for the Hebrew preposition *min,* hence "from Arah" (JB) or "'depuis' Méara" (Gelin). Some need is felt for a "from" clause to complement "as far as," which follows. The LXX has: *enantíon Gázēs;* NEB "from the low-lying land." It seems that every attempt to restore this name must remain purely conjectural; thus Aharoni, *op. cit.,* p. 216.

Hittite sources. If so, Aphek was located thus on the southern border of that region.[11]

5 The country yet to be occupied also includes that of *the Giblites*, a name derived from the ancient city of Gebal (Byblos) on the Phoenician coast north of Sidon. It is frequently mentioned in Egyptian sources. Egypt entertained busy commercial relations with Gebal. Moving eastward the description refers to *the entire Lebanon*. *Eastward* may be understood as referring either to the Lebanon which is to the east of the territory of the Giblites, or to the Antilebanon, which was east of the Lebanon. The latter view appears to provide a better background for what follows: *from Baal-gad under Mount Hermon to Lebo-hamath*. For Baal-gad, cf. 11:17; 12:7. Lebo-hamath has also been rendered "entrance to Hamath" or "on the road to Hamath" (Heb. *bô'*, "to come," "to enter").[12] Lebo-hamath is believed to have been an important city on the border of the kingdom of Hamath, to the northeast of Palestine.

6 We have treated the first part of this verse as the conclusion of the enumeration of the land yet to be occupied.[13] Understood in that way, v. 6a focuses on *the inhabitants of the mountain regions*, who live *from the Lebanon to Misrephoth-maim*. They are designated as living in the mountain regions because they inhabit the promontory of Naqurah. For Misrephoth-maim see 11:8. It is meant as the western terminus of the region described and may be modern Khirbet el-Mushrefeh, below Râs en-Naqurah.[14]

If our understanding of v. 6a has been correct, the assurance that the Lord himself *will drive them out from before the Israelites* is applicable to the inhabitants of all the "land that remains," in the south as well as in the north. The idea underlying the entire book of Joshua remains the same in this second part (cf. 3:10; 10:42; 11:6). All Joshua must do is to

11. J. Simons believes that vv. 4b, 5a must be transposed to make the enumeration at this point understandable; *GTT*, p. 112. Aharoni, *op. cit.*, p. 217, argues for no such transposition.

12. There was a city called Hamath on the Orontes River. But it hardly seems suitable as a *border* designation to speak of a *point* "where one goes to Hamath"; see Aharoni, *op. cit.*, pp. 65f. JB renders "to the Pass of Hamath." See on this question also *GTT*, pp. 100f.

13. Other translations, e.g., NEB, F.-M. Abel, and A. Gelin take v. 6a with v. 6b: "I will drive out . . . all the inhabitants of [etc.]." According to our understanding of the verse the words "I myself will drive them out . . ." apply to all of the land that remains and not just to what precedes immediately.

14. See *GTT*, p. 113.

allot[15] *it to Israel as an inheritance* (for this significant word see 1:6; 11:23).[16]

7 The words *and now*, with which this verse opens, sometimes occur in a legal, juridical setting.[17] The activity at hand may be a formal land grant, establishing legal claims to the country. This verse again uses the word *inheritance* (see previous verse). Joshua is to *divide this country*[18] among the nine tribes and the half tribe of Manasseh. The Hebrew root of the verb translated "divide" *(ḥālaq)* yields the noun *ḥēleq*, "allotted portion," sometimes parallel to *gôrāl*, "lot" (17:14; see also 18:5-6, 9; 19:9, etc.). For the spiritual dimension of this terminology see Ps. 16:5; 119:57; 142:6 (Eng. 5); Isa. 61:7.[19]

B. THE DISTRIBUTION OF TRANSJORDAN RECALLED (13:8-33)

8 *Half the tribe of Manasseh and with them the Reubenites and the Gadites had received their inheritance which Moses had given them on the other side of the Jordan eastward, as Moses, the Lord's servant, had given it to them:*
9 *from Aroer, which is on the edge of the Arnon Valley, and the city that is in the center of the valley and the entire tableland of Medeba as far as Dibon;*

15. Heb. lit. "cause to fall," i.e., the lot. For the division of the land by lots see also Isa. 34:17; Mic. 2:4-5. The lot was ruled by God (Prov. 16:33). R. de Vaux, *Ancient Israel*, p. 165, rightly sees in the sharing-out by lot an expression of God's sovereign domain over the land.
16. The NEB renders the word with "patrimony." The word "inheritance" continues to play a part in NT vocabulary and it describes there the blessings of salvation in Christ.
17. See M. G. Kline, *WTJ* 32 (1969–70), pp. 49–67, 179–200; 33 (1970–71), pp. 45–72; and cf. C. Vonk, *Inleiding op de Profeten: Jozua*, pp. 200f.
18. The boundaries of the country described in vv. 2–6 were ideal and hence contained a program of action to be carried out by Israel with the Lord's help. Y. Kaufmann, *The Biblical Account of the Conquest of Palestine*, pp. 46f., rightly chides Higher Critics for not having paid attention to the ideal nature of Israel's proposed boundaries as presented in Joshua and elsewhere.
19. According to the OT the land of Canaan in which Israel lived was the Lord's land (Lev. 25:23). This theocentric way of looking at the land also had social implications, as Naboth seems to have understood at the cost of his life (1 K. 21:3). Possession of the land and assurance of God's covenant favor went hand in hand, but they were not automatically connected. As redemptive history proceeds, Israel learns that the latter can be enjoyed without the former.

10 *and all the cities of Sihon king of the Amorites, who ruled in Heshbon, to the territory of the Ammonites;*

11 *then Gilead and the territory of the Geshurites and the Maacathites, and all of Mount Hermon and all Bashan as far as Salecah;*

12 *the whole kingdom of Og in Bashan who ruled in Ashtaroth and in Edrei; he was a survivor of those that remained of the Rephaim; Moses had put them to death and had driven them out.*

13 *But the Israelites did not drive out the Geshurites and the Maacathites, so that Geshur and Maacath continued to live among Israel until this day.*

14 *Only to the tribe of Levi Moses gave no inheritance; the offerings by fire to the Lord God of Israel are their inheritance, as he said to them.*

15 *Moses had made allotments to the tribe of Reuben according to their families as follows:*

16 *They obtained the territory from Aroer which lies on the edge of the valley of Arnon, the city that was in the middle of the valley and the whole tableland near Medeba;*

17 *Heshbon, and all its dependent villages which were on the tableland, Dibon, Bamoth-baal, Beth-baal-meon,*

18 *Jahaz, Kedemoth, Mephaath,*

19 *Kiriathaim, Sibmah, Zereth-shahar on the mount of the valley;*

20 *Beth-peor, the slopes of Pisgah, Beth-jeshimoth,*

21 *and all the cities of the tableland, and the whole kingdom of Sihon the king of the Amorites who ruled at Heshbon, whom Moses put to death together with the princes of Midian, Evi, Rekem, Zur, Hur, and Reba, vassals of Sihon who lived in that country.*

22 *Balaam also, the son of Beor, the soothsayer, the Israelites killed with the sword, as one of those slain by them.*

23 *The border of the Reubenites was the Jordan and its bank. This was the inheritance of the Reubenites according to their families with the cities and their villages.*

24 *Moses then made allotments to the tribe of Gad, the Gadites, according to their families.*

25 *They obtained this territory: Jazer, and all the cities of Gilead, and half the country of the Ammonites as far as Aroer which lies over against Rabbah,*

26 *from Heshbon to Ramath-mizpeh and Betonim, and from Mahanaim to the border of Lidbir;*

27 *and in the valley: Beth-haram, Beth-nimrah, Succoth, and Zaphon, the rest of the kingdom of Sihon the king of Heshbon; the Jordan with its bank to the tip of the Sea of Chinnereth, on the east side of the Jordan.*

28 *This was the inheritance of the Gadites according to their families,*
   with the cities and their villages.
29 *Moses then made allotments to the half tribe of Manasseh: this was*
   meant for the half tribe of Manasseh, according to their families.
30 *Their territory stretched from Mahanaim; all of Bashan, the whole*
   kingdom of Og the king of Bashan, and all the encampments of Jair
   which are in Bashan, sixty towns;
31 *half of Gilead, Ashtaroth and Edrei, the royal cities of Og: this was*
   for the children of Machir, the son of Manasseh, that is for the half
   of the children of Machir, according to their families.
32 *These are the inheritances which Moses assigned in the plains of*
   Moab on the east side of the Jordan at Jericho.
33 *But to the tribe of Levi Moses did not give an inheritance; the Lord*
   God of Israel is their inheritance, as he promised them.

Grammatically v. 8 belongs to the immediately preceding section,[1] but the difference in subject matter warrants a new division. There may be a special reason why the writer returns once again to Israel's holdings east of Jordan, which have already been mentioned (12:1–6, esp. v. 6). It probably is part of his design, observed elsewhere in the book,[2] to stress the basic ccherence and unity of the entire people, and to emphasize that those on the east side of the river are fully entitled to their inheritance. Moreover, this section serves as a suitable parallel to the much longer section dealing with the distribution of the land west of Jordan.[3]

The division of vv. 8–33 is simple and perspicuous. Verses 8–12 present a survey of all of Transjordan. Verses 13–14 contain two additional comments. Verses 15–23 describe Reuben's inheritance, vv. 24–28 that of Gad, and vv. 29–31 that of the half tribe of Manasseh. Verses 32–33 contain concluding comments. The description of the Transjordanian area contains both geographical and historical elements. Some cities are described by their geographical names; others are simply referred to as those originally belonging to Sihon and Og.

8–13 It is through *Moses* that the Transjordanian tribes have received their inheritance. Verse 8 mentions him twice (see also vv. 14–15, 24, 29, 32–33). Moses is *the Lord's servant* (see 1:1–2). The description of Transjordan in vv. 9–13 follows similar passages such as 12:2–6; Deut.

---

1. The verse begins with the preposition *'im*, "with," followed by the suffix of the third masculine singular pronoun, therefore lit. "with him the Reubenites . . . received." To be supplied are the words "half the tribe of Manasseh and. . . ."
2. See 1:12–18; ch. 22. Israel is to be viewed as a union of twelve tribes, each of which receives an inheritance.
3. For the author's concern to portray Joshua's role as parallel to Moses see G. J. Wenham, *JBL* 90 (1971), pp. 145f.; see also 5:15; 12:1–6, 7–24.

3:8– 17, and moves from south to north. *Aroer*[4] is a city *on the edge of the Arnon Valley*, with the Arnon forming the southern boundary of Israelite Transjordan (see 12:2). South of the Arnon was the country of Moab.

Then follows *the city that is in the center of the valley* (see also 12:2). "In the center of" probably means "halfway along." This city may have been Ar of Moab (Num. 21:28); it was not close to the river, but could still be described as lying in the center of its valley. The area also involved *the entire tableland of Medeba as far as Dibon*. This refers to the elevated plateau between the Arnon in the south and Heshbon in the north, 2000–2400 feet high (vv. 16–17, 21; 20:8; Deut. 3:10; 4:43). Its main cities were Medeba in the north and Dibon in the south. Medeba is 7 miles south of Heshbon (v. 10). Dibon, modern Dhībân on the north side of the Arnon, was Moab's capital in later times (Isa. 15:2; Jer. 48:18, 22). This territory further included *all the cities of Sihon . . . to the territory of the Ammonites* (see 12:2). Sihon's territory had been acquired in part from that of Moab. It extended down to the Arnon and reached to Ammon's border, which was formed by the Jabbok.

With *Gilead* (v. 11) the description turns northward. For the geographical meaning of that name, see 12:2 and commentary. It stands here for that part of Gilead situated north of the Jabbok. *The territory of the Geshurites* was northeast of the Sea of Galilee, and that of the Maacathites was still farther north (see 12:5). It lay west of Bashan and east of the sources of the Jordan. *Mount Hermon*, *Bashan*, and *Salecah* all have been mentioned in 12:4– 5. Bashan offered good opportunities for agriculture, because part of the area was particularly fertile. For *the kingdom of Og* and his two residencies, *Ashtaroth and Edrei*, and for the *Rephaim* of which Og was a *survivor*, see 12:4. These Rephaim had been put to death by Moses (v. 12).

The brief description of Transjordan is concluded by the information that *the Israelites did not drive out the Geshurites and the Maacathites*. Thus these original inhabitants continued to live among the Israelites until the time the book was written (v. 13). The book of Joshua shows impartiality in this respect, reporting similar failures on the part of the Cisjordonian tribes (15:63; 16:10). This account of failure occurs in the same chapter in which God promises that he himself will drive out the inhabitants

---

4. There is some discussion as to the possible existence of more than one Aroer. G. Lisowsky, *Konkordanz zum hebräischen AT* (²1966) lists no fewer than three: (a) 12:2; 13:9, 16; (b) 13:25; Judg. 11:33; and (c) 1 Sam. 30:28. But E. G. Kraeling, *The Rand McNally Bible Atlas*, p. 161, calls the matter of even a second Aroer "uncertain."

from before Israel (v. 6). Such assurances do not automatically take effect, but presuppose Israel's readiness to carry out God's will in expelling the inhabitants.

A special point is made in vv. 14, 33 of *the tribe of Levi*, to whom *Moses gave no inheritance*. From a purely mathematical viewpoint this information was necessary in order to account for the figures 9½ and 2½ within the twelve-tribe arrangement. The tribe of Levi simply is not counted among the twelve for this purpose. The writer considered this chapter, which deals with the Transjordanian settlements, the most appropriate place to convey this information. He does not repeat it after the record of Cisjordanian boundaries (e.g., at the end of ch. 19; but see 14:4). Since Levi also would receive cities in Transjordan (21:27–41), it would be natural to point to their exceptional position at this juncture. Levi's *inheritance* consisted of *the offerings by fire*[5] *to the Lord God of Israel* (see Lev. 1:9, 13, 17). In v. 33 Levi's inheritance is said to be the Lord. Most of the offerings by fire as mentioned in Leviticus were wholly for the Lord (Lev. 3:3–5, 9, 14; 23:18, 25; but cf. 6:10 [Eng. 17]). Perhaps the term must be understood more broadly to include the tithes to which Levi was entitled (Num. 18:21–32).

15   In this and following verses the allotment[6] made by *Moses* to Reuben[7] is set forth. This allotment is made *according to their families*,

5. This expression is omitted in JB and NEB, probably in line with the LXX which does not have it and which omits all of v. 33. The Hebrew construction is somewhat harsh: a plural noun is followed by a singular pronoun which refers back to the plural noun. The translation and etymology of Heb. *'iššê* is disputed. Cf. P. C. Craigie, *Deuteronomy*, p. 258. If the form actually does represent a Hebrew word, the derivation from *'ēš*, "fire," seems called for. R. de Vaux observes that "there is no doubt that the editors of the Bible thought the word applied to any offering which was wholly or partly destroyed by fire (*'ēsh*)"; *Ancient Israel*, p. 417. See also W. H. Gispen, *Het Boek Leviticus Verklaard*. Commentaar op het OT (Kampen: 1950), p. 42, on Lev. 1:9; and G. J. Wenham, *Leviticus*, p. 56.
6. The Hebrew formulation is the same in vv. 15, 24, 29: *wayyittēn* ("and he gave") without a direct object.
7. There is widespread critical opinion that Reuben's actual place in history is more complex than a first reading of the biblical record would indicate. For a summary of this discussion cf. J. A. Soggin, *Joshua*, pp. 154–57. See also Y. Aharoni, *The Land of the Bible*, p. 190; R. de Vaux, *Early History*, pp. 576–581; and M. Noth, *History*, pp. 63-67. Some believe, on the basis of passages such as 15:6; 18:17, that Reuben was originally settled in Cisjordania as well. As a tribe, Reuben is supposed to have had far greater significance than is now obvious from the biblical record. Part of the argument is based on passages such as Gen. 49:3–4; Deut. 33:6, which are taken as a *vaticinium ex eventu* rather than as a

a formula used also in the distribution of Cisjordanian land (15:1, 20; 18:11; 19:1), but not in every case (16:1, Ephraim and Manasseh). For the tribe and its subdivisions, cf. 7:14. Reuben, one of the sons of Leah, Jacob's first wife (Gen. 29:32), lost his preeminence amongst his brothers (Gen. 35:22; 49:3). In later history Reuben's significance as a warrior tribe disappears. The Mesha inscription, c. 830 BC, while referring to Gad, does not mention Reuben among the adversaries of Moab. In prophecy Reuben retains his place (Ezek. 48:7, 31; cf. Rev. 7:5). For a postexilic summary of Reuben's vicissitudes see also 1 Chr. 5:1–10.

16–17 Reuben's territory lay in the southern part of Israelite Transjordan. The line is drawn from *Aroer* (v. 16) on *the edge of the valley of Arnon* to *Heshbon*, farther north (v. 17; see v. 9). Most of the towns listed as belonging to Reuben lie on a line from Aroer to Heshbon. This does not mean that Reuben possessed only a narrow strip of land. The list simply does not trace the eastern frontier.[8] For *the tableland near Medeba*[9] see v. 9. *Heshbon* was Sihon's capital (v. 10; 12:2). Reuben's allotment consisted mainly of Sihon's former kingdom (v. 21). Heshbon lay almost midway between the Arnon and the Jabbok (21:39; Num. 32:37; 1 Chr. 6:81). Heshbon also had *dependent villages*.[10] *Dibon* is the most important city north of the Arnon, called Dibon of Gad in Num. 32:34 because the Gadites fortified it. Later in history it is a Moabite town (Isa. 15:2; Jer. 48:18, 22), indicating Reuben's decline. *Bamoth-baal*, literally "the heights of Baal," was in the vicinity of Medeba. Balaam ascended its heights to curse Israel (Num. 22:41). Its name occurs on the Mesha inscription as Beth-bamoth. *Beth-baal-meon*, also called Baal-meon (Num. 32:38), is modern Maʿîn (cf. also Jer. 49:34).

18–19 Reuben's territory also included *Jahaz, Kedemoth, and Mephaath* (v. 18). Jahaz was the point where Sihon attacked Israel and

---

prophetic statement. Thus these statements, attributed in the Bible to Jacob and Moses respectively, are thought by certain scholars to reflect much later events, such as a decline of the tribe of Reuben after an earlier prominence. But the biblical record places these utterances, at least that of Gen. 49, before the tribe of Reuben was actually in existence. E. A. Speiser, *Genesis*, admits in commenting on Gen. 35:22 that "tangible evidence about the events in question is unfortunately lacking" (p. 274) with regard to precise information about the supposed vicissitudes of the Reuben tribe. De Vaux's critical analysis of Noth's and C. Steuernagel's position is helpful, but his own solution does not satisfy.

8. So J. Bright, *IB* II, p. 624.

9. "Near" is the translation of Heb. *'al*, which some interpreters have emended to *'aḏ*, "as far as." No preposition is used in v. 9.

10. Heb. *'ārîm*, plural of *'îr*, ordinarily "city" but also used of other permanent settlements without regard to size or rights; so KB.

was defeated by them. It has been variously identified[11] with Khirbet Libb or with el-Medeiyineh. Its general location was east of Medeba. Kedemoth, literally "east villages," has been identified with Qaṣr ez-Zaʿferân, a site about 7.5 miles northeast of Dibon, quite near the eastern border of Sihon's kingdom (see also Deut. 2:26). Mephaath, later a Levitical city (21:37; 1 Chr. 6:79), was also in the eastern region (cf. Jer. 48:21).

Other cities mentioned are *Kiriathaim*, *Sibmah*, and *Zereth-shahar on the mount in the valley* (v. 19). Kiriathaim was conquered and strengthened by the Reubenites (Num. 32:37). Later it was a Moabite city (Jer. 48:1). Its name occurs in the Mesha inscription. Sibmah was not far from Heshbon, but its precise location is uncertain. It was known for its vine culture (Isa. 16:8–9; Jer. 48:32). Zereth-shahar lay *on the mount of the valley*, probably the Jordan Valley. This is the only OT passage where its name occurs.

20–21 *Beth-peor* was the place where Israel received Moses' farewell address (Deut. 3:29), and Balaam uttered one of his prophecies from the top of Mount Peor (Num. 23:28). It was within easy reach of Shittim, for it was at the latter site that Israel followed Baal-peor (Num. 25:3; Deut. 4:3).[12] For *the slopes of Pisgah*, cf. 12:3.[13] *Beth-jeshimoth* (lit. "steppe-dwelling") may be modern Tel el-ʿAzeimeh near the northern shore of the Dead Sea (see 12:3). The phrase *and all the cities of the tableland* could also be rendered "That is, all the cities . . . etc.," for the cities just mentioned were located on the tableland. The phrase, however, may also be an indication of all the *other* cities located in the tableland.[14]

The expression *And the whole kingdom of Sihon* should be taken in a qualified sense, for in v. 27 part of Sihon's kingdom goes to Gad. Here it stands for that part which extended over the tableland. (On Sihon, king of the Amorites, see 12:2 and commentary.) The author of this list briefly pauses to relate the event of Sihon's death at the hand of Moses *together with the princes of Midian* (Num. 31:8).[15] Their names were *Evi, Rekem,*

11. Cf. J. R. Bartlett, *VT* 20 (1970), p. 259.
12. See Kraeling, *op. cit.*, p. 126. Eusebius speaks of Beth-peor close to Mount Peor, six miles east of Livias (Tell er-Râmeh).
13. The translation "slopes" is not entirely certain; see KB, p. 91, s.v. *ʾāšeḏ*. A. Gelin, *Josué*, p. 84, treats it as a proper name: Asedoth ha-Pisga.
14. So, e.g., KD, p. 141; C. Steuernagel, *Das Buch Josua*, p. 259.
15. They are called "kings" in Numbers. M. Noth, *Das Buch Josua*, p. 74, considers this "transformation" a sign of a later hand, but offers no reasons for his opinion. It would seem that in this kind of society such functions would not be separated very precisely. For another theory concerning an alleged "conflation" of two supposedly different strands of tradition at this point, cf. J. M. Miller and G. M. Tucker, *The Book of Joshua*, p. 110.

Zur, Hur, and Reba, and they are called *vassals of Sihon*. Zur is also mentioned in Num. 25:15, where he is called "head of the people of a father's house." The translation "vassals" for Heb. $n^e s \hat{\imath} k \hat{e}$ is not certain.[16] The death of these men is recorded here, although it did not take place at the time Sihon himself was slain.

22–23 Still another historical remark in Reuben's boundary list concerns the death of *Balaam . . . the son of Beor*, here called *the soothsayer* (Heb. *qôsēm*), a title assigned only in this passage. The story of how the Lord frustrated Balaam's intended curse and turned it into a blessing is told several times (24:9–10; Deut. 23:4–5; Neh. 13:2; Mic. 6:5), for this had been an outstanding act of God's deliverance. The present verse recalls Balaam's death at the hand of the Israelites (Num. 31:8). Was this also intended as an indirect warning against a possible repetition of the apostasy in which Balaam had played an infamous role (Num. 31:16)? See also 22:17.

The translation of v. 23a has been difficult. This is caused by the twofold occurrence of Heb. $g^e \underline{b} \hat{u} l$, "border," "territory." The present translation renders it the second time by "bank."[17] Thus understood the passage indicates that *the border of the Reubenites was the Jordan and its bank*. Apparently, Reuben's allotment reached as far as the Jordan, though the bulk of it was east of the Dead Sea, with its northern point reaching the northern tip of the Sea where the Jordan flowed into it. The verse concludes with the summary statement that this was indeed Reuben's *inheritance* (cf. vv. 28, 33; 14:2, 14, etc.).

24 Gad's territory is described next. It was situated to the east of the Jordan, north of Reuben's domain[18] and to the south of that of the half tribe of Manasseh (see also Num. 32:33–36). The description of this area begins in a manner identical to that of Reuben (v. 15). The emphasis on *Moses'* role, repeated throughout this chapter, recurs (cf. v. 8). The transjordanian tribes are fully entitled to their possession, for no less a person than Moses had distributed it to them. The words *the Gadites* after *the tribe of Gad* appear tautological and are not found in some of the ancient versions, but the Hebrew text maintained them without apparent difficulty.

---

16. Probably derived from *nāsak*, containing the meaning of "consecration," hence obligation to a suzerain, and so vassaldom. See KB, s.v. *nāsîk* II, where the meaning "vassal" does not occur.

17. So rendered by Gelin, *op. cit.*, p. 85 ("avec sa rive").

18. De Vaux, *Early History*, p. 576, contends that Num. 32:34–38 presents a more fluid picture of the boundary between these two. But Numbers speaks only of the "building," i.e., strengthening, of certain cities by the two tribes. It does not speak of final allotment.

Gad was the son of Jacob by Zilpah, Leah's maidservant (Gen. 30:10–11). For the blessings of Gad, cf. Gen. 49:19; Deut. 33:20–21. In the prophetic redistribution of territory in Ezek. 48:27–28 Gad receives the southernmost zone in the land.

The distribution of Gad's territory occurred *according to their families*[19] (cf. v. 15).

25 Gad's territory comprised almost the entire Jordan Valley, east of the river. From the valley it ran eastward as far as the south-north course of the Jabbok. On the north it had for its border the east-west course of that river. At two points it extended beyond that line: in the Jordan Valley it stretched to the Sea of Galilee, and in the northeast it included the district of Mahanaim and the strategic city of Ramoth-gilead.

Verse 25 seems to be dealing with districts rather than with cities. *Jazer* is the name of a region (Num. 32:1) as well as of its principal city (Num. 32:3). The site may be Khirbet Gazzir on the Wâdī Sha'ib near Es-Saat (cf. also 21:39).

The second region was that comprising *all the cities of Gilead* (cf. v. 11; 12:2). It refers here to southern Gilead.[20] The northern part was to belong to Manasseh (v. 31). A further region consisted of *half the country of the Ammonites*. This was the western part of Ammon's land, between the Arnon and the Jabbok. The other half of Ammon had been left unharmed by Israel (Deut. 2:19). The line at this point ran *as far as Aroer which lies over against Rabbah*. The expression "over against" is taken to mean "east of" by some, and "west of" by others.[21] Rabbah was the capital of Ammon. It is modern Amman, situated 22 miles east of the Jordan. Aroer must be different from the city assigned to Reuben (v. 16). Its location is unknown.

26–27 These verses contain first a list of cities, followed by an apposition and a reference to Gad's western border. Two approximately parallel lines are drawn south to north. One runs from Heshbon to Mahanaim on the Jabbok, while the other is roughly parallel with it but

---

19. For a discussion of the "family-clan-tribe" relationship in Israel, cf. C. H. J. de Geus, *The Tribes of Israel*, pp. 133–156; and Gottwald, *The Tribes of Yahweh*, pp. 243–337. Gottwald admits that some of his theses need reexamination in light of de Geus' critique, especially his theory concerning the origins of the house of Joseph (p. 898).
20. Simons, *GTT*, p. 120, thinks of a restricted area above Jazer.
21. Aharoni, *op. cit.*, p. 232, and Steuernagel, *op. cit.*, p. 259, belong to the former; Simons, *idem*, to the latter. The Hebrew reads '*al p^enê*, lit. "in front of." Noth, *Das Buch Josua*, p. 81, definitely rejects the translation "east of" and opts for the more neutral "angesichts, gegenüber."

remains in the valley, starting from *Beth-haram* and ending at *Zaphon*.[22] On the location of Heshbon see v. 17; 12:2. *Ramath-mizpeh*, also called Ramoth in Gilead (20:8),[23] was one of the cities of refuge. *Betonim*, in the vicinity, is the present Khirbet Baṭneh. *Manahaim*'s location is still uncertain. It is to be found on the border between Gad and Manasseh (v. 30). From that point the line ran to *Lidbir*. The translation, however, is difficult at this point. Some read this name as Lo-debar,[24] others as Debir.[25] No city by the latter name is known east of the Jordan. Lo-debar is described as being in this region (2 Sam. 9:4; 17:27), but its location is otherwise unknown. In v. 27 the description deals with locations in the Jordan Valley to the west side of Gad. Two cities south of the Jabbok are *Beth-haram*, the location of which is unknown, and *Beth-nimrah* ("house of leopards" or "house of pure water"), which Eusebius located 5 miles north of Livias (Beth-horon). Two cities north of the Jabbok are *Succoth*, generally identified with an impressive tell north of the Jabbok at the point where that stream turns sharply southward toward Jordan,[26] and *Zaphon*, Tell es-Saʿîdîyeh,[27] just north of Succoth. Archaeological excavations have taken place at both sites.

Verse 27b is an apposition. It calls the areas just described *the rest of the kingdom of Sihon*. The other part of Sihon's kingdom had been allotted to Reuben (vv. 15–23). Then follows a second addition, v. 27c dealing with *the Jordan with its bank*. As noted earlier, Gad's domain extended up the Jordan Valley as far as the Sea of Galilee, here called *Sea of Chinnereth* (see also 12:2–3).

28 The conclusion of this description is identical to that of Reuben (v. 23).

---

22. So J. Simons, *GTT*, p. 121. Aharoni, *op. cit.*, p. 78, believes that in v. 26 several points are designated in different directions; see also p. 232. The "from–to" construction should not be taken as a formal description of boundary lines, consisting of reference points in a fixed order.

23. This identification is doubted by Simons, *GTT*, *idem*.

24. Proposed by BH, and found also in the translations of Abel, Gelin, and Hertzberg.

25. So ASV and RSV.

26. N. Glueck, *AOTS*, p. 431, states that Succoth is "probably" Tell Deir ʿAllā, excavated by H. J. Franken. But see Franken, "Heilig Land en Heilige Huisjes" (inaugural address, Leiden: 1962), pp. 29f., who challenges Glueck's methods of identification.

27. This site, however, is considered to be Zarethan by Glueck, *op. cit.*, p. 431, on the basis of J. B. Pritchard's work at this place. Zaphon has also been identified with Tell el-Qôs, or in late Jewish tradition with Tell ʿAmmatā, but this is judged unsuitable by Simons, *GTT*, p. 300.

29   Now follows a description of the territory of the half tribe of Manasseh. Manasseh was the oldest son of Joseph, son of Jacob (Gen. 41:50–51). Two prominent members of the tribe, Jair and Machir, are mentioned in this pericope (vv. 30–31).[28] Although the name Machir occurs chiefly for the Transjordanian part of Manasseh, in Judg. 5:14 it appears to be used for the entire tribe, and more particularly for its western half. The description of Manasseh's territory consists of little more than an enumeration of districts, the nucleus of which consists of all of Bashan and half of Gilead. Verse 29 again reminds the reader that it was *Moses* who *allotted* this area (vv. 8, 15, 24).

Twice the author reports that the third allotment in Transjordan was for *the half tribe of Manasseh.*[29] The division of this tribe over two distinct territories on different sides of the Jordan may account for this seeming redundancy.

30–31   Manasseh's territory *stretched from Mahanaim*, which was also one of the northernmost points of Gad's territory (see v. 26). In general terms the description proceeds to mention *all of Bashan* (see v. 12; 12:4 and commentary), a rich and fertile land north of the Yarmuk, reaching to Mount Hermon and eastward to the northern slopes of the Hauran. It also mentions *the whole kingdom of Og* (see 12:5). Manasseh's domain included *all the encampments*[30] *of Jair*, a prominent member of the tribe of Manasseh (see above; cf. Deut. 3:14). These were encampments of tent villages. (For their capture by Jair cf. Num. 32:41.) There were *sixty* of these encampments (cf. also 1 Chr. 2:22), and they were located *in Bashan* (in Num. 32:39 they are said to be in Gilead, the name being used in an extended sense to stand for all of Transjordan including Bashan).

The enumeration concludes with *the children of Machir*, another descendant of Manasseh. Their territory consists of *half of Gilead* plus the royal residences of *Ashtaroth and Edrei* that had belonged to king Og. (For Machir, see 17:1; Gen. 50:23; Num. 26:29; 1 Chr. 7:14, where he is called the "son" of Manasseh. For Machir's conquest of Gilead, see Num. 32:39–

---

28. About supposed difficulties in the genealogies of Manasseh and a suggested solution, see R. J. A. Sheriffs, "Manasseh," in *NBD*, pp. 778f. M. Noth, *The OT World*, p. 73, considers Machir to have been the original name of one of the branches of the house of Joseph. But 17:1ff.; Judg. 5:14 are capable of a different interpretation than Noth gives; see also 17:1ff. and commentary.

29. Two different words for "tribe" are used in this verse: *šēḇeṭ* and *maṭṭēh*. On the difference in meaning see KD, p. 75; cf. 7:1, 18; 22:1, 14, where *maṭṭēh* is used; and 3:12; 4:2; 7:14, 16, where *šēḇeṭ* occurs. In the present verse the difference is negligible.

30. Heb. *hawwâ*. See Craigie, *op. cit.*, p. 122, n. 5.

40.) In Judg. 5:17 the name Gilead appears to be used for that part of Manasseh living in Transjordan, and the name Machir is applied to the Cisjordanian part of the tribe (Judg. 5:14). The half of Gilead received by the Machirites is north Gilead. That this area was for only half of the children of Machir is said with a view to the events recorded in 17:3.

32–33 A summary statement concerning *the inheritances which Moses assigned* to the 2½ tribes concludes the section. (No separate summary for Manasseh is given, unlike vv. 23b, 28.)

In conclusion, a second note about the Levites' not receiving an inheritance, inasmuch as the Lord is their inheritance (see v. 14), is appended to the Transjordanian list. The second statement about Levi is more direct and richer than that of v. 14. The language differs from that of the Pentateuch. Num. 18:20; Deut. 10:9 resemble this verse; Num. 18:24; Deut. 18:1 refer to offerings, as in v. 14. In Ps. 16:5 this language is applied to the believing Israelite in general.

The stage now is set for the much longer description of the allotments on the west side of Jordan.

C. THE DISTRIBUTION OF WEST JORDAN INTRODUCED (14:1–15)

1. THE LORD'S COMMANDS EXECUTED (14:1–5)

1 *Here follow the inheritance portions which the Israelites received in the land of Canaan. Eleazar the priest, Joshua the son of Nun, and the heads of the fathers' houses of the tribes of the Israelites divided them as an inheritance.*

2 *Their inheritance was by lot, as the Lord had commanded through Moses concerning the remaining nine and a half tribes.*

3 *For Moses had given the inheritance of two and a half tribes beyond the Jordan; and to the Levites he had not given an inheritance among them.*

4 *For the Josephites formed two tribes, Manasseh and Ephraim. And to the Levites they gave no portion in the land, but cities to live in, with their pasture lands for their cattle and their substance.*

5 *As the Lord commanded Moses, so the Israelites did as they divided the land.*

Chapters 14–19 contain a description of the allotment of Canaan west of the Jordan. Ch. 14 is introductory in two ways. Verses 1–5 set forth the circumstances of the allotment procedures, the number of tribes concerned, and the authorization for this activity. The rest of the chapter, vv. 6–15, is probably also meant to be introductory. It describes one instance of outstanding faith, that of Caleb, who claimed a portion of land that was inhabited by redoubtable foes. The story may be meant as an indication of what faith and loyalty to the Lord can do in possessing "the land that yet remains" (13:2; see also Introduction, p. 15). If so, the concluding words "and the land had rest from war" (v. 15c), words which also occur at the end of the story of the Conquest proper (11:23c), can be understood readily.

1–2 "The inheritance portions" to be described are *in Canaan*. That word had not been used previously for the territory received by the Transjordanian tribes. Canaan was rightfully Israel's land on the basis of divine promise (see 13:3) made to the patriarchs. The similarity in wording with 13:32 shows that the writer again is concerned to draw a parallel with what Moses had done on the east side of the Jordan.

Joshua, however, is not the first of the authorities undertaking the distribution of the land to be mentioned. *Eleazar the priest* takes priority in this matter.[1] He is the son and successor of Aaron, the former high priest (Exod. 6:23; Num. 3:4; Deut. 10:6). Then comes the military leader *Joshua*, here designated by his additional epithet *the son of Nun*, probably to give full weight to this new undertaking. Finally, the *heads of the fathers' houses* are mentioned. This threefold division reflects Num. 34:16–29 (see also 32:28–32).

The parallel of Moses and Joshua is also shown in the use of the *lot* as the means for distributing the land (see Num. 26:52–56; 33:54). This lot, which was directed by divine guidance (Prov. 16:33), was to determine the general area and size of the tribal allotments, allowing for more precise fixing of boundaries at a later point (see 19:9). Some of the boundaries had been established at an earlier time (18:4–5). Even so, the lot was used to mark the divine apportionment of the land in question. The author stresses the divine command behind this procedure as it has been communicated to Moses, and leads up to the point where he now will explain once again that this was meant for the *nine and a half tribes* which had not yet received their lot.

3–4 Starting from the basic figure of the twelve-tribe arrange-

---

1. The presence of Eleazar is why those adhering to the Documentary Hypothesis ascribe this part of Joshua to the "P" document; see, e.g., O. Eissfeldt, *The OT: An Introduction*, pp. 251f. Other alleged "P" sections are chs. 15–16; 17:1–11; 18:11–28; 19. J. Bright, while not rejecting this classification, nevertheless points out that the presence of a priest at the casting of lots, a religious ceremony, is something to be expected. The constructions of Wellhausen continue to influence many a scholar's views concerning the role of the priesthood in Israel's religion and in religion in general.

ment,² these verses explain the relationship between the 2½ tribes east of the Jordan and the 9½ west of the river. Apparently it was necessary to make even more clear that which was obvious from the preceding chapter (13:7–8). Special concern is shown to emphasize that the tribes on the east side of the Jordan indeed did belong to Israel.³ This is also the reason for repeating what had been said about Levi, who had not been *given an inheritance among them* (13:14, 33). With Levi eliminated from the twelve-tribe arrangement it became necessary to point out that *the Josephites formed two tribes*. The additional remark that the *Levites* received *no portion in the land, but cities to live in* is less cultically oriented than the earlier explanation where the offerings of the Lord (and even the Lord himself) are said to be Levi's share. Levi will have the benefit of *pasture lands for their cattle and their substance*, which consisted at that point of other livestock.

5 The introductory significance of this pericope also becomes clear from this verse, which indicates Israel's strict adherence to the Lord's command to Moses in the division of the land. Since the account of this division actually does not begin until ch. 15, it is clear that what follows in vv. 6–15 is meant to be a further introduction to chs. 15–19.

2. CALEB'S PORTION CLAIMED IN FAITH (14:6–15)

6 *Now the people of Judah had come to Joshua at Gilgal; and Caleb son of Jephunneh the Kenizzite said to him: "You know what the Lord said to Moses the man of God at Kadesh-barnea concerning you and me.*

7 *Forty years old I was when Moses the servant of the Lord sent me from Kadesh-barnea to spy out the land; and I brought back to him a conscientious report.*

8 *While my brothers who had gone up with me made the heart of the people melt, I remained completely loyal to the Lord my God.*

---

2. The tribal system of Israel has been subjected to much critical scrutiny, e.g., by M. Noth, *History*, pp. 85–97. Noth approaches the "traditions" preceding Israel's settlement in Palestine with a good deal of scepticism. Such traditions, so he holds, while basic for Israel's faith and self-consciousness, were nevertheless shaped by presuppositions which arose from Israel as a settled nation in Canaan; see also pp. 68–84. A study based on Noth's approach, while critical of some of his findings, is C. H. J. de Geus, *The Tribes of Israel, passim*, esp. pp. 69–119. Popular commentaries such as J. M. Miller and G. M. Tucker, *The Book of Joshua*, also reflect this opinion. See also N. K. Gottwald's discussion of Noth's theories; *The Tribes of Yahweh*, pp. 345–386, and *passim*.
3. C. Vonk, *Inleiding op de Profeten: Jozua*, pp. 216–18, enumerates not fewer than ten references in the Pentateuch and Joshua where the 2½ tribes are given special mention.

9 *So Moses declared under oath on that day: Surely the land on which your foot has gone will be yours and of your children as an inheritance forever, for you have been completely loyal to the Lord my God.*

10 *Well, the Lord has kept me alive, as he has promised. It is now forty-five years since the Lord spoke this word to Moses, during which time Israel journeyed through the desert. Here I am today, eighty-five years old!*

11 *I am still as strong today as on the day when Moses sent me out; I have the same vigor now as I had then for warfare and for daily duties.*

12 *Give me therefore this hill country of which the Lord spoke at that time; for you yourself heard at that time that the Anakim are there with large fortified cities. It may be that the Lord will be with me; then I shall drive them out even as the Lord has promised."*

13 *Then Joshua blessed him; and he gave Hebron to Caleb the son of Jephunneh for an inheritance.*

14 *Therefore Hebron has been the inheritance of Caleb the son of Jephunneh the Kenizzite to the present day, because he was completely loyal to the Lord, the God of Israel.*

15 *Hebron's name was previously Kiriath-arba; this Arba was the greatest man among the Anakim. And the land had rest from war.*

6 The story of how Caleb obtained his inheritance is linked with *the people of Judah*, who *had come to Joshua at Gilgal*. What precisely is the link between Judah's coming to Gilgal and Caleb's request that follows is not clear. *Caleb* often is linked with the tribe of Judah (Num. 13:6; 34:19), but his precise ethnic origin is a matter of debate since he is also called a *Kenizzite* (vv. 6, 14; Num. 32:12). Kenizzites are listed among the original, non-Israelite population of Canaan (Gen. 15:19). It may be that this name here simply stands for a descendant of Kenaz, which name occurs among Caleb's descendants (1 Chr. 4:13, 15).[1] Upon that supposition Caleb was Judahite by descent.

---

1. Other solutions have included the following: (a) The Kenizzites were an ethnic group first incorporated into Edom and subsequently into Judah. This must have taken place early, for Caleb was born in Egypt. (b) Jephunneh, Caleb's father, was a Kenizzite, but married a woman from the house of Caleb whose name occurs in 1 Chr. 2:18–20. A son of that marriage would be the Caleb of Josh. 14. Jephunneh had two more sons by a second wife, Othniel and Seraiah, called sons of Kenaz, or Kenizzites (cf. 1 Chr. 4:13). (c) The Kenizzites were always a Judahite clan but never left Canaan to go to Egypt; so, e.g., J. Steinmann, *Josué*, p. 81; cf. also F.-M. Abel, *Le Livre de Josué*, p. 69, n. b, but this presupposes a view of the Conquest different from that of Joshua.

The place where the people of Judah gathered was *Gilgal*, probably the place near Jericho (see 5:9; 10:43).[2]

Caleb's conversation and request are reported masterfully, and because of the vividness of presentation would seem to reflect an eyewitness account. Caleb begins by reminding Joshua[3] of what *the Lord said to Moses . . . concerning you and me*. This recalls the events of Num. 14:24, 30. The story of the twelve spies and its aftermath mentions Caleb alone at first (see also Num. 13:30; Deut. 1:36). Apparently the role of Joshua, Moses' special servant, was too obvious to mention at every point. Caleb calls Moses the *man of God*. Subsequently (v. 7) he calls him the *servant of the Lord* (cf. 1:1). The designation "man of God" is particularly frequent in the case of Moses (Deut. 33:1; Ezra 3:2; Ps. 90:1), but it is also used of prophets in general (e.g., 1 Sam. 9:6; 1 K. 17:18; 2 K. 4:7; also of David, 2 Chr. 8:14; Neh. 12:24, 36).

7–9 Caleb's account of past events goes back to the time he was sent by Moses *to spy out the land*. He recalls the *conscientious report* (lit. "a word as was with my heart") he had rendered, a report which had not just emphasized the threatening aspects of Canaan's conquest. Caleb's role had been different from that of his *brothers* (the use of the independent personal pronoun is emphatic). While these others *made the heart of the people melt*, he had been *completely loyal to the Lord my God*.[4] The writer of this account may have told the story with special concern for his later readers, who would be tempted, as were the Israelites during their desert journey, to lose heart in the face of great odds. The account of Caleb's courageous stand would then serve to remind God's people of how the promised land had been won.

Caleb speaks of an *oath* made to him by *Moses*. This supplements what is reported in Num. 14:24; Deut. 1:36, where no such oath is recorded. *The land on which your foot has gone*: the southern part of Palestine in which Hebron was located had been the special focus of the mission of the twelve spies, although they had explored the whole land (Num. 13:21). The language Caleb uses could therefore be applied to Hebron, the city he now claims for himself. That Caleb was *completely loyal* to God is the reason for Moses' assurance to him. The book of

2. Much discussion centers on the possible location of Gilgal (see also Deut. 11:29–32; 27:1–8). Some believe the Gilgal meant here is that near Shechem.

3. The Hebrew uses the independent personal pronoun in connection with Joshua: "you yourself know."

4. Other translations: Zürcher Bibel "während ich unwandelbar zum Herrn hielt"; A. Gelin "j'ai accompli pleinement la volonté de Yahweh"; BDB "I wholly followed the Lord."

Joshua stresses the gratuitous giving of the land to Israel by God (e.g., 1:3), but this giving is closely connected with Israel's faith (compare 13:6b with 13:13).

10–12   Caleb's speech is marked by great vividness and animation. Three times the Hebrew uses the particle w^e '*attâ*, twice in v. 10 and once in v. 12. This usage may point to a juridical aspect of the words of Caleb. *Forty-five years* have elapsed since Caleb received God's promise, which took place in the second year after Israel's departure from Egypt (Num. 10:11). About the length of the actual conquest of Canaan, see also 11:18. Caleb praises God for granting him the vigor he possesses at the age of *eighty-five*. The long and wearisome trek through the desert has left his strength undiminished (v. 11). This applies to the waging of war and to *daily duties* (lit. "going out and coming in"), for which an aged person normally has no strength (Deut. 31:2). The specific request is: *Give me therefore this hill country* (v. 12). Hebron is situated in the mountain region. Does Caleb's use of the pronoun "this" indicate a location other than Gilgal which was near the Jordan? Is the Caleb episode an insertion into a narrative which originally spoke only of the allotment given to Judah? These are possibilities, although the pronoun "this" in Hebrew grammar does not always denote close proximity.[5] Without mentioning Hebron by name Caleb nevertheless has that city in mind. But he explicitly refers to the redoubtable *Anakim* who lived in that region with their *large fortified cities* (Num. 13:28, 33). It may not be without reason that these Anakim are mentioned both at the conclusion of the story of the actual Conquest (11:21–22) and at the beginning of the story of the allotment (v. 15), for it was their presence in Canaan which had made Israel fainthearted in the desert. That is why the story of the Conquest concludes fittingly with a reference to their being driven out, while the story of the allotment begins equally fittingly with Caleb's desire to obtain their territory in order that, with the Lord's help, he may drive them out. Joshua himself had heard about the Anakim's presence when he was with Caleb on the spying mission.[6]

The relationship between the account of Joshua's exploits vis-à-vis the Anakim (11:21–22), Caleb's desire to drive them out at this point, and the story of Judg. 1:10 is a matter of continuing debate. Joshua's defeat of the Anakim may not have been as definitive as might appear at first

5. See GKC § 136 b; cf. "this" Lebanon in 1:4.
6. Verse 12a can also be combined as follows: ". . . at that time, for you yourself heard (it); for the Anakim are there. . . ." So, e.g., C. F. Keil and F. Delitzsch, C. J. Goslinga.

sight from 11:21–22. Some, indeed, did escape and lived elsewhere. This may account for their relatively early resurgence. The same applies to the city of Hebron, which had been captured earlier (10:36–39). See also the story of Jebus (15:63; Judg. 1:21; 2 Sam. 5:6).[7]

It may be that the Lord will be with me. Heb. *'ûlay* ("maybe") need not express fear or doubt. Usually it signifies hope (Gen. 16:2; Num. 22:6, 11).[8] The outcome of Caleb's hope is as sure as his faith is strong. The Anakim will be driven out. Faith in what *the Lord spoke at that time* and in what he *has promised* makes Caleb speak as he does. Is not this one of the obvious reasons why this story occurs at this point, namely at the beginning of the land allotment process, a procedure which has as its background 13:1–7, especially v. 6?

13-14 *Then Joshua blessed him*: he bestowed upon Caleb power to be successful in his undertaking, which would be begun and ended in faith. Blessing is not a magical conferment of potency, yet it is more than the mere utterance of a pious wish.[9] It is done in the name of the Lord, who is the source of all power and prosperity, both material and spiritual. Blessing often involves material prosperity such as numerous offspring (Gen. 1:28; 28:3) or land (Gen. 26:3; 28:4; Ps. 37:22). See also Deut. 15:4, 14; 16:10, 17. In the NT it is those "blessed of my Father" who will "inherit the kingdom" (Matt. 25:34); the word "inherit" is derived from OT usage concerning the possession of Canaan. For a rather "material" understanding of the blessing, see also 15:19, where the word translated "gift" (Heb. *berākâ*) means literally "blessing"; cf. Judg. 1:15.

Joshua, who here acts alone (cf. v. 1; 17:14), gives *Hebron to Caleb the son of Jephunneh for an inheritance*. The phraseology may be deliberately fulsome to emphasize the legal transaction of this land grant. As 15:13 shows, the Lord's command to Joshua was behind this granting of Hebron to Caleb. Hebron was to become one of the cities assigned to the Levites (21:11).

Though the chief purpose of the story follows the lines indicated

7. Another attempt to relate the various accounts is to suppose that Caleb's capture of Hebron and his expulsion of the Anakim was also attributed to Joshua, and rightly so, for this feat took place under his over-all military leadership.

8. See BDB. KD, p. 150, quote Masius to the effect that this particle "does not express a doubt, but a . . . 'hope mixed with difficulty; and whilst the difficulty detracts from the value, the hope stimulates the desire for the gift.' "

9. See KB, s.v. *bāraḵ*, where it is defined "mit heilvoller Kraft begaben," i.e., to "gift somebody, something with fortunate power," i.e., full of wholeness, well-being, salvation. See also H. W. Beyer, "εὐλογέω," *TDNT* II (E.T. 1964), pp. 754–765.

above, it has a further purpose, namely to inform the readers that *Hebron has been the inheritance of Caleb . . . to the present day*. But this is not just another etiological tale to explain how a supposedly non-Israelite clan came to have an inheritance amidst the Israelites. For one thing, Caleb's non-Israelite origins are not established (see v. 6 and commentary). In addition, all historiography has an etiological element, in that it seeks to preserve those memories of the past that make the present meaningful. That is the kind of etiology that is squarely rooted in fact, and not in a fictitious composition invented by an author. On the expression *till the present day*, see 4:9 and commentary. Verse 14 contains the third reference to Caleb's complete loyalty to the Lord (see vv. 8-9), the key to the story's main purpose.

Care should be taken not to make Caleb into a mere example. Exemplars of faith can be gathered from church history and the history of missions as well. The example element is present, but it is embedded in a story which conveys the history of the progress of God's redemption. The events that happen in that historical context are nonrepeatable and unique. They cannot simply be lifted out of that context for purposes of a message for today. God uses Caleb's loyalty and faith to bring about the realization of his promise of the land. The story begun here has for its ultimate fulfilment the inheriting of salvation in Christ (see also Matt. 25:34; Eph. 1:14; Col. 3:24; Heb. 9:15). This provides the Joshua material with the necessary perspective as well as with eschatological depth, and it leads to a much more dynamic and effective "application" than the example method would be able to provide.[10] At stake is the ability of the reader and interpreter to listen to what the text has to say. The main thrust of the biblical text, here or elsewhere, is the development of the line of the history of redemption. Within that larger context, "examples" of faith may be given due prominence.

15 The story ends with a note concerning *Hebron* and its previous name, *Kiriath-arba* (Gen. 23:2). Hebron was one of the cities of the southern coalition defeated by Joshua (10:3). The name Kiriath-arba may mean "tetrapolis," literally "city of four" (quarters, districts, confederated cities),[11] but Arba is here taken as a proper name (cf. 15:13; 21:11). He is called *the greatest man among the Anakim*, which probably refers to his

---

10. On the matter here mentioned see also B. Holwerda, "De Heilshistorie in de Prediking," in *Begonnen Hebbende Van Mozes* (Terneuzen: 1953), pp. 79-118; and S. Greidanus, *Sola Scriptura* (Kampen: 1970), *passim*.

11. Very different is Jerome's opinion: Kiriath-arba is the city of four famous men, Adam, Abraham, Isaac, and Jacob. Jerome understood Heb. *'āḏām*, "man," to be a reference to Adam, and translated: "Adam was great among the Anakim."

unusual height.[12] He was a giant among giants. This historical note lends emphasis to the story's main concern, Caleb's heroic faith used by God for the conquest of this area of the promised land.

Concerning the concluding words, *the land had rest from war*, see the introduction to this pericope. The story of Caleb's acquisition of Hebron, an instance of what could and should be done with the whole land allotted to the tribes, concludes with the same words as were used for the conclusion of the conquest stories (11:23). As such this information also leads naturally to the story of the allotment. The peaceful condition of the country allowed Israel to engage in this activity without fear of hostile interference.

D. JUDAH'S ALLOTMENT (15:1–63)[1]

1. JUDAH'S BOUNDARY LINES (15:1–12)

1 *The lot for the tribe of Judah according to their families extended to the territory of Edom, to the desert of Zin southward, in the extreme south.*

2 *Their southern border ran from the end of the Salt Sea, from the bay which faces southward;*

3 *then it ran on to what is south of the ascent of Akrabbim, passed on to Zin, and went up south of Kadesh-barnea; then it ran past Hezron, ascended to Addar, and turned about to Karka;*

4 *then it passed along to Azmon, and came out at the brook of Egypt, so that it ended at the sea. This will be the southern border for you.*

5 *The east border was the Salt Sea to the mouth of the Jordan.*
The border on the north side began at the bay of the sea at the mouth of the Jordan;

6 *the border went upward to Beth-hoglah and passed then on north of Beth-arabah; then the border ran upward to the stone of Bohan the son of Reuben;*

7 *the border then ascended to Debir from the valley of Achor and turned northward toward Gilgal, which lies opposite the ascent of Adummim, south of the valley; the border then passed along to the waters of En-shemesh and ended at En-rogel.*

---

12. The LXX must have read *hā'ᵃḏāmâ haggᵉḏôlâ* (lit. "the great country") instead of *hā'āḏām haggāḏôl*, "the great man," and rendered it with *mētrópolis*. Several interpreters prefer that understanding of the text.

1. The scholarly debate concerning a possible date of the lists of boundaries and cities contained in these allotment chapters is referred to in the Introduction to this commentary.

8 *Then the border ran by the valley of the son of Hinnom, and up to the southern slope of the Jebusite, that is, of Jerusalem; then the border ran up to the top of the mountain which lies westward opposite the valley of the son of Hinnom, at the northern end of the valley of Rephaim.*

9 *The border then turned from the top of the mountain to the spring of the Waters of Nephtoah, and came out at the cities of the mountain of Ephron; it then turned to Baalah, that is, Kiriath-jearim.*

10 *Then the border bent westward from Baalah to Mount Seir; it ran on to the slope of Mount Jearim, that is, Chesalon, northward; it ran down to Beth-shemesh, and passed along to Timnah.*

11 *The border then went northward to the ridge of Ekron; the border turned to Shikkeron, passed along to the mountain of Baalah, and came out at Jabneel. The border then came to its end at the sea.*

12 *The western border was the Great Sea with its coastline. This is the border round about the people of Judah according to their families.*

The purpose of this chapter, along with the other chapters dealing with the distribution of the land to the tribes, is to give concrete shape to the leading idea of the book of Joshua, the fulfilment of the promise to the forefathers (see the writer's concluding comment in 21:43-45). The special significance of the chapter dealing with Judah is the fact that his lot is mentioned first. Under the superintending providence of God this is an indication of Judah's future prominence. From him was to come the "scepter" of which Gen. 49:10 had spoken.[2]

This chapter, dealing with Judah's territorial allotment, consists of four parts: (1) a description of Judah's boundaries (vv. 1-12); (2) a short account of the conquests by Caleb and Othniel (vv. 13-19); (3) a list of Judahite cities (vv. 20-62); and (4) a concluding note (of warning?) concerning Judah's inability to drive out the Jebusites from Jerusalem (v. 63).

1 This verse continues the action of 14:6a, in which the people of Judah have presented themselves to receive their allotment. The story of Caleb's acquisition of Hebron (vv. 6b-15) must be viewed as somewhat paradigmatic of God's purpose for the land of promise and of Israel's role in occupying that land.

Each tribe's territory was designated by *lot* (14:2). As had been the case with the tribes east of the Jordan, this took place *according to their families* (see 13:15, 24, 29). The lot served to ensure the divine guidance of this undertaking. Sometimes the lot was preceded by a description of the land to be allotted (18:4, 9). The delineations of the borders which resulted from the casting of lots vary considerably in the amount of detail

2. See J. Calvin, *Commentaries on the Book of Joshua*, ad loc.

233

they include.[3] The Bible gives no details as to the precise manner in which the lot settled a given boundary.[4] Various expressions are used in Hebrew to describe the transaction. In the present verse the expression reads literally "and the lot *was* for the tribe . . ." (cf. 16:1 "and the lot *went out* for the children of Joseph"; 18:11 "and the lot of the tribe of the children of Benjamin *went up*").

Judah's southern border is given first (vv. 1–4); the line moves from east to west. Judah's lot extended *to the territory of Edom, to the desert of Zin*, the points where Judah's territory began. Edom's territory was to the south of Moab, east of the Dead Sea, and it extended as far as the Gulf of Aqaba.[5] The desert of Zin, on the other hand, may have been a part of the promised land (see Num. 13:21). This desert is often identified with the area of Kadesh-barnea (Num. 20:1; 27:14), but here it is distinguished from that area and placed between the ascent of Akrabbim and the area of Kadesh (v. 3).

2–4 Here begins the detailed description of Judah's southern border. This border is the same as that of the promised land (Num. 34:3–5). It begins at *the end of the Salt Sea*, i.e., the southernmost tip of the Sea, and more exactly, at *the bay which faces southward*. The Hebrew for "bay" is *lāšôn* (lit. "tongue"). Customarily, the tongue area in the Dead Sea region is identified with the flat peninsula-platform that juts out from its eastern shore. Here, however, it must refer to a region on the west side. (Other references to the "tongue" are in v. 5b; 18:19.)

The Hebrew tenses used in vv. 1–2 differ from those in vv. 3–4.[6] Some modern translations seek to express this difference;[7] the translation offered here continues the tenses of the opening verses throughout. The

---

3. See Y. Aharoni, *The Land of the Bible*, pp. 228–230. Aharoni assumes that the original lists may all have been quite detailed but that they were "simplified and shortened in varying degrees" for the present lists. This is a possibility, but we cannot be sure.

4. The rabbis believed that there were two urns, containing the names of the tribes and the divisions of the land respectively. First, a slip was taken out of one urn, then out of the other.

5. Edom's domain may have extended to the west side of the Arabah (the deep rift in which the Jordan Valley is found); see Num. 20:16. If so, the final words of v. 1 would apply to both Edom and the desert of Zin.

6. Verses 1–2 contain *waw* consecutive with imperfects; vv. 3–4 have perfects with *waw* copulative.

7. These translations use the present in vv. 3–4 (e.g., RSV, Zürcher Bibel, M. Noth, *Das Buch Josua*). Others (ASV, NAB, F.-M. Abel, DNV) continue the past tenses of vv. 1–2.

southern border *ran on*[8] *to what is south of the ascent of Akrabbim*, which has been identified with modern Naqb eṣ-Ṣafā. *Zin* may have been a water point or oasis east of Kadesh. It was from the desert of Zin (v. 1) that the spies left for the land of Canaan (Num. 13:21), and Miriam died there (Num. 20:1). The next border point is *Kadesh-barnea* (cf. 10:41). This was the center of Israel's extended sojourn in the desert (Deut. 1:46), south of the Amorite mountain country (Deut. 1:20) and east of Gerar (Gen. 20:1), in the southern extremity of the land which Joshua conquered (Josh. 10:41). Proposed identifications are 'Ain Qedeis, or, more probably, 'Ain el-Qudeirât.[9] This city did not play a part in Israel's subsequent history, but its name recurs in the prophetic delineation of Israel's borders (Ezek. 47:19), a passage with eschatological overtones. Perhaps this is an indication that the allotment of the land contains theoretical features as well. The boundary lists were not necessarily founded on actual historical conditions, as many scholars assume. Despite the programmatic element they contained, the event of the allotment is historical.

The towns of *Hezron*, *Addar*, and *Karka*, mentioned next, cannot be identified with certainty (cf. Num. 34:4–5). Three wells found in the vicinity of 'Ain el-Qudeirât may serve as possible identifications. The location of *Azmon* (v. 4) is uncertain. The border then came out at *the brook of Egypt* (see commentary on 13:3), and *it ended at the sea*,[10] i.e., the Mediterranean Sea. The concluding words (*This will be the southern border for you*) may suggest a public reading of the boundary lines aimed at an audience, hence *for you*. The LXX reads "for them"—possibly a simplification?

5a The description now moves back to its starting point in the east. Judah's eastern border was *the Salt Sea to the mouth* (lit. "the ex-

---

8. The boundary description uses a variety of verbs depending on local topography, e.g., "to go up," "to go down," vv. 6, 10; also "to pass along," "to turn about." "It is not always possible to distinguish the narrow shades of meaning"; Aharoni, *op. cit.*, p. 228, n. 136.

9. Arabic *qedeis* is not the same as the root from which Kadesh is derived. The second location has been called "the richest and most centrally located of a group of springs on the southern edge of the Negeb" (*idem*, p. 65).

10. More literally "and the goings out of the border were at the sea" (ASV). Other translations: NEB "and its limit was the sea"; NAB "before coming out at the sea"; Noth "und die Ausgänge der Grenze führen zum Meer"; J. H. Kroeze "de uitlopers van de grens waren zeewaarts." The Hebrew expression used here often takes together several segments in the border.

tremity") *of the Jordan*. The rest of the eastern border coincided with
Edom's western border (see above).[11]

5b–6 Judah's northern border began *at the bay of the sea at the
mouth of the Jordan*. For "bay" (Heb. *lāšôn*, "tongue") see v. 2. The Dead
Sea at that time had a higher shoreline than at present,[12] and this had
caused a bay to be formed extending to a point level with *Beth-hoglah*, the
first town mentioned in the northern border. Beth-hoglah was a border
town between Benjamin and Judah. The town was actually allotted to
Benjamin (18:19, 21).[13] The same holds for the next town *Beth-arabah*
(18:22), but in 15:61 it is also assigned to Judah, which points to certain
adjustments in the boundaries between the tribes.[14]

The location of *the stone of Bohan the son of Reuben* is not known.
The words *ran upward* (for the opposite expression see 18:17b) suggest
that this may have been the point where the boundary reached the slopes
of the hill country. Nothing further is known about Bohan, Reuben's son.[15]
Reuben's territory is placed entirely in Transjordan.

7–8 The description of v. 7 presents several uncertainties. The
border *ascended to Debir from the valley of Achor*. These words do not
occur in the description of Benjamin's border, corresponding to that of
Judah (18:15, 17). The LXX lacks the reference to Debir, and reconstruction of the Hebrew text has been attempted.[16] The city of Debir is not that
mentioned in v. 15; 10:38. Perhaps it is modern Thogret ed-Debr, east-
northeast of Jerusalem near Adummim. Also considerable dispute centers

11. The NEB reads v. 5 as follows: "The eastern boundary is the Dead Sea as far
as the mouth of the Jordan and the adjacent land northwards from the inlet of the
sea, at the mouth of the Jordan," leaving one to wonder where exactly the description of the northern border begins.
12. Thus *GTT*, p. 138. Others assume that there has been no such change in the
shoreline.
13. Most of the same border will be described again in connection with Benjamin's
allotment and some also in connection with that of Dan (18:14–19; 19:40–48).
14. Aharoni, *VT* 9 (1959), pp. 225–246, esp. p. 230, has pointed out that the
double appearance of Beth-arabah is actually an argument against A. Alt's theory
that the Benjaminite list of 18:22 was originally a Judahite list. See also F. M.
Cross, Jr., and G. E. Wright, "The Boundary and Province Lists of the Kingdom
of Judah," *JBL* 75 (1956), pp. 202–226, esp. p. 209, who observe, against Alt:
"One does not cut apart a list leaving the same place name on both sides of the
Document."
15. About Reuben's role in Israel's early history see also 13:8, 15. A. Gelin,
Josué, p. 91, calls attention to 22:10 as another sign of possible Reubenite influence west of the Jordan.
16. *GTT*, p. 137, n. 113.

on the situation of the *valley of Achor* (see 7:24).[17] A further difficulty lies in the fact that the border is said to be turning *northward to Gilgal*, whereas the general direction of the line being drawn appears to be southward (see the conclusion of v. 7). The reference to Gilgal itself also presents a problem. Although the location of the Gilgal mentioned in 5:9 is not certain, its general position was farther north. The solution may lie in reading *gᵉlîlôṯ*, "circles of stones," or "districts."[18]

The last part of v. 7 is less problematical. The *ascent of Adummim* (lit. "the ascent of blood") is the present Talʿat ed-Damm, which conveys the same notion of "redness" as does Adummim. This was *south of the valley*, meaning the Wâdī Qelt. *En-shemesh*, to which the border then *passed along*, is a well near Jerusalem, also known as Gihon (cf. 1 K. 1:33). Many identify it with ʿAin el-Hôd, along the Jericho road, east of the Mount of Olives and northeast of Bethany. *En-rogel*, presently Bir Ayyūb ("Job's well") is located where the Kidron Valley east of Jerusalem joins the valley of Hinnom, to the south of it.

As is clear from v. 8, Judah's boundary did not include Jebus, the later capital of David's kingdom.[19] It ran through the valley south of that city, called the *valley of the son of Hinnom, and up to the southern slope*,[20] said to be that *of the Jebusite*. (For the Jebusites, see 3:10.) The city of the Jebusites is identified here with *Jerusalem*.[21] Leaving the valley, the border climbed to the crest of the Judean hill country, i.e., *to the top of the mountain which lies westward opposite the valley of the son of Hinnom*. This mountain shuts off *the valley of Rephaim*, west of Jerusalem, on the

---

17. One suggestion identifies it with el-Buqeiʿah; see J. P. U. Lilley, "Achor," in *NBD*, pp. 9f.

18. The helpful translation found in NAB (". . . in the direction of the Gilgal that faces the pass of Adummim") avoids the impression that the other, and better known, Gilgal is meant.

19. Is not this circumstance an indication of an early date for this list?

20. Heb. lit. "shoulder." Aharoni, *The Land of the Bible*, p. 235, defends the translation "slope" on the basis of an inscription from Silwan, carved in the slope opposite the site of ancient Jerusalem.

21. On Jerusalem see 10:1 and commentary. The name Urusalim occurs in the Amarna tablets (*ANET*, p. 488). R. North, *Bibl* 54 (1973), pp. 43–62, observes that the Amarna city is "unhelpfully never related to Jebusites; but we can hardly doubt its identity with Jerusalem." The identity of Jebus with Jerusalem is questioned for several reasons in J. M. Miller and G. M. Tucker, *The Book of Joshua*, p. 121, but this assumes that the note in v. 8 is in error. The Jebusites "probably belonged to the Amorite tribes which occupied the hill country, with the Canaanites in occupation of the plains" (K. M. Kenyon, *Digging up Jerusalem* [New York: 1974], p. 41).

northern end. How the name Rephaim came to be associated with this valley, the present Baqa', is not clear. (On the Rephaim see 12:4; 13:12.)

9–11 Judah's boundary then ran *from the top of the mountain to the spring of the Waters of Nephtoah*,[22] in a northwesterly direction. Nephtoah is considered to be identical with modern Liftā, 2 miles northwest of Jerusalem. The border then *came out at the cities*[23] *of the mountain of Ephron*. (For Ephron see also 2 Chr. 13:19, but note the difference between the Ketib and the Qere; cf. 2 Sam. 13:23.) *Baalah, that is, Kiriathjearim*, is identified with Deir el-Azhar, a "mound representing an ancient city of five to six acres, with debris of a depth of over twelve feet on the summit."[24]

From this point Judah's border, which previously corresponded to that of Benjamin, begins to coincide with Dan's border. The latter is not enumerated minutely in terms of boundary points. Hence vv. 10–12 are not duplicated elsewhere in Joshua.[25] Judah's border now runs westward, *to Mount Seir* (v. 10). This name is not to be confused with the site which was Edom's domain east of the Dead Sea. The present Seir may be perpetuated in the name Sarid, near Chesalon, southwest of Kiriath-jearim. The border continues *to the slope of Mount Jearim*, which some consider just another name for Seir.[26] On the northern slope was *Chesalon*, modern Keslā. The boundary then runs down to *Beth-shemesh*, identified with Tell er-Rumeileh,[27] and called Ir-shemesh in 19:41. The next point, *Timnah*, is the present Khirbet Tibnah,[28] southeast of Beth-shemesh and well known from the Samson stories (Judg. 14:1–5).

22. The opinion is widespread that this name (Heb. *mĕneptôaḥ*) was originally a reference to Pharaoh Merneptah. Cf. *ANET*, p. 258c, where the "Wells of Merne-Ptah" occur in the journal of an Egyptian frontier official. There is no unanimity on this theory.

23. The word "cities" does not occur in the LXX. Abel omits it, and Aharoni observes that cities in this indefinite manner cannot designate a point in a borderline. B. J. Alfrink, *Josué*, p. 82, suggests that the word be read "forests" (*yᵉārê* for *'ārê*).

24. Kraeling, *op. cit.*, p. 175.

25. For a discussion of Alt's opinion concerning the Danite borders and their alleged omission from the original list of boundary descriptions, see Y. Kaufmann, *The Biblical Account of the Conquest of Palestine*, pp. 15–19.

26. E.g., G. E. Wright and F. V. Filson, eds., *The Westminster Historical Atlas of the Bible*, p. 125. Similarly, W. H. Gispen et al., eds., *Bijbelse Encyclopaedie*, s.v. Seir.

27. For the result of the excavations at this site during the years 1911–13 and 1928–33, see J. A. Emerton, "Beth-shemesh," in *AOTS*, pp. 197–206.

28. Aharoni, *The Land of the Bible*, p. 235, identifies it with Tell Batashi. Simons, *GTT*, p. 141, states: "If hirbet tibnah preserves only the ancient name, a site in its vicinity has to be looked for."

The border then ran *northward to the ridge of Ekron* (lit. "to the shoulder of the hill north of Ekron"). Ekron was one of the five principal cities of the Philistines who later would settle in Palestine. For its location, see 13:3 and commentary. If Khirbet el-Muqenna' is the site, then the shoulder of the hill north of the city may be the steep incline north of this town. A fortified Iron Age city has been discovered at this site, but the allotment took place before the beginning of the Iron Age. *Shikkeron*, Judah's next border point, has been identified by some with Tell el-Fûl, 3½ miles northwest of Ekron, but this is not certain. *The mountain of Baalah* to which the border passes next is probably the ridge of el-Mug-hâr.[29] The presence of a mount in this flat coastal area has been judged intrinsically impossible by some. El-mughâr is a steep slope 2 miles northwest of Shikkeron, which may explain the name "mountain." The last place on this east-to-west boundary line is *Jabneel*, the Jamnia of later times (1–2 Maccabees). Eusebius' *Onomasticon* places it between Diospolis (NT Lydda) and Ashdod. Its present name is Yebnā. Jabneel was later a Philistine city and was captured by Uzziah (2 Chr. 26:6). The border *came to its end* (lit. "had its goings-out") at the Mediterranean *Sea*.

12 Just as the eastern border of Judah's lot was the Dead Sea, so the *western border* was formed by the Mediterranean Sea.[30] A summary statement concludes this border list.

2. CALEB'S GIFT TO HIS DAUGHTER (15:13–19)

13 *To Caleb son of Jephunneh, however, they gave a portion among the Judahites, namely Kiriath-arba, according to the Lord's command to Joshua. (Arba was the father of Anak.) This is Hebron.*

14 *And Caleb drove out from there the three Anakim: Sheshai, Ahiman, and Talmai, the descendants of Anak.*

15 *From there he marched up against the inhabitants of Debir. The name of Debir was previously Kiriath-sepher.*

16 *Then Caleb said: "Whoever attacks Kiriath-sepher and captures it, to him I will give Achsah my daughter as wife."*

17 *Othniel, son of Kenaz, the brother of Caleb, took it; so Caleb gave him his daughter Achsah as wife.*

---

29. So Aharoni, *The Land of the Bible*, p. 235.
30. Verse 12 offers a translation difficulty, caused by the second occurrence of *$g^eb\hat{u}l$*, "border," "territory." The ASV renders literally "And the west border was to the great sea, and the border *thereof*." Simons, *GTT*, p. 141, reads "The Great (or Mediterranean) Sea and 'its' coastland," assuming that the suffix has been omitted from *$g^eb\hat{u}l$* (second occurrence); see also GKC § 90f.

18 *When she arrived she urged him to ask her father for a field. Then, as she alighted from her donkey, Caleb asked her: "What do you want?"*

19 *She said to him: "Give me a marriage gift. You have assigned to me land from the Negeb; give me also springs of water." Then he gave her the upper springs and the lower springs.*

The purpose for inserting this story at the present point in the description of Judah's lot may have been the same as that of the earlier Caleb story (14:6–12). Apparently the author wishes to complete the story of Judah's allotment with an account of how Caleb actually did drive out the Anakim from the area he had claimed as his own. Note also the similarity in wording of v. 12b, at the conclusion of Judah's border list, and v. 20. The Caleb episode concludes the account of Judah's borders, just as the earlier Caleb story stood at its beginning.

For the possible time sequence of the events reported in 11:20; 14:6–12; the present pericope, and Judg. 1:10–15, see 14:10–12 and commentary. Since Caleb made his request for Hebron at the advanced age of eighty-five, one must assume that the conquest of the area now described took place at an early point after the granting of his request. This would mean that the events recorded in Judg. 1:10–15 actually took place during Joshua's lifetime.[1]

13–14 Following several translations and commentaries the translation presented here has rendered the opening *waw* with *however*. The story does not just mean to continue the description of Judah's boundaries, but harks back to what had been reported earlier. Hebrew narrative is paratactic. Caleb's *portion* was *Kiriath-arba*, which he received *among the Judahites*. (About Caleb's ethnic derivation see 14:6.) That Caleb's portion had been given him *according to the Lord's command to Joshua* is said to supplement the story of 14:6, where only the Lord's command to Moses is mentioned.[2]

For other details of v. 13, see 14:15 and commentary.

On the *Anakim*, driven out by Caleb, see 11:21–22; 14:12, 15. The names *Sheshai, Ahiman, and Talmai* may be designations of family units (see also Num. 13:22). The meaning of the names is not known. The expulsion of these redoubtable inhabitants of Canaan (Deut. 9:2), who had

1. A. E. Cundall, *Judges*, argues that *all* the events recorded in Judg. 1:1–2:5 took place during Joshua's lifetime and are to be connected with the invasion under his command. This position can only be defended by considering Judg. 1:1a to be a heading over the entire book, not over that which immediately follows.
2. The two do not necessarily exclude each other. As this commentary has noted frequently, e.g., in chs. 3–4, later accounts supplement earlier ones.

inspired fear in Israel's heart (Num. 13–14), must be seen as a singular instance of the Lord's help. This lends a paradigmatic nature to the story told here. With like faith, but exercised at the successive stages of redemption history, all of God's promises would be fulfilled equally.

15–16 Caleb also takes *Debir*, a city captured earlier (10:36–39) by Joshua. This presupposes a subsequent loss of some of the cities taken in the southern campaign. (On Debir's location see commentary at 10:38.[3]) Debir's name *was previously Kiriath-sepher*, which has been understood as "scribe town" (from Heb. *sôpēr*), also "city of books" or "city of records." Perhaps the city was the repository of a library like those of the great Mesopotamian cities. Referring to Debir by its ancient name, Caleb offers his daughter *Achsah* ("woman's anklet") to the person who will capture the city. (For a similar offer cf. 1 Sam. 17:25; 18:17.) This procedure conformed to oriental custom.

17–19 *Othniel, son of Kenaz, the brother of Caleb*, takes the city and obtains Achsah as his wife. (About Caleb's relation to Kenaz see 14:6 and commentary.[4]) Othniel was Caleb's younger brother (Judg. 1:13; 3:9).

Achsah's request was made when *she arrived*, probably when she entered the new family relations implied in her marriage to Othniel. She incites her husband[5] to request of her father *a field* in addition to the city of Debir. Achsah must have let it be known that she had this matter on her mind even though she had spoken about it only to Othniel. As she alights from her donkey[6] her father, who apparently perceived her state of mind, asks *"What do you want?"* She then remarks forthrightly that she desires a *marriage gift* (lit. "a blessing").[7] The *Negeb* is known for its relative scarcity of water. What she desires is *springs of water* (Heb. *gullōṯ*). The meaning of the word is not entirely certain. Some suggest the idea of

3. Albright's identification of Debir with Tell Beit Mirsim (see "Debir," *AOTS*, pp. 207–223) is denied by M. Noth, who opts for a less important site nearer to Hebron, Khirbet Terrameh. See also A. F. Rainey, "Debir," in *ISBE* I, pp. 901–4; *GTT*, p. 282; and J. P. U. Lilley, "Debir," *NBD*, pp. 302f. with bibliography.
4. According to the Masoretic accentuation "son of Kenaz" is to be separated from "the brother of Caleb."
5. Some modern translations, e.g., NEB, read "he incited her." This is based on the LXX of Judg. 1:14.
6. The translation of the Hebrew is uncertain. Most translations use a word suggesting "to come down from," "to descend." The NEB is a notable exception! Another rendering is "And she clapped in her hands."
7. See also 14:13 for the meaning of "blessing." The following translations have been offered: Zürcher Bibel "parting gift"; JB "favour"; NAB "an additional gift"; DNV "dowry."

"pool" or "basin."[8] Achsah's request is granted, for her father gives her the upper and the lower springs.[9]

3. CONCLUDING STATEMENT (15:20)

20 *This is the inheritance of the tribe of the people of Judah according to their families.*

20 The translations display no unanimity as to the place of this verse with respect to what precedes and follows. Some consider it to be the heading of the material in vv. 21–63 (e.g., RSV, NEB, NAB, NIV). Others treat it as an independent statement, leaving the reader to make his own combination as he sees fit. A third possibility is to draw it closely to what precedes. This approach helps the reader to see the Caleb-Othniel episode as a concrete instance of how Judah received its inheritance according to its families. In all but one of the descriptions of the various inheritances (Manasseh, 17:7–10) this formula is used, and always by way of conclusion (18:28b; 19:16, etc.).

4. CITY LIST OF JUDAH (15:21–62)

a. In the South (15:21–32)

21 *The cities of the tribe of the Judahites that were farthest removed, toward the border of Edom, in the South, were Kabzeel, Eder, Jagur,*
22 *Kinah, Dimonah, Adadah,*
23 *Kedesh, Hazor, Ithnan,*
24 *Ziph, Telem, Bealoth,*
25 *Hazor-hadattah, Kerioth-hezron (that is, Hazor),*
26 *Amam, Shema, Moladah,*
27 *Hazar-gaddah, Heshmon, Beth-pelet,*
28 *Hazar-shual, Beer-sheba, Biziothiah,*
29 *Baalah, Iim, Ezem,*
30 *Eltolad, Chesil, Hormah,*
31 *Ziklag, Madmannah, Sansannah,*
32 *Lebaoth, Shilhim, Ain, and Rimmon.*
   Twenty-nine cities in all, with their villages.

Along with the description of Judah's boundaries (vv. 1–12) this chapter

8. W. F. Albright, basing his remarks on the identification of Debir with Tell Beit Mirsim, thinks of "underground basins fed by springs" (*AOTS*, p. 208).
9. See JB, Zürcher Bibel.

presents a lengthy list of cities located in Judah's allotted territory. An exhaustive treatment of these would require topographical expertise which only specialists can bring to the task.[1] The discussion given here is based on the work of others who have examined the materials in the light of direct topographical investigations. For an understanding of the total "message" of Joshua, a minute discussion of the geographical details of these chapters is of relatively little value.[2] At the same time, the total impact of these lengthy enumerations is such as to give concrete expression to the fulfilment of God's promises regarding the land (see 21:43–45). Moreover, the Bible is not a treatise of philosophy or theology, nor is it a manual of abstract ethics. Rather, the Bible tells of God's actions in time and space. At no point can its message be adequately understood without at least some knowledge of the setting in which God's redemptive acts took place.[3]

The list of Judah's cities is given in four parts: those in the South (Negeb) (vv. 21–32); in the Shephelah; the area between the mountainous center and the coastal plain (vv. 33–47); in the Judean hill country (vv. 48–60); and in the desert toward the Dead Sea (vv. 61–62).

21 This verse and those which follow describe the cities that *were farthest removed* (Heb. *miqṣēh*, lit. "at the end of ").[4] Their center lies roughly in Beer-sheba (v. 28), their northern extent is marked by Madmannah (v. 31) and Hormah (v. 30), and in the west they extend as far as Shilhim (v. 32), assuming that this stands for Sharuhen.[5]

The list begins in the area of Edom's border *in the South* (Negeb), as did the boundary list above. A great many of the cities mentioned cannot be identified with certainty. The commentary presents some representative views gathered from leading handbooks and atlases.

The exact location of *Kabzeel*, near Arad, is unknown. It was the home of one of David's heroes (2 Sam. 23:20). *Eder* is possibly modern

---

1. In this respect we are in the company of others who likewise indicate a lack of topographical skills; see J. A. Soggin, *Joshua*, p. x.
2. Calvin refrains from extensive comment on these lists, partly because of a lack of necessary skills, partly because he judges that "great labour would produce little fruit to the reader"; *Commentaries on the Book of Joshua*, p. 200.
3. See G. E. Wright and F. V. Filson, eds., *The Westminster Historical Atlas of the Bible*, p. 5.
4. Other translations: ASV "uttermost cities"; RSV "cities . . . in the extreme South"; NEB "cities . . . , the full count"; Gelin "à l'extrémité (du territoire)."
5. See J. Bright, *IB* II, pp. 630f.

Tell 'Arâd.[6] *Jagur* is another city whose location is unknown; Khirbet Gharrah, 11.2 miles from Beer-sheba, has been suggested.

22 *Kinah* is of uncertain location, but is probably somewhere near Arad, on the Wâdī el-Qeini. *Dimonah*, near Aroer (1 Sam. 20:28), also has not been located, but some have identified it with Tell ed-Dheib. *Adadah* is held to be the same as Aroer. Others suggest the name be read Ararah,[7] identified with Khirbet 'Ar'arah, almost 12.5 miles southeast of Beer-sheba.

23 Some consider *Kedesh* to be Kadesh-barnea, but this is doubted by others,[8] since other towns were also called Kedesh (12:22). *Hazor* is of unknown location. In any event, it is not the same as that of 11:10. Some combine this name with the following, resulting in Hazor-ithnan, tentatively identified with el-Jebarîyeh on the Wâdī Umm Ethnân.[9] The location of *Ithnan* also is unknown.

24 *Ziph* is to be distinguished from the town in v. 55. Probably it is modern ez-Zeifeh. *Telem* is held by some authorities to be the same as Telaim (1 Sam. 15:4), but its location is uncertain. One suggestion is Umm es-Salafe. *Bealoth* ("goddesses") is probably Baalath-beer (cf. 19:8).

25 *Hazor-hadattah* ("New Hazor") was located perhaps near Maon, but this is uncertain. *Kerioth-hezron* is read as one name by the LXX, although some take it to be two names, Kerioth and Hezron.[10] Kerioth may be Khirbet el-Qaryatein, about 5 miles north of Arad. For Hezron, see v. 3.

26 *The location of Amam* is uncertain, but was perhaps near Beer-sheba. *Shema* has been held to be the same as Jeshua (Neh. 11:26), probably Tell es-Sa'wī or Khirbet el-Faras. *Moladah* may be Tell el-Elith or Tell el-Milḥ.[11]

27 *Hazar-gaddah* was near Beer-sheba, but the precise location

---

6. See Y. Aharoni, *The Land of the Bible*, p. 105. B. Mazar thinks it refers to a town other than Arad; "The Cities of the Priests and the Levites," *VTS* 7 (1960), pp. 192-205. See C. F. Pfeiffer, ed., *The Biblical World* (Grand Rapids: 1966), p. 51.

7. See Aharoni, *op. cit.*, p. 106; cf. LXX (Codex B), which has *Arouēl*.

8. In the description of Judah's southern boundary this is the most southerly situated city; see *GTT*, p. 143. See also Aharoni, *op. cit.*, p. 298.

9. The name does not occur in the LXX (Codex A), and it occurs in a longer form in Codex B. This may support the combination of the two names.

10. Aharoni, *idem*, n. 49: "It is difficult to determine whether some names refer to one town or more."

11. A. Alt, "Beiträge zur historischen Geographie und Topographie des Negeb," *KS* III, p. 432, does not consider the identification with Tell el-Milḥ sufficiently supported (see also Neh. 11:26; 1 Chr. 4:28).

is unknown. *Heshmon* has not been located either. *Beth-pelet* was at one time identified with Tell el-Fâr'ah,[12] but this has been doubted strongly.[13] Tell es-Saqati has been suggested as an alternative.

28 Some suggest Khirbet el-Watan as the location of *Hazar-shual*. This town later belonged to Simeon (19:3; see Neh. 11:27). *Beer-sheba* ("well of the oath" or "well of the seven"; Gen. 21:31) is known by the modern name Bir es-Sab'. The present city is built on a site which contains remains from only the late Roman and Byzantine periods. East of this town lies Tell es-Seba', also called Tell el-Masah, which has a good claim to be the town that the patriarchs knew.[14] Some suggest that *Biziothiah* be read *ubᵉnôṯeyhā* ("and its dependencies"),[15] but others retain the reading as a proper name. If it actually is the name of a town, it must be sought near Beer-sheba.

29 *Baalah*[16] and *Iim* are both unknown. *Ezem* was possibly the present Umm el-'Aẓam (cf. 19:3; 1 Chr. 4:29).

30 The location of *Eltolad* is unknown. *Chesil* is possibly the same as Bethul (19:4); the modern site may be either Khirbet er-Râs or Khirbet el-Qaryatein. *Hormah*, also called Zephath (Judg. 1:17), near Ziklag, is also of uncertain location (cf. 12:14; Num. 14:45; 21:3; 1 Sam. 30:30). Suggestions include Tell el-Meshash and Tell es-Sebeta.

31 *Ziklag* is possibly Tell el-Khuweilfeh, which has been called "a natural candidate."[17] *Madmannah* ("dungheap") is now known as Umm Deimneh. *Sansannah* ("date cluster" [?]; "fruit stalk of date" [?]; "thorn" [?]) is modern Khirbet esh-Shamsanīyât. This town may be the same as Hazar-susah (19:5), a name which suggests a garrison town for cavalry (cf. 1 Chr. 4:31).

32 *Lebaoth* ("lair of lioness") is another town of unknown lo-

12. See J. Garstang, *The Foundations of Biblical History: Joshua, Judges* (London: 1931), p. 285.

13. See Alt, "Barsama," *KS* III, p. 472, n. 3.

14. So E. G. Kraeling, *The Rand McNally Bible Atlas*, p. 75. Aharoni, *op. cit.*, p. 184, distinguishes between Tell es-Seba' (Beer-sheba) and Tell el-Meshash (Hormah). Wright and Filson, *op. cit.*, and L. H. Grollenberg, ed., *Atlas of the Bible* (E.T. 1963), prefer Tell es-Seba'.

15. NEB, Gelin, DNV. But B. J. Alfrink, *Josué*, points out that such an expression, common in other lists, fails completely in the rest of the present list. C. Steuernagel, *Das Buch Josua*, p. 267, considers it a late addition. RSV retains the form as a proper name.

16. On the relation between Baalah, Balah (19:3), and Bilhah (1 Chr. 4:29), cf. Aharoni, *op. cit.*, p. 104.

17. Kraeling, *op. cit.*, p. 188. Another proposed identification is Tell esh-Sheri'a; Aharoni, *op. cit.*, p. 298.

cation. In 19:6 it is called Beth-lebaoth.[18] *Shilhim* is probably the same as Sharuhen of the Simeonite list (19:6), and located at Tell el-Fâr'ah. Otherwise the town is unknown (cf. 1 Chr. 4:31). *Ain* and *Rimmon* appear in the Hebrew text as two names. In 19:7 they are apparently considered to be one name (see also 21:16 where Ain stands alone). If only one name, En-rimmon, actually is intended, the site may be the present Khirbet Umm Ramāmīn.

Twenty-nine cities in all: The actual total of the list, regardless of some possible combinations of names, exceeds the number twenty-nine by six. Some interpreters suggest that the additional names were later interpolations which did not affect the original tally. More plausible is the suggestion that some of the names mentioned actually represent localities too small to be counted as cities, although a completely convincing explanation cannot be given.[19]

b. In the Shephelah (15:33–47)

33 *In the Lowland: Eshtaol, Zorah, Ashnah,*

34 *Zanoah, En-gannim, Tappuah, Enam,*

35 *Jarmuth, Adullam, Socoh, Azekah,*

36 *Shaaraim, Adithaim, Gederah, Gederothaim;*
fourteen cities with their villages.

37 *Zenan, Hadashah, Migdal-gad.*

38 *Dilean, Mizpeh, Joktheel,*

39 *Lachish, Bozkath, Eglon,*

40 *Cabbon, Lahmam, Chitlish,*

41 *Gederoth, Beth-dagon, Naamah, and Makkedah;*
sixteen cities with their villages.

42 *Libnah, Ether, Ashan,*

43 *Iphtah, Ashnah, Nezib,*

44 *Keilah, Achzib, and Mareshah;*
nine cities with their villages.

45 *Ekron, with its towns and villages.*

46 *From Ekron toward the sea, everything that was by the side of Ashdod, with its villages,*

47 *Ashdod, its towns and villages; Gaza, its towns and villages to the Brook of Egypt, the Great Sea, and the coast.*

18. In the LXX (Codex B) the name is *Labōs*; in Codex A it is *Labōth*.
19. S. Talmon, "The Town Lists of Simeon," *IEJ* 15 (1965), p. 235, suggests that the solution may lie in the twelve cities which also occur in Simeon's list.

33 The list containing the cities in the Shephelah, i.e., the lower hills between the coastal plain and the central ranges, is divided into four parts. The fourth area represents cities which were only theoretically under Judah's control. In this part of the list the movement is from north to south, unlike the first list.

Eshtaol is possibly the village of Arṭûf. Together with *Zorah*, it was later allotted to Dan (19:41). This was the area in which Samson was to operate later (Judg. 13:25; 16:31; cf. also 2 Chr. 11:10). Zorah, modern Ṣar'ah, is the highest point in the Shephelah; its name also occurs in the Amarna tablets. *Ashnah* may be 'Aslîn.

34 *Zanoah* is modern Khirbet Zanû'. *En-gannim* ("well of the garden") is of unknown location. One suggestion puts it close to Beth-shemesh, possibly Beit Jemâl, while another locates the town at Umm Gina, 1 mile southwest of Beth-shemesh. *Tappuah* is yet another site that cannot be identified. It could be Beit Nettûph, but according to some scholars it could be Umm Gina. Another Tappuah is situated in the mountain district (v. 53; cf. also 12:17; 16:8; 17:8). The location of *Enam* is unknown.

35 *Jarmuth*, one of the cities of the southern coalition (10:3), was 16 miles west of Jerusalem. It dominated, and offered a view of, the coastal plain and the sea.[1] Its present name is Khirbet Yarmûk. *Adullam*, an ancient Canaanite city, was located at Khirbet esh-Sheikh Madhkûr, on a hill west of the valley that leads to Wâdî eṣ-Ṣûr, the place where David encountered Goliath.[2] *Socoh* ("thorn hedge") is Khirbet 'Abbâd (1 Sam. 17:1). A second town by this name is listed in v. 48. Iron Age sherds and remains of walls of Israelite days have been found at the Khirbet 'Abbâd site, which is in an ideal position for controlling the valley below. *Azekah*, Tell ez-Zakarîyah, is a bold site filling a strategic position below Jarmuth, where the Wâdî es-Sanṭ opens as it emerges from the hills.[3]

36 *Shaaraim* ("two gates") lies in the neighborhood of Ashkelon. It is mentioned in 1 Sam. 17:52, but its location is uncertain. *Adithaim* cannot be identified, though some believe it may be el-Ḥadîtheh, north of Aijalon. *Gederah* ("stone wall") is modern Jedîreh. Some doubt that *Ged-*

---

1. A tablet from the Amarna period found in Palestine testifies to the fact that the king of Lachish gave assistance to the king of Jarmuth; see Y. Aharoni, *The Land of the Bible*, p. 162.
2. J. Garstang, *Joshua, Judges*, p. 176, calls Adullam "a fortress strongly placed on a rounded hilltop with a very copious supply of water at the foot."
3. *Idem*, p. 360; E. G. Kraeling, *The Rand McNally Bible Atlas*, p. 138. See also 10:10–11.

erothaim ("two walls") is a place name,[4] but others take it to be a town near Gedarah. If it is not a place name, then the number *fourteen* of the final tally agrees with the number of towns listed.

37 The first city in the second group[5] in the Shephelah is *Zenan*, possibly modern 'Arâq el-Kharba near Lachish, though some consider its site uncertain. Zenan may be the same as Zaanan (Mic. 1:11). *Hadashah*, the precise location of which is unknown, lay perhaps between Lachish and Gath. *Migdal-gad* is probably Khirbet el-Mejdeleh, east of Ashkelon.

38 The site of *Dilean* is unknown. Some have suggested an identification with Tell en-Najileh, south-southwest of Tell el-Ḥesī. The location of *Mizpeh* is also unknown, though the name is borne by many Israelite localities (e.g., 11:3; cf. 13:26). *Joktheel* is likewise unknown, but it was not far from Socoh and Zanoah.

39 *Lachish*[6] was one of the largest cities in ancient Judah, and its king was one of the five slain by Joshua (ch. 10). It is located at Tell ed-Duweir. The site of *Bozkath* is unknown. *Eglon* was another of the cities joining in the southern coalition (10:3). There is no unanimity about its identification, though Tell el-Ḥesī, formerly considered to be Lachish, may be the site. This tell lies 7 miles southwest of Lachish at the edge of a group of foothills which jut out into the coastal plain due west of Hebron.[7] The span of occupation extends from about 2600 BC to 400 BC.

40 Nothing is known with certainty about the location of *Cabbon, Lahmam, and Chitlish*. Lahmam may be Khirbet el-Laḥm. Chitlish is not identified.[8]

41 The site of ancient *Gederoth* ("walls") is unknown, as is also the case with *Beth-dagon*. *Naamah* ("the lovely") may be Khirbet Fered near Timnah. However, other scholars suggest Ni'amah. *Makkedah* (cf. 10:10) is possibly Khirbet el-Heishum, but another suggestion places it at Tell Magdun, 7 miles southeast of Beit Jibrîn.

This group of *cities with their villages* totals *sixteen* (see v. 36 and commentary).

---

4. The LXX understood it to mean "and her sheepfolds" (other translations of the Greek: "and her dwellings" or "and her vine-walls"). J. Bright calls the validity of this emendation "questionable" (*IB* II, p. 632).
5. KD, p. 166, state that this second group contains "the towns of the actual plain in its full extent from north to south, between the hilly region and the line of the coast held by the Philistines."
6. For its location see Garstang, *op. cit.*, pp. 173, 391.
7. See C. Pfeiffer, *The Biblical World*, p. 566.
8. The LXX (Codex B) reads *Maachōs*.

42   The third group of towns in the Shephelah which begins here comprises settlements in the southern half of the hilly region. *Libnah* (see 10:29) may be Tell eṣ-Ṣâfî, excavated in 1879 by F. J. Bliss and R. A. S. Macalister, or perhaps Tell Bornat.[9] *Ether*, subsequently assigned to Simeon (19:7), is Khirbet el-'Ater. *Ashan*, the precise location of which is unknown, was northeast of Beer-sheba.[10]

43   *Iphtah*'s location is uncertain. *Ashnah* is the present Idhnah near Maresha, while *Nezib* is located at Khirbet Beit Neṣib, 8 miles northwest of Hebron.

44   *Keilah* is Khirbet Qîlā, on the east side of the Wâdî eṣ-Ṣûr, known from the encounter between David and Goliath. It was located in the eastern part of the Shephelah. *Mareshah*, the last town in this group, lay in the southwest of that same area of the Shephelah. Keilah is mentioned in the Amarna tablets.[11] It lay on a hill between two valleys that come down to the wadi (see also 1 Sam. 23:6). Also mentioned by Micah (1:14), Mareshah is Tell Sandaḥanna. (For King Asa's fight with the Ethiopians, see 2 Chr. 14:9-15; cf. 1 Chr. 4:21; 2 Chr. 20:37.) *Achzib* occurs in a list of towns mentioned by Micah (1:10-15), but its location is unknown.

The total of the cities of this group is *nine*.

45   The fourth group (vv. 45-47) consists of towns in what was to be the Philistine territory, although the northern part of it was afterward given to the tribe of Dan (19:43). It remained almost entirely in Philistine hands (see also 13:3 and commentary).

The way the information is listed in this fourth group differs notably from the preceding three. Is this an evidence of a later insertion, as many claim? Was this a list of Philistine cities which David actually incorporated into his kingdom?[12] However, of at least one of the cities listed here, *Ekron*, it is known that David did not incorporate it (see 1 Sam. 17:52). In Jer. 25:20 Ekron is still a part of the Philistine land. (See also 2 K. 1:2-3, where Ekron is the seat of the worship of Baal-zebub.) A possible reason for this difference in format is the fact that some of the territory

---

9. Cf. Kraeling, *op. cit.*, p. 286. Aharoni, *op. cit.*, p. 77, considers identification with Tell eṣ-Ṣâfî impossible, because, so he observes, the city is mentioned alongside Mareshah, Keilah, and Nezib in the southeastern Shephelah and not in association with towns adjacent with Tell eṣ-Ṣâfî.

10. The cities of Ether and Ashan, listed here among the Shephelah cities, occur elsewhere at the end of the Negeb list (19:7).

11. See *ANET*, p. 489.

12. See Bright, *op. cit.*, p. 632, for this suggestion.

described here subsequently was assigned to Dan and receives a fuller description at that point (19:40–46).[13]

Ekron (13:3; 15:11) is probably 'Aqîr, a town on the lower course of the Wâdī eṣ-Ṣarâr.[14] It had various dependencies (lit. "daughters"), which are not listed. Ekron was the northernmost of the five principal cities of the Philistines.

46 *Ashdod* was about 3 miles from the coast, just south of the latitude of Jerusalem. Josh. 11:22 reports that some Anakim remained in Ashdod. Judah's claim also included the area *from Ekron toward the sea, everything that was by the side of Ashdod*. This was the entire territory occupied by the Philistines. Because it belonged to the land that remained (13:2), allotting it to Israel meant a constant challenge to the people, a challenge which was met only imperfectly (see Judg. 1:18; but compare v. 19).

47 *Gaza* (10:41; 13:3) lay in the extreme south of the coastal plain near the sea. In Gen. 10:19, a description of Canaan's borders, it marks the southwest limit of the land. On the identity of the *Brook of Egypt*, toward which Judah's allotment extended, see 13:3 and commentary. It also extended *to the Great*[15] *Sea* (the Mediterranean Sea) *and the coast*.[16]

c. In the Hill Country (15:48–60)

48 *And in the hill country: Shamir, Jattir, Socoh,*
49 *Dannah, Kiriath-sannah (that is, Debir),*
50 *Anab, Eshtemoh, Anim,*
51 *Goshen, Holon, and Giloh;*
   eleven cities with their villages.
52 *Arab, Dumah, Eshan,*

13. M. Noth, *Das Buch Josua*, pp. 96f., although for a different purpose and in support of a theory which is not accepted in this commentary, connects the present list with that of Dan in order to explain its different format.
14. Kraeling, *op. cit.*, p. 174, prefers this site to that of Qaṭrâ, which some authorities have favored. The difficulty with 'Aqîr is that sufficiently ancient occupational remains seem to be absent. See *GTT*, p. 148. Yet another suggested identification (see 13:3 and commentary) is Khirbet el-Muqenna' (see T. C. Mitchell, "Ekron," *NBD*, pp. 354f.).
15. Substituting *gādôl* for *geḇûl* (Qere for Ketib).
16. The translation of the last few words of the verse is not certain. It reads lit. "and the Great Sea and the border." Some recent translations include JB "the Great Sea marks the boundary"; RSV "and the Great Sea with its coast-line"; NEB "and the Great Sea and the land adjacent"; Zürcher Bibel "Und das Grosse Meer bildet die Grenze." A similar translation difficulty was encountered in v. 12.

53 *Janim, Beth-tappuah, Aphekah,*
54 *Humtah, Kiriath-arba (that is, Hebron), and Zior;*
   nine cities with their villages,
55 *Maon, Carmel, Ziph, Juttah,*
56 *Jezreel, Jokdeam, Zanoah,*
57 *Kain, Gibeah, and Timnah;*
   ten cities with their villages.
58 *Halhul, Beth-zur, Gedor,*
59 *Maarath, Beth-anoth and' Eltekon;*
   six cities with their villages.
60 *Kiriath-baal (that is, Kiriath-jearim) and Rabbah;*
   two cities with their villages.

48 This verse commences the third part of Judah's city list (see v. 21). This part consists of five districts, but if the LXX reading is followed, which has an additional verse between 59 and 60, there are six. The cities listed here are *in the hill country*, the central mountain area of Palestine between the Shephelah in the west and the "desert of Judah" in the east.[1]

Shamir has been identified with el-Bîreh, northeast of En-rimmon. *Jattir*, subsequently a Levitical city (21:14), is the present Khirbet 'Attîr (see also 1 Sam. 30:27; 1 Chr. 6:42 [Eng. 57]). *Socoh* is at Khirbet Shuweikeh (v. 35 mentions a different city by the same name).

49 *Dannah*'s location is uncertain, but it was not far from Debir. *Kiriath-sannah (that is, Debir)*: Debir's other name is Kiriath-sepher (v. 15). For its localization see commentary at v. 15.[2]

50 *Anab* (see 11:21) is Khirbet 'Anâb. *Eshtemoh* may be es-Semû'. It is also called Eshtemoa (1 Sam. 30:26–31; cf. 1 Chr. 4:17, 19; 6:42 [Eng. 57]). *Anim* was possibly Khirbet Ghuwein et-Taḥta, 7 miles southwest of Hebron.

51 *Goshen* is unknown as a place name, but it is used for an area in 10:41. It has been linked with Tell el-Khuweilifeh in the center of the Negeb.[3] *Holon* is located at Khirbet 'Illîn near Beth-sur. *Giloh*, home city

---

1. It consists of a "large rugged range of limestone mountains, with many barren and naked peaks, whilst the sides are for the most part covered with grass, shrubs, bushes, and trees, and the whole range is intersected by many fruitful valleys"; KD, p. 169. At this point the term hill country "stands for little more than the narrow mountainous area on both sides of the line Jerusalem–ez-Zahiriyeh, with Teqoa . . . as its most eastern and Qirjath-Jearim . . . as its most northern settlement"; *GTT*, p. 53.
2. The LXX, which renders Kiriath-sepher with *Pólis grammátōn* (15:15) does the same with Kiriath-sannah.
3. See Y. Aharoni, *The Land of the Bible*, p. 184.

of Ahithophel, David's counselor (2 Sam. 15:12), has been linked with Khirbet Jâlā.[4]

The above cities add up to *eleven*. As in previous tallies, the *villages* belonging to the cities are also mentioned.

52 *Arab* heads the list of the second group in the hill country. The nine cities in this group lie to the north of the first, in the country around Hebron. Arab has been located at er-Râbiyeh. *Dumah* is placed at Deir ed-Dômeh,[5] and *Eshan*[6] was west of Dumah, but its location is unknown.

53 *Janim* was near Hebron, but its location is unknown. *Beth-tappuah* is modern Taffûḥ, more than 3 miles west of Hebron. *Aphekah* is of unknown location.

54 *Humtah* is also unknown. *Kiriath-arba* was the alternate designation of *Hebron* (v. 13; 14:15). The precise relation between these two names remains uncertain.[7] The settlement was a Levitical city and a city of refuge (20:7; 21:11). *Zior* is modern Ṣiʿir, 5 miles east-northeast of Hebron.

55 *Maon*, later the home town of Nabal (1 Sam. 25:2), has been linked with Tell Maʿîn, south of Hebron. The extensive wasteland east of it might well be called "the desert of Maon" (1 Sam. 23:24). *Carmel* is also mentioned in the Nabal story (1 Sam. 25:2; cf. 1 Sam. 15:12). It is the present Khirbet el-Kermel. *Ziph* is identified with Tell Ziph (cf. 1 Sam. 23:19). The preceding three towns were all southeast of Hebron, bordering on the wilderness that surrounds En-gedi and Masada. *Juttah*, assigned to the priests in 21:16, is modern Yaṭṭā.

56 *Jezreel*, not to be confused with a town of the same name in the valley of Esdraelon, was the residence of David's wife Ahinoam. Its location remains unknown. *Jokdeam* and *Zanoah* also remain unknown, although the latter has been linked with Khirbet Beit ʿAmra or with Zanûtā, close to Jattir.

---

4. E. G. Kraeling, *The Rand McNally Bible Atlas*, p. 204, makes the following observation: "Its (i.e., Giloh's) connection with Khirbet Jāla, a mile and a half west of *Beit Ummar*, receives some support from the fact that the town Holon mentioned before it in Joshua 15:51 may be linked with *Khirbet ʿĀlin*. However, some scholars seek both places farther south."

5. A. Alt, *KS* III, pp. 401–9, links the Udumu of the Amarna letters (see *ANET*, p. 486) with Dumah. Alt also discusses other proposed identifications, particularly M. Noth's identification of Goshen (v. 51) with Gari, mentioned in the Amarna letters (spelled Garu in *ANET*, p. 486).

6. The LXX (Codex B) reads *Sōma*; in Codex A the order differs.

7. See the discussion by J. M. Miller and G. M. Tucker, *The Book of Joshua*, p. 197.

57 *Kain* (the Hebrew adds the definite article) may be Khirbet Yaqîn, almost 2 miles northeast of Ziph.[8] *Gibeah* was southwest of Jerusalem, probably el-Jeba'. *Timnah* is also the name of other towns (cf. v. 10). It may be the same as that mentioned in Gen. 38:12[9] and located southeast of Hebron.

The total of this list is *ten*.[10]

58 This verse begins the fourth group of cities in the hill country. *Halhul* is modern Halhûl, near Hebron. *Beth-zur* is the same as Khirbet et-Tubeiqah, 4 miles north of Hebron (cf. 2 Chr. 11:7). *Gedor* has been identified with Khirbet Jedûr (cf. 1 Chr. 4:4; 12:7).

59 Two of the cities listed here, *Maarath* and *Eltekon*, have not been located. *Beth-anoth* is Khirbet Beit 'Ainûn. One suggestion for Eltekon is Khirbet ed-Deir, west of Bethlehem.

At this point, the LXX contains an additional list of eleven names, some of which stand for well-known cities, the omission of which from the list would cause surprise. Jerome considered this an arbitrary interpolation on the part of the LXX. Others are inclined to consider the omission in the Hebrew text to be a copyist's error, which may well be the case.[11]

60 The last group of cities in the hill country consists of only *two* towns, *Kiriath-baal (that is, Kiriath-jearim) and Rabbah*. For Kiriath-baal, see v. 9 and commentary. *Rabbah* may be the same town as that mentioned in lists of Egyptian Pharaohs as *rbt*, also called Rubutu in the Amarna correspondence.[12]

---

8. M. Noth, *Das Buch Josua*, p. 92, suggests that originally the name stood in genitive relation to Zanoah (v. 56), hence "Zanoah of the Kenites," but admits that this would be contrary to the tally of ten for the list. See also *GTT*, p. 150.
9. The list of Judahite cities contains several names that play a role in the life of Judah, Jacob's son: Enam (v. 34), Adullam (v. 35), and Achzib (v. 44); cf. Gen. 38:1, 5, 14, 21.
10. In the LXX, which combines Zanoah (v. 56) with Kain (v. 57), this is nine. See n. 8 above.
11. KD, p. 172, accept the authenticity of the list contained in the LXX, as do many others. The LXX reads as follows: "Tekoa and Ephrathah (that is, Bethlehem), and Peor, and Etam, and Koulon and Tatam, and Zobah (Codex A: *Sōrēs*; Codex B: *Eōbēs*), and Karem, and Gallim, and Bether, and Manathah; eleven cities with their villages." For the location of these cities, if known, see Aharoni, *op. cit.*, p. 300.
12. See *ANET*, pp. 488–89, nos. 287, 289–290.

d. In the Desert (15:61–62)

> 61 *In the desert: Beth-arabah, Middin, Secacah,*
> 62 *Nibshan, the City of Salt, and En-gedi;*
> *six cities with their villages.*

61–62   The last of the four major groups of cities belonging to Judah is
located *in the desert*. The extent of this "desert of Judah" (so mentioned
only in Ps. 63:1) is rather limited. It consists of a narrow tract of land
along the Dead Sea. The Hebrew name used here is *miḏbār,* also translated
"wilderness" at times. The eastern slopes of the Judean mountains are an
almost complete desert because of the steep descent of more than 3000
feet over a distance of only 10–15 miles.[1] With few exceptions the region
never possessed any permanent habitation.

The line drawn runs from north to south. *Beth-arabah* (see v. 6)
may be the present 'Ain el-Gharabeh. In 18:22 it is mentioned as one of
the cities of Benjamin. *Middin, Secacah, Nibshan,*[2] *the City of Salt*[3] (or Ir
Hammelach), and *En-gedi* are all of uncertain location, with the exception
of En-gedi, which is Tell ej-Jurn near 'Ain Jidi on the Dead Sea.

5. JUDAH'S FAILURE TO TAKE POSSESSION OF JEBUS (15:63)

> 63 *The Judahites, however, could not drive out the Jebusites who lived
> at Jerusalem, so that the Jebusites have continued to dwell at Je-
> rusalem with the Judahites until this day.*

The concluding note about Judah's inability to drive out the Jebusites from
Jerusalem shows the true nature of the "prophetical" historiography contained in this book. A warning note is implied in this and similar notices
(see also chs. 16–17; cf. Judg. 2:1–5). The description of Judah's lot,
begun with the story of Caleb and his claim, made in faith and loyalty to

---

1. See Y. Aharoni, *The Land of the Bible*, p. 27.
2. Some hold that the first three names can be identified respectively with Khirbet
Abū Ṭabaq, Khirbet es-Samrah, and Khirbet el-Maqârî, three sites discovered in
the Buqei'a region; so G. E. Wright and F. V. Filson, eds., *The Westminster
Historical Atlas* and Aharoni, *op. cit.*, p. 302.
3. Some have tried to identify this city with Khirbet Qumrân, famous for the
discovery of the Dead Sea Scrolls, but its remains are no older than the Roman
period; cf. M. Noth, *Das Buch Josua*, p. 100.

God (ch. 14), is concluded on a different note.[1] Israel had been told that it was to make no peace with Canaan's earlier population (Num. 33:52–56; Deut. 7:1–2). Although the elimination of this original population was to take place gradually (Exod. 23:29), Israel was to expel them eventually (Deut. 20:16–18). The failure to do so would have evil consequences, as is amply borne out by the events recorded in the book of Judges.

The statement made in this verse concerning Judah's failure is repeated almost verbatim in Judg. 1:21 with respect to Benjamin. Yet, in the same chapter, v. 8, Judah is said to have fought against Jerusalem and to have taken it. Actually, Jerusalem did not belong to Judah's territory, but was allotted to Benjamin (Josh. 18:16, 28). These data seem to be contradictory at first sight, and many have regarded them so.[2]

The fact that in Judg. 1 the two "viewpoints" stand side by side (vv. 8, 21) should caution against glibly assuming a contradiction. To postulate such a situation certainly casts aspersions on the intellectual ability of the one finally responsible for the shape of that chapter in its present form. Of course, the solution might be sought in the statement that it was of no concern to the Primary Author to iron out these apparent contradictions since his purpose was not to present a perfectly harmonious account of all that ever happened. However, such a solution may lead to an undermining of faith in the trustworthiness of Scripture.

Jerusalem, though assigned to Benjamin, was actually a border town between the two tribes. Actually, Judah's boundary made a sudden detour to the south and ran through the valley just south of the city. Thus it easily could have become a sort of enclave, a "no man's land"[3] between the two, which either could legitimately acquire, and for the conquest (or non-conquest) of which either could be held responsible. Judah's capture of the town, recorded in Judg. 1, may have been ineffective if it was not followed by subsequent occupation. In the time of the Judges Jerusalem was rated as unsafe territory (Judg. 19:10–12).

Verse 63 states that the Jebusites and the Judahites *have continued to dwell* together *at Jerusalem until this day* (see also Judg. 1:21). Perhaps this can be understood best as a form of habitation in which common pasturage was enjoyed outside the city's walled part. Others suggest that

---

1. For these insights into the structure of chs. 14–15, see C. Vonk, *Inleiding op de Profeten: Jozua*, pp. 238f.
2. E.g., M. Noth, *Das Buch Josua*, p. 100; J. A. Soggin, *Joshua*, p. 180. F.-M. Abel, *Le Livre de Josué*, p. 76, considers this to be simply a matter of "rival claims" on the part of the two tribes, but it would seem that more than that is at stake here.
3. This is the term used by A. E. Cundall, *Judges*, p. 1153.

even after the city's capture a non-Israelite element continued to live in its vicinity; witness the presence of Araunah the Jebusite in 2 Sam. 24:16.[4]

E. JOSEPH'S ALLOTMENT (16:1–17:18)

1. GENERAL BOUNDARY DESCRIPTION (16:1–4)

1 *Then the lot for the Josephites came out. [The boundary ran] from the Jordan at Jericho, east of the waters of Jericho, by the desert, which runs up from Jericho through the hill country to Bethel.*

2 *From Bethel it ran on to Luz; then it passed on to the territory of the Archites, to Ataroth.*

3 *It then descended westward to the territory of the Japhletites, to the region of Lower Beth-horon and on to Gezer; and it ended at the Sea.*

4 *Here the Josephites, Manasseh and Ephraim, received their inheritance.*

Chapters 16–17 offer a description of the territory of the Joseph tribes, Ephraim and Manasseh. The descendants of Joseph drew one lot, but their territory was divided between the two separate tribes. The sequence of 16:4–5 reflects the background given in the blessing of Jacob (Gen. 48). Manasseh is mentioned first in v. 4, but Ephraim's borders are listed before those of Manasseh. Ephraim received the southern portion. The opening verses of this section, 16:1–4, describe the southern boundary of the whole territory of the Joseph tribes, the part that bordered on Benjamin (18:11–14) and the part that bordered on Dan (19:40–48). Then follows a description of Ephraim's territory (16:5–10), which in turn is followed by the territory assigned to Manasseh (17:1–13). In the north Manasseh's boundaries are not described precisely, the only indication being that they touched on those of Asher and Issachar and that some of Manasseh's cities were actually located in the territory of those tribes (17:10–11).

These chapters long have been known to be notorious for their difficulties of interpretation. At points the author's scheme is extremely difficult to establish.[1] Some have felt the need for textual emendation, and

---

4. For a suggestion that Jebus should not be equated with Jerusalem, a suggestion which contradicts explicit biblical testimony, see J. M. Miller and G. M. Tucker, *The Book of Joshua*, pp. 121, 196.

1. See *GTT*, p. 158. J. P. Lange quotes C. F. Keil to have said with respect to 16:6: "With v. 6 I know as little as my predecessors how to begin"; *A Commentary on the Holy Scriptures* 4, p. 142.

others have rearranged the text.[2] In the present work an attempt is made to understand the text as handed down.

1 *Then the lot for the Josephites came out* refers to the "coming out" of the actual lot, which was probably contained in an urn.[3] The house of Joseph is considered here to be a unit (see v. 4; 17:14). This is in accord with the situation reflected in Gen. 48 (cf. 49:22–26).

The line of Joseph's southern boundary overlapped with Benjamin's northern frontier, but some elements found in the Benjamin list do not occur in that of Joseph (compare 18:12–13 with 16:1–3). Similarly, the references to the Archites and the Japhletites (vv. 2–3) are missing in the Benjamin list. Another unique feature is the reference to Upper Beth-horon (v. 5), which occurs neither in Judah's boundary description nor in that of Benjamin.

An explanation of the difficulties of understanding referred to above may be the fact that the boundaries of the Joseph tribes were handed down in an abbreviated form. It is apparent that no extensive city lists such as were given for Judah have been preserved.

Joseph's southern boundary, starting from the east, begins *from the Jordan at Jericho* (lit. "the Jordan of Jericho"). Judah's boundary also began at that point, but somewhat more to the south, immediately north of the Dead Sea (15:5). A short stretch of the Jordan bank formed Benjamin's eastern border (18:19–20). *East of the waters of Jericho*: Benjamin's border included Jericho (18:12). Hence Ephraim's boundary ran north of that city and reached the waters of Jericho, i.e., 'Ain Nu'eimeh

2. Among them, M. Noth, *Das Buch Josua*, p. 96. Following K. Elliger, Noth arranges the text as follows: 16:1–3; 17:1–13; 16:5–10. Noth's views of these boundary lists have been critically discussed by Y. Kaufmann, *The Biblical Account of the Conquest of Palestine*, pp. 28–40; and by J. Simons, "The Structure and Interpretation of Josh. xvi–xvii," *Orientalia Neerlandica* (1948), pp. 190–215, a study not available to this author. See also *GTT*, pp. 159–169, where the positions taken are in some respects "notably different" from those in the earlier article. C. H. J. de Geus also is critical of Noth's approach in several respects; *The Tribes of Israel*, pp. 75–83. De Geus agrees with Kaufmann and Simons at significant points.

3. See also 14:2; 15:1. In 18:11 the lot is said to have "come up." Some translators, e.g., F.-M. Abel, regard the verb "to come out" (Heb. *yāṣā'*) to have reference to the beginning of the boundary line ("Leur limite . . . partait du Jourdain [18:12]"); see also RSV. NAB reads "The lot that fell [Heb. *yāṣā'*] to the Josephites extended from. . . ." This rendering appears to be preferable.

and 'Ain Dûq, at the foot of the Judean hills. It then ran *by the desert*[4] *which runs up*[5] *from Jericho*.[6] This desert, in the region bordering upon the Jordan Valley, is also mentioned in 15:61, although at that point the description is of territory farther to the south. More specifically, the desert intended here is that also called the desert of Beth-aven (18:12).[7] It rises precipitously out of the Jordan Valley.

2 *From Bethel it ran on to Luz*. These two sites are clearly distinguished, but in 18:13; Gen. 28:19; Judg. 1:23, they are identified. One suggestion for a solution of this apparent discrepancy is that the name Bethel was given originally not to the city of Luz itself but to the site near it which had been Jacob's resting place. Later, however, this spot became so important that the name Bethel was also applied to the city of Luz itself.[8] The site of Jacob's Bethel would then have been Burj Beitin, located between Ai and Beitin, while the site of ancient Luz would be modern Beitîn.[9] From Luz the border *passed on to the territory of the Archites*. The only other biblical reference to this apparently well-known clan is 2 Sam. 5:32, where Hushai, David's counselor, is said to be an Archite.[10] *Ataroth*, next mentioned, has been identified with Khirbet 'Aṭṭārûs, a site which at least perpetuates the ancient name although the original settlement

4. Taking the word "east" (lit. "eastward") with the word "desert," the NAB renders v. 1b "to the waters of Jericho east of the desert." Abel omits any reference to the "waters" and translates ". . . en face de Jéricho à l'orient." The translation offered here agrees with RSV and NEB.
5. The article has been restored in front of the participle *'ōleh*. Others supply a conjunction; e.g., NEB ". . . and goes up." This agrees with the LXX and has been adopted by the critical apparatus of BH. The difference is minor and does not affect the sense.
6. On the possible location of Jericho see 2:1 and commentary, n. 6.
7. This is the opinion of KD, p. 176, and agrees with Y. Aharoni, *The Land of the Bible*, p. 236. Some commentators prefer to move the word *miḏbār*, rendered here "by the desert," to immediately in front of Bethel. This results in the translation ". . . up from Jericho to the mountains, to the desert of Bethel." So, e.g., C. J. Goslinga, *Het Boek Jozua*, p. 131; A. Gelin, *Josué*, p. 97 (". . . vers le desert de Béthel-Luz . . ." [sic]); and JB. The translation difficulties arise from the fact "that the whole of vv. 1–3 is a mixture of fragmentary boundary descriptions and asyndetically recorded border-points"; *GTT*, p. 163.
8. Some translators, e.g., Abel and Gelin, apparently unable to accept the juxtaposition of the two cities, translate "Bethel-Luz."
9. For Bethel and Beth-aven see also 7:2 and commentary.
10. Were this the name of an Israelite clan, it would have been used proleptically of the later settlement of the clan at this point. However, it may also have been the name for an indigenous group to which Hushai held some connection.

must have been elsewhere.[11] In the description of Benjamin's border it is called Ataroth-addar (18:13).

3 The boundary then *descended westward to the territory of the Japhletites*, an otherwise unknown segment of the population.[12] Going still further west the boundary came to *Lower Beth-horon* (10:10–11) and *Gezer* (10:33). For their respective locations see commentary on ch. 10. Gezer formed the southwest boundary point. From there it continued till *it ended at the* (Mediterranean) *Sea*.[13] The exact course through the coastal area which was only theoretically within Israel's domain is not indicated further.

4 Some take this verse to be the beginning of the description of Ephraim's borders, but this would make it difficult to explain the sudden shift in the order of the two sons, *Manasseh and Ephraim* (see introduction to this chapter). Obviously, vv. 4–5 follow each other in order. The effect of the switch, however, can best be understood if v. 4 is taken with the preceding material. The author states the genealogical order first. He then (v. 5) calls attention, implicitly to be sure, to God's sovereign arrangement which had given Ephraim the priority.[14]

---

11. Another suggestion for Ataroth is Tell en-Naṣbeh; see D. Diringer, "Mizpah," in *AOTS*, pp. 331f. This involves the identification of Ataroth with Mizpah. For this suggestion and an extensive critique of it see *GTT*, p. 164.

12. Reference is sometimes made to 1 Chr. 7:32–33, but the name Japhlet used there occurs among Asher's descendants.

13. J. Gray, *Joshua, Judges and Ruth*. Century Bible (London: 1967), p. 152, calls the reference to the sea at this point "unrealistic." In the view of many interpreters, including Gray, the boundaries of the tribes were drawn up in terms of actual historical situations which at one time or other prevailed in Palestine. In that light a reference to the sea and the coastal zone, held largely by the Philistines, is indeed unrealistic. See also 13:2 and commentary. According to the biblical view the entire allotment is unrealistic. It is projected against the background of 13:1–7 and presupposes a further subjugation of the land allotted. On the other hand, the boundary lists of the tribes are also a case of *divine realism* (cf. K. Gutbrod, *Das Buch vom Lande Gottes*, p. 116: "biblischen Realismus"). This biblical realism means to give concrete expression to God's work upon earth, a work which finds embodiment in the geography of the promised land.

14. Noth, *op. cit.*, p. 102, seeks to understand the question of the relative order of Ephraim and Manasseh (see also 17:1ff.) in the light of the "law of primogeniture" which would have influenced the writer of Joshua at this point. But Y. Kaufmann, *op. cit.*, p. 31, points out that this principle was not operative among Israel, not even in common inheritance law, still less in the matter of the distribution of the Land. Kaufmann's viewpoint is strongly endorsed by C. H. J. de Geus, *The Tribes of Israel*, p. 77.

2. EPHRAIM'S INHERITANCE (16:5–10)

5 *The territory of the Ephraimites by their families was as follows: the border of their inheritance was from Ataroth-addar in the east as far as Upper Beth-horon;*

6 *then the border went out westward to the north of Michmethath; the border then turned eastward to Tanaath-shiloh and passed along eastward to Janoah.*

7 *Then it went down from Janoah to Ataroth and to Naarah; it touched Jericho and came out at the Jordan.*

8 *From Tappuah the border went westward to the brook Kanah and ended at the sea. This was the inheritance of the tribe of the Ephraimites by their families,*

9 *including the cities which were set aside for the Ephraimites within the inheritance of the Manassites: all those cities and their villages.*

10 *However, they did not drive out the Canaanites who lived in Gezer. These Canaanites have lived among the Ephraimites until this day, but they have been made to do forced labor.*

5 The description of Ephraim's border, called *inheritance* whereas that of Manasseh is called "lot" (17:1), begins with the southern boundary. This boundary was already described in vv. 1–3 and is given in abbreviated form, mentioning two points, *Ataroth-addar*, possibly identical with Ataroth (v. 2), and *Upper Beth-horon* (cf. v. 3; 10:11).

6 Considerable uncertainty concerns the meaning of this verse. The words *then the border went out westward* also have been taken to mean "the border went from there to the sea." Heb. *yāmmâ* here can mean both "westward" and "toward the sea." In Palestine these were identical directions. The fixed point in v. 6 is *Michmethath*, which was a point on Ephraim's northern border, near Shechem, the precise localization of which is still a matter of dispute.[1] With this northern town as the central reference point the description in v. 6 moves in both directions, east and west. Verses 6–7 deal with the eastward direction, while in v. 8 the westward direction is traced briefly. Ephraim's border ran *to the north of Michmethath*,[2] a

---

1. Two candidates are Khirbet Makhneh el-Fôqā (Aharoni) and Khirbet Juleijil (Kraeling).
2. See KD, p. 177. Y. Aharoni, *The Land of the Bible*, p. 236, states that Ephraim's northern border, i.e., the border which it had in common with Manasseh, "began just south of Shechem and descended on a sharp diagonal line in each direction, south-east to Jericho and westward along the Wâdī Qânah which runs into the Yarkon."

place before (or "opposite") Shechem (17:7). Going east, the boundary ran to *Tanaath-shiloh*[3] and then *passed along*[4] *eastward to Janoah*.[5]

7 Going further in a southeasterly direction the border *went down from Janoah to Ataroth and to Naarah*. Ataroth may be Tell Sheikh ed-Diab, and Naarah has been identified with Tell el-Jisr, close to 'Ain Dûq (cf. commentary on v. 1) and to Jericho. The border then *touched Jericho*. This city was not in Ephraimite territory, belonging instead to Benjamin (18:21). Finally the border ended at the river *Jordan*.[6]

8a The description of the western half of Ephraim's northern boundary starts with *Tappuah*. Although its exact localization remains a matter of debate, a strong contender is Sheikh Abū Zarad. Some further indication about its general area in 17:7–8 is given. From Tappuah the boundary ran *westward to the brook Kanah and ended at the* Mediterranean *Sea*.

8b–9 The description of Ephraim's boundary is concluded with the statement that this was indeed Ephraim's *inheritance* (see v. 5b; 13:23, 28). It is added, however, that *cities were set aside*[7] *for the Ephraimites within the inheritance of the Manassites*. This may be due to Ephraim's privileged position which it had received when Jacob blessed the sons of Joseph (Gen. 48), but see 17:11 where Manasseh is assigned certain cities in Issachar and Asher.[8]

10 As with Judah (15:63), Ephraim is mentioned for its failure to drive out some of the original inhabitants, probably for a similar reason. According to Deut. 7:1–5 failure to eradicate the original population of

3. Probably Khirbet Ta'nah el-Fôqā.
4. The Hebrew has an additional '*ôtô* (ASV "Along it"), which has not been translated.
5. I.e., Khirbet Yānûn.
6. Some believe that v. 7 describes Ephraim's eastern boundary rather than its northeastern limits. See, e.g., J. M. Miller and G. M. Tucker, *The Book of Joshua*, pp. 131, 191; the accompanying map makes the border come out not at the Jordan but at a point west of the Jordan. *GTT*, p. 167, considers the reference to the Jordan to have been the result of thoughtlessness on the part of the author.
7. Heb. *hammibdālôt* may be either the plural of a noun meaning "separate place" or, with slightly different pointing, a verbal participle with definite article. The conjunction *waw* is taken here in the sense of "including" or "and in addition." See also n. 8 below.
8. M. Noth, *Das Buch Josua*, p. 100, considers the *waw* to be explicative and understands v. 9 to say that Ephraim's cities were all set aside within Manasseh's territory. This is then used to bolster the position that originally the Joseph materials knew only of a Joseph-Manasseh group, with Ephraim being secondarily inserted. For a rebuttal of Noth's position, see Y. Kaufmann, *The Biblical Account of the Conquest of Palestine*, p. 31, and C. H. J. de Geus, *The Tribes of Israel*, p. 76.

Canaan would have serious consequences for the life of God's people. But Ephraim *did not drive out the Canaanites* at *Gezer*. Gezer's king was defeated originally by Joshua (10:33), but the city had remained independent (cf. Judg. 1:29). Gezer was in Ephraim's extreme southwest portion, some 18 miles west of Jerusalem. During Solomon's days it became part of the kingdom of Israel (1 K. 9:16–17). It would seem, therefore, that this notation has a bearing on the date at which Joshua was written (see Introduction to this commentary).

3. MANASSEH'S ALLOTMENT (17:1–13)

1 *And this was the lot for the tribe of Manasseh, for he was the first-born of Joseph. (To Machir the first-born of Manasseh, the father of Gilead, had been allotted Gilead and Bashan, because he was a capable warrior.)*

2 *So the lot was for the rest of the Manassites, by their families, for the sons of Abiezer, Helek, Asriel, Shechem, Hepher, and Shemida; these are the male descendants of Manasseh the son of Joseph, by their families.*

3 *Now Zelophehad the son of Hepher, son of Gilead, son of Machir, son of Manasseh, had no sons, but only daughters. These are the names of his daughters: Mahlah, Noah, Hoglah, Milcah, and Tirzah.*

4 *They presented themselves before Eleazar the priest, before Joshua the son of Nun, and before the princes, and said: "The Lord commanded Moses to give us an inheritance along with our brothers." So according to the Lord's command, he gave them an inheritance among the brothers of their father.*

5 *Thus there fell to Manasseh ten portions, besides the land of Gilead and Bashan on the other side of the Jordan,*

6 *because the daughters of Manasseh received an inheritance along with the sons. But the land of Gilead belonged to the rest of the Manassites.*

7 *The boundary of Manasseh reached from Asher as far as Michmethath, which is opposite Shechem; then the boundary ran southward to the inhabitants of En-tappuah.*

8 *The land of Tappuah belonged to Manasseh, but Tappuah itself on the border of Manasseh belonged to the Ephraimites.*

9 *The boundary then ran down into the brook Kanah, south of the brook; the cities there belonged to Ephraim although they lay among the cities of Manasseh. The boundary of Manasseh then ran north of the brook and ended at the sea.*

10 *In the south the land belonged to Ephraim, in the north to Manasseh. Its boundary was the sea; in the north they touched on Asher, and on the east on Issachar.*

11 *In Issachar and in Asher the following belonged to Manasseh: Beth-shean and its villages, Ibleam and its villages, the inhabitants of Dor and its villages, the inhabitants of En-dor and its villages, the inhabitants of Taanach and its villages, the inhabitants of Megiddo and its villages, the three-heights country.*

12 *The Manassites could not take possession of these cities while the Canaanites persisted in dwelling in that land.*

13 *But when the Israelites grew strong, they put the Canaanites to forced labor; but there was no question of driving them out.*

1 Before describing *the lot for the tribe of Manasseh* the author provides some genealogical observations. First, he reiterates that Manasseh was Joseph's *first-born*. This is not meant to explain why Manasseh's portion is listed in second place, as might be assumed.[1] The particle "for" (Heb. *kî*) should not be given much stress, and may virtually be ignored.[2] Rather, the author simply recalls this fact with a view to the information which follows.

Machir, called *the first-born of Manasseh*, was actually Manasseh's only son (see Gen. 50:23; Num. 26:29). To Machir, who was *the father of Gilead*,[3] had been allotted *Gilead and Bashan* (see 13:29–31). This was done because Machir *was a capable warrior* (lit. "a man of war"), and reflects the fierce fighting in which the Transjordanian tribes had engaged before occupying their territory (Num. 32:39).

2 The *rest of the Manassites* mentioned in this verse are Manasseh's descendants via Gilead, the son of Machir (see also Num. 26:30–

1. Many interpreters consider the information about Manasseh's status as first-born son to be an indication that originally the relation Manasseh-Ephraim, even during their settlement in Canaan, was different from what now appears due to supposed later hands reworking the text. About this suggestion see also the commentary on 13:29, n. 29.
2. Cf. A. Gelin's translation in *Josué*, p. 98: "Le sort tomba pour la tribu de Manassé: c'était l'aîné de Joseph"; and also J. P. Lange, ed., *A Commentary on the Holy Scriptures* 4, p. 143, where Keil is quoted as follows: "The *kî* is not to be pressed. . . ."
3. KD suggest this be understood as *"lord (possessor) of Gilead,"* with Gilead the district in Transjordan. Note the use of the definite article with Gilead, since it is not used in v. 3 where Gilead clearly represents a personal name. See also H. Freedman, *Joshua, ad loc.*, who believes the clan of Gilead is meant here. This would then agree with Deut. 3:14, which relates that it was Jair who captured Bashan and that Gilead was assigned to Machir. For a discussion of critical theories about a Gilead clan see also R. de Vaux, *Early History*, pp. 574–76.

32).[4] These received their lot on the west side of the Jordan *by their families*, a term used in other boundary descriptions as well (15:20; 16:5). The Manassites on the west of Jordan comprise the *sons of Abiezer, Helek, Asriel, Shechem, Hepher, and Shemida*. In anticipation of the story told in vv. 3–4 these are called Manasseh's *male descendants*. The genealogical information provided for Manasseh is more complete than that given for the other tribes where the names of individual descendants are not listed.

3–6 Background for the story here told is Num. 26:33; 27:1–11. *Zelophehad, the son of Hepher*, whose name is listed in v. 2, had only daughters. Their names are mentioned in full, as in Num. 27:1.[5] They had been promised inheritance rights along with their male relatives. Faith in that promise makes them appear *before Eleazar the priest, before Joshua . . . , and before the princes*, i.e., those appointed to supervise the distribution of the land (14:1; 19:51: 21:1; Num. 34:17). Their appeal to the Lord's earlier command given to Moses is granted.[6] The word "brothers" should be understood here in the broader sense of tribal relations.

Therefore, altogether *there fell to Manasseh ten portions* besides the land obtained on the east side of the Jordan. Five of these were for those mentioned in v. 2, excluding Hepher, the father of Zelophehad. The other five were for Hepher's daughters.[7] With great explicitness v. 6 sums up the situation as it prevailed among Manasseh's descendants. The arrangement was apparently in need of such explicitness in view of its unusual nature.

7 The actual boundary description of Manasseh's lot which begins here does not excel in precision, in contrast, for example, to those of Judah and Benjamin (15:2–63; 18:12–28). Manasseh's territory lay to the north of that of Ephraim mentioned in ch. 16. The description of Manasseh's portion begins with its northern boundary. The opening statement that the border *reached from Asher as far as Michmethath, which is opposite Shechem*, has been understood variously. If, as some think, Asher is the

---

4. For a somewhat different scheme of listing the genealogical table see 1 Chr. 7:14–17. R. J. A. Sheriffs, *NBD*, pp. 778f., assumes that the Chronicles text is corrupt.

5. The names Hoglah and Noah also occur in the inscriptions of the Samaritan ostraca, as does the name Shemida (v. 2). Cf. Y. Aharoni, *The Land of the Bible*, p. 322; *ANET*, p. 321.

6. The chief agent in this appears to have been Joshua ("he gave"). Some take this to be an indefinite "he" and translate with the passive, "it was given."

7. J. Gray, *Joshua, Judges and Ruth*, p. 155, suggests that the concern of Zelophehad's daughters was not so much for land possession as for a status in the sacral confederacy. But this presupposes the existence of an amphictyonic arrangement, a theory the validity of which has been critically assailed in recent publications.

name of the tribe which inherited land north of Manasseh, then the line drawn runs from north to a point on the south boundary to Michmethath, opposite[8] Shechem. Some have looked for a locality by the name of Asher in the vicinity of Shechem.[9] Others, however, point out that Michmethath follows upon Asher without any syntactic connection or transition. In the translation offered here, the words "as far as" have been supplied on the basis of the understood meaning. Thus understood, the text is first making a statement about Manasseh's northern boundary near Asher, and it then proceeds to speak of the southern boundary at Michmethath, where it coincides with the northern border of Ephraim.[10]

Verse 7b states that *the boundary ran southward to the inhabitants of En-tappuah*. The reason why the inhabitants are specified here lies in the fact that the city itself was given to Ephraim, but the general district belonged to Manasseh.[11]

8–9 While the land of *Tappuah*, a Canaanite city (12:17), belonged to Manasseh, the city was in the possession of the Ephraimites. The boundary then continued westward and *ran down into the brook* (or "gorge") *Kanah* (v. 9). There is no unanimity about the way in which the Hebrew clauses should be combined at this point. Some prefer to take the words "south of the brook" with what follows concerning the cities belonging to Ephraim.[12]

As in 16:9 certain cities of the Ephraimites are said to lie in Manasseh's territory. The last part of v. 9 may also be rendered: "The territory of Manasseh was north of the brook." One possible meaning of this difficult passage[13] is that the boundary ran from Tappuah toward the brook

---

8. This "opposite" (Heb. *'al p^enê*, "to the face of") is often understood as "to the east of," but cf. R. L. W. Cleave, "Student Map 'A'," *Pictorial Archive of Near Eastern History* (Jerusalem: n.d.), where it is placed to the south-southwest of Shechem.

9. E.g., KD, *ad loc.*

10. H. W. Hertzberg, *ATD* IX, p. 103, considers the words "from Asher" to be due to textual corruption. Gray, *op. cit.*, p. 156, states "the north-east [sic] limit is given vaguely as Asher." Asher, however, was in the northwest.

11. Some prefer to emend the Hebrew text slightly, changing "the inhabitants of" to the place name Yashub (Yashib). So, e.g., F.-M. Abel, *Le Livre de Josué*, p. 79, and JB; see also *GTT*, p. 167; B. J. Alfrink, *Josué*, p. 89. Some support is given by the LXX. See also Aharoni, *op. cit.*, p. 325, n. 101, who observes that Jashub was also a clan in Issachar. However, this is not the only time this list refers to the inhabitants of a city rather than the city itself (cf. v. 11).

12. So RSV, JB, NAB. The translation offered above agrees with NEB, DNV, and Freedman, *Joshua*.

13. See also Y. Kaufmann, *The Biblical Account of the Conquest of Palestine*, pp. 34–36. Kaufmann assumes "textual confusions and omissions" (p. 35), as in ch. 16. This solution hardly commends itself.

and then to the other side. This would mean that the south side of the brook belonged to Manasseh, although the cities located there belonged to Ephraim.

10–11 The relative location of Ephraim and Manasseh was such that the former's territory lay to the south of the latter. The western boundary of Manasseh[14] was the Mediterranean Sea, while on the north the Manassites *touched on Asher, and in the east on Issachar*. Manasseh also held cities in the territories of Issachar and Asher, respectively. This corresponds to what was said about Ephraim having cities amidst Manasseh. The cities mentioned are *Beth-shean, Ibleam, Dor, En-dor, Taanach*, and *Megiddo*, although in the case of several of them it is the inhabitants of these cities rather than the cities themselves that are specified (see v. 7). With the exception of Dor the cities mentioned are located in the plain of Esdraelon. The line runs from the east (Beth-shean, or modern Tell el-Ḥuṣn near Beisan) to the west (Megiddo or Tell el-Mutesellim). Ibleam lies north of modern Nablus. The cities, the inhabitants of which are mentioned, remained Canaanite (see also v. 16). Dor was located on the coast, south of the Carmel mountain range. En-dor is 7 miles southeast of Nazareth.[15] Taanach and Megiddo are also mentioned in 12:21. Heb. *šᵉlōšet hannāpet* has been rendered "the three-heights country." Although a number of different translations have been proposed,[16] this rendering does correspond accurately to the geographical situation of the last three cities mentioned, each of which was situated near a mountain ridge.[17]

12–13 These verses are in harmony with the information given in 15:63; 16:10 (cf. 13:13). Within the scope of the "prophetical" historiography of the book of Joshua these notes alert the reader to the threatening danger that comes from a failure to eliminate the Canaanite population (Deut. 12:29). Israel's inability to take possession of these cities created dangerous enclaves and set the stage for the developments contained in the book of Judges (compare 15:63 with Judg. 1:21; 17:11–13 with Judg.

14. The Hebrew uses a singular suffix, although in actual fact Ephraim's border also was formed by the Sea.
15. Some hold the reference to this city to be a later addition. Gray judges it too far north of Manasseh to be part of the original text; *op. cit.*, p. 157. Aharoni, *op. cit.*, p. 212, believes it was added because of the name Dor, which does not occur in Judg. 1:27 and does not seem to have been a Canaanite center. However, none of these reasons is compelling enough to consider the name a later addition.
16. E.g., RSV "the third is Napheth"; JB "and a third of the Nepheth"; Freedman "the three regions," "the triple region." Part of the difficulty lies in the uncertainty of the meaning of *nepet*. KB render it with "Anhöhe? hill?," indicating uncertainty.
17. The word translated "villages" in v. 11 differs from that used in other passages, such as 15:51, 54, 59. "Surrounding settlements" would be another possible translation.

1:27–28; and 16:10 with Judg. 1:29). *Forced labor* was imposed on the Canaanite population, but the text makes it clear that this was not the same as eradication. Thus the seeds were sown for later syncretism and apostasy.

4. COMPLAINT OF THE JOSEPHITES (17:14–18)

14 *But the Josephites had a discussion with Joshua. They said: "Why have you given me only one lot and one portion as an inheritance? I am a numerous people, since the Lord has blessed me hitherto."*

15 *Joshua said to them: "If you are a numerous people, go up to the forest, and there clear a space in the land of the Perizzites and the Rephaim, since the hill country of Ephraim is too narrow for you."*

16 *The Josephites replied: "That hill country is not enough for us, and the Canaanites who live in the plain region have iron chariots, both those in Beth-shean and its villages and those in the valley of Jezreel."*

17 *Then Joshua said to the house of Joseph, to Ephraim and Manasseh: "You are a numerous people, and you have great power; you will not have one lot,*

18 *but the hill country shall also be yours. It is forest land. Clear it. It will be yours to its farthest reaches. You will surely drive out the Canaanites, though they have chariots of iron and are powerful."*

There is a formal similarity between this section and 14:6–15, but the spirit is contrasting. Caleb's request proceeded from his great faith in God's previous word to him. The Josephites take issue with the "lot" they have received, whereas in actual fact this lot was ruled by God. Moreover, their fearful attitude toward the Canaanites was anything but commendatory. The purpose of inserting this episode at the conclusion of the description of Joseph's portion may be to alert the reader to the fact that the promised land, if it is to be possessed, requires the activity of the tribes, who must not be deterred by the threats of Canaan's superior military force.

14 Joshua alone is the leading figure in this episode (cf. vv. 3–6). Precisely when this request on the part of the Josephites was made is not immediately clear. It may well have been that enough time had elapsed to acquaint the Josephites with the nature of the land they had been given and to provide them with a basis for their complaint.

There is a formal justification for Joseph's complaint. In 16:1 the fact that Joseph received only one lot is clearly stated. However, they had in fact received part of Transjordania plus two portions on the west side of Jordan, one for Ephraim, the other for the half tribe of Manasseh. The Josephites appeal to the fact that they are *a numerous people* and ascribe this to the blessing of the Lord (cf. Gen. 1:28; 12:2). Comparative census figures from the book of Numbers (26:34, 37) indicate that Ephraim numbered 32,500 and Manasseh 52,700. Manasseh, however, was spread over two territories, and some of the other tribes were actually more numerous.

15 Joshua takes them at their word. If they are as numerous as they say, what prevents their taking proper measures to extend their territory? The *forest* to which they are urged to go covered a considerable portion of the northwest of the mountain of Ephraim. They are urged to clear a space there. It is *the land of the Perizzites and the Rephaim*. Some interpreters think this proposed transaction is a sign of a push by the Josephites from the west to Transjordan. This is suggested in the light of 2 Sam. 18:6, which speaks of a forest of Ephraim, probably located east of the Jordan. Another reason for this suggestion is found in the reference to the Rephaim, who are generally placed east of the river (12:4; 13:12), but not exclusively so (see 15:8). As to the forest of Ephraim east of the Jordan, this name may have originated from the defeat Ephraim suffered in that area during the time of the Judges (Judg. 12). Moreover, the Perizzites, also mentioned by Joshua, are firmly embedded in accounts describing activity west of the Jordan (3:10; 9:1; 11:3; 12:8; 24:11).

Joshua appears to recognize that the *hill country of Ephraim* is too restricted for the Josephites. This hill country could be so designated proleptically, since it had been assigned to Ephraim. The use of this expression may also be due to the fact that the episode recorded here took place some time after the actual allotment.[1]

16–18 The Josephites do not consider Joshua's suggestion to be a sufficient answer to their complaint.[2] They object that *the hill country is not enough*[3] for them. But there is a second reason, namely the *iron chariots* of *the Canaanites who live in the plain region*. These were iron-plated war chariots. The plain region (lit. "the land of the valley") is the area of *the valley of Jezreel*,[4] and also that of the Jordan. *Beth-shean*,

1. For a description of this central mountain region of Palestine, also called "hill country of Israel" (11:16), cf. Y. Aharoni, *The Land of the Bible*, pp. 26f.; see also KD, p. 183.
2. Some consider vv. 16–18 to be but another version of the same story, a duplicate. However, these same interpreters admit that the redactor has woven these two together into one consecutive story; see, e.g., H. W. Hertzberg, *ATD* IX, p. 104.
3. Heb. *māṣā'*, as in Num. 11:22; Zech. 10:10. It may also be rendered "is not available."
4. This is the largest valley bisecting the central mountain range of Palestine and the only one which connects the coastal area with the Jordan Valley; see Aharoni, *op. cit.*, pp. 21f. Some of its main cities, Megiddo, Taanach, and Ibleam, are mentioned in v. 11.

which formed the connecting link between these two regions, is the present Tell el-Ḥuṣn near modern Beisan.[5] Although this further reaction on the part of the Joseph tribes betrays lack of confidence and faith, Joshua's reply does not rebuke their cowardly attitude in so many words. Nevertheless, his utterances are solemn (note the writer's introduction: *Then Joshua said to the house of Joseph, to Ephraim and Manasseh*) and emphatic.[6] He reminds his fellow tribesmen (he himself was of Ephraimite stock) that they are indeed *numerous* as they themselves have said. Though at the allotment they had been treated as one and had received one lot, they will in actual fact have more than one if they only assert themselves and do what he suggests.

Thus Joshua assures them that they will have *hill country* (the Hebrew lacks the article). This refers to that which had already been allotted to them, but it must have special reference to what they themselves are to *clear*. When this is done the land will be theirs *to its farthest reaches*.[7] The hortatory, parenetic purpose of inserting this episode becomes clear from Joshua's final words concerning the certainty of the expulsion of the Canaanites, be they ever so powerfully equipped with the dreaded *chariots of iron*.[8]

F. LAND DISTRIBUTION CONTINUED AT SHILOH (18:1–10)

1 *Then the whole congregation of the Israelites assembled at Shiloh and set up the tent of meeting there, since the region was subdued before them.*

5. For a description of the archaeological finds at this site see G. M. Fitzgerald, "Beth-shean," in *AOTS*, pp. 185f.
6. The Hebrew particle *kî*, which v. 18 uses several times, can have an asseverative meaning, "truly." In our translation we have sought to achieve the effect by using short sentences.
7. Heb. *tōṣeʾōṭāyw*, lit. "its goings out," may also be taken in a more figurative sense, namely "that which comes of it," "its results." The NAB renders "its adjacent land." We understand it in the sense of "furthest extent," meaning probably the forested mountain area plus the adjoining valleys.
8. For a discussion of scholarly speculation concerning the "original" form of the story here recounted see also C. H. J. de Geus, *The Tribes of Israel*, p. 82. Whereas M. Noth considers the existence of a unified "house of Joseph" to be early and the separation between Ephraim and Manasseh to be late, de Geus considers the collective name "Joseph" to be late! See also p. 221, n. 14.

2 *Seven tribes were left among the Israelites which had not yet apportioned their inheritance.*

3 *So Joshua said to the Israelites: "How long will you be slack in going to take possession of the land which the Lord, the God of your forefathers, has given you?*

4 *Supply three men for each tribe and I will send them out. They will get up, walk through the land and make a record of it, according to the inheritance of each, and come back to me.*

5 *Let them divide it into seven portions. Judah stays in his territory in the south, and the house of Joseph stays in their territory in the north.*

6 *But you are to make a record of the land in seven portions and bring that to me here. Then I will cast lots for you here in the presence of the Lord our God.*

7 *The Levites have no portion among you, for the priesthood of the Lord is their inheritance. And Gad, Reuben, and half the tribe of Manasseh have received their inheritance east of the Jordan, which Moses the servant of the Lord gave them."*

8 *Then the men made ready for the journey. And Joshua commanded those who were about to undertake the journey for the purpose of making a record of the land: "Go, traverse the land and make a record of it. Then you are to come back to me, and right here I will cast the lot for you, in the presence of the Lord at Shiloh."*

9 *So the men went, traveled through the land and, in a book, they made a record of it by cities, in seven portions. They they came to Joshua to the camp at Shiloh.*

10 *Joshua thereupon cast lots for them at Shiloh in the presence of the Lord. That is where Joshua divided the land to the Israelites according to their tribal divisions.*

Chapters 18–19 contain the boundary descriptions of the remaining seven tribes. The writer first repeats a number of points already made in earlier chapters; see for example v. 7, where Levi's exceptional position is once again described (cf. 13:14; 14:4) and the assignment of Transjordan to the 2½ tribes is recalled (see 13:8–32; 14:3). This is not needless redundancy[1] but proceeds from the writer's thematic interest in the twelve-tribe scheme

1. J. Gray, *Joshua, Judges and Ruth*, p. 59, considers the information of v. 7 to be needless repetition, but this overlooks the thematic interest the writer may have had and forces the account into the straightjacket of a mere chronicle. Gray, for that matter, considers the entire story of a systematic survey and apportionment by lot for tribes he believes already partly settled in their respective regions (such as Issachar and Zebulun) to be redactional and due to an unrealistic conception. However, 17:11–13 does not say clearly that these tribes were already settled in their regions.

and in the unity of Israel as it participates equally in the Conquest (cf. 1:12–18) and as it shares alike in the distribution of the promised land.

1 *Shiloh* is chosen as the location for the continued distribution of the land to the remaining tribes.[2] This city belonged to Ephraim's territory and is located at the site of modern Seilûn, 12 miles south of Shechem. Its choice as the place where the tent of meeting was to be set up was probably due to its central location.[3]

Joshua is not mentioned as the chief agent responsible for the transfer to Shiloh, although in the light of the entire book this transfer must be assumed to have taken place under his direction and under that of the priest Eleazar. *The whole congregation* (Heb. *'ēḏâ*) is said to have come together at Shiloh and to have *set up the tent of meeting there*. This is the second time the notion of the congregation of Israel occurs in the book (see 9:15, 18–19, 21, 27; for later occurrences see 20:9; 22:12, 16–17, 20, 30).

The tent of meeting[4] occurs here for the first time in the book. The only other reference is in 19:51. What is meant is the sacred tent in which the ark of the covenant was kept (Exod. 25:8; 27:21). It was the appointed meeting place between God and his people and could also be referred to as "the house of the Lord" (see 6:24; cf. Exod. 34:26). Possibly the setting up of the tent at this central site was meant to counteract the tendencies toward disintegration which had shown themselves in the episode of the complaint of the Josephites reported in the previous chapter. At that time self-interest threatened to overshadow national unity,[5] a tendency even more pronounced at a later point in Israel's history (cf. Judg. 5:16–18).

---

2. H. Holzinger, *Das Buch Josua*, p. 73, following J. Wellhausen, believes that the reference to the Shiloh location originally stood in front of 14:1, in view of v. 1b; see also 19:51, which is then understood as applying to the whole allotment process; see also C. Steuernagel, *Das Buch Josua*, p. 277. Others consider Shiloh to be an interpolation; see J. A. Soggin, *Joshua*, p. 189. It is held that if Shiloh were the orientation point, v. 5 could not have referred to Joseph being on the north. But cannot this have been a reference to the relative location of Judah and Joseph?

3. This choice of a city which had no previous cultic associations is puzzling to those who attempt to explain the choice of Israel's cult centers (Gilgal, Jerusalem, Bethel) in the light of earlier pre-Israelite occurrences. In the case of Shiloh, God simply chose to cause his name to dwell there (cf. Deut. 12:11; Jer. 7:12). That was the only justification for Israel's choice of this city.

4. Heb. *'ôhel mô'ēḏ* has also been rendered "Tent of the Presence" (NEB) and "tent of reunion" (F.-M. Abel). The word "tabernacle" is the English form of Latin *tabernaculum*, which is a translation of *'ôhel*. Another Hebrew word used for the tent is *miškân*, "tent," "dwelling."

5. See H. Freedman, *Joshua*, ad loc.

Israel's relocation of the sanctuary at Shiloh was made possible inasmuch as that *region was subdued before them*. Perhaps this refers to what the Josephites, in whose territory Shiloh was located, had done with the land allotted to them. It may also be that motifs such as that expressed in Deut. 12:10, where the erection of a sanctuary in Palestine is connected with God's giving of "rest" to Israel, play a part in this information (see also 2 Sam. 7:1–2).[6]

2–4 Since Judah and the two branches of the house of Joseph had received their inheritance, there were now *seven tribes* left of the 9½ mentioned in 13:7. The author is concerned to present his material in terms of the twelve-tribe system. He does not weary to relate the pertinent facts needed to understand that system (see also v. 7; cf. 14:3).

Taking possession of the land which has been subdued was meant to be an act of faith. Not to do so, as was the case with the seven remaining tribes, therefore is called slackness by Joshua. After all, was it not *the Lord, the God of your forefathers* who had *given* the land to them? This notion of the "giving" of the land had been the writer's concern from the very beginning of the book (1:2, 6, 13; 2:24, etc.). To fail to act upon this gracious gift was tantamount to an attitude of ingratitude. The other significant word used is *inheritance* (v. 2; see 1:6 and commentary). Thus in Joshua's words as recorded, and in those of the writer himself, the neglect of the seven tribes assumes a serious character. Judah earlier had shown a more commendable attitude (14:6), although the same initiative is not mentioned in connection with the Josephites (16:1).

Joshua orders *three men for each tribe*[7] to be picked so that they may be sent out through the land to *make a record of it*. Verse 9 indicates that this record would consist chiefly of a list of the towns in the area to be possessed. This list must be made *according to the inheritance of each* (lit. "according to their inheritance"). Since in v. 2 the writer has reported that the inheritance had not yet been taken possession, he cannot mean to say here that the description had to prepare a record of the portions already settled. The description is to be done with a view to, and hence also according to, the inheritance each will eventually acquire.[8]

6. The word rendered "region" (Heb. *'ereṣ*) may also be translated "land." This would agree with summary statements such as made in 11:16, but in 13:1–7 the incomplete nature of the Conquest is stressed. This seems to favor the word "region" as the best translation at this point.
7. Probably only the seven tribes are intended, although abstractly it is possible that all the tribes participated, to show the national unity which has been stressed at other points (1:12–18; 4:12). The latter view is held by A. Gelin, *Josué*, p. 103.
8. Other translations of this phrase are "with a view to its apportioning" (JB) and "for purposes of inheritance" (NAB).

The men appointed are to come back to Joshua (v. 4; cf. v. 6), who is here seen as the sole agent of the allotment (cf. 14:1, where others also participate). Silence about the others does not necessarily preclude their participation, however. This participation is explicitly asserted in 19:51.

5–7 Judah and Joseph had received their respective territories already, the one in the south, the other to the north of that southern territory. There is no need to think here of a Gilgal perspective, as is done by some interpreters (see above). The land is to be recorded in seven portions, corresponding to the seven tribes mentioned earlier. Joshua then will receive the record and *cast lots . . . in the presence of the Lord our God*. This presence was made tangible by means of the tent of meeting mentioned earlier, and especially by the ark which was the most central emblem of the Lord's indwelling (cf. 7:6; cf. also 2 Sam. 6:14). It is clear that the continued allotment for the remaining tribes will be no less significant than that of those already completed.

If v. 1 meant to say no more than that the region around Shiloh was subdued, the question arises as to whether the recorders to be sent out could actually do their work unhindered by Canaanite interference. Some have considered this to be an unrealistic feature in the proposed transaction. But it should be kept in mind that, according to 11:16–17, the writer intends to depict that the land had been subdued, at least in principle. This would allow the men a certain freedom of movement. One may also think of the dread of which 2:9, 11 speaks. Moreover, the description intended did not require a penetration into every corner of the land.

With a reference to two well-known facts, that of the exceptional position of the Levites (cf. 13:14, 33; 14:3–4) and that of the allotment of the Transjordanian tribes (cf. 1:12–18; 13:8–33), the report of Joshua's words is concluded. For its significance in light of the total emphasis of the book, see the introduction to this chapter. Apparently everything must be done to bring before the mind of the reader the twelve-tribe system. With a slight variation from what 13:14, 33 stated, the author now reports that the exceptional position of the Levites is because *the priesthood of the Lord is their inheritance*.

8–10 The account does not mention explicitly the selection of the men to carry out Joshua's command, but it is assumed that they were picked. These now *made ready for the journey*[9] and were given more

---

9. Others, e.g., B. J. Alfrink, *Josué*, p. 92, followed by J. H. Kroeze, *Het Boek Jozua*, p. 199, prefer to translate v. 8 as follows: "the people (Heb. *hā'ᵃnāšîm*) arose and went away." In other words, the meeting of the assembly was dismissed.

specific instructions as to what to do. Renewed emphasis (*right here . . . , in the presence of the Lord at Shiloh*) is placed on the sacredness of the future casting of the lot for the remaining seven tribes. Their slackness to possess the land intended for them shows that they were in need of this added incentive. The writer may also have desired to stress that the remaining tribes, though at a later time to play a less significant role than some of the others, were all treated equally at that stage and had received their inheritance no less officially than the rest. The *book* (*sēper*) into which the record of the *cities* was entered consisted of some sort of written material, but the word should not be taken in its modern sense. The *portions* into which the description was divided were probably of about equal size so that at the drawing of the lot each remaining tribe would receive a fair share. When Joshua had received the report[10] from the tribal representatives, he *cast lots*. The whole procedure was a combination of what had been done for the Transjordanian tribes (no lots, but land distribution) and what had been done in the case of Judah and Joseph, where the lot had determined the inheritances of each without prior description of the land to be allotted. That this was done *at Shiloh in the presence of the Lord* (vv. 6, 8) is asserted once more. The final words of v. 10, translated *according to their tribal divisions*, indicate smaller subdivisions of the tribes. No precise formula is used in each instance[11] (see also 11:23; 12:7).

G. BENJAMIN'S ALLOTMENT (18:11–28)

1. BENJAMIN'S BOUNDARY LINES (18:11–20)

11 *The lot of the tribe of the Benjaminites came up according to their families; the territory of their allotment extended between the Judahites and the Josephites.*

The NAB quite clearly chooses the approach followed in the present commentary by translating "When those who were to map out the land were ready for the journey, Joshua instructed them. . . ."

10. Joshua is said to be "in the camp" when the report is rendered. This language reminds one of Israel's earlier location at Gilgal (cf. 10:43) but is not as such inappropriate for the new location at Shiloh, where some sort of military establishment may have been maintained during the allotment procedures.

11. Instead of tribal divisions some translations see in the word *maḥlᵉqôt* the meaning "portions, shares." GB render it with "Abteilung, des Volkes" in all but one instance, but see KB for the other meaning.

12 *Their northern border began at the Jordan; then the border went up to the flank of Jericho northward and went up westward into the hill country, and came out at the desert of Beth-aven.*

13 *From there the border ran on to Luz, southward in the direction of the mountain flank of Luz, which is Bethel; then the border ran down to Ataroth-addar on the mountain that lies to the south of Lower Beth-horon.*

14 *Then the border made a turn on the west side and swung south from the mountain that lies opposite Beth-horon southward and it ended at Kiriath-baal, that is, Kiriath-jearim, a city of the Judahites. This was the west side.*

15 *The southern border began at the limits of Kiriath-jearim; it then ran westward and reached the well of the waters of Nephtoah.*

16 *The border then went down to the limits of the mountain that lies facing the valley of the son of Hinnom north of the valley of Rephaim. It continued down to the valley of Hinnom, along the flank of the Jebusite southward, and then went down to En-rogel.*

17 *Then the border extended northward and went as far as En-shemesh and Geliloth, which is opposite the ascent of Adummim. It then went down to the stone of Bohan the son of Reuben.*

18 *It then continued in the direction of the flank over against the Arabah northward and ran down into the Arabah.*

19 *The border then continued in the direction of the mountain flank of Beth-hoglah, northward, and the extreme end of the border was at the northern bay of the Salt Sea, at the south end of the Jordan. This was the southern border.*

20 *The Jordan formed its border on the east side. This was the inheritance of the Benjaminites, according to their families, with its borders round about.*

The description of the boundaries of the seven remaining tribes, which begins at this point, serves the same purpose as that of the earlier tribes. Israel is entering upon its "inheritance" according to a promise made by God to the forefathers. Verse 3 has once again recalled the significance that the allotment has within the scheme of the book of Joshua. The rationale for more lengthy boundary descriptions lies therefore in the awareness that these boundaries give concrete shape to the promises of God. The promise of the land was one of the recurring features of the covenant undertakings given to the patriarchs and others (Gen. 12:7; 13:15; 15:18; see also the introduction to ch. 13 in this commentary). The essentially spiritual nature of the "lot" which Israel received from its Lord comes to beautiful expression in Ps. 16:5–6.

11 Benjamin, the first to receive his lot, was Jacob's second son by Rachel.[1] Benjamin's lot *came up*, but the precise manner of how the lot was determined is not stated anywhere (cf. 14:2; 16:1). Benjamin's territory was north of that of Judah and south of that of Joseph. For a complete understanding of Benjamin's borders, see 15:5–11; 16:1–3.

12–13 The description begins with the northern boundary, which is contiguous with Ephraim's southern boundary (16:1–3). It is described from east to west. Hence it *began at the Jordan*. It then ran up to the *flank* (lit. "shoulder") *of Jericho*. This is the high ground north of Jericho. Going *westward* from that point it ran through the *hill country*. The course is only vaguely indicated when it is said to come out *at the desert of Beth-aven*. (For the location of this city and the meaning of its name, cf. 7:2 and commentary).[2]

The boundary then ran in a southerly direction toward the *mountain flank of Luz*. This has been taken to mean that it followed the ridge south of Bethel, otherwise known as Luz (for the relation of Bethel to Luz see 16:2). The line continued to run down to *Ataroth-addar*, which is said to be *on*[3] *the mountain that lies to the south of Lower Beth-horon*. Beth-horon itself belonged to Ephraim. For its location cf. 10:10; 16:3.

14 At Beth-horon the border turned southward, *from the mountain that lies opposite Beth-horon*. This means, therefore, that v. 14 describes Benjamin's western border (cf. *the west side*). A space is thus created for the territory allotted to Dan.[4] The southern boundary of Ephraim and

---

1. The order in which the lots were determined follows the order which prevailed in Jacob's household. The children of Jacob's two wives receive their share first, namely Benjamin, Simeon, Zebulun, and Issachar; subsequently those of Jacob's concubines, that is to say, Asher, Naphtali, and Dan. The allotment of territory in Transjordan is not taken into account here. This may indicate something of God's concern for established rights. In the case of Isaac, the son of the wife, over against Ishmael, the son of the concubine, this concern is apparent from the account of Gen. 21:8–16; cf. 25:6. For possible further theological implications of God's procedures, see C. Vonk, *Inleiding op de Profeten: Jozua*, pp. 254–56. Vonk also sees a parallel between this concern for established rights and the lesser and greater prominence among Jesus' disciples, and among Christians in general.
2. Y. Aharoni, *The Land of the Bible*, p. 236, tentatively identifies it with Tell Maryam, and seems to treat it as an independent locality, different from Bethel.
3. Heb. *'al*. Some translations take this to mean "by." J. Simons, *GTT*, defends the translation "before" (p. 172, n. 155). The versions and commentaries are divided. RSV, NAB, JB have "on"; ASV "by"; Hertzberg "auf den Berg zu"; Zürcher Bibel "gegen den Berg." One of the difficulties stems from the verb "to go down" (*yāraḏ*), but its use is sometimes ambivalent, as Simons admits.
4. For a discussion of Benjamin's boundaries in conjunction with those of Dan, see also Y. Kaufmann, *The Biblical Account of the Conquest of Palestine*, p. 16, in which issue is taken with A. Alt's theories.

Benjamin's border, which had been contiguous to this point, now part company. The former runs on toward the sea, whereas the latter does not. The only other point in this western boundary is its terminus, *Kiriath-baal*, another name for *Kiriath-jearim* (cf. 9:17). The city itself belonged to Judah (cf. 15:9, 60).

15–19 Benjamin's southern boundary *began at the limits* (lit. "the end") *of Kiriath-jearim*. This refers to the edge of the city's surrounding territory. This southern border coincides with Judah's northern border (cf. 15:5–9). But from the description the movement of the two is in opposite directions, since in Benjamin's case the movement is from west to east. For this reason the words which have been translated *it then ran westward* pose a difficulty. Perhaps the intention is that the border first ran westward.[5] For *the waters of Nephtoah*, cf. 15:9. The border then followed a downward course and came to the *limits*, i.e., the foot or edge, of the mountain facing the valley of Hinnom. It then ran through that valley, which means that Jerusalem, which was north of that line, belonged not to Judah but to Benjamin (cf. 15:8, 63). For *En-rogel*, see 15:7. Turning *northward* the border then ran *as far as En-shemesh* (15:7) and *Geliloth* (lit. "stone circles"). In 15:7 the name Gilgal is used for this. For the *stone of Bohan* cf. 15:6. The border ran in the direction of the mountain flank opposite *the Arabah*, that is to say, the deep depression in which the Jordan winds its way. It then went into the Arabah itself. Going in the direction of the mountain flank of *Beth-hoglah* (15:6), the border finally ended at the point where the Jordan empties into the Dead Sea.

As one compares the present passage with 15:5–11, both the similarities and the differences meet the eye, which can be taken as an indication of the fact that there was no question of a slavish copying from one list to the other.

20 Because the east border was formed by *the Jordan*, there was no further need for specifics. The description ends with the customary statement that this was Benjamin's *inheritance* and that it was allotted to them *according to their families* (13:23, 28; 15:12).

2. CITY LIST OF BENJAMIN (18:21–28)

21 *Now the cities of the tribe of the Benjaminites according to their families were Jericho, Beth-hoglah, Emek-keziz,*

---

5. Some have followed emendations, based in part on the LXX. JB reads "towards Gasin." NEB omits the phrase. RSV reads "to Ephron"; but see J. Gray, *Joshua, Judges and Ruth*, p. 162.

22 *Beth-arabah, Zemaraim, Bethel,*
23 *Avvim, Parah, Ophrah,*
24 *Chephar-ammoni, Ophni, and Geba.*
   Twelve cities with their villages.
25 *Gibeon, Ramah, Beeroth,*
26 *Mizpeh, Chephirah, Mozah,*
27 *Rekem, Irpeel, Taralah,*
28 *Zelah, Eleph, the Jebusite (that is, Jerusalem), Gibeath, and Kiriath.*
   Fourteen cities with their villages.
   This was the inheritance of the Benjaminites, according to their families.

As was the case with Judah, the lot of Benjamin is provided with a rather extensive city list. The list divides into two groups; the first comprises twelve cities in the eastern part of the territory (vv. 21–24), and the second contains those in the western portion, totalling fourteen cities (vv. 25–28).

21–24 For *Jericho* and its probable location, cf. 2:1. For *Beth-hoglah*, cf. 15:6. *Emek-keziz* is unknown, and its name occurs only here. Jericho was in ruins at this time, but Beth-hoglah was actually a border town (see 15:61).

For *Beth-arabah*, see 15:6 and commentary. *Zemaraim*, otherwise unknown, is mentioned in 2 Chr. 13:4.[1] *Bethel* (7:2) is also mentioned in connection with the Joseph tribes (Judg. 1:22–23), and is apparently a later development. It definitely belonged to the northern kingdom after the division and then became the site of a sanctuary (1 K. 12:29). *Avvim* (in Hebrew with the definite article) may be another name for Ai. *Parah*, also with the definite article, is Khirbet el-Fârah, northeast of Anathoth, the birthplace of Jeremiah. *Ophrah* is identified with eṭ-Ṭaiyibeh, a village 4 miles northeast of Bethel. *Chephar-ammoni* defies identification so far as some scholars are concerned, but others identify it with the modern Kefr 'Anā, 3 miles north of Bethel. *Geba* has tentatively been identified with Khirbet et-Tell, about 7 miles north of Bethel. The total of twelve cities agrees with the names listed in the Hebrew text.[2]

25–28 The second group of cities was in the western part of Benjamin's territory. *Gibeon* is well known from 9:3, 17. For possible identification see 9:3–5 and commentary. The other three cities, which belonged to a common league with Gibeon, namely Chephirah, Beeroth,

1. Y. Aharoni, *The Land of the Bible*, p. 287, suggests that it "must be sought in the vicinity of Ramallah and el-Bireh on the Judean border" and refers to 2 Chr. 13:4. *GTT*, p. 174, looks for the approximate location at Râs ez-Zeimara.
2. In the LXX (Codex A) the total is also twelve, but Codex B lists thirteen names.

and Kiriath-jearim, also were allotted to Benjamin. *Ramah* is the present er-Râm, 5 miles north of Jerusalem. For the discussion about *Beeroth*, see 9:17 and commentary. *Mizpeh* may be the same as Mizpah.[3] It is then to be identified with Tell en-Naṣbeh. *Chephirah's* location has been discussed in the commentary on 9:17. *Mozah*, mentioned only here, may be Khirbet Beit Mizze, west of Jerusalem.[4] *Rekem's* location is uncertain, as is that of the following two cities, *Irpeel*[5] and *Taralah*.

The city of *Zelah* is mentioned as Saul's burial place (2 Sam. 21:14). Its location is unknown. Since *Eleph* is preceded in the Hebrew by the definite article, it is combined by some with the preceding name. such as in the NAB, which translates Zelah-eleph. However, this interferes with the tally of cities. Eleph's location is unknown. The next few words present certain difficulties.[6] Some question the identification of Jebus with *Jerusalem* (see 15:8 and commentary; cf. 10:1; 15:63). *Gibeath*, or Gibath, has been identified with Tell el-Fûl.[7] *Kiriath* is possibly Kiriath-jearim.[8]

The total of the cities listed is *fourteen*.

H. SIMEON'S ALLOTMENT (19:1-9)

1 *The second lot came out for Simeon, namely for the tribe of the Simeonites, according to their families. Their inheritance was an enclave in that of Judah.*

2 *As their inheritance they had Beer-sheba, Sheba, Moladah,*

3 *Hazar-shual, Balah, Ezem,*

4 *Eltolad, Bethul, Hormah,*

3. This Mizpah is mentioned in 1 Sam. 7:5; 10:17; 1 K. 15:22; 2 K. 25:23. P. R. Ackroyd, *The First Book of Samuel*. Cambridge Bible Commentary (Cambridge: 1971), p. 236, considers its location uncertain. About questions of identification see D. Diringer in *AOTS*, pp. 329-342.

4. Others, e.g., *GTT*, pp. 176f., suggest Qalunyah as the possible site; likewise G. E. Wright and F. V. Filson, eds., *The Westminster Historical Atlas*; Aharoni, *op. cit.*, pp. 225, 301.

5. Some identify it with Rafah, north of ej-Jib.

6. Gibeath and Kiriath are, strictly speaking, construct states, but no absolute follows the construct. For a possible adjustment of the text see Aharoni, *op. cit.*, p. 301, n. 53.

7. But see H. J. Franken, "Heilig Land en Heilige Huisjes," *passim*, for a critical discussion of this identification and the general method followed in archaeological work related to the Bible.

8. This name is also written Kiriath-arim (Ezra 2:25). Heb. *'ārîm* is at the same time the word for "cities." Hence it has been suggested that the second part of the name is missing through haplography; see *GTT*, p. 177.

5 *Ziklag, Beth-marcaboth, Hazar-susah,*
6 *Beth-lebaoth, and Sharuhen.*
   Thirteen cities with their villages.
7 *Ain, Rimmon, Ether, and Ashan.*
   Four cities with their villages,
8 *and all the villages that were round about these cities as far as
   Baalath-beer, Ramah of the Negeb.*
   *This was the inheritance of the tribe of the Simeonites according to
   their families.*
9 *The inheritance of the Simeonites came out of the share of the Judahites, for the share of the Judahites was too much for them. Therefore the Simeonites received their inheritance in the midst of that of
   the latter.*

Simeon, whose lot is now described, was the second son of Jacob by Leah
(Gen. 29:33). Concerning the order in which the lots came out, see the
introduction to ch. 18. Although by no means a small tribe (the census
number given in Num. 1:23 is 59,300), Simeon was not given an independent portion, but its inheritance fell within that of Judah. The biblical
background for this dispersion is Jacob's utterance in Gen. 49:7.[1] Judah
and Simeon act closely together in Israel's later history (see Judg. 1:3).
Simeon appears to have lost its tribal identity at an early point in history.
A comparison between Num. 1 and 26 shows declining figures for Simeon.
See also 1 Chr. 4:24–43, which mentions Simeon's smallness (vv. 27, 31,
34–43).

   The cities assigned to Simeon divide into two groups, the first (vv.
2–6) consisting of thirteen names (or fourteen, depending on how v. 2 is
read), all in the Negeb, and the second (v. 7), consisting of four cities,
two in the Negeb and two in the Shephelah. The great majority of the
cities listed for Simeon have been discussed earlier in 15:21–32, 42. See
also 1 Chr. 4:24–43 where they occur in the same order. Simeon's territory
did not form a contiguous whole.

   1–6 For *Beer-sheba*, see 15:28. As to the next name, *Sheba*,
some hold this to be a scribal error for Shema, which occurs in the cor-

---

1. Scholarly speculation, disregarding the patriarchal stories and the background
information they provide, has attempted to explain the unusual treatment Simeon
received along other lines. A. Alt, *KS* II, pp. 285f., believes that the information
concerning Simeon reflects the fact that the people of the Negeb in Joshua's time
still remembered a primitive settlement by the Simeonites. M. Noth, *History*,
p. 58, ascribes the present passage to a late redactor. See also R. de Vaux, "The
Settlement of the Israelites in Southern Palestine and Origins of the Tribe of Judah," in H. T. Frank and W. L. Reed, eds., *Translating and Understanding the
OT* (Nashville: 1970), pp. 108–134.

responding list of 15:26.[2] Others believe its occurrence is due to dittography, i.e., the second part of the name of Beer-sheba was repeated inadvertently. The Hebrew text treats it as a separate place name preceded by the conjunction "and."[3] For *Moladah*, see 15:26.

Eltolad is mentioned in 15:30; *Hormah* in 12:14; 15:31; and *Ziklag* in 15:31. *Bethul's* location is uncertain. It has been suggested that *Beth-marcaboth* and *Hazor-susah*, neither of which occurs in ch. 15, are other names for Madmannah and Sansannah respectively (see 15:31). This is a plausible suggestion. Both Beth-marcaboth (lit. "house of chariots") and Hazar-susah (lit. "village of horses") here have functional names, which may have been used as substitutes for the real place names, to be found in 15:31.[4] *Beth-lebaoth* is called Lebaoth in 15:32. *Sharuhen* is thought by some to be the same as Shilhim (15:32).[5] The total number of cities is *thirteen*, but if Sheba is treated as a separate town the actual count is fourteen.

7 The second group consists of four cities. *Ain* and *Rimmon*[6] were located in the Negeb, while *Ether* and *Ashan* are found in the Shephelah.

8 Although the cities mentioned each had their *villages* (see v. 7), still more of these villages were given to Simeon. They extended to *Baalath-beer* ("mistress of the fountain"), called Bealoth in 15:24, and located near Rehoboth. Another name for it was *Ramah* ("the height") *of the Negeb*.[7] The closing statement concerning Simeon's *inheritance* resembles those of 18:28; 19:16, 23, 31, 39, 48.

9 This verse repeats what had been said in v. 1 above, namely that Simeon received an inheritance out of that of Judah because the latter's share *was too much for them*. No reference is made here to the events described in Gen. 34 (cf. 49:7). Much of the early history of the relation between Judah and Simeon remains obscure. Though the dwindling significance of Simeon may be seen in the comparative census figures (see above), 1 Chr. 12:25 speaks of an important contingent of Simeonites belonging to David's army. The blessing of Moses, Deut. 33, makes no

2. This is how the question is treated in NAB, JB, and A. Gelin, *Josué*, p. 106. The ASV translates "or Sheba." H. Freedman, *Joshua*, renders "with Sheba."
3. KD, p. 191, appeal to 15:26, and retain it as another name for Shema.
4. Y. Aharoni, *The Land of the Bible*, p. 266, does not mention this as a possibility.
5. The city of Sharuhen is known from Egyptian records; cf. *ANET*, p. 233. It was the city to which the Hyksos fled upon their expulsion from Egypt.
6. Treated as the name of one town, En-rimmon, by *GTT*, p. 153; RSV. When this is done the total of v. 7 does not tally.
7. Because of the meaning of the names of the last two towns it has been suggested that they fulfilled a cultic function; see also 1 Sam. 30:27.

mention of this tribe, but in Deut. 27:12, Simeon, together with some of the other tribes, is assigned a place among those who are to stand upon Mount Gerizim to bless the people. For other references to this tribe cf. 2 Chr. 15:9; Rev. 7:7.

Although Judah's territory had been indicated by lot, and hence under divine direction, it was not fixed so inflexibly that Simeon could not receive certain parts of it. This second apportionment was also done by lot (v. 1). Some of the cities belonging originally to Simeon were reckoned later on as Judahite, e.g., Beer-sheba (1 K. 19:3).

I. ZEBULUN'S ALLOTMENT (19:10–16)

10 *The third lot came up for the Zebulunites according to their families. The border of their inheritance reached as far as Sarid.*

11 *Their border ran up in a westward direction and on to Mareal; it reached to Dabasheth and to the brook opposite Jokneam.*

12 *From Sarid the border turned in the opposite direction eastward toward the sunrising to the territory of Chisloth-tabor; it came out at Dobrath and went up to Japhia.*

13 *From there it passed along eastward toward the sunrising to Gath-hepher, to Eth-kazin, and came out at Rimmon, which stretches toward Neah.*

14 *Then the border turned around it northward of Hannathon and ran out into the valley of Iphtah-el.*

15 *Included were Kattath, Nahalal, Shimron, Idalah, and Bethlehem. Twelve cities with their villages.*

16 *This is the inheritance of the Zebulunites according to their families, these cities with their villages.*

Zebulun,[1] who received the third lot of the remaining seven, had descended from Jacob's youngest son by Leah (Gen. 30:20). Though Issachar was older, he is mentioned after Zebulun, as also in Gen. 49:13–14. This treatment is comparable to that of Manasseh and Ephraim, and shows an element of divine sovereignty in the unfolding of Israel's history.[2] Although during the desert journey the order of encampment placed Issachar and Zebulun close to Judah, east of the tabernacle, the lot which Zebulun now

1. It has been suggested that the name Zebulun can also be detected in the Egyptian Execration Texts and in the Ugaritic Keret legend. The Keret reference can also be rendered "young men," "nobles."
2. The protracted barrenness of the wives of the patriarchs, and the reversal in the position of Esau and Jacob are an indication of the same thought.

receives is far removed from that of Judah. It lies to the north of the valley of Jezreel in northern Palestine. It is bounded by Asher on the west and northwest, by Naphtali on the north and northeast, and by Issachar on the southeast and south. It touches neither the Mediterranean Sea nor the Jordan.

10 *The third lot came up*; for this and other terminology, cf. 18:11; 19:1, 17, 24, 32, 40. *According to their families*: this is a much-used expression in the allotment chapters (cf. 13:23 and elsewhere). The first point to which Zebulun's border *reached* was *Sarid*, which has been widely associated with Tell Shadûd,[3] 5 miles southeast of Nazareth and thus situated at the southeastern extremity of Zebulun's inheritance.

11 With Sarid as its starting point the description now moves west. The point the border is said to have *reached* ("touched") eventually is *the brook opposite Jokneam*. For Jokneam see 12:22; it is the present Tell Qeimûn. The brook opposite it is probably the Wâdī Mughrârah, which joins the brook Kishon opposite Jokneam.[4] In other words, the border in its westward direction ran along the course of the Kishon. Two points are mentioned in between Sarid and the end point, namely *Mareal* and *Dabasheth*. Mareal has been identified with Tell Thorah[5] and Dabasheth with Tell esh-Shamman.

12 Returning now to Sarid (v. 10), the description moves from that point in an easterly direction.[6] The border ran *to the territory of Chisloth-tabor*.[7] This may have been the same as the Chesulloth mentioned in v. 18, modern Iksâl. If so, then this is a point where Zebulun and Issachar shared a single boundary. This point is 2 miles southeast of Nazareth. *Dobrath* (Daberath) is the present Dabûriyeh at the northwest foot of Mount Tabor. *Japhia* to which the border *went up* is modern Yâfâ, southeast of Nazareth. No precise boundary description is intended. Dobrath is farther northeast, Japhia to the southwest.

13–14 The Hebrew of these verses is worded obscurely. It seems that the eastern border is intended. Only one of the places mentioned,

---

3. Sarid is then supposed to be a scribal variant for Sadud, on the basis of some of the ancient versions.

4. J. Simons, *GTT*, p. 181, thinks that the brook referred to here can only be the Kishon itself.

5. This and the following identification are from Y. Aharoni, *The Land of the Bible*, p. 237. Mareal has also been identified with Tell Ghalta. G. E. Wright and F. V. Filson, eds., *The Westminster Historical Atlas*, consider the location of both points to be "uncertain."

6. Heb. *qēḏmâ* may also be translated "in the east."

7. Instead of the preposition "to" some prefer to render Heb. *'al* with "over" or "past." J. Gray, *Joshua, Judges and Ruth*, p. 166, states: "the border runs eastwards along the foothills to Chisloth-tabor."

Rimmon, can be identified with certainty. The border actually runs north-ward[8] to *Gath-hepher*, which has been identified with Meshhed or with Khirbet ez-Zurrâ', a site close to Meshhed. It is the place from which the prophet Jonah came (2 K. 14:25). *Eth-kazin* is unknown. *Rimmon, which stretches toward Neah*,[9] is the present Rummâneh, 6 miles northeast of Nazareth and about 12 miles west of Tiberias. *Neah* is unknown.

Then the border turned around, probably in a westerly direction, since the *valley of Iphtah-el* was between the territory of Zebulun and that of Asher to the west (19:27). *Hannathon* to the north of which the line ran is Tell el-Bedeiwîyeh. The valley of Iphtah-el has been identified by some scholars with Wâdī el-Melik, but others prefer Ṣahl el-Baṭṭof.

The boundary description is herewith concluded. What follows is a list of cities. Zebulun's territory does not at any point touch on the sea. Yet both Jacob's and Moses' blessings (Gen. 49:13; Deut. 33:18–19) speak of Zebulun in connection with the sea. These blessings do not indicate Zebulun's future place in Canaan but point to the prosperity which it would derive from the sea, by means of fishing, maritime commerce, and from products yielded by the seashore, such as shellfish and dye made from shellfish, as well as glass made from sand.[10]

15–16 The group of cities now listed roughly links up with Dabasheth in the southwest corner of Zebulun's land. *Kattath* has not been identified positively, any more than the Kitron of Judg. 1:30 from which Zebulun did not drive out the inhabitants.[11] *Nahalal*, also spelled Nahalol, has been identified by some with Tell en-Naḥl in the plain south of Acre. Both these places testify to Zebulun's westward orientation and may give added force to what was said above about Zebulun's connections with the sea.[12] For *Shimron*, cf. 11:1.[13] *Idalah* is identified tentatively with Khirbet

---

8. The border itself runs northward although it does so on the eastern side of the territory.

9. The words "which stretches toward" are a translation of Heb. *hammᵉṭō'ār*, the meaning of which is not entirely certain. Some translators take this to be part of a proper name; e.g., BDB translate "and it inclined to Ne'a" (p. 1061).

10. See P. C. Craigie, *Deuteronomy*, p. 399.

11. A. Gelin, *Josué*, p. 108, considers the two to be the same and places them (it) 8 miles southeast of Kartah, otherwise known as 'Atlit (21:34).

12. *GTT*, p. 182, is not sure of this alleged expansion toward the sea.

13. The LXX reads *Symoōn* in Codex B, but *Semrōn* in Codex A. Shimron is known from the Egyptian Execration Texts and from the list of Thutmose III in the form *šm'n*. In the Amarna tablets it occurs as Shamhuna. See Aharoni, *op. cit.*, p. 106. On the basis of this and other spellings of the name, including Codex B of the LXX, but omitting Codex A, Aharoni concludes that the name of the city was originally Shim'on.

el-Ḥawârah near the Bethlehem mentioned next, although others list it as unknown. *Bethlehem*, not to be confused with the Bethlehem in Judah, lies northwest of Nahalal.

The total of *twelve* in v. 15 does not tally, nor do other totals in vv. 30, 38. The LXX omits the totals.[14] Possibly a gap must be assumed in the list, as in 15:59; 21:39. Perhaps other cities, not found in the present enumeration, belonged to the twelve referred to here (cf. 21:34; Judg. 1:30). This suggestion achieves some plausibility in light of the fact that Nazareth, one of the cities in Zebulun, is not mentioned here.

Verse 16 concludes with a final statement similar to 15:20; 18:28.

J. ISSACHAR'S ALLOTMENT (19:17–23)

17 *For Issachar the fourth lot came out, for the Issacharites according to their families.*
18 *Their territory included Jezreel, Chesulloth, Shunem,*
19 *Hapharaim, Shion, Anaharath,*
20 *Rabbith, Kishion, Ebez,*
21 *Remeth, En-gannim, En-haddah, and Beth-pazzez.*
22 *The border also touched on Tabor, Shahazumah, and Beth-shemesh; and the border ended at the Jordan.*
Sixteen cities with their villages.
23 *This is the inheritance of the tribe of the Issacharites according to their families, the cities with their villages.*

Issachar, whose lot came out next, was the fifth son of Jacob by Leah. About Zebulun's preferment above his older brother, see the introduction to vv. 10–16. In Issachar's case the description of his lot consists mainly of a list of cities, with the exception of the eastern portion of the northern boundary and the boundary line.[1] Issachar's territory lay north of Manasseh, east of Asher, southeast of Zebulun, and south of Naphtali. It consisted for the most part of the large and very fertile plain of Jezreel,[2] of which Zebulun also received a part. Issachar's role in later history is quite

---

14. J. Bright, *IB* II, p. 645, suggests that this may have been done "to get rid of the difficulty."
1. So KD, p. 195.
2. M. Noth, *The OT World*, p. 61, also includes the mountain country between the valley of Jezreel, the valley of the Nahr Jālûd, and the Jordan Valley. Of the other part, that of the valley of Jezreel itself, he points out that it remained largely in Canaanite hands, although it was allotted to Issachar.

undistinguished (but cf. Judg. 5:15). Issachar's mood is also aptly described in Gen. 49:14–15.[3]

17 Issachar was the *fourth* of the seven remaining tribes (18:2) to receive its lot. This lot was fixed *according to their families* (13:23, 28; 15:20, etc.).

18 The enumeration of Issachar's cities does not observe specific geographical locations. Not many of the cities mentioned can be located with any degree of certainty. *Their territory included Jezreel*. Since Jezreel has the so-called *he*-locative behind it, some understand this to mean "their territory extended beyond Jezreel."[4] The *he*-locative, however, does not always express direction. It sometimes occurs in a weakened form[5] and thus may be ignored at this point. Jezreel, modern Zer'în, lay on the northwest of the mountains of Gilboa.[6] For *Chesulloth*, cf. v. 12. *Shunem*[7] is modern Sôlem, 3 miles east of 'Affûleh, northeast of Jezreel.

19 *Hapharaim*, not listed elsewhere in the OT, may be eṭ-Ṭaiyibeh, northeast of the hill of Moreh.[8] *Shion*, also mentioned only here, is unknown. *Anaharath* is considered to be the same place as a town mentioned on the topographical list of Thutmose III, where it occurs as *inḫrt*.

20 *Rabbith* may be the same as Dobrath (Daberath) mentioned in

---

3. A. Alt, "Neues über Palästina aus dem Archiv Amenhophis' IV," *KS* III (1959), pp. 169–175, seeks to connect the sentiments attributed to Issachar in Gen. 49:14–15 with the fact that Issachar was settled in land which had been depopulated by Egypt after the suppression of a native revolt in the region. About the theories of Alt and Noth see also Weippert, *The Settlement of the Israelite Tribes in Palestine*, p. 43, n. 136. For a further evaluation of the approach of Alt (and also of S. Mowinckel) and for a discussion of the evidence one may gain from Gen. 49:15, cf. also Y. Kaufmann, *The Biblical Account of the Conquest of Palestine*, pp. 25f., where issue is taken with the position that Issachar had no fixed boundaries or that the author of Joshua did not know of the tribe's boundaries. Kaufmann rightly points out that 17:10 makes the northeastern border of Manasseh touch on Asher and Issachar, implying some sort of fixed boundaries for both. Cf. also A. Saarisalo, "Issachar," in *NBD*, p. 589.
4. So KD, p. 195.
5. Cf. J. H. Kroeze, *Het Boek Jozua*, and GKC §§ 90f, g.
6. Various notable events took place in or near this city in later history; cf. 1 Sam. 29:1; 2 Sam. 2:2. In Solomon's time it became an administrative district (1 K. 4:12), and it was the scene of tragedy during Ahab's reign (1 K. 21:1).
7. It is called Shunama in the correspondence of Amenhotep IV; see Alt, *op. cit.*, p. 169. It is also mentioned in the time of Thutmose III; see *ANET*, p. 243.
8. So Y. Aharoni, *The Land of the Bible*, p. 241, and G. E. Wright and F. V. Filson, eds., *The Westminster Historical Atlas*. It is called "unknown" by L. H. Grollenberg, ed., *Atlas of the Bible*. H. Freedman, *Joshua*, suggests "Perhaps now the ruins of Prieh, between Megiddo and Jokneam"; p. 113.

v. 12.[9] *Kishion* may be Khirbet Qasyun. The name occurs in the list of Thutmose III. *Ebez* is unknown.

21 *Remeth* is listed only here in the OT. From a stele of Pharaoh Seti I discovered at Beth-shean it is known that the Habiru, a people whose precise identity is still a matter of debate, made an attack from a mountain called Yarmuta. This Mount Yarmuta may be associated with Jarmuth, otherwise known as Remeth.[10] *En-gannim* is modern Jenîn, west of Beth-shean in the southern extremity of the plain of Jezreel. *En-haddah*, which some regard as unknown, also is said to be el-Hadetheh. *Beth-pazzez* remains unknown.

22 This verse presents a form of boundary line. Since the terminal points are *Tabor* and the river *Jordan*, this must be the northern boundary. Tabor, also mentioned in v. 12, is probably a city near Mount Tabor. *Shahazumah* and *Beth-shemesh* both are of uncertain location.[11]

23 The description ends with the usual formula (cf. vv. 16, 31).

K. ASHER'S ALLOTMENT (19:24– 31)

24 *The fifth lot came out for the tribe of the Asherites, according to their families.*

25 *Their territory included Helkath, Hali, Beten, Achshaph,*

26 *Allammelech, Amad, and Mishal. And it reached to Carmel west-ward and to Shihor-libnath.*

27 *Then it turned toward the sunrising to Beth-dagon; it touched on Zebulun and the valley of Iphtah-el northward, Beth-emek, and Neiel. It then went on to Cabul northward,*

28 *and Ebron, Rehob, Hammon, and Kanah, to Sidon the Great.*

29 *The border turned to Ramah and to the fortress Tyre. The border then turned to Hosah and came out at the sea: Meheleb, Achzib,*

30 *Ummah, Aphek, and Rehob.*

Twenty-two cities with their villages.

31 *This is the inheritance of the Asherites according to their families, these cities with their villages.*

---

9. This is the suggestion of Wright and Filson, *op. cit.*; and Grollenberg, *op. cit.*
10. Thus Aharoni, *op. cit.*, pp. 168, 175.
11. Issachar's territory forms roughly a square, with Jezreel forming its southwest corner and Chesulloth its northwest corner. The northern border ran from Tabor to the Jordan, which it reached just south of the Sea of Galilee. In the south the border ran from Jezreel east to the Jordan at some point northeast of Bethshean; cf. J. Bright, *IB* II, p. 645.

Asher was the second son of Leah's maid-servant Bilhah (Gen. 30:13). His future prosperity is spoken of in Gen. 49:20. Asher's territory was principally the plain of Acre, the western slopes of the Galilean hills behind it, and the coast from the tip of Carmel northward to Tyre and Sidon.[1] This was, in fact, all the territory west of Zebulun and Naphtali. (For the cities from which Asher failed to drive out the original inhabitants, cf. Judg. 1:31–32.)

24–25 The description begins in the customary fashion (cf. vv. 1, 10). The exact identity of *Helkath*, located somewhere in the Kishon Valley, is disputed. Candidates for the site are Tell el-Harbaj and Tell el-Qassis. In Egyptian lists the name occurs as *hrqt*. With the present level of information it is impossible to state whether Helkath is a boundary point or simply a settlement inside Asher's territory. *Hali* is unknown. *Beten*, probably modern Abṭûn, is on the Gulf of Acre. For *Achshaph*, cf. 11:1. In the Thutmose III lists it occurs as *îksp*.

26 *Allammelech* is *rtmrk* in the list of Thutmose III. Its location is unknown, as is that of *Amad*. *Mishal* (called Mashal in 1 Chr. 6:59 [Eng. 74]) is *mšîr* in the list of Thutmose III. It must be sought near the Carmel, but its precise location is unknown. The border then *reached to Carmel westward and to Shihor-libnath*. Carmel is a range of hills extending from northwest to southeast, from the Mediterranean to the plain of Dothan. Mount Carmel more narrowly is the main ridge at the northwest end, running some 12 miles inland from the sea.[2] The word rendered *westward* (Heb. *hayyāmmâ*) may also be rendered "toward the sea." There is no unanimity about the identification of Shihor-libnath.[3]

27 The description now turns *toward the sunrising* and traces Asher's eastern border, which touches the area of *Zebulun* and the *valley of Iphtah-el* (v. 14). *Beth-dagon* is the only specific point mentioned on the eastern border, for the next two names are cities inside the territory.[4] Beth-dagon must be sought somewhere between Helkath (v. 25) and the valley of Iphtah-el. *Beth-emek and Neiel* are both of uncertain location,

1. So K. A. Kitchen, "Asher," in *NBD*, p. 95.
2. See K. A. Kitchen, "Carmel," *NBD*, p. 200.
3. It is rendered "the swamp of Libnath" (NEB) and "the streams of the Libnath" (JB). Some hold it to be a small river on Asher's southern boundary, probably modern Nahr ez-Zerqā. M. Noth, *Das Buch Josua*, p. 117, suggests it is the swampy region of the rivers Nahr ed-Difleh and Nahr ez-Zerqā. Y. Aharoni, *The Land of the Bible*, p. 237, finds this "impossible to accept." He suggests that Tell Abū Hawām, at the mouth of the Kishon, is ancient Libnath.
4. It is possible, however, to take Cabul to be one of the boundary points as well.

but well within Asher's territory. *Cabul* is modern Kābûl, northwest of the Ṣahl el-Baṭṭof.

28 The four cities mentioned in this verse represent a group still farther north. *Ebron* appears as Abdon in the list of Levitical cities (21:30; 1 Chr. 6:59 [Eng. 74]). Identification with Khirbet 'Abdeh, a site 10 miles north-northeast of Acco, is strongly suggested. *Rehob*, also mentioned in the list of Canaanite cities which Asher failed to conquer (Judg. 1:31), is located in the plain of Acre. *Hammon* cannot be identified positively. *Kanah* is at present a village by that name located 7 miles southeast of Tyre. The name also appears in a series of reliefs from the reign of Ramses II, describing the capture of certain Palestinian cities.[5]

The rest of Asher's territory, namely that bordering upon Naphtali, is not given in the present list. All one reads is that this territory ran *to Sidon the Great*, that is to say, it went to the Sidonian border somewhere near the river Litani. One must assume that the cities up to Sidon (cf. 11:8) were included in Asher's lot. The reference to Sidon once again shows that the lines drawn here in the lists of allotments are all somewhat theoretical. Its occurrence here should not be attributed to a later redactor.

29 This verse contains two clauses, both indicating a change in direction. *Ramah*, toward which the border *turned*, may be er-Ramiah, a city in Asher's interior, going in a southerly direction. Another Ramah is in Naphtali (v. 36). The *fortress of Tyre* (or "the fortified city of Tyre") appears to be the coastal town opposite Tyre called Ushu in ancient non-biblical sources. It is the present Tell Rashidiyeh by the main watercourse of Tyre.[6]

The border then *turned* again, to *Hosah*, the identity of which remains unknown. One suggestion is that the Ushu mentioned above is Hosah. This would mean that the text should be reconstructed to read: "The border turned to Ramah and to the fortress Tyre (which is) Hosah, and came out at the sea," but much must remain uncertain about this suggestion.[7]

The last few words of the verse rendered *Meheleb, Achzib* (Heb.

5. For the information concerning the cities mentioned in this verse cf. Aharoni, *op. cit.*, pp. 46, 106, 169.
6. This is Aharoni's suggestion, *op. cit.*, p. 238. J. de Groot, *Het Boek Jozua*, p. 141, suggests that the fortress of Tyre (Ṣûr) is probably Râs el-'Ain, south of Tyre; de Groot refers to the Papyrus Anastasi III, dating from Pharaoh Merneptah, which mentions a fortress on the way to Tyre.
7. See J. M. Miller and G. M. Tucker, *The Book of Joshua*, p. 150, who state that "there is some reason to believe that Hosah was an on-shore suburb of the same city" (i.e., Tyre).

mēḥeḇel 'aḵzîḇâ, with locative *he*) have been rendered in various ways. The ASV reads "by the region of Achzib," adding a marginal note, "or, from Hebel to Achzib." In both suggestions the prefix *me*- is taken to be from the preposition *min*, "from," "by." Other suggestions are "Mahalab, Achzib" (RSV, JB, NAB); "Mehalbeh, Achzib" (NEB); "Mehalleb and Achzib" (M. Noth).[8] A growing consensus regards these as two proper names. Meheleb would then be a Phoenician coastal city, Ahlab-Helbah (cf. Judg. 1:31, where this name occurs as two separate names). Today this city is Khirbet el-Maḥâlib, about 4 miles north of Tyre.[9] The second city, *Achzib*,[10] is on the coast, between Acco and Tyre. It is the present ez-Zîb.

31 *Ummah* perhaps may be identical with Acco, otherwise known as Ptolemais (cf. Judg. 1:31).[11] The name *Aphek* occurs frequently in widely scattered areas of Palestine. Here it may stand for Tell Kurdâneh, near the sources of the river Namain on the plain of Acco. Heb. *'ᵃpēq* means "wadi," "streambed." *Rehob*, at the end of the list, is not the place mentioned in v. 28. It has been identified tentatively with Tell el-Gharbi, 7 miles east of Acco.

The tally of this list as given in the text is *twenty-two*. If Tyre and Sidon are included, the total should be twenty-four, but these sites may have been left out.[12]

32 This verse contains the customary summary statement (cf. vv. 16, 23, 39).

L. NAPHTALI'S ALLOTMENT (19:32–39)

32 *For the Naphtalites the sixth lot came out, for the Naphtalites according to their families.*

33 *Their border ran from Heleph, from the oak at Za-anannim and Adami-nekeb and Jabneel to Lakkum, and ended at the Jordan.*

8. The LXX (Codex B) treats this as the name of two cities: "from Leb and Achzib."
9. So Aharoni, *op. cit.*, p. 214.
10. The Hebrew word has another *he*-locative, but the original meaning of direction appears to be lost; see GKC §§ 90f.
11. An appeal to Judg. 1:31 does not necessarily settle this matter.
12. KD, p. 201, arrive at an actual tally of twenty-three. They suggest that no certainty can be obtained, since other cities which are definitely assigned to Asher are wanting in the list.

34 *Then the border turned westward to Aznoth-tabor; from there it came out at Hukkok and reached to Zebulun on the south; to Asher it reached on the west and to Judah at the Jordan on the east.*

35 *The fortified cities were Ziddim, Zer, Hammath, Rakkath, Chinnereth,*

36 *Adamah, Ramah, Hazor,*

37 *Kedesh, Edrei, En-hazor,*

38 *Yiron, Migdal-el, Horem, Beth-anath, and Beth-shemesh. Nineteen cities with their villages.*

39 *This is the inheritance of the Naphtalites according to their families, the cities with their villages.*

Naphtali was the youngest son of Rachel's servant Bilhah (Gen. 30:8). His territory was located between that of Asher and the river Jordan's upper course. Northward its border coincided with that of Canaan itself, and on the south it touched on Zebulun and Issachar. Few of the sites mentioned in the following description can be determined with certainty. The lot of Naphtali consisted of fairly fertile land.

32 The beginning of the account resembles that of the others (see vv. 1, 10, 17).

33 The description begins in the south of Naphtali's territory[1] at *Heleph*, probably Khirbet 'Arbathah at the foot of Mount Tabor. *Adami-nekeb*[2] is the present Khirbet et-Tell, above Khirbet Dâmiyeh; *Jabneel* corresponds to Tell en-Na'am, and *Lakkum* to Khirbet el-Manṣûrah. Thus the border generally followed the course of Wâdī Fajjas. That the border *ended at the Jordan* is by itself a significant point in favor of a southern understanding of the verse, for in the north Naphtali's territory turns away from the river Jordan.[3]

34 *Aznoth-tabor*, a town at the foot of Mount Tabor, was actually a point where the remaining three tribes met (cf. vv. 12, 22). *Hukkok*, presently Yâqûq, lies west of the Sea of Tiberias.[4] It is not clear how Hukkok fits in at this point. The meeting-point between Naphtali and *Zebulun on the south* was farther to the south than Hukkok's assumed location.[5] That Naphtali *reached to Asher on the west* makes geographical sense, but that it touched on, or *reached . . . Judah at the Jordan on the*

1. For a defense of this position as opposed to a northern orientation, see *GTT*, p. 195, n. 185; and Y. Aharoni, *The Land of the Bible*, p. 204. At stake in this problem among other things is the location of the oak of Za-anannim and that of Kedesh, which, according to Judg. 4:11, were in each other's vicinity.
2. This is treated as two names in *GTT*, p. 195.
3. See M. Noth, *Das Buch Josua*, p. 119.
4. The identification with Yâqûq is not accepted universally.
5. *GTT*, pp. 196f., believes that what is being said is that the part of the boundary in the south as described touched, after Hukkok, the territory of Zebulun.

east, has caused great difficulty to interpreters. Many consider it to be due to textual corruption. Judah's territory was much farther south, and Naphtali's territory did not touch it. In an effort to make sense out of the text as it stands some have pointed out that the Hebrew text has a slight disjunction between the word Judah and the following word. Thus the translation has been proposed: "to Asher it reached in the west, and to Judah; the Jordan (was) on the east," but this does not explain the curious reference to Judah as such. Others, disregarding the Hebrew accentuation which they believe obscures the text, think that "Judah" stands in apposition to "Jordan." Thus the translation which results is: "and to Judah of the Jordan on the east." The Judah here referred to, in this view, stands for the sixty towns of Jair, east of Jordan (13:30), with Jair belonging on the paternal side to Judah (1 Chr. 2:21–22).[6]

35 The first of the *fortified cities* in Naphtali's territory is *Ziddim*. Its location is unknown, and as a result scholars prefer to read this name with the following one, thus Ziddim-zer. Others identify *Zer* with Madon, west of Tiberias. *Hammath*, the name of which suggests the proximity of warm springs such as are found in the neighborhood of Tiberias, has been equated with Ḥamman Tabaríyeh, but with no unanimity on the matter. *Rakkath* is identified in rabbinical writings with Tiberias, but Tell Eqlāṭíyeh is the preferred site.[7] *Chinnereth* is Khirbet el-'Oreimeh, northwest of the Sea of Tiberias.

36 *Adamah* may be Ḥajar ed-Damm, 2.5 miles northwest of the point where the Jordan enters the Sea of Galilee. *Ramah* has been identified with er-Râmeh, on the road from Safad to Akkad. For *Hazor*, cf. 11:1.

37 *Kedesh*, also mentioned among the cities of refuge (20:7), was in Naphtali's hill country, in the northeast. *Edrei* occurs as *ìtr'* in the roster of Thutmose III. Its location, however, is unknown. *En-hazor*, according to some scholars, is to be located to the southwest of Kedesh, on the border between Naphtali and Asher. Others hold that it may be Khirbet Hazireh, west of Kedesh.[8]

38 *Yiron* is the present Yārûn, on the modern border between Lebanon and Israel. *Migdal-el*, mentioned here only, is not known. Some

---

6. This is the solution of KD, pp. 203f. In the LXX the words "and Judah" do not occur. Aharoni, *op. cit.*, p. 239, only comments that the passage is "obscure."
7. Since Hammath and Rakkath stand asyndetically, some would read the two as one name. Most newer English versions, however, treat them as two names (NAB, NEB, JB, RSV).
8. J. Gray, *Joshua, Judges and Ruth*, p. 169, holds that the cities in this verse mark the boundary with Dan's territory, later situated in the north.

identify it with Mejdel-Islim, near Kedesh-naphtali. *Horem*, the name of which occurs only here, is unknown. *Beth-anath* has not been identified as yet.[9] *Beth-shemesh*, held by some to be the same town as that mentioned in v. 22,[10] is otherwise of unknown location. The last two cities mentioned were left unconquered by Naphtali as appears from Judg. 1:33.

The tally, absent from the LXX text here and elsewhere, is *nineteen*. The actual count of the cities listed is sixteen. Perhaps some of the missing names can be taken from the border towns mentioned in vv. 33–34. The tally probably concerns only the fortified cities of vv. 35–38, not those mentioned earlier. Apparently not all the cities that qualified were included in the list. One might think of Kartan which, according to 21:32, was one of the cities of Napthali, yet is not mentioned here.

M. DAN'S ALLOTMENT (19:40–48)

40 *The seventh lot came out for the tribe of the Danites, according to their families.*

41 *The territory of their inheritance comprised Zorah, Eshtaol, Ir-shemesh,*

42 *Shaalabbin, Aijalon, Ithlah,*

43 *Elon, Timnah, Ekron,*

44 *Eltekeh, Gibbethon, Baalath,*

45 *Jehud, Bene-berak, Gath-rimmon,*

46 *Me-jarkon, and Rakkon, with the territory over against Joppa.*

47 *The territory of the Danites was too small for them. So the Danites marched up and attacked Leshem, took it, and put it to the sword. Then they took possession of it, settled in it, and called Leshem Dan, after the name of Dan their ancestor.*

48 *This is the inheritance of the tribe of the Danites, according to their families, these cities with their villages.*

Dan was the elder of the two sons borne to Jacob by Rachel's maidservant Bilhah (Gen. 30:1–6). Dan's territory was west of that of Benjamin, between Judah and Ephraim.[1] It takes in the coastal region, from the Brook Sorek to the Yarkon opposite Joppa. No boundaries are given, but these

9. This town may occur also in some Egyptian lists; see Aharoni, *op. cit.*, pp. 99, 153, 166.
10. The name may also occur in the Thutmose roster (no. 89) and in the Execration Texts; *idem*, p. 133.
1. For a discussion of Dan's boundaries in answer to certain theories of A. Alt, cf. Y. Kaufmann, *The Biblical Account of the Conquest of Palestine*, pp. 15–19.

could be inferred from the adjoining territories.[2] Some of Dan's cities were taken from the territory of other tribes (compare v. 41 with 15:33). The Danites were under continual pressure from the Amorites, who forced them into the hill country (Judg. 1:34). Laxness and fear on Dan's part were probably part of the problem. In Judg. 5:17 Dan is said to have had some association with ships, probably through its proximity to Joppa (v. 46).

40 The *seventh* and last *lot came out* for Dan. The introductory formula is similar to that of the other tribes (vv. 1, 10, etc.).

41 Although no formal boundaries are given in Dan's case, most of the cities listed are located on or near the boundaries of the tribe's allotment. *Zorah* and *Eshtaol* were received from Judah (see 15:33). These cities play a role in the later stories of the Danite Samson (Judg. 13:2, 25). *Ir-shemesh* is mentioned as a border town among the list of Judah, under the name of Beth-shemesh (15:10). Today it is Tell er-Rumeileh, situated on the saddle of a hill spur to the west of the later settlement of 'Ain Shems. Ir-shemesh ("sun city") is the same as Har-heres ("sun mountain") in Judg. 1:35. Dan probably never took possession of it. It was given subsequently to the Levites, but as one of the cities belonging to Judah (21:16).

42 *Shaalabbin*, also written Shaalbim (Judg. 1:35), was located in the valley of Aijalon east of Gezer, as was *Aijalon* itself. Selbît has been suggested by some as the present site of Shaalabbin, but others doubt this. (For *Aijalon* see 10:12; cf. 21:24; Judg. 1:35; 1 Sam. 14:31; 1 Chr. 8:13; 2 Chr. 28:18). Its present site is at Yâlô. *Ithlah* has not been identified positively.

43 *Elon*, mentioned only here, is of uncertain location, but Khirbet Wâdī 'Alin has been suggested as the possible site.[3] *Timnah* (cf. 15:10) was on Dan's boundary with Judah, as was *Ekron* (cf. 13:3; 15:11, 46).[4]

44 *Eltekeh* may be Tell esh-Shalaf, although some scholars identify it with Khirbet el-Muqenna', also suggested to be ancient Ekron. *Gibbethon*, which appears as *qpt* in the roster of Thutmose III, may be

2. This could also be done in Benjamin's case. Nevertheless the latter's boundaries are described fully, but not those of Dan.

3. In 1 K. 4:9 the name occurs with the addition of Beth-hanan. See E. G. Kraeling, *The Rand McNally Bible Atlas*, p. 214.

4. For those who, like the majority of scholars, believe the lists of chs. 13–19 to "reflect" some sort of actual possession of the cities mentioned during the period of the monarchy, the inclusion of a city like Ekron poses great difficulty, for there is no evidence of Ekron ever having been conquered. Cf. Y. Aharoni, *The Land of the Bible*, p. 266, who suggests that the "original" text "perhaps" read "Timnath-Ekron."

Tell el-Melât. *Baalath* is considered by some to be the same as Baalah mentioned in 15:11, which in turn is another name for Kiriath-jearim.[5]

45 *Yehud* is not mentioned elsewhere. In the LXX (Codex B) it is called Azōr, for which reason it has been held identical with the city of Azuru, mentioned in the annals of Sennacherib.[6] *Bene-barak*, also found in Sennacherib's annals, is the present Ibn-ibrâq, west of Yehud. *Gath-rimmon* has tentatively been identified with Tell ej-Jerisheh,[7] a site where strong fortifications from the Hyksos period have been found. It was also a Levitical city (21:24).

46 *Me-jarkon*, not mentioned elsewhere, is unknown.[8] It was in the vicinity of Joppa. *Rakkon* is possibly Tell er-Reqqeit. Included in Dan's inheritance was also *the territory over against Joppa*. Joppa itself was not in Israel's hands during the early centuries of its settlement of Palestine. The city is referred to in 2 Chr. 2:15 (Eng. 16); Ezra 3:7; Jon. 1:3.

47 The story of Dan's migration to the north and the subsequent capture of Leshem, which later was to be renamed Dan, is told more fully in Judg. 18. The reason stated for this northward move is that their territory *was too small for them* (lit. "went out from them"). This could mean also that the land passed from the possession and control of Dan, either in the sense that the tribe did not fully conquer it, or that after a brief tenure it was reconquered (cf. Judg. 1:34–36, where it is recorded that it was the house of Joseph, not Dan, that prevailed over the Amorites in this area).[9] For further reasons for Dan's northern conquest, see Judg. 18:1.

The city of *Leshem* (Laish) lies at the headwaters of the Jordan. It is an ancient city, already mentioned in the Palestine list of Thutmose III. The Danites conquered it and renamed it after their ancestor.[10] This event, which took place later in history, is inserted here to complete the survey of the allotment of the various tribes. The story is added without comment.

---

5. *GTT*, p. 201, rejects the suggested connection between this city and that in 15:11.
6. These were annals of a campaign through Palestine in 701 BC (see *ANET*, p. 287).
7. Aharoni, *op. cit.*, p. 136; *GTT*, p. 201. M. Noth, *Das Buch Josua*, p. 121, however, calls this identification "unfounded."
8. For a discussion of this name and the following, see *GTT*, p. 201. Simons assumes that the name Rakkon slipped in through dittography with the preceding Jarkon.
9. This is the opinion of H. Freedman, *Joshua*, *ad loc*. The RSV translates "when the territory of the Danites was lost to them"; NAB "was too small for them."
10. The location of this northern Dan corresponds to Tell el-Qâḍī, on the Nahr Lītânī ("river of Dan"). *Qâḍī* is the Arabic word for "judge," corresponding to Hebrew Dan, which also means "judge"; see Kraeling, *op. cit.*, p. 167.

Perhaps the writer meant to indicate that the northern location of Dan was theirs as lawfully as had been their previous one assigned to them by lot. But the fact that the migration took place during the period of the Judges, a period not known for lawful behavior, puts that view in jeopardy. More plausibly, the writer wanted to record this later development in order to round off his record.

48 The description of Dan's lot is concluded in the customary fashion (vv. 16, 23, 31, 39).

N. JOSHUA'S INHERITANCE: THE ALLOTMENT CONCLUDED (19:49–51)

49 *Now when the Israelites had finished dividing the land as inheritance, by its respective territories, they gave an inheritance to Joshua the son of Nun in their midst.*

50 *According to the command of the Lord they gave him the city which he asked, Timnath-serah in the hill country of Ephraim. He rebuilt the city and settled in it.*

51 *These are the inheritances which Eleazar the priest, Joshua the son of Nun, and the heads of the fathers' houses of the tribes of the Israelites distributed as inheritance by lot at Shiloh before the Lord at the door of the tent of meeting. So they completed the dividing of the land.*

49 The report concerning the tribal allotments is completed with an account of Joshua's inheritance, given to their leader by the Israelites. Structurally, within the total compass of the book, the placement of this story at this point is of great importance. Together with the account of Caleb's inheritance, placed at the beginning of the allotment chapters (14:6–15), this account frames the entire proceedings in their present literary form. Joshua and Caleb had risked their lives initially by bringing out a good report concerning the land which they had explored with ten others (Num. 14:6). Their courage and faith continue to be the focus of "the book of the land," called Joshua.[1]

50 Some prefer to take the words *according to the command of the Lord* with the preceding verse. This avoids the difficulty of finding a specific command indicating the exact place of Joshua's inheritance, but a combination with the preceding verse does not remove the difficulty

1. For this insight cf. K. Gutbrod, *Das Buch vom Lande Gottes*, *ad loc.*; cf. also C. Vonk, *Inleiding op de Profeten: Jozua*, p. 264. For a summary of other structural elements in Joshua, see Introduction, pp. 14ff.

altogether. All one can say is that the Scripture did not record the command to which reference is made. This is also the case with the story of Caleb's inheritance (14:9). In general, the promise made in Num. 14:30 may be understood to have as its concrete implication the allotment of a specific portion of the promised land, assigned upon the special request of both Caleb and Joshua.

Timnath-serah, also called Timnath-heres (Judg. 2:9) is the present Khirbet Tibneh, about 16 miles southwest of Shechem. Some authorities place it at Kafr Ḥaris in the same vicinity. (For Joshua's burial here, cf. 24:30.) Joshua *rebuilt* (lit. "built") the city and took up residence there.

51 At the conclusion of the entire section concerning the allotment is a rather full statement indicating the participants and the place where the allotment had occurred (cf. 14:1; 17:4; 18:6, 10). This final summary has a certain solemnity about it, quite in keeping with the crucial role which the possession of the promised land played within the covenant dealings between the Lord and Israel. For further comments, see the introduction to chs. 13–19.

O. GOD'S JUSTICE IN GOD'S COUNTRY: SETTING ASIDE CITIES OF ASYLUM (20:1–9)

1 *The Lord spoke to Joshua and said:*
2 *"Tell the Israelites: 'Designate the cities of asylum about which I spoke to you through Moses,*
3 *cities to which a person who has killed someone unintentionally, without premeditation, may flee, so that they may be to you for a place of asylum from the avenger of blood.*
4 *When a man has fled to one of these cities he shall halt at the entrance of the city gate, and he shall present his case in the hearing of the elders of that city. Then they shall take him with them into the city and assign a place to him; and he will live with them.*
5 *When the avenger of blood pursues the killer, they shall not hand him over to him, because he struck down that other person without intent, without having hated him beforehand.*
6 *So he shall live in that city until he has stood before the assembly for the decision, until the death of the high priest who will function in those days. Then the killer may go back to his own city and his own house, to the city from which he had fled.' "*
7 *So they set apart Kedesh in Galilee in the hill country of Naphtali, Shechem in the hill country of Ephraim, and Kiriath-arba (that is, Hebron) in the hill country of Judah.*

297

8 *And on the other side of the Jordan, east of Jericho, they designated Bezer in the desert on the tableland, from the tribe of Reuben, Ramoth in Gilead from the tribe of Gad, and Golan in Bashan, from the tribe of Manasseh.*

9 *These were the cities designated for all the Israelites and for the stranger who sojourns among them, so that a person who has killed someone unintentionally may flee there and not die by the hand of the avenger of blood till he has stood before the assembly.*

The chapter dealing with the setting aside of the cities of asylum[1] follows naturally upon the account of the distribution of the promised land to the tribes. This land was the Lord's land (cf. Lev. 25:23). How to conduct oneself in the land and how to obtain justice in it are questions following logically upon the record of the tribal inheritances. Unjust shedding of blood would be a blot upon the land the Lord had given. To prevent this from happening the writer presents a final record of the disposition of this matter. Earlier references are found in Num. 35:6, 9–34; Deut. 4:41–43; 19:1–13. (Cf. also Exod. 21:12–21, which speaks of the Lord's promise to "appoint a place" where the manslayer may flee.)

1–2 *The Lord spoke[2] to Joshua*: The assignment of the cities of asylum is traced back to a special injunction given by the Lord to Joshua. While in other instances of the divine communication to Joshua the verb *'āmar*, "to say," is used (1:1; 3:7; 4:15; 6:2; 7:10; 8:1, 18; 11:6; 13:1), the verb used here is *dibbēr*, "to speak." The Talmud attributes special significance to its use, stressing the unique emphasis which it implies.[3] Joshua is to remind the Israelites of the Lord's earlier word to them through Moses with respect to the cities of asylum. In the earlier parts of the book Joshua's strict adherence to the Lord's commands as given to Moses had been stressed (see 11:15, 20, 23). This trend of reporting is continued here. The main reference is Deut. 19:1–13, which speaks of the setting aside of cities yet to be done on the west side of the Jordan.

3 The cities of asylum were meant for those who had *killed un-*

---

1. Heb. *'ārê hammiqlāṭ* is composed of *'îr*, "city," and *miqlāṭ*, a noun from the verbal root *qlt*, "to draw in," "to draw together." Its exact meaning cannot be ascertained on purely linguistic grounds, but its usage suggests that of asylum or refuge, with possibly the notion of reception being more prominent than that of refuge; see N. H. Ridderbos, "Cities of Refuge," in *NBD*, pp. 234–36. Other works dealing with the subject include B. van Oeveren, *De Vrijsteden in het OT* (diss., Amsterdam: 1968); M. Greenberg, "The Biblical Conception of Asylum," *JBL* 78 (1959), pp. 125–132; R. de Vaux, *Ancient Israel*, pp. 160–61.
2. About the possibility of divine speech being communicated to humans, cf. 1:1 and commentary.
3. See H. Freedman, *Joshua, ad loc*.

intentionally[4] (*biš*ᵉ*gāgâ*, lit. "through error") and *without premeditation* (lit. "without knowing").[5] The latter term is used in Deut. 4:42; 19:4. It was for this unintentional killing that the law was meant. The underlying assumption is that of the *avenger of blood*,[6] the person who in Israelite society was held responsible for carrying out a primitive form of justice by pursuing the manslayer and putting him to death. Excesses which might result from this system of retribution were to be curbed by the appointment of cities to which the unintentional killer could flee.

The idea of vengeance was by no means foremost in the institution here described. The avenger (Heb. *gō'ēl*) is a person who acquits himself of a certain obligation resting upon him (cf. Lev. 25:25; Num. 5:8; Ruth 3:13; Jer. 32:7). The avenger of blood was called upon to restore the balance in the family relations which had been upset by the slaying of one of its members. Retribution, not vengeance, is the leading thought (cf. Exod. 21:23–25; Lev. 24:17). This avenger was not expected to make a distinction between intentional and unintentional slaying. The cities of asylum were meant to introduce that distinction and to make it a workable feature in the system of retribution (see also Exod. 21:13).

4 The rules for what one had to do when approaching a city of asylum are specified only here, and are not found in Num. 35; Deut. 19.[7] The manslayer was to *halt at the entrance of the city gate* and *present his case* to *the elders*[8] *of that city*. The latter then were to receive him into the

4. Other translations: RSV "without intent"; JB "accidentally"; NEB "inadvertently." For sins committed this way, cf. Lev. 4:2, 22, 27; 5:15; 22:14. In themselves these involuntary sins, which still require atonement, constitute an important category, and shed light on the biblical sin-concept in more than one way; see G. Quell, *TDNT* I, pp. 279f.

5. This phrase is supposed to be "older" than the one which precedes it. For a critical evaluation of this supposition cf. van Oeveren, *op. cit.*, p. 142.

6. This is generally thought to have been the nearest male relative of the one slain. But cf. P. C. Craigie, *Deuteronomy*, p. 266, where a different theory is evaluated critically. This theory considers the avenger to have been an official, a representative of the elders of the city in which the death took place. Craigie himself favors a possibility "somewhere between these two alternatives."

7. On the precise relation of ch. 20 to Num. 35; Deut. 19 and an evaluation of the various theories concerning this question, see van Oeveren, *op. cit.*, pp. 119, 126ff.

8. Those who incline toward the Documentary Hypothesis with respect to the Pentateuch (and Joshua) consider the feature of the elders' role to be older than that of the assembly, mentioned in vv. 6, 9. For a summary of this approach, cf. de Vaux, *Ancient Israel*, pp. 162f.

city and *assign* him *a place* where he could live, at which place he was to remain.[9]

Though the details of this legislation concerning the cities of asylum are not fully perspicuous, it may be assumed that first came a provisional hearing before the elders, who were the local authorities. (About the role of such persons in the case of manslaughter (murder) by an unknown person, see also Deut. 21:3–9.) The elders were also the ones to hand over the manslayer to the avenger of blood in the case of premeditated killing (cf. Deut. 19:12). Verses 6, 9; Num. 35:12, 24 seem to suggest a more formal trial before the assembly (Heb. *'ēḏâ*). Whether such a trial was always held in the city of the homicide or in the city of asylum is not clear.[10]

5 If the avenger of blood demands the surrender of the manslayer, the latter shall not be handed over. This, however, is upon the clear assumption of unintentional manslaughter. How this fact is to be established apart from the hearing by the elders is not specified. In any case, the assembly's role is not mentioned until v. 6. Verse 5 first describes in some detail the principle of safety and refuge for which the cities of asylum were instituted.

6 The manslayer may remain in the city until he has stood trial before the *assembly*.[11] Here this takes place in the city of asylum, although in Num. 35:24–25 it appears to occur in the city where the manslayer lives. The relative guilt or innocence of the person in question is thus established. Two time limits are specified in this verse which establish the length of the interval that the manslayer may stay in the city. One is the meeting of the assembly. The other, placed in juxtaposition with it, is *the death of the high priest* in power at the time. This arrangement raises problems of understanding. In Num. 35:12, 25, 28, the two are mentioned separately, but here they occur side by side. Some have tried to solve the problem by considering the two in an either-or position.[12] Others simply

---

9. Since the cities of asylum were also cities in which the Levites were permitted to dwell (see ch. 21), the manslayer living in one of these would have found not only refuge but also a means of subsistence, something which a mere place of refuge would not have provided. This is an indication of an advanced social consciousness typical of the whole OT; cf. J. A. Soggin, *Joshua*, p. 198.

10. In Deut. 19:12 the elders of the city of the manslayer are to fetch the latter and bring him back so that the avenger of blood may exercise his rights.

11. The RSV renders this word as "congregation"; JB, NEB, NAB as "community." No precise distinction between "congregation" and "assembly" has been attempted in this commentary. For the range of meaning of the term (also used in 9:15, 18–19, etc.), see van Oeveren, *op. cit.*, pp. 85ff.

12. DNV; C. J. Goslinga, *Het Boek Jozua*, p. 148, who refers to Num. 35:24 by way of justification. Cf. H. W. Hertzberg, *ATD* IX, p. 114, where a *"beziehungsweise"* is inserted between the two clauses.

juxtapose the two clauses (e.g., RSV, JB). Still others look upon the two limits as representing two successive stages of the entire process. The NEB translates: "The homicide may stay in that city until he stands trial before the community. On the death of the ruling high priest, he may return. . . ."[13]

Another question concerns the precise significance of the high priest's death. Perhaps a certain atoning effect was produced by the death of the chief sacerdotal functionary.[14] Although it was actually the sacrifices, and not the high priest, that provided atonement for sin, yet the latter's central role in the sacrificial cultus may have given his death some sort of atoning significance. The fact that the high priest had been anointed with the holy oil (Num. 35:25) is also important.[15] An alternate explanation (besides those mentioned in note 14) links the life and hence the death of the high priest, who was of the tribe of Levi, with the representative function that this tribe had among Israel (cf. Exod. 32:28–29). The high priest in turn, so this theory maintains, was as it were the substitute for his tribe. His death therefore loosens the bond between the manslayer and the city of asylum, which is also a Levitical city.[16]

7 What Joshua had ordered Israel to do was carried out. Six cities were *set apart*.[17] The verb used indicates a setting aside for special use.[18] The principle of selection appears to have been general accessibility.

Most of the cities set apart belonged to Israel only during the early period of its national existence in Palestine and Transjordan. This has been

---

13. Equally clear is NAB: "once he has stood judgment before the community, he shall live on in that city till the death of the high priest who is in office at the time."

14. Others think of a kind of amnesty proclaimed at the time of his death. If the death was thought to conclude an epoch, it may have served as a statute of limitations. Still another view points to the significance of the altar as the chief and original place of refuge (cf. Exod. 21:12–14). The priest's death would have effected a certain freedom enabling the manslayer to return; see van Oeveren, *op. cit.*, pp. 162–68 for an extensive discussion.

15. Both KD, p. 209, and J. H. Kroeze, *Het Boek Jozua*, p. 224, call attention to this fact.

16. For this explanation, endorsed by van Oeveren, see W. H. Gispen, *Het Boek Numeri* II. Commentaar op het OT (Kampen: 1964), p. 304.

17. Heb. *qāḍaš*, a play on the name of the first city mentioned, Kedesh. This is no *terminus technicus*, as appears from the use of other verbs in v. 8; Deut. 4:41–43.

18. Other translations include "dedicated," "sanctified," "declared inviolate." There is no reason to assume that the use of the root *qāḍaš* stems from a supposed earlier sacredness of the cities chosen. The Deuteronomic background to the law on asylum would prevent rather than favor such associations; cf. Deut. 12:1–14.

used as an argument in favor of placing this arrangement at an early point in history.[19]

Kedesh is *in Galilee* (Heb. *gālîl*, "district," from which the name Galilee has been derived; see also Isa. 8:23 [Eng. 9:1][20]). On this city see 12:22; 19:37. In 734 BC Kedesh was taken by Tiglath-pileser III. *Shechem* was in the central region, *in the hill country of Ephraim*. On this city, see 8:30 and commentary. Shechem is also mentioned in 21:21; 24:1. Today it is Balâṭah, near Nablus. *Kiriath-arba* was located *in the hill country of Judah*, hence in southern Palestine (cf. 14:15; 15:13; 21:11).

8 As had been the case with the allotment of the tribes (ch. 13:8–33), so also in this instance the earlier choice of cities by Moses in Transjordan is recalled, although not explicitly mentioned. The writer's concern for Transjordan and his consequent concern for the unity of all the tribes, a "motif" of the book (see 1:12 and commentary), may have something to do with this. Two of the cities in Transjordan are mentioned only here and in the list of Levitical cities. They are *Bezer*,[21] *from the tribe of Reuben*, possibly modern Umm el-'Amad, and *Golan*, the capital of *Bashan*, in Manasseh's territory.[22] The third city mentioned in Transjordan is *Ramoth in Gilead from the tribe of Gad*. This is usually identified with Tell Rāmîth, 22.4 miles south of Ashtaroth (see also 1 K. 4:13; 22:3ff.; 2 K. 8:28; 9:1).

9 The final verse summarizes what has been stated earlier in the chapter. A new element is that the law on asylum applied not only to the native born but also to the stranger, a feature commonly found in the laws of the Pentateuch. The cities are now referred to as *'ārê hammû'āḏâ*, lit. "cities of appointment," "of designation."[23]

---

19. Some scholars for a variety of reasons consider the material on the cities of asylum to be postexilic. Others suggest a preexilic, monarchic date; see J. A. Soggin, *Joshua*, pp. 198f., where a monarchic date (David or Josiah) is held possible.

20. The phrase "Galilee of the nations" may refer to Canaanites in the plain of Esdraelon, the plain of Acre, in Phoenicia, and in the Mount Hermon area; see E. G. Kraeling, *The Rand McNally Bible Atlas*, p. 29.

21. This place is mentioned in the Moabite Stele. It was conquered by Moab's king Mesha about 850 BC. Other identifications are (a) Bosor (1 Macc. 5:36); and (b) Bozrah (Jer. 48:24).

22. The name survives in Saḥem el-Jōlân, although the Golan district is closer to the Jordan and to the Sea of Galilee.

23. As noted above, there may be a possible connection between cities of asylum and the presence of sanctuaries in such cities. In addition, the fact that a Levitical city was also a city of asylum may have been due to the following considerations. (a) The priestly nature of such cities may have served as a restraining influence upon the avenger of blood. (b) Living in a Levitical city allowed the offender to

P. THE LEVITICAL CITIES CLAIMED AND ASSIGNED (21:1–42)

1. THE LEVITES CLAIM THEIR RIGHTFUL SHARE (21:1–3)

1 *The heads of the Levite families approached Eleazar the priest, Joshua the son of Nun, and the heads of the families of the other tribes of the Israelites,*

2 *and said to them at Shiloh in the land of Canaan: "The Lord issued a command through Moses to give us cities to live in with their pasture grounds for our cattle."*

3 *Then the Israelites, according to the Lord's command, gave to the Levites out of their own inheritance these cities and their pasture lands.*

The story of the assignment of cities to the priests and Levites is not only a natural complement to the account of the allotments for the other tribes, but it is also demanded by the frequent references to the Levites earlier in the book (13:14, 33; 14:3; 18:7). Moreover, as was the case with Caleb in 14:6, an appeal could be made to what Moses had stated with respect to this matter (Num. 35:1–8).

The tribe of Levi was divided into three branches, the Gershonites, Kohathites, and Merarites (Num. 1–4). Each of these received its own cities, the location of which was determined by lot, and hence by God. Since some of the cities of asylum also were to be designated Levitical cities, chs. 20–21 follow logically upon each other.[1]

1 In their approach to *Eleazar*, *Joshua*, and *the heads of the families of the other tribes*, the Levites show the same initiative of faith as

---

become a virtual part of the community in which he lived. The presence of a sanctuary at such a point is, to cite M. Haran, "Studies in the Account of the Levitical Cities. I. Preliminary Considerations," *JBL* 80 (1961), p. 53, nothing more than "a purely accidental combination of two characteristics in one place." See also van Oeveren, *op. cit.*, p. 182.

1. The existence of Levitical cities, some of which were important centers of population (e.g., Hebron, Shechem, Libnah, Gibeon, Gezer, etc.), has been assailed as unrealistic and utopian. It should be remembered, however, that the cities so assigned remained in the possession of the tribe. The Levites received them "to dwell in" along with the use of the adjoining pasture land; see v. 2. Cf. A. Noordtzij, *Het Boek Numeri* (Kampen: 1941), p. 346. B. Mazar, "The Cities of the Priests and Levites," *VTS* 7 (1959), pp. 193-205, maintains that the list of Levitical cities "must be understood against the background of the Israelite kingdom" (p. 195). But this ignores the setting in which the book of Joshua places them. Mazar holds that the list fits the period of Solomon. However, such reasoning is based, not on the allotment pattern, but on the assumption of actual possession.

did Judah (and Caleb) in ch. 14. Some of the other tribes needed prompting (see 18:2–3). Those to whom the request for cities is made are the same persons as the ones responsible for the general allotment (cf. 14:1; 19:51; Num. 34:16–29).

2–3 The request was made *at Shiloh*,[2] hence subsequent to the time when Joshua had established the tent of meeting there (18:1), and possibly also after the distribution of the land to the seven remaining tribes. A precise indication of time is lacking, however. The request recalls the Lord's words to *Moses* that the Levites receive *cities to live in* (see introduction) and the *pasture grounds*[3] related to these cities. The request appears to have been granted readily. The Levites receive cities out of the inheritance of the other tribes.[4]

2. THE LEVITICAL CITIES[1] DETERMINED BY LOT (21:4–8)

4 *The lot came out for the families of the Kohathites; those Levites who were descendants of Aaron the priest received by lot thirteen cities out of the tribe of Judah, out of the tribe of the Simeonites, and out of the tribe of Benjamin.*

5 *The remaining Kohathites received by lot ten cities out of the families of the tribe of Ephraim, out of the tribe of Dan, and out of the half tribe of Manasseh.*

6 *The Gershonites received by lot thirteen cities out of the families of the tribe of Issachar, out of the tribe of Asher, out of the tribe of Naphtali, and out of the half tribe of Manasseh in Bashan.*

7 *The Merarites received, according to their families, twelve cities, out of the tribe of Reuben, out of the tribe of Gad, and out of the*

---

2. The additional words *in the land of Canaan* may carry over from the original instructions in Num. 34:29; 35:10 concerning these matters; so KD, p. 210.

3. Heb. *migrāš*. BDB translate "common," "common-land"; GB "Weideplatz." It may also have a wider reference to open land or space about a temple (Ezek. 45:2). For this reason A. Gelin, *Josué*, p. 114, translates "banlieues."

4. K. Gutbrod, *Das Buch vom Lande Gottes*, may be right in suggesting that the "dispersion" of the Levites among the tribes reflects something of the sojourner status which the patriarchs had while in Canaan; cf. also Heb. 11:9; 1 Pet. 1:1.

1. For a discussion of J. Wellhausen's view of this chapter, see J. A. Soggin, *Joshua*, pp. 202f.; and Y. Kaufmann, *The Biblical Account of the Conquest of Palestine*, pp. 40–46. As Soggin points out, both Wellhausen and his critic Kaufmann use the concept of a utopian dream to explain the existence of a list of Levitical cities. The former places it in postexilic times, the latter during the time of the Conquest. Although Kaufmann's use of the word "utopian" is subject to some criticism, his fundamental notion that the list of Levitical cities was set up without regard to the possession or non-possession of the cities assigned is in agreement with the emphasis of this chapter, which speaks of an assignment based on the *lot*, and not on the actual conquest of the cities mentioned.

tribe of Zebulun.

8 *So the Israelites gave by lot these cities and their pasture lands to the Levites, as the Lord had commanded through Moses.*

In the enumeration the following features are of special significance. (a) The writer makes a special point of the fact that the lot determines the assignment of these cities (note the frequency of the words "by lot"). By this stylistic device he means to alert the reader to the divine appointment underlying the assignment.[2] (b) The Kohathites receive their lot first. They are the family from which the priestly line descended via Aaron. From the Kohathites the priests receive their cities in the territory of Judah, Simeon, and Benjamin—in other words, in areas closest to the city of Jerusalem where, at a much later time, they would be expected to function.[3] (c) The usual grouping of Reuben and Gad with the half tribe of Manasseh, who together received territory in Transjordan, is not followed, but Reuben and Gad are grouped with Zebulun (v. 7). (d) The terminology used to describe the falling of the lot differs slightly. In one instance (v. 4) the lot "comes out"; in the others the Levites "receive" the cities by lot; and yet another contains no reference to the lot (v. 7). Thus the impression is created of a natural narrative style, which would argue against a late utopian schematization.[4]

4-5 For *the Kohathites* and the other branches of the tribe of Levi, see above.[5] The priestly descendants are mentioned first because the

2. Those who consider this list to be a late postexilic fabrication or who, while rejecting the late dating, seek to base their theories on alleged occupation of the cities assigned are in fundamental contradiction of this basic feature of the list. Neither case allows any chance for a real interpretation of the text. Yet this is what historical-grammatical exegesis is expected to provide.

3. Some would see this as a reflection of the times when Jerusalem actually functioned (or had functioned) as the country's central cult site. Others, e.g., Calvin, see this as an extraordinary sign of God's providence. The latter view does justice to the true meaning of the text in its present form. For a third view regarding the assignment for the priestly line, cf. H. W. Hertzberg, *ATD* IX, p. 119, who points out that the cities in Judah-Simeon are all south of Hebron, in other words not in the immediate vicinity of Jerusalem. Hertzberg believes this to be a mixture of earlier and later traditions. The earlier ones represent ancient "memories" when there were Levites in those southern towns.

4. Other less significant variants are suggested. (a) In two instances (Ephraim [v. 5] and Issachar [v. 6]) it is specified that the cities were taken *out of the families* of these tribes. (b) In the case of the Merarites (v. 7) the words "by lot" are omitted.

5. A widespread scholarly opinion is that the Levites in the Bible do not originally represent a tribe among the other tribes but were a social group of functionaries. See for a discussion of the question D. A. Hubbard, "Priests and Levites," in *NBD*, pp. 1028–1034; cf. R. de Vaux, *Ancient Israel*, pp. 369–371.

lot *came out* first for them. The remaining Kohathites, that is to say, those not of the priestly line, receive their lot in *Ephraim*, *Dan*, and the *half tribe of Manasseh*. As is clear from the cities listed later, this is the part of the tribe of Manasseh that lived west of the Jordan.

6–7 The descendants of Gershon received by lot *thirteen cities*, located in *Issachar, Asher,* and *Naphtali*, all in the districts of Galilee, as well as in the territory of *the half tribe of Manasseh* that lived *in Bashan*. The Merarites receive twelve cities from the tribes of *Reuben, Gad,* and *Zebulun*. (About this order of enumeration see above.)

8 This verse reiterates what had been stated in v. 3. It also may be taken immediately with vv. 9–40.

The fact that *the pasture lands* which went with the cities were given in precise measurements in Num. 35:4–5 which seem to ignore the terrain surrounding a given Levitical city has been cited as another indication of the alleged lateness and lack of realism pertaining to the arrangement.[6] This assumes also that the lands around the cities destined for Levitical use were contiguous. Such a situation, however, is not stated in the legislation of the book of Numbers.[7]

3. THE LEVITICAL CITIES LISTED BY NAME (21:9–40)

a. The Cities of the Aaronites (21:9–19)

9 *They gave out of the tribe of the Judahites and out of the tribe of the Simeonites these cities which are mentioned by name*

10 *(these were for the Aaronites, out of the families of the Kohathites who belonged to the Levites, for the lot was first for them):*

11 *They gave them Kiriath-arba (this Arba is the father of Anak), which is Hebron in the hill country of Judah, with its pasture land round about it.*

12 *But the fields of the city and its open lands they had given to Caleb the son of Jephunneh as his possession.*

13 *To the sons of the priest Aaron they gave Hebron, the city of asylum for the manslayer, with its pasture lands, Libnah with its pasture lands,*

14 *Jattir with its pasture lands, Eshtemoah with its pasture lands,*

15 *Holon with its pasture lands, Debir with its pasture lands,*

---

6. This opinion can be traced to J. Wellhausen and is echoed in contemporary writing; see Hertzberg, *op. cit.*, p. 118, who states that this feature indicates that the law was formulated at the "green table," i.e., the boardroom table.
7. See B. van Oeveren, *De Vrijsteden in het OT*, p. 181.

16 *Ain with its pasture lands, Juttah with its pasture lands, Beth-shemesh with its pasture lands: nine cities out of these two tribes;*

17 *then out of the tribe of Benjamin, Gibeon with its pasture lands, Geba with its pasture lands,*

18 *Anathoth with its pasture lands, and Almon with its pasture lands: four cities.*

19 *The cities of the Aaronites, the priests, were in all thirteen cities with their pasture lands.*

The following should be noted in the city list now presented (vv. 9–40). (a) The list contains names of cities which only later came into Israelite hands, such as Gezer (cf. 1 K. 9:16), Gibbethon (cf. 1 K. 15:27), Taanach (Judg. 1:27; 5:19), Nahalol, and Rehob (Judg. 1:30–32). (b) The non-schematic (and hence noncontrived?) nature of the lists appears from the fact that, while in most cases four cities are taken from each tribe, Naphtali yields only three, and Judah plus Simeon together produce nine.[1] (c) The stipulation laid down in Num. 35:8 (the number of cities to be allotted is to be proportionate to the size of a given tribe) is not closely adhered to. Naphtali was at this time larger than both Ephraim and Gad (see the census of Num. 26), yet it yields only three towns. On the other hand, though Issachar and Dan are larger than Ephraim, they all yield the same number of cities.

9–10 After the cities had been designated by lot they were given to the Levites.[2] The Aaronites received cities in the Judah-Simeon area.[3] As noted earlier, the Aaronites lived generally in the southern region of this district, with Hebron the northernmost of the Judahite towns allotted. Some of the Benjaminite cities were closer to Jerusalem, for example Gibeon and Anathoth. The writer makes a special point that *the lot was first* for the Aaronites (see above). Another feature to be noted is the reference to the "sons of Levi" (here translated "Levites" [v. 10] according to standard procedure), as distinct from the customary designation *lᵉwiyyim* (properly "Levites") used elsewhere in this chapter. The expres-

---

1. It would seem that this approach, stressing the nonschematic nature of the list, is truer to fact than the approach of F.-M. Abel, *Le Livre de Josué*, p. 91, who on the basis of the same data emphasizes its schematic nature.

2. Cf. KD, pp. 210f.: "The towns in which the different families of Levi were to dwell were determined by lot; but in all probability the towns which each tribe was to give up to them were selected first of all, so that the lot merely decided to which branch of the Levites each particular town was to belong."

3. The list of Levitical cities also occurs in 1 Chr. 6:54–81, in a version which shows significant variations from the Joshua list.

sion "sons of Levi" obviously means to stress the genealogical, tribal
connection rather than that of function or status.[4] (On this question see
above.)

11–12 The first city mentioned is *Kiriath-arba* (see 14:15; 15:13).[5]
The other name for it was *Hebron*. While the pasture lands of this city, as
well as all other cities mentioned, go to the Levites, in this case it is
recalled that the *fields* and *open lands* (others translate "villages"[6]) of
Hebron had gone *to Caleb*. This, then, is supplementary information to
that found in 14:13–15; 15:13.

13–18 Verse 13 paraphrases v. 11. This repetition became necessary because of the parenthetical remark about Hebron in the preceding
verse. An additional point of information concerns the status of this city
as a *city of asylum*. (On the connection between Levitical cities and cities
of asylum, see the previous chapter and commentary.) Most of the cities
mentioned have occurred in other lists and have been discussed there; at
the present stage little more than a reference to the earlier discussion
appears called for. *Libnah* (10:29; 12:15; 15:42) was so near the Philistine
plain that it could be regarded as a frontier town. It was never quite a part
of Judah (cf. also 2 K. 8:22; 19:8). *Jattir*, *Eshtemoa* (15:50), *Holon* (15:51;
written Hilen in 1 Chr. 6:58), and *Debir* (15:49) all occur in earlier lists.
The latter city was given to Othniel (15:17). On *Ain*, cf. 15:32; 19:7; on
Juttah, cf. 15:55. *Beth-shemesh* is one of Judah's boundary points (cf.
15:10). Significant omissions from the list are Bethlehem, which had a
connection with the Levites during the time of the Judges (Judg. 17:7) and

---

4. H. W. Hertzberg, *ATD* IX, p. 118, believes that the reason for the change may
lie in the fact that the same context refers to the "sons of Aaron," but it is his
opinion that the predominant use of *halleʷwiyyîm* supports the thesis that the Levites
were a social rather than a tribal entity. This shows how tenacious a certain theory
can be. Is there not much more reason to let the more specific "sons of Levi"
determine the general "Levites" than vice versa? On Levi as a "secular" tribe see
also C. H. J. de Geus, *The Tribes of Israel*, pp. 97–108.
5. *Arba* is called *the father of Anak* (Heb. *hāʾᵃnôq*, otherwise *hāʾᵃnāq*, variants
of the plural *ʾᵃnāk̲îm*, "Anakites").
6. Heb. *ḥāṣēr*; GB define this word "eig. das umhegte Lager . . . Dann aber auch
jede Ortschaft ohne Mauer, im Ggs. zu befestigten Ortenoder grösseren Städten";
KB "permanent settlement, court without walls." Although "villages" is abstractly speaking a good translation, the diminutive size of the actual cities of
Palestine makes the presence of villages (plural) around such a small city somewhat
unreal in terms of modern notions. Hence we have here rendered the word with
"open lands," although that too has its drawbacks. It does stress, however, the fact
that the settlements intended had no walls around them. In other parts of the
commentary the word "villages" has been used.

Jerusalem, the omission of which causes surprise only if the theory of the list's late origin is accepted.[7] Its omission may well plead in favor of exactly the opposite position, that of an early date.

Thus far the cities from Judah have been listed. Out of Benjamin came *Gibeon* (cf. 9:3; 18:25), the inhabitants of which had been given certain duties to perform at the sanctuary (9:21), *Geba* (18:24), *Anathoth*, not mentioned in earlier lists and later the home town of Jeremiah, and *Almon*, called Alemeth in 1 Chr. 6:45 (Eng. 60), located northeast of Anathoth.[8]

19 Thus the total number of cities for the Aaronites came to *thirteen* (cf. vv. 4, 16, 18).

b. The Cities of the Remaining Kohathites (21:20–26)

20 *As to the families of the Kohathites, the Levites who still remained of the Kohathites, the cities of their lot came out of the tribe of Ephraim.*

21 *To them were given Shechem with its pasture lands in the hill country of Ephraim, the city of asylum for the manslayer, Gezer with its pasture lands,*

22 *Kibzaim with its pasture lands, Beth-horon with its pasture lands: four cities;*

23 *and out of the tribe of Dan, Elteke with its pasture lands, Gibbethon with its pasture lands,*

24 *Aijalon with its pasture lands, Gath-rimmon with its pasture lands: four cities;*

25 *and out of the half tribe of Manasseh, Taanach with its pasture lands and Gath-rimmon with its pasture lands: two cities.*

26 *The cities of the families of the rest of the Kohathites were ten in all with their pasture lands.*

20 The remaining Kohathites who were not in the priestly line received ten cities, four each from Ephraim and Dan, and two from that part of Manasseh settled west of the Jordan. The list of Levitical cities does not exhibit dull uniformity. Its mode of expression varies, as is clear from a comparison of v. 20 with vv. 9, 13.

21 Among the cities taken out of *Ephraim*, *Shechem* is first because it, like Hebron, was a city of asylum (see v. 13; cf. vv. 27, 32,

---

7. See on this point of Jerusalem's omission Y. Kaufmann, *The Biblical Account of the Conquest of Palestine*, p. 42, who asks pointedly how it would be possible for the later "programmers" to omit a city of such significance.

8. Both Anathoth and Alemeth occur as personal names in 1 Chr. 7:8; 8:36.

36).[1] *Gezer* was one of those cities in the list not conquered until a much later time (10:33; cf. 16:10; Judg. 1:29; 1 K. 9:16). The list of Levitical cities therefore contains an element of unreality, not because of its utopian lateness but because the Israelites, in distributing the land and allotting these cities in the land, acted in the belief and expectation that conquest would be made if the tribes only put their faith in what the Lord had promised (13:6b). Without taking note of the faith perspective, or of the lack of it (cf. 13:13 and elsewhere), one cannot do justice to the biblical text or interpret it according to its true grammatico-historical meaning.[2]

22–25 Other cities from Ephraim were *Kibzaim*, of unknown location, the name of which does not occur in the parallel list of 1 Chr. 6 which has Jokneam at this point. But Jokneam occurs later in the present list (v. 34; cf. also 19:11). For *Beth-horon*, see 10:10; 16:3, 5.

From Dan's allotment were taken *Elteke* and *Gibbethon* (cf. 19:44). They were located in Dan's original allotment, which was never quite possessed (see 19:47 and commentary). David conquered this area, but later on it fell into Philistine hands again (cf. 1 K. 15:27; 16:15). These two cities do not occur in the list of 1 Chr. 6. *Aijalon* and *Gath-rimmon* were also in Dan (19:42, 45). They are considered Ephraimite cities in 1 Chr. 6, but Dan probably no longer was holding land by the time the Chronicles list was made.

From Manasseh, west of the Jordan, came *Taanach* and *Gath-rimmon*. The former was not subdued during the Conquest period (cf. 17:12; Judg. 1:27). As to Gath-rimmon, some hold this to be a copyist's error repeating the name from v. 24, whereas the real name was Bileam

1. Since most of the cities listed here belong to the northern and not the central part of Ephraim's territory, some scholars think the list represents a moment in Israel's history when the central area was occupied by the Samaritans. See, e.g., H. W. Hertzberg, *ATD* IX, p. 119. Cf. also A. Alt, "Festungen und Levitenorte im Lande Juda," in *KS* II (1953), pp. 310–15. It was Alt who pointed out that the Levitical cities are either in frontier regions or in areas that had formerly been Canaanite, while there are no Levitical cities in central Judah or Mount Ephraim. See also Y. Aharoni, *The Land of the Bible*, p. 270. However, Shechem is definitely on Mount Ephraim. The view of Alt "strangely ignores the inclusion of Shechem" (J. Gray, *Joshua, Judges and Ruth*, p. 27) or it considers its presence in the list an insertion caused by its status as city of asylum (Aharoni, *idem*). But is this not begging the question?
2. We therefore find it impossible to endorse J. Gray's suggestion (*idem*) to the effect that cities to the west of Gezer such as Gibbethon, Elteke, and Gath-rimmon (vv. 23–24) can only be accounted for in the list on the supposition that it was composed after Gezer had passed into Solomon's possession. This bases an understanding of the list on assumed facts rather than on what the list strongly suggests: the exercise of faith.

(cf. 1 Chr. 6:55 [Eng. 70]). Others retain it by appealing to the Amarna correspondence, where the name is said to occur.[3]

26 The total of cities for the remaining Kohathites is *ten*.

c. The Cities of the Gershonites (21:27–33)

27 *To the Gershonites, of the families of the Levites, were given, out of the half tribe of Manasseh, Golan in Bashan with its pasture lands, the city of asylum for the manslayer, and Be-eshterah with its pasture lands: two cities;*

28 *and out of the tribe of Issachar, Kishion with its pasture lands, Daberath with its pasture lands,*

29 *Jarmuth with its pasture lands, En-gannim with its pasture lands: four cities;*

30 *and out of the tribe of Asher, Mishal with its pasture lands, Abdon with its pasture lands,*

31 *Hilkath with its pasture lands, and Rehob with its pasture lands: four cities;*

32 *and out of the tribe of Naphtali, Kedesh in Galilee with its pasture lands, the city of asylum for the manslayer, Hammoth-dor with its pasture lands, and Kartan with its pasture lands: three cities.*

33 *Altogether the Gershonites, according to their families, received thirteen cities with their pasture lands.*

27–33 Verse 27 first identifies the Gershonites as being *of the families of the Levites*. Different designations are used in vv. 20, 34, so the writer apparently is duly concerned to make the proper distinctions. Official documents of this sort may be expected to be specific to the point of redundancy. Another matter to be noted is that the order of the tribes followed in v. 6, where Gershon's cities are first mentioned, is altered.

The cities from Transjordanian *Manasseh* are *Golan* (20:8), another city of asylum, and *Be-eshterah*, called Ashtaroth in 1 Chr. 6:56 (Eng. 71). The name may be a contraction of Beth-eshterah, "house of Astarte." Most probably it is Tell 'Ashtarah. Both these cities suggest a regular frontier situation. The cities in *Issachar* are *Kishion* (19:20), called Kedesh in 1 Chr. 6:57 (Eng. 72), *Daberath* (19:12), and *Jarmuth*, which may be the Remeth of 19:21 (called Ramoth in 1 Chr. 6). It is probably near Jabbul, north of Beisan. *En-gannim* also is mentioned in 19:21. Issachar gave *four cities*.

---

3. So H. Freedman, *Joshua, ad loc.* Cf. also *GTT*, p. 205, which substitutes Ibleam for Bileam but also allows for the Masoretic Text to contain the authentic reading.

The cities of *Asher* are *Mishal* (19:26), *Abdon* (cf. Ebron in 19:28), *Helkath* (19:25), and *Rehob* (19:28). Rehob was not subdued by the Israelites (Judg. 1:32).

In Naphtali the following cities were given to the Levites: *Kedesh in Galilee*, another city of asylum (20:7; cf. 12:22; 19:37); *Hammoth-dor*, called Hammath in 19:35 and Hammon in 1 Chr. 6:61 (Eng. 76); and *Kartan*, which occurs as Kiriathaim in 1 Chr. 6. It is perhaps the present Khirbet el-Qureiyeh, north of the present boundary of Israel.

The total of the cities given to the Gershonites is *thirteen*.

d. The Cities of the Merarites (21:34–40)

34 *As to the families of the Merarites, the remaining Levites, they obtained, out of the tribe of Zebulun, Jokneam with its pasture lands, Kartah with its pasture lands,*

35 *Dimnah with its pasture lands, Nahalal with its pasture lands: four cities;*

36 *and out of the tribe of Reuben, Bezer with its pasture lands, Jahaz with its pasture lands,*

37 *Kedemoth with its pasture lands, and Mepha-ath with its pasture lands: four cities;*

38 *and out of the tribe of Gad, Ramoth in Gilead with its pasture lands, the city of asylum for the manslayer, Mahanaim with its pasture lands;*

39 *Heshbon with its pasture lands, and Jazer with its pasture lands: four cities in all.*

40 *All these cities the Merarites, those remaining of the families of the Levites, received according to their families. Their lot was twelve cities.*

34–40 The *Merarites*, rather elaborately called *the remaining Levites*, received their cities out of Zebulun, Reuben, and Gad. (See the introduction to this chapter on this unexpected combination of one West Jordanian and two Transjordanian tribes.) *Jokneam*, a name which fails to appear in the list of 1 Chr. 6, is mentioned in 12:22 (cf. 19:11). *Kartah*, here listed as a town in Zebulun, does not occur in Zebulun's list in 19:11–16, although Kattath occurs in 19:15. *Dimnah*, which occurs here only, is held by some to be the same as Rimmono in 1 Chr. 6:62 (Eng. 77). Perhaps it is the same as Rimmon of 19:13, a town in Zebulun. For *Nahalal*, cf. 19:15. This is the extent of Zebulun's cities given to the Merarites.

Out of Reuben's territory the following cities are taken: *Bezer* (20:8), one of the cities of asylum, a fact which is not recorded this time (but cf. vv. 13, 21, 27, 32, 38); *Jahaz*, also called Jahzah (13:18); *Kedemoth*, and *Mephaath* (13:18).[1]

From Gad the following are taken: *Ramoth in Gilead*, a city of asylum (cf. 20:8); *Mahanaim* (cf. 13:26); *Heshbon* (cf. 9:10; 13:17); *Jazer* (cf. 13:25 and Num. 21:32). The total number of Merari's cities was *twelve*.

e. Concluding Statement (21:41-42)

41 *The total of the cities of the Levites in the midst of the possession of the Israelites was forty-eight cities with their pasture lands.*

42 *These cities consisted each of a city with its pasture land round about it. Thus it was with all those cities.*

41-42 Altogether the number of Levitical cities totaled forty-eight, as Num. 35:6 had specified. A special point is made of the fact that the cities assigned *consisted each of a city with its pasture land round about it*. The fact that this already much-repeated information is mentioned once more at the end indicates the functional purpose that the cities had. The Levites were not to possess them (see above), but to be users of them. They did not receive an "inheritance" in the proper sense of the word because the Lord was their inheritance. The cities were meant for them to dwell in. The Levitical cities were a constant reminder to Israel that the land they had received was different from that of other lands. This helped every believing Israelite to say as he reflected on his blessings: "the Lord is my portion" (Ps. 16:5).

Q. GRATEFUL RECOGNITION OF THE LORD'S FAITHFULNESS (21:43–45)

43 *So the Lord gave to Israel the whole country which he had promised by oath to give to their forefathers; they took possession of it and settled in it.*

44 *And the Lord gave them rest round about, exactly as he had promised by oath to their forefathers. Not a single one of all their enemies was able to stand up to them. All their enemies the Lord gave into their hand.*

1. The list of Reuben's cities is left out of the *masora magna* and does not occur in many manuscripts; see also BH. However, it does occur in the ancient versions. Moreover, the four Reubenite cities are required to attain the number of forty-eight (v. 41). Inclusion of them appears warranted.

45 *Not a word failed of all the good words which the Lord had spoken to the house of Israel; everything came out.*

This passage constitutes one of the key sections of the entire book, for one may learn from it the revelational purpose that the Holy Spirit had in inspiring the human author to compose this book. This purpose is to let the full light of revelation fall upon the faithfulness of the covenant God who keeps his word once given to the forefathers. As such, this passage summarizes the first part of the book and points out its basic message. Verse 43 refers primarily to the distribution of the land described in chs. 13–21; v. 44 reflects on the actual stories of the Conquest as told in chs. 1–12; and v. 45 places the entire book under the perspective of God's faithfulness.

The book of Joshua views the conquest of Canaan as both complete and incomplete. In 23:4–5 these two lines run side by side, an indication that the author means them to be equally valid, although the emphasis on the completeness of the Conquest is predominant. Summaries stressing the completeness of the Conquest are found also in 10:40–42; 11:23; 12:7–24; cf. also 23:1, 4. From time to time a hint is given that more needs to be done (13:2–6; 14:12; 17:12–18; 18:2; 23:5, 7, 12). The present passage completes the cycle begun in 1:2–6. The promise that God would give the whole land to Israel is now fulfilled. But another emphasis occurs in ch. 1, the insistence upon covenant obedience and adherence to Moses' law (vv. 5–6, 9). The covenant, the laws of which must be obeyed, is one of grace. This is a truth which is written large over Israel's antecedent covenant history and should not be forgotten at this point.

43 This verse first of all recalls God's promise that he would *give* the land to Israel, one of the leading motifs of the book (1:2–3, 6, 11, 13, 15; 2:9, 24; 5:6; 6:2, 16; 8:1, 7; 10:8, etc.). This giving of the land was in keeping with the *oath* sworn by God to the forefathers (1:6; cf. Gen. 24:7; 26:3; 50:24). This oath is also recalled in other books of the Pentateuch (Num. 11:12; 14:16, 23; Deut. 1:8, 35; 6:10, etc.).

The view of a completed conquest and settlement in the land which God had given must also be seen against the background of the patriarchal stories which first mention the oath made to the forefathers. These patriarchs could not call any part of the land that God promised them their own except a grave or two in which to bury their beloved dead. Compared to that, how rich the fulfilment of the promise now appeared!

44 This verse reintroduces the concept of *rest*, mentioned in the Pentateuch (Exod. 33:14; Deut. 12:9–10) and in Joshua (1:13, 15; 22:4; 23:1). It is a notion with ever expanding horizons, as is clear from the way the thought reappears in the stories of David (e.g., 2 Sam. 7) and Solomon (1 K. 5:4). It assumes NT and eschatological meanings in Heb. 4. The rest obtained for Israel had as its necessary corollary the defeat of Israel's *enemies*.[1] Israel is not only meant to be a blessing for the nations (Gen. 12:3). God also states that he will curse those who curse Abraham (*idem*), and that he will be an enemy to Israel's enemies (Exod. 23:22). This is why Joshua was so dismayed when Israel was beaten by the men of Ai (cf. 7:8, 12). But what Joshua feared would happen next did not come about, for God did put down the enemies of his people. Mighty coalitions in the south (ch. 10) and the north (ch. 11) were defeated with his help. None *was able to stand up to* the Israelites, as had been promised (1:5).

45 No wonder, then, that the final word of this passage is one of thankful recognition of the faithfulness of God. Instead of failing to come to pass (Heb. "fall to the ground"), *the good words* of the Lord, spoken to *the house of Israel* (viewing the people as a unity, another leading motif), have all come out[2] (cf. 23:14). This note of thanksgiving reverberates in the NT as well (cf. Rev. 11:16–18).

R. JOSHUA'S FAREWELL ADDRESS TO THE TRANSJORDANIAN TRIBES (22:1–8)

1 *Then Joshua called the Reubenites, the Gadites, and the half tribe of Manasseh,*

2 *and said to them: "You have observed everything Moses the Lord's servant commanded you, and you have listened to me in everything I have commanded you.*

3 *These many days, down to this day, you have not forsaken your brothers, but you have performed the task laid on you by the Lord your God.*

4 *But now the Lord your God has given rest to your brothers as he promised them. Therefore, turn back and go to your tents, to the land of your possession, which Moses the Lord's servant gave you beyond the Jordan.*

5 *Only take good care to do the commandment and the law which Moses the Lord's servant laid on you, to love the Lord your God,*

1. In 23:1 these two are placed in immediate conjunction: God gives rest *from* the enemies.
2. The OT speaks concretely about the word of the Lord, which word can either "fall to the ground" (cf. Rom. 9:6 for a similar use) or "come out" (Heb. *bô*', lit. "come"; cf. Jer. 17:15).

> *to walk in all his ways, to keep his commandments, to hold firmly to him, and to serve him with your whole heart and soul."*
>
> 6 *So Joshua blessed them and let them go. And they went to their tents.*
>
> 7 *(To the one half of Manasseh Moses had given a share in Bashan. But to the other half Joshua gave a share with their brothers west of the Jordan.) When Joshua let them go to their tents he blessed them,*
>
> 8 *and said to them: "Return to your tents with much wealth and with very many cattle, with silver, gold, bronze, and iron, and with a very large supply of clothing. Divide the spoil of your enemies with your brothers."*

Materially, there is a close connection between the present passage and that immediately preceding.[1] The occasion for dismissing the Transjordanian tribes, the subject matter of the present passage, is the rest which God has granted Israel (v. 4). The previous pericope also spoke of this rest (21:44). Both passages hark back to the beginning of the book, where the rest concept is mentioned (1:15) and the keeping of the law given by the Lord to Moses is enjoined (1:7–8).

At the same time, the story of the dismissal of the Transjordanian tribes forms the natural preamble to what follows in the rest of the chapter concerning the building of an altar in the Jordan region.

The evident reason for including Joshua's words of farewell to the 2½ tribes is the fact that ch. 1 began with the story of Joshua's solemn charge to the same tribes to participate with their fellow Israelites in the conquest of Canaan (1:12–18). Thus the story has come full cycle. At both points in the narrative the writer pursues his theme of the unity of Israel (cf. vv. 2–3).

1–3 *The Reubenites, Gadites, and the half tribe of Manasseh* have occupied the writer's attention at several points in the book (besides ch. 1, cf. 12:1–6; 13:8–32; 14:3). Here they are noticed again. As is clear from the rest of the chapter, they are to be considered an integral part of the covenant nation, even though a distinction is made between Israelites and others (cf. v. 13). Joshua here commends them for observing faithfully the commands of the Lord with respect to participation in the Conquest. In this respect they have been obedient to Moses and Joshua alike,[2] as had been promised (cf. 1:17). The juxtaposition of Moses and Joshua, giving

---

1. H. W. Hertzberg, *ATD* IX, p. 120, links the two closely together, as does B. Holwerda, *Jozua*, p. 40.
2. For the relationship between Joshua and Moses, cf. G. J. Wenham, *JBL* 90 (1971), pp. 145f.

equal authority to both, also is typical of other parts of the book (cf. 1:5; 3:7). Looking back upon the entire period of the Conquest, Joshua speaks of *many days* (cf. 11:18) during which they have *performed the task laid on* them *by the Lord* (lit. "have kept the charge of the commandment of the Lord"). These are generous words of commendation. The writer, who has shown so much concern for the tribes on the east side of the river, must have been delighted to write them. They could only bolster his feelings for the unity of the people.

4–5 Since the *rest* of which 1:15 had spoken now also had been achieved for those on the west side of the Jordan, the 2½ tribes may now go back[3] to the *land of their possessions* (cf. Lev. 14:34; 25:24), elsewhere called their inheritance (13:23, 28). Nevertheless, past obedience to the commands of Moses and of Joshua must be followed by a continued keeping of *the commandment and the law which Moses . . . laid on* them. In other words, the enjoyment of the rest in Transjordan will be assured only if there is covenant faithfulness on the part of the people. Although these words were first spoken to one part of the people of Israel, their significance in this chapter is wider. Chs. 23–24 will return to that theme.

The words urging obedience to the law are couched in the language of Deuteronomy (cf. Deut. 4:4, 29; 6:5; 10:12; 11:13, etc.). The "first and great commandment" is that people love God (cf. Deut. 6:5; Matt. 22:37).[4] This is to express itself in the way in which the people live. A wealth of biblico-theological material can be found in the expressions used to augment the basic requirement of love. The figure of walking in *the ways* of the Lord is widely used in Deuteronomy and elsewhere (Deut. 5:33; Ps. 27:11). No mere externalities are expected, for keeping the *commandments* must go hand in hand with holding *firmly* to the Lord and with a service to him which involves the *whole heart and soul*.[5] This earnest admonition following upon the generous words of praise may be understood if it is kept in mind that the tribes addressed here were to live primarily in a somewhat isolated location. The possibility of apostasy,

3. The expression "go to your tents" is nothing more than a standard mode of speech, without implications for the kind of dwelling intended; cf. Deut. 16:7; Judg. 7:8; 1 K. 12:16.
4. The entire book of Deuteronomy may be regarded a commentary on this central command of love. See P. C. Craigie, *Deuteronomy*, pp. 169f., who also points to parallels in extrabiblical treaty language and in the father-son relationship in the ancient Near East.
5. The full range of these significant biblical key words may be learned from consulting lexicons and OT theologies.

always and everywhere present, was especially great under these circumstances.[6]

6 Assuming the function of a father in a patriarchal family, or that of a king in later times, *Joshua blessed them and let them go.* (On the biblical idea of blessing, see 14:13 and commentary; cf. vv. 7–8).

7–8 The writer deems it necessary to inform the reader of the unusual arrangement which had been made for the tribe of *Manasseh,* one half of which was given a place *in Bashan* by no less than *Moses* himself, and the other half a *share*[7] *with their brothers* west of the river. The reference to Manasseh[8] at this point is probably due to the purpose of the later part of the chapter, in which the unity of the tribes east and west of the Jordan is emphasized. Nevertheless, the information, already well known to the reader, interrupts the flow of the account of the dismissal and makes it necessary to resume the thread of the narrative with a rather laborious *gam kî* (lit. "moreover when") in v. 7b.[9]

The present structure of the text amounts to an anticipatory statement about the tribes going back to their tents (v. 6b), followed by a further elaboration of the circumstances under which they went, namely Joshua's words of blessing recorded in v. 8. This narrative structure is not unusual and has been encountered already in the early chapters.

Joshua's words of blessing are put in the form of imperatives. (For this format cf. Gen. 1:28.) They are to return *with much wealth,*[10] *cattle,*

---

6. Simply to say, as does H. Holzinger, *Das Buch Josua*, that this kind of "anxious admonition" does not quite fit after the words of praise that precede it (p. 91) and hence to conclude a "deuteronomistic" insertion does not do justice to the true state of affairs. Biblical religion is not anxious, but it is realistic.

7. The Hebrew has no direct object. The word "share" is supplied both times, as it seems implied in the verb "to give."

8. Manasseh's place in the allotment of the Transjordanian territories is different from that of Reuben and Gad. In Num. 32 Reuben and Gad are mentioned first; then in v. 33 that of the half tribe of Manasseh is added. In the present chapter Manasseh's name is sometimes omitted (vv. 25, 32–34). To think that the "redactor" inserted the name at some spots but failed to do so at other points is casting an unnecessary aspersion on his astuteness and assumes a process of inscripturation about which the last word has not been said.

9. The LXX presents a smoother reading of vv. 7b–8. Holzinger, *op. cit.*, p. 119, is probably right in saying that this is another example of a "kritische Korrektur" on the part of the LXX, and that the more difficult reading of the MT is to be preferred. For a similar judgment on the LXX of Joshua, see J. Bright's discussion of 20:6b, where the LXX simply avoids the difficulty by omitting the verse; *IB* II, p. 650.

10. The Hebrew uses a word (*kesem*) which is only encountered in Ecclesiastes and Chronicles. Some argue from this to the lateness of the account. However,

precious metals, and *clothing.* These bounties are the result of the completed Conquest of which 21:43–45 had spoken. Their enumeration serves to remind the reader of what God has wrought.[11] In keeping with Num. 31:27, they now are to *divide the spoil* with their *brothers.*[12]

S. THE PEOPLE'S UNITY PRESERVED (22:9–34)

1. UNAUTHORIZED ALTAR DEEMED THREAT TO UNITY (22:9–12)

9 *So the Reubenites, Gadites, and the half tribe of Manasseh returned and departed from the Israelites at Shiloh in the land of Canaan, to go to the land of Gilead, to the land of their possession, which they had seized according to the command which the Lord had given through Moses.*

10 *Having come to the circles of stones of the Jordan which are in the land of Canaan, the Reubenites, Gadites, and the half tribe of Manasseh built there an altar by the Jordan, an altar of conspicuous appearance.*

11 *And the Israelites heard the report: "See, the Reubenites, Gadites, and the half tribe of Manasseh have built an altar in front of the land of Canaan, at the circles of stones of the Jordan, toward the other side of the Israelites."*

12 *When the Israelites heard this, the whole assembly of the Israelites gathered together at Shiloh to march against them in war.*

The obvious purpose of the story of the altar near the Jordan is to warn Israel against the danger of losing sight of its unity, a unity which can be disrupted when unauthorized cult places are erected. The law of Deut. 12 did not insist on the limitation to one central sanctuary, although this is

---

conclusions based on the relative earliness or lateness of Hebrew words must be handled with great caution. The range of literature is too limited to make binding conclusions.

11. See also what Hertzberg, *op. cit.,* p. 122, says about the "Seitenblick auf die Leser und Hörer späterer Zeit" for which this passage is meant also.

12. The expression "divide the spoil with someone" also can be understood in the sense of an achieving of victories with someone; see J. H. Kroeze, *Het Boek Jozua,* p. 237; and cf. Isa. 53:12. However, within the present context, which stresses a common sharing of lot, it would seem that the dividing of booty obtained in the conquest west of the Jordan is intended here. The words have also been understood as applying to the tribes west of the Jordan with whom the Transjordanian tribes were to experience a true brotherhood shown in the dividing of the spoils. This view appears rather strained, however.

the way that the law has been widely understood. The chief concern of Deut. 12:5 was to set the place where the Lord was to be worshipped in sharp antithesis to the places where Canaanites practiced their fertility rites. A plurality of sanctuaries does not seem to have been frowned upon in the OT prior to Josiah's reforms. Neither was such a plurality ruled out by the law of Deut. 12.[1] It was the arbitrary choice of cult places without prior divine authorization (the "causing of his name to dwell" there) that was prohibited.[2]

9 This verse links up closely with what precedes. It reports the return of the 2½ tribes to *the land of their possession* (v. 4). In doing so they *departed from the Israelites*, an expression which in this context quite obviously must mean the *other* Israelites. Nevertheless, both at this point and others the possible bifurcation of the nation into two more or less isolated groups appears to have influenced the narrative. The purpose of the story is to remind the reader of the danger which threatened once and may threaten again. It is the obvious intent of the narrator to prevent this danger from becoming a reality. Hence the "West Jordanian" terminology employed should not be pressed. The tribes are said to have departed from *Shiloh in the land of Canaan* (21:2), an expression which may have been used here to suggest that this departure to parts on the other side of the Jordan did have possibilities for future trouble.

On the other hand, the writer seems concerned to stress once again (cf. 13:8–32; 14:3) that the tribes east of the Jordan are no less entitled to their inheritance than are those on the west side of the river. Their territory is the *land of their possession*, which they have because of *the command which the Lord had given* to them *through Moses*[3] (cf. v. 4). This is another reason not to press the language, which seems to consider the western parts to be Canaan. The leading concern is to stress the need for religious and national unity, to be expressed in the choice of sanctuaries duly authorized by divine appointment lest apostasy soon set in.

The land to which the tribes return is called *the land of Gilead*, here used in a comprehensive sense of all the land to the east of the Jordan (cf. Num. 32:29; Deut. 34:1; Judg. 5:17).

10 *Having come to the circles of stones*: the translation "circles

---

1. See on this matter P. C. Craigie, *Deuteronomy*, p. 217. The present writer agrees with the position of M. H. Segal, *The Pentateuch: Its Composition and Authorship and Other Biblical Studies* (Jerusalem: 1967), mentioned by Craigie, p. 217, n. 11.
2. This is the position of B. Holwerda, *Jozua*, p. 43.
3. The words "which they had seized" translate an unusual Hebrew form, called Nuphal in KB; see also GKC § 68 i.

of stones" is uncertain (Heb. $g^e l \hat{\imath} l \hat{o} t$). This name occurs as a geographical name in 18:17 (cf. 13:2) and is so rendered by some of the versions, e.g., NEB and Zürcher Bibel. Others, on the basis of the LXX and the Syriac version, take this to be another name for Gilgal.[4] The place is further defined, but not sufficiently, by the phrase *of the Jordan*, and the altar is said to be *by* ("at") *the Jordan* (Heb. *'al hayyardēn*).[5]

Neither can one be perfectly sure whether the altar was built on the west side or on the east side of the river. Since the $g^e l \hat{\imath} l \hat{o} t$ are said to be *in the land of Canaan*, many believe that the position must have been on the west side. However, some of the expressions of v. 11 could be interpreted as speaking of an altar across the river from the Israelites who heard about it on the west side. This would argue for an eastern location.[6]

What is known for certain is that the altar was *of conspicuous appearance*.[7]

11 The report of this altar built without due authorization reaches *the Israelites*, meaning the other Israelites. In view of the ambiguities in the text, the translation of the report is as literal as possible. Even so, one might differ about some of the details. Neither is it of great exegetical moment to establish the exact location of the altar. It may well be that the ambiguities stem in part from the fact that rumors reached Israel which

---

4. F.-M. Abel, *Le Livre de Josué*, states that this identification has "assez de vraisemblance," but in his translation he prefers "sur le bord du Jourdain." Was Gilgal actually on Jordan's banks? Others have thought of the $g^e l \hat{\imath} l \hat{o} t$ as Jordan's terraces; e.g., B. J. Alfrink, *Josué*; J. H. Kroeze, *Het Boek Jozua*, p. 237. The RSV translates "region." Still others render "districts."

5. J. Gray, *Joshua, Judges and Ruth*, p. 183, rejects the rendering of this term as "Gilgal," since it was not on Jordan's bank. But does the Hebrew actually say that much? Heb. *'al* need mean no more than "by" or "near."

6. J. Bright, *IB* II, states: "The altar was east of the Jordan, facing the land," but he feels that "the sense of the verses is against this (cf. vss. 10, 11, 19)." See also H. Freedman, *Joshua*, ad loc., who with Josephus believes the altar to have been east. Was the altar's function to express unity with the western part? If so, a western location seems plausible. But others think it was meant for giving purity to a land which otherwise might be held to be impure (cf. v. 19). At least this is what the tribes west of the river allege. But how could this have been maintained if the altar was on the west side?

7. Lit. "large to look upon." The opinion is fairly widespread that the story of this large altar was combined with the story of the large monument erected by Jacob and Laban (Gen. 31:44–48); e.g., H. W. Hertzberg, *ATD* IX, pp. 125f. It then is pointed out that the witness character of the altar would agree with the witness of the monument in Genesis, for it was called "heap of witness" (Heb. *gal'ēd*, a play on words with Gilead?). For such traditio-historical speculations, however intriguing, the story of the book of Joshua does not leave sufficient room for serious consideration.

321

were themselves somewhat indefinite.[8] If this is the case, then one need not analyze too precisely the words of the present verse.[9]

12 Upon receiving the report the *assembly* ("congregation"; Heb. *'ēḏâ*; see 9:15, 18; 20:6, 9) is called together. The terms used to describe this calling together of the assembly are precisely those used for this process in the books of Exodus, Leviticus, and Numbers. The Israelites consider what has happened to be a potential breach of the purity of religious worship and hence a threat of apostasy. The background for their reaction is found in Lev. 17:8–9; Deut. 13:12–15. For this reason, they are prepared to go to war against their brothers.

2. THE ALLEGED OFFENSE INVESTIGATED (22:13–20)

13 *The Israelites sent to the Reubenites, the Gadites, and the half tribe of Manasseh, to the land of Gilead, Phinehas the son of Eleazar the priest,*

14 *and with him ten princes, one prince from each of the families of the Israelite tribes. Each of them was the head of his family among the clans of Israel.*

15 *And they came to the Reubenites, the Gadites, and the half tribe of Manasseh, in the land of Gilead, and said to them:*

16 *"Thus says the whole congregation of the Lord: 'What trespass is this which you have committed against the God of Israel, in that you today are turning away from following the Lord by building yourselves an altar, and thus today are rebelling against the Lord?*

17 *Is the iniquity of Peor not enough for us, from which to this day we have not cleansed ourselves and through which a plague came on the Lord's congregation,*

18 *that you should this day turn from following the Lord? When you rebel against the Lord today, tomorrow he will be angry with the whole congregation of Israel.*

19 *If the land of your possession is unclean then pass over to the land of the Lord's possession where the Lord's tabernacle stands, and settle among us. But do not rebel against the Lord nor rebel against us in building yourselves an altar besides the altar of the Lord our God.*

8. This is pointed out by Kroeze, *op. cit.*, p. 237. Perhaps Keil and Delitzsch are right when suggesting that the word Canaan is used here in a restricted sense, namely of the valley of the Jordan. If so, an eastern location still could be maintained.
9. To demonstrate the ambiguities of translation, attention is called to two contrasting renderings of the last part of the verse: RSV "on the side that belongs to the people of Israel"; NEB "opposite the Israelite side" (Heb. *'el-'ēḇer bᵉnê yisrā'ēl*).

20 *When Achan the son of Zerah committed a trespass concerning the accursed thing, did not wrath descend upon the whole congregation of Israel? Neither did he himself alone perish for his iniquity.' "*

In addition to what was said about the motivation for inserting this narrative into the book of Joshua (see the introduction to this chapter), another reason can be noted now for locating this account at this place. The purpose lies in the use of Heb. *ma'al* ("breach of faith, trespass"), in both the Achan story (ch. 7) and the present chapter (vv. 16, 20). After the story of the first city to be conquered in the promised land had been told, the Joshua narrative focused on this corporate trespass which, though initially committed by one man, was in effect a sin held against all Israel (see 7:1). Now, after all the cities in the promised land have been taken and those who took part in this conquest have returned to their possessions, the cry of another breach of trust occurs. Thus on both sides of the conquest narratives one sees this concept looming up, first as an actual reality, then as a potential danger. This is meant to inculcate the lesson that the promised land can be truly possessed only if the people of God adhere to his commandments (see also Introduction, pp. 14ff.).

13–15   Before carrying out their intent of making war with their brothers, the Israelites decide upon an on-the-spot investigation. The delegation they send is headed by *Phinehas the son of Eleazar the priest*. His priestly functions make him a natural choice for this mission. His zeal for the service of the Lord had been shown earlier in the episode of Baal Peor (Num. 25:7), an incident which will be recalled in the message that the delegation addresses to the suspected offenders (v. 17).[1]

The remainder of the delegation consists of *ten princes* (9:15), who were men prominent in tribal affairs. The number indicates that they were meant to represent the ten tribes west of the Jordan.[2] The delegation reaches *the land of Gilead* (cf. v. 9).

16   The message which is delivered on the part of *the whole congregation of the Lord* is solemn and searching. Its serious nature shows both to Israel and also to later readers the gravity of a suspected departure

---

1. Apart from certain entrenched theories concerning a Priestly document dating from postexilic times, there appears to be no reason to think of the figure of Phinehas as representing priestly influences upon this account.

2. The terminology used to describe tribal functions is not uniform in the OT; cf. R. de Vaux, *Ancient Israel*, p. 8. Those functionaries called "princes" ("chiefs," "leaders") at this point may be called "heads" (*rāšîm*) elsewhere (Num. 1:16; 10:4). Moreover, the expression "families of the Israelite tribes" usually designates smaller subdivisions of a clan (Num. 17:18, 21 [Eng. 3, 6]), but here it appears to be co-terminous with the tribe itself (cf. also Num. 17:17 [Eng. 17:2]).

from God's law. The message opens with the customary messenger formula, *thus says* . . ., a mode of address particularly prominent in prophetic writings where the speaker is the Lord. At this point the speaker is the congregation of the Lord, but they have met at Shiloh where God is visibly present in tabernacle and ark (cf. v. 19).

The perspective under which the building of the altar is viewed is that of a breach of faith (Heb. *ma'al*), a term used to describe the offense that Achan committed, also found in the Pentateuch (cf. Lev. 5:15, 21 [Eng. 6:2]; Num. 5:6, 12) and later in the prophets (cf. Ezek. 14:13; 15:8) as well as in Ezra, Nehemiah, and 1–2 Chronicles. Its basic meaning is that of a breach of trust, or faithlessness. The use of this word bespeaks the fear that, as was the case with Achan's offense, so also now the whole congregation will be held guilty on the basis of the principle of corporate solidarity (v. 18).

The offense committed was, so the delegation charges, directed against *the God of Israel*, and consisted in *turning away from following the Lord*. To follow the Lord means to adhere to his will and precepts. Not to do this is tantamount to an act of rebellion against him. The verbal background for these charges is found in Lev. 17:8–9; Deut. 12:4, 11–14, 26.

17 *Is the iniquity of Peor not enough for us:*[3] this recalls Num. 25, which speaks of idolatry coupled with immorality. This altar, erected without authorization and in a seeming disregard for the Lord's service, will lead, so the delegation thinks, to similar things. Also implied is the sentiment that the root evil which caused "Peor" to happen has not been eradicated, and that its seeds are still present among the people. Of that iniquity of the past they have not *cleansed* themselves. The consequences now will be as severe as they were then, when a *plague* (lit. "blow") was inflicted on *the Lord's congregation*. (For the word plague cf. Exod. 12:13; Num. 8:19; 17:11–12 [Eng. 16:47–48].) Both in this verse and the next the corporate element in human sin and punishment is stressed duly. This element has not ceased completely even in modern society; it is implicit in the human situation.

18 Here is a repetition of thoughts expressed previously for purposes of making the message more urgent. A new element in this context is the reference to the Lord's anger, a reality which Israel had experienced again and again during the desert journey (cf. Deut. 1:34; 9:19). This

3. Heb. *ham^e'aṭ-lānû* means "is it not more than enough?" It is construed with a following accusative; cf. GKC § 117 aa.

anger, unlike that of the gods of heathendom, the so-called *ira deorum*, was not capricious or whimsical, but ethically motivated.

19-20   Did the tribes east of the Jordan build the altar because they deemed their land of possession to be *unclean*? The notion of uncleanness involves unfitness for worship. It is not the same as pollution, but it is a ritual category established by God to make the people conscious of the close tie between daily conduct and the worship of him. Violation of the laws of the clean and unclean barred a person from the sanctuary. The offense committed might not have been an intrinsically sinful act, but it was declared to be sin by the divine Lawgiver to inculcate the important lesson of the connection between religion and ethics.[4] If the tribes that had built the altar had been so impressed by their country's uncleanness, they could have passed over to the other side *where the Lord's tabernacle stands*. The language used to describe the land west of the Jordan (*the land of the Lord's possession*) should be understood within the present context of conflict and suspected breach of faith. The book of Joshua does not disparage the qualities of the land in which the Transjordanian tribes settled. On the contrary, it stresses constantly the divine authorization for settling there (1:15; 14:2).

As it now appears, the building of *an altar besides the altar of the Lord our God* must be deemed an act of rebellion against both the Lord and his congregation[5] as it is settled on the west side of the river.

3. APOLOGY AND RECONCILIATION (22:21-34)

21 *Then the Reubenites, the Gadites, and the half tribe of Manasseh answered and said to the heads of the clans of Israel:*
22 *"The Mighty One, God, the Lord! The Mighty One, God, the Lord! He knows, and Israel will also know: if it is out of rebellion or out of faithlessness against the Lord (save us not today!)*
23 *that we have built ourselves an altar to cease from following the Lord, or if to offer on it burnt offering or meal offering, or to bring on it sacrifices of peace offerings, let the Lord himself take vengeance.*
24 *But truly, it is from a certain concern that we have done it, reasoning*

---

4. For this biblico-theologically important concept cf. G. Vos, *Biblical Theology*, pp. 199f.
5. The use of "rebel" (Heb. *māraḏ*) with the direct object (Heb. *'ōṯānû*) has caused difficulty to some translators. The RSV changes the verb form to a Hiphil ("make us rebels"). J. H. Kroeze, *Het Boek Jozua*, p. 239, points to Job 24:13 as another example of *māraḏ* in the Qal with direct object.

that in time to come your children might say to our children: 'What have you to do with the Lord, the God of Israel?

25 For the Lord has made the Jordan as a border between us and you, Reubenites and Gadites; you have no portion in the Lord.' So your children would cause our children to cease fearing the Lord.

26 Therefore we said: 'Let us do something by building an altar for ourselves, not for burnt offering, nor for sacrifice.'

27 But it shall be a witness between us and you, and between our generations after us, that we will observe the service of the Lord before his face with our burnt offerings, our sacrifices, and our peace offerings, so that your children in time to come may not say to our children: 'You have no share in the Lord.'

28 We said: 'When they will say this in time to come, to us and to our descendants, we will say: Look at the model of the altar of the Lord which our forefathers made, not for burnt offering or for sacrifice, but that it be a witness between us and you.'

29 Far be it from us that we should rebel against the Lord and turn today from following the Lord by building an altar for burnt offering, meal offering, or sacrifice, besides the altar of the Lord our God that is before his tent."

30 When Phinehas the priest and the princes of the congregation, the heads of the Israelite clans who were with him, heard the words which the Reubenites, the Gadites, and the half tribe of Manasseh spoke, it pleased them.

31 And Phinehas the son of Eleazar the priest said to the Reubenites, the Gadites, and the Manassites: "Today we know that the Lord is among us, because you have not committed this trespass against the Lord. Now you have delivered the Israelites out of the Lord's hand."

32 Then Phinehas the son of Eleazar the priest and the princes returned from the Reubenites and the Gadites, out of the land of Gilead, to the land of Canaan, to the Israelites, and brought back word to them.

33 The report pleased the Israelites. The Israelites praised God and spoke no longer about going against them in war to destroy the land in which the Reubenites and the Gadites were living.

34 And the Reubenites and Gadites called the altar: "It Is a Witness Between Us That the Lord Is God."

21–23 The form in which the reply of the Transjordanian tribes is reported shows the weightiness attached to their words by the author. The answer is addressed *to the heads of the clans of Israel* ("princes" in v. 14). Phinehas is not the dominating figure. This is a truly national concern. The words used in the reply show by their very construction something of the excitement which the author wishes to convey. A solemn appeal is made, not once but twice, to the all-knowing God, called *The Mighty One, God, the Lord*.[1] Israel will know what this God already knows, namely that *rebellion* and *faithlessness*, as charged, have been far removed from their minds. The very thought makes them utter the wish that the Lord may not *save* them if their words are untrue.

Negatively phrased, they have had no desire *to cease from following the Lord* (cf. v. 16). Neither has the altar been constructed to bring regular sacrifices. Several forms of sacrifices are mentioned, but this is done for rhetorical purposes, since the categories are not distinguished clearly (for the various categories of sacrifice, cf. Lev. 1-3). If all of these things had been their hidden aim, then may *the Lord himself take vengeance* (cf. Deut. 18:19; 1 Sam. 20:16).

The vivid report of this obviously sincere reaction on the part of the accused tribes must have been intended to leave a deep impression on the readers. Both the accusers and the accused stand together in their outright condemnation of anything remotely resembling a form of worship practice other than that of the Lord alone.

24-27   After these strong denials follows an equally strong asseveration.[2] The *concern* expressed about the building of the altar was prompted by a fear of possible future disparagement which coming generations might suffer at the hand of those west of the Jordan. Just now (cf. v. 16) they had heard the words *"the God of Israel."* It was, however, no imaginary danger to suppose that those on the west bank somehow would begin to think they could lay a stronger claim to that God than their brothers in the east. Was not *the Jordan* an ever present barrier? Would it not also be a terrible thing if the one part of the covenant nation were to tell the other that they had *no portion* ("share") *in the Lord*? This hypothetical case nevertheless points up a very real truth. Possession of the land, as the Israelite knew well, was ultimately centered in the Lord in whom they had their portion and lot (cf. Ps. 16:5-6). This deeply spiritual outlook had determined the writing of the book of Joshua thus far. It again plays a vital part here.

The building of the altar is therefore not a way of ceasing to fear the Lord, as had been alleged. Indeed, the opposite is true. Disparaging the claim of the Transjordanian tribes to being God's people surely would

---

1. Heb. *'ēl 'ᵉlōhîm yhwh*. Other possible renderings are: God, God the Lord; God of gods, the Lord; El, God, the Lord. When used alone in the OT *'ēl* never stands for the true God except in poetic literature.

2. Heb. *'im lō'*, which in oath-like formulas is the same as a strong affirmation; cf. GKC § 149.

lead to a forsaking of the fear of the Lord. Yet that fear of the Lord was what was expected of Israel (Deut. 4:10; 6:2, 13, 24, etc.). Indeed, it was at the very heart of their relationship to the Lord. No wonder, therefore, that a vigorous attempt had to be made to prevent this from happening: *Let us do something by building an altar*.[3] As had already been asserted strongly, this particular altar was not meant for sacrificial service. Rather, the altar is intended as a *witness*. Surely sacrifices will be brought also by the tribes of Transjordan, but this will be done in *the service*[4] *of the Lord* and *before his face*. While both of these expressions could be taken as referring to the service at one central sanctuary, they do not necessarily compel such an interpretation. If, as can be maintained, Deut. 12 allowed for other altars besides the altar at Shiloh, or wherever the tent of meeting was located, then the sacrifices brought upon such altars also would be the Lord's service and would be done before his face.

What the answer does not make very clear is how precisely the building of this altar was meant to serve as the desired witness.[5] The main point is obvious, however: the tribes east of the Jordan want it to be a reminder of their equal sharing in the Lord with their brothers on the opposite side.

28–29 Still fearing future disparagement because of their location beyond the river, the tribes point out that if that should occur they would have a *model* (Heb. *taḇnît*[6]) *of the altar of the Lord* to point to as a silent and yet (at least so it was intended) eloquent *witness between us and you*. Again the question of how this would happen exactly is not made clear. Apparently the altar's format and conspicuous size were meant to establish the claims of the Transjordanian tribes to be truly a part of God's people and entitled to his service. Moreover, the very fact that it resembled the altar of the Lord was enough to express therewith their loyalty to him whose altar they copied. The word *witness* (Heb. *'ēḏ*) is a term used in covenant making. It had been used also in the covenant made between Jacob and Laban in this same country of Gilead (Gen. 31:48) and would

---

3. Lit. "Let us do for ourselves to build an altar." The infinitive is used here to describe attendant circumstances or otherwise to define them more exactly; cf. GKC § 114 o.

4. Heb. *'aḇōḏâ*, primarily regarding the outward worship of Yahweh (cf. Exod. 27:19; 30:16; Ezek. 44:14), although the OT also knows of the inward condition of the hearts and lives of those worshipping; cf. Ps. 15. Sometimes *'aḇōḏâ* is used of an individual act of worship (cf. Exod. 12:25–26; 13:5).

5. H. W. Hertzberg, *ATD* IX, p. 127, calls the defense of the altar builders, "awkward" (*"nicht eben geschickt"*).

6. From *bānâ*, "to build," hence "construction," "pattern," "figure."

again be used in the covenant ceremony recorded in 24:26–27. Under no condition should the tribes west of the river think that the altar was meant to be a rival to the true worship of the Lord. Rebellion and forsaking the Lord were no part of the original intent.

30–31 The author's report of the reaction of *Phinehas the priest and the princes of the congregation* shows as much genuine joy as his earlier report of the accusation and the defense had exhibited concern. Thus the reader is helped to see the great things that were at stake for the continuity of the service of God. One might almost speak of a spirit of euphoria coming to expression in the response to the defense just delivered. A serious threat has been averted. A calamity which might have plunged the whole people into ruin had been avoided. *Today we know that the Lord is among us.* Thus the true cause of this happy turn of events is seen to lie in the Lord's presence with his people. While in times of spiritual decline and apostasy this awareness can wreak havoc and stem from a false sense of security (cf. 1 Sam. 4:3), in other times it is a perfectly wholesome and legitimate expression prompted by thankfulness to God. This is one of these times.[7]

32–33 The amicable outcome of the dispute is now reported to the tribes on the other side of the Jordan. As before, *Gilead* is distinguished from *Canaan*, as is natural in terms of geographic considerations. Moreover, as before, Manasseh's name is omitted from the list of Transjordanian tribes. Perhaps its share in the altar building episode was not as great as that of the others (see above). The mood of thanksgiving which had been felt by the members of the delegation is shared by the tribes in general. Praise to God is the natural expression of this gratitude. Naturally, the earlier plan to make war against those who were held at fault is abandoned. Judg. 20 shows that intertribal war was necessary on occasion to discipline a tribe, but that was when the times were different.

34 The final verse of this rather vivid account contains a reference to a name-giving ceremony. It was the Transjordanian tribes, of whom again only two are mentioned, who gave the altar a name. Some think that the actual name has dropped out of the text. From the context it is then supposed that the name was "Witness." For example, the AV supplies this word. In the ASV the passage reads: "And the children of Reuben . . .

---

7. Cf. also the conclusion that J. Calvin draws from this joyful exclamation, to the effect that "we never revolt from God, or fall off to impiety unless he abandon us, and give us up when thus abandoned to a reprobate mind"; *Commentaries on the Book of Joshua*, p. 261.

called the altar *Ed* " (marginal note: "That is, Witness").[8] Others, however, prefer to take the final sentence to be the actual name of the altar.[9] Since the names of other altars also consist of short sentences (see Exod. 7:15; Judg. 6:24) this approach has been taken here. The name would then be "It Is a Witness Between Us That the Lord Is God."[10]

In this way the altar with its name would answer to its intended purpose. It was not meant to be a novel way of worshipping the Lord but rather as a reminder, made within the covenant context (witness!), of the exclusive nature of the covenant God. Alien religious influences must be kept far from Israel if it is not to perish. The possession of the land, the main subject of chs. 13–22, can only be a blessing if the people of the land observe the covenant statutes of the Lord whose land it is (Lev. 25:23). Further instructions and admonitions will follow in chs. 23–24.

Christians today are no longer bound to such externalities as land and altar (cf. John 4:21–26). Yet the story of how the Israel of God was kept pure from pagan intrusions is significant for them also, since out of Israel the world's Redeemer was to come and did come.[11]

8. JB leaves a blank where it is thought that the name originally occurred, and refers to Gen. 31:47–48.
9. Cf. C. Steuernagel, *Das Buch Josua*, p. 295: "Der Name des Altars besteht in einem ganzen Satz." The particle *kî* with which the name is introduced need not be more than a particle of asseveration; cf. GKC § 157 b. This is also the approach taken by JPS and DNV, and by KD, C. J. Goslinga, J. H. Kroeze, B. Holwerda, Cf. also the Vulgate: "*vocaveruntque . . . altare quod extruxerant Testimonium nostrum quod Dominus ipse sit Deus.*"
10. The LXX sees in this verse a reference to Joshua, who is not mentioned by name in the entire account outside the story of the dismissal of the tribes (vv. 1–8), and renders the verse as follows: "And Joshua gave to the altar of Reuben, Gad, and half Manasseh a name and said: 'It is a witness between them that the Lord is their God.'"
11. For a discussion of the many problems OT scholarship encounters in interpreting this chapter, cf. R. de Vaux, *Early History*, pp. 581–84.

III. THE PROMISED LAND TO BE KEPT IN COVENANT OBEDIENCE (23:1– 24:33)

A. JOSHUA'S PROVISIONAL FAREWELL (23:1– 16)

1. FIRST CALL TO COVENANT OBEDIENCE (23:1–8)

1 *A long time later, after the Lord had given Israel rest from all its enemies round about, and when Joshua was old and well advanced in years,*

2 *Joshua summoned all Israel, its elders, its chiefs, its judges, and its officers, and said to them: "I am old and well advanced in years;*

3 *and you have seen all that the Lord your God has done to all these nations because of you; it has been the Lord your God who has been fighting for you.*

4 *Behold, I have assigned to you by lot these nations which remain as an inheritance for your tribes, together with the nations I have already destroyed, from the Jordan to the Great Sea in the west.*

5 *The Lord your God will himself make them retreat at your advance and drive them out before you, and you will take possession of their land as the Lord your God has promised you.*

6 *Be therefore very steadfast to keep and to do all that is written in the book of the Law of Moses, so that you do not depart from it to the right or to the left,*

7 *neither associate with these nations who remain among you. Do not invoke the name of their gods nor swear an oath by them, neither render them worship or obeisance.*

8 *But cling firmly to the Lord your God as you have done to this day.*

The dominant note of the concluding two chapters of the book is hortatory. In this respect they correspond to the first part of the opening chapter. (See

331

also "Unity of Composition" in the Introduction for other structural features in the book.) This hortatory section, together with the exhortations at the beginning of the book, forms a fitting frame around the bulk of the book and shows its true nature.

Throughout the book have been many occasions where Joshua was compared with his great predecessor Moses, or where words spoken to and by Moses were recalled (cf. 1:5, 9, 17). Several events of Joshua's life may be compared with similar events in Moses' life: both cross a body of water with the people of Israel; both have a "burning bush" experience (in Joshua's case the outward phenomena differ but the essence is there; 5:13–15); both hold out a staff (javelin) at a crucial time during the battle (8:26; Exod. 17:8–16); and both build an altar to the Lord (8:30; Exod. 17:15–16). The farewell addresses recorded of Joshua conform to this same pattern (cf. Deut. 31–32).[1]

Though there is great similarity between chs. 23–24, the emphasis of each is somewhat distinct. In both chapters exhortations are made to remain faithful to the Lord of the covenant. However, while ch. 24 stresses particularly God's acts in the past, ch. 23 also speaks of what he will still be doing in the future.

Perhaps the scope of the first assembly, that of ch. 23, was more limited than that of the second, and perhaps the former was meant to be somewhat preparatory to the latter. The location of the two assemblies also may have been different. Shechem is clearly mentioned as the location of the second meeting. On the basis of earlier references (18:1; 21:2; 22:1–9), one is led to believe that the first took place at Shiloh.

1 Chronologically the events of this chapter need not be placed much later than those of ch. 13. In both, Joshua is portrayed as a man *well advanced in years*. If the events reported here took place shortly before his death at age 110 (24:29), this description would be accurate. The *long time* of which this verse speaks is to be viewed from the book's starting point, not from the events recorded in ch. 13. The *rest* which the Lord had given to Israel was accomplished during the period that had elapsed between the beginning of the book and its end. By using this concept of rest the author reverts to a motif already mentioned at the beginning (see 1:13 and commentary; cf. also 21:43–44). Thus the two lines which run through the book of Joshua, that of a completed conquest and that of further conquest yet to take place (see "Date and Authorship" in the

---

1. KD put it strongly: "Joshua, in this last act of his life, was merely treading in the footsteps of Moses" (p. 223). For the same emphasis, cf. also H. W. Hertzberg, *ATD* IX; C. Steuernagel, *Das Buch Josua*.

Introduction) are found side by side in this chapter (compare v. 1 with
v. 5; cf. vv. 4, 7, 12–13). These are two compatible ways of viewing the
same events.

The nations that the Lord dispossessed on Israel's behalf are called
enemies, a word which is very significant theologically (cf. also 7:8; 10:25;
Exod. 23:27; Judg. 5:31). The use of this word is not out of accord with
the mission of Israel to be a blessing for the nations (Gen. 12:3). Rather,
it represents a supplementary thought, also developed very fully in the
prophecies "against the nations" found in almost all of the latter prophets.
While Israel was meant to be a channel of salvation for the nations, it was
also called to represent provisionally the kingdom of God on earth. This
meant that those who were not of Israel were the nations who knew not
the Lord (Ps. 79:6). In the full consciousness of its theocratic role as God's
representative on earth, Israel was justified in considering those who opposed it as enemies of God (Exod. 23:22) and God identified with Israel
in that respect.[2] To be freed from one's enemies and to look for their
destruction thus becomes a part of the OT eschatological perspective and
hope (Num. 24:18; Isa. 62:8; Obad. 17; Mic. 5:9), an emphasis which
also carries over into the NT (Luke 1:71). By having rest from its enemies
Israel thus was enjoying a foretaste of the Messianic kingdom.

2 Those summoned to this assembly are first designated as *all
Israel* (see 3:7, 17; 4:14). However, it may well be that at this point only
certain representatives assembled. The language in 24:1 is slightly more
comprehensive: "all the tribes of Israel." *Elders* also play a role in 8:33.
In the future envisaged by 20:4 they will also function in connection with
the cities of asylum. "Elder" is a general term for representatives of the
people (cf. Exod. 3:16; Deut. 21:3–4, 19; 22:15; 25:7). For *chiefs*, see
22:14, 30. *Judges*, also mentioned in 8:33, are not to be equated with the
later charismatic leaders. For *officers*, see 3:2; 8:33.

Calling attention to his advanced years, Joshua intends his words
to be understood as a last will and testament.

3 This verse expresses a leading thought of the book. The Lord
did something to the *nations* because of Israel, and it was he *who has been
fighting for them*. Israel was in some respect only an onlooker (note Heb.

---

2. See the worthwhile discussion of W. Foerster, *TDNT* II, pp. 811–15. The en-
mity relationship between Israel and the nations is not one of its own choosing
and cannot be abandoned at will. Certain mission theologies, e.g., J. Blauw, *The
Missionary Nature of the Church* (Grand Rapids: 1962), p. 38, tend to give this
adversary relation too subordinate a place.

$re^{,}\hat{u}$, "behold," v. 4). This is as the Lord had promised (1:9), and it agrees with other emphases in the book (cf. 10:14).

The frequent use of the word *nations* in this chapter is also to be noted (cf. vv. 4, 7, 12). It does not occur very often elsewhere in the book. The expression *the Lord your God* is also frequent here. It is common in the book of Deuteronomy (3:21; 4:3, 21, etc.). Joshua's address consists to a large extent of reminiscences from the Pentateuch, especially Deuteronomy.

That the Lord would fight for Israel had been promised in Deut. 1:30; 3:22; 20:4 (cf. Exod. 14:14), and this had actually come to pass.[3]

4–5 Joshua recalls the allotment of the land to the tribes. The land had become their *inheritance* (see 1:6 and commentary; cf. Deut. 32:8; Ps. 16:5), so Israel rightly may lay claim to the land. A greater inheritance awaits the believer in the new dispensation.

The land of promise is described here as to its western (Jordanian) part only. Throughout the book much emphasis is placed on the fact that the tribes east of the river also belonged to the people of God and that they had received their land from Moses (e.g., 13:8–33; cf. ch. 22), although there appears to be no need to stress this fact here. Joshua not only recalls the blessings of God's past deliverance, but he also assures the people of the Lord's future help in driving out the nations that remain. (For a similar promise cf. 13:6; Deut. 6:19; 9:4.) Thus the background is provided for the exhortation to covenant loyalty, which involves following God's commands. These are evangelical commands, and come within the framework of grace.

6–8 The exhortation to be *steadfast* (lit. "be strong") has its parallel in 1:7–9; cf. also 8:31, 34. The possession of the land, both that which Israel already has and that which it will yet receive, is conditional upon covenant obedience. This condition should not be seen as contrary to the principle of gratuitous giving which is so prominent throughout the book. Nevertheless, it is a condition just the same. It consists of keeping and doing all that which is *written in the book of the Law of Moses* (cf. 1:7). This law (Heb. *tôrâ*) is God's gracious provision for a life of covenant fellowship between himself and the people. They are to do what Joshua had been commanded to do in the beginning of the book; that is to say, they are not to *depart from it to the right or to the left* (cf. 1:7).

Viewing the nations as Israel's enemies (v. 1), the account of

---

3. Heb. *hannilḥām* (lit. "the fighting one") indicates a durative aspect. The definite article indicates that it is the Lord and no one else who is doing this; cf. P. Joüon, *Grammaire de l'Hébreu biblique* (Rome: 1923, repr. 1965), § 137 l.

Joshua's farewell speech enjoins strict separation from them. Israel was to develop its own identity as the people of God. The powerful attraction of the fertility worship, with rites that were degrading for the worshippers of the Lord, must be avoided at all cost.[4] For this reason any semblance of adherence to Canaanite religion is ruled out. Four outward forms accompanying worship are here listed. Similar injunctions may be found in Exod. 20:24; 23:13; Deut. 6:13; 10:20; 12:3. Following these negative injunctions might easily lead to a form of legalism, which did not involve the heart. However, Ps. 16 (see esp. v. 4) shows that the believing Israelite knew how to combine the negative with the positive side of heart attachment and godly fear.[5]

The word rendered *invoke* means lit. "make mention of." Possibly the prohibition went beyond the formal invoking of the name of the other god. Theophoric names, names compounded of the name of a deity, were common. In Saul's family the name Baal served as such a compound (cf. 1 Chr. 8:33; 9:39; cf. 2 Sam. 2:8, where the name is compounded with -*bosheth*, meaning "shame"; cf. also Hos. 2:18-19 [Eng. 16-17]). Swearing an *oath* was a religious act, and doing so by a false god was tantamount to recognition of that deity. Swearing by the Lord's name, on the other hand, is sometimes described as the sum of true religion (Ps. 63:12 [Eng. 11]). This shows the centrality of these prohibitions (cf. Jer. 12:16). The other nations are teaching Israel to swear by the name of their gods. However, when they turn to the Lord they themselves will begin to swear by his name. Thus the separation enjoined here may have a positive end in providing an ethnic entity in which the true name is revered, so that others may come to acknowledge it.

Next to the negative stands the positive. Israel is to *cling firmly*[6] *to the Lord your God*. Clinging or cleaving to God is frequently mentioned in Deuteronomy (4:4; 10:20; 11:22; 13:4; cf. also Josh. 22:5). The verb often occurs in a sequence of verbs, all of which express the idea that the believer adheres to his covenant God.[7]

The favorable evaluation of Israel's past relationship to the Lord

---

4. As more knowledge is obtained of the cultures of the ancient Near East our eyes have been opened to the polemic thrust which some of Israel's legislation at times possesses. This should caution against making Israel's laws *ipso facto* binding codes of moral behavior for today.

5. Some critical scholars would assign this attitude to the postexilic period, but this would leave the earlier period without a norm.

6. Heb. *dābaq* is also used of the man-to-wife relationship (Gen. 2:24).

7. Others verbs in such sequences include "to love," "do the commandments," "walk in the Lord's ways."

should be noted. Joshua indicates they have been clinging to him *to this day*. No gross, wholesale apostasy such as would mark later phases of Israel's history had yet occurred, although there had been occasional lapses, as recorded in Exodus and Numbers. The prophets too will sometimes view Israel's pristine relationship to God favorably (cf. Jer. 2:2), although they will also look at Israel's early history as one concatenation of failure to keep God's will (cf. Ezek. 20, 23). The historical record provides reasons for both the positive and the negative view, and Joshua's emphasis is on the positive (cf. 24:31).

2. SECOND CALL TO COVENANT OBEDIENCE (23:9–13)

9 *The Lord has driven out from before you great and mighty nations; no man has been able to hold his ground before you to this day.*

10 *One of you chased a thousand, because the Lord your God, he it is who has been fighting for you, as he promised you.*

11 *Take good care therefore that you love the Lord your God.*

12 *For if you should become apostate and cling to the remnant of these nations who still remain among you, if you should make marriages with them and associate with them and they with you,*

13 *you may be sure that the Lord your God will not continue to drive out these nations before you. They will become a snare and a trap for you, a scourge on your backs and thorns in your eyes, till you perish from this good land which the Lord your God has given you.*

This section resembles in formal structure the former call to covenant obedience. First is a recalling of past favors received from the covenant Lord, followed by an exhortation to be faithful to him, and this is combined with the threat of ultimate destruction.[1]

9–10 The Lord's promise made in 1:5; Deut. 7:1; 11:23, 25, that he would drive out the other nations has come true. The emphasis placed on the greatness and the power of these nations enhances the greatness of the Lord's deliverance and is added reason for serving him. Elsewhere in the book the expulsion of the Anakim, who had inspired such fear in Israel's mind in the desert (cf. Num. 14), is given prominent mention (11:21; 14:6–15; 15:13–14). The rest of the population had also breathed hatred against Israel (cf. 9:1–2), but God's promise (1:5) had been kept (21:44). The point of view is that of the completed Conquest (cf. 11:23–

1. Some would consider this pattern to reflect the treaty forms that have been discovered among the cultures of Israel's neighbors; see K. Baltzer, *Covenant Formulary*, p. 63. More about that question will be found in ch. 24 and commentary. It may well be that the shape of ch. 23 was influenced by a free application of this treaty pattern.

24; 21:43–45). This emphasis stands side by side with that of an only partial Conquest (v. 5; 13:1–4; 15:63). Initial fulfilment followed by a greater fulfilment at some point in the future make up the total picture of the book.

The language of v. 10 is reminiscent of Deut. 32:30, and also reflects promises made in Lev. 26:7–8; Deut. 28:7. Formulas of blessings and curses such as those just cited were part of the treaty patterns of the ancient Near East.[2] In Samson's case (Judg. 15:15–16), the chasing of *a thousand* by one man was fulfilled literally.

11–13 That Israel should *love[3] the Lord* had already been stated in Deut. 6:5; 10:12; 11:13. Love for God is an exclusive thing; it is a conscious devotion to him, based on what he has done for Israel. It has for its corollary the hating of evil. This love is enjoined here again upon Israel. The words translated *take good care therefore* read lit. "take care for your very souls" (cf. Deut. 4:15). Heb. *nepeš* ("soul") is not to be taken in quite the same way as it is used in the NT. It strengthens the intensity of the command to love. The Israelites are to love for their life's sake.[4]

Apostasy (Heb. *šûḇ*)[5] is a constant possibility. It consists of a turning from God. When this happens, Israel, instead of clinging firmly to God (v. 8), will *cling to the remnant of these nations*. Intermarriage was one form that this clinging to the nations could take. Therefore it was strictly forbidden (cf. also Exod. 34:12–16; Deut. 7:3).[6]

When Israel turns from God, he *will not continue to drive out these*

---

2. Comparative studies of these blessings and curses in the OT and its "Umwelt" have been made in recent years. See F. C. Fensham, *ZAW* 74 (1962), pp. 1–9; S. Gevirtz, "West-Semitic Curses and the Problem of the Origins of Hebrew Law," *VT* 11 (1961), pp. 137–158. D. R. Hillers, *Treaty-Curses and the OT Prophets*, especially pp. 69f.

3. The Hebrew word for "love," *'aheḇ*, covers the whole range of human affection: sexual love, love of friendship, and love for God. It is more than a voluntary expression of the emotions. It can be commanded, and it expresses itself in concrete acts of obedience to law. The discussion of this concept by G. Quell, *TDNT* I (E.T. 1964), pp. 21–35, suffers from a one-sided emphasis. Quell appears to have difficulty with the fact that love can be the subject of divine command, but this is judging the biblical love concept by an extraneous standard.

4. H. W. Hertzberg, *ATD* IX, translates: "So haltet denn streng darauf, um euer selber willen, den Herrn . . . zu lieben."

5. This phrase is very frequent in Jeremiah (31:22; 49:4), where the nation is called *šoḇēḇ*, "apostate"; cf. Jer. 3:14, 22. It may also be used of a positive turning to the Lord.

6. Perhaps the special focus of this prohibition is the making of marriages for political alliances with other nations. See Exod. 34:12–16, where the making of a covenant is the context in which the intermarriage prohibition occurs.

nations. God's punishment will be in accord with the people's wishes. They desire to cling to the nations that *remain* (v. 12), and God will make it possible for them to do so by letting these nations live in the land.[7] There is a point when God abandons sinners to their wicked desires (cf. Rom. 1:28).

An accumulation of terms describes the evil effect that the nations will have upon Israel. The words *snare*, *trap*, *scourge*,[8] and *thorns* are used to impress the people with the dire consequences of their departure from the Lord[9] (see also Exod. 23:33; 34:12; Num. 33:55). Ultimately Israel will *perish from this good land*. Captivity will then be their lot in a place far from the land of the fathers.

3. THIRD CALL TO COVENANT OBEDIENCE (23:14–16)

14 *Now I am about to go the way of all the earth. Know therefore with your whole heart and soul that not a single thing has failed of all the good things which the Lord your God promised with respect to you. Everything has been fulfilled to you; not one thing has remained unfulfilled.*

15 *But just as all the good things which the Lord your God promised concerning you have been fulfilled for you, so will the Lord bring on you all the evil things until he has destroyed you from off this good land which the Lord your God has given you.*

16 *When you transgress the covenant of the Lord your God which he has laid upon you, and you go and worship other gods and do obeisance to them, then the Lord's wrath will be kindled against you, and you will perish quickly from off the good land which he has given you.*

This is the third exhortation to remain loyal to the Lord, Israel's covenant God. As with the previous two charges, first comes a reminder of what God has done, followed by the exhortation to be faithful, an appeal which at this point consists entirely of threats of punishment if such faithfulness will not be rendered.

7. The OT looks upon the nations that remain in Canaan in a variety of ways. In Exod. 23:30 it is stated that the Lord will drive them out little by little, lest the land become desolate. In Judg. 3:4 the nations are permitted to live in Canaan in order to test Israel, to know whether it will obey the Lord.

8. Heb. *šōṭēṭ* occurs only here in the OT. The word's meaning is not entirely clear. F.-M. Abel, *Le Livre de Josué*, calls it "unintelligible."

9. Hillers, *op. cit.*, pp. 69f., calls attention to the Esarhaddon Treaty, 672 BC, where similar curses can be found. For the imagery of a bird caught in a trap or snare, cf. also Isa. 8:14; 28:13; Jer. 48:43–44; 50:24; Ezek. 17:19–20; Hos. 7:12.

14–16 Joshua reminds the people of the fact of his impending death. He is *about to go the way of all the earth*. This whole chapter is meant to be a word of farewell, a last will and testament (cf. vv. 1, 2b).

The viewpoint here is of a complete fulfilment of all God's promises (cf. 21:45). Israel ought to perceive this fulfilment with all its faculties (*with your heart and soul*). Recognition of the Lord's complete faithfulness ought to dominate their lives and their thoughts.

A certain degree of repetition characterizes this chapter, but this is designed to drive home a few central thoughts. Following the style of the book of Deuteronomy, which has this same earnest tone of exhortation and appeal, Joshua urges the people to be mindful of the Lord's great acts on their behalf.

The good which God promised will turn into its opposite should *the covenant* be transgressed (v. 16). The word "covenant" is used sparingly in Joshua, even though its idea is present everywhere. It occurs in the expression "ark of the covenant" in chs. 3–4, 6, 8, and is also used with respect to Achan's sin (7:11, 15). In ch. 9 it is used of a treaty between Israel and Gibeon, and it occurs again in 24:25.

The word used for the violation of the covenant is *transgress* (Heb. *'ābar*).[1] Since covenant is closely connected with law (cf. Deut. 4:13), failure to keep the covenant is tantamount to transgressing the law of the covenant. This law had been given within the context of grace and redemption. It provided, by means of the sacrificial system, for the expiation and removal of sin. Nevertheless, it was a law that should be kept.

Transgression of the covenant could assume various forms. It is linked with the service of other gods, as in Deut. 17:2. This transgression will provoke the Lord's anger (Heb. *'ap*), resulting in expulsion from the land which the people have received as fulfilment of the covenant promise. One need not think only of the two major captivities of the northern and the southern kingdoms. Earlier in Israel's history, national sin also resulted in severe national affliction (cf. 1 K. 14:25; 2 K. 13:1–17; 2 Chr. 33:11). One may also think of the immediate neighbors of Israel who frequently harassed it.

The earnest exhortations of this chapter, combined with those of ch. 24, form a fitting conclusion to the book. Together with the hortatory section of 1:1–9 they form a frame around the rest of the book and help the reader to understand its purpose and goal (see also p. 15).

---

1. Other words for covenant disobedience are *pārar*, "break," *'āzaḇ*, "forsake," and *šiqqēr*, "be false to."

B. COVENANT RENEWAL AT SHECHEM (24:1–28)

1. AN ASSEMBLY CALLED AT SHECHEM (24:1)

1 *Joshua assembled all the tribes of Israel at Shechem. He summoned the elders of Israel, its chiefs, its judges, and its officers, and they stationed themselves before God.*

The relation between this chapter and ch. 23 has been noted in the introduction to the previous chapter. We have called ch. 23 Joshua's provisional farewell, thereby suggesting a relation of "earlier" and "later," but the chronological sequence is not explicitly stated. The Hebrew text of ch. 24 begins with a simple conjunction, which some render "afterwards."

It would seem, however, that the nature of the two assemblies certainly differs. The second bears a more official character. The use of the word "stationed themselves" (cf. also Deut. 29:9 [Eng. 10]) points to a formal covenant ceremony, the transaction of which is described in vv. 25–27. The phrase *before God* should be noted also. The use of "God" as a single designation of the deity in Joshua occurs only in 22:34 (cf. also 14:6, "the man of God"). The significance of the phrase at this point will be examined below. The unusual character of this gathering at Shechem appears to be indicated by the words used to describe it.

Many recent expositors have claimed to detect various elements of ancient suzerainty treaties in this last chapter of Joshua. These treaties date from both the second and the first millennia BC. Scholarly debate is still continuing on the question as to which kind most closely resembles the biblical materials.[1] The treaties referred to usually follow a fixed format which included the following elements: 1. preamble (corresponding in this case to 24:2); 2. historical prologue (vv. 2–13); 3. stipulations (vv. 14–15, followed in 16–25 by the people's response); 4a. deposition of the treaty text (v. 26); 4b. public reading of the covenant document (no parallel in ch. 24); 5. witnesses (v. 27; cf. also v. 22; in pagan treaties the witnesses were the gods of the contracting parties, so quite naturally this could find no exact correspondence among Israel); 6. curses and blessings (implicit in vv. 19–20).[2]

---

1. Much has been written on this question of possible parallels between biblical and extrabiblical treaty patterns. See G. E. Mendenhall, "Ancient Oriental and Biblical Law," *BA* 17 (1954), pp. 26–46; *idem*, pp. 50–76; J. A. Thompson, *The Ancient Near Eastern Treaties and the OT*; M. G. Kline, *Treaty of the Great King*. 2. We follow the division of the materials as presented by K. A. Kitchen, *Ancient Orient and OT*, pp. 96f. Commentators who have applied this scheme to their interpretation of ch. 24 include J. J. De Vault, *The Book of Joshua*. Pamphlet

It is clear from the suggested distribution of the materials over the various treaty categories that ch. 24 does not present a perfect example of such a treaty. If the treaty scheme has been applied, it must have been done so in a narrative adaptation. Deuteronomy in its entirety presents a more suitable model.[3]

1 The assembly called by Joshua takes place *at Shechem*. This is the only passage where this city is explicitly mentioned (cf. 8:30). It was an ancient city, known also from extrabiblical documents.[4] Upon his arrival in Canaan, Abraham built an altar here. Jacob purchased a parcel of ground from the Shechemites (Gen. 33:18–20) and built an altar at this site. Thus, the place had hallowed associations. Its capture by the Israelites is not mentioned anywhere in the book.[5] The choice of Shechem as the site of this solemn assembly probably was motivated by the ancient traditions reaching back to patriarchal times.[6]

Joshua summons *all the tribes of Israel* to this sacred site ("all

---

Bible Series (New York: 1960); J. Gray, *Joshua, Judges and Ruth*; J. Rea, "Joshua," in C. F. Pfeiffer and E. F. Harrison, eds., *The Wycliffe Bible Commentary* (Chicago: 1962); and C. Vonk, *Inleiding op de Profeten: Jozua*.

3. P. C. Craigie, *Deuteronomy*, is structured entirely around the covenant-treaty pattern described here.

4. Cf. G. E. Wright, *AOTS*, p. 356. The earliest datable reference to Shechem is by an officer of the Egyptian Pharaoh Sesostris III, c. 1878–1843 BC; another reference is found in an Egyptian Execration Text from c. 1800 BC.

5. From the Amarna tablets it is known that the city was ruled by Labayu during the first half of the 14th century BC. This king was in confederation with the Habiru, a group of people whose precise identity continues to be a matter of scholarly debate; see, e.g., M. G. Kline, *WTJ* 20 (1957–58), pp. 46–70; and cf. the survey of opinions in L. Wood, *A Survey of Israel's History* (Grand Rapids: 1970), pp. 104–6. For a discussion of a possible equation of Habiru with Heb. *'ibrî*, cf. also C. H. Gordon, *Ugaritic Textbook*. Analecta Orientalia 38 (Rome: 1965), 19.1899. The discovery of the name Ebrum among the ancient kings of Ebla has provided new material for a possible derivation of *'ibrî*, but no certainty has as yet been attained; cf. P. C. Maloney, "Assessing Ebla," *BAR* 4 (1978), pp. 4–10, especially p. 8.

6. Combining materials from the patriarchal stories (Gen. 34–35) with the present chapter, A. Alt considers ch. 24 to be an "aetiological explanation of a regularly repeated act in the sanctuary of Yahweh at Shechem"; "Die Wallfahrt von Sichem nach Bethel," *KS* I, pp. 79–88; and cf. *Essays on OT History and Religion*, p. 162, n. 112. M. Noth, *History*, p. 92, also thinks of a regularly enacted ceremony, involving the promulgation and proclamation of the Lord's judgments. Noth regards Shechem as the original site of Israel's tribal amphictyony. For newer literature on this subject and a critique of the amphictyony hypothesis, cf. S. Herrmann, *A History of Israel in OT Times*, p. 127, n. 41. See also J. R. Vannoy, *Covenant Renewal at Gilgal* (Cherry Hill, N.J.: 1978).

Israel" in 23:2) with its *elders, chiefs, judges,* and *officers.* The phrase *before God* need not mean that the ark and the tabernacle were actually present at Shechem, although such a temporary transfer from Shiloh is not to be ruled out completely (cf. Judg. 20:18, 26). The LXX makes the whole event take place at Shiloh in the presence of the ark, but this may be because a difficulty was felt with the phrase *before God.* As such, the expression is sufficiently accounted for through Shechem's sacred associations going back to patriarchal times. See also v. 26, which mentions a sacred place or sanctuary.

2. PROPHETIC SURVEY OF REDEMPTIVE HISTORY (24:2–13)

2 *Joshua then said to all the people: "Thus says the Lord, the God of Israel: 'Long ago your forefathers lived on the other side of the River: Terah, the father of Abraham and the father of Nahor, and they served other gods.*

3 *I took your father Abraham from beyond the River. I led him through the whole land of Canaan, multiplied his descendants, and gave him Isaac.*

4 *And to Isaac I gave Jacob and Esau. To Esau I gave Mount Seir, to take possession of it, while Jacob and his children went to Egypt.*

5 *Then I sent Moses and Aaron, and I plagued Egypt according to that which I did among them. Thereupon I led you out.*

6 *I led your forefathers out of Egypt, and when you came to the sea, the Egyptians pursued your forefathers with chariots and with horsemen to the Red Sea.*

7 *Then they called to the Lord and he put darkness between you and the Egyptians, and made the sea come over them, which covered them. Your own eyes saw what I did to Egypt. You stayed a long time in the desert.*

8 *Then I brought you in the land of the Amorites, who lived on the other side of the Jordan. They fought against you, and I gave them into your hand. You took possession of their land, while I destroyed them before you.*

9 *Then Balak, son of Zippor, the king of Moab, arose to make war against Israel. He sent to summon Balaam the son of Beor to curse you.*

10 *But I would not listen to Balaam, so he did nothing but bless you; and I delivered you out of his hand.*

11 *Then you crossed the Jordan and came to Jericho, and the men of Jericho fought against you: the Amorites, Perizzites, Canaanites, Hittites, Girgashites, Hivites, and Jebusites. But I gave them into your hand.*

342

12 *And I sent hornets ahead of you, which drove them out before you, the two kings of the Amorites, not by your sword or by your bow.*

13 *So I gave you a land on which you had not expended any effort, cities which you did not build, but in which you now may live, vineyards and olive yards which you did not plant, though you eat their fruit.'*

According to the division into treaty elements offered above, this section contains both the preamble and the historical prologue. Other suggested approaches to this chapter speak of it as the oratorical development of an ancient confession, such as is believed to be preserved in Deut. 6:21–24; 26:5–9.[1] M. Noth believes this chapter constitutes the account of the extension of the covenant relationship, which was originally established with some of the tribes only, to the entire twelve-tribe league which Noth claims is being constituted here;[2] this is an unproven hypothesis.[3]

Taken in its present form and regarded as Joshua's review of redemptive history, this section offers a very useful insight into the way in which this redemptive history is to be understood. This can be of service for a broader understanding of the various historical materials which the OT contains, and may serve as a useful guideline for sermonic treatment of such materials. All too often the historical materials of the Scripture are treated as so many examples of moral or immoral behavior, to be either copied or shunned. Joshua's survey puts God in the center, and points to the dynamic progress which binds the various stories together. (For similar surveys, cf. 1 Sam. 12; 2 K. 17.)

2 This verse introduces the Lord of the covenant, who identifies himself in this preamble to the covenant. The formula *thus says the Lord*

---

1. F.-M. Abel, *Le Livre de Josué*; cf. JB. J. H. Kroeze, *Het Boek Jozua*, pp. 251f., discusses extensively this creedal approach, which is found also in the works of G. von Rad. It usually presupposes a separation between a Sinai tradition, which is supposed to be legal in orientation, and a historical tradition including the Exodus and the Conquest. Moreover, confessed events and "real" events are separated. See also M. H. Woudstra, in S. Kistemaker, ed., *Interpreting God's Word Today*, pp. 49–72. Kroeze points out that the so-called confessions in Deuteronomy are not really confessions in the accepted sense. Moreover, Josh. 24:2 begins with the words "Thus says the Lord," and is a prophetic survey of redemptive history. In Neh. 9:13, Sinai references occur side by side with historical materials. Moreover, the Sinai tradition contains references to the Exodus; cf. Exod. 19:3b–4.
2. See M. Noth, *History*, pp. 93f.
3. K. A. Kitchen, "Historical Method and Early Hebrew Tradition," *TB* 17 (1966), p. 87, points out that the role of "all Israel" in the conquest under Joshua is not a mere preconception to be dismissed as secondary, as is alleged by certain scholars, but that it is primary and universal in Hebrew tradition.

THE BOOK OF JOSHUA

anticipates the language of the prophets. It is the so-called messenger formula, constituting an integral part of the message though introductory to it. According to Gen. 20:7, Abraham was a prophet (cf. also Deut. 34:1–12), and here Joshua joins these ranks. As *God of Israel* the Lord is described by the name which Jacob also had used when building his altar at Shechem (Gen. 33:20).

Following the preamble the covenant form usually includes a review of the relations between suzerain and vassal.[4] Such reviews may include a reference to the land which the suzerain bestows upon his vassal or which he confirms in his possession. Similarly, vv. 2–13 contain a review of Israel's story of salvation.

Joshua first looks back to the time when Abraham was as yet living beyond the river Euphrates. At that time, the forefathers *served other gods*. Terah is singled out, but he is viewed also as the father of Abraham and Nahor. To what extent Abraham himself was implicated in the serving of other gods is a question on which scholars are not agreed. It would seem that, as was the case later among Abraham's distant relatives in Haran, there may have been a mixture of true and false religion (see Gen. 31:19, 34, 35). Joshua's reference to the former idolatry of the fathers serves to underscore the gracious character of God's call to Abraham.[5]

Verse 14 speaks of foreign gods which must be put away by Israel at this very moment. Does this mean that some idolatrous worship actually existed in Israel's midst at this time? Or does the injunction to put away these gods refer to the gods of the nations still among them?[6]

The fathers dwelt *on the other side of the River*. This suggests the city of Ur, Abraham's original home.[7] Haran, to which he migrated with

---

4. While formal similarities between extrabiblical and biblical covenants may be noted, their material differences should likewise be stressed. Cf. R. de Vaux, *Ancient Israel*, p. 148: ". . . the Israelite law, for all its resemblances in form and content, differs radically from the clauses of the Oriental 'treaties' and the articles of their 'codes.' " De Vaux also points out that in the Bible "God was not merely a guarantor of the Covenant, he was party to it, and no Oriental code can be compared with the Israelite law, which is ascribed in its entirety to God as its author" (pp. 148f.).

5. Cf. J. Calvin: "For God gathered them together to be his peculiar people, from no respect to anything but his mere good pleasure"; *Commentaries on the Book of Joshua*, p. 272.

6. About the God the patriarchs worshipped, see T. E. McComiskey, "The Religion of the Patriarchs: An Analysis of *The God of the Fathers* by Albrecht Alt," in J. H. Skilton, ed., *The Law and the Prophets* (Phillipsburg, N.J.: 1974), pp. 195-206.

7. There is no complete unanimity about the location of Ur. Most scholars place it in southern Mesopotamia, but a northern hypothesis is proposed as well. This hypothesis has been strengthened by the discoveries at Tell Mardîkh (Ebla).

Terah his father, was west of the Euphrates. It may also be that the expression was actually a term used by the Babylonians with reference to regions *west* of the river.

3 Joshua now summarizes briefly the patriarchal stories as recorded in Gen. 12–21. This greatly condensed mode of representation helps to point out the leading concern of these stories, and should caution against taking biblical history as a collection of incidents from which to derive moral lessons by way of example. The emphasis is rather on what God did.

Joshua's words are God's words. Hence, he can use the first person singular (but cf. v. 7, where the third person [*"the Lord"*] is used.) Such usage is not uncommon in prophecy.

First to be mentioned is God's taking *your father Abraham from beyond the River*. In just those few words an immense occurrence is succinctly set forth: God makes a new beginning with Abraham. He takes him from the environment described in v. 2. This provides the background for the later exhortation (v. 14) to abandon the very gods which were served by the forefathers. Abraham's seed must walk in the footsteps of Abraham. *I led him through the whole land of Canaan*: the divine activity is central in Joshua's description of the past. (For Abraham's going through the land, cf. Gen. 12:6, 8–9; 13:17.) As did their ancestor in the time of the promise, so may the Israelites now do in the time of the fulfilment (cf. v. 13).

Central to the patriarchal stories is the promise of the numerous offspring (Gen. 12:2; 17:6). The struggle to obtain the promised seed is a crucial datum of the stories of Abraham, Isaac, and Jacob. This is why the fulfilment of that promise is put first here, even before the birth of Isaac is recalled. (See also the brief backward-looking summary of Abraham's life in Gen. 25:19 before the story of Isaac and the birth of the twins is presented.) God's gracious activity underlies the very existence of Israel.

4 The element of election, already present in the pre-patriarchal narratives (Cain-Abel and Seth; Noah and the rest of mankind; Shem as compared to Japheth and Ham), is particularly strong in the story of the birth of Jacob and Esau, although the Isaac-Ishmael stories also contain that emphasis. By stating that the Lord gave to Isaac *Jacob and Esau*, Joshua's prophetic summary of past events brings into clear focus the divine choice that was operative in the distinction made between these twins, of whom the older was to serve the younger. This was another reminder to the Israel of Joshua's day of the unmerited divine choice underlying their national existence.

Another deliberate contrast, but now in reverse, may be intended by the recalling of the twofold experience which Esau and Jacob had. To Esau God *gave Mount Seir, to take possession of it*, whereas *Jacob and his children went to Egypt*. Thus, while election was stressed at the beginning of the verse, the course of history, which often seems to conflict with God's design, also is given ample recognition. In Egypt Jacob and his descendants would appear for centuries to be anything but the elect people of God, suffering cruelly as they did at the hand of Egypt's kings. Still, in all its brevity, this summary contains a strong undercurrent of divine guidance which triumphs in the end.[8]

5–6a Passing over the actual oppression suffered by Israel when in Egypt, Joshua's prophetic survey takes note of it indirectly by making mention of God's sending *Moses and Aaron*, and by speaking of the plagues[9] with which he afflicted the Egyptians.

The details of the Egyptian sojourn are assumed as known. This accounts for the broad reference to that *which I did among them*.[10] The deliverance from this fiery furnace of affliction formed a highpoint of Israelite history, which is why the text mentions this great fact twice in quick succession: *Thereupon I led you out* (v. 5); *I led your forefathers out of Egypt* (v. 6).[11] This, then, constitutes the great event of the Exodus, lit. "the going out."

6b–7 Now follows a brief account of the deliverance at the Sea. The alternation between the various ways of describing those who experienced that event should be noted. Sometimes Joshua refers to what happened to Israel's forefathers, but then again he includes also the present generation in the events of the past (*when you came to the sea* [v. 6b]; *your own eyes saw* [v. 7]). There is a unity between past and present generations of believers. That which was experienced in the past was in effect expe-

---

8. The LXX expands the text by giving further details about Israel's affliction in Egypt, but the succinctness of the remaining part of this prophetic survey amply justifies the summary character of the MT text at this point. The LXX omits the reference to Moses and Aaron in v. 5.

9. Heb. *nāgap* is also used in the actual account of the Exodus deliverance; see Exod. 7:27 (Eng. 8:2); 12:23, 27.

10. The phrase has been considered obscure by some, e.g., Noth, who suggests that it be emended to read "the signs which . . ."; *Das Buch Josua*, p. 136; see also C. H. Giblin, *CBQ* 26 (1964), p. 58.

11. This dual reference is considered a doublet by some; cf., e.g., A. Gelin, *Josué*, p. 129. But J. Muilenburg, "The Form and Structure of the Covenantal Formulations," *VT* 9 (1959), p. 357, warns against the assumption of such doublets here on the basis of ancient Near Eastern texts, where, according to Muilenburg, "repetitions are much more profuse than in their biblical counterparts."

rienced by all. One must allow also for those who had in actual fact gone through the Sea and who were now still standing before God at Shechem.

The distress the Israelites experienced as they were faced with the pursuing forces of Pharaoh by the Sea made them call to the Lord. This feature of Israel's calling, or crying, to the Lord, is frequent in the Exodus narratives (Exod. 8:8; 14:10, 15; 15:25). Because of this appeal to the Lord and the resultant deliverance, Israel was to show mercy to the oppressed in its own midst. If these, the widows and orphans, should call to the Lord (Exod. 22:23), he would certainly hear their cry.

Having recounted the deliverance from the Egyptians by means of the miracle of the Sea, Joshua's summary now speaks in a strongly condensed form about the desert sojourn: *You stayed a long time in the desert*. Forty years of triumph and of tragedy, of obedience and of rebellion, are thus mentioned briefly. The design of the prophetic summary concerns the more recent past, and the story hastens to recall it.

8 Although at many points in the book the writer has been at pains to point out that the territory east of the Jordan was lawfully occupied by part of the Israelite tribes, he also seems to be aware that the true conquest of the promised land did not start until the crossing of the Jordan. The events described in vv. 8–10 must be seen to be somewhat preliminary to that great moment. Nevertheless, there can be no doubt about the fact that the eastern regions were given into Israel's hand by God, no less than would subsequently be the case on the other side of the river. The emphasis is once again on what God did. He *brought* Israel into *the land of the Amorites*[12] and *destroyed* them, while Israel occupied their land.

The events to which Joshua refers are related in Num. 21:21–35; Deut. 1:4; 2:24–3:3; 4:47; 31:4; see also 2:10; 9:10; Ps. 135:10–12; 136:17–22. About linking Sihon and Og with the Amorites, see also 2:10 and commentary. Note the "giving" of the land of the Amorites into Israel's hand, which is a consistent emphasis of the book of Joshua (see 1:2 and commentary; cf. 11b).

9–10 Joshua's summary now refers to what *Balak . . . the king*

---

12. About the Amorites, cf. 3:10 and commentary; 5:1. This term is used in both a broader and a narrower sense. In v. 15 it stands for the whole population of Palestine; cf. also Gen. 15:16; Judg. 1:34–35. In other cases they are regarded as having been confined to the mountain regions (7:7; Num. 13:29). Their relationship to the Amurru, frequently mentioned in extrabiblical sources, is a subject of ongoing debate. So is the question of the precise identity of the Amurru themselves. The biblical Amorites are listed among Canaan's descendants (Gen. 10:16) and continued to dwell in Palestine during the days of Samuel and David (cf. 1 Sam. 7:14; 2 Sam. 21:2; Ezra 9:1–2).

of Moab did as he *arose to make war against Israel*.[13] Balak summoned from the east the celebrated soothsayer Balaam, known for the powerful curses he could deliver (Num. 22–24). This episode left a deep mark upon Israel's memory; even the NT speaks of Balaam (2 Pet. 2:15; Rev. 2:14). Balak wants Balaam to curse Israel. (On the nature of a curse in ancient society, see 6:26 and commentary.) Curses are not to be treated lightly, even within the pale of special revelation, where God, and not magical forces, is seen as the bearer of the powerful word. Had God allowed Balaam to curse Israel, this curse would have had its effect. But God did not allow such a thing (cf. Num. 22:12; 23:8, 23).

Instead of cursing there was nothing but blessing. This almost ironical way of speaking shows the complete mastery of the God of Israel over all forces that would seek to harm his people. Nevertheless, the seriousness of a possible curse pronounced by Balaam is not minimized. Since God *would not listen to Balaam*, he *delivered* Israel out of Balaam's hand. The power of evil that would have been embodied in Balaam's curse was thwarted by God's intervention. At this point the reader is probably to think of a demonic influence that might have been operative in the curse. Later books of the OT, for example, the latter part of Daniel, show more of the spiritual side of the battle on Israel's behalf (Dan. 10:12–13).

11 Joshua now proceeds to recall some of the leading elements in the conquest of the territory west of the river Jordan. Again emphasis is placed on the giving of the land into Israel's hand (v. 11b). Moreover, the Lord is the one to send the *hornets* to drive out Canaan's inhabitants (v. 12).

You crossed the Jordan: compared to the lengthy description of this mighty miracle in chs. 3–4, a great economy of words is shown at this point. Yet the fact of the miraculous crossing is recognized.

The men[14] *of Jericho fought against you*. This is a new element not mentioned in the earlier conquest stories. At this point Joshua's prophetic summary combines whatever resistance Jericho may have offered with the resistance experienced later, when Israel was already well inside Canaanite territory (cf. 9:1). Jericho's resistance thus is viewed as part of the concerted efforts by the seven nations of Canaan (3:10) to thwart Israel's occupation of the country. But again the outcome was victorious: *I gave*

---

13. This can also be translated "arose and made war against Israel," but the biblical record is silent on a war between Balak and Israel (cf. Judg. 11:25).

14. Heb. *ba'ᵃlê*, lit. "lords," "possessors." Although the word *ba'al* can also be used in a more general sense of one who is characterized by certain features (cf. BDB), here it may stand for the free citizens, the landowners (cf. Judg. 9:2, 20, 23; 20:5; 1 Sam. 23:11–12; 2 Sam. 21:12).

them into your hand. This survey of the Lord's redemptive acts is indeed calculated to cause Israel to choose for him and not for the other gods who had been worshipped by the nations that were driven out before them.

12 There is no unanimity about the identity of the *hornets*[15] which the Lord is to have sent ahead of Israel to drive out the Canaanites before them. Some think that the Hebrew word does not refer to insects but to a condition of irrational fear or panic. The LXX renders it by "hornet." As was pointed out by Kroeze,[16] the activity attributed to the instrument of God, that of "driving out," agrees quite well with the latter meaning and not quite so well with that of fear or panic, although the notion of great fear experienced by the nations of Canaan is not absent from the book (cf. 2:9; 5:1).

In spite of some uncertainty as to detail, the main thrust of the verse is clear. It means to stress once again the divine monergism displayed in the work of the Conquest. Other parts of the book sometimes present a more composite view, as for example the story of the battle of Gibeon, but the book's main emphasis lies on the gratuitous nature of the gift God gave to his people in granting them the land. This is also the purpose of the concluding words: *not by your sword or by your bow.*[17]

13 The prophetic summary, characterized by an emphasis upon the undeserved nature of the gifts that the Lord of the covenant has bestowed upon Israel and its forefathers, now comes to its conclusion. The present possession of the *land*, of its *cities*, *vineyards*, and *olive yards*, is once more said to be due entirely, not to Israel's efforts but to the goodness

---

15. Heb. *ṣir'â*. KB see in the word meaning "downcast," "discouraged." J. Garstang, *Joshua, Judges*, pp. 258-260, thinks of the power of Pharaoh, one of whose symbols was a bee or hornet. This would imply Egyptian campaigns that had weakened the Canaanites before Israel's arrival. This view is adopted by J. Bright, *IB* II, but W. H. Gispen, *Het Boek Exodus*, rejects it in his commentary on Exod. 23:28, where the word also occurs.

16. Cf. Kroeze, *op. cit.*, p. 254. J. Gray, on the other hand, accepts the suggestion of KB. See also Hertzberg, Noth, for similar solutions.

17. According to the present text, the hornets were used to drive out "the two kings of the Amorites." Hence the setting is once more the east side of Jordan. The LXX reads "twelve" instead of "two." Some scholars believe that the kings of Canaan proper are meant, but these number thirty-one in the enumeration of ch. 12. Others consider the phrase to be a gloss, but to remove a difficulty in that manner is unsatisfactory. J. A. Soggin, adhering to the LXX's figure twelve, suggests that this may reflect a formula also employed in Assyrian annals, in which are found, in stereotyped form, twelve kings for the region consisting of Syria and Palestine; *Joshua*, p. 235. However, this does not explain how the obviously more difficult MT reading could have come into the text. Giblin, *op. cit.*, p. 64, suggests that v. 12c may have been added in light of v. 18a.

of Israel's God. (The same thought is expressed in Deut. 6:10–11.) Thus the stage is set for the exhortations that follow.

3. EXHORTATION AND RESPONSE (24:14–24)

14 *"Now therefore fear the Lord and serve him sincerely and faithfully, and put away the gods whom your forefathers served beyond the River and in Egypt and serve the Lord.*

15 *If it does not look good to you to serve the Lord, choose then today for yourselves whom you will serve, whether the gods your fathers served who were beyond the River or the gods of the Amorites in whose land you live. As for me and my house, we will serve the Lord."*

16 *Then the people answered: "Far be it from us to forsake the Lord for the purpose of serving other gods.*

17 *The Lord our God, he it was who brought us and our fathers up out of the land of Egypt, from the house of bondage, and who did great signs before our eyes. He kept us all along the way on which we traveled and among all the nations through which we passed.*

18 *The Lord drove out ahead of us all the peoples, and the Amorites who lived in the land. We too want to serve the Lord, for he is our God."*

19 *But Joshua said to the people: "You cannot serve the Lord. He is a holy God; he is a jealous God. He will not forgive your transgressions and your sins.*

20 *If you forsake the Lord and serve strange gods, then he will turn and do evil to you and destroy you, after he has been good to you."*

21 *But the people answered Joshua: "No, but we will serve the Lord."*

22 *Then Joshua said to the people: "You are witnesses against yourselves that you have chosen the Lord as the one you will serve." "We are witnesses," they said.*

23 *"Now, therefore, put away the strange gods which are among you and turn your hearts to the Lord, the God of Israel."*

24 *Then the people promised Joshua: "The Lord our God we will serve, and to his voice we will listen."*

Earlier it was suggested that ch. 24 is a narrative adaptation of the ancient treaty form which has survived in several extrabiblical documents now extant. If this assumption is correct, then v. 14 may be the equivalent of the basic declaration demanded of the vassal in relation to his lord.

14 Previously, in vv. 2–13, Joshua functioned as the prophetic spokesman for the Lord. At this point, however, follows an exhortation by Joshua himself presented against the background of the prophetic survey just offered. The words *Now therefore* indicate the legal setting of covenant within which the exhortation is to be seen.

Israel is to *fear the Lord*. Fearing the Lord sums up the religious attitude expected of the OT believer. The term occurs frequently in Deuteronomy (4:10; 6:2, 13, 24). Fear of the Lord is the attitude of awe and of filial reverence which befits the child of God over against his Maker and Redeemer. This fear is desired and approved by God (Deut. 4:10). It is not inconsistent with, but flows from, the experience of forgiveness (cf. Ps. 130:4). This fear is to be rendered *sincerely*[1] *and faithfully*.[2] It should be without hypocrisy, but should be expressed with simplicity and truth of heart.

Service of the Lord is meant to be exclusive service. It involves putting away *the gods whom your forefathers served* (v. 2). The same demand is made at other points in Israel's history (Gen. 35:2; 1 Sam. 7:4). The cultus of other deities is forbidden in much the same way that in ancient Near Eastern treaties the vassal was forbidden to have any other overlord except the lord to whom he was bound in treaty.[3] This antithetical nature of Israel's relationship to the Lord must also be kept in mind when reading the laws of the Pentateuch. Whatever resembled an alliance other than that with the Lord, be it in manner of dress, sacrificial practices, common mores, and the like, was forbidden. Some things prohibited by law were not necessarily immoral when viewed by themselves, but their connection with the cultus of foreign gods rendered them unusable for Israel. A literal application of these laws today may do them serious injustice.

The gods to be put away were served not only beyond the Euphrates but also *in Egypt*. This addition need not be considered suspect as do some. It is true, in the earlier prophetic summary given in vv. 2–13, that Egypt was the place where the people cried to the Lord and were delivered. But the OT also presents another facet of the situation in Ezek. 20:7; 23:3, 8. According to that viewpoint, Israel is seen as having played the harlot while in Egypt. Thus there is no need to eliminate this reference in order to streamline the account.[4] Some form of idolatry was found among Israel also during the desert journey (cf. Lev. 17:7, which suggests goat

---

1. Heb. *tāmîm*, suggesting "fullness," "completeness," "integrity." This word expresses the harmony that should exist between man's external and internal qualities.
2. Heb. *'emet*, another theologically fruitful word. In 2:12 it is used of a sign on which Rahab can rely. Cf. A. Jepsen, "'āman," *TDOT* I, pp. 292–323.
3. Examples of this are given in K. Baltzer, *Covenant Formulary*, p. 21.
4. Cf. also the favorable opinion of the early relation between the Lord and Israel as expressed in Jer. 2:2, as contrasted with the Ezekiel passages mentioned above. Both traditions have basis in biblical fact.

[satyr?] worship). Nevertheless, 23:8b states that Israel has been cleaving to the Lord unto this day. The author of Joshua saw no difficulty in letting these emphases stand side by side.

15 The choice which Joshua presents to Israel (either the gods *beyond the River* or *the gods of the Amorites*) can hardly be regarded a real choice in the light of the Bible's resolute rejection of all deities except the Lord.[5] On the other hand, the choice between serving the Lord and the serving of all other deities was real, and that is Joshua's main concern. If the service of the Lord *does not look good to you* (lit. "is evil in your eyes"), then the way is open to that other choice which really is no choice, even though the possibilities are many and seemingly a choice is there. Local and regional gods, or ancestral gods, the Israelites may choose to their hearts' content. Joshua himself, however, wants it to be known that *as for me and my house,*[6] *we will serve the Lord*.

16-18 Responding to the basic covenant demand as laid down in the words of v. 14, the people vehemently deny any intention of disloyalty to the Lord. They will not *forsake* him, so they solemnly and emphatically declare. The term "forsake," Heb. *'āzaḇ*, contrasts with the demand of "clinging" to the Lord made by Joshua at the earlier assembly (23:8; cf. Deut. 28:20; 31:16; Judg. 2:12-13; 10:6, 10). This forsaking of the Lord, so Israel knew, would bring about the curse of the covenant (cf. Deut. 28:20).

In language reminiscent of the prologue to the Ten Commandments, the people recall their deliverance from Egypt. The prophetic survey presented to them by Joshua (vv. 2-13) has had its impact. It is the God of their deliverance and of their safekeeping in the desert that they wish to serve. Later in their history Israel would forget these great acts of the Lord (Jer. 2:4-8).

The people continue to recount the past blessings received. They reflect on the driving out of *all the peoples* ahead of them. Possibly this refers to various hostile encounters in the desert (Exod. 17:8; Num. 31:2), but the use of the term "drive out" for the defeat of desert dwellers is surprising. When Israel came to Canaan *the Amorites* were a threat (cf. vv. 8, 15), but these too the Lord drove out. In light of these manifest

---

5. G. Quell, "ἐκλέγομαι B," *TDNT* IV (E.T. 1967), pp. 144-168, suggests that Joshua is using irony at this point. On the meaning of *bāḥar*, "choose," see H. Seebass, *"bāchar,"* *TDOT* II, pp. 73-87, especially p. 86.
6. The solidarity in evil between a man and his house had been stressed in ch. 7. Here this same solidarity is expressed in a favorable sense. Joshua's choice affects his descendants (cf. the baptisms of Lydia and the Philippian jailer, together with their "houses" in Acts 16:15, 31-34).

blessings in redemptive history the people state that they do not want to be any less loyal to the Lord than Joshua had vowed to be (v. 15). They too *will serve the Lord, for he is our God*.[7]

19 *You cannot serve the Lord*: it is evident from other parts of the book (e.g., 23:8) as well as from this chapter (v. 31) that these words, although their seriousness should not be minimized, should nevertheless not be taken in an absolute sense. Joshua simply wants to confront Israel with the seriousness of the solemn promise it has just uttered.

Two things are said about God, both of which are meant to impress Israel with the weightiness of the moment. God is *holy*, and he is *jealous*. God's holiness (Heb. *qōdeŝ*) is that which makes him incomparable (1 Sam. 2:2). There is something of the unapproachable about the holy. Nevertheless, in later literature God is also the Holy One of Israel (frequently so in Isaiah), who in spite of his holiness dwells *with* Israel. Here, however, the unapproachable sanctity of God is in the foreground. When that holiness is violated by sinful man it expresses itself in "jealousy," God's zeal for the maintenance of his honor. This zeal can be shown through acts of punishment upon evildoers or through acts of vindication on behalf of God's people (cf. Exod. 20:5; 34:14; Deut. 5:9). Stress upon the "jealousy" of God does not conflict with his status as the redeeming God. In the Decalog both features occur side by side (Exod. 20:2, 5). Hence Joshua's words must not be considered to be in conflict with the people's earlier reference to the Exodus redemption (v. 17).

Continuing his solemn words of warning, Joshua now tells the people in absolute terms that the covenant God, once his "jealousy" is provoked, *will not forgive your transgressions and your sins*. These words must be understood in their proper context, yet their force should not be diminished to the point of complete diminution. Forgiveness of sins is something on which a sinner cannot count. The fact that sins are forgiven at all is due to a miracle of grace, for always sin calls for punishment by a holy God.[8]

Two words are used here for sin. The second word used (Heb. *ḥēṭ'*) is the more common, designating the sinful act as the missing of a mark, the righteousness demanded by God's law. The other word, rendered

---

7. This solemn declaration is repeated in vv. 21, 24. Baltzer, *op. cit.*, considers this an indication of the juridical nature of the document here incorporated into the sacred text. For some of the stylistic and rhetorical features of this dialogue, cf. also C. H. Giblin, *CBQ* 26 (1964), pp. 50–69.

8. The sin of idolatry, which was a rupture of the covenant bond, was to be punished severely (cf. Deut. 13).

"transgression" (Heb. *peša'*), views sin from its wilful side. Sin is rebellion, insurrection.

20 Joshua tells the people that the covenant blessings that are promised to the obedient will turn into the covenant curses when disobedience is shown. Serving strange gods and forsaking the Lord will cause the Lord to *turn and do evil to you and destroy you*. The Pentateuch contains both the blessings and the curses of the covenant (cf. Deut. 28; Lev. 26). The Bible speaks nonsystematically about God, hence it speaks freely of the "turning" of God in case of covenant breaking (cf. 23:15). In order to arrive at a complete picture of what God is like, one also would have to take into account the passages where God is said to be unchangeable, or *nonturning*. Sometimes the two thoughts may occur in one and the same chapter (e.g., 1 Sam. 15:11, 29).

The gods that Israel may want to serve instead of the Lord are called *strange gods*. This recalls Gen. 35:2, 4; cf. also Judg. 10:16; 1 Sam. 7:3; Jer. 5:19. For the singular, cf. Deut. 32:12; Ps. 81:10 (Eng. 9). Evil and ultimate destruction will be Israel's lot when it turns after these other gods. It is left to other parts of Scripture, which also contain the curses of the covenant (e.g., Lev. 26:41b–42), to speak of the possibility of Israel's repentance and God's turning again, this time in grace and forgiveness. At the present moment, however, Israel must be confronted with the full weight of its decision.

21 For the second time in this dialogue setting, the people respond with a clear affirmation of loyalty to their covenant Lord. They will serve him. The message of the book of Joshua is essentially very positive and hopeful. The seriousness of Joshua's challenge only serves to enhance this positive aspect of the people's response. The many accounts of covenant apostasy which Israel preserved for later generations to ponder upon should not obscure this affirmative and encouraging element.[9]

22–24 As in all judicial procedures so also here in this covenant context the need for witnesses arises. Joshua calls on the people to be witnesses against themselves. This means that they thereby will take upon themselves the curses of which he has been speaking, should they become unfaithful to their Lord. Again, the readiness of the people to enter into this solemn compact should be duly noted (cf. also Exod. 19:8). It is this

9. It seems to this observer that the sentiment of Amos 3:2 receives greater stress in current biblical theology than thoughts such as Ps. 147:20a embodies. Both need stress. Both are equally legitimate. Perhaps in the present age of uncertainty and discouragement among Christians the latter thought should be given special attention.

spirit of covenant adherence which also underlies some of the sentiments of the Psalms, where the believer knows himself to be on the Lord's side (e.g., Pss. 17, 26, etc.). Pharisaism must not be attributed to this sentiment.

By informing the reader of Israel's undertaking of the covenant obligation the writer of this book makes it clear that Israel's later calamities can not be laid to God's charge. The Lord himself is beyond reproach (cf. also Jer. 2:5).[10]

Verse 23 begins with another *now therefore* (cf. v. 14). Because of the rather solemn nature of that introduction, the writer omits mention of the fact that it is Joshua who utters these words. Again the demand to put away the strange gods is repeated (cf. v. 14). The people's positive response to the covenant demands must find its counterpart in a negative putting away of the strange gods (cf. vv. 14, 20), although no merely negative attitude is expected. There also must be a turning of the heart to the Lord. For the involvement of the "heart," including not only the emotions but also the mind and will, see Deut. 6:5; 10:16. By using the expression *the Lord, the God of Israel*, this significant passage returns to its starting point (v. 2).[11]

Nothing is said about the execution of the demand to remove the idols. Some would hold that the idolatry meant here is only an inward one. Others believe that the putting away of idols refers not to those still found among Israel, but to those of the nations in whose midst Israel now lived. On the other hand, one need not insist on an explicit account of how this demand was actually put into effect.

With another unambiguous statement of their willingness to *serve the Lord our God* and to listen to *his voice* (v. 24) the people respond to this final call on Joshua's part. They do so after they have undertaken to be witnesses against themselves (v. 22), which is tantamount to taking an oath. Hence this solemn declaration forms a final attestation on the people's part.

4. COVENANT DOCUMENTATION (24:25–28)

25 So Joshua made a covenant with the people on that day, and there in Shechem he laid down for them a statute and an ordinance.
26 Joshua recorded these things in the book of the law of God, and he

10. The LXX lacks the emphatic "We are witnesses" of the MT. But, as Baltzer, *op. cit.*, p. 26, rightly remarks, these words are necessary at this point of solemn oath taking.
11. Giblin, *op. cit.*, calls attention to this *inclusio*.

took a large stone and set it up under the oak that was in the holy place of the Lord.

27 *Then Joshua said to all the people: "This stone will be a witness against us, for it has heard all the words of the Lord which he spoke to us; it will be a witness against you so that you do not betray your God."*

28 *Then Joshua sent the people away, each to his own inheritance.*

The ancient treaty pattern which one encounters in extrabiblical documents usually includes a clause concerning the deposition of the treaty text and the calling of witnesses. The latter element, the covenant witness, has received attention already in v. 22, and it recurs in these final verses. The covenant document is mentioned here for the first time.

25 Although the entire transaction described in this chapter must be seen within the context of covenant renewal, the first explicit reference to "covenant" does not occur until this verse. *Joshua*, so it is recorded, *made a covenant* (Heb. *berît*)[1] *with the people.* Some interpreters, wishing to stress the unilateral origin of this covenant, and taking note of the fact that the Hebrew uses a preposition (*le-*) which usually means "for," translate accordingly "a covenant for the people." When King Nahas imposes a covenant on the people of Jabesh-gilead the same preposition is used (cf. 1 Sam. 11:1–2). However, regardless of the one-sided imposition of a particular covenant, each covenant involves some form of mutuality. This is certainly clear from the present context. In a few instances, however, the word "covenant" in the OT is almost identical with "disposition."[2]

At this point, the covenant made by Joshua was tantamount to laying down for Israel *a statute and an ordinance* (Heb. *ḥôq*, *mišpāṭ*). (For the use of these terms in the plural, cf. Deut. 4:1, 45; 6:1.) In some instances they are used in a triad, together with "commandments." In the present verse the two terms are virtually synonymous. At any rate, the writer does not elaborate as to their precise nature. Some interpreters believe the reference here is primarily to the ritual ordinances to be used

---

1. The etymology of *berît* is not certain. A variety of suggestions has been made, including "to eat" and "to bind." The Hebrew expression for "making" a covenant means literally "cutting" a covenant. The use of that verb (Heb. *kārat*) suggests the cutting of animals in the covenant ceremony.

2. C. Steuernagel, *Das Buch Josua*, p. 301, in translating v. 25, omits any reference to the word "covenant" and places all stress on the notion of obligation: "So verpflichtete denn Josua das Volk. . . ." For the terminology of covenant making cf. M. Weinfeld, *TDOT* II, pp. 259f. The Hebrew particles used with the making of a covenant are *le*, *'im*, *'et*, and *'al*. The idea expressed by *le*, "for," can also be expressed by *'et*, "with," an indication of the rather imprecise way in which the OT uses its terms.

in worship. However, it would seem from the context, which speaks of Israel's total commitment to its covenant Lord, that more specifically ethical commands were not to be excluded. Essentially all of covenant law, whether "civil," "ceremonial," or "ethical," is held together by one underlying spiritual principle, that of the Lord's redemption of his people, a redemption which obliges the people to serve and love their Lord with heart, mind, and soul. This principle pervaded all of Israel's laws and was operative in the smallest minutiae of these laws. In summary, it may be said that the statute and the ordinance were the rule by which the covenanting parties were to live.

26 Joshua then writes down *these things* (or "these words") in a book. Among Israel's neighbors, a covenant document usually accompanied the making of a treaty.[3] This provided for the treaty proceedings and allowed the document to be deposited at a safe place, often at the foot of some idol statue, indicating symbolically that the god would watch over the treaty. A similar recording of covenant proceedings is found in Deut. 31:24–27.

The book, or document, which Joshua wrote is solemnly called *the book of the law of God*. God had been the witness to all that had been said and done, and the people had presented themselves before him (v. 1). The treaty document therefore could be properly called by his name.[4] The word translated "law" (Heb. *tôrâ*) has a wider meaning than the English word itself would suggest. It may also mean "direction," "teaching."

Joshua also erects *a large stone*. Ceremonies in the OT world were often accompanied by the erection of such a stone (cf. Gen. 28:18; 1 Sam. 7:12). This stone was set up under *the oak that was in the holy place of the Lord*. One should not think of this holy place as a formal structure but rather as a sacred precinct within which a tree could be found. The sanctity of the place near Shechem goes back to Abraham's time (Gen. 12:6; cf.

---

3. Cf. K. Baltzer, *Covenant Formulary*, pp. 26f., who shows that in ancient treaty making the treaty and its corresponding document belonged inseparably together: "The treaty document is an inseparable part of the treaty."

4. For a different understanding, cf. J. H. Kroeze, *Het Boek Jozua*, p. 259. Kroeze takes the book of the law of God to be the same as that mentioned in Deut. 31:26. This would mean that Joshua actually wrote in the book of the law of Moses which, so Kroeze infers, was not yet completed in Joshua's days. J. Gray, *Joshua, Judges and Ruth*, p. 198, considers the expression "book of the law of God" to be late. He suggests that what Joshua originally wrote was more probably a series of laws on a standing stone. For this he refers to 8:32. But this is clearly not what the text says, and to introduce the idea of lateness here may well be begging the question.

also 35:2, 4). In both these instances in Genesis mention is made of a significant tree.

27–28 The stone is to serve as *a witness against us*. Joshua here includes himself with the people as those who have entered into covenant and who must adhere to its statutes. However, he also distinguishes himself from them (*against you*). The stone has been a silent witness of the words the Lord spoke to Israel. The emphasis falls on what the Lord has said rather than on what the people have said. Through Joshua, the Lord had set the stage for the covenant ceremony by presenting to his people a summary of his great acts of deliverance (vv. 2–13). This was done to motivate the people to show true covenant loyalty. Whatever Israel would do with the covenant would be done against the background of the record of God's deeds in the past. When, therefore, this stone would witness against them, this would be tantamount to God's redemptive acts witnessing against them. For other witnesses to the words of the Lord, cf. Deut. 32:1; Isa. 1:2.

C. THREE GRAVES IN THE PROMISED LAND (24:29–33)

29 *After these things, Joshua, son of Nun, the servant of the Lord, died. He was 110 years old.*

30 *They buried him in the territory of his own inheritance, at Timnathserah, which is in the hill country of Ephraim, north of Mount Gaash.*

31 *Israel served the Lord during the entire lifetime of Joshua and that of the elders who outlived Joshua and who had known all the work of the Lord which he had done for Israel.*

32 *And Joseph's bones, which the Israelites had brought up from Egypt, were buried in the plot of ground which Jacob bought for a hundred pieces of money from the sons of Hamor, father of Shechem. And this became the inheritance of the Josephites.*

33 *Eleazar, son of Aaron, also died. They buried him in the hill of Phinehas his son, which had been granted him in the hill country of Ephraim.*

The book of Joshua concludes with three reports about the deaths and/or burials of some prominent persons in Israel's history: Joshua, Joseph, and Eleazar. Since Joseph's bones probably had been buried several years before the Shechem assembly described in this chapter, it would appear that the listing of these facts at the conclusion of the book serves a thematic purpose. The purpose of the book now has been accomplished. God's complete fulfilment of the promise in granting Israel the land of Canaan has been set forth. Solemn exhortations to remain loyal to the Lord of the covenant have been given. Now, for symbolical reasons, the author must tell finally about the death and/or burial of these three men.

Joshua was instrumental in helping Israel to obtain the promised land. Joseph, at the time of his death, had looked forward in faith to the future fulfilment of God's promise (Gen. 50:24–26), and in that confidence he had ordered his bones to be taken out of Egypt, once the promised deliverance had come. Eleazar had played a part in the distribution of the promised land to the tribes. The remains of all these men, so the writer means to indicate, were now laid to rest in the land that God had promised to the fathers.[1]

29–30   The report of the death and burial of Joshua parallels a similar report concerning Moses, whose death and burial are recorded at the conclusion of Deuteronomy. This is consistent with many other parallels which the book of Joshua makes between these two: the crossing of the Red Sea and that of Jordan; the appearance of a mysterious figure at the beginning of their respective ministries, and several other features (cf. 1:17; 4:14). In keeping with this, the honorary title *servant of the Lord* now is bestowed upon Joshua, previously having been reserved for Moses (cf. 1:1, 7, 15). Looking back upon the sacred history in which Joshua had played such a valiant part, the writer, guided as he is by the Spirit, senses that Joshua's place is equal to that of his great predecessor. Hence he accords him the title "servant of the Lord," a title held by only a few individuals in the history of OT redemption. Joshua's age, 110 years, is the same as that of Joseph, whose name is mentioned next. In OT times a long life was a sign of God's blessing (Ps. 91:16). Thus Joshua dies as one of the blessed ones.

The place of burial is given as Timnath-serah,[2] presently Khirbet

---

1. There is a parallel between 24:29–31 and Judg. 2:6–10 (cf. also Judg. 1:1). This serves to link together these two books in the canon. Similarly, Josh. 1:1 links up with Deut. 34. C. Vonk, *Inleiding op de Profeten: Jozua*, p. 25, correctly sees in this interlinking of the various OT books a testimony to the unity of the Bible and also to the canonicity of these books.

2. In Judg. 2:9 this is written Timnath-heres. Some believe that this is the original name, but that the association of this place with a pagan sun cult (*heres* means sun) caused the author to change the name. A simpler explanation is that a scribe copying Judges reversed the consonants (*serah* to *heres*) and that the Joshua version is the original.

Tibneh, about 12 miles northeast of Lydda.[3] The writer emphasizes the fact that this was Joshua's *own inheritance*, lending further support to the earlier suggestion concerning the symbolical role that these burial stories fill in the book. Joshua is not buried in a strange land in which, as did the patriarchs earlier, a grave had to be purchased from the real inhabitants (cf. v. 32). Instead, he is buried in his own inheritance. (On the words "inheritance" and "inherit," see 1:6 and commentary.) *Mount Gaash* has not been identified, but its general location is in the *hill country of Ephraim*, in which Joshua had received his portion (cf. 19:49–51).[4]

31 *Israel served the Lord*: the positive significance of this statement should not be overlooked, particularly since earlier in the chapter the reader had been reminded of the (virtual) impossibility of serving the Lord (v. 19). At the conclusion of his book the writer wishes to make this ringing testimony to Israel's loyalty to the covenant. This accords properly with the spirit of joyful optimism which pervades the book. The fact that the writer goes on to add that this service was rendered *during the entire lifetime of Joshua and that of the elders* who outlived him must serve to prepare the stage for what follows in the book of Judges (cf. Judg. 2:7). Still, it would be erroneous to overlook the positive aspect of this laudatory comment in its entirety. Temporal closeness to the great *work*[5] *of the Lord* which he had done for Israel appears to be given as a reason for this show of loyalty. Nevertheless, the book which is now brought to its conclusion will help Israel throughout its history to participate in that work as well. Thus there is no excuse at any time in Israel's subsequent history for not serving the Lord in the way that it was done in Joshua's time.[6]

3. A. Alt, "Josua," *KS* I, p. 186, considers this part of the Joshua "tradition" to be characterized by *"Unerfindlichkeit"* and *"Tendenzlosigkeit"* (not invented and not showing a bias), a scant recognition in light of the many etiologies Alt claims to have discovered in the rest of the book.
4. The LXX also speaks of the burial of the flint knives with which Joshua performed the rite of circumcision (5:2). Was this an attempt to embellish the story, or does it represent a true tradition?
5. By using the singular the author probably wants to present the various acts of God on his people's behalf, namely the Exodus, the giving of the law, wilderness experience, and the possession of the promised land as so many manifestations of God's one work of redemption.
6. On the role of biblical narration and biblical narrative, see also C. Westermann, *Genesis*. BK I/2, pp. 32–40. Westermann's rejection of what he calls "argumentative theology" in favor of narrative theology is subject to criticism. Yet his plea to see the theological relevance of narrative per se should be heeded. Westermann points out that through narration things are being disclosed (p. 39). One is enabled to participate by means of narration.

32 The report of the burial of Joseph's bones is meant to alert the reader to the faith that Joseph expressed at the time of his death (Gen. 50:25). This faith has now been rewarded. In other words, God has fulfilled his promises. It is not Joseph's faith but God's faithfulness that should be uppermost in interpreting this passage.

Joseph's bones are buried at Shechem in *the plot of ground which Jacob bought* (Gen. 33:19). Here again the story suggests the giant step forward that has been made since the days of Jacob. No longer is there need to buy a parcel of land! To be sure, Jacob's purchase had established a lawful claim to the land where Joseph's bones were put to rest. Nevertheless, today this claim was exercised on a different basis. The whole land is now lawfully Israel's. The conquest of the land in the neighborhood of Shechem is not mentioned explicitly anywhere in the book. Yet the book of Joshua presents the possession of Canaan as essentially complete, though in need of further implementation (cf. 13:1ff. and commentary).

The exact significance of Heb. $q^e \hat{s} \hat{t} \hat{a}$, "piece of money," is not known.[7] Exact precision probably was not the point of the story. What is important is that by means of this monetary transaction Jacob became owner of the plot where the bones of Joseph are now interred.

Moreover, this same plot has become the *inheritance of the Josephites*.[8] This is the second time that the word "inheritance" occurs in this concluding section (cf. v. 30).

33 The report of Eleazar's death and burial concludes the book in a fitting manner.[9] Eleazar had played a role with respect to Joshua similar to that fulfilled by Aaron with respect to Moses (cf. Num. 27:21). It has been suggested that Eleazar's death marks the end of the period of elders who outlived Joshua (cf. v. 31), but this is not certain. Eleazar is mentioned in 14:1; 17:4; 19:51; 21:1.

The place where Eleazar is laid to rest is called *the hill of Phinehas*, which may also be rendered Gibeah of Phinehas. More than one town by

---

7. H. W. Hertzberg, *ATD* IX, p. 139, surmises that it was a gold coin, on the basis of Job 42:11, where the term occurs in conjunction with a gold ring. However, this is not certain.

8. Heb. lit. "and they became the inheritance. . . ." "They" can only refer back grammatically to the antecedent "sons of Hamor." It would seem, however, that the reference must be to the plot of land. This is how it was understood by the Vulgate: *et fuit in possessione filiorum Ioseph*. The LXX reads "and he gave to Joseph as a portion."

9. No historical value is attributed to this story by J. A. Soggin, *Joshua*, p. 245, who holds it to be an etiology of the place Gibeah of Phinehas. We fail to see how a book so obviously showing marks of deliberate composition should have ended so ingloriously.

the name of Gibeah is attested (15:57; 1 Sam. 13:2; 15:34). Phinehas may have been given this hill (or "town") as a recognition of his zeal for God (cf. 22:13; Num. 25:7). Its location is not known, except that it too is said to be in the "hill country of Ephraim" (cf. v. 30). Aaron's descendants, to whom Eleazar belonged, received their cities in Judah, Benjamin, and Simeon (21:9-19). No mention is made of Ephraim. Perhaps the "hill country of Ephraim" at this point must be understood in a wider sense, to include certain areas belonging to Benjamin (cf. Judg. 4:5). If so, then the Gibeah here mentioned may have been the same as Geba cited in 21:17.[10]

10. The LXX, at least in some manuscripts, presents additional information which touches on the movements of the ark from place to place, on Eleazar's succession by Phinehas, and on Israel's apostasy with Astarte and the Ashtaroth.

I. INDEX OF SUBJECTS

II. INDEX OF PROPER NAMES

Astharoth 203, 216, 223
Ataroth (Kh. 'Aṭṭārûs, Ataroth-addar, Tell en-Naṣbeh?) 258, 260, 276
Avvim (city) 278
Avvim (people) 211
Azekah (Tell ez-Zakarîyah) 173, 247
Azmon 235
Aznoth-tabor 291

Baal 335
Baalah 238f., 245, 295
Baalath-beer (see Bealoth) 244, 281
Baalbek 195
Baal-gad 195, 205, 212
Baal-peor 219
Baal-zebub 249
Babylon (Babylonia) 345
Balaam 219f., 348
Balah 245
Balak 347
Balâṭah (see also Shechem-city) 302
Bamoth-baal 218
Barak 187
Bashan 202, 216, 223, 263
Bealoth (Baalath-beer) 244, 281
Beeroth 161, 278
Beer-sheba 245, 280
Be-eshterah (Tell 'Ashtarah) 311
Beirut 211
Beisan 311
Beitîn (see also Luz) 122
Beit Jamâl 247
Beit Mirsim 22, 242
Beit Ummar 252
Bene-berak (Ibn-ibrâq) 295
Ben-hadad 188
Benjamin 236, 255, 275, 293, 305
Beor 220
Beten 288
Beth-anath 293
Beth-anoth (Kh. Beit 'Ainûn) 253
Beth-arabah ('Ain el-Gharabeh) 236, 254, 278
Beth-aven 122, 258, 276
Beth-baal-meon (Ma'în) 218
Beth-dagon 248, 288
Bethel (Burj Beitîn) 122, 205, 258, 278
Beth-emek 288
Bether 253
Beth-haram 222
Beth-hoglah 236, 277f.
Beth-horon 172, 257, 259, 276, 310
Beth-jeshimoth (Tell el-'Azeimeh) 202

Beth-lebaoth 281
Bethlehem (in Judah) 253, 308
Bethlehem (in Zebulun) 285
Beth-mar-coboth (see Madmannah)
Beth-nimrah 222
Beth-pazzez 287
Beth-pelet (Tell el-Fâr'ah? Tell es-Saqati?) 245
Beth-peor 219
Beth-shean (Tell el-Ḥuṣn) 266, 268
Beth-shemesh (in Issachar) 287, 293
Beth-shemesh (in Judah) 238, 308
Beth-tappuah (Taffûḥ) 252
Bethul 281
Beth-Zur (Kh. eṭ-Ṭubeiqeh) 253
Betonim (Kh. Baṭneh) 222
Bezer (Bosor? Bozrah?) 302, 312
Bilhah 245, 288, 291, 293
Bizjothjah 245
Bohan 236, 277
Bozkath 248
Burqa 122
Byblos (Begal) 211

Cabbon 248
Cabul (Kābûl) 289
Cain 345
Caleb 15f., 209, 225, 240f., 254f., 308
Canaan, boundaries 59f., 320, 329; inhabitants 84, 189, 205; kings 98, 200; promised to patriarchs 59, 110; typological significance 209
Canaanites, defeat 178; dread/fear 71, 99, 164, 168; extermination 38, 42, 154, 193, 196, 266; religion 320; identity 84, 98, 189, 211
Captain of the Lord's Army 105
Carmel (Mount) 189, 266, 288
Carmel (town; Kh. el-Kermel) 252
Chemosh 57
Chephar-ammoni (Kefr 'Anā?) 278
Chephirah 161
Chesalon (Keslā) 238
Chesil (Bethul? Kh. er-Râs? Kh. el-Qaryatein?) 245
Chesulloth 283
Chinnereth (Chinneroth; Kh. el-'Oreimeh) 189, 202, 222
Chisloth-tabor (Chesulloth? Iksâl?) 283
Chitlish 248
Cisjordan 204, 224
City of Salt 254
Crete (Caphtor) 210

III. INDEX OF AUTHORS

IV. INDEX OF
SCRIPTURE REFERENCES

INDEX OF SCRIPTURE REFERENCES